From Time to Time

From Time to Time
JOURNEYS IN THE JEWISH CALENDAR

Rabbi Dalia Marx, PhD

Foreword by Rabbi David Ellenson, PhD
Translated by Rabbi Peretz A. Rodman

Reform Judaism Publishing, a division of CCAR Press
Central Conference of American Rabbis
5784 NEW YORK 2023

Copyright © 2023 by the Central Conference of American Rabbis.
All rights reserved. No portion of this book may be copied in any form for any purpose without the written permission of the Central Conference of American Rabbis.

Published by Reform Judaism Publishing, a division of CCAR Press
Central Conference of American Rabbis
355 Lexington Avenue, New York, NY 10017
(212) 972-3636 | info@ccarpress.org | www.ccarpress.org

Originally published in Hebrew as בזמן: מסעות בלוח השנה היהודי–ישראלי
by Miskan - Yedioth Ahronoth Books and Chemed Books, Rishon LeZion, Israel, 2018.
Cover and interior art by Elad Lifshitz, Dov Abramson Art and Design Studio.
Used by permission.

Library of Congress Cataloging-in-Publication Data
Names: Marx, Dalia, 1966—author. | Rodman, Peretz, translator. | Ellenson, David Harry, 1947—writer of foreword.
Title: From time to time: journeys in the Jewish calendar / Rabbi Dalia Marx, PhD; foreword by Rabbi David Ellenson, PhD; translated by Rabbi Peretz A. Rodman.
Other titles: Ba-zeman, masa'ot be-luaḥ ha-shanah ha-Yehudi-Yiśre'eli. English
Description: New York: Central Conference of American Rabbis, CCAR, 5784= 2023. | Summary: "The book is an exploration of the treasures of the Jewish year. It blends traditional and contemporary perspectives on each Hebrew month and its holidays. Each month features a selection of poetry and prayers"—provided by publisher.
Identifiers: LCCN 2023022738 (print) | LCCN 2023022739 (ebook) | ISBN 9780881236132 (hardcover) | ISBN 9780881236149 (ebook)
Subjects: LCSH: Prayer—Judaism. | Jewish religious poetry. | Jewish calendar.
Classification: LCC BM669 .M37513 2023 (print) | LCC BM669 (ebook) | DDC 296.4/5—dc23/eng/20230513
LC record available at https://lccn.loc.gov/2023022738
LC ebook record available at https://lccn.loc.gov/2023022739

English edition designed and composed by Scott-Martin Kosofsky at The Philidor Company, Rhinebeck, NY.

Printed in U.S.A.

10 9 8 7 6 5 4 3 2 1

Rabbi Aaron D. Panken, *z"l*, taught:

"We use our power for good in the world and utilize it for what is sacred, peaceful, and wonderful in the world." (2017)

"Reform Judaism envisions the possibility that the potential for holiness exists in every human being." (2015)

Rabbi Dalia Marx, PhD,

the Rabbi Aaron D. Panken Professor of Liturgy and Midrash
at Hebrew Union College-Jewish Institute of Religion,
sustains the legacy of Rabbi Panken with her teaching and research.

∾

This book is dedicated with admiration by
Patty Beck
Joy Greenberg
Lisa Messinger
Carole and Jay Sterling

CONTENTS

Foreword
    Rabbi David Ellenson, PhD ... xi
Translator's Preface
    Rabbi Peretz A. Rodman ... xv
Preface ... xvii
Tov L'hodot: How Good It Is to Give Thanks ... xxi

Tishrei ... 1
    Kavanah: A Meditation for Tishrei ... 3
    At the Gates of Tishrei ... 4
    Poem of the Month: *Achot K'tanah* ("Little Sister") ... 5
        Human Time, Cosmic Time ... 6
        "Let Us Proclaim the Power of This Day": Human Being, Nation, and World ... 9
        Is Forgiveness Possible? ... 15
        Kol Nidrei and Babylonian Incantation Bowls ... 19
        Sukkot: "We've Stepped Out. Be Back Soon!" ... 23
        Simchat Torah: There Is No Joy Like the Joy of Torah ... 28
    Prayers of the Month:
        A Blessed Meal of Symbols ... 31
        Ashamnu, Bagadnu: Old and New Confessions ... 35
        Ushpizin and *Ushpizot:* Heavenly and Earthly Guests ... 40
        Praying for Rain: Old and New *Geshem* Prayers ... 44

Marcheshvan ... 47
    Kavanah: A Meditation for Marcheshvan ... 49
    At the Gates of Marcheshvan ... 49
    Poems of the Month: Songs of Rain and Realization
        Geshem ("Rain") and *Geshem B'ito* ("Rain in Its Proper Time") ... 50
        A Toast to the Blessing of Routine ... 53
        What Shall We Remember on Yitzhak Rabin Memorial Day? ... 56
        Jeroboam Demands Social Justice (and Religious Freedom) ... 60
        Sigd: The Holiday of the Ethiopian Jews ... 63
    Prayer of the Month: *Egzio sema'ane*—"Eternal, Hear Us" ... 67

Kislev ... 71
    Kavanah: A Meditation for Kislev ... 73
    At the Gates of Kislev ... 73
    Poem of the Month: *Maoz Tzur* ("Rock of Ages") ... 74

Kislev: To Be Most at Home in the Entire World	76
"Open the Gate, Open It Wide"	80
Two Chanukah Menorahs, Two Worldviews	82
The "December Dilemma"	84
We Celebrate, We Eat . . . and We Argue	87
Prayer of the Month: Dedication of a Home (*Chanukat HaBayit*)—Not Just for When You Move In	91

Tevet — 95

Kavanah: A Meditation for Tevet	97
At the Gates of Tevet	98
Poems of the Month:	
Lailah ("Night") and *Mizmor Lailah* ("A Night Psalm")	99
Rosh Chodesh Tevet: The Festival of the Women	100
A Candle for Rabbi Regina Jonas	105
A Fast (or Fasts) during Tevet and the Danger of Translation	108
Hebrew, Revived—Part I	111
Prayer of the Month: Bedtime *Sh'ma*	115

Sh'vat — 119

Kavanah: A Meditation for Sh'vat	121
At the Gates of Sh'vat	121
Poem of the Month: *Efnt dem Toyer* ("Open the Gate")	122
Tu BiSh'vat: A Growing Holiday	123
They Didn't Try to Kill Us, So How Can We Celebrate?	128
The Connection between Gardening and Parenting	130
Shabbat Shirah: The Shabbat of Song	133
Family Day	137
Prayer of the Month: Prayers for the Welfare of Our Families	141

Adar — 143

Kavanah: A Meditation for Adar	145
At the Gates of Adar	145
Poem of the Month: *Shir Samei-ach* ("A Happy Song")	146
Must We Be Happy? Always?	148
The Joy in Incompleteness	150
The Faces of Janus	154
A Matter of Time: Adar I	156
Everything Turned Upside Down: Switching Gender on Purim	160
Purim Sheini: A Second Purim	163
Prayer of the Month: Esther Does *T'shuvah*	166

Nisan — 169
- *Kavanah:* A Meditation for Nisan — 171
- At the Gates of Nisan — 172
- Poem of the Month:
  - When Taharlev Met Ibn Ezra: *Kotnot Pasim Lavash HaGan* ("The Garden Donned Coats of Many Colors") — 173
    - Why Is This Night Different—and What Is Still the Same? — 177
    - O Brother, Where Art Thou? — 181
    - Women at the Seder: Speaking Out of Order? — 184
    - Lots of Flavors of Mimouna — 189
    - How (and Where) Are We to Remember the Holocaust? — 193
    - "They Must Be Whole": *S'firat HaOmer* / The Counting of the Omer — 198
- Prayer of the Month: The Prayer for Dew (*Tal*) — 205

Iyar — 207
- *Kavanah:* A Meditation for Iyar — 209
- At the Gates of Iyar — 209
- Poem of the Month: HaTikvah ("The Hope") — 210
  - The Twilight Hour: Between Yom HaZikaron and Yom HaAtzma-ut — 213
  - Who Are the Ones Who Remember—and Who Is Remembered? — 216
  - The Farmer and Chagall's Floating Jews — 221
  - How Many Types of Food Bless the Land of Israel? — 225
  - Hebrew, Revived—Part II — 229
  - Lag BaOmer: *Yahrzeit*, Might, and New Light — 232
- Prayer of the Month: *Al HaNisim* for Yom HaAtzma-ut — 236

Sivan — 239
- *Kavanah:* A Meditation for Sivan — 241
- At the Gates of Sivan — 242
- Poem of the Month:
  - *Saleinu Al K'teifeinu* ("Our Baskets Are on Our Shoulders") — 243
    - Shavuot: It Grows on You — 246
    - First Fruits, Many Words — 250
    - "Honey and Milk Are Under Your Tongue": Food for Body and Soul — 255
    - Ruth and Joining the Jewish People — 258
  - "And the Torah in One's Mouth Shall Be Sweet":
    - Rites of Initiation into Torah Study — 262
  - The (Forgotten) Fast of the Twentieth of Sivan:
    - Three Stops on the Journey of Mourning — 266
- Prayer of the Month: *Akdamut Milin* — 269

Tammuz	275
Kavanah: A Meditation for Tammuz	277
At the Gates of Tammuz	278
Poem of the Month: *Atanu L'cha* ("We Have Come before You")	279
On the Importance of Taking a Break	281
To Die in Tammuz: Some Thoughts on Alienation and Identity	285
Crying Over You, Tammuz	288
Long Live the Protest!	291
Prayer of the Month:	
Prayer for the Welfare of Schoolchildren on Vacation	295
Av	297
Kavanah: A Meditation for Av	299
At the Gates of Av	299
Poem of the Month: *Eish Tukad B'kirbi* ("A Fire Is Kindled within Me")	301
"The Face of Tishah B'Av": The Tenacity of Memory	305
By the Rivers of Babylon, We Were Like Dreamers	309
Jewish Phantom Pain: On the Temple That Was Destroyed	313
We Want *Mashiach* (Messiah) Now?	317
Tu B'Av (Fifteenth of Av): Celebrating in the Vineyards	321
Prayer of the Month: Praying for Love	325
Elul	329
Kavanah: A Meditation for Elul	331
At the Gates of Elul	332
Poem of the Month: The Stuff of Which Life Is Made:	
Psalm 27, "The Eternal Is My Light and My Deliverance"	334
An Unapologetic Look at *S'lichot*	338
Lamaze for Creation: Shofar during Elul	342
The First of Elul: Rosh HaShanah for the Animals	346
Prayer of the Month: The Thirteen Attributes,	
"Which Do Not Come Back Empty-Handed"	351
Afterword	355
Glossary	357
Diagram of the Hebrew Calendar Year	363
Sources, Permissions, and Notes	365
About the Author	377

FOREWORD
Rabbi David Ellenson, PhD

MARTIN BUBER once observed that a teacher is simply one who has trod further down a path than the student. The hope of the teacher is that the student will master that path and one day create pathways of their own. As one who taught Dalia Marx, I can say that this hope is realized in *From Time to Time: Journeys in the Jewish Calendar*. She was my student. Dalia Marx is now my teacher. She will become yours as well as you read and are inspired by this book.

I first met Dalia Marx twenty-five years ago, when I was a professor at Hebrew Union College–Jewish Institute of Religion in Jerusalem. At that time, she enrolled in a class I was teaching in Jewish liturgy at HUC–JIR. As a "typical Israeli," her background in Jewish liturgical traditions was limited. However, her intellectual curiosity, her natural drive, her brilliant mind, and a native proficiency in Hebrew that gave her access to the classical, literary, and cultural traditions of Judaism and the Jewish people soon showed me how irrelevant the oft-cited binary dividing "secular" and "religious" in Israel was. A tenth-generation Israeli, Marx was clearly exceptional by any standard. Her term paper on the *Aleinu* prayer still stands out in my mind as one of the most outstanding seminar papers I ever read in almost five decades of teaching. Her talents were such that within six years she was ordained as a rabbi at HUC-JIR in both Cincinnati and Jerusalem and completed a doctorate in Jewish liturgy in the Hebrew Literature Department of Hebrew University under the direction of Avigdor Shinan, one of the premier scholars of Jewish studies in the world. Rabbi Dalia Marx, PhD, was then and is now extraordinary by any standard.

Rabbi Marx is currently the Rabbi Aaron D. Panken Professor of Midrash and Liturgy at HUC-JIR in Jerusalem. A prolific author and lecturer who writes and speaks in Hebrew, English, German, and Spanish, she is the chief editor of *T'filat HaAdam: Israeli Reform Prayer Book*, the official siddur of Israeli Reform Judaism. Her fame is now pronounced in both Israel and throughout the world, and her authorship of *From Time to Time* will only enhance that fame.

Rabbi Marx is arguably the foremost student of Jewish liturgy of her generation, and this book reflects her unique genius. No one could be more qualified or able than she to describe and mine the holidays and calendar of the Jewish people. *From Time to Time: Journeys in the Jewish Calendar* in many ways expresses and captures the most noble ambitions that informed both religious and cultural Zionism. This work fully represents the highest hopes both Rav Kook and Achad HaAm had for the Zionist enterprise. Rav Kook dreamt of Jewish national renewal in religious terms and believed that a newborn Zion is where the "old would be renewed and the new would be made holy." Complementing this religious vision was the notion Achad HaAm put forth that the future Zion would be a *merkaz ruchani*, a spiritual center that would facilitate the revival of Jewish culture in Israel and breathe life into Jewish existence in the Diaspora. He believed that the opportunity for the rejuvenation of Hebrew culture and the Jewish prophetic spirit was dependent upon the creation of a Jewish community in *Eretz Yisrael*, the Land of Israel, the ancient homeland of the Jewish people, that would preserve and foster new forms of Hebraic culture and Jewish tradition even as it would nurture the future organic development of the culture and the spirit of the Jewish people in both Israel and the world.

In the pages of *From Time to Time*, Marx covers the entirety of the Jewish year and the full gamut of celebrations and remembrances that are observed today by *Am Yisrael* in *Eretz Yisrael* and beyond. She opens old doors to traditional observances and holidays such as the High Holy Days, the Pilgrimage Festivals of Sukkot, Passover, and Shavuot, as well as Purim and Chanukah even as she shines new light and original perspectives that allow these occasions to be approached in novel and rich ways. For example, in keeping with contemporary insights and sensibilities regarding sexuality and gender, Rabbi Marx highlights how a deeper appreciation of Purim can emerge from an understanding that the holiday of Esther and Mordecai involves notions of gender transitions and crossings.

In addition, Rabbi Marx wrote for an Israeli audience in a way that is mindful of what the State of Israel and its diverse populations have contributed to the Jewish rhythm of life both within and beyond the borders of the State of Israel. Consequently, she brilliantly and movingly captures the poignancy of how the Memorial Day that marks the assassination of Prime Minister Rabin can be observed, and she sweetly introduces the reader to how Beta Israel (Ethiopian Jews) have introduced the holiday of Sigd into the Israeli calendar. However, rather than celebrating the Sigd as Jews in Ethiopia once did by praying in the direction of Jerusalem, the Ethiopian community in Israel now goes to Jerusalem and prays for the Ethiopian Jews who are yet to come, even as they lovingly recall their sisters and brothers who died while engaging in the hazardous journey that they had hoped would culminate in their *aliyah*. Of course, the Moroccan Mimouna at the conclusion of Passover and Yom HaZikaron and Yom HaAtzma-ut are also included, as are other rites and ceremonial occasions that mark the Israeli year. Given her feminist commitments, Rabbi Marx also presents a ceremony of candle lighting commemorating the ordination of Regina Jonas, the first woman rabbi privately ordained in Germany, on December 27.

Marx marks these and other occasions in the Jewish year by setting up a fixed pattern that informs the entire book. She treats each month of the year as the unique time it is and begins each chapter with a prayer of *kavanah* (intention) that captures its special spirit. Rabbi Marx then offers her own introduction to the month, selects a poem from either classical or modern sources that speaks to the special nature of the month, and then adds an additional overarching reflection on the different topics (*iyunim*) that she will take up as she approaches each month.

The range of sources cited to accomplish these tasks and realize and promote her understandings of the holidays is surely breathtaking. Rabbi Marx displays an encyclopedic knowledge of classical and modern sources, midrashim and *piyutim*, and offers commentary drawn from every era of Jewish tradition and every corner of the Jewish world in pursuit of her goals. She cites so-called religious and secular sources with equal facility, and the divisions one might normally expect to separate these two approaches to life collapse as she mines the spiritual depths found in each. Her ability to draw on academic resources and her talent for speaking in a personal voice abound in these pages and make this a book to savor throughout the year. *From Time to Time* offers the opportunity for reflection on the nature and rhythm of the Jewish year and provides for an unparalleled and rich journey through the Jewish year and its holidays.

Originally, this book was written by an Israeli for an Israeli audience. However, this translated edition not only provides insight into Israeli culture and religious expression, but also speaks more broadly to Jewish culture and Jewish religious expression as a whole. In this volume, Rabbi Marx instinctively grasps, as Rabbi Abraham Joshua Heschel wrote in his spiritual classic *The Sabbath*, that "Judaism is a religion of time aiming at the sanctification of time." Jewish religion "teaches us to be attached to holiness in time, to be attached to sacred events, to learn how to consecrate sanctuaries that emerge from the magnificent stream of a year."

Marx's book achieves what Heschel has here characterized as the thrust of Jewish holiday observance. *From Time to Time* constitutes a riveting panorama of the Jewish year and its holidays. Rabbi Marx consistently presents diverse perspectives and insights that often surprise and always engage the reader. Her sources highlight and extend familiar pathways by illuminating Jewish tradition in innovative ways. This book genuinely "renews the old and sanctifies the new" by approaching the Jewish calendar from angles old and new. It constitutes a treasure trove of the spirit that marks both modern Israel and present-day Judaism in all their fullness and diversity. It indicates that a Torah that renews and sanctifies Judaism and the Jewish people in both *Eretz Yisrael* and the *T'futzot* (Diaspora) continues to come forth from Zion.

From Time to Time displays the modesty and contains the wisdom to carve out multiple paths to Jewish life and meaning. In this volume, Rabbi Marx proves herself a matchless spiritual guide for Jews and others who look to the Jewish year for meaning. This work displays Jewish creativity and depth at its best.

> **Rabbi David Ellenson**, PhD, is chancellor emeritus of Hebrew Union College–Jewish Institute of Religion, where he also served as president from 2001 to 2013 and again from 2018 to 2019. He was the director of the Schusterman Center for Israel Studies and is currently professor emeritus of Near Eastern and Judaic studies at Brandeis University. Rabbi Ellenson was ordained by HUC-JIR in 1977 and received his PhD from Columbia University in 1981. A scholar of modern Jewish thought and history, he has written extensively in these areas. His books include *After Emancipation: Jewish Religious Responses to Modernity* (2005), *Jewish Meaning in a World of Choice* (2014), and *American Jewish Thought Since 1934: Writings on Identity, Engagement, and Belief* (2020).

TRANSLATOR'S PREFACE
Rabbi Peretz A. Rodman

No one gets to know a book the way a translator does. It has been a pleasure and an education to render this work by my friend and colleague Rabbi Dalia Marx, PhD, into an English edition. While my assignment from the publisher was to adapt the book for an English-speaking readership, I have labored not to shed or even dim the Israeli character of the work, because that is its greatest value for non-Israeli readers: its voice is that of an Israeli rabbi and scholar, and her perspective should enrich readers' appreciation for both the Jewish calendar cycle and the unique nature of Jewish life in contemporary *Eretz Yisrael*.

The translations from the Torah are from CCAR Press's 2005 Plaut edition, and other translations from the Hebrew Bible are based on the 1986 edition of the *Tanakh* by the Jewish Publication Society, those from the Mishnah are based on Herbert Danby's 1933 translation for Oxford University Press, and those from the Babylonian Talmud are based on the Soncino Press edition in English—but all have undergone adaptation for reasons of style and context. Other translations from classical sources are largely my own, as are those from medieval and modern texts for which no other translator is credited.

Rafael Chaiken and Rabbi Anne Villarreal-Belford of the CCAR Press have demonstrated patience, encouragement, and good humor throughout the months during which the translation has been produced. The staff of the Zalman and Ayala Abramov Library at HUC-JIR's Jerusalem campus, headed by Rabbi Dr. Tamar Duvdevani, provided their usual kind and gracious assistance. The assistance of a number of relatives and friends (too numerous to mention here) as readers and hosts is much appreciated, and even more so the patience and encouragement of my wife, Miriam Laufer.

Throughout this tour of literary sources from the ancient Near East, the Eastern Mediterranean world of late antiquity, medieval Jewish communities, and modern Hebrew culture, I have been aware of the privilege I have enjoyed of acquiring skills and knowledge from many of the world's finest scholars and teachers of Jewish studies at Brandeis University, Hebrew College, the Hebrew University of Jerusalem, and the Schechter Rabbinical Seminary. One instructor in particular, Dr. David Simha Segal, taught me to let go of the linguistic features of a source text and remake it in a new language, a daunting and exhilarating practice. To him I am especially grateful.

None of those who helped enable me to undertake this work bear responsibility for any errors of interpretation or language, of course. Those errors are the components of this book that are uniquely mine.

Rabbi Peretz A. Rodman is an American-Israeli rabbi, teacher, writer, and translator who was educated in Jewish studies and Hebrew linguistics at Brandeis University, Hebrew College, the Hebrew University, and the Schechter Rabbinical Seminary. He has been a visiting rabbi and scholar at congregations from Los Angeles to Beijing, a lecturer at Brandeis University, Hebrew College, Hebrew Union College–Jewish Institute of Religion (Jerusalem), and the Hebrew University, and a contributor to My Jewish Learning (myjewishlearning.com), TheTorah.com, and numerous popular and academic publications. He serves as *av beit din* (chair) of the Masorti (Conservative) rabbinical court in Israel.

PREFACE

Summer and winter, spring and fall,
Wide open sea and rivers all,
Mountain and forest, flower and bush,
Limber grasses green and lush,
The wand'ring light like a prince enthralled,
The chill of silver, the heat of gold,
Turn round and round in the wheel of the year,
Drift on and on in the seasons of the year,
Along with you in the seasons of the year.
—DAHLIA RAVIKOVITCH[1]

WHAT IS TIME? What is this slippery, uncontrollable element in our lives? The thing that sometimes flies at top speed and sometimes refuses to budge? The thing that moves babies to start turning over on their bellies, sit up, stand, and grow into children, that causes the young to grow tall and adds the graceful touch of silver hair to older people? How can we define the constant, inscrutable flow that we call "time"?

Ever since ancient times, people have endeavored to understand time and control it by dividing it into measurable units: hours, days, months, and years. This division grants us a certain sense of control over our lives and that unrestrainable demon we call time. Holidays and observances enable us to focus attention on experiences and memories, to sort and store them in particular emotional and intellectual drawers. Taking stock of our lives is what Jews do on Yom Kippur, but Purim should have a good measure of lighthearted celebration. How would our lives look if every day were Purim or, alternatively, Yom Kippur? There has to be some kind of order. Measuring time and subjecting it to discipline is the basis of all culture. "Teach us to count our days rightly," says King David, the sweet singer of Israel, "that we may obtain a wise heart" (Psalm 90:12).[2]

༄

The goal I have set for myself with this book is to open windows and doors to our calendar, to air out rooms that have been closed for a long time, to illuminate hidden places, and to do my part in broadening our shared tent, as the prophet Isaiah put it, "Enlarge the site of your tent, let the cloths of your dwelling extend. Do not stint! Lengthen the ropes, and then drive the pegs firm" (Isaiah 54:2).

Each month in the year has its own character, its own special flavors and aromas. I have tried to bring them into these pages. **Each chapter** is a deep dive into one of the Hebrew year's twelve months, according to a fixed structure: a *kavanah* (intention) prayer, an introduction, a "Poem of the Month," sections (which I call *iyunim*)

At the beginning of each **monthly chapter**, I have cited information about the name of the month. I have also noted the month's zodiac sign, the tribe of the month, and the stone of the High Priest's breastplate associated with that month.³

Songs are part of the way so many of us think about the world around us. Many Hebrew songs—folk melodies, old and new popular Israeli tunes, religious melodies—are referenced throughout this book. Since it is not possible for us to include a recording of every song discussed, we encourage you to look for recordings of these songs online.

Iyun literally means "study, deliberation, meditation, reflection." The plural of *iyun* is *iyunim*. In this book, an *iyun* signifies a unique section devoted to a specific topic about the Hebrew month.

that examine a series of topics, and a "Prayer of the Month." The *kavanah* is an intention-setting prayer or meditation that spells out my wishes for all of us during each particular month. The short introduction to each chapter, labeled "At the Gates of . . . ," previews the *iyunim* sections. In each chapter, I have highlighted a **poem**, song, or *piyut* (liturgical poem) written for or mentioning the month's events. The *iyunim* sections address various subjects that arise from the nature or events of the month. The Prayer of the Month might be a prayer recited during a particular month or another prayer that illuminates an aspect of the month. There are numerous sidebars alongside the text, where I have placed midrashim (exegesis), supplementary *piyutim*, thoughts, and additional materials.

Friends who read drafts of the various chapters commented that I adopt different styles and voices in the different *iyunim* sections. I was happy to receive those responses. Pluralism and diversity are important elements in the message of the book. I profoundly believe in the power of these values. Different topics require different voices and varied approaches. By design, the narrative voice in this book is sometimes personal and sometimes academic. Sometimes the perspective is historical, and sometimes it is cultural and religious.

It is also important to me to challenge the supposed contradiction between what is considered "religious" and "secular," presenting the entire range of the Jewish discourse in Israel and beyond. Even if there is a degree of criticism here and there, it was always written out of love and belonging.

As a Jewish woman born in Jerusalem, a rabbi and a scholar of liturgy, and a professor at Hebrew Union College–Jewish Institute of Religion, it is important to me to weave together both old and new, feminine and masculine, Western and Eastern, familiar and less familiar throughout the book. I sought to include Jewish voices from different eras and places that express a range of positions and trends of thought. The criterion for focusing on specific subjects, additional texts, and poetry was first and foremost the quality of the material rather than a technical attempt to present all voices. I was happy to see that what emerged from my keyboard reflected the beneficial and fruitful diversity I had hoped for. I have not attempted to encompass everything. After all, this is not an encyclopedic work. I merely wanted to offer suggestions for thought, conversation, and even healthy debate.

Originally, this book was written by an Israeli for Israelis, but this translation attempts to offer insight not only into Israeli culture and religious expression but also more broadly into Jewish culture and Jewish religious expression. This English volume also seeks to be inclusive of the experiences of people who live in English-speaking countries. At the same time, many of the prayers and poems appear in both English and Hebrew, because I want to share the power and beauty I find in the Hebrew language. Even if you cannot read the Hebrew, I hope that the image of the original text is powerful in and of itself.

Where does this book fit in one's life? What is its place? I envision it near the family dining table or next to the bed, in the synagogue or community center or office, in a bookcase at home or the backpack on a trip, in the informal educator's drawer or on the teacher's desk.

I invite you to come along on this journey through our calendar year—the Jewish one, the Israeli one—ancient but always in the process of renewal. You can read the book from cover to cover, take it month by month, or even *iyun* to *iyun*, reading about each month's special days and events as they arrive. I do not expect you to agree with everything I wrote. In fact, I will be happy if what you read stimulates your own new thoughts and encourages you to set off on additional journeys to ancient and modern destinations, both far and near.

From Time to Time is dedicated to the loving memory of our teacher, leader, and friend, Rabbi Dr. Aaron D. Panken, *z"l*, the former president of Hebrew Union College–Jewish Institute of Religion, who was taken from us too early.

TOV L'HODOT
How Good It Is to Give Thanks

Work on this book was spread out over nearly a decade. How good and how pleasant it is to express my thanks to all the people who helped the book emerge into the light of day!

Thanks are due to my teacher and friend Rabbi Dr. David Ellenson, who introduced me to the world of Jewish prayer. He has been and remains a dear and beloved presence in my life and that of my family for almost three decades. David—I thank you for the abundant wisdom and knowledge I acquired from you and for the (way too) generous introduction you wrote for this book.

There is no doubt the dedicated and skilled effort of Rabbi Peretz Rodman was essential to the creation of the English version of the book. His work was profound and thorough and his translation of poetry exemplary. People keep stopping me on the street to let me know he contacted them about their contribution to this volume! Thank you, Peretz, for this beautiful translation.

The English edition would not have been possible without the leadership of Rabbi Hara Person, chief executive of the Central Conference of American Rabbis (CCAR); thank you, Hara, for your friendship and vision. I am grateful to Rafael Chaiken, director of CCAR Press, who proved to be a valuable and insightful partner as we navigated the (somewhat long!) process of English publication. Thank you also to Rabbi Annie Villarreal-Belford, editor at CCAR Press, for your wisdom, friendship, and dedication, for our many and sometimes hilarious WhatsApp exchanges, and for your extremely professional and patient care and attention in being able to express and reflect in English what my heart and mind say in Hebrew. I cannot wait to meet you in person! Assistant editor Chiara Ricisak provided enormous assistance in securing permissions and checking all the sources—not an easy task!—and keeping all the pieces moving. Raquel Fairweather-Gallie, marketing and sales manager, helped make sure this book reached far into the world, and Deborah Smilow, CCAR Press operations manager, made sure everything behind the scenes flowed as smoothly as possible; thank you both. Debra Hirsch Corman carefully copyedited, Michelle Kwitkin thoroughly proofread, and Scott-Martin Kosofsky elegantly adapted the original design into the English edition. Thank you all for your incredible work.

In particular, I want to thank Lisa Messinger, whose tireless work to honor Rabbi Dr. Aaron D. Panken, *z"l*, led to the funding to support this book and indeed my professorship as the Rabbi Aaron D. Panken Professor of Liturgy and Midrash at HUC-JIR in Jerusalem. It is an honor to carry Rabbi Panken's name in my professorship and in the publication of this book, and I am grateful beyond measure for your support.

One of the most pleasant things about writing this book was the encounters with people who contributed their own writing and the conversations that took place with them. I wish to extend unbounded thanks to the people who read and commented on parts of the manuscript, adding to the manuscript and, when necessary, chastising me. Many thanks to Rabbi David Ariel-Joel and Rabbi Dr. Tamar Duvdevani, who read the manuscript. Thanks to all those who read individual chapters of the book and shared their comments with me and to those who have contributed their works for the enhancement of this book: Talma Alyagon-Rose, Rabbi Dr. Yehoyada Amir, Orit Amiri, Rabbi Talia Avnon-Benveniste, Maya Bartal, Shoshana Ben-Dor, Yochi Brandes, Rabbi Gila Caine, Rabbi Naama Dafni-Kellen, Rabbi Tamar Elad-Appelbaum, Dr. Marcia Falk, Dr. Netanel Fisher, Rabbi Dr. Shlomo Fox, Vicky Franco Sharzman , Yehudit Ginger, Rabbi Esteban Gottfried, Dr. Melila Hellner-Eshed, Dr. Yizhar Hess, Anat Hoffman, Rabbi Myra Hovav Katz, Dr. Anat Israeli, Zeev Kainan, Tamar Katzir, Rabbi Naamah Kelman, Dr. Admiel Kosman, Rabbi Dr. Binyamin Lau, Dr. Jacqueline Laznow, Rabbi Maya Leibovich, Rabbi Alona Lisitsa, Sheikha Ibtisam Mahmid, Dr. Yaakov Maoz, Shira Marx-Sapunar, Rabbi Noa Mazor, Rabbi Ofek Meir, Rabbi Oshrat Morag, Dr. Vered Noam, Anat Ophir, Rabbi Dr. Renana Peres, Dr. Avner Peretz, Rabbi Orna Pilz, Rabbi Dan Prath, Shanni Reiff Profesorsky, Rabbi Mira Regev, Rabbi Uri Regev, Dahlia Reich, Rabbi Amnon Ribak, Dr. Ruvik Rosenthal, Rabbi Moti Rotem, Rabbi Chaya Rowen-Baker, Rabbi Ofer Sabath Beit Halachmi, Rabbi Rinat Safania, Rabbi Noa Sattath, Rabbi Dr. Shalom Sharon, Dr. Avigdor Shinan, Dr. Yoav Silbert, Rabbi Ariel Tovlev, Aharon Varady, Rabbi Ari Vernon, Dr. Zvia Walden, Dr. Ruhama Weiss, Sharona Yekutiel, and Rabbi Gili Zidkiyahu. Thanks are due as well to Beit Avi Chai, which published earlier versions of several of the *iyunim* sections. Prayers and *kavanot* that are unattributed are my own compositions.

The Hebrew version of the book was published with the generous support of the Hebrew Union College–Jewish Institute of Religion, with the participation of the International Movement of Progressive Judaism. I want to express my deep appreciation to Rabbis Naamah Kelman, Dr. Michael Marmur, Gilad Kariv, and Mira Regev. Thanks are due as well to the people of Yediot Books, the publisher of the original Hebrew version, and especially Amichai Berholz, Sarit Blonder, and Zeev Kainan. I am grateful to the people of Dov Abramson Studio: Nava Ghiat, Aharon Friedman, Noa Imbar, Elad Lifschitz, and, of course, Dov Abramson himself.

Thanks as well to the websites that have made the treasures of our people's wisdom accessible to all: The Piyut and Tefillah Website (maintained by the National Library of Israel, nli.org.il), Project Ben-Yehuda (benyehuda.org), Zemereshet (zemereshet.co.il), and others. I have endeavored to give credit to all those quoted here and to receive their permission, but if errors have crept in, I would be happy to correct them in future editions. I would also be very glad for readers to share additional insights.

Finally, I want to share a special thanks that words are unable to fully encompass: to my husband, Roly, and my children, Tom and his wife Iris, Niv, and Noam. Thank you for being you. How good and how pleasant it is to traverse with you the paths of life and the course of the days and the years.

TISHREI

Zodiac Sign: Libra | Tribe of the Month: Dan | Breastplate Stone: Jacinth/*Leshem*

The Hebrew name of this month, Tishrei, is derived from its Babylonian name, Tashritu, an Akkadian word meaning "beginning." As the months are counted in our time, Tishrei is indeed the first month of the year, but in the biblical count, it is the seventh month. Perhaps the name indicates the beginning of the second half of the year or the onset of the rainy season in the Land of Israel.

This month has other names as well. In the Torah, it is called *HaChodesh HaSh'vi-i*, "the seventh month" (Leviticus 23:24). At the time of Solomon, or perhaps even earlier, each month was given its own name, aside from its ordinal number. Our month was called *Yerach HaEitanim*, "the month of power/powerful ones," one of the five months whose ancient Hebrew names we still know.

Kavanah: A Meditation for Tishrei

"Eternal, our God, make this a blessed year . . . and fill our hands with Your blessings and the abundant gifts of Your hands" (from the ninth blessing of the winter *Amidah*, according to the Sephardic rite).

With the start of a new year, I give thanks for the ability to choose, to change things, to change and be changed. Rosh HaShanah is a reminder of the marvelous gift we have been given—the ability to make a change. Along with the recognition that there are things that have happened that cannot be changed, we are reminded that much is still in our hands, subject to our choice.

Everything Changes
   Bertolt Brecht

Everything changes. You can
Begin anew with your very last breath.
But what has been, has been. And the water
You once poured into the wine, you can never
   drain off again.

What has been, has been. The water
That you poured into the wine, you can
Never drain off again. But
Everything changes. You can
Begin anew with your very last breath.[1]

תְּהֵא הַשָּׁנָה הַזֹּאת	**May This Year Be**
שְׁנַת אַהֲבָה	A year of **a**mple sustenance
שְׁנַת בְּרָכָה	A year of **b**lessing
שְׁנַת גְּדִילָה	A year of **c**reativity
שְׁנַת דְּרִישַׁת טוֹב	A year of **d**eep breaths
שְׁנַת הַשְׁרָאָה	A year of **e**nergy and concentration
שְׁנַת וִתּוּר	A year of **f**riendship
שְׁנַת זִכְרוֹנוֹת יָפִים	A year of **g**rowth and **g**oodness
שְׁנַת חֲבֵרוּת אֱמֶת	A year of **h**ealth and **h**ope
שְׁנַת טוֹב	A year of **i**nspiration and **i**ndependence
שְׁנַת יְצִירָה	A year of **j**ustice
שְׁנַת כֹּחוֹת חֲדָשִׁים	A year of **k**eeping faith
שְׁנַת לִמּוּד	A year of **l**ove and **l**earning
שְׁנַת מֶרֶץ וְנִמְרָצוּת	A year of **m**emories to savor
שְׁנַת נְשִׁימָה עֲמֻקָּה	A year of **n**ew energy
שְׁנַת סַבְלָנוּת	A year of **o**pportunity
שְׁנַת עַצְמָאוּת	A year of **p**atience
שְׁנַת פַּרְנָסָה טוֹבָה	A year of **q**uestions asked and **q**uestions answered
שְׁנַת צֶדֶק	A year of **r**estoration and **r**epair
שְׁנַת קוֹר רוּחַ	A year of **s**incerity
שְׁנַת רְפוּאָה	A year of **t**rue friendship
שְׁנַת שָׁלוֹם	A year of **u**nderstanding
שְׁנַת תִּקְוָה	A year of well-being and peace
שְׁנַת תִּקּוּן	A year of **e**xtending our hands to others
שְׁנַת תֹּם לֵב	A year of **y**ielding to others
	A year of **z**estful living.
תְּהֵא הַשָּׁנָה הַזֹּאת	May this year be
שְׁנַת רַחֲמִים	a year of mercy
וְעֵת רָצוֹן מִלְּפָנֶיךָ	and divine goodwill
לָנוּ וּלְכָל בָּאֵי עוֹלָם	for us and for all who dwell in this world.

Tishrei Marcheshvan Kislev Tevet Sh'vat Adar Nisan Iyar Sivan Tammuz Av Elul

AT THE GATES OF TISHREI

FRESH NEW NOTEBOOKS, white, foreshadowing good things to come. Long, empty lines with the promise of being filled with wisdom and knowledge. That is Tishrei. The scent of the new books whose corners haven't yet been bent and wrinkled and in whose margins there not yet any doodles from boring classes. The new pencils still unsharpened, with their ends not yet gnawed and nibbled. That is Tishrei. Tishrei is the squill lilies flowering along the roads, the ripe pomegranates and quinces. Tishrei is the sky changing right before the farmers' eyes. Tishrei is the heart that is not yet tired of hoping and yearning, it is the song *Lu Y'hi*, "all that we ask for—let it be." That's it. We are starting a new year.

Tishrei is a month of rapid transitions. We go from the festivity of Rosh HaShanah to the gravity of Yom Kippur, and from there we go out into nature—to Sukkot and Simchat Torah. Tishrei invites us to move from the family's holiday table to the synagogue and on to the sukkah and the street and finally to folk dancing on Simchat Torah.

The Sages of the Talmud debate about when the world was created. Rabbi Eliezer ben Horcanos says, "In Tishrei the world was created" (Babylonian Talmud, *Rosh HaShanah* 10b). In his view, Tishrei is the original month of the world's birth, the time of its creation. Creation was not a one-time event, but rather the world is created anew each day, day after day; we along with it are created and create, renew and are renewed. In Tishrei we mark the first Creation—the original creation. Tishrei is an opportunity to take stock of ourselves and to take responsibility for our lives, to expand our circle of responsibility with ripples that grow ever wider across our community, our country, and our world.

Each month in this book explores a number of different topics or themes, which I call *iyun* or *iyunim* (plural). On the next few pages, you will find *iyunim* of six dimensions of the holidays in Tishrei (with no claim to it being an exhaustive list). The first *iyun* addresses that most slippery of concepts, time, and examines its connection to the Tishrei holidays. The second *iyun* examines *Un'taneh Tokef*, a hair-raising liturgical poem that invites us to grapple with the fragile elements of our lives as Jews and as human beings. In the third *iyun* we will explore whether forgiveness—real forgiveness—is at all possible, and a practical suggestion will be offered. In the fourth *iyun*, we will seek out the ancient sources of the *Kol Nidrei* ritual enacted just before Yom Kippur and will inquire into the secret of that dry-as-dust legal formula that has become so central to the Yom Kippur experience. The fifth *iyun* addresses the holiday of Sukkot and the sukkah itself, aiming at a "reading" of that temporary structure as a cultural and spiritual symbol. In the sixth and last *iyun*, we turn our attention to Simchat Torah, a relatively late holiday that took shape in the Diaspora.

Because Tishrei is replete with holidays, we offer a few prayers in this chapter, each one connected to a different holiday: the special blessings on foods for Rosh HaShanah evening, new and surprising confessional prayers for Yom Kippur, suggestions for special new *ushpizin* guests on Sukkot, and ancient and modern prayers for rain for Sh'mini Atzeret.

POEM OF THE MONTH

Achot K'tanah ("Little Sister")

The *piyut* (liturgical poem) "Little Sister," composed by Rabbi Avraham Chazan of Gerona, a Sephardic poet of the thirteenth century, brings us across the abyss between the year that was and the year that will be. Rabbi Avraham was one among a group of kabbalists in that city, which was then a prominent center of Jewish mystical teachings. This *piyut* is sung at the beginning of the Rosh HaShanah evening service, most commonly in Sephardic synagogues. This is a dramatic moment, one that helps us to separate from the year that has passed and welcome the new year as it arrives.

The phrase "little sister" is a code name for the people Israel, based on a common Rabbinic interpretation of the line "We have a little sister" in Song of Songs 8:8. Here, the sister who recites her prayers and addresses her Creator in song says goodbye to the passing year, with its difficulties and problems, and prays, "Let the year end, with its curses" (based on the Babylonian Talmud, *M'gillah* 31b). In the final stanza the little sister now greets the new year, and the refrain shifts its gaze to the future: "Let the year begin, with its blessings."

These are the first two and final stanzas of this poem, in which the poet discreetly displays his name in an alphabetical acrostic at the beginning of each stanza:

In a poem cycle "My Little Sister" (אֲחוֹתִי קְטַנָּה, *Achoti K'tanah*), poet and Holocaust survivor Abba Kovner describes the fate of a young girl, a little sister, in the Holocaust. Kovner, too, borrows the image of a little sister from the Song of Songs, but this image could not be more different from the one in the *piyut*. Kovner concludes one of the poems with a question:

> My home carried its roots
> to the stake.
> With what—
> with what, little sister,
> shall we spin and weave the dream now?²

Yet there are similarities between the two poems: the *piyut* refers to the Jewish people's tribulations—and that is also the central topic of Kovner's poem. And both Kovner and Rabbi Avraham look toward the future: a bit of warmth that will "spin and weave the dream," making continued life possible.

Little Sister
  Rabbi Avraham Chazan of Gerona

The little sister—her prayers
she proclaims and voices her praises:
Please, O God, please cure her ailments.
  Let the year end, with its curses.

Sweetly she calls out to You
and with song and praises, as befits You.
When will you stop averting Your eyes
  and see?
Strangers are devouring her patrimony.
  Let the year end, with its curses.
. . . .
Be strong and rejoice for the plunder has
  ended;
place hope in the Rock, who keeps the
  covenant.
You will ascend to Zion and God will say:
Pave! Pave its paths!
  Let the year begin, with its blessings!

אֲחוֹת קְטַנָּה
רִבִּי אַבְרָהָם חַזָּן גְרוֹנְדִי

אֲחוֹת קְטַנָּה תְּפִלּוֹתֶיהָ
עוֹרְכָה וְעוֹנָה תְּהִלּוֹתֶיהָ
אֵל נָא רְפָא נָא לְמַחֲלוֹתֶיהָ
תִּכְלֶה שָׁנָה וְקִלְלוֹתֶיהָ.

בְּנֹעַם מִלִּים לְךָ תִּקְרָאֶה
וְשִׁיר וְהִלּוּלִים כִּי לְךָ נָאֶה
עַד מָה תַּעְלִים עֵינְךָ וְתֵרָאֶה
זָרִים אוֹכְלִים נַחֲלוֹתֶיהָ
תִּכְלֶה שָׁנָה וְקִלְלוֹתֶיהָ.
. . . .
חִזְקוּ וְגִילוּ כִּי שֹׁד גָּמַר
לָצוּר הוֹחִילוּ בִּרִיתוֹ שָׁמַר
לָכֶם וְתַעֲלוּ לְצִיּוֹן וְאָמַר
סֹלּוּ סֹלּוּ מְסִלּוֹתֶיהָ
תָּחֵל שָׁנָה וּבִרְכוֹתֶיהָ.

Human Time, Cosmic Time

THE SHIFTS IN NATURE between day and night, summer and winter, the dry and the rainy seasons are all evident. Much less evident, though, are the precise moments when they occur—the moment when the day begins, the moment when the summer is over.

For example, during the British Mandate era (1920–48), there were roiling debates in Israel over **daylight saving time**, demonstrating that the nexus between the clock and the seasons is much less obvious and unequivocal than we may think. While these debates are largely in the past and now there is greater agreement over daylight saving time in Israel, the debate continues in the United States. Two states opt out of changing their clocks twice a year, and general resistance to the practice seems to be growing. The debates in both countries reflect the ongoing tension between the seasons, the time on the clock, and the pages of the calendar.

Daylight saving time is the practice of changing clocks according to the seasons of the year, usually by moving the clock an hour ahead during the summertime. The goal of this summertime practice is greater overlap of the daylight hours with common hours of activity, for the sake of saving energy. Daylight saving time, first introduced in practice in North America and Central Europe during the early years of the twentieth century, was established in pre-state Palestine in 1940 and applied only intermittently from then until the establishment of the State of Israel, when the new Ministry of the Interior put it in place in 1948. Since then, various changes have been made in the length of Israel's *shaon hakayitz* (literally "timepiece of the summer," as daylight saving time is known in Hebrew), and there were a few years during which it was suspended entirely. Those changes stemmed in part from debates about its economic benefit and the opposition of the religious parties in the Knesset, whose members were concerned the time change might lead to the desecration of Shabbat or holidays. At the time of this book's publication, Israel's daylight saving time begins at the end of March, when Israelis lose an hour of sleep, only to gain it back with the return to standard time at the end of October.

Still, when Elul arrives, we hope that the cooling autumn winds will begin to blow on us; however, we are likely to be disappointed, because nature is not disciplined and does not always heed the markings of the calendar. Still, the sun shines each day (because after all, the sun does not really rise or set but stays in place!), day follows day, and night follows night; the hours of light grow shorter and then again grow longer; the seasons change, and a coat, a scarf, and gloves replace a thin shirt and sandals, and then they return again in an endless cycle.

It is precisely at the time of the transition between seasons, when our human nature seems especially fragile and ready to crumble, that we recognize—perhaps desperately so—that there is a special dimension to our existence as humans. We remind ourselves, in Ecclesiastes's words, that "humans have no advantage over beasts" (Ecclesiastes 3:19). We try to believe that we can seek out the exalted and the sanctified, that it is possible to have our social nature rule over and control our animal nature. Every culture expresses this in its own way.

Rosh HaShanah is a festive moment in which we mark both endings and beginnings. It is a liminal moment, a moment that places us on the threshold or border. We are no longer in the year that was, nor really in the year that is now beginning—and at the same time we are in both. By their very nature, liminal moments cause discomfort and even anxiety, and such feelings seek out relief and release. Perhaps the Rabbis were speaking about precisely this "in-between" feeling when they said, "The Adversary [*satan*, the angel who challenges our faith] makes accusations only at a time of danger" (*B'reishit Rabbah* 91:9).

At moments of transition, when we are suspended from the usual flow of life, we gain an opportunity to examine the everyday reality of our lives and remember that it should not be taken for granted. These are times set aside and intended for reflection and creative thought. Rosh HaShanah and the Days of Awe are such times. Instead of starting the year with fireworks and bottles of champagne, the Jewish tradition invites us into a month of preparation, reflection, and introspection by taking stock of our lives. It is a month of examining what we have done right and what we need to correct, especially in our relations with others. The *Tashlich* ceremony, for example, helps us define what we want to get rid of in our behavior and relationships, and helps us refine our intentions for the new year. So, too, Yom Kippur's confessional prayer, *Vidui*, invites us to conduct a similar self-assessment. The *Vidui* is phrased in the first person plural—*ashamnu, bagadnu, gazalnu*, "We have incurred guilt, we have been unfaithful, we have robbed" (see pp. 35–39)—and is an invitation to join with those around us in acknowledgment that we are part of a community, a congregation. Leaving the warmth of our houses and its comforts for the temporary setting of the sukkah is a similar acknowledgment.

> The British anthropologist Victor Turner (1920–83), who studied rites of passage in many cultures, said that those who experience such rites are in a state he called "sacred poverty." The person undergoing a rite is like raw matter that has lost its earlier form but has not yet taken on its new form. That situation, Turner said, has an important cultural function: it removes the individual from the continuous flow of daily life and offers an opportunity to test life's realities, which are normally taken for granted.³

Gatekeepers in the Face of Chaos

Like mushrooms proliferating after rain, what fills the streets of my home city Jerusalem just after Yom Kippur are the sukkot: sukkot with walls of wood or waterproof materials or impromptu walls of bedsheets, sukkot kits ready to be raised, and family sukkot that have been passed down for generations. The holiday of Sukkot is a holiday of exploring boundaries—between home and outdoors, between private and public, between permanent and temporary.

The Mishnah lists Sukkot as one of the four times a year when the world is judged: "On the holiday [of Sukkot] judgment is issued regarding water" (*Mishnah Rosh HaShanah* 1:2). This holiday is umbilically connected to water through the water libation in the ancient Temple, the way dwelling in the shade of the sukkah evokes the clouds that shaded the Israelites in the wilderness, and of course the Prayer for Rain recited with great fanfare on Sh'mini Atzeret. On the opposite side of Sukkot in the circle of the Jewish year is Passover, when we start reciting the counterpart to the Prayer for Rain, the Prayer for Dew (see pp. 205–6). Those two holidays, Sh'mini Atzeret and Passover, stand as the gatekeepers of the natural seasons in Israel, dividing the year into two nearly equal parts: the rainy season that begins around the autumnal equinox (when day and night are of equal length) at Sukkot, and the dry season that begins around the time of the vernal equinox at Passover (see pp. 76–79).

These two "gatekeepers"—the ritual moments of the prayers for rain on Sh'mini Atzeret and dew on Passover—both separate the seasons and bind them together. Our expectations for how nature will conduct itself find expression in the references to rain in the prayers of the rainy season. Those references organize what is lived by the community of worshipers, providing a response to their existential experience in the world around them.

In some parts of the world, of course, rain falls during very different seasons. The timing of the prayers for rain and for dew reflects the seasons most familiar to the Rabbis who lived in or near ancient Israel. Israelis today remain deeply aware of these ancient seasons.

Tishrei   Marcheshvan   Kislev   Tevet   Sh'vat   Adar   Nisan   Iyar   Sivan   Tammuz   Av   Elul

"Chaos, Be Gone!" Chaos as an Opportunity

The people who established Jewish prayer were entirely and directly dependent upon rain. In *Eretz Yisrael*, the ancient Land of Israel, a year of drought brought with it poverty and hunger; rain out of season, the kind that gets the crops wet and makes them rot, could bring about severe famine. The summer and the winter are distinct from each other, but the transitional periods between them are far less distinct: the winter arrives bit by bit, and we often find ourselves looking upward and asking whether the drops falling on our head are the first spring rain, known as the *yoreh*; only in retrospect can we say when we experienced the *malkosh*, the last rain. One of the important functions of ceremonies is their ability to channel chaotic and anarchic forces for the benefit of the social order and the individual's sanity. In this instance, the ritual moments of the prayers for rain and for dew sung with such festivity in many synagogues help us to "turn the page," announcing as they do: Behold, it is winter! Behold, it is summer!

These ceremonies, prayers, and ritual moments grant clothing, as it were, to the naked human experience, giving it both religious and existential meaning. They enable us to grapple with the sense of chaos that is an inherent part of living in a confusing world. In the Prayer for Rain, we ask, "Let [this season] be marked by a blessing and not a curse, for life and not for death, for satiety and not for hunger." Inherent in this statement is a quiet, dark awareness of the fact that what we pray for may not come to pass and that its absence may sadly mean the fulfillment of the dark side of that prayer's counterpoint.

Rituals recognize the power of disorder and its destructive potential. But that chaotic and anxiety-producing recognition is also a creative and productive force. The purpose of the ritual is also to expose us to chaos in a controlled manner, so that we can sample its threatening taste, in order to then bring us to a safe place where our reality can once again be grounded.[4] It is like the injection of an attenuated vaccine so that the body learns to fight the disease. Going out to the sukkah, with the rain that drips into the *Kiddush* cups, the evening chill, the wind that tugs off the decorations, the neighborhood critters that come into the sukkah at night and wreak havoc—all these are experiences of a controlled dose of chaos, of emerging from our comfortable, familiar places precisely to return to them fortified.

Praying for Rain While Desalinating Water

Israel desalinates over 500 million cubic meters (over 17.6 trillion cubit feet) of water a year in five different treatment plants. Undoubtedly, Israel leads the world in recycling water, treating wastewater from washing and bathing (known as "gray water") so it may be reused. Israel has considerably outpaced other countries in its use of recycled water for agricultural use. Ze'ev Kainan, an Israeli expert in water resources, explains that treated and desalinated water needs to be mixed with fresh water from nature, because the desalinated water lacks minerals needed by humans and essential for agriculture. Although there is much we can control, there are nonetheless elements we cannot produce on our own; we must still rely on nature.

The Sukkah: Between Nature and Culture

The sukkah, like other ritual symbols, is a cultural construction within nature, but it also preserves the character of nature and connects us to it. So, for example, the *s'chach* (thatch or branches) that forms the covering over the sukkah must be made from vegetation, but only if it is not still connected to the tree in the ground and thus no longer an organic part of nature. The *s'chach* must create more shade than it yields sunlight, but must nevertheless not obscure the view of the stars at night. It should, then, simultaneously separate and connect those who sit in the sukkah and the natural phenomena around them (see pp. 23–24).

"Let Us Proclaim the Power of This Day": Human Being, Nation, and World

ONLY WHEN I SPEND TIME outside Israel do I pay attention to what a unique and special atmosphere permeates Yom Kippur in Israel. The roads are silent and the air is suffused with sanctity, and that holiness is felt in the conversations among people who have slowed their pace. One sees children riding in circles on their bicycles on streets that have emptied of all vehicular traffic. This is not the only difference, though, between the experience of Yom Kippur inside and outside of Israel. If you ask Israelis to share the first thing that comes into their mind when they think of Yom Kippur, many of them will mention the Yom Kippur War (1973). The harsh shock of that war, which shattered the euphoria of invincibility sensed by Israelis in the years after the Six-Day War (1967), has not been forgotten. The trauma of 1973 enabled the voicing of long-suppressed doubts and existential questions that had been simmering under the surface of Israelis' consciousness; certainty about Israeli life was shown to rely on false feelings.

Un'taneh Tokef is one of the central *piyutim* in the High Holy Day liturgy, primarily in Ashkenazic congregations. At first it was recited on Rosh HaShanah; today it appears on Yom Kippur as well. Its chilling lines "Who will live and who will die, who will reach the ripeness of age, who will be taken before their time, who by fire and who by water . . ." express generations of our people's suffering and anxieties; in 1973, those words suddenly took on new and frightful meaning. Seventeen years after the Yom Kippur War smashed its way into our lives, Israeli composer Yair Rosenblum— impelled by his war experience—premiered new music for *Un'taneh tokef*.

Yair Rosenblum's *Un'taneh Tokef*

Yair Rosenblum (1944–96) was best known in Israel as the composer of songs performed by the military entertainment troupes. Among them are *Givat HaTachmoshet*, a popular ballad about the battle for Jerusalem's Ammunition Hill in 1967, and the widely known *Shir LaShalom*, "Song for Peace." In 1988, Rosenblum was invited to Kibbutz Beit HaShita in northern Israel to serve as musical director for the kibbutz's sixtieth anniversary. While there, he was deeply impressed by the memorial ceremonies that are customary at Beit HaShita, especially the profound grieving for the eleven members and young residents of the kibbutz who had been killed in the Yom Kippur War. The kibbutz had held memorial services on the eve of Yom Kippur since 1944. As part of the ceremonies that took shape over the 1980s, two kibbutz members, Shula and Hanoch Albalak, would sing some *piyutim* from the Yom Kippur prayers. The next day, a discussion would be held in the kibbutz dining hall about pressing communal and national concerns.

Rosenblum, along with Aryeh Ben-Gurion, the founder of the archive of inter-kibbutz holiday materials, chose specific texts to be set to music, among them *Un'taneh Tokef*, which Rosenblum composed while playing on a small electric keyboard. Hanoch Albalak premiered Rosenblum's melody for the *piyut* in 1990, and that performance

Un'taneh Tokef

Let us proclaim the power of this day—
a day whose holiness awakens deepest awe
and inspires highest praise for Your dominion;
may Your throne be established with grace,
for Your reign is a reign of truth.

In truth,
You are judge and plaintiff, counselor
 and witness.
You inscribe and seal. You record and recount.
You remember all that we have forgotten.
And when You open the Book of Memories,
it speaks for itself—
for every human hand leaves its mark,
 an imprint like no other.

And so a great shofar will cry—*t'kiah*.
A still small voice will be heard.
Angels, in a whirl of fear and trembling,
 will say:
"Behold the day of judgment"—
for they too are judged;
in Your eyes even they are not blameless.

All the inhabitants of the world pass
 before You like sheep before their shepherd.
As a shepherd considers the flock,
when it passes beneath the staff,
You count and consider every life.
You set the bound; You decide destiny;
You inscribe judgments.

On Rosh HaShanah it will be written;
on the Fast of Yom Kippur this is sealed:

How many will pass away from this world,
how many will be born into it;
who will live and who will die;
who will reach the ripeness of age,
who will be taken before their time;
who by fire and who by water;
who by war and who by beast;
who by famine and who by drought;
who by earthquake and who by plague;
who by strangling and who by stoning;
who will rest and who will wander;
who will be tranquil and who will be troubled;
who will be calm and who tormented;
who will live in poverty and who in prosperity;
who will be humbled and who exalted—
continued

---

stirred a strong emotional response among kibbutz members. Rosenblum's *Un'taneh Tokef* weaves together Ashkenazic and Sephardic musical motifs—some of which the composer recalled from his childhood synagogue—with motifs from Israeli folk songs. It was not guaranteed that a composition so complex and so theologically and emotionally demanding would become an Israeli standard, an instant classic—especially among those who labeled themselves as "secular"—but that is exactly what happened: the public perceived it as authentic because it emerged from real people and their lived experiences. Rosenblum repeatedly expressed concern that his setting for a liturgical poem might not be well received by members of the secular kibbutz.[5] His concern was for naught: his setting of the *piyut* was greeted warmly, and appreciation for Rosenblum's composition grows from year to year, in wider and increasingly diverse circles.[6]

In fact, its power was so great that in many synagogues, cantors began to sing *Un'taneh Tokef* to Rosenblum's melody. Thus the "secularized" composition, as it were, returned to its natural source. The *piyut* set to Rosenblum's music has almost become the theme song of the Days of Awe, not only because of the work's beauty and profundity but also because the composition unites three disparate worlds: the Jewish, the Israeli, and the human. In other words, Rosenblum's *Un'taneh Tokef* brings together elements from the historical, the local, and the existential planes.

In a similar vein, many English speakers might be familiar with Leonard Cohen's evocative retelling of *Un'taneh Tokef*, "Who by Fire?" This song was written after Cohen spent time on the front lines of the Yom Kippur War, guitar in hand.[7] Released in 1974, it includes powerful and difficult questions akin to those in the classic *piyut*: "Who in her lonely slip, who by barbiturate? Who in these realms of love, who by something blunt?" Its chorus is simply a repetition of the line "Who shall I say is calling?" This is widely understood as an expression of spiritual doubt. Rather than offending listeners, the song remains beloved—so much so that it is included in the Reform Movement's High Holy Day prayer book *Mishkan HaNefesh* as a commentary on *Un'taneh Tokef*.

The Jewish *Un'taneh Tokef*: In my elementary school days (in a non-religious public school in Israel), every year we learned the frightening tale of the martyrdom of Rabbi Amnon of Mainz, ending with his composing the words to *Un'taneh Tokef*. In his thirteenth-century book *Or Zarua*, Rabbi Yitzchak ben Moshe of Vienna quoted Rabbi Ephraim of Bonn's story of the famous *piyut* and the events behind it. He wrote, "I heard that Rabbi Amnon of Mainz established it on the basis of something awful that happened to him, for Rabbi Amnon was very wealthy, from a good family, and handsome, and the local ruler and his ministers asked him to adopt their mistaken religion, which he refused to do."[8] The ruler tortured Rabbi Amnon, demanding that he abandon his religion and become a Christian, while chopping off his fingers and toes one by one. Rabbi Amnon continued to refuse, and on the evening of Rosh HaShanah he was carried recumbent to his loved ones in the synagogue, along with all the severed pieces of his extremities. He recited the words of the *Un'taneh Tokef* and then disappeared before everyone's eyes—"and he was no more, for God had taken him," just like Elijah the Prophet. Rabbi Ephraim of Bonn then continued:

> After these things, wherein Rabbi Amnon was elevated and called to the Academy on High, on the third day after his sanctification, he appeared in a dream of Rabbi Kalonymos ben Rabbi Meshullam ben Rabbi Moshe ben Rabbi Kalonymos, and he taught him this prayer, *Un'taneh Tokef*. And he commanded him to send it to the entire Diaspora, that it should serve as a testimony and a remembrance. And the rabbi did this.[9]

According to this tradition, Rabbi Amnon appeared three days after he was "elevated"—in other words, three days after he was miraculously taken up to heaven—and instructed that all Jewish communities recite the *piyut*. However, this is a not a historically true tale. The figure of Rabbi Amnon is apparently invented; we know of him from no other source. The *piyut* itself is more ancient than the story, having been found in the Cairo Genizah. It was apparently written in the Land of Israel no later than the seventh century. Nevertheless, the suffering and persecution endured by Jews throughout history resound in the *piyut*.

The Israeli *Un'taneh Tokef*: Rosenblum's composition for *Un'taneh Tokef* is quintessentially Israeli, not only because of the Israeli musical motifs that it contains, but because it was composed under the direct influence (even if—or perhaps precisely because—it was somewhat belated) of the Yom Kippur War and its horrors, and it stands as a symbol of the price Jews pay to exist in the Land of Israel. Despite the inherent difference between the generations of suffering of the Jews and the difficulties of life in a sovereign Jewish state, the trauma of the Yom Kippur War swept up the memory of all previous disasters. Perhaps it also redefined the sense of loss and the status of "victim," a status that is also the foundation of *kiddush HaShem*, the sanctification of God's name by martyrdom. That war may have been the first time that Israeli Jews felt pursued and hunted in their own land, weak, almost as though we were exiled from our own home. Indeed, as tension mounted before the 1967 Six-Day War, there had been an anxious sense of peril, but that war's quick, resounding victory made it disappear from memory. Moreover, the Yom Kippur War provoked anger and indignation against Israel's political leadership, which until that point was considered

---

Un'taneh Tokef, continued
But through return to the right path,
through prayer and righteous giving,
we can transcend the harshness of the decree.

You are everything that we praise You for:
slow to anger, quick to forgive.
You do not wish the death of sinners,
but urge them to return from their ways
   and live.
Until the day of death, You wait for them;
You accept them at once if they return.
Since You created us, You know our impulses;
we are but flesh and blood.

We who are mortal—our origin is dust, and so
   is our end.
We wear out our lives to get our bread—
like broken vessels, like withered grass,
like a flower that must fade,
a shadow moving on, a cloud passing by,
mere dust on the wind, a dream that flies
   away.

But for You, ever-living Sovereign, time has
   no limits.
Your presence, unbounded by days and years,
   is everywhere—
a glorious mystery none can decipher.
Your name is worthy of You, and You are
   worthy of Your name.
And our name You have linked with Yours.[10]

nearly sacrosanct; after the war, political leadership fell from grace and earned public rebuke for its hubris, which had sealed the fate—for life or for death—of so many. That point of fracture was salient when Rosenblum composed his *Un'taneh Tokef*.

Rosenblum's setting also brought *Un'taneh Tokef* into the world of Sephardic and Mizrachi Jews, whose liturgical traditions had not emphasized the *piyut*. Now, it is something shared by all Israeli Jews. This is not the full extent of *Un'taneh Tokef*'s significance, though; its full meaning comes from its ability to speak to all humankind, dealing as it does with the fragility of our existence in this world.

The Human *Un'taneh Tokef*: Rosenblum concluded his work by referring to the *piyut*'s powerful images describing the frailty of human beings: "We who are mortal—our origin is dust, and so is our end." He did not include the *piyut*'s final passage (greatly emphasized in settings by traditional cantors), beginning "But for You, ever-living Sovereign, time has no limits." This final passage speaks of God's greatness in contrast to humankind's minuscule status. By eliminating that passage, Rosenblum's setting allows the idea of humankind's tiny stature and ephemeral nature to remain, since in the final analysis a human being is nothing more than "a dream that flies away." Perhaps *Un'taneh Tokef* was the composer's requiem for himself; he wrote it at the end of his life, reminding himself and others of the fragility and mortality of every human being.

Some have argued that Rosenblum secularized the *piyut* by leaving out its final section, which stresses God's eternality in contrast to human ephemerality. I, for one, don't agree. In my view, his work reflects a spiritual struggle and does in fact relate to the Exalted and Eternal, which some call God and some call by other names. Rosenblum employs religious tools to raise questions with religious dimensions, namely human mortality and an individual's purpose in the world. Rosenblum's composition is an elegy for the fragility of life, displaying not an acceptance of but rather a penetrating debate about the individual's fate. He deviates from the original *piyut* that ends with praise of God because that is not his focus; instead, he leaves *Un'taneh Tokef* unresolved and open for reflection on the suffering and fear that are inherent elements of human existence.

This *piyut* provides tools for dealing with the uncertainty of human existence. Its intent is to claim not that *t'shuvah* (return/repentance), *t'filah* (prayer), and *tzedakah* (righteous giving) work magic in this world, but rather that our efforts to do what is good before God and our fellow humans are itself a form of amelioration of the "divine decree"—that is, the painful realities of life.

A Message for Israel and World Jewry

The pioneers of the first waves of modern immigration to the Land of Israel abandoned the Eastern European synagogue by conscious choice. In their eyes, Zionism and making *aliyah* were inextricably connected to leaving behind the parental home, with all that leave-taking entails. Later, many *olim* (immigrants), especially from the Near East, were forced to abandon some important and beloved aspects of their tradition, sacrificing them in an attempt to make Israel a melting pot of worldwide Jewish communities gathering together again. The formation of a New Jew—an Israeli—was considered a heroic undertaking, but it was accompanied by a sense of something lost, something missing. The descendants of the *olim* from both West and East are, in many instances, devoid of even the most basic knowledge that would give them a familiarity with the immense cultural treasures of the Jewish people. Unpleasant as it is, we must admit that the new Israeli tree is planted, to a large extent, in shallow Jewish soil; in Israel we see many Jews who have allowed their important religious decisions to be made in complete ignorance of their religious heritage and tradition, rather than on the basis of knowledge and free choice.

The phenomenon of religious ignorance is not limited to Jews in Israel. Indeed, many Jews around the world are less grounded in their Jewish roots and less knowledgeable about Judaism than Jews in previous generations. The Pew Research Center's 2020 study on religion shows that roughly one-quarter of American Jews are "Jews of no religion."[II] In other words, they have a cultural, ethnic, or familial connection to Judaism but do not participate in any of Judaism's religious aspects. World Jewry has experienced its own set of challenges including assimilation, antisemitism, and disengagement, and it could be argued that many Jews around the world share the same "shallow Jewish soil" of the New Israeli Jew. This is ironic because many Jews around the world assume that Israelis are well informed about their Jewish identity, which is not always the case. Fortunately, it is not too late to ensure our plantings are more deeply rooted.

Since the 1990s, Israelis have shown a growing interest in Jewish texts and a range of Jewish experiences. I am not referring to the phenomenon known as *chazarah bi-tshuvah*, "return" to traditional religious observance, but to the fact that many people are choosing to examine Jewish tradition and its sources both lovingly and critically and adapting Judaism for themselves. The flourishing of secular and liberal *batei midrash* (places for Torah study), for example, which began back in the 1990s, led to the establishment of many places of worship that call themselves "secular." Some nationwide projects, too, are contributing to this trend; the 929 Project, for example, invites Israelis (and now English speakers as well) to study one chapter of the *Tanach* (the Hebrew Bible) every day, reminding everyone that the *Tanach* belongs to all Jews. Other projects attempt to bring classic works of liturgy and religious poetry into the public sphere. Now, disparate Jewish communities from the breadth of Israel's population find representation when their unique *piyut* musical traditions are available to all. Similar projects in North America include Moishe House (a communal Jewish living space for young people), JewV'Nation (Union for Reform Judaism's Jews of Color Leadership

One example among many of supposedly "secular" poems that really function as prayers is the poem cycle "Songs of the End of the Road" ("Shirei Sof HaDerech") by Lea Goldberg (1911–70), especially the second poem in the collection.[12] Its popularity spans the globe, so much so that it was included in the Reform Movement's prayer book *Mishkan T'filah* as well as the Israeli Reform siddur *T'filat HaAdam*:

> Teach me, O God, a blessing, a prayer
> on the mystery of a withered leaf,
> on ripened fruit so fair,
> on the freedom to see, to sense,
> to breathe, to know, to hope, to despair.
>
> Teach my lips a blessing, a hymn
> of praise,
> as each morning and night
> You renew Your days,
> lest my day today be as the one before;
> lest routine set my ways.[13]

Cohort), Yeshivat Maharat (a modern Orthodox seminary for women), and Svara (a "traditionally radical" yeshivah for queer and trans people. These programs seek to elevate traditionally marginalized people within the Jewish community, thereby broadening the tent of connection and enriching the entire Jewish community.

Yet expanding the tent of belonging is just one part of deepening Jewish roots. Similarly, making classic *piyutim* accessible is just one side of the *piyut* revival. In recent years we have enjoyed having the works of many "secular" poets not only read as prayers but also sung as prayers. And, as we have seen, prayers and *piyutim* have gained great popularity among wide audiences, sometimes when set to new melodies. Rosenblum's *Un'taneh Tokef* is a prime example. The choice of a "secular" composer such as Rosenblum to take on such a theologically challenging and religiously prominent liturgical text—and then to have that work performed by a singer without cantorial training—is not to be taken for granted. Rosenblum remarked that he did not compose the piece for a *chazan* to chant in synagogue, as a popular music performance, or even as a regular recording; rather, it was the communal setting of the kibbutz that gave birth to the arrangement. Only in retrospect do we see that his composition brought the *piyut* to public attention in Israel. He removed it from the synagogue's sole possession and offered it to the broader Israeli society, which was grappling in various ways with the spiritual challenges of the Days of Awe.

The fact that Rosenblum's *Un'taneh Tokef* became popular among professional *chazanim* and prayer leaders in many synagogues reflects a complex web of relationships between the "religious" (*dati*) and what Israelis call the "secular" (*chiloni*) communities. In many instances, the direction of influence flows from religious to secular, but here the *chiloni* segment of society has exerted influence within *dati* circles—on the holiest of holiday periods no less! Perhaps this indicates that Rosenblum's definition of *beit k'neset* (synagogue; literally "house of gathering") was too narrow. Perhaps, too, we can learn that despite the hard-fought ideological debates in Israel, our enduring cultural treasures are insatiable sources of inspiration and innovation for us all.

🍎 Is Forgiveness Possible?

> *For transgressions between the individual and God, Yom Kippur atones. But for transgressions by one individual against another, the Yom Kippur atones only if they have appeased the other person.*
>
> (Mishnah *Yoma* 8:9)

ANGER IS AN UNDERSTANDABLE EMOTION, often even a justifiable one. But it is also a destructive emotion, a gnawing and consuming feeling that brings harm to those who harbor it no less than to the objects of their fury. The arrival of the new year, when we seek to turn over a new leaf, invites us to consider another equally complex emotion: forgiveness, the emotion that seeks to bring about peace with someone who has harmed us and within ourselves.

Forgiveness is an interpersonal process that occurs between two people: one seeking forgiveness and the other granting it. Beyond such an act, though, forgiveness is also an inner reflective process, one that may take an extended period of time and be accompanied by difficult and contradictory feelings. Not infrequently, even when we know it is best to forgive, we find ourselves having trouble doing so. Can it be that pardoning others and forgiving in our hearts are two totally different things? Is it even possible to genuinely forgive someone who has caused us deep pain?

Forgiveness becomes a possibility only after there is harm, insult, or injustice. Paradoxically, the greater the harm suffered, the greater the need for forgiveness, and the harder it is for the victim to really forgive. It is easy to forgive someone who knocks into us gently on the street, and concurrently the need for forgiveness is not great. However, when the offense is harsh and serious, forgiveness—although even more essential—is much more difficult.

An offense by one person against another (when the offender recognizes the offense) creates a world in which both parties are trapped in isolation and alienation on opposite sides of the painful event. Even after the request for forgiveness has been made and accepted, both the victim and the offender wrestle alone with the painful encounter, its aftermath, and its implications. It is not always clear whether the two sides—offender and victim—can really overcome the divide between the harm and the forgiveness. In this dynamic, the offender is rightly dependent upon the injured party in the process of forgiveness. One cannot forgive oneself for an offense committed on another (even though in our postmodern world there are those who consider it possible). Instead, the victim is put into a position to forgive the perpetrator precisely because of the harm the perpetrator has caused. This is a unique connection between two private individuals, both of whom carry the burden of the relationship in need of repair.

We may feel there are acts for which there is no forgiveness. Even if the request for forgiveness is made sincerely with a broken heart, we cannot be forced to forgive. Conversely, the question arises as to how much one should request forgiveness if it is not forthcoming from the victim; is there a point at which the offender can throw up their hands and cease their efforts? Following the Talmud, Maimonides (twelfth century) teaches that after a person asks to be forgiven three times, and after friends have made a plea on the offender's behalf, the obligation to seek forgiveness is relieved, and "the one

Tishrei Marcheshvan Kislev Tevet Sh'vat Adar Nisan Iyar Sivan Tammuz Av Elul

who has not forgiven is the sinner" (*Mishneh Torah, Hilchot T'shuvah* 2:13). Sometimes the damage sustained by the victim is so great that the offenders themselves cannot do proper *t'shuvah* (repentance) and enter the forgiveness process. So it was, for example, with the biblical Pharaoh of the Exodus narrative. After describing his cruelty, the Torah tells us that "the Eternal hardened Pharaoh's heart" (Exodus 9:12), and he was not even afforded the right to repent and mend his ways. Rather than dwelling on this painful possibility, let us examine some instances in which forgiveness is possible and both the offender and the victim long for it.

"Forgiveness through Dialogue"

A few years ago, I happened to discover that a friend—a person with whom I worked for many long years—held an inappropriate conversation about me with a third person neither of us knew well. When I confronted my coworker about this, he offered what was, as far as I can tell, a sincere apology. On the day before Yom Kippur I even received a detailed letter from him, in which he once again requested forgiveness for what he had done. I honestly wanted to forgive him, but I had a hard time doing so, and I was pained by the fact that it was so hard. It was a feeling of loneliness and helplessness.

Dr. Yotan Benziman, who teaches philosophy at the Hebrew University, suggests a useful direction for dealing with the loneliness and alienation inherent in the process of forgiveness. In his book *Forgive and Not Forget: The Ethics of Forgiveness*, Benziman argues that the only way to mend an injury is through "dialogic forgiveness."[14] One's attempts at forgiveness can never remove the pain caused, and even if the offender feels remorse and is forgiven by the injured party, the relationship cannot be restored unless the offender and offended integrate the memory of the transgression into their lives and grow from that place of pain. Rather than attempting to "forgive and forget" or "leave the anger behind us," Benziman suggests a forgiveness process based on remembering, responding to, and growing from the transgression. The offender must take responsibility for the harm they caused and make significant efforts to atone. The offended must share their experience, feelings, and expectations. Of course, both individuals are not equally culpable. The offender cannot force forgiveness, but can only ask for it.

The expression "to ask for forgiveness" reflects the interdependence of the offender and the injured party. Forgiveness cannot exist without the offender's readiness to begin the process of requesting forgiveness; the offender is dependent upon the injured party for granting that forgiveness. The offender cannot be forced to request forgiveness, just as the victim cannot be forced to grant it.

Forgiveness, in "dialogic forgiveness," is built upon the offender's acceptance of responsibility and efforts to create new relationship dynamics grounded in benevolence; this effort benefits both those requesting forgiveness and those granting it. This is not an egalitarian arrangement, because forgiveness is possible only if the victim agrees to engage with the offender in an interpersonal way. In this process, a person who in the past chose to do something hurtful (or did so unknowingly or unintentionally) recognizes that fact and now chooses to correct the injustice.

An example of Benziman's approach is the worldwide movement seeking to rectify the often abusive power dynamics between men and women—especially in regard to men's sexual harassment and assault of women—widely known as "#MeToo." We have seen women and other disempowered people powerfully express the injustices they have endured and continue to face, and many workplaces where the abuses occurred are taking corrective action. Ideally, these changes derive from a dialogue that acknowledges the harassment, abuse, discrimination, or injustice, in which the perpetrator accepts that their actions were wrong and then works together with those impacted to create a new dynamic that benefits all.

This way of dealing with offense and hurt was manifested in the Truth and Reconciliation Commission that was established in South Africa in 1991, in the spirit of Nelson Mandela's teachings, as part of the process of healing and rehabilitation after the end of apartheid. In the commission's sessions, people who had taken part in crimes committed during apartheid were invited to speak frankly about their actions and to admit guilt, for which they suffered no punishment. This was an attempt at atonement, even with no claim to exercise judgment over those who had committed the crimes. One may argue, perhaps, that this way of doing justice is unfair, but in practice it gave the victims—and the perpetrators—a chance to achieve some tranquility, to put the painful past behind them, and to move forward with their lives.

Benziman's approach speaks to me. Today, one might hear that "every one of us is responsible" for the damage and pain incurred, which might easily lead a victim to assume their own actions have brought suffering upon them. To my mind, this is dangerous and damaging. We all navigate our lives as best we can, but not every damage we have suffered is our own fault. Counter to this is the populist approach, according

Restorative Justice

My friend Vicky Franco Sharzman is a social worker who specializes in mediation between victims and offenders, based on the concept of restorative justice. Vicky explains that the system draws its values from, among other sources, the conflict resolution traditions of the natives of New Zealand, Australia, and America and is based on the concept that the offender takes responsibility for their actions and deals with the implications in dialogue with the person whom they have wronged. The process takes place only if the victims want it to, and it is directed toward their needs. As the first step in the process, the offender listens to the victim, who describes the ramifications of the offender's actions. In the second step, the aggressor details their own actions and answers any of the victim's questions. In the third step, a discussion takes place, and when the aggressor feels ready, they request forgiveness from the victim. It should be pointed out that the victim is under no obligation to forgive; that is their own choice. At the end of the process, victim and aggressor decide together what recompense is appropriate. The concept of restorative justice is built on the belief that something must be done to repair the rupture, bringing the two sides together again.

Tishrei Marcheshvan Kislev Tevet Sh'vat Adar Nisan Iyar Sivan Tammuz Av Elul

to which "I alone am responsible for my suffering," which also clouds the concepts of responsibility and misdeed. If we follow this approach to its logical end, we will reach a point at which no one is responsible for anything.

In the end, true forgiveness is possible only between two people who believe that we are responsible for the choices we make and that we have the ability to mend our ways; thus we are also able to choose to forgive. Mutual commitment to change through forgiveness builds a bridge, fragile and tentative as it may be, over the abyss separating the one who caused injury and the one who was injured. This itself is an act of creation, recalling Genesis 1:2, "The spirit of God hovered over the face of the waters." In a sense, God is the third partner in a complex relationship between offender and forgiver. Over those who truly seek justice and forgiveness, the Divine Presence hovers. Our relationships matter because there is an intrinsic *k'dushah* (sanctity) in them.[15]

Kol Nidrei and Babylonian Incantation Bowls

How did *Kol Nidrei*—a dry, technical legal text—become the most prominent and beloved of all the Yom Kippur prayers? How did a passage that was not an integral part of the ancient Yom Kippur observance become the very essence of the day for so many? What follows is my attempt to address the question: What is the secret behind the *Kol Nidrei*'s charm and fascination?

The Jews of antiquity were no strangers to magic, and some of them were even intimately familiar with its deepest secrets. Commentators and halachic authorities, along with many scholars of the Mishnaic and the Talmudic periods, have refrained from ascribing a belief in demons and demonic forces to our ancestors, but it is evident that Jews—no less than their non-Jewish neighbors—did indeed believe in evil forces and sought protection from them. Even in the Talmud there are references to supernatural forces. To defend against dangerous forces, our ancestors consulted experts who composed spells, oaths, and curses against enemies, illnesses, and the damages that might befall them.

Many such spells were created in the years 300–700 CE and have been discovered in many places in Mesopotamia, most notably in the Babylonian city of Nippur (in today's Iraq). They were written in Aramaic on clay bowls, which were generally buried upside down, under the floor inside or around one's home, in an attempt to trap the demons—both male and female—and evil spirits threatening the house and its inhabitants. Written on them were magical formulas that included the use of names of God and angels. Using these bowls promised prosperity, health, and protection, especially for young children. The discovery of the incantation bowls and research into them has revealed a rich world of ancient popular culture that was almost completely absent from the mainstream writings of that time, the literature of the Rabbis of classical Judaism.

Kol Nidrei in a Bowl

Contrary to common belief, *Kol Nidrei*—that text that pulls at our heartstrings, the one sung before the open ark right before Yom Kippur begins—is not a prayer at all. It is a somewhat dry legal formula that serves to cancel any vows we have made (or that we might make in the future). Of course, this refers to personal vows undertaken before the Creator, and not legal contracts (whether commercial or of any other sort) that we have made with other people. Aside from the significance of *Kol Nidrei* under Jewish law, it has an

---

The making of vows and oaths is a controversial topic. On one hand, our biblical ancestors made such vows. The patriarch Jacob, for example, vowed that if he enjoyed divine protection, the stone he had put down at his head "shall be God's abode; and of all that You give me, I will set aside a tithe for You" (Genesis 28:22). By contrast, other vows were perceived negatively, such as Jephthah's vow to sacrifice whatever emerged first from his home if he won the battle against the Ammonites (Judges 11:30–31). The Torah warns us to demonstrate alacrity in fulfilling our vows: "When you make a vow to the Eternal your God, do not put off fulfilling it" (Deuteronomy 23:22). The early Rabbinic Sages regarded the making of vows and oaths as a very serious business—an act of cosmic significance with palpable influence on reality—and so they did not particularly encourage the practice. Rabbi Yosef Karo, author of the *Shulchan Aruch*, wrote, "Do not get used to making vows. Everyone who makes a vow, even if he keeps it, is called an evildoer and a sinner" (*Yoreh Dei-ah* 103:1).

Kol Nidrei is intended to cancel all the vows we make rashly or without serious consideration, across the board, in this language:

> All vows—
> resolves and commitments, vows of abstinence and terms of obligation,
> sworn promises and oaths of dedication—
> that we promise and swear to God, and take upon ourselves,
> from this Day of Atonement until next Day of Atonement,
> [and/or: from the last Day of Atonement until this Day of Atonement,]
> may it find us well:
> we regret them and for all of them we repent.
> Let all of them be discarded and forgiven, abolished and undone;
> they are not valid and they are not binding.
> Our vows shall not be vows; our resolves shall not be resolves;
> and our oaths—they shall not be oaths.[16]

important psychological significance: it helps us to part ways with mistaken commitments, to overcome choices made in error, and to recognize that even if we have made mistakes, we can still set them right.

Scholars have noted fascinating parallels between the texts on some incantation bowls and *Kol Nidrei*, both in vocabulary and in style—for example, "Reversed [literally 'turned upside down'] are all the vows and curses and oaths and spells and curses and magic and terrible plagues that exist on those people."

Kol Nidrei is known to us only from the ninth century on, while the incantation bowls predate it by hundreds of years. On some bowls one can see strings of expressions of bans and interdictions, such as "Forbidden, captured, bound up, suppressed, thrown aside, [and] rotted away are all . . ." and there follows a list of evil forces.[18] The bowls and the text of *Kol Nidrei* as we recite it are similar in that both employ a list of Aramaic nouns and verbs related to vows, resolves, commitments, promises, oaths, and the like. It is fascinating to realize that formulas like those said in *Kol Nidrei* were used by Jews centuries before they entered the pre–Yom Kippur liturgy, even if they were composed and employed in a very different context.

The linguistic and stylistic similarity between the formulas on the bowls and those in our High Holy Day *machzor* (prayer book) suggests that the original meaning of *Kol Nidrei* may have been drawn from the realm of magic. If so, it is not surprising to discover that there were Babylonian rabbis from the time of the *Geonim* (seventh to eleventh century) who were **opposed to that text**. Despite these linguistic and stylistic similarities, however, we need to be mindful of the psychological and cultural differences between *Kol Nidrei* and the incantation bowls.

Kol Nidrei, as we have said, is a legal text employed within the liturgy to express requests and desires, while the bowls are magical texts, meaning that they try to influence and almost force God to act in a particular way. *Kol Nidrei* is performed aloud and in public; the bowls were private written texts connected to a person's home. *Kol Nidrei* is tied to a particular date on the calendar, while the incantation bowls had no fixed date and were set up as

There has been opposition to *Kol Nidrei* since as far back as the Middle Ages. Rav Amram, a *Gaon* (head of a major Torah academy) in ninth-century Babylonia, even wrote of its recitation: "This is a ridiculous custom and it is forbidden to do so."[17] And yet, in his siddur—one of the earliest Jewish prayer books—we find a Hebrew version of *Kol Nidrei*, largely parallel to the original Aramaic. Rav Amram's version speaks of release from vows from the previous year. Rabbeinu Tam (1100–1171), Rashi's grandson, changed the wording based on the authority of his father Rabbi Meir; his version related to vows we have not yet made and canceled them in advance: "from this Day of Atonement to next Day of Atonement." This is the wording that remains in most High Holy Day prayer books today.

The purpose of canceling all the vows we have not yet made is to emphasize that this ceremony will not actually cancel vows (a ceremony undertaken in the daytime before three witnesses). The wholesale cancellation of oaths aroused many objections over the centuries from Jews and others, even serving as an argument in the mouths of antisemites to "prove" that Jews lack credibility and reliability—despite the fact that the passage speaks only of vows made to God rather than of commercial deals and the like. The fact that we still recite *Kol Nidrei*, despite all these objections, indicates the strength of popular will, which sometimes overcomes the views held by the rabbis.

needed. *Kol Nidrei* is usually led by cantors and trained prayer leaders, but any adult Jew could sing it; incantation bowls are the work of experts in casting spells. *Kol Nidrei* is an all-purpose text for canceling all the vows and oaths made by those present; the incantation bowls were generally created to defend the clients who ordered them from dangerous demons and enemies. Perhaps most important, *Kol Nidrei* cancels the vows of those physically present in the synagogue, while the incantation bowls arrest and imprison external forces outside the home. To recite *Kol Nidrei*, one needs no esoteric technical knowledge at all; the text deals with vows made by the person reciting the prayer and references their own words. In contrast, the incantation bowls were made by experts at magic and those familiar with mystical lore, in order to deal with external damaging forces that threatened their clients. What then is the point in comparing these two very different phenomena? What can we learn from comparing the bowls and *Kol Nidrei* and the common source they seem to share?

First, the similarity between them helps us sketch out an experimental, provisional map of a text that was originally domestic and private, then later became a public ceremony on the holiest day of the year. Second, both texts illustrate the seriousness and resolution necessary for making a vow and, more broadly, the deep reverence toward the significance of words and their function in the world. No less important is the fact that the two texts—the words on the bowls and of *Kol Nidrei*—address basic, profound aspects of human nature, particularly at a time of encounter with the unknown. Both reveal responses to human frailty and to the sense of powerlessness that results from living in a complex world that affords us only limited control. Both reflect human anxieties about things that lie beyond human control. In other words, both *Kol Nidrei* and the incantation bowls are ways of using ritual texts to achieve desired results, and the goal of each of them is to liberate us from the chains that bind.

Is Success Guaranteed?

Did the people who ordered those incantation bowls from an expert in magical spells in Babylonia a millennium and a half ago really stop worrying about dangerous enemies once the bowls had been set properly in their intended place? I dare to venture that they did not. Do those who come to pray on the eve of Yom Kippur depart the synagogue having discarded their remorse, guilt, and embarrassment over their misguided decisions, unfulfilled promises, unattained expectations, and maybe even for things they had neglected the entire year? Here too, the answer is almost certainly no. Existential worries and fears are tenacious; they don't easily melt away.

If we are honest, do we really believe that the variety of modern means we employ to overcome our anxieties and our fears have an absolute effect? The self-help books, presentations, experts, diets, psychological therapies, exhausting training

Before *Kol Nidrei*, the following sentence is recited:

> With one voice, assembled Sages past and present declare:
> all may pray as one on this night of repentance;
> let none be excluded from our community of prayer.[19]

The Hebrew text is a bit more direct: "we give our permission to pray with the transgressors [*avaryanim*]." Some claim this phrase was added as a preface to *Kol Nidrei* to grant permission for Spanish Jews—who had been forced to convert to Christianity but still clung to their Jewish practices in secret—to join the congregation in prayer. The term *avaryanim* (transgressors) appears in some prayer books in a variant that looks more like *abirinim* (Iberians), which may allude to the Spanish and Portuguese residents of the Iberian Peninsula. This touching explanation may be historically inaccurate, though. It was Rabbi Meir ben Baruch of Rothenberg (1219–93) who added this passage to the liturgy, two hundred years before the forced expulsion of Jews from Spain, to announce that it is permissible for Jews who had been placed in *cherem*—that is, banned by rabbinic authorities from participation in Jewish life—to join the congregation in prayer on Yom Kippur. I understand this passage as a call to recognize that we are all transgressors, that all of us bear some measure of disrepute, but nevertheless we permit ourselves to stand in prayer on this holy and awesome day.

regimens, spiritual practices from East and West, and of course the medicines and the chemical support that many of us turn to—do any of these completely wipe out the anxiety and the tension inherent in human existence? I think we can assume that in most cases, the answer to this question is also no.

Our ability to find real answers to such open-ended questions is limited. The existential fears remain, and we can only hope and pray we figure out how to achieve a measure of control over them. Yom Kippur is a day devoted to taking stock of ourselves, but every time we examine our lives or stand in prayer—not only on the Days of Awe—we have an opportunity for personal reflection. *Kol Nidrei* provides us with language and tools that might help us to grapple with our frail and mortal nature. Its liberating language offers a small measure of comfort and an opportunity for growth.

The days spent preparing for Yom Kippur provide an excellent opportunity to ask: What are the vows that bind and constrain us, and what shall we seek to unbind this year?

🍎 Sukkot: "We've Stepped Out. Be Back Soon!"

WHY DOES THE TORAH command us to go out to a sukkah, of all things, and why at harvest time, when our ancestors sat in their homes with their grain-filled silos? Maimonides's answer is that "a person should always recall the bad days during the good days."[20] Other commentators offered similar reasons. There were some who argued that the role of the sukkah is to remind the Children of Israel of the life of their ancestors in the wilderness before they entered the Promised Land. Rabbi Mordecai Kaplan (1881–1983) thought the reason was that the Torah wanted to make the memory of the wilderness journey present in the lives of later generations:

> Having the Israelites relive their Wilderness experience on the festival of Sukkot was bound to place them in a frame of mind which enabled them to detach themselves from the order of life which they had come to accept as normal and to view it critically. This call of "Back to the wilderness!" was the first articulation of that call which is familiar to us under the slogan "Back to nature!" It, too, was a call to self-emancipation from the artificialities and injustices of current civilization, and like the latter, it assumed the character of a yearning for an idealized past.[21]

In Kaplan's view, then, Sukkot is an opportunity to reexperience unsettled life in the wilderness and to return to ancient, formative times—the infancy of the people Israel.

Wilderness as Wedding

The Hebrew words *midbar* (wilderness) and *D'vir* (a synonym for the Holy Temple) have the same root (*dalet-bet-reish*, ד-ב-ר), and similarly, the word *tziyah* (dry territory) and *Tziyon* (Zion) are closely related to each other. In many cultures, the wilderness is perceived as a poor, dry place and (for that very reason) as pure and unsullied. When the prophet Jeremiah describes the pure early days of the relationship between God and the people Israel, he mentions the days in the wilderness with tender longing: "I accounted to your favor the devotion of your youth," says the Eternal to the Israelites, "your love as a bride—how you followed Me in the wilderness, in a land not sown" (Jeremiah 2:2). Israel's travels through the wilderness are seen as the beginning of a fresh, pure marriage, a time to prove love and fidelity. For the prophet Hosea as well, God's reconciliation with God's people is described in terms of the renewal of a damaged marriage through a couple's travel through the wilderness. God's reconciliation with God's spouse—that is, with God's people—is bound up with remembering their youth and the covenant that God would make with all of nature, "with the beasts of the field, the birds of the air, and the creeping things of the ground" (Hosea 2:20). The renewed covenant is a renewal of the engagement period before their marriage, a

---

Mark, on the fifteenth day of the seventh month, when you have gathered in the yield of your land, you shall observe the festival of the Eternal [to last] seven days: a complete rest on the first day, and a complete rest on the eighth day. On the first day you shall take the product of elegant trees, branches of palm trees, boughs of leafy trees, and willows of the brook, and you shall rejoice before the Eternal your God seven days. You shall observe it as a festival of the Eternal for seven days in the year; you shall observe it in the seventh month as law for all time, throughout the ages. You shall live in booths [sukkot] seven days, all citizens in Israel shall live in booths [sukkot], in order that future generations may know that I made the Israelite people live in booths [sukkot] when I brought them out of the land of Egypt, I the Eternal your God.

(Leviticus 23:39–43)

That is when I will entice her to Me,
lead her into the wilderness
and speak to her heart. . . .
There she will respond as when she was young,
when she came out of Egypt.
And on that day—says the Eternal One—
you will call Me *my Spouse* [*Ishi*, a neutral
male-gendered term for "my spouse"]
and no longer call me *my Baal* [*Baali*, a term for
"my husband" tainted by idolatry and ownership].
For I will erase the names of the Baals from
 her mouth,
and they shall no longer be mentioned by name.
On that day I will make a covenant for them
with beasts of the field, birds of the air,
and with creeping things on the ground;
I will remove the bow, the sword,
and war from the land,
and make them lie down in safety.
I will betroth you to Me forever;
I will betroth you to Me
in righteousness and justice,
in steadfast love and compassion.
I will betroth you to Me
in faithfulness,
and you shall know the Eternal.
(Hosea 2:16–22)

The last three verses of that passage are said as one wraps *t'fillin* (phylacteries) on one's hand. It is customary to wind the leather strap three times around one's middle finger, reciting with each time around one of the "I will betroth you" lines. In that way, the laying on of *t'fillin* becomes a daily symbolic ceremony of being wed to God. This passage is also part of the haftarah of the weekly portion of *B'midbar*, the beginning of the Book of Numbers.

time of righteousness, justice, mercy, and faithfulness born of deep familiarity: "then you shall know the Eternal" (Hosea 2:21–22).

The Bible also tells another story, though, about those days of wandering. It tells of a stiff-necked people who fell into anger and despair over and over, a people that presented demands and had no faith. The Torah's description of Israel's wanderings in the wilderness, one has to admit, is a far cry from a time of fresh and loyal youth. In the Book of Psalms too, that period is described in unflattering terms: "Do not harden your hearts as you did at Meribah, the Waters of Strife, when you stormed at Moses to strike the rock; nor that day at Massah, the Testing Place in the wilderness, when all you could think of was your thirst. How your ancestors tried Me, tested Me, though they had seen My work! For forty years I loathed that generation, I called them, 'People of a Wandering Heart,' for they did not know My paths. And so in anger I took an oath: 'They shall not enter the land where My rest is to be found'" (Psalm 95:8–11). The wanderings are described here as a period of estrangement, distance, and bickering, during which God almost gives in to the temptation to prevent the people from entering the Promised Land. This is a case of every story having more than one side, and unlike the famous Japanese legend of Rashomon, in which each character narrates the tale from their own perspective, here the protagonists recall the events in different and contradictory ways on different occasions. That, apparently, is human nature. Nevertheless, despite the mixed memories of the period of wandering, the sukkah also symbolizes a longing for a primal, pure past. The sukkah is something of a chuppah, a wedding canopy, which evokes memories of the wilderness wedding period, when property and possession did not weigh us down and slow our steps individually or collectively.

The anthropologist Claude Levi-Strauss (1908–2009) claimed that humans think in a system of pairs of contradictory and opposite terms, and he focused on the basic antinomy of nature versus culture. To Levi-Strauss, nature is emotional, impulsive, and close to the animal world, while nurture—or culture—is cerebral and rational.[22] To a great extent, the project of humankind is a transition from nature to culture, from the unruly and untamed to the defined, social, and controlled (or seemingly controlled). By contrast, on Sukkot we receive a taste of the opposite transition—from culture to nature, from the permanent to the temporary, from the built to the bosom of nature. But that is only part of the story.

From Time to Time → Dalia Marx

From the Temporary Sukkah to the Great and Holy House of the Eternal

Imagine ancient Israel and the astonishment of a young Galilean girl from a small village, accompanied by the hardscrabble farmer with an elevated pulse, as they made their way up to Jerusalem on foot, with the glory of the city and its Temple slowly coming into view. In addition to the temporary transition from culture to nature that the sukkah provides, the holiday of Sukkot was characterized by the transition from the quotidian to the extraordinary. As long as the Temple still stood, the Israelites ascended to Jerusalem on the Three Pilgrimage Festivals—Sukkot among them. It is easy to picture the many pilgrims on their path, leaving their villages and little towns, setting off for Jerusalem—the city of the Temple. They gathered to experience the direct sanctity of the great and holy house of the Eternal with both body and soul.

Thus, we have a dual existence on Sukkot: we emerge from our comfortable homes into nature—our temporary sukkah—and from home into the Temple, which until its destruction was understood to be a stable, eternal institution. On the surface, these seem to be two opposite sorts of "emergences" in every way. They share the essential commonality of **leaving the place that is comfortable** and familiar for a place that is new and unfamiliar. What is important is the *moving*.

An Arabic proverb teaches: *Fi l'charake—barake*, meaning "In motion there is blessing." And so it is: stagnation is death; in motion, there is learning, growth, and change; in learning and change, there is indeed blessing. When we step outside of all that is familiar and safe and look on reality and our lives from another vantage point, we return to our lives enriched by new insights.

Moreover, staying someplace out of the ordinary and uncomfortable enables us to realize that even those things that are consistent and stable in our lives are not impervious to sudden, wrenching changes. Even during times of stable, blessed routine, once in while a small, dark demon raises its head and asks, "What if . . . ?" Tragedies, illnesses, wars, accidents, and crises might—heaven forfend—bring about the collapse of that beneficial routine in our inner lives and expose us to terror, orphanhood, and bereavement. Who can guarantee that our reality won't be upended in a single moment? Perhaps to spend time in a sukkah, then, is to recognize that there can be blessing in uncomfortable situations, that there is a measure of certainty and satisfaction even in a life of uncertainty.

Splendid and Green

Tens of thousands of sukkot are constructed each year in Israel. Urban neighborhoods are dotted with these temporary buildings. Israeli children decorate them, hoping the rain will not come and destroy their creations. When we go out into the sukkah, we encounter our neighbors and acquaintances in a special way. We hear their singing, smell their foods, peek in and give holiday greetings to those inside the sukkah. A family who forgot to bring out salt is easily passed a saltshaker from the next sukkah. The sukkah builds our awareness that property and a comfortable and protective home—air-conditioned and fully equipped—are not the critical components in life. One can make do without them. Even without relocating our lives into a sukkah, even if most of us do not actually sleep in them, the sukkah makes us aware that we can imagine our lives without quite so many creature comforts. Building that temporary home and spending time in it summons us to examine our lives, the choices we make, and our relationships with others from a new perspective. The sukkah's purpose is not to negate our life of routine and its comfort, but to invite us to examine our lives from a different angle and vantage point, as though we had gone out for a time into the wilderness, from which we'll return soon.

Feeling Like a Stranger, Feeling at Home

Sukkot contains another possibility as well—for Israeli Jews, it presents a special opportunity to think about our place on the soil in the Land of Israel. Yes, the holiday gives expression to being uprooted from one's regular place, but for Israelis it is a very local, *Eretz Yisrael*-oriented holiday. Sukkot invites us to take hold of both sides of the dichotomy of both feeling like a stranger and also feeling at home. This is not dissimilar to the familiar experience throughout Jewish history of living in a strange land and longing for a return to "home"—that is, *Eretz Yisrael*—while also creating full and often fulfilling lives wherever Jews found themselves. For world Jewry and Israelis, summoning both ends of that rope, holding them together in one strong but gentle grasp, is an invitation to understand the Jewish experience across history. At the same time, this is also a warning to the Jews living on their land. So wrote Rav ShaGaR (Rabbi Shimon Gershon Rosenberg, 1949–2007):

> What happens when the balance of power shifts, when the nation that had been exiled and dispersed around the world . . . becomes sovereign in a defined territory . . . ? Must we necessarily become evil when the power shifts to us . . . ?
>
> One can see that the desire to establish a "softer" nationalism of a type that makes space for the other, that does not hold itself up above other nations and does not make itself a stranger to them, can already be found in the verses of the Torah: "The stranger who resides with you shall be to you as one of your citizens; you shall love each one as yourself" (Leviticus 19:34). . . .
>
> The Torah's intent in commanding that the Exodus from Egypt be remembered is to establish solidarity among the vanquished, not among the victors. . . . The enticement to brutally wield power is strong, and the Torah is worried, warning us about it incessantly. . . .
>
> Therefore, it is the very exilic nature of the sukkah, the sukkah that God had us dwell in when we left Egypt . . . that can give rise to the positive attitude . . . to welcome all the nations of the world.²³

In what follows, Rav ShaGaR emphasizes the importance of holding onto both the universal and the national. It is precisely the awareness of our "at-homeness" in all its fragility that requires us to recognize the value of home—for others as well as for ourselves.

"Spread over us the sukkah of your peace." Those protective words are said in the *Hashkiveinu* blessing recited after the evening *Sh'ma*, under the cover of God's sukkah of peace.

It is not a tough, resistant fortress that symbolizes divine protection in our tradition, nor a well-guarded, isolated bastion. Instead, it is the frail and temporary sukkah, which is the place of beneficent protection. At the conclusion of the *Hashkiveinu* prayer, which is all about God guarding and protecting us, we say on Shabbat evenings:

> And spread over us Your sukkah of peace.
> Blessed are You, Eternal, Guardian of Israel,
> whose shelter of peace is spread over us,
> over all Your people Israel, and over Jerusalem.

If only there could be peace both outside and inside our homes. Shalom Bayit (meaning "peace in the home"), an American nonprofit organization dedicated to ending domestic violence in Jewish homes, calls on people to tie a purple ribbon on the sukkah, in honor of all those who do not get to dwell in security and peace in their homes, and to recite this special prayer when dwelling in the sukkah:

> We bless the Divine Presence, whose wings shelter us with peace.
>
> Redeemer of Israel who brought us out of Egypt, on this festival of Sukkot,
>
> our thoughts turn to those who dwell in fear and danger in their own homes.
>
> With compassion and an outstretched arm, bring them forth into freedom,
>
> and shelter them in Your sukkah of peace.[24]

A short time after the 2014 Gaza War, Dr. Gili Zivan of Sa-ad, an Orthodox kibbutz near the Gaza border, wrote:

> This past summer taught us about the experience of ephemerality in our lives. From the rulers of the land, we turned into a people in exile. We came to know the experience of refugees forced to abandon their own place because of a raging war that has overcome them. It taught us that a sense of security and rootedness can quickly give way to a sense of uprootedness and fear of what might happen. . . . The violent shake-up we experienced here in the area around Gaza taught us once again a lesson in how to be human. We learned that impermanence dwells here in our secure and complacent surroundings, more than we dared admit. Paradoxically, though, it also strengthened our sense of being at home.[25]

The feeling of foreignness and the feeling of being at home are intermingled, and they cannot really be teased apart. But Dr. Zivan's words teach us that despite ephemerality and insecurity, the feeling of being at home is a profound sense that cannot be undermined. We may add that this is the case not only for us, but for all people who dwell on this soil.

Simchat Torah: There Is No Joy Like the Joy of Torah

LAST AUTUMN I wore white; I was a bride. I stood under a festive chuppah, a large tallit held aloft above me, and to the sound of joyful song from all those assembled, I was led to the bimah in my synagogue. My husband and children surrounded me. Last autumn, on Simchat Torah, I was given the great honor of being the *kallat Torah* (bride of the Torah). This means that I had the honor of reciting an *aliyah* Torah blessing for the reading of the final verses of Deuteronomy, which marks the end of a full annual cycle of Torah reading. I had no idea that I would be so moved hearing the voice of Ittai, the cantor, calling me in formal, traditional language "with the consent of this entire holy congregation, to complete the Torah!"

On Simchat Torah, there is a custom to invite a designated person to complete the reading of the Torah. This person is called *chatan Torah* (groom of Torah), and today we also have *kallat Torah* (bride of the Torah). Another person is called to begin the Torah anew. This person is called *chatan* or *kallat B'reishit* (groom or bride of Genesis).

An Emotional Roller Coaster

Simchat Torah is unusual among Jewish holidays: it was created in the Diaspora and not the Land of Israel. To each of the Three Pilgrimage Festivals—Pesach, Shavuot, and Sukkot—the Rabbis added an additional day of holiday observance for those people outside of Israel, a "second *Yom Tov* [holiday]." That extra day was added before the calendar became fixed according to rules and was instead based on observation of the moon, which led to some doubt about the precise date of each holiday. Traditionally, in the Diaspora, Sh'mini Atzeret is the day after the seven days of Sukkot and is entirely focused on the Prayer for Rain, while Simchat Torah is celebrated on the day after that—the "second *Yom Tov*" of Sh'mini Atzeret. When Simchat Torah "made *aliyah*" and began to be celebrated in Israel, it was combined with Sh'mini Atzeret; now in Israel the two are celebrated on the same day. Most Reform Jewish congregations in the Diaspora follow Israel's calendar, likewise combining the two holy days into one.

From Time to Time → Dalia Marx

Because of this history, Simchat Torah (as we usually call the one day of combined festivities) in Israel is a day rich in content when the atmosphere shifts radically, back and forth, over and over. For me, the day spent in synagogue is an emotional roller-coaster ride. After the joyous, energetic *hakafot*—when we circle the synagogue in song and dance with Torah scrolls in hand—it is time to read from the Torah. In many congregations, it is customary to give an *aliyah* (Torah blessing) to every person present on Simchat Torah. The *chatan* (groom) or (in progressive communities) *kallah* (bride) of the Torah is called up to offer blessings over the final portion of the Torah, and then right away we call up another *chatan* or *kallah* to offer blessings over the reading of the beginning of Genesis, since we Jews refuse to spend even a moment outside the cycle of reading from the Torah. From there we move to the Prayer for Rain (see pp. 44–45). When we recite that prayer, the atmosphere is completely different, because its text refers to the fragility of our lives, the existential dangers we face, and our hopes for a year of blessing. In Ashkenazic synagogues, *Yizkor* (the memorial service)—the prayer service that recalls and honors our relatives who have passed on from this world—is also observed on Simchat Torah. It is no surprise that I get home from synagogue that day entirely exhausted, not only from the length of the service, but also because of the liturgical mood that oscillates so sharply.

The Eighth One: Nature above Nature

Simchat Torah, celebrated in Israel together with Sh'mini Atzeret, concludes the Sukkot holiday. Sukkot—a holiday of going out into nature, of returning to the primal, unformed, the cosmic—is celebrated for seven days. The Torah gives instructions for Sukkot that seventy bulls be sacrificed, representing the seventy nations of the world. This suggests that the connection to nature is also a connection to what is common to all humankind, to what came before the division into peoples and nations. Simchat Torah is made of an entirely different cloth. It is a holiday that is all about the people Israel's Torah, the foundational text that belongs intimately to the Jewish people. It is a return from the universal back to the particular, to the unique aspect of the people Israel.

The number eight in Jewish culture indicates something above or outside nature. A classic example is circumcision. After the first seven days of the male baby's life—which symbolize the fullness of Creation—comes the eighth day, on which a ceremony takes place that symbolizes the unique creation of that child as a Jew—a creation beyond Creation. So too with Sh'mini Atzeret: if the seven days of Sukkot symbolize nature, Sh'mini Atzeret—along with Simchat Torah—positions itself at their culmination as the day that marks the unique Jewish nature. This is a nature that loves study and debate, profound analysis and examination—the nature of Torah. By the way, the musicians in my family point out that it is the same in the world of music: a musical octave is built on seven notes (*do, re, mi, fa, sol, la, ti*), and the following eighth note in the series is the return of *do* from another octave, another place.

Tears of Simchat Torah | Dr. Michal Wosner

The following text reflects the feelings of an Orthodox woman, Dr. Michal Wosner, after realizing the impact of exclusively experiencing services from the woman's section of synagogue:

> Rabbi Ovadiah of Bertinoro (1450–1515) describes the custom of Jewish women in Sicily who enter the synagogue and kiss the Torah scrolls on the eve of Yom Kippur: "The women come, family by family, to bow down and kiss the *sifrei Torah*," he writes, "entering from one doorway and leaving from the opposite one, and all night, as one comes in, one goes out." When I read these words, I suddenly realized with amazement that I had never had the privilege of bowing down to a Torah scroll and that I could count on the fingers of one hand the number of times I had kissed one. Throughout my life, I have been to a synagogue countless times, on Shabbat and *Yom Tov*, and countless times I have looked at it from afar, but I had never seen a Torah scroll open before me, I have never read the formative words of my life directly from it; I never rolled it or opened it, never picked it up, felt its weight, or heard near my ears the soft ringing of the bells on its crown.[26]

The Torah Belongs to All

I recall very well a Simchat Torah service that I participated in many years ago. Present in the synagogue was the grandmother of one of the worshipers. That grandmother, who had made *aliyah* (immigrated) in the 1950s from North Africa, hugged the Torah scroll with great excitement and shed tears as she kissed the mantle covering it. She told me she was the widow of a rabbi who had served his community for dozens of years, yet she herself had never touched a Torah scroll, nor even had the privilege of getting close to one. That woman's excitement remains in my memory, as do the memories of many other experiences with other mothers, grandmothers, and aunts from a variety of communities and backgrounds—none of whom had ever been given the opportunity to touch a Torah scroll. Each of these women's faces filled with light as they held Torah in their arms for the first time.

Simchat Torah is a holiday that reminds us that **the Torah belongs to all**, to anyone who chooses to love it, study it, and make it into the light that illuminates our path and slakes our thirst for knowledge.

That's it, the holidays are over, and . . . back to the routine!

From Time to Time → Dalia Marx

Prayers of the Month

A Blessed Meal of Symbols

THE CANDLES ARE BURNING, and we are sitting around a lovely holiday table. My grandfather, Moreno Levi, an eighth-generation Jerusalemite, his eyes flashing, takes a date in his hand and in his strong, emphatic voice calls out an imprecation over the date (*tamar*): "May all our enemies and all those who wish us harm be doomed [*yitamu*]!" When he gets to the word *yitamu*, he raises his voice even more and gives a frightening look. As a young girl, I didn't understand the meaning of *yitamu* or why anyone might wish us harm, but it was clear to me that this was a dramatic moment of great importance.

Blessings and good wishes for the new year on Rosh HaShanah take many forms, and one of the most mysterious of them is the meal of *simanim* (symbols, signs) and the "May it be . . ." lines that accompany them on the holiday evening. The custom is to offer special blessings over certain kinds of food before eating them. Those blessings focus mainly on sweet foods, and they play on the shape or name of each one. As far back as the Bible we find an instruction to eat sweet, enjoyable foods on Rosh HaShanah, although in that context the consumption of the foods is not accompanied by blessings: "Go eat choice foods and drink sweet drinks, and send portions to whoever has nothing prepared. For the day is holy to our Eternal. Do not be sad, for your rejoicing in the Eternal is the source of your strength" (Nehemiah 8:10).

Unrelated to that verse and in a rather unexpected context, the Talmud cites a **recommendation of Abaye**, the fourth-century head of the Babylonian academy of Pumbedita, regarding the foods one should eat on Rosh HaShanah: "Since you hold that a symbol [Aramaic: *simana/simanim*] is meaningful, every person should make it a habit to eat on Rosh HaShanah pumpkin, fenugreek, leek, beet, and dates" (Babylonian Talmud, *K'ritot* 6a). Abaye's suggested practice of eating five symbolic foods on Rosh HaShanah, which forms the basis for our ceremony today, is similar to the one I encountered in my childhood and which is observed mainly in families of Sephardic or Middle Eastern origin. Can we conclude from the context of Abaye's *simanim* that the symbolic foods of Rosh HaShanah have, or at least once had, a magical significance? By eating them, can we gain power to figure out the future or perhaps even to influence it? Abaye's terse comment about the holiday *simanim* is not enough for us to learn whether he believed eating the food

Abaye's recommendation appears as part of Talmudic suggestions for divining the future through symbols or indicators. The first is cited in the name of Rav Ami, who says that if a person wants to know if they are going to live and not die in the year to come, they should light an oil lamp during the Ten Days of Repentance (from Rosh HaShanah to Yom Kippur). If the lamp continues to burn, then they will live through the year. Other directions are given to someone who wants to know whether they will be successful in business affairs: they should raise a rooster; if it fattens up beautifully, then business will prosper. If someone is about to begin a journey and wants to know whether they will return home safely, they should go into a dark building and look for their shadow. If they see it, they will return home safely. Here the Talmud adds a warning: "But it is not proper [to make these tests], for one might be discouraged and mar one's fortune." The Talmud recognizes that luck is in part—or perhaps, mostly—dependent on one's perspective. The reality is that every *siman* can be interpreted in any direction. It is the individual who endows the sign with its meaning, and thereby influences reality to some degree as a self-fulfilling prophecy. In a similar way, the interpretations of our dreams influence our reality, thereby allowing our dreams to be "prophetic."

"All Dreams Follow the Mouth"

Many centuries before the dream theories developed by Sigmund Freud (1856–1939), father of psychoanalysis, our Sages wrestled with the meaning of dreams in a fascinating deliberation that cites many different opinions. To my mind, one particularly important statement is that of Rabbi B'naah, which emphasizes the creative power of the dream in deciphering reality:

> There were twenty-four interpreters of dreams in Jerusalem. Once I dreamt a dream and I went around to all of them. They all gave different interpretations, and all were fulfilled, thus confirming that which is said: "All dreams follow the mouth [i.e., what is said about them by interpreters]." (Babylonian Talmud, *B'rachot* 55a)

That is to say, a dream has no intrinsic meaning of its own; alternatively, it contains a wealth of interpretations. Those who interpret the dream grant it meaning by their interpretations.

Tishrei Marcheshvan Kislev Tevet Sh'vat Adar Nisan Iyar Sivan Tammuz Av Elul

is what brought about the blessing or whether its meaning is only symbolic and educational. In another place in the Talmud (*Horayot* 12a), Abaye's statement appears with one small but significant change: instead of eating the *simanim*, a person is just supposed to look at them! The difference between the two versions is fascinating. Looking at something, thinking about its form, its taste, or its name, is not at all the same as actually tasting, chewing, swallowing, and making the food part of one's own body. Eating combines different senses—sight, touch, smell, and of course taste—and thus brings a person to become intermixed with that symbolic food. It transforms the *siman* into something tangible, a very real part of one's body—something beyond mere words.

The Talmud does not mention anything about saying blessings in the context of the *simanim*. We first hear about this custom later, in the literature of the *Geonim* and early medieval authorities. Rabbi Menachem HaMeiri, who lived in Provence in the thirteenth to fourteenth century, addressed the idea that the *simanim* are intended to have a supernatural effect on reality:

> Many things have been permitted at times that look like expressions of magic, not—heaven forfend—as actual magic but as a sign [*siman*] to stimulate one's heart to proper conduct. Therefore, on the night of Rosh HaShanah we are told to place pumpkin, fenugreek, leek, beet, and dates—some of which grow quickly and some of which grow very large—on our table. However, to prevent anyone being led astray into magical practices, a custom was established of saying over them things that arouse us to repentance [*t'shuvah*]. (HaMeiri on Babylonian Talmud, *K'ritot* 12a)

HaMeiri chose to emphasize the educational aspects of eating the *simanim*. For him, eating them stirs our hearts to the meaning behind our wishes and prevents us from regarding them as magical. The blessings we recite over them transform this special consumption of foods into a holy act.

Different Jewish ethnic communities around the world developed their own unique customs of which symbolic foods are eaten on the night of Rosh HaShanah. The wording of the prayers of supplication recited over those foods, marking them as *simanim*, also differs by community. It is interesting to note that the most common and widely known customs—the consumption of apples and honey, a pomegranate, and the head of a fish—are not found in the Talmud, but appear only later in the works of the *Geonim* and scholars of the Middle Ages. Rabbi Yosef Karo (1488-1575) codified the custom, including the recitation of blessings and prayers of supplication. Karo writes:

> Everyone should make it a habit to eat on Rosh HaShanah fenugreek, leek, beet, dates, and pumpkin. And when one eats the fenugreek [*rubya*], one should say, "May it be [Your] will that our merits increase [*yirbu*]"; leek [*kartei*]—"…that those who hate the Eternal be cut off [*yikaretu*]"; beet [*silka*]—"…that our enemies disappear [*yistaleku*]"; dates [*tamrei*]—"…that those who hate the Eternal be ended [*yitamu*]"; pumpkin [*kara*]—"…that the verdict against us be torn up [*yikara*] and be called merits by You." One eats a lamb's head and says, "May we be the head and not the tail"; this is also done in memory of Isaac's ram. (*Shulchan Aruch, Orach Chayim* 583:1-2)

Perhaps the most widely known custom regarding symbolic foods eaten on Rosh HaShanah was first described by Rabbi Moshe Isserles (the Rema, 1520–72) in his glosses to this passage of the *Shulchan Aruch*, which detail Ashkenazic practices:

> And there are those who are accustomed to eating a sweet apple with honey, and saying, "Make this new year a sweet one for us," and so should one do. And some eat pomegranates and say, "May our merits be as multitudinous as [the seeds of] a pomegranate." And it is customary to eat fatty meat and all sorts of sweets.

While there are many descriptions of recommended foods to eat on Rosh HaShanah, there are also foods that are considered inappropriate for the day. Rabbi Isserles, for example, recommends not eating nuts. He bases this by determining that the combined numerical value (*g'matria*) of the letters in the Hebrew word *egoz* (nut) is equal to the *g'matria* of the word *cheit* (sin) (if one ignores the final letter *alef* in *cheit*, following a variant spelling). Additionally, the *Geonim* instruct us not to eat meat cooked in vinegar.

A "Little Sister" and a Big Blessing

Earlier I introduced this month's poem, the *piyut* "Little Sister" (*Achot K'tanah*), by the *chazan* Rabbi Avraham of Gerona. Sephardic congregations begin the Rosh HaShanah evening service, and thus the entire period of the Days of Awe, with this *piyut*. Its words, then, are the first words uttered in the new year. Each stanza of the poem ends with the refrain to "Let the [past] year and its curses come to an end," based on a passage in the Babylonian Talmud (*M'gillah* 31b). The last stanza ends with a positive refrain: "Let the new year and its blessings begin!" The poem communicates the expectation that as the year fades, melting away with the setting sun, its "curses" and stains will fade as well; only in successfully parting from the old year can we greet the new one with hope for its blessings.

We have seen that many of the traditional "May it be . . ." blessings of the ceremony of *simanim* on the night of Rosh HaShanah are in fact curses or requests for the removal of curses. I distinctly recall that as I got a little bit older, I wondered about the contrast between the sweetness of the date and the curse hurled at our enemies calling for their destruction, and about the tension between the wonderful taste of my aunt's leek patties and the request that it be God's will for "all our enemies and all those who seek our misfortune be cut off."

Curses have a clear psychological and cultural purpose. The need to curse is understandable, and even more so the Jews' need to do so after so many historical periods that left us vulnerable and defenseless. In those situations, words were the only power our ancestors could wield. But do we still feel so vulnerable that we require expressions for others—Jews or non-Jews—to suffer misfortune? Is our benefit inextricably bound up with others' loss? In our imperfect world, it may feel that we must curses others in order to feel blessed ourselves, but is that really true? Perhaps our task at the outset of a new year is to wish for our own good without connecting it to others' doom. Maybe we should focus solely on the sweetness of the date and wish for such sweetness to be our lot in the new year, without wishing for others' doom.

Maybe, in fact, we should think about updating all the *simanim* blessings. After all, these are unstructured wishes, not pleas that have a formal and binding structure, so they can shake off one form and adopt another. Here are some suggestions:

Over a date: "May it be Your will that this year be as sweet as a date."
Over pumpkin (*kara*): "May it be Your will that we be called [*nikarei*] and answered, that we may answer and call [*nikra*]."
Over leeks (*kartei*): "May it be Your will that we recognize [*nakir*] that we have not come into this world for contentiousness and divisiveness" (borrowing from a prayer of Rabbi Nachman of Bratzlav (1772–1810).

Perhaps we can add blessings and pleas over additional foods, being as creative as possible. For example:

Over a cup of liquor: "May it be Your will that this be a year of blessed rainfall."
Over quinoa: "May it be Your will that this be a year without envy [*kinah*]."
Over grapes and figs: "May it be Your will that we sit, each under their own grapevine and under their own fig tree" (adapted from Micah 4:4).
Over eggplant (*chatzil*): "May it be Your will that this be a year without pressure [*lachatz*]."
Over *t'chinah* (tahini, sesame paste): "May it be Your will that our pleading [*t'chinah*] be heard."
Over an apple (*tapuach*): "May it be Your will that our hearts remain always open [*patuach*]."
Over tofu: "May it be Your will that the mountains drip [*yatifu*] wine" (based on Amos 9:13).
Over ice cream (*g'lidah*): "May it be Your will that all our wounds, physical and spiritual, heal over [*yaglidu*] and we all find relief."[27]

And what wish shall we make at a Rosh HaShanah meal over shepherd's pie, pasta, lemon mousse, or chocolate cake? The possibilities are endless!

The dinner table on Rosh HaShanah (and other holidays as well, of course) can become a creative workshop for children and adults, where smiles and heartfelt good wishes are all part of the experience.

Ashamnu, Bagadnu: Old and New Confessions

TWELVE-STEP RECOVERY PROGRAMS were created to assist people suffering from addictions address and overcome those addictions. It involves a dozen steps, each of which is built on the preceding steps. The first step is "We admitted we are powerless over our addiction, that our lives have become unmanageable." Admitting to damaging behavior is a necessary, basic step in every change we seek to make. Without awareness of our errors, no change can take place. This truth, discovered in the twentieth century by those who sought to deal with problems of alcohol, smoking, gambling, or compulsive eating, was also known to our Sages long ago.

"I Acknowledge My Sin to You"

In the Book of Psalms we find a synopsis of the idea of a *vidui* (confession): "My sin I made known to You; my crookedness I did not cover up" (32:5). The sinner admits the sin and makes a confession, assured that God will accept and forgive the one who committed it.

As far back as the Torah we find the requirement of confession on Yom Kippur, though that was required only of the High Priest: "Aaron shall lay both his hands upon the head of the live goat and confess over it all the iniquities and transgressions of the Israelites, whatever their sins, putting them on the head of the goat; and it shall be sent off to the wilderness through a designated agent" (Leviticus 16:21). By the laying on of his hands, the High Priest transfers—through confession—all the sins, misdeeds, and transgressions of the people Israel onto the goat that is to be sent away. It was the High Priest who offered confession on behalf of the people. While the Torah does command the individual to confess their sins (see Leviticus 5:5, for example), the Rabbis added their own innovation: not only that each individual was required to confess, but also to commit not to repeat their transgression. The Rabbis believed everyone should perform *vidui* as a periodic and recurring practice.

The formal confession was originally a private text recited silently by the person making confession; over time, the wording of the confession became fixed (although people continued to say their personal confessions alongside the official formulas). Thus, two confessions—one short, one long—were developed, both worded in the first-person plural. This enables sinners to confess their sins more easily and also reinforces the idea that if one person in a community has transgressed, all bear some responsibility. The shorter confession—the Hebrew term is *Vidui*—is an alphabetical acrostic.

It is interesting to note that most of the listed sins are moral transgressions related to misdeeds in one's relationships with other human beings, and not related to ritual transgressions. There is nothing in the confession about eating nonkosher food, missing required prayers, or even a lack of faith; rather, it is almost entirely about mistreating others or ourselves.

Originally, the wording of *Vidui* was relatively short, and the text grew longer over time. It is worded in the plural. Over time both the long and a **short *Vidui*** were fixed as part of our Yom Kippur liturgy.

Mishkan HaNefesh, the High Holy Day *machzor* published by the Central Conference of American Rabbis, includes the following translation of the short *Vidui*:

> *Ashamnu, bagadnu.* . . .
> Of these wrongs we are guilty:
> We betray. We steal. We scorn. We act perversely.
> We are cruel. We scheme. We are violent. We slander.
> We devise evil. We lie. We ridicule. We disobey.
> We abuse. We defy. We corrupt. We commit crimes.
> We are hostile. We are stubborn. We are immoral.
>   We kill.
> We spoil. We go astray. We lead others astray.[28]

In addition to that translation, *Mishkan HaNefesh* also includes a confessional using the twenty-six letters of the English alphabet:

> We **a**buse, we **b**rutalize, we **c**ovet, we **d**eceive, we **e**nslave, we **f**eud,
> we **g**ossip, we **h**umiliate, we **i**njure, we **j**udge unfairly, we **k**ill, we **l**ie,
> we **m**anipulate, we **n**eglect, we **o**stracize, we **p**lagiarize, we **q**uarrel,
> we **r**age, we **s**hame, we **t**urn away, we **u**ndermine, we **v**ilify, we **w**aste,
> we e**x**ploit the earth, we **y**earn too much for yesterday—and too easily forget **Z**ion.

Our sins are an alphabet of woe.

This is what young Bialik wrote:

> My heart has died within me . . . and I too am going to die. . . . I'm disgusted with my life, which has become a burden for me. . . . But let me say, before I die, I acknowledge my errors and my sins, for one who confesses and abandons his mistaken ways is forgiven. I smack my thigh and beat upon my heart and say: "For the sin which my ancestors have sinned before me by force or by choice, and for the sin which they have sinned before me through hardening their hearts. . . . For the sin they have committed before me knowingly and deceitfully, and for the sin which my parents and teachers have committed before me by scorning me. . . . And for the sins for which I have been punished by lashes and beatings, whether deserved or undeserved. . . . For all these, forgive and pardon and grant atonement for them, for you are a forgiving and pardoning [God], etc., etc."[29]

The Confession of a Sensitive, Troubled Boy

In the month of Elul in the early autumn of 1889, a sensitive seventeen-year-old young man from a village in the Pale of Settlement (in today's Ukraine) wrote a despairing, even suicidal letter to his parents and friends. He had just arrived at the Yeshivah of Volozhin, the prestigious "mother of all yeshivot," but he was lonely and disappointed with his studies. Toward the end of that long letter, he wrote a confession about his situation that cannot but stir up compassion in the reader.

The author of this stirring letter and blistering "confession" is Chayim Nachman Bialik, who came to be considered Israel's national poet. Bialik chose to employ the structure of the traditional *Vidui*, which he knew well, to express his extremely personal pain. Yet Bialik's *Vidui* is largely the opposite of the traditional one, since rather than beating his own chest in a plea for forgiveness, he uses the confessional formula to beat on the chests of those who caused him suffering and pain. Despite the sense of impending death expressed in Bialik's words, a short time after writing his letter he left the yeshivah and moved to Odessa, the cultural capital of Eastern European Jewry; later still he came to the Land of Israel.

As one of the founders of Modern Hebrew poetry, Bialik holds a special place in the hearts of most Israelis. Yet his experience is relatable to anyone who was once a teenager. Feeling at times that the world is against you and that your situation is desperate is universal, as is the experience of moving from the darkness of despair to the light of a new beginning.

New Versions of *Vidui*

A number of new versions of the *Vidui* have been written in recent decades. Most of them follow the traditional alphabetical structure but add new, more contemporary content. One of those is the social change *Vidui* written by Israeli rabbi Moti Rotem:

אָטַמְנוּ We closed our ears to the cry of the poor and wretched.
בַּזְנוּ We disdained people of honesty and integrity.
גָּבַהּ לִבֵּנוּ Our heart was haughty.
דְּחִינוּ We excluded good manners from our lives.
הִסְכַּמְנוּ We agreed with entrenched power holders.
וְתַרְנוּ We gave up on holiness.
זִבַּחְנוּ We sanctified the Golden Calf.
חָרַטְנוּ We set our sights on "only by might and only by power."
טַחְנוּ We daubed with plaster the flimsy chambers of our hearts.
יָכֹלְנוּ We were able but unwilling.
כָּרִינוּ We dug a pit for those who walk in innocence.
לָטַשְׁנוּ We stared with enmity at others.
מִהַרְנוּ We were quick to raise our voices and our hands in aggression.
נִצַּלְנוּ We took advantage of every opportunity to exploit.
סָמַכְנוּ We were self-satisfied.
עָבַדְנוּ We worshiped foreign idols.
פָּחַדְנוּ We were afraid to proclaim the truth out loud.
צָחַקְנוּ We laughed at and mocked the unfortunate.
קִדַּשְׁנוּ We sanctified the unholy and the materialistic.
רָאִינוּ We saw and did not testify.
שָׁכַחְנוּ We forgot what was not convenient to remember.
תָּפַשְׂנוּ We reached for more but ended up with less.[30]

Many new versions of the *Vidui* have been written in recent years, some with a political slant and some as parodies. There is a confession from the anti-Occupation group Yesh Gvul, one from Rabbis for Human Rights, and one from L'hava to prevent "assimilation" in the Holy Land. There is an ecological confession, a driving infraction confession, a confession for not having done one's homework, as so on. Let's have a look at two examples, one political and one a parody.

A very caustic political *Vidui* was written by Rabbanit Rivkah Lubitch, a rabbinical court "pleader" (advocate but not attorney), who works for the Center for Women's Justice representing women in Israel's official Orthodox rabbinical courts (*batei din*). Her *Vidui* cites the difficulties women face within that institution and includes her suggestion that rabbinical court judges beat their chests over offenses committed against women and all

Vidui for the Rabbinical Court Judge
Rabbanit Rivkah Lubitch

What shall we say before You, who sit on high, and what shall we tell You, who dwell in the upper worlds? Are not all hidden things and all revealed things already known to You?

For the sin which we have committed before You by duress and by our will. By duress—because we looked over our right shoulder and saw rabbis issuing stringent, draconian rulings and felt under duress to be stringent. And by our will—because sometimes, even without looking over our shoulder, we chose to be stringent and demanding of people.

For the sin which we have committed before You unknowingly—in that we did not always comprehend the extent of the suffering of family members when we hesitated and took our time, dragging a case on for years.

For the sin which we have committed before You through forbidden sexual relationships—as, for example, that time when we said there is no basis to require a husband to issue a divorce, because the things he did to his daughter are not connected to the relationship between husband and wife, and they do not constitute sufficient grounds for divorce. . . .

For the sin which we have committed before You by levity—because we sometimes laughed at Jews-by-choice and asked them ridiculous questions. Such as, for example, when we asked an artist seeking to convert what would happen if we took down a picture of hers from the wall and served a cup of coffee on it as if it were a tray—would that be something forbidden to touch on Shabbat (ha ha ha!).[31]

the people who come before them for judgment. She obviously does not anticipate that the judges will act according to her suggestions. Instead, her goal is to raise public awareness of the injustices she is railing against. The text is strong and powerful even if it does not meet the criteria for a true *Vidui* in which people confess their own sins.

Confessions That Empower

A few years ago, I discovered a new type of *Vidui* that reflects a completely different theology—a theology of empowerment. Here, the basic character of the confession undergoes change. Instead of beating one's chest in contrition for sin, we are asked to embrace our weaknesses in order to bring about change and to recognize what cannot be changed. At the same time, we are asked to recognize our merits. Here are two versions of such a text. The first, "A Parallel Vidui," is from the *machzor* of the Nava Tehila community in Jerusalem. It was composed by Rabbis Ruth Gan Kagan and Nachshon David Carmi.[32]

אָהַבְנוּ, בֵּרַכְנוּ, גָּמַלְנוּ חֶסֶד, דָּרַשְׁנוּ אֱלֹהִים,
הִשְׁתָּאנוּ, וְהִקְשַׁבְנוּ, זָכַרְנוּ טוֹב, חִבַּקְנוּ, טִפַּלְנוּ, יָרֵאנוּ חֵטְא,
כָּבַשְׁנוּ יֵצֶר, לָמַדְנוּ מִטָּעוּיוֹת, מָחַלְנוּ, נוֹלַדְנוּ, סָעַדְנוּ, עָזַרְנוּ, פָּתַחְנוּ דֶּלֶת,
צָחַקְנוּ, קֵרַבְנוּ, רָקַדְנוּ, שָׁמַרְנוּ תּוֹרָה, תָּמַכְנוּ.

We **a**wakened, we **b**lessed, we **c**ared, we **d**anced in Your presence,
  we **e**mpathized, we **f**ought for justice, we were **g**rateful, we **h**ealed, we **i**magined,
we were **j**oyful, we were **k**ind, we **l**istened,
  we **m**ended our ways, we **n**urtured, we **o**pened doors to others,
we **p**raised, we **q**uestioned, we **r**eflected, we were in **s**ervice, we **t**aught, we **u**nified,
we **v**eered from evil, we **w**elcomed strangers, we e**x**alted, we **y**earned,
  we remembered **Z**ion.

The second empowering *Vidui* was written by Professor Vered Noam, a Talmud professor at Tel Aviv University. Her *Vidui* reflects an approach that is at once demanding and forgiving, recognizing that sometimes we have been successful, sometimes not. We are imperfect, but we ask that our efforts be considered.³³

Vidui for Adults   וִדּוּיֵי לַמְבוּגָּרִים

We loved,   אָהַבְנוּ,

we built,   בָּנִינוּ,

we brought up,   גִּדַּלְנוּ,

we worried,   דָּאַגְנוּ,

we tried, and we partially succeeded.   הִשְׁתַּדַּלְנוּ, וְהִצְלַחְנוּ חֶלְקִית.

We faked it sometimes.   זִיַּפְנוּ לִפְעָמִים.

We sinned, we erred, we extricated ourselves somehow.   חָטָאנוּ, טָעִינוּ, יָצָאנוּ מִזֶּה אֵיכְשֶׁהוּ.

We felt pain, we learned, we stumbled, we tried.   כָּאַבְנוּ, לָמַדְנוּ, מָעַדְנוּ, נִסִּינוּ.

We forgave ourselves and others too little.   סָלַחְנוּ מְעַט מִדַּי לְעַצְמֵנוּ וְלַאֲחֵרִים.

We got something done anyway.   עָשִׂינוּ מַשֶּׁהוּ בְּכָל זֹאת.

We provided a living.   פִּרְנַסְנוּ.

We were right, infrequently.   צָדַקְנוּ לְעִתִּים רְחוֹקוֹת.

We received much,   קִבַּלְנוּ הַרְבֵּה,

We wanted too much.   רָצִינוּ הַרְבֵּה מִדַּי.

We were happy less than was possible and necessary.   שָׂמַחְנוּ פָּחוֹת מִמַּה שֶׁהָיָה אֶפְשָׁר וְצָרִיךְ.

We give thanks for it all.   תּוֹדָה עַל הַכֹּל.

The approach underlying these confessionals is that it is not enough to stop doing evil; rather, one must actively do good. Rabbi Y'hudah Aryeh Leib Alter (1847–1904), the author of the Chasidic Torah commentary *S'fat Emet*, commenting on the verse "Negate evildoing; rather do good—seek peace and harmony—pursue them!" (Psalm 34:15), wrote that if we turn away from what is bad and focus on doing what is good, evil will consequently disappear.³⁴

Ushpizin and *Ushpizot*: Heavenly and Earthly Guests

THE WALLS of the sukkah are thin. The conversation and singing of those sitting inside can be heard by passersby and people in nearby sukkot. It is easy to smell the aroma of the food and hear approaching footsteps. It is no surprise that particularly on Sukkot we are supposed to invite guests into our sukkah, to share our tasty foods with them, and to spend time with them in that home-outside-home.

The mitzvah of dealing graciously with guests, known as *hachnasat orchim*, is one of the six activities of which the Talmud says, "These are things that are limitless, of which a person enjoys the fruit of this world, while the principal remains in the world to come" (*Shabbat* 127a). The Sages of the Talmud discuss the greatness of this mitzvah, saying:

> Rabbi Yochanan said: Hospitality to wayfarers is as great as early attendance at the *beit midrash* [house of study]. . . .
> Rav Dimi of Nehardea said: It is *greater* than early attendance at the *beit midrash*. . . .
> Rav Y'hudah said in Rav's name: Hospitality to wayfarers is greater than welcoming the presence of the *Shechinah*, for it is written, "He said, 'My lords, if it please you, do not go on past your servant'" (Genesis 18:3).

Aside from inviting guests from among our family and friends, the kabbalistic tradition teaches about the seven historical guests—*ushpizin* in Aramaic—whom we are to invite into our sukkah throughout the seven days of Sukkot. Each day of the holiday, a different guest is invited to spend time with us in our sukkah.

Those seven *ushpizin* are Abraham, Isaac, Jacob, Joseph, Moses, Aaron, and David. This list of patriarchs and leaders are ordered by generation, according to the Ashkenazic custom. In Sephardic tradition, though, they are arranged according to the order of the kabbalistic *s'firot*, the successive divine emanations related to distinct qualities of the Divine. In this tradition, each one of the seven *ushpizin* is connected to a particular *s'firah* in the following order: Abraham, Isaac, Jacob, Moses, Aaron, Joseph, and David.

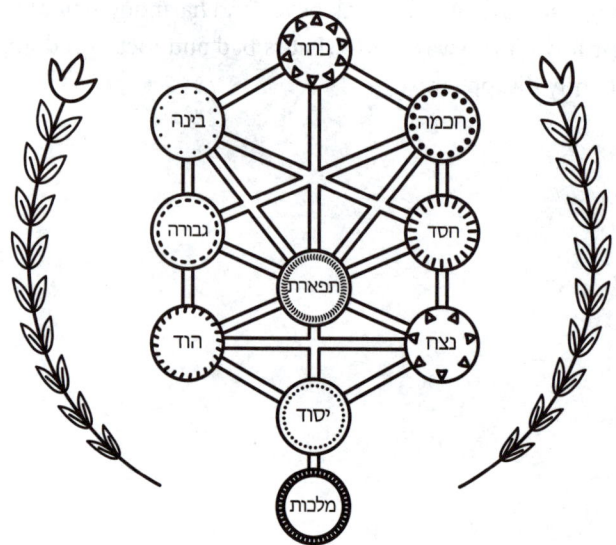

The *ushpizin* are greeted with a *piyut* in Aramaic:

Come in, exalted and holy guests!	עוּלוּ אוּשְׁפִּיזִין עִלָּאִין קַדִּישִׁין
Come in, exalted and holy ancestors,	עוּלוּ אַבָהָן עִלָּאִין קַדִּישִׁין
to sit in the shadow of the exalted Faithful One,	לְמֵיתַב בְּצִלָּא דִמְהֵימְנוּתָא עִלָּאָה
in the shadow of the blessed Holy One!	בְּצִלָּא דְקוּדְשָׁא בְּרִיךְ הוּא.

The *piyut* continues by inviting one guest in succession to enter the sukkah each day, accompanied by the other six. Many customs have arisen in connection with figures of the *ushpizin*. Some people decorate the sukkah with pictures of them. Some relate each one to the quality represented by a particular kabbalistic *s'firah*: Abraham represents *Chesed*, "kindness"; Isaac represents *G'vurah*, "strength"; Jacob—*Tiferet*, "adornment"; Moses—*Netzach*, "eternity"; Aaron—*Hod*, "splendor"; Joseph—*Y'sod*, "foundation"; and David represents *Malchut*, "kingship." Each one of the *ushpizin* brings his particular quality into the sukkah with him.

Ushpizot—Don't Forget the Female Guests!

A few years ago, we bought a nice new sukkah, on the cloth walls of which are inscribed the names of the *ushpizin*. I was industrious; I bought a set of permanent markers and added to those seven names the names of women I wanted to greet as *ushpizot* in my sukkah.

In recent years, an increasing number of women have sought to take a more active part in the Jewish religious experience, and indeed almost all streams of Judaism are now involved with the inclusion of women. As part of those efforts, many people have brought to the fore female role models from the Jewish tradition. We are learning that it is not enough to be engaged only with the figures of our three Patriarchs; we also need to take a deep dive into the figures of the four Matriarchs. When the liturgy includes the Song at the Sea, sung by the Moses and the Israelites as they passed through the sea on dry land, some now add the Song of Miriam (Exodus 15:20–21). The purpose of including women is to present female role models (even if they are not always perfect, since the mothers of the nation—like the fathers—were human, with all that entails). In this context, suggestions have been made to add seven female guests to the seven *ushpizin* invited into the sukkah on Sukkot.

Since this suggestion was first made, it has attracted many supporters; little by little, in many parts of the Jewish world, people have begun to include seven female guests alongside their male counterparts. As opposed to the traditionally established list of the male *ushpizin*, active choices must be made for the seven *ushpizot*.

Who are the seven female guests we would like to bring inside the sukkah with us? The need to choose seven ancient female role models has resulted in some interesting answers.

One suggestion was to add the female partner of each of the male *ushpizin*. Abraham, then, would be joined by **Sarah**, Isaac by **Rebekah**, and Jacob by **Leah**, while **Rachel** would join her son Joseph; **Zipporah** would join Moses, **Miriam** would join her brother Aaron, and with David would come one of his wives (**Bathsheba**, **Michal**, or **Abigail**—with no illusion about that being a fraught decision) or with his great-grandmother, that paragon of faith, **Ruth**.

Here are three more ideas that have been proposed. Dr. Anat Yisraeli has suggested including the seven female prophets that arose among the people Israel: "'Seven female prophets [prophesied for Israel].' Who were these? Sarah, Miriam, Deborah, Hannah, Abigail, Huldah, and Esther" (Babylonian Talmud, *M'gillah* 14a). Yisraeli ascribes to each of the seven female prophets a beneficent quality and suggests embracing that quality during that day: Sarah had endurance and an ability to protect and shield others. Miriam had vitality and exuberance. Deborah modeled leadership and bravery; Hannah—faith and willpower; Abigail—resourcefulness and mercy; Huldah—powers of prophecy and rebuke; and Esther—self-sacrifice and courage.

The psychologist Judith Jungman Saadon has suggested a different *ushpizot* journey:

> On **the first day of Sukkot**—representing the *s'firah* of *Chesed*, "kindness"—we invite the four Matriarchs, **Sarah, Rebekah, Rachel, and Leah**, to stimulate in us the qualities of generosity, hospitality, and consideration.
>
> On **the second day**—representing the *s'firah* of *G'vurah*, the realm of law and justice—we invite **Deborah the prophetess**, to bring to the fore our inner leader and pursuer of justice.
>
> On **the third day**—representing the *s'firah* of *Tiferet*, "adornment"—we open our hearts to **Jochebed, mother of Moses**, the Jewish people's midwife, to learn from her maternal wisdom, whose essence is a delicate balance between *Din* (law, justice) and *Chesed* (kindness), a balance learned in this *s'firah*, which represents the quality of mercy.
>
> On **the fourth day**—representing the *s'firah* of *Netzach*, "eternity," the *s'firah* of creation and imagination—we would like to invite **Serach, daughter of Asher,** and **Miriam the prophetess**, to stimulate our imagination with the power to see beyond the present reality—to see redemption, to see the exodus from slavery to freedom, to see the divine overflow that is present in our lives every moment. And to know, like Miriam the prophetess, how to animate the creative potential within us to give thanks and praise to the Blessed Holy One.
>
> On **the fifth day**—representing the *s'firah* of *Hod*, "splendor," which is the *s'firah* of action connected to truth—we invite **Batyah, Pharaoh's daughter**, and **Ruth the Moabite**, to teach us how to choose the correct path and dare to follow it despite any difficulties along the way. This is the palace of women who act, the repentant ones who walk along the path.
>
> On **the sixth day**—representing the *s'firah* of *Y'sod*, which connects the spiritual word to the terrestrial world—we encounter **Hannah the prophetess**, who knows how to make the connection between the world of faith and prayer and the fulfillment of our requests in the world of *asiyah*, "action": realizing our dreams in a manner that contributes to us and also to the world around us, as did Hannah, who had her request for a child of her own granted by giving birth to Samuel—Samuel, who also became a prophet, a messenger for the entire people Israel.
>
> On **the seventh day**—representing the *s'firah* of *Malchut*, which is the *s'firah* of actual life on earth, the *s'firah* of God's revelation in this world—we will ask **Queen Esther** to direct us to recognize and reach for our destiny in this world, so that each of us may be a vessel for discovering the light of the Holy One in this world.[35]

Other interesting suggestions have been offered for including the *ushpizot*, such as that of the Dov Abramson Studio, a Jerusalem graphic design firm, which produced a series of twenty-six posters (and little flags and magnets) of *ushpizot* from the Bible through today. In this case, it is precisely the absence of women from an ancient tradition that makes it possible to exercise some measure of contemporary creativity. And when we seek to bring our ancient female forebears into traditions we are creating, we are invited to answer some fascinating questions.

Your Own *Ushpizin* and *Ushpizot*

In our sukkah we have started a new custom. Each one of those seated at a holiday meal names a guest, regardless of gender, they would like to invite into the sukkah. Some invite relatives who are no longer with us, while others invite figures from ancient history or from more recent times. The rule is that you can invite anyone, from any walk of life, including fictional characters. Vicky invited Golda Meir, to ask her what it was like to function in such a male environment. Ulrike invited Hannah Arendt, so she could debate with her about her theories. Noam invited David Ben-Gurion. (We carefully pointed out that he and Golda might not get along so well.) Sarah invited Rabbi Regina Jonas (see pp. 105–107), the first woman to receive rabbinic ordination. Niv invited his basketball hero LeBron James. Orna invited Theodor Herzl, so she could ask whether he is satisfied with the outcome of the Zionist movement. And Danny invited a service technician—any service technician—who wouldn't let him down (that is, if he could find one by next year).

Inviting *ushpizin* and *ushpizot* from Jewish tradition alongside actual flesh-and-blood guests—and the unique guests each of them would like to encounter and talk with—transforms Sukkot into a holiday of surprising encounters with ourselves and others; it spreads out a sukkah of peace that brings together past, present, and future, brings distant people near, and offers endless opportunities for conversation.

Who are your *ushpizin* and *ushpizot*?

My friend Rabbi Shlomo Fox offered a teaching about the custom of hanging pictures of the *ushpizin* or their names on the walls of the sukkah:

> Making the *ushpizin* present in the sukkah is in accord with the verse "Then your eyes will see your guides" (Isaiah 30:20). Our choice of who we invite into our sukkah defines our aspirations and hopes. Those figures symbolize not only the walls—the borders of home—but also our identity.
>
> Tell me who the guests in your sukkah are, and I'll know a good deal about your world.

May an opening be made in our sukkah, through which we can view the horizon.[36]

Praying for Rain: Old and New *Geshem* Prayers

In the Jewish tradition, rain—*geshem*—in season is a sign of blessing. The rain enables the "bringing forth of bread from the earth," as the blessing puts it. It symbolizes our connection with the Divine and makes it possible for life on earth to be sustained. This request for rain is especially salient in Israel, where there is always a danger of drought. With rising global temperatures and changing climate patterns, this is becoming an increasingly common experience around the world. Deeply sensitive to drought and its negative impacts, our tradition considers rain to be an expression of the connections among humanity, the land, and God.

Sh'mini Atzeret, the day after Sukkot, is the moment when Jewish liturgical tradition brings us into an autumnal mood. That mood is expressed when the "summer" addition of the prayer for rain (or dew) changes to the "winter" version with the addition of a line to the *Amidah* prayer: "You cause the wind to shift and the rain to fall." That transition is made with great festivity in synagogues as the Prayer for Rain (*T'filat HaGeshem*) is recited during or just before the *Musaf* (additional prayers).

In many synagogues, particularly among Ashkenazim, the melody for *T'filat HaGeshem* is borrowed from the Days of Awe, and the cantor or prayer leaders dons a white robe (kittel), as some people do on Yom Kippur. These customs stem from the understanding of the vital importance of rain. In the past, when rain has not come in its proper season, the impact has been famine and death; in our time too, and despite the sophisticated water desalination efforts, rain is still of critical importance.

The *piyutim* written to be part of the Prayer for Rain are quite long, and in many synagogues only parts of them are recited. In Ashkenazic synagogues, it is customary to recite a poetic version of the prayer penned by Rabbi Elazar HaKalir (sixth to seventh century)—the greatest of the liturgical poets (*pay'tanim*) of late antiquity. Each stanza of the *piyut* is dedicated to one of the Patriarchs and emphasizes his connection to water. Through the merit of our ancestors, the *piyut* asks, may we too be granted water. A somewhat abridged version, but one that includes female figures alongside male figures from the Bible, appears in the Reform siddur for the English-speaking world, *Mishkan T'filah*:

Remember those whose hearts poured out to You like water,
who trusted that the journey would lead to You:
    For Abraham and Sarah's faith, do not withhold water.
Remember the one chosen for her words, "Please take some water";
and remember the one whose blood was almost spilled like water:
    For Rebecca and Isaac's righteousness, grant water.
Remember how Jacob crossed the river to wrestle in the waters of his conscience; recall
the sisters' tears, their waters of birth, their tents of peace.
    For Jacob, Rachel and Leah, fill the earth with needed water.

The poem, whether in its classical or modern form, ends with a three-part call for life and sustenance:

For blessing and not for curse.	לִבְרָכָה וְלֹא לִקְלָלָה
For life and not death.	לְחַיִּים וְלֹא לְמָוֶת
For abundance and not for want.[37]	לְשֹׂבַע וְלֹא לְרָזוֹן

May there be abundant, blessed rainfall for us and for everyone on earth!

MARCHESHVAN

Zodiac Sign: Scorpio | Tribe of the Month: Naphtali
Breastplate Stone: Agate/*Sh'vo*

The Hebrew name of this month, Marcheshvan, is apparently a corruption of *warchu shamnu*, an Akkadian phrase meaning "eighth month." Indeed, in the biblical count, Marcheshvan is the eighth month. Curiously, it is also the month of the olive harvest, when *shemen*, olive oil, is produced; the word *shemen* is related to *sh'mini*, "eighth." Some suggest the name comes to us from the Persian calendar, whose eighth month is Markashan. In the Middle Ages, Jews began to refer to the month in a truncated form, as Cheshvan. That may have been the result of a misunderstanding: the first syllable, *Mar*, is also an honorific title, meaning "Sir" or "Mr.," and as such may have been considered an unnecessary addition. Referring to the month as "Cheshvan" persisted, and in fact most Jews throughout the world are more familiar with Cheshvan than Marcheshvan.

In the Bible, this month is called simply "the eighth month," using the count that begins with Nisan. In the books of the Prophets we find the name *Bul* (I Kings 6:38) to describe this month, which may be related to the words for "crop harvest" (*y'vul*) or "flood" (*mabul*).

Kavanah: A Meditation for Marcheshvan

May we know how to discern blessing even in the yoke of the mundane,
joy even in simple moments, beauty even amidst everyday distress.
May we accept what life rains down on us as children find joy in rainfall.
May we be as numerous as the innumerable raindrops.
May we accept abundance so that we may be abundant.
> *Imagine a small attic in which you will preserve the beauty of this moment.*
> *May you have a small corner for sanctity from which you can inhale on difficult days.*
> *As the Shunamite woman was granted a miracle, so may you be as fortunate.*
> *It is not a major miracle you've asked for;*
> *a small, everyday miracle too can bring great joy.*
> *Amen, so may it be God's will.*[1]

This prayer, written by Rabbi Maya Leibovich, is based on the story of the woman of Shunem in II Kings, chapter 4. The biblical story presents an independent, strong-willed woman of wisdom and foresight. As we read, we learn that she is childless. Due to her talents and her generosity toward the prophet Elisha, she is granted a son, and a miracle is performed for her as well: her child is rescued from danger thanks to her initiative and intervention.[2]

At the Gates of Marcheshvan

THE MONTH OF MARCHESHVAN is a month of routine. It contains no holidays, and the special events marked in it are few. Marcheshvan is an opportunity to celebrate our blessed routine days. The regularity of Marcheshvan is familiar to students in Israeli schools, colleges, and universities. After the long summer break and the holidays that punctuate Tishrei, students settle into the everyday routine of studies. During Marcheshvan I want to ask, *Shigrah zeh ra*? "Is routine so bad?"—a question familiar from a favorite old Israeli advertisement. Marcheshvan, almost all of which is regular routine, offers us an excellent chance to consider our lives in this world, especially as Jews, and to ponder the questions related to the essence of our lives.

Here is what is waiting for us in this chapter on Marcheshvan: Our first *iyun* will take a look at routine and the significance of the passage of time in our lives; our next *iyun* will examine the creation of new holidays, their legitimacy, and our need for them. That discussion will begin with a close look at the holiday invented (or, as the Bible puts it, "contrived by his own mind") by Jeroboam son of Nebat. The *iyunim* that follow deal with the introduction of two new holidays into the Jewish-Israeli calendar and how they have been accepted. One of those is the Memorial Day for Prime Minister Yitzhak Rabin (twelfth of Marcheshvan). The other, quite different from the first, is the Sigd festival introduced into Israel by the Beta Israel, the Jews of Ethiopia (twenty-ninth of Marcheshvan). In the *iyunim* exploring the two holidays, we will explore the place of these two new events on the calendar and imagine in what directions they might develop.

During the month of Marcheshvan, we begin praying for rain, and so the Poems of the Month section will address the topic of rain and its fulfillment. We will look at two poems that mark a broad arch of Israeli attitudes about living on the beautiful and difficult soil of *Eretz Yisrael*. The Prayer of the Month will feature a special prayer recited by the Beta Israel community on the day of the Sigd festival.

Poems of the Month

Songs of Rain and Realization:
Geshem ("Rain") and *Geshem B'ito* ("Rain in Its Proper Time")

During the month of Marcheshvan, we begin reciting the **Prayer for Rain**.[3] In the climate of the Land of Israel, the summer is long and arduous, and by the end of that season, the people and the soil are crying for life-giving waters to rain down. It is no surprise, then, that our sources describe rain as a blessing from God, and the anticipation of rain is like anticipating a revelation of blessing and bounty over the surface of the earth. To this very day, we anticipate rain from infancy through adulthood. In preschools (which in Hebrew are called *ganim*, literally "gardens"), children sing these words from a song based on a Lea Goldberg poem: *Bo-u ananim, havu geshem laganim!*—"Come on, clouds! Make rain for the gardens/preschools." In adulthood, this child's song transforms to the words of a popular song by Meir Banai, and we continue to ask that rain come "since everything needs to be rinsed off." Rain songs are actually a special genre in Hebrew popular song and in Hebrew poetry.

I have chosen to present here two Israeli poems about rain written by women, both worded as modern prayers for rain: *Geshem* ("Rain") by Esther Raab and *Geshem B'ito* ("Rain in Its Proper Time") by Talma Alyagon-Roz.

Esther Raab (1894–1981), the first prominent woman poet born in the Land of Israel, wrote this poem of prayer for rain:

An elaborate Prayer for Rain (*T'filat HaGeshem*) is recited on Sh'mini Atzeret, and from that day on until Passover, when the dry season begins, we mention rain in our prayers. Many *piyutim*, both ancient and new, accompany the prayers for rain. (See the previous chapter for an example.) Quite different is the seventh day of Marcheshvan, when in Israel we not only mention that this is the season for rainfall but actively begin asking for rain. (The prayers asking for rain begin later outside Israel, on December 4 or 5. That day goes unmentioned by the Diaspora poets who wrote *piyutim*; it gets no special attention.)

Perhaps Sh'mini Atzeret, which is already a festival day for reasons besides rain, is a natural magnet for the poets' attention, while the seventh of Marcheshvan is just an ordinary weekday. But an ordinary weekday is also reason for celebration, and in the month of Marcheshvan we celebrate routine and ordinary weekdays.

Rain

   Esther Raab

Open, please, the floodgates of the heavens—
one floodgate!
A cluster of swollen, moist clouds—
for which all the seedlings are thirsting.
Send big drops,
round and sweet—
to the soil, the parched soil.
Drive away the evil winds running about,
and dry, rustling brambles.
Make soft groundsel flowers sprout up for us,
yellow as egg yolks,
on the plates of the hillsides;
anemones smiling in the wadis,
wood sorrel and tulip
among greenish retama bushes,

גֶּשֶׁם

אֶסְתֵּר רָאב

אָנָּא פְּתַח אֲרֻבּוֹת־שָׁמַיִם —
אֲרֻבָּה אַחַת!
סִיעַת עֲנָנִים תְּפוּחִים, לַחִים —
לָהֶם כָּל הַזֵּרְעוֹנִים צְמֵאִים.
שְׁלַח טִפּוֹת גְּדוֹלוֹת,
עֲגֻלּוֹת וּמְתוּקוֹת —
לָאֲדָמָה אֲדָמָה צְחִיחָה.
גָּרֵשׁ רוּחוֹת רָעוֹת מִשְׁתּוֹלְלוֹת
וְחַרוּלִים מְרַשְׁרְשִׁים יְבֵשִׁים.
הַעֲלֵה לָנוּ סַבְיוֹנִים רַכִּים,
צְהֻבִּים כְּחֶלְמוֹנִים,
עַל צַלָּעוֹת הַגְּבָעוֹת;
וְכַלָּנִיּוֹת מְחַיְּכוֹת בַּוָּאדִיּוֹת
וְחַמְצִיץ וְצִבְעוֹן
בֵּין שִׂיחֵי־רֹתֶם יְרַקְרַק,

and make the wheat stalks sprout and the oats turn green, and let there be food for human and beast and grasses too for the sparrows so gray, so hungry— wallowing and calling out in the dust. Open the locked gates of the heavens. Send down big, sweet drops upon the human heart and that of the earth.[4]	וְתִנְבֹּט הַחִטָּה וְתוֹרִיק הַשְּׂעוֹרָה וְלֶחֶם יִהְיֶה לָאָדָם וְלַבְּהֵמָה, וּדְשָׁאִים גַּם לָאַנְקוֹרִים אֲפֹרִים, רְעֵבִים — בָּאָבָק מִתְפַּלְּשִׁים וְצוֹוְחִים. פְּתַח שַׁעֲרֵי שָׁמַיִם נְעוּלִים שְׁלַח טִפּוֹת גְּדוֹלוֹת, מְתוּקוֹת עַל לֵב אָדָם וַאֲדָמָה.

Raab's poem is all blessing and joy, with nature revealing itself before our eyes in all its colorful and attractive splendor, due to those "big drops, round and sweet" that will suffuse the land and renew it. The poem begins with a specific request for rain: "Open, please, the floodgates of the heavens," a petition that may remind us of the Flood in Genesis, in which the floodgates of the heavens did open (Genesis 7:11). This is deliberate; Raab's poem is in dialogue with the prayers for rain in the Sephardic rite. The request for the gates of heaven to open appears at the beginning of an ancient *piyut* sung on Sh'mini Atzeret in Middle Eastern communities. It begins:

> May the Living God open the storehouses in the sky.
> May God's winds blow! Let the waters flow!
> With desired rain, bless our sacred band,
> trapped in sorrow like a bird in hand,
> by the merit of Abraham who prepared a meal for those who came onto his land
> and said, "Let a bit of water be offered them,"
> May God's winds blow! Let the waters flow!

Here, the poet is asking for a "flood" that will be gentle and beneficial. The poem ends with a broad, inclusive request that goes beyond asking simply for rain: "Open the locked gates of the heavens" is intended not only for the land but for "the human heart" as well, in hopes that big, sweet drops quench and sweeten our parched and bitter hearts.

The second poem is by Talma Alyagon-Roz (born in 1944). It is a poetic prayer but with a decidedly different tone.

Rain in Its Proper Time **Talma Alyagon-Roz** Rain in its proper time, so much sadness comes with it. Everything has stopped, everything has stood still; only the rain comes on time. It doesn't care that the nights there are very cold, that in the dunes it is hard to cry, that there's no one's shoulder to fall on, that outside the rainfall is knocking.	גֶּשֶׁם בְּעִתּוֹ תַּלְמָה אֱלִיגוֹן-רוֹז גֶּשֶׁם בְּעִתּוֹ כַּמָּה עֶצֶב בָּא אִתּוֹ הַכֹּל עָצַר, הַכֹּל עָמַד רַק הַגֶּשֶׁם בָּא לוֹ בַּזְּמַן לוֹ לֹא אִכְפַּת — שֶׁבַּלֵּילוֹת שָׁם קַר מְאוֹד שֶׁבַּחוֹלוֹת קָשֶׁה לִבְכּוֹת שֶׁאֵין עַל מִי לְהִתְרַפֵּק כְּשֶׁבַּחוּץ הַגֶּשֶׁם דּוֹפֵק.

Grant some of your warmth, grant some of your light,	תֵּן מֵחֻמְּךָ וְתֵן מְאוֹרְךָ
give the fields only proper, blessed rain.	תֵּן לַשָּׂדוֹת רַק גֶּשֶׁם בְּרָכָה
Share your loaf of bread generously,	תֵּן מִפִּתְּךָ בְּיָד רְחָבָה
and give us a time for love.	וְתֵן לָנוּ זְמַן לְאַהֲבָה.
Rain in its proper time,	גֶּשֶׁם בְּעִתּוֹ
they say it's good that way,	וְאוֹמְרִים שֶׁכָּכָה טוֹב
over summer clothes—an old sweater,	עַל בֶּגֶד קַיִץ סְוֶדֶר יָשָׁן
and in a pocket—an old letter from somewhere.	וּבַכִּיס מִכְתָּב מֵאֵי־שָׁם
Sweet rain,	גֶּשֶׁם מָתוֹק
rain, kiss him for me,	גֶּשֶׁם, נַשֵּׁק אוֹתוֹ בִּשְׁמִי
rain, caress his face.	גֶּשֶׁם, לַטֵּף אֶת הַפָּנִים
You brought rain in its time,	הֵבֵאתָ גֶּשֶׁם בְּעִתּוֹ
so bring him, bring him to me.[5]	אָז הָבֵא, הָבֵא לִי אוֹתוֹ.

This poem was written during that awful winter after the Yom Kippur War in 1973. Kobi Oshrat set it to music, and it is most widely known in Israel in the version recorded by Ruthi Navon. Rain is described in the poem as something difficult, with which comes "so much sadness." It uncovers the feelings of grief and loss that overcame Israeli society in the wake of that war, with rain turning into weeping (or perhaps teardrops falling like rain). But rain can also express hope and connection: "Rain, kiss him for me, / rain, caress his face." Longing for the return of a loved one is intertwined, in this poem, with a prayer for blessing: "Grant some of your warmth, grant some of your light, give the fields only proper, blessed rain."

Our ancestors also made a connection between women and rain. Rabbi Shimon ben Lakish says, "When the heavens are shut up so that neither dew nor rain falls, it is like a woman who is in labor but cannot give birth" (Babylonian Talmud, *Taanit* 8a). According to this description, seasonal rain—like pregnancy and childbirth—involves painful anticipation. Moreover, there is something hidden and mysterious with both rain and childbirth. Neither is taken for granted, nor do we have control over them. Our waiting and hoping for rain is somewhat akin to waiting for the end of labor pains, which is perhaps one of the most difficult parts of anticipating the birth of a baby.

The Talmud goes on with its comparison between childbirth and rainfall. We read the words of Reish Lakish in the name of Bar Kappara:

> "Block up" is applied to rain, and "block up" is applied to a woman. "Block up" is applied to a woman, as it is said, "For the Eternal had blocked up every womb" (Genesis 20:18), and "block up" is applied to rain, as it is written, "And God will block up the skies" (Deuteronomy 11:17). "Birthing" is applied to a woman, and "birthing" is applied to rain. "Birthing" is applied to a woman, as it is written, "And she conceived and gave birth to a son" (Genesis 30:23), and "birthing" is applied to rain, as it is written, "making the earth bring forth [literally 'give birth'] and sprout" (Isaiah 55:10). (Babylonian Talmud, *Taanit* 8a–b)

🌂 A Toast to the Blessing of Routine

AT THIS TIME OF YEAR, my grandfather, Moreno Levi, used say in Ladino, "*Si chuei Sukkot, vino falakot*," meaning "Sukkot is gone, the beatings are on," referring to blows from the *melamed*, the teacher, since studies begin in earnest after all the Tishrei holidays.[6] Tucked away between the spiritually stormy and emotional Days of Awe and the other Tishrei holidays, and the anticipated pleasures of Chanukah, with its lights, doughnuts, and gifts, is the modest month of Marcheshvan. When I was a child, my preschool teacher said that the month of Cheshvan was sad and bitter (*mar*), because it contains no holidays or festivities like those in Tishrei before it and Kislev after it, and that is how it got the name Marcheshvan. This story is only a popular etymology, a playful take on the name of the month. While in fact Marcheshvan does symbolize the yoke of routine, there is blessing and goodness to be found in everyday life. During Marcheshvan, we can celebrate the blessing of routine and the minor celebrations and gifts of daily life.

Marcheshvan offers a good opportunity to ask general existential questions, and if we look carefully, we will see that it offers a wide range of contrasts marking the contours of our lives as Jews. Here are three such complex, thought-provoking contrasts.

I. Rain—From Blessing to Curse to Blessing

Water shortages are increasingly common throughout the world, and it is something with which Israel has long been familiar. The Land of Israel does not have many rivers, nor does it have many sources of water. Agriculture and life in Israel—as in many places around the world—are dependent upon the blessing of rain. In Israel, we begin to recite the blessing that asks for rain on the seventh day of Marcheshvan. The blessing requesting a good year, which originally meant a successful agricultural year, is amended by adding the words "and grant dew and rain as a blessing." The particular date on which we begin this petitionary prayer was selected because those who established the liturgical cycles calculated that by the seventh of Marcheshvan, all the pilgrims who had come to the Temple in Jerusalem for Sukkot and Sh'mini Atzeret would have arrived home. Waiting until the seventh of Marcheshvan to begin the prayer would thus, in theory, prevent the ancient pilgrims from getting caught in the rain during their arduous journey home (*Mishnah Taanit* 1:3). This short prayer encapsulates our ongoing hope for a rainy winter in the face of anxiety about a possible drought, which could threaten the delicate fabric of life. Our ancestors knew that without water, there is no harvest and no food. Even today in Israel, as well as in many places in the world, water is a source of concern and, not infrequently, the basis of bitter conflicts.

The concern for the ancient pilgrims also reflects the need for balance between different populations—between the needs of Jews

---

During the rainy season, Sephardic Jewish communities add much more to the prayer for a good crop year (in the *Amidah*) than the short addition "and grant dew and rain as a blessing" added by Ashkenazim. They recite a long, detailed blessing that connects rainfall with a life of protection and hope:

Bless our year and its various harvests for good,
and grant dew and rain as a blessing throughout the earth,
and grant abundant water to the soil,
and satiate the entire world with Your bounty,
filling our hands with Your blessings and the rich gifts from Your hand.
Guard and rescue this year from every evil
and from every destructive force and any sort of disaster.
Make this a year full of good hope and a peaceful destiny.
Grant mercy and kindness to all its yield and its produce,
and bless it with the gift of proper rain,
and may its conclusion be life and fullness and peace,
like the best years of blessing.
Blessed are You, Eternal, who blesses the years.[7]

around the world, some of whom come from places with abundant water, and the needs of the residents of the Land of Israel. The life of routine requires some compromises and consideration of complex needs.

On the other hand, in the weekly Torah portion of Noah, the first weekly portion read during Marcheshvan, we read about the Flood: "Forty days the flood was upon the earth; the waters increased" (Genesis 7:17). The flood threatened to wash the world away and return it to primordial chaos. After the flood came God's promise of proper order in the world (Genesis 8:22) and that the earth would never again be so cursed. Along with anxiety about a lack of water, then, is the fear of being swept away by too much water. Between these two extremes we find a longing for balance and a quiet flow of the river of life.

II. The Sacred—and the Beginning of Disaster

On the first of Marcheshvan, according to tradition, the construction of the First Temple, Solomon's Temple, was completed (I Kings 6:38). That occasion was celebrated with a glorious and impressive ceremony. If we approach holiness and holy places from a very different angle, we arrive on the sixteenth of Marcheshvan, just after the full moon, as the anniversary of the Nazi pogroms known collectively as Kristallnacht (November 9, 1938), during which hundreds of synagogues were destroyed and innumerable Torah scrolls and synagogue objects were desecrated. That day marks, for many people, the beginning of the destruction of European Jewry during the Holocaust. The beginning of the month is about building, high spirits, and the institutionalization of the sacred, and mid-month its monstrous unraveling.

III. "The First Flowering of Redemption"[8]—and Concern for the Country's Future

Marcheshvan also marks two events in modern times that have influenced the lives of those of us who live in the State of Israel. During Marcheshvan in the Hebrew year 5778, on November 2, 1917, the Balfour Declaration was issued. The declaration states that Great Britain, then a major world power, would support the establishment of "a national home for the Jewish people" in Palestine. Lord Balfour's statement is a significant cornerstone, the first important political achievement of the Zionist movement, and, even more significantly, the genesis of a reasonable hope to create an organized Jewish life in the Land of Israel.

Marcheshvan is also when we mark a danger to the integrity and continuity of that national home—not danger emanating from the weapons of our foreign enemies, but a danger from within. This danger is marked in red ink on the calendars of the lives of many Israelis as the Memorial Day for Prime Minister Yitzhak Rabin, observed on the twelfth of Marcheshvan (see pp. 56–59). Those two events mark the range of feelings from the hope of creating a stable, sustainable Jewish national home in the Land of Israel to the recognition of how fragile that society is and how much we need to be wary of the dangers it faces.

A Colorful Weave of Jewish-Israeli Life

We have now seen three important circles of attention that the month of Marcheshvan summons us to think about: the **cosmic**, with its petition for rain and life, and a desire to achieve a balance in life and in nature; the **Jewish**, ranging from the quest for sanctity and nearness to God by building a Temple to mourning over the violation of sanctity during the darkest days our people has known; and the **Israeli**, moving forward from the beginning of achieving our dreams of building a national home in the Land of Israel to anxiety about the danger of its being overthrown, God forbid.

In the present Israeli reality, variety and diversity are regarded as blessings, a reason to rejoice: in addition to the general Jewish and Israeli calendar events, we mark holidays of Jewish ethnic groups such as Maimuna, Saharana, and, on the twenty-ninth of Marcheshvan, the Sigd holiday of Beta Israel, which is all about the renewal of the covenant between the people and their God.

The Book of Kings describes an ancient Marcheshvan holiday that was established by Jeroboam son of Nebat (see pp. 60–62) and was celebrated on the fifteenth of the eighth month—the fifteenth of Marcheshvan (I Kings 12:32). Jeroboam, who established the independent northern Kingdom of Israel, which encompassed ten of the twelve Israelite tribes, threatened the Kingdom of Judah to the south. The establishment of the holiday was understood (apparently correctly) as a sign of rebellion and of an intention to break away from the Jerusalem-based regime. Understandably, this holiday is not part of our calendar today.

In the month of Marcheshvan, there are indeed many great occasions, but it is also a time that marks the edge of the colorful weave of which our lives are stitched as Jews in Israel. "Does anyone scorn a day of small things?" asks the prophet Zechariah (4:10). Moving beyond Tishrei and the Days of Awe enables us to pay attention to "a day of small things," with its slow and patient signs on which our lives are inscribed.

Tishrei *Marcheshvan* *Kislev* *Tevet* *Sh'vat* *Adar* *Nisan* *Iyar* *Sivan* *Tammuz* *Av* *Elul*

What Shall We Remember on Yitzhak Rabin Memorial Day?

"THE GOVERNMENT OF ISRAEL announces in shock, with great sadness and deep sorrow, the death of Prime Minister and Defense Minister Yitzhak Rabin, who was murdered by an assassin, tonight in Tel Aviv."[9] I get goosebumps and shivers every time I hear the words of that announcement, given by Eitan Haber—a noted Israeli journalist and longtime friend of Rabin—on that bitter autumn night in November 1995. The murder of Yitzhak Rabin (1922–95) shaped a whole generation, and to a considerable degree continues to shape us.

In 1997, the Knesset established the official Yitzhak Rabin Memorial Day, to be observed on the twelfth of Marcheshvan. Despite that provision of the law, many Israelis continue to mark a Memorial Day for Rabin on the civil date of his murder, November 4. The law states that a memorial service is to take place on Mount Herzl (the national cemetery of Israel), at Rabin's grave, with an emphasis on Rabin's life and legacy, and with discussions about democratic values in the public schools. We have promised not to forget, but just what is it that we must not forget? What exactly do we need to remember? How should modern events be formed into national, public memory to be shared by us as Jews in Israel, especially when we are dealing with events of political significance?

Let us consider how best to shape the national Memorial Day of Rabin's assassination. (The murder itself and the public atmosphere that led up to it—and the implications of both—deserve a separate discussion.) The significance of these questions is much broader than the treatment of remembering the victim, the murder, and their meaning. These questions touch the very heart of the pulsing nerve of our existence, and they are instructive as to how we perceive ourselves as a Jewish-Israeli society.

When? How? What? Where?

Every family has its seder night traditions—the way they sing the Four Questions and the special recipe for *charoset*—but the general outline is similar in every home.

From Time to Time → Dalia Marx

Different synagogues have different liturgical traditions, *piyutim*, and a variety of customs for the holidays—but the basic prayers are similar in all of them. When we add a new observance to the calendar, we cannot rely on existing traditions, and many questions arise about the character we should give such a day. So it was with the need to institutionalize a memorial to the Holocaust, a memorial to fallen Israeli soldiers, and the celebration of Israel's independence, all of which are still in search of their unique expression in Israel. For Yitzhak Rabin Memorial Day, this is even more true, given Israel's segmented and divided society. In fact, there is not even unanimous agreement that it should take place at all. I will not issue a ruling or suggest cut-and-dried answers about how we should observe this Memorial Day. Instead, let us address the questions that it raises: (a) when to observe it, (b) what content it should have, and (c) in what context it should be marked.

I. When to Observe It: Should the Knesset or the Public Decide?

A bitter debate took place between the Pharisees and Sadducees, the two main sects of the Second Temple period, about how the calendar and its dates of various holidays and observances should be set (see p. 247). Both groups understood that whoever controls the calendar controls everything. While one might exhibit tolerance for different holiday customs, the date of the holiday itself is its identity card, and that must be a matter of consensus. Two years after Rabin's assassination, the Israeli Knesset established the twelfth of Marcheshvan as the official Yitzhak Rabin Memorial Day, but the public has more widely accepted the civil date of his assassination on November 4. So when should we mark Rabin's murder?

The example of Yitzhak Rabin Memorial Day is just an illustration of the fact that Israeli Jews exist in a kind of calendrical schizophrenia, living according to two different calendars—the Hebrew calendar and the civil calendar of the wider world. Jewish holidays are observed on their Hebrew dates, while meetings and professional events follow the civil calendar. The question remains: How are other days—like someone's birthday or conversely the anniversary of someone's death—to be marked? How do our days flow? The question of when to have a memorial to Yitzhak Rabin is a classic example of the tension between the official decisions "from on high"—here, the Hebrew date—and the demand "from below"—the civil date. For many people, the civil date represents the nation's actual experience. This is the tension between what is official and what is seared into the collective memory.

II. What Should We Remember on the Memorial Day for Rabin?

The content of Yitzhak Rabin Memorial Day, too, is caught up in controversy. Rabin was a political man and the architect of the Oslo Accords, the first set of peace accords that sought to establish peace between Israel and the Palestinians. His political activity earned him hero status among some people, while at the same time it made him a despised figure among other segments of the Jewish population of Israel. His assassination was an extreme and violent expression of the political opposition to the process he was leading. As a result, there is no agreement about the nature of his Memorial Day. In the eyes of part of the public, the focus should be on the man and his legacy,

The Yitzhak Rabin Memorial Day Law, 5758/1997

1. The twelfth of Marcheshvan, the anniversary of the murder of Prime Minister and Minister of Defense Yitzhak Rabin, will be a national Memorial Day; this day will be marked in government institutions, IDF camps, and schools. . . .
2. The flags at government institutions and IDF camps will be lowered to half-staff.
3. Alongside Yitzhak Rabin's grave on Mount Herzl, a memorial ceremony will take place.
4. In IDF camps, the chief of staff will proclaim an order of the day.
5. In schools, this Memorial Day will be marked by:
   - activities that will highlight Yitzhak Rabin and his achievements;
   - activities devoted to the importance of democracy in Israel and the danger to society and the state presented by violence.[10]

while for others, it is a day to consider Israeli democracy and discuss the dangers that lurk at its door by warning against political, nationalist, and religious extremism and learning about the dangers of hatred and violence. Still others call for the day to be one on which we focus on Jewish unity and *ahavat Yisrael*, love for all Jews, while others stress human dignity and the sanctity of life. Some have suggested that the day should serve as a day of national self-reflection (this just one month after Yom Kippur, when we do our individual self-reflection). Even the wording of the law establishing Yitzhak Rabin Memorial Day reflects this indecision.

The larger framework of the day is also a matter of controversy. Some argue that it should have Jewish content, such as prayers and a fast; others see it as a civil and essentially secular observance. The curricula, assemblies, and lessons that have been created to mark Yitzhak Rabin Memorial Day represent a range of content and approaches. The question arises as to whether to make Yitzhak Rabin Memorial Day into a civil holiday, given that part of the public essentially opposed Rabin's actions and views. Additionally, the question remains of whether we should properly educate against the violence and rhetoric that led to the assassination. These questions have only grown more pressing in the decades since Rabin's assassination.

Where to Remember and with Whom?

"Where were you when Rabin was murdered?" Most adult Israelis—along with many Jews around the world—can answer that question, reporting in detail on the events of that evening and the days that followed. In the aftermath of the assassination, many spontaneous gatherings took place in what was Kings of Israel Square (later renamed Rabin Square) the site of the assassination in Tel Aviv, and in the streets of other cities. Teenagers and young adults lit candles and sang songs together, in what appeared then to be the beginning of a tradition. Those gatherings faded away over the next few years though. A central mass gathering was held annually over many years in the square where the assassination took place. Ceremonies continue to take place in schools and youth movements, and various groups and organizations hold public dialogue events to mark the Memorial Day each year. The Israeli public, however, has not yet settled on a pattern for this memorial. Underlying all our questions about this day, one question still gnaws at us: What will happen to Yitzhak Rabin Memorial Day when most of the public no longer recalls that fateful evening in the autumn of 1995? Will Yitzhak Rabin Memorial Day become securely established, entering the Jewish-Israeli calendar in one form or another for generations, or will Rabin's memory fade as the years pass? Will these memorial observances become empty rituals devoid of the emotional force they had in the early years?

From Time to Time → Dalia Marx

Days That Are Magnets

In the Hebrew calendar there are days that attract meanings as though they were magnets for events. Tradition tends to cluster important events onto special days, which draw in new meaning over the generations and create clusters of significance. The most famous example is the cluster of fast days in the summer, of which the Mishnah (*Taanit* 4:6) says, "Five things happened to our ancestors on the seventeenth of Tammuz and five on the ninth of Av" (see pp. 277, 305–6). Those two fast days are difficult days, and naturally other difficult and sad events that occurred on or close to those dates have been linked to them. So it was in ancient times, and so it is even now, in our time. One of the days connected to Yitzhak Rabin Memorial Day is the Fast of Gedaliah.

The Fast of Gedaliah marked on the third of Tishrei, just after Rosh HaShanah, recalls the murder of Gedaliah son of Achikam, who was the governor of Judah in the period after the destruction of the First Temple when most Judeans were exiled to Babylon. Gedaliah strove to ensure the existence of Jewish life even after the destruction, acting pragmatically in his relations with the Babylonian conquerors. Groups of extremist nationalists (or perhaps just those who wanted to rule themselves) conspired to murder him, which led the remnant of the Jewish settlement in Israel to completely disappear. The assassination of Gedaliah signifies the complete and utter destruction of the First Jewish Commonwealth, and it became a fast day for later generations.

Some people have pointed to similarities between these events and the murder of a prime minister. During the first years after Rabin's murder, there were in fact some who offered a special prayer on the Fast of Gedaliah at the site of Rabin's assassination. After a few years this custom dwindled, perhaps because Gedaliah ben Achikam was perceived by some of the public as someone too willing to kowtow to the enemy, which was precisely the accusation hurled against the prime minister by the circles from which Rabin's assassin emerged. The timing of the Fast of Gedaliah is also not close to the date of Rabin's assassination, and the religious nature of the day may have been unattractive to many people.

Israeli society has not yet provided an answer to the questions of when, what, and where we should observe Yitzhak Rabin Memorial Day. It has not yet found an appropriate and widely accepted framework that will grant the day meaning and establish a solid historical, ideological, and theological pattern for it. Only time will tell how we will recall the day of that tragic murder, what the day's content will be, and when we will mark it. Time will tell whether Rabin's memory will crystallize and become an essential part of our consciousness or if it will fade and slowly disappear from public awareness. I believe that it would be better not to focus the day's events on the victim's personality alone; instead, we would be wise to lift our sights and use this difficult day to ask questions of principle related to our very existence—as people created in the divine image, and as Jews in the State of Israel.

The Assassination of Gedaliah

The officers of the troops in the open country, and their men with them, heard that the king of Babylon had put Gedaliah son of Achikam in charge of the region, and that he put in his charge the men, women, and children—of the poorest of the land, those who had not been exiled to Babylon. . . . Gedaliah son of Achikam son of Shaphan swore to them and their men, saying, "Do not be afraid to serve the Chaldeans. Stay in the land and serve the king of Babylon, and it will go well with you." . . . Ishmael son of Nethaniah and the ten men who were with him arose and struck down Gedaliah son of Achikam son of Shaphan with the sword and killed him, because the king of Babylon had put him in charge of the land. (Jeremiah 40:7–41:2)

Jeroboam Demands Social Justice (and Religious Freedom)

AT EXACTLY MID-MONTH when the moon is full, on the fifteenth of Marcheshvan, comes the holiday that Jeroboam son of Nebat "contrived by his own mind" (I Kings 12:33) and that is long forgotten. However, this is a good opportunity to reflect on a king who is considered in Jewish tradition to be an entirely negative figure, one of the three kings who according to the Mishnah have no place in the world-to-come (*Mishnah Sanhedrin* 10:2). When we read his story, though, it is hard to understand why he was so reviled. According to the biblical account, Jeroboam was a tool in the hands of God, the one who carried out Solomon's divinely foretold punishment that warned the kingship would be torn away from his descendants. He is also the recipient in the dramatic prophecy of Ahijah of Shiloh, who ripped his garment into twelve shreds as a sign of the kingdom's dissolution. Ahijah put ten of those shreds into Jeroboam's hand, assuring him that he would be king over ten tribes.

Jeroboam was a charismatic leader in his own right. He was not born into a family with a dynastic pedigree. He was a leader with a social conscience, who refused to submit to the cruel system of taxation imposed by Solomon and his heir Rehoboam. Jeroboam's rebellion broke out after Rehoboam refused to alleviate his pressure on the people, who were being crushed by taxes. Rehoboam even threatened the people: "My father made your yoke heavy, but I will add to your yoke; my father flogged you with whips, but I will flog you with scorpions" (I Kings 12:14).

Before Rehoboam's rule, Jeroboam had publicly protested King Solomon's policy of using public funds to build a house for Pharaoh's daughter and closed up openings in the city wall in order to levy onerous taxes on pilgrims to Jerusalem. This was a protest against Solomon's corruption, as he was more concerned about his foreign wives than his own people. Jeroboam's revolt against the Kingdom of Judah was political, social, and religious as well, and unlike other biblical rebellions (such as David's rebellion against Saul), it was nonviolent.

The Prophecy of the Kingdom's Division

During that time Jeroboam went out of Jerusalem and the prophet Ahijah of Shiloh met him on the way. He had put on a new robe; and when the two were alone in the open country, Ahijah took hold of the new robe he was wearing and tore it into twelve pieces. "Take ten pieces," he said to Jeroboam, "For thus said the Eternal, the God of Israel: 'I am about to tear the kingdom out of Solomon's hands, and I will give you ten tribes. . . . And to [David's] son I will give one tribe, so that there may be a lamp for My servant David before Me in Jerusalem—the city where I have chosen to establish My name. But you have been chosen by Me; reign wherever you wish, and you shall be king over Israel.'"
(I Kings 11:29–37)

A "Contrived Holiday"?

The holiday that Jeroboam invented, or, as the Bible puts it, "contrived," was celebrated exactly a month after the holiday of Sukkot, "just like the festival in Judah" (I Kings 12:32). Jeroboam did not invent a new holiday; he instead declared a sort of "leap month"—an extra month added to the calendar—and declared that Sukkot would occur not in its normal month of Tishrei but would instead be marked in this added leap month. There are some who claim that Jeroboam restored an ancient northern harvest festival celebrated a month after the one observed in the south by the people of Judah, since the colder climate of the north delayed the ripening of the crops. Making this change had a critical influence: whoever holds the keys to the calendar, so to speak, holds the mechanism by which the people's collective lives are lived. By creating an independent calendar for the Northern Kingdom, Jeroboam severed that kingdom from the Kingdom of Judah; from that point forward, the calendar of Israel was distinct from the calendar of Judah.

Jeroboam's protest was expressed not only in the temporal dimension but in the spatial dimension as well: he created an alternative cultic center. His political goal was to make pilgrimage to Jerusalem unnecessary, thereby diminishing the centralization of religious—and thus economic—power in Jerusalem. We do not know very much about Jeroboam's religious motivation, but it is clear he was a bold innovator. He had no compunction about creating (or renewing) one of Israel's festivals. Jeroboam worked to undermine the priesthood as well, which the Torah had given to the tribe of Levi: "He appointed priests from the ranks of the people who were not of Levite descent" (I Kings 12:31). And he himself ascended the altar to offer incense. We know almost nothing about the nature of that cult, but the Bible tells us that Jeroboam made two golden calves, which are particularly fraught symbols. The golden calves obviously evoke the sin of the Golden Calf. Jeroboam then called, "You have been going up to Jerusalem long enough. This is your god, O Israel, who brought you up from the land of Egypt!" (I Kings 12:28), which is reminiscent of the people's response before the Golden Calf that Aaron made (Exodus 32:4).

Did Jeroboam intend to create a cult of calf worship and to rebel against the God of Israel? Perhaps, but that is by no means the only way to understand the passage. Keep in mind that our Book of Kings was composed by people who were supporters of the southern Kingdom of Judah, and its author clearly sought to make an evildoer of Jeroboam, king of the northern realm. Jeroboam's actions can be read as a demand for cultural and religious pluralism among the people, for the decentralization of authority, or for a more democratic approach to holiness, and not necessarily as a rebellion against faith in the one God. After all, in the Temple in Jerusalem there were statues too—the two cherubim over the Ark of the Covenant, and according to at least some interpretations, their faces were those of calves. There seems to be something about these particular animal figures that was understood to be related to sanctity, to God's chariot. In Ezekiel's vision of the chariot, for example, there are four creatures, and "the feet of each were like a single calf's foot" (Ezekiel 1:7). On this basis, perhaps we can infer that Jeroboam's wish was to observe the revelation of the Divine Presence, rather than to institute idolatry. He set up the calves in the borderlands of the north, one at Dan and the other at Bethel. Bethel, it should be recalled, was the place where Jacob had received divine revelation. Jeroboam's act of subversion against Judahite authority in Jerusalem may symbolize a return to that more ancient revelation, a reversion to the people's ancient foundation. In *The Secret Book of Kings*, popular Israeli novelist Yochi Brandes portrays Jeroboam as an enlightened leader with an unusual monotheistic and pluralistic vision. Brandes's interpretation earned her some sharp condemnation, and in fact her story is inconsistent with the reading we

On Jeroboam's Religious and Ritual Initiative

So the king took counsel and made two golden calves. He said to the people, "You have been going up to Jerusalem long enough. This is your god, O Israel, who brought you up from the land of Egypt!" He set up one in Bethel and placed the other in Dan. This proved to be a cause of guilt, for the people went to worship [the calf at Bethel and] the one at Dan. He also made cult places and appointed priests from the ranks of the people who were not of Levite descent.... And Jeroboam established a festival on the fifteenth day of the eighth month; just like the festival in Judah, he established [an altar] at Bethel, and he ascended the altar [there]. On the fifteenth day of eighth month—the month in which he had contrived of his own mind to establish a festival for the Israelites ... and he ascended the altar to present an offering. (I Kings 12:28–33)

In the coronation speech that Yochi Brandes places in the mouth of Jeroboam in her book *The Secret Book of Kings*, he calls out to the assembled masses:

"My brothers, my loved ones, my people, on this day, thirty-three years after that company of soldiers ruined the Festival of Rain in Zeredah, I hereby proclaim the restoration of the ancient festivals of all the tribes of Israel. God loves the holidays of all of us: the rain festival of Ephraim, the fire festival of Manasseh, the dairy festival of Benjamin, the sun festival of Dan, the rainbow festival of Naphtali, the shearing festival of Simeon, the fertility festival of Reuben,

Tishrei **Marcheshvan** *Kislev Tevet Sh'vat Adar Nisan Iyar Sivan Tammuz Av Elul*

the fish festival of Zebulun, the oil festival of Asher, the moon festival of Issachar, and the wine festival of Gad. And God also loves the ingathering festival of Judah, just as he loves the holidays of every other tribe—no less, but also no more. We will all continue to celebrate the Festival of Freedom, the Festival of Harvest, and the Festival of Booths, the three major holidays of Israel, while each tribe will celebrate its own holidays separately, as our ancestors did before us. These separate holidays do not harm our unity as a nation....

"I am directing this call from the top of Mount Gerizim to the mountains of Judah.... My brothers, my loved ones, people of Judah, do not split off from us. Return to us, and we will be one people and one kingdom together, just as God promised our patriarchs."[11]

Innovation without Overthinking

About a month before Passover, as Purim approached in 1930, a member of Kibbutz Ginegar named David Omnitsky wrote to Chayim Nachman Bialik to ask the nation's poet for advice and direction regarding a meaningful observance of that holiday and of the seder night in the young kibbutz. Bialik replied:

"It is impossible to put a holiday or a holiday ceremony in order. Real, reliable celebration comes from the heart and comes into this world with divine inspiration. If it doesn't have these, what long-distance advice can be useful?

My advice is: celebrate your ancestral festivals and add to them something of your own, according to your own ability, taste, and conditions. The important thing is that you do everything wholeheartedly and with a sense of live emotion and spiritual need, without overthinking it."[12]

have been accustomed to. But if someone can read the story with fresh eyes, this subversive retelling is not unreasonable.

Every religious behavior, and every religious text or ritual, has sociopolitical dimensions. In general, the rituals and prayers create a sense of togetherness that characterizes a worship community and at the same time sets it apart from others. Jewish prayer primarily addresses God but additionally addresses other worshipers and even other "others" who are not present. For example, the prayer calling for God to destroy "sectarians" was created in the first century CE at Yavneh, a major center of Torah learning after the destruction of the Second Temple (Babylonian Talmud, *B'rachot* 28b). This prayer is actually a curse against "sectarians"—those people who seem to be part of the Jewish covenant with God but have different beliefs. This prayer was created to distinguish between proper worshipers and "others." Similarly, when the *Geonim* instituted that the Mishnaic passage about kindling Shabbat lamps be recited on Fridays just before Shabbat begins, their goal was to make a religious and political statement against the Karaites, who were opposed to the kindling of Shabbat lamps at all. When Diaspora Jews historically created prayers for the welfare of the government, they did so to show loyalty to the countries in which they lived. In the case of the holiday that Jeroboam instituted, it is hard to distinguish between a social and political agenda and authentic religious sentiments. In other less extreme instances, many complex factors coalesce in a search for a sustainable religious experience.

What turns a ceremony or ritual into part of a people's canon? What gives it a stamp of approval to enter the calendar? Jeroboam supplied an interesting model, resurrecting a preexisting holiday and including ancient tribal traditions to create something new, rather than creating an entirely new holiday *ex nihilo*. The holiday that Jeroboam instituted came to an end with the loss of the Northern Kingdom, but centuries later, another holiday came into being as a sort of postponed Sukkot, and this holiday is still celebrated by the Jewish people with great fanfare. I am referring to Chanukah. According to the apocryphal book of II Maccabees, Chanukah was celebrated after the Hasmonean victory as a sort of correction or second chance to observe the Sukkot holiday that the Jews had been unable to observe in its season, when the Temple was still in a state of defilement. There we read:

> They celebrated it for eight days with rejoicing, in the manner of the Festival of Sukkot, remembering how not long before, during the Festival of Booths, they had been wandering in the mountains and caves like wild animals.... They decreed by public edict, ratified by vote, that the whole nation of the Jews should observe these days every year. (II Maccabees 10:6–8)

The spontaneous holiday that marked the Hasmoneans' victory became, through a "public edict," a holiday observed "every year."

Sigd: The Holiday of the Ethiopian Jews

SIGD IS A SPECIAL HOLIDAY of the Ethiopian Jewish community, known as Beta Israel, which confirms and celebrates the renewal of the covenant between God and the people of Israel. It is celebrated on the twenty-ninth of Marcheshvan, exactly fifty days after Yom Kippur, just as Shavuot is celebrated exactly fifty days after the first day of Passover. In both instances, this specific period of time indicates a profound spiritual process: the counting of the Omer between Passover and Shavuot, and the process of *t'shuvah* between Yom Kippur and the Sigd festival. Sigd forms "a sort of 'upper level' of communal self-assessment, constructed over the 'ground floor of individual stocktaking done by each individual on Yom Kippur.'"[13]

Before their *aliyah* (immigration to Israel), the members of the Beta Israel community lived among Christian and Muslim populations in hundreds of small villages scattered across a broad territory in the north and northwest of Ethiopia. They zealously preserved their pre-Rabbinic Jewish traditions and developed unique customs, since Rabbinic literature and law had never reached their community. Sigd was an opportunity for these small, widely dispersed communities to gather and celebrate together.

Ethiopian Jews report that the preparations for the holiday lasted many days. As in the ancient pilgrimage to the Temple, the residents of distant villages gathered around the mountain on which Sigd was celebrated. Several mountains were located near some central places where the Beta Israel lived, and those were chosen by the religious leaders, the *kessoch*, for celebrating Sigd. In preparation for the holiday, the people immersed in a river for purification.

On the day of Sigd, everyone fasted and wore festive white clothes. The *kessoch* donned white headdresses, and the dignitaries held festive parasols, symbols of status and honor. The priests, singing at the head of a procession that ascended the mountain, carried the *Orit* (a Torah scroll in the ancient Ge'ez language, whose name is a cognate for the Aramaic term for Torah, *Oraita*), which was wrapped in a colorful cloth. A few of the pilgrims carried a stone on their backs or heads, which symbolized either their submission before God or the sins that weighed on them. When they reached the top of the mountain, they placed the stones on a fence that demarcated the site where the *kessoch* would stand; each year, that fence grew taller. The way the Beta Israel cast off the stones forms an interesting parallel to the medieval *Tashlich* ceremony of Ashkenazic Jewry, during which sins are symbolically cast off by throwing bread crumbs into water.

At the top of the mountain, the *kessoch* stood in a purified compound and spread out the books of *Orit* on multicolored cloths. As far as I have been able to learn from Ethiopian *olim*, there was no barrier (as in Orthodox communities) separating the men and the women, but a separation was maintained according to age and status, with the women standing at the periphery all around.

The Sigd ceremony itself was crafted in large part on the image of the Revelation at Mount Sinai. After the people gathered and the dignitaries ascended the moun-

> The meaning of the word *sigd* (ስግድ) in Ge'ez is "genuflection." Ge'ez, Ethiopian Jewry's holy tongue, and Amharic, their spoken language, are both Semitic languages. The word *sigd* is from the root *s-g-d*, which in Hebrew also refers to worship of God; *sagad* in Hebrew means "to bow down in worship," and the root is understood similarly in both Aramaic and Arabic. The term *misgad*, the Hebrew term (with an Arabic cognate) for a mosque, is derived from the same root.

Recognition of the Beta Israel community as Jews had been an issue in Israel since 1973, when Rabbi Ovadia Yosef (Sephardic chief rabbi from 1973 to 1983) ruled that the Ethiopian Jews are descendants of the biblical tribe of Dan. His ruling relied on an earlier ruling by Rabbi David ben Zimra in the sixteenth century after he had met Jewish prisoners from among the Jews of Ethiopia.

Nonetheless, when they came to Israel in modern times, the Ethiopian immigrants were met with suspicion by the religious establishment. Israel's chief rabbinate took the position that although the group as a whole was recognized as Jewish, not every individual person could be considered a Jew. The fact that Ethiopian Jews were unfamiliar with Rabbinic literature and law led the chief rabbinate to doubt the word of the *kessoch*, the religious leaders of the Beta Israel community, as to the Jewish status of individual members (for purposes of conversion or divorce). As a result, the chief rabbinate demanded that the Ethiopian immigrants of the 1970s and early 1980s undergo an accelerated conversion process that included an immersion in a *mikveh* (ritual bath), a declaration of acceptance of Rabbinic law, and for men, a symbolic re-circumcision. With Operation Moses, the covert Israeli mission to airlift thousands of Ethiopian Jews to Israel, in 1984, an internal movement rose in opposition to that conversion process, accompanied by a string of demonstrations; this gradually led to the removal of the chief rabbinate's demands—although the rabbinate never formally changed its requirements. This demand—that the Ethiopian *olim*, who saw themselves as Jews in every way, undergo conversion—left a stain on their experience of coming to Israel. The Ethiopian Jewish community in Israel now numbers about 155,000 people.

tain and laid out the *Orit* on the raised platform covered with colorful cloth, the official ceremony took place. It included prayers performed by the *kessoch* and the reading of the Torah in Ge'ez—the ancient holy language—and its translation into the vernacular Amharic. The *kessoch* called on the participants to forgive each other and encouraged them to cling to the mitzvot. At the end of their exhortations, they blessed the assembled congregation for having taken the covenant upon themselves and expressed hope that all of them would reach Jerusalem.

In the afternoon, the atmosphere would undergo a total reversal, and the sobriety, the fast, and the serious and somber atmosphere of taking stock of oneself transformed into the joy of purity and release, as the celebrants descended to the bottom of the mountain in song and dance and in anticipation of a great feast.

The Covenant Renewed

In the Bible we read about many covenants established between people, such as Abraham's covenant with Abimelech in Genesis 20 and, of course, covenants between God and Abraham, such as the Covenant of the Pieces in Genesis 15. What they have in common is that they are both a onetime occurrence and last for eternity. Even when Israel sins and violates the terms of the covenant, they might receive punishment—but the covenant remains intact. The belief of Beta Israel "reflects a different, more stringent approach to the covenant, according to which the covenant between the Eternal and the people is not fixed and eternal, but instead dependent on the acts of each and every person."[14] The idea that the covenant is conditional is expressed, for example, in the insistence that if someone leaves the village and is later exposed as abandoning the tradition, they need to convert in order to be readmitted. Thus, there was a need for a seasonal renewal of the covenant and people's commitment to it.

The basis for Sigd is the ancient communal covenant renewal arranged by Ezra and Nehemiah for the Babylonian returnees to ancient Israel on a date close to Sigd:

> On the twenty-fourth day of this month, the Israelites assembled, fasting, in sackcloth, and with earth upon them. Those of the stock of Israel separated themselves from all foreigners and stood and confessed their sins and the iniquities of their ancestors. Standing in their places, they read from the scroll of the Teaching of the Eternal their God for one-fourth of a day, and for another fourth they confessed and prostrated themselves before the Eternal their God.... "May Your glorious name be blessed, exalted though it is above every blessing and praise!" ...
>
> And they take an oath with sanctions to follow the Teaching of God, given through Moses, the servant of God. (Nehemiah 9:1–3, 5, 10:30)

Similarly, we can find a few precedents from the Second Temple period that indicate there were some who thought the covenant with God needed an annual renewal. In the Book of Jubilees, for example, we read that Shavuot marks Noah's exit from the ark, so that holiday can also be considered a holiday of covenant renewal (Jubilees 6:1).

From the Holy Mountain to the Holy City

The Sigd holiday expressed the Beta Israel community's longing for Jerusalem and redemption. After Operation Moses and the first wave of *aliyah* by Ethiopian Jews in the 1980s, they began to observe Sigd in Israel and included in the celebration a pilgrimage to Jerusalem. In the early years, Sigd was observed on Mount Zion and at the Kotel (the Western Wall), but since 1984, in the middle of Operation Moses, the ceremony has taken place on the Sherover Promenade in Talpiyot, overlooking the Temple Mount from the south. In 2008, Sigd was accepted as an official holiday of the State of Israel.

The promenade is divided into many sections for the day's celebrations. In a large tent, the members of the community offer explanations of the holiday to visitors who come to show respect for the Ethiopian community on its holy day. Stands offer information about the history of the community and about its struggle to attain a recognized place in Israeli society. Dialogue groups invite passersby to converse and learn about the holiday. Youth movement members, most of them members of the Ethiopian community, have a salient presence at the gathering and a notable effort is made to give them a sense of belonging and pride and to involve them in the Sigd ceremony from the old country, which they never experienced firsthand. The prayers, Torah reading, and the glow on the faces of the community elders who listen with one ear to the melody of the *kessoch*'s prayers and with the other to the curiosity of the young people who did not know Sigd as it was in Ethiopia—I find all this particularly moving. After the prayers are completed, the celebrants go to a broad tent to break their fast with the holy bread called *berekete*.

When I took part in the Sigd celebration, I asked one of the leaders of the Ethiopian community why the choice was made to hold the central celebration at the promenade overlooking the Old City rather than by the Western Wall (although there is a group whose festivities take place there). His answer was, "We have come to Jerusalem, but we are still not fully there, so we chose a place from which to look out on the site where the Temple stood. Our redemption is not yet complete." His answer stirred up many thoughts for me about the place of Zionism in our lives. This is, perhaps, the story of Zionism as a whole—a culture that was founded on yearning for an unattained land that achieved its dream; that fulfillment, conversely, led many powerful historical symbols and ceremonies to lose their power and has forced us to give them new meaning or to adopt new symbols.

> An additional day on the calendar that marks the heritage of the Beta Israel community is the Memorial Day for those lost in the Ethiopian Jewish *aliyah*, observed on the twenty-eighth of Iyar—which is also Yom Y'rushalayim (Jerusalem Day).
>
> Some four thousand members of the community lost their lives during the exhausting overland trek to the refugee camps in Sudan that served as the gathering point for flights to Israel, or during the long wait for those flights from the camps. Many others experienced indescribable suffering as they waited to realize their dream and come to Israel.

∽

Sigd—and similarly the Mimouna festival of North African Jewry (see pp. 189–92), the Saharana of the Jews of Kurdistan, the Novy God of *olim* from the (former) Soviet Union, and the Thanksgiving holiday of the *olim* from the United States—enrich the Jewish-Israeli calendar and thicken it with local and ethnic holidays. These holidays enable members of the various Jewish ethnic groups in Israel to honor their uniqueness and invite the larger Jewish Israeli community to come, taste, and participate in their culture.

Prayer of the Month
Egzio sema'ane—"Eternal, Hear Us"

THE PRAYER I HAVE CHOSEN for the month of Marcheshvan is taken from one of the prayers said by the *kessoch*, the religious leaders of the Beta Israel Ethiopian Jewish community, on the morning of the Sigd festival (see above). Shoshana Ben-Dor has collected, transcribed, and translated into Hebrew the prayers of the Ethiopian community from the oral traditions of the *kessoch* who came as immigrants, some of whom have now passed away; this is part of a larger effort to preserve the heritage of the Beta Israel community.[15] The community's prayers are offered in Ge'ez, the ancient sacred language of Ethiopian Jews. Today that language is known only by a few, which makes it difficult to pass the prayers on to the community's younger members.

Egzio sema'ane is a petitionary prayer of fourteen stanzas recited on Sigd and other holidays and also during a drought or in times of trouble. One *kes* would take turns reciting the stanzas, and between stanzas a refrain was recited by all of the *kessoch* in unison: *Egzio sema'ane, sema'ane! Egzio sema'ane, sema'ane amlakne!* ("Eternal, hear us, hear us! Eternal, hear us; hear us, our God!").

The first stanzas of the prayer recall God's kindness and care for such biblical figures as Moses, David, Solomon, Elijah, and Elisha. Each of these figures shares the experience of praying to God and having their prayers answered.

The second part of the prayer includes requests for protection and rescue, and forgiveness of sins. These are stanzas nine through eleven:

> Eternal, *Egzio sema'ane, sema'ane*—redeem us, redeem us, Eternal!
> Redeem us, our God, with Your power,
> just as, with Your power, You took [us] out of Egypt,
> with the great power of Your uplifted arm, redeem us.
> Eternal, God of justice, like them—redeem us.
>
> Eternal, guard over us, guard over us, Eternal!
> Guard over us, our God, guard over us,
> just as You guarded over them, You were a shepherd for Israel.
> Like a flock alongside Joseph
> who saw Ephraim, Benjamin, and Manasseh before him,
> in Your power, and heal us!
> Forgive us as You forgave them.
> Like them, guard over us.
> Eternal, guard over us, guard over us, Eternal!
> Eternal, guard over us, my God!
> The Eternal will guard over you, the Eternal will protect you.
> The Eternal by day will call to you and will see you at night.
> The Eternal will guard over you from all disaster
> and place your life under guard.
> The Eternal is on your path and in your home.
> Amen, God's name from eternity to eternity.

Tishrei **Marcheshvan** Kislev Tevet Sh'vat Adar Nisan Iyar Sivan Tammuz Av Elul

It is exciting to see the similarity of style and themes between this prayer and prayers from the liturgy of Jewish communities around the world. Interestingly, some words in Ge'ez are closely related to Hebrew terms they know, since both are Semitic languages.

The Mishnah (*Taanit* 2:4) describes the prayers, fasts, and ceremonies that were arranged during periods of drought. Such observances were scheduled for the seventeenth of Marcheshvan if the autumn rain had not yet begun, and they would become increasingly serious and stringent if the drought continued. On a declared fast day (*taanit*), the ark containing a Torah scroll would be brought out into the public square, as those observing the fast covered it and their own heads with ashes, all the while praying. As part of those prayers, they recited special blessings that recalled the merit of our ancient forebears:

> For the conclusion of the first blessing, "Redeemer of Israel," one recites: "God who answered Abraham on Mount Moriah [Genesis 22:11–18], God will answer you and hear the sound of your cry on this day. Blessed are You, Eternal, Redeemer of Israel."
>
> For the second blessing, to which are added the verses of Remembrances (*Zichronot*), one recites: "God who answered our ancestors at the Sea of Reeds [Exodus 14:15–31], God will answer you and hear your cries on this day. Blessed are You, Eternal, who remembers the forgotten."
>
> For the third blessing, which includes the verses of *Shofarot*, one recites: "God who answered Joshua at Gilgal, when they sounded the shofar in Jericho [Joshua 6:5], God will answer you and hear the sound of your cry on this day. Blessed are You, Eternal, who hears the *t'ruah* [sound of the shofar]."
>
> For the fourth blessing, one recites: "God who answered Samuel in Mizpah [I Samuel 7], God will answer you and hear the sound of your cry on this day. Blessed are You, Eternal, who hears cries."
>
> For the fifth, one recites: "God who answered Elijah on Mount Carmel (I Kings 18), God will answer you and hear the sound of your cry on this day. Blessed are You, Eternal, who hears prayer."
>
> For the sixth blessing, one recites: "God who answered Jonah from within the innards of the fish [Jonah 2:2–11], God will answer you and hear the sound of your cry on this day. Blessed are You, Eternal, who answers in a time of trouble."
>
> For the seventh blessing, one recites: "God who answered David and Solomon his son in Jerusalem [I Kings 53–8:12], God will answer you and hear the sound of your cry on this day. Blessed are You, Eternal, who has mercy on the Land."

Making mention of the merit accumulated by our ancestors who were shown kindness by God along with a petition for our own salvation is a combination that forms the basis for the *Mi She-anah* (May God who answered) prayers recited by many Jewish communities on Yom Kippur. It is interesting to note that the prayers of Beta Israel known as *Egzio sema'ane*, which were also recited during droughts, also recall the kindnesses shown to prominent biblical figures, accompanied by a request that we too be saved. For example:

> Eternal, hear us, hear us!
> Eternal, hear us; hear us, our God!
> And Elijah and Elisha,
> who prayed to You on Mount Carmel—
> Let them say, "The Eternal was and will be, the Eternal is the Sovereign
>   of our ancestors."

KISLEV

Zodiac Sign: Sagittarius | Tribe of the Month: Gad
Breastplate Stone: Crystal/*Achlamah*

Kislev got its Hebrew name from the Babylonian name of the month, Kisilimu, a word whose meaning is unclear. The *m* sound in the Babylonian name was replaced by the Hebrew letter *vav* (pronounced today as *v*).

The name of the month appears in the opening verse of the Book of Nehemiah: "The narrative of Nehemiah son of Hacaliah: In the month of Kislev of the twentieth year, when I was in the fortress of Shushan" (Nehemiah 1:1). It is also known in the Bible by its ordinal number: "the ninth month" (Jeremiah 36:22).

Kavanah: A Meditation for Kislev

For the miracles,
and for the redemption,
and for the mighty deeds
and for the saving acts,
and for the wonders,
and for the consolations,
and for the efforts,
and for the surprises,
and for the loves,
and for the mercies,
and for the recoveries.
For the miracles
large and small,
rare and ordinary,
You brought about for our ancestors
for us and for our loved ones
in days of old at this season,
in these days, and in times to come.[1]

At the Gates of Kislev

THE TASTE OF THE MONTH of Kislev is that of sweet *sufganiyot* (fried jelly-filled doughnuts), *sfinj* (traditional Moroccan doughnuts), and *latkes* (Eastern European potato pancakes)—the taste of oily satisfaction and guilty feelings about overeating. Its aroma is that of burning candles, rain-swept wind at the window, mulled wine with cinnamon and cloves, and sweet baked goods. The sounds of Kislev are the voices of children confused by the timing of the round *Mi Y'maleil G'vurot Yisrael*, the special melody for the blessings over candle lighting, and the quiet popping of melting candles. Kislev is a spinning *dreidel*—known in Israel as a *s'vivon*—and the outline of a cellophane cruse of oil that we made in school and taped onto a window. It's chocolate coins. Kislev's dark shadows remind us of the longing for light—for many lights, but also for the periods of darkness between them; in short, it makes us long for the elusive materials from which our lives are woven.

Kislev is a month of home, of the feelings of warmth and comfort in the home we have always loved, which may or may not have existed. Kislev celebrates another home too—the Eternal's home on earth, the *Mikdash* (Temple)—which was the heart of the ancient people Israel and the place where pilgrimage was made even after it was desecrated and defiled. And now that it has been destroyed, our sanctity has been fragmented and is drawn to every place where a Jewish soul longs for holiness. The synagogue is sometimes called a "miniature Temple" (*mikdash m'at*), as is any community gathering-place where people come in search of value and meaning. Of course, our own homes can also be sacred spaces, if we guard their purity and the holiness of the relations inside.

Kislev is the ninth month in the biblical count, which begins with Nisan. Kislev brings us to the shortest day of the year, and in a sense it can be said to complete nine months of gestation, since right afterward, in the month of Tevet, daylight is "reborn"—the days begin to lengthen and the nights shorten.

The Poem of the Month is *Maoz Tzur*. The first *iyun* will explore the position of Kislev in the Jewish and cosmic calendars. Our second *iyun* will be about the Temple, with a new understanding of that ancient institution. The third *iyun* will explore the dispute between the camps of Hillel and Shammai over how to kindle Chanukah lights, which appears as a technical legal question but in fact reflects different perceptions of the meaning of life. Our fourth *iyun* is the "December Dilemma" and the different ways Jews in Israel and around the world approach Chanukah. A fifth *iyun* looks at the special holiday foods, and the distinct meanings that accompany their equally distinct flavors. The Prayer of the Month is the one said at the dedication of a new home, *chanukat habayit*.

Chanukah invites us to reflect on questions about our personal and national homes, about identity and belonging, and about the different challenges posed by living as a minority in the Diaspora versus life in Israel within a Jewish majority.

Poem of the Month

Maoz Tzur ("Rock of Ages")

Maoz Tzur is the central *piyut* of Chanukah. It is customary to sing it each night of the holiday after lighting the menorah. But was this song—so widely enjoyed, the soundtrack for Chanukah in so many homes—really written specifically for Chanukah? If we read it attentively, we discover that it is not necessarily a Chanukah song. Instead, it marks the rescue of the people Israel in a series of central events over the course of history.

The first stanza is a song of praise for the dedication of the altar, but it is not explicitly said that it refers specifically to the rededication commemorated on Chanukah. The second stanza refers to the Exodus from Egypt ("Pharaoh's army and all his offspring dropped into the depths like a stone"), so it could also be sung at Passover. The next stanza addresses the Babylonian exile ("the end of Babylon, Zerubavel, at the end of seventy [years] I was saved"), so the song could be sung on Tishah B'Av, and fourth stanza speaks of the victory over Haman ("The Aggagite, son of Hammedatha, sought to cut down the cypress [symbol of the Jews]"), so the song could be sung on Purim. Only the fifth stanza addresses the Chanukah story—"Greeks ganged up against me"—and the miracle of the oil is mentioned—"and from what was left of the cruses [of oil], a miracle was performed for [the Jews]." In many homes, the practice is to sing only the first stanza.

Unlike the first five stanzas of the *piyut*, the sixth and last stanza does not relate historical events but instead offers a plea for future rescue and revenge against our

From Time to Time → Dalia Marx

foes. The call in that last stanza to "Subdue *admon* [the red one] in the shadow of *tzalmon* [darkness, Gehenna]" has been interpreted by many as a reference to Frederick Barbarossa (meaning "red beard"), the Holy Roman emperor who was killed in 1190 during the Third Crusade; others believe that *admon* could be simply a reference to Edom, Esau's descendants, who became identified with Christendom.

The last stanza first appears in printed editions only in the eighteenth century. Some scholars believe that it was a late addition (and indeed it does not form part of the acrostic spelling the author's name, Mordechai, in the first words of the first five stanzas); others argue that it is indeed original but had not appeared in print because of censorship and that the request regarding the future is an organic part of the original *piyut*, which naturally moves from recounting divine favors in the past to a request for future redemption.

It is important to remember that *Maoz Tzur* was composed in Europe during the era of the Crusades, when Jews were suffering brutal attacks. We do not know just when it was written or by whom, but the author's name seems to have been Mordechai, based on that acrostic signature. Some have speculated that he may be Rabbi Mordechai ben Hillel of Nuremberg, who was murdered during the Rindfleisch massacres of 1298. More recently, researchers believe *Maoz Tzur* may have been written even earlier, perhaps in the twelfth century.

In many newer prayer books, such as the Israeli Reform siddur *T'filat HaAdam*, alternative words are suggested for some lines of the lyrics, such as replacing the call for God to arrange a slaughter of our enemies with a call for putting an end to the slaughter of humans by other human beings.

Maoz Tzur has several musical settings, though the most widely known is thought to be an adaptation of a Bohemian folk tune. The melody seems to have been well-known in Bohemia and was applied to Lutheran prayers and other religious melodies, just as it was to the words of *Maoz Tzur*. This is a characteristic example of the way a particular musical style becomes part of the cultural public domain and illustrates the adoption of music by different ethnic groups—in this case Bohemian, Polish, German, and also Jewish—for different uses, including liturgical music.

Rock of Ages

Rock of Ages let our song
    praise Your saving power.
You amidst the raging foes
    were our sheltering tower.
Furious they assailed us,
    but Your arm availed us.
And Your word broke their sword
    when our own strength failed us.[2]

מָעוֹז צוּר

מָעוֹז צוּר יְשׁוּעָתִי
לְךָ נָאֶה לְשַׁבֵּחַ.
תִּכּוֹן בֵּית תְּפִלָּתִי
וְשָׁם תּוֹדָה נְזַבֵּחַ.
לְעֵת תָּכִין מַטְבֵּחַ
מִצָּר הַמְנַבֵּחַ,
אָז אֶגְמֹר בְּשִׁיר מִזְמוֹר
חֲנֻכַּת הַמִּזְבֵּחַ.

Kislev: To Be Most at Home in the Entire World

A SEASON COMES TO ITS END. In classical Hebrew, the month of Kislev concludes "the Tishrei period," the first quarter of the Hebrew year, and takes us straight into the winter and the shortest days of the year. The division of the calendar year into four quarters, or "periods" (*t'kufot*), is not specific to the Hebrew calendar. It is shared by many cultures and is accomplished by dividing the year along two axes, which are defined by the earth's relative position to the sun. One axis joins the two days—one in the spring and one in the autumn—when daylight and nighttime hours are equal in length; these are the equinoxes. The other axis joins the longest day of the year in the summer with the longest night of the year in the winter; these are the solstices. Those two axes bisect each other, dividing the year into four periods of three months each.

Solstice, Equinox, and the Land of Israel

In Jewish culture, **the two equinoxes** are emphasized and marked by holidays, as we have noted: Passover occurs around the time of the vernal **equinox**, and Sukkot falls around the time of the autumnal equinox. In Second Temple times, the Chanukah holiday was added near the time of the winter solstice, but the summer solstice is not specifically marked by a holiday. We know of an ancient pagan festival that took place in the Near East during the month of Tammuz, around the summer solstice (see pp. 286–87), and perhaps that is the reason Jewish culture paid no attention to that point on the calendar. It may also be, though, that the fast of the seventeenth of Tammuz is the way we mark the summer solstice.

In the region that includes Israel, the basic division of the year is between the rainy season and the dry season. The axis of the **equinoxes** cuts across the year and divides it between them. Both periods begin with a major holiday: Sukkot in the autumn and Passover in the spring. The two holidays are similar in many respects, including that they both begin when the moon is full and are both celebrated for seven days. The division along the axis of equinoxes finds expression in our liturgy as well. In the winter rainy season, beginning on Sh'mini Atzeret, we mention the rains in the second blessing of the *Amidah*, saying, "Praised are You . . . who causes the wind to blow and the rain to fall." In the dry spring season, beginning on the first day of Passover, we in the Land of Israel (and according to some rites outside the Land of Israel too) say, "You rain dew upon us."

Might the Earth Revert to Chaos?

In ancient times, the ever-shortening days and growing darkness engendered anxiety. Even today, there are those who suffer from some degree of **depression during the winter**. There is a touching midrash that relates to that experience and describes Adam's response when he noticed, with considerable anxiety, that the days were growing shorter during that season:

> When the original human, Adam, saw the day getting gradually shorter, he said, "Woe is me! Perhaps because I have sinned, the world around me is darkening and returning to its state of chaos and confusion; this, then, is the kind of death to which I have been sentenced from heaven!" So he began observing an eight-day fast. But as he noticed the winter equinox and noted the day getting increasingly longer, he said, "This is the world's course," and he set forth to keep an eight-day festival. In the following year he appointed them as festivals. (Babylonian Talmud, *Avodah Zarah* 8a)

In this midrash, Adam was concerned that the shortening days were a result of his sins and that Creation would unravel and the world would return to the primeval chaos described at the beginning of Genesis. That existential anxiety led him to consider his actions and do *t'shuvah* (repentance, return), and when he then saw the days starting to become longer, he concluded that his prayers had been answered. As a sign and memorial to his answered prayers, Adam "set forth to keep an eight-day festival," which he declared an annual observance.

This story has a distinctly legendary character, but it reveals real human distress and at the same time provides an ancient reason for the holiday of Chanukah—a reason that predates the story of Judah the Maccabee and the miraculous cruse of oil. This is an example of the ancient layer of the Jewish holidays that reflects a pre-Israelite era marking the seasons and forces of nature. Those ancient observances were so completely absorbed into Jewish thought that it is hard to recognize that they represent an ancient layer that may predate Judaism.

The Jewish people are not alone in their winter festivals of light; many other cultures also have celebrations connected with light and fire during this time of year. The darkness and cold of winter create a need for some sort of assurance and hope for the rebirth of the sun.

SAD

For some individuals, the winter doldrums and the lack of light lead to the development of a type of depression known as seasonal affective disorder (SAD). Also known as "winter depression," it causes fatigue and feelings of sadness and tends to dissipate in the spring with increased sunlight and warmth. (Interestingly, there are some who experience SAD in the summer, which is characterized by insomnia and anxiety.)

Cosmic Banking

A picturesque midrash describes the celestial relations between day and night in the four seasons of the year as a kind of banking system, in which night and day borrow from each other and pay off their loans:

> "Day pours out speech to day, night transmits knowledge to night . . ." (Psalm 19:3): Beginning with the winter solstice [*t'kufat Tevet*] and up until the vernal equinox [*t'kufat Nisan*], the night yields time to the day; beginning with the vernal equinox and up to the summer solstice [*t'kufat Tammuz*], the day borrows time from the night. How much does the night yield to the day? And how much does the day borrow from the night? One-thirtieth of an hour [i.e., two minutes].
>
> From the beginning of the summer solstice up until the autumnal equinox [*t'kufat Tishrei*], the day yields time to the night; and from the autumnal equinox up until the winter solstice, the night borrows time from the day. From this it follows that a day in the vernal equinox equals the length of a day in the autumnal equinox. Now they borrow and yield, the one from the other, in trust, and none hears any speech between them because they do not quarrel as humans do. (*Midrash T'hillim* 19:10)[3]

The process of loans and repayments between day and night takes place calmly, in exemplary order and agreement. The month of Kislev, which closes out *t'kufat Tishrei*, during which the night "borrows" from the day, brings us to the shortest day of the year—and from that point, the night begins to repay its debt to the day, which starts to lengthen.

This celestial banking may take place in harmony and calm, but throughout generations the shortening days and lengthening nights caused discomfort and even anxiety for humanity, lest the world gradually return to chaos and Creation slowly unravel. That was certainly true in ancient times, when the shortening daylight hours and the growing darkness were more palpable than they are now, when we surround ourselves with electric light and innumerable distractions. Yet, even in our time—so rich with

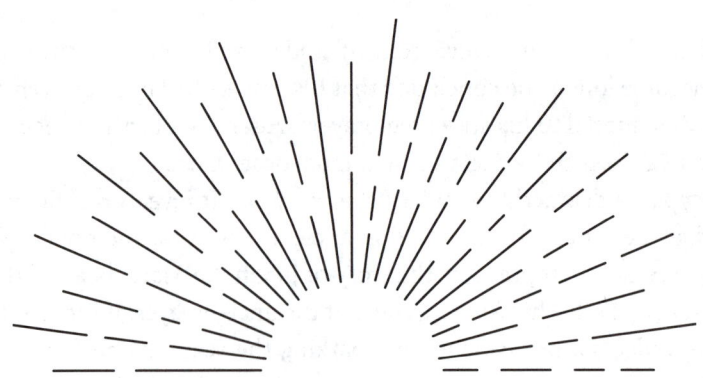

electronic comforts—those winter days with clouds and howling winds sometimes bring up melancholy thoughts and existential questions.

The Hindus celebrate Diwali by lighting lamps that are placed on the verandas of homes and by lighting pots decorated with flowers then set afloat on rivers, with many fireworks bursting overhead. The holiday marks the return of Rama to his city after a fourteen-year exile and the victory of good (light) over evil (darkness).

Western Christians light a special candle on Sundays during Advent, the four weeks before Christmas, and the Christmas tree that adorns every home is decorated with many candles (or today, electric bulbs).

The Swedes celebrate Santa Lucia Day, when children dressed in robes hold long candles or torches and are led by a girl playing the part of Santa Lucia, wearing a white dress and a crown adorned with candles.

In many African American communities in the United States, Kwanzaa is celebrated for the seven days between December 26 and January 1, with a candle lighting every evening. The holiday was created in 1966 by Dr. Ron "Maulana" Karenga, out of a desire to give Black communities their own holiday with the purpose of empowering and strengthening their identity.

Everyone's Holiday

Every Jewish holiday has multiple layers and diverse meanings. This is especially clear when it comes to Chanukah: in the Books of Maccabees, the main emphasis is the military heroism of the Hasmoneans (the priestly family, led by Mattathias and his children, who started the Maccabean Revolt of 167–160 BCE). The Rabbis later deemphasized the military victory gained by force and instead placed the miracle of the cruse of oil at the center of the holiday, which represented divine intervention on the nation's behalf (Babylonian Talmud, *Shabbat* 21b). With the rise of the Zionist movement, Chanukah became a holiday of prime significance. The movement's leaders regarded the Maccabees' victory as a useful model for Jewish sovereignty in their era. Ben Zion Dinur, a Zionist historian and, during the 1950s, Israel's minister of education, wrote:

> With the Chibat Tziyon ["Love of Zion," a precursor to political Zionism] movement, a new era began for the holiday of Chanukah. The revival of feelings for our homeland . . . Chanukah is a holiday that is close to us in soul and spirit . . . . The holiday of the victory of national, political, and socialist activism, of freedom and of war on its behalf, the days of Chanukah again became festival days of salvation and victory.[4]

In this spirit, the Jewish sports organization Maccabi was founded, the Young Maccabi youth movement was established, and the international Maccabiah games were organized—all contributing to the enhancement of the heritage of the Maccabees, the ancient fighters who served as examples for those in our time.

Chanukah has come once again, then, to represent bravery and heroism in opposition to a foreign ruler. This meant emphasizing an unwillingness to rely upon miracles and an insistence instead on taking our fate into our own hands. Many observe Chanukah today as a holiday of liberty and religious freedom. And in the Diaspora, there are those who take advantage of its proximity to Christmas for interreligious dialogue (see pp. 85–86).

From Time to Time → Dalia Marx

Just as the holiday candles are multicolored, so is its meaning variegated; one meaning does not cancel out or even cast a dark shadow on the others. On the contrary, the holiday's multiplicity of meanings enhances it. Many people report that Chanukah is their favorite holiday, and in Israel and the rest of the world, even many secular families light candles and eat traditional Chanukah treats.

This holiday, celebrated at the end of Kislev and the beginning of Tevet, marks the transition away from darkness and cold and toward the gradual return of sunlight and warmth; it is the most home-oriented holiday on the calendar. The celestial payments of day and night morph into Chanukah *gelt*, the money (traditionally coins, now often made of chocolate) given to children on the holiday. The longing for light is expressed in the light of the Chanukah candles or oil lamps dancing in the window; the wind and rain outside transform into oil-fried potato pancakes, attempts at inserting jelly into doughnuts, and snuggling with one's family.

On this family-centered holiday, we are invited to think about the shifting time of nature and to feel, as the El Al (the national airline of Israel) advertisements put it, "to be the most at home in the entire world."

The emphasis on **bravery and valor** as Chanukah themes found expression in the poem by Aharon Zeev (1900–1968), set to music by the popular composer Mordechai Zeira (1905–68). The song became an anthem of Zionism, which challenged the passive anticipation of divine intervention, typified by the miracle of the oil lasting eight days. In this song, it is the Zionists who make the miracle occur with their own bare hands:[5]

We are carrying torches
in the dark night.
The paths shine beneath our feet,
and whoever is brave
who thirsts for light—
let them lift eyes and heart to us,
toward the light, and come along.
No miracle happened for us.
No cruse of oil did we find.
We walked through the valley,
ascended the mountain,
the springs of hidden light—
we uncovered.
No miracle happened for us.
Through the rock we hewed until we bled –
And there was light!

אָנוּ נוֹשְׂאִים לַפִּידִים
בְּלֵילוֹת אֲפֵלִים.
זוֹרְחִים הַשְּׁבִילִים מִתַּחַת רַגְלֵינוּ
וּמִי אֲשֶׁר לֵב לוֹ
הַצָּמֵא לָאוֹר –
יִשָּׂא אֶת עֵינָיו וְלִבּוֹ אֵלֵינוּ
לָאוֹר וְיָבוֹא!
נֵס לֹא קָרָה לָנוּ –
פַּךְ שֶׁמֶן לֹא מָצָאנוּ.
לָעֵמֶק הָלַכְנוּ, הָהָרָה עָלִינוּ,
מַעְיְנוֹת הָאוֹרוֹת
הַגְּנוּזִים גִּלִּינוּ.
נֵס לֹא קָרָה לָנוּ –
פַּךְ שֶׁמֶן לֹא מָצָאנוּ.
בַּסֶּלַע חָצַבְנוּ עַד דָּם –
וַיְהִי אוֹר!

"Open the Gate, Open It Wide"

I ADMIT, I have always felt a certain hesitancy toward dealing with questions related to the ancient Temple and to animal sacrifices. (Adding to my own sense of discomfort, I am a vegetarian!) In the past, I was only comfortable recognizing the Temple cult as a religious expression more appropriate to an earlier age in Jewish history. Recently, I have become more open to understanding its place and centrality for Jews, both when it still stood in Jerusalem and in the space that opened after it was destroyed. To be sure, I do not hope for the rebuilding of the Temple and the restoration of sacrificial worship, but I am moved by the place it occupied—and still occupies—in our people's heritage and studies. Today I understand that in order to grasp the historical Jewish experience in full, I have to try to draw closer—even if only a little bit—to the experience of the Israelite pilgrims who were privileged to enter its gates. In the text below I will explain why I believe the month of Kislev is an excellent month to place the Temple at the forefront of our consciousness.

Toward Destruction, Toward Rebuilding

In retrospect, Kislev in the year 588 BCE, the eleventh year of the reign of King Zedekiah, marks the end of an era. That was the last month in which the usual regimen of worship took place in the First Temple in Jerusalem. In the following month of Tevet, King Nebuchadnezzar of Babylonia set siege to the city, which ended when he destroyed Jerusalem and sent most of its population into exile.

About seventy years later, the Second Temple was built. The prophet Haggai reports that the establishment of that Temple took place during the month of Kislev, the ninth month in the biblical count that begins with Nisan: "Take note, from this day forward—from the twenty-fourth day of the ninth month, from the day that the foundation was laid for the Eternal's Temple—take note" (Haggai 2:18).

Almost four hundred years after that prophecy (in the year 164 BCE), and again during the month of Kislev, the Temple was cleansed and purified. Judah the Maccabee recaptured the Temple from its Seleucid occupiers, destroyed the altar that had been defiled by the sacrifice of a pig, and built in its place a new altar dedicated to the Eternal, to the sound of cheering from the people. The holiday of Chanukah was declared to memorialize the purification of the Temple and the rededication of the altar.

And again in Kislev, more than two thousand years after the Maccabees rededicated the Temple, which had since been destroyed again (this time in 70 CE), the United Nations decided on November 29, 1947—the seventeenth of Kislev in the Hebrew year 5708—to establish a Jewish state in the Land of Israel. Two years later, on the fourteenth of Kislev in the year 5710, David Ben-Gurion, prime minister of the young State of Israel, proclaimed Jerusalem its capital.

The First Chanukah
This is the description of the eight days of celebration that followed the re-purification of the altar, in I Maccabees:

> Early in the morning on the twenty-fifth day of the ninth month, which is the month of Kislev, in the 148th year, they rose and offered sacrifice, as the law directs, on the new altar of burnt offering that they had built. At the very season and on the very day that the gentiles had profaned it, it was dedicated with songs and harps and lutes and cymbals. All the people fell on their faces and worshiped and blessed God of heaven, who had granted them prosperity. So they celebrated the dedication of the altar for eight days and joyfully offered burnt offerings; they offered a sacrifice of well-being and a thanksgiving offering. (I Maccabees 4:52–56)

From Time to Time → Dalia Marx

Our month of Kislev, then, gathers together many hopes for redemption: the hopes that were reflected in the building of the Temple in the past, first at its inception and then its rededication after its defilement; the hopes for a new independent Jewish life, with the declaration of Jerusalem as the capital of the modern State of Israel serving as a symbol of the Jewish people's return to its land and the realization of Jewish sovereignty; the hopes for commitment to a life of peace and wholeness.

The Temple in Our Minds

Like the destruction of the First Temple, the destruction of the Second Temple was an experience of shock and devastation to the Jews of that era. In its aftermath, however, the Jewish people burst forth with powerful and vital creativity. The Rabbis led a tremendous religious revolution, which forever changed Judaism and even influenced broader Western culture. It was a democratic and nonviolent revolution. From this point forward, there was no need for priests to conduct worship on our behalf; instead, every Jew of any gender can stand in prayer and serve as a prayer leader. Today, every time we seek out holiness in our lives—in the synagogue, at home, at work, in public places—we are making a metaphorical pilgrimage to the Temple. And if, in the past, pilgrimage involved extended travel that was expensive and often dangerous, today everyone can make the pilgrimage in a symbolic fashion, at any time.

The destruction of the Temple created the conditions that led to Judaism as we know it today. Unlike other peoples who faded away after the destruction of their cultic center, the people Israel was reborn as the People of the Book, a people of social justice and eternal longing.

The person most identified with the Rabbis' intellectual revolution is Rabban Yochanan ben Zakkai, who lived during the time of the destruction of the Second Temple and, according to tradition, set up the Jewish center at Yavneh (see pp. 221–22). Here we read about his response to the situation after the disaster:

> Once Rabban Yochanan ben Zakkai went out of Jerusalem, and Rabbi Y'hoshua was walking behind him, and he saw the ruins of the Temple.
>
> Rabbi Y'hoshua said, "Woe is us, for it has been destroyed—the place where atonement is made for Israel's transgressions."
>
> He [i.e., Rabban Yochanan ben Zakkai] said to him, "My son, let this not bother you so. We have another [means of] atonement that is like it. And what is that? Acts of kindness [*g'milut chasadim*], as the Bible says, 'For I desire goodness, not sacrifice' (Hosea 6:6)." (*Avot D'Rabbi Natan* A, chap. 4)

The month of Kislev, the month of the rededication of the Temple, invites us to renew ourselves and to open the gates to holiness, to justice, and to kindness—to open them wide for all those who want to enter.

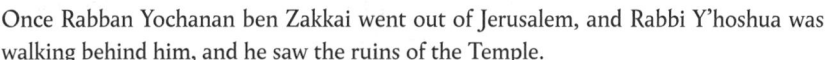

Two Chanukah Menorahs, Two Worldviews

DOES EVERYONE WHO LIGHTS a Chanukah menorah (known in modern Hebrew as a *chanukiyah*), every man and woman, girl and boy, know that they are not only doing the mitzvah in grand fashion, but in the grandest of grand fashions—in Hebrew, *m'hadrin min ham'hadrin*? After all, the Talmud teaches us:

> Our Rabbis taught: The precept of Chanukah [demands] one candle for a person and the household; the zealous [*m'hadrin*] [light] a candle for each member [of the household]; and the extremely zealous [*m'hadrin min ham'hadrin*] [light even more]. The House of Shammai maintains: On the first day eight lights are lit and thereafter they are progressively reduced. Those of the House of Hillel say: On the first day one is lit and thereafter they are progressively increased. (Babylonian Talmud, *Shabbat* 21b)

That is to say, the basic commandment is to light a Chanukah light in the home, and just one light is enough for the whole household. Those who wish to enhance the performance of the *mitzvah*, the Talmud tells us, kindle one light for each person in the house, and only those most eager to enhance the performance of the *mitzvah* kindle a large number of lights. But how many, and exactly how? On that point, two contrasting systems are presented, that of the House of Shammai and that of the House of Hillel. According to Shammai's view, they would light eight lights on the first night, seven on the second night, and continue to reduce the number by one each night, until the last night they would light only one light. According to Hillel's view, familiar to us because it is the view that was accepted, we start with one light and add one a day, until on the last night the entire *chanukiyah* is filled with lights. The Talmud recounts some explanations for the two different systems. One suggests that the House of Shammai are counting off the number of remaining days each time, while the House of Hillel are counting the number that have passed. According to another explanation, the House of Shammai are counting off the days following the model of the bulls sacrificed on Sukkot, whose number was reduced by one each day—on the first day thirteen bulls, on the second day twelve, and so on, while the House of Hillel's reasoning was "one rises in holiness rather than reducing it" (Babylonian Talmud, *Shabbat* 21b).

Competing Worldviews

The two systems for lighting Chanukah lights represent different worldviews, at the base of which stand two competing perceptions of reality. According to Shammai, the world was created whole and perfect, and ever since then, "the generations are successively diminished." Following this approach, human beings are born with their full potential, with all their lives ahead to achieve it, but each passing day brings them closer to the end and serves as a depressing reminder of what they will not manage to achieve. So too the Chanukah menorah is lit at first in its full glory and slowly loses its light until only one light remains. Shammai's approach sets up a picture of a reality of fullness and perhaps perfection that is progressively marred, each day lowering the bar and coming to terms with our limited abilities.

Sidebar:

The holidays that appear in the Torah earned enough attention from the Rabbis that they dedicated a tractate of the Mishnah, and later of the Talmud, to each of them—*Rosh HaShanah*, *Yoma* (Yom Kippur), *Sukkah*, *P'sachim*, and *Bikurim* (about Shavuot). Purim too, which is absent from the Torah and mentioned only in the Writings section of the Hebrew Bible, in the Book of Esther, earned itself a tractate, *M'gillah*. Chanukah is not mentioned in the Bible, because the events it commemorates took place after the biblical period, and so it does not merit a tractate of its own. Some matters pertinent to Chanukah are mentioned, though, in the tractate *Shabbat*.

Hillel's approach reflects a more optimistic view of life. One starts off small, with just one light, and from there one adds progressively more light. Every new thing that we learn and every action we perform in the world empowers us and enhances our light. This approach by Hillel reminds us of the words of the thinker, poet, and teacher Aaron David Gordon (1856–1922), a Second Aliyah pioneer, who mentioned that the victory of light over darkness comes from our magnifying the light (see p. 97). Hillel reminds us to strive for the good and the worthy and to increase light in the world.

As is well-known, Hillel's approach was accepted as normative halachah, and it is customary to light our Chanukah candles according to this approach. However, the Talmud, as is its wont, does not obliterate the rejected opinion, bringing it into the discussion instead.

The reduction of light in the *chanukiyah* teaches that military victory and sovereignty are important but insufficient; they have to be the basis on which a just society is created. When they exist on their own, they are barren and even dangerous. According to historian Ely Ben-Gal, the educational goal of the approach that would have us reduce the number of lights each night is to remind us of the danger in exercising the power of might and the state. Ben-Gal concludes his teaching by saying that "whenever Jews remind themselves and warn themselves that light is not assured, that it can sputter and be in danger of being extinguished, it will continue to shine. Such is the power of freedom."[6]

Rising in Holiness and Recognizing the Danger of Power

In recent years, my family has joined in the custom of a few families and communities to light two *chanukiyot* on Chanukah—one following the approach of Shammai, reducing the number of lights each night, in recognition of the danger of the diminishing light and a warning against bowing down to power, and another according to Hillel's approach of adding a light each day, thus emphasizing the desire for growth and for increasing light in the world and in our hearts. The two menorahs are placed side by side, and they can help us keep the forces in balance and consider the complexity of our lives. May we be privileged to kindle many lights on Chanukah and all year round.

The Torah instructs us to sacrifice a total of seventy bulls on the seven days of Sukkot: thirteen on the first day, twelve on the second day, and so on until on the seventh day, seven bulls are sacrificed. The total is thus seventy: 13 + 12 + 11 + 10 + 9 + 8 + 7 = 70. The Talmud explains, "These seventy bulls are numbered like what? The seventy nations of the world" (Babylonian Talmud, *Sukkah* 55b).

Chanukah, the festival of purifying the Temple, is a kind of "second Sukkot," a delayed celebration of the Sukkot holiday, which the Jews were unable to celebrate while the Temple remained defiled. So we read in the apocryphal book II Maccabees:

> It happened that on the same day on which the sanctuary had been profaned by the foreigners, the purification of the sanctuary took place, that is, on the twenty-fifth day of the same month, which was Kislev. They celebrated it for eight days with rejoicing, in the manner of the Festival of Sukkot, remembering how not long before, during the Festival of Sukkot, they had been wandering in the mountains and caves like wild animals. Therefore, carrying ivy-wreathed wands and beautiful branches and also fronds of palm, they offered hymns of thanksgiving to God, who had given success to the purifying of God's own holy place. They decreed by public edict, ratified by vote, that the whole nation of the Jews should observe these days every year. (II Maccabees 10:8–11)

The "December Dilemma"

"It's not fair that Jewish kids get eight presents, and we get only one!" grumbled the young American cabdriver, not much more than a child himself, as he drove me to the airport in Cincinnati after I told him I was Jewish. I was a bit perplexed, and I hesitantly asked him what eight presents he was talking about. "Chanukah," he replied immediately, "Chanukah presents." He said this as though it were obvious and looked at me with some suspicion, as though maybe I was faking being Jewish. "Eight presents? What is he talking about?" I thought. "Maybe I've missed something?" In my house growing up, we received symbolic Chanukah gelt, sometimes in the form of chocolate coins, and that is what my husband and I do with our own children. And now you're telling me there is a different Chanukah? The driver was right. We spent two years in the United States, and we learned from our (somewhat frustrated) children that their friends received valuable presents for Chanukah. Grandmothers and grandfathers living far from their grandchildren send special packages, with instructions inside as to which box to give to each of the children on each night of the holiday. New trendy gadgets, rollerblades, and fancy sneakers appeared each day in school. Jewish homes were decked out with colored lights no less impressive than those of their neighbors, and in the Jewish schools the holiday was observed with great fanfare. Weeks before Chanukah, the preparations began, and they reached their zenith at a gigantic "Chanukah fair" that drew a large crowd. I found myself buying special tools for making *latkes* in a variety of shapes, *dreidels*, pitcher-shaped gift bags, and glittery decorations—not one of which I had bought in any previous year's Chanukah.

In Israel too, Chanukah is a fun, lively holiday: lighting candles with family and community, singing *Maoz Tzur*, eating sweet *sufganiyot*, and recounting the tale of the amazing holiday miracle. But there is no comparison between the centrality of Chanukah in the Diaspora—and especially in the largest Jewish Diaspora community, the United States—and the holiday's place in Israel. The reason is clear: the need to grapple with Christmas, celebrated so close to Chanukah not only in churches but in public spaces—shopping malls and restaurants and even the public school system. The magic worked by Christmas, especially on children, forces Jewish leaders, teachers, and parents to offer an especially attractive alternative to the majority Christian culture. This book is mostly about Israeli Judaism, but Chanukah is an excellent test case for examining the influence of the non-Jewish environment on a Jewish holiday in comparison with its observance in Israel.

Life as a Minority: Deliberate Inattention, Emphasis on Difference, and Partial Adoption

For most of the years of our existence as a people, we Jews have lived exclusively as a minority within a larger non-Jewish society. Minority status, whether in a hostile environment or a tolerant one—and sometimes even an amicable one—invites different reactions, and so it is with Chanukah as well. There are those who think Jews should ignore the Christian holidays taking place around them, not relate to them at all. The storm may rage, the advertising run rampant, the rehearsals in schools and preschools garner lots of attention, parties take place at work, and holiday songs ring out in every store and mall—but we will act as though none of that is happening. This approach bears the danger that the children, once they understand something is being kept from them, will be especially interested in that well-guarded secret, so interesting and hidden, and as a result they may develop a sense of bitterness at being denied all the fun that their Christian classmates get to have during the Christmas season.

Others choose to embrace the general holiday atmosphere but to keep away from its explicit Christian content, in order to emphasize and strengthen Jewish identity. Parents and educators feel that they must give an appropriate response to the enticements of the Christian holiday, which is understood by many as an aspect of American culture, and so they emphasize Chanukah. The custom of giving eight presents, first introduced to me by my non-Jewish taxi driver, is one result of those efforts. Another example of this is the now-famous Chanukah song by the American Jewish actor Adam Sandler, which aims to support kids who may feel "a little left out" during the Christmas season.[7] The song, which became very popular and spawned a number of versions, lists the names of famous Jews in an attempt to arouse pride and identification at that very time of year when Jews do not join in widespread Christmas festivities.

Another accepted mode of response is the deliberate partial adoption of the trappings of the Christian holiday while avoiding the religious Christian content of the celebration of the birth of their Messiah. So, for example, my grandmother Ruth's family had a very strong secular Jewish identity, but nevertheless, her parents would place a "Chanukah tree" in their living room in Düsseldorf, Germany, and decorate it with Chanukah menorahs, Jewish stars, and other symbols of the holiday. This is the custom in many Jewish homes in the Diaspora. To be honest, in Israel too, the emphasis placed on the custom of Chanukah gelt and presents is a partial adoption of the non-Jewish holiday's contours.

A Counter-Celebration

It is fascinating to see how Jews of the past who lived among a Christian majority "celebrated" the Christian festival in order to grapple with the cultural threat (and in early periods, the actual threat) of the majority culture against the Jewish minority. Despite the great importance of studying Torah, Chasidim used to refrain from Torah study on Christmas Eve. One of the explanations given for that was that the study of Torah hastens the coming of the Messiah, and despite their fervent hope to witness the great redemption, they did not want it to be on that very night of the non-Jewish holiday, which they referred to as Nitelnacht, that the Redeemer would arrive (lest the Christians regard that as proof that Jesus is the Messiah). It seems, however, that the real reason Jews closed their study halls (*batei midrash*) was that they feared attacks by the holiday revelers. Instead of studying, Chasidim spent that evening engaged in card games or chess. Other customs included symbolic acts of an insulting nature, such as cutting up toilet paper for use on Shabbatot during the year and frying smelly foods.

Moving away from religious war to more lighthearted Jewish customs

> The name **Nitelnacht** (Nitel Night) comes from the Latin *Natale Dominus*, "the birth of God." However, other explanations have been suggested regarding the source of the name. For example, some want to connect "Nitel" to the Hebrew *nitleh* (hanged), since Jesus was called "the hanged one" in medieval times. Alternatively, some suggest a connection to the Hebrew *nital*, "taken," referring to Jesus having been taken from this world.

In a famous (and probably invented) letter widely circulated in social media, "the Chinese Restaurant Association of the United States" is said to "extend our thanks to the Jewish People. We do not completely understand your dietary customs. . . . But we are proud and grateful that your God insists you eat our food on Christmas."

regarding Christmas, we find this story: When Elana Kagan, a Jewish U.S. Supreme Court justice, was asked during her Senate confirmation hearings where she had been one particular Christmas Eve, she replied, "Like all Jews, I was probably at a Chinese restaurant."[8] For whatever reason, American Jews do tend to go out on Christmas Eve to Chinese restaurants, followed by a movie. Why specifically a Chinese restaurant? Maybe because that is an encounter between minority cultures—or maybe because all the other restaurants are closed.

From Threat to Opportunity

During many periods in history, relations between Jews and Christians were hostile and sometimes devolved into violence against the Jewish minority. Jewish holidays were sometimes a source not only of joy and contentment, but also of fear of attack; especially dangerous were those times when Jewish holidays overlapped with Christian holidays. Hatred-fomenting sermons and blood libels sometimes brought angry mobs of Christians into the Jewish neighborhoods in order to exact revenge.

One of the after-school programs in which I participated as a child took place next to the YMCA building in Jerusalem. At Christmastime, the YMCA sported a gigantic tree, decorated with shining multicolored balls and gigantic snowflakes. That tree looked dazzling to me, beautiful—but also frightening.

I was born in the State of Israel, I grew up there, and I was educated there—far from the Christian world and any sense of living as a religious minority. I never felt that anyone forced a Christian holiday on me, and the public space was not filled with its symbols. So what was it that nonetheless scared me about the YMCA Christmas tree?

Maybe it was the memory of the stories that my grandmother told me about antisemitism in Germany? Maybe it was what we learned in school about Jewish persecution by their Christian neighbors? Or maybe I was worried by a sense that there was something primeval and dark about the lovely tree that might entice me? Were those worries connected to my familial and national wounds from the past? Or was it some deeper aversion—a perception that the beauty and splendor of the decorated tree hid something seductive and threatening?

Fear is an understandable emotion (even if its roots are not always understood), but a dangerous one as well. Most acts of hatred and violence are generated by that corrosive emotion. Familiarity and recognition can be a corrective to the disturbances that fear engenders. Is it possible to be amazed by the beauty of a foreign holiday without being afraid of it? Can the light of the *chanukiyah* be shared with followers of other religions without instilling fear in them?

So it was in the past, but we have the privilege of living in a time when there can be interreligious encounters of conversation and connection—not out of a desire to impose anything on anyone else or even attempt to convince them of anything, but simply out of interest and friendship. The close or even overlapping dates of Christmas and Chanukah (and sometimes one of the Muslim festivals) can be an opportunity for meeting and learning about life in a multicultural community. I am not talking about syncretistic customs combining Chanukah and Christmas into one holiday (sometimes called "Chrismukah" or "Chanukamas"). I am not in favor of blurring one's identity, but I am in favor of deepening our familiarity with the values and practices of each religion. For example, the city of Haifa makes an effort at deepening connections during December, when the city holds its Festival of Festivals to mark the holidays of the three religions that fall at that time of year.

Chanukah has national and religious dimensions—the rededication of the Temple that was despoiled by Antiochus's soldiers, the miracle of the cruse of oil—and also general human dimensions—fear of the dark, the striving for light, and the hope for restoration of the light. The holiday of Chanukah is also a good opportunity to present Jewish tradition to non-Jews in a homey, comfortable atmosphere.

🕎 We Celebrate, We Eat . . . and We Argue

Jews take food seriously—*profoundly* seriously. There is almost no event—happy or sad, occurring once or on a regular basis, private or public—in which food does not play an important part. The taste of Passover in our mouths is the taste of matzah and *charoset*, with each community preparing its own unique recipe. The taste of Rosh HaShanah is the taste of the apple, the honey, and the other foods at the meal of symbolic foods (see pp. 31–33). Even on our fast days, food is significant—in its absence. In this culinary mix, Chanukah is no different. Weeks before the holiday, the children—and maybe not only the children—begin to dream about Chanukah's calorie-rich, cholesterol-laden foods.

The Murderous *Latke*

Take the potato pancake, for example. It is known in Yiddish as a *latke* and in Hebrew as *l'vivah*. *L'vivot* are mentioned as far back as the Bible, when Amnon, son of King David, pretends to be ill and asks his sister Tamar to prepare "a couple of *l'vivot*" in front of him (II Samuel 13:6), in a ploy to take advantage of her kindheartedness and attack her. The word *l'vivot* appears again in medieval Hebrew literature. Rashi thought the *l'vivah* in Samuel were cakes made of "choice flour soaked first in water and then in oil" (Rashi, *ad loc.*). The *l'vivah* shows up in the medieval *M'gillat Y'hudit* as well, a medieval version of the story of the apocryphal Book of Judith (see p. 101), the brave woman who saved her city from an enemy army.[9] According to this version, Judith is Judah Maccabee's sister, which explains her special connection to Chanukah. The *m'gillah* relates that Judith asked her maidservant to cook her two *l'vivot*: "She made her the *l'vivot*, and she salted them heavily." Judith brought the steaming food to Holofernes, the invading Assyrian general, fed it to him, gave him wine to drink—and when he fell asleep, sated and satisfied, she decapitated him. The *m'gillah* ends with a description of the celebrations that the Jews used to hold in memory of Judith's bravery:

> Then Judith became queen over the land and judged Israel. Because of this the Children of Israel shall make a very great feast in their pots and cauldrons, with pieces of cheese, gladness and feasting, a good day, of sending portions to one another, baked pieces, food from the frying pan and dough kneaded until it is leavened so its glory will grow with honey, all manner of baked goods. . . . And the drinking was according to the law: none did compel, for thus Queen Judith had appointed to all the officers of [his] house, that they should do according to every man's pleasure. The Jews ordained and took it upon themselves to confirm this letter to make a day of feasting and joy and a good day.

The text's description of a feast and sending portions of food "to one another" in the liberated city make the celebration of Chanukah into a kind of second Purim, which is also a holiday that recalls rescue from persecution by an enemy (and in a moment we will see another, unexpected connection of a culinary sort between Chanukah and Purim). The tradition of consuming dairy foods during Chanukah took on an air of permanence once it was mentioned in some works of Jewish law, including the run-

*Tishrei   Marcheshvan   **Kislev**   Tevet   Sh'vat   Adar   Nisan   Iyar   Sivan   Tammuz   Av   Elul*

ning commentary by Rabbi Moshe Isserles (1520–72) to Rabbi Yosef Karo's *Shulchan Aruch*. Isserles writes, "Some say that one should eat cheese on Chanukah, since the miracle was accomplished through the milk that Judith fed the foe" (gloss to *Shulchan Aruch, Orach Chayim* 570:3).

The Children of Jerusalem Offer Blessings and Chow Down

Yosef Yoel Rivlin, the father of Israel's tenth president, Reuven (Ruvi) Rivlin, documented a lovely custom, according to which the children of Israel, before the holiday, would circulate among the homes accompanied by their teachers, singing songs in Ladino (Judeo-Spanish), and asking the residents for food items. They would bless the donors, reciting *Birkat Kohanim* (the Priestly Blessing) three times for them. They arranged a big festive meal from the donated food, and in a grand ceremony they brought very large pots to a traditional elementary school (*talmud Torah*) in the Old City. The Sephardic chief rabbi, whose title was *Rishon l'Tziyon*, would stand on a bimah, and in his presence the children would read the Song of Songs, pray for rain, sing in Ladino, and recite over and over the verse "Their father said to them, 'Go back and buy us a bit of food'" (Genesis 43:2). That verse appears in the weekly portion of *Mikeitz*, which is read during Chanukah. A teacher would use beans to count out the number of times the children repeated the verse, and on that day hundreds of beans would be collected. Later, the children would circle the bimah seven times, with the pots on their heads. The head teacher would stand and ask questions, and the children would answer:

> "Do you desire bread?"—and all of them would answer aloud in unison: "Yes!"
> And he would add, "Beans as well?"— "Yes!"
> "Rice as well?"— "Yes!"
> "*Pastilla* too?"— "Yes!"
> "And lashes too?"— "No, no, no!"¹⁰

In large pots they would cook rice and beans. In addition, they would cook *pastillas* (meat pies) and give them out to all the poor and needy. After all the poor had received their portions, the teachers would distribute food to their pupils. The atmosphere was fun and even silly; the teachers would fill some of the *pastillas* with cotton batting instead of meat, and every time such a *pastilla* would be discovered, the children would be doubled over with laughter. At the end of the event, the teachers too would partake of the food and sing many songs. In that way a multi-age celebration combined gifts for the poor, words of Torah and prayer, and joyous celebration. In Ladino, the festive meal was called *miranda di Chanukah*.

"*Latkes* or *Hamantaschen*?"

Let us leave the Sephardic community of Jerusalem of olden days and approach the halls of an American university in the middle of the last century. Generations of Jews who downed plates of *latkes*—fried potato pancakes, sometimes served with applesauce or sour cream—never dreamed that their warm, oil-soaked comfort food would gain profound academic attention and be forced to defend its honor against another

---

Sidenote: The custom of **collecting food for the needy** is reminiscent of the custom of *kimcha d'pascha* ("flour for Passover" in Aramaic), the collection of food for the needy before Passover. Oddly enough, it is also a little reminiscent of American Halloween customs, based on a pagan practice, of going from house to house and asking for sweets with the refrain "Trick or treat!" In the Jewish holiday tradition, though, the approach is communal, with the children asking for basic foodstuffs in order to prepare a meal for the poor and the needy.

comfort food, also connected to a Jewish holiday: the *hamantaschen* (triangular pastries of cookie dough, open at the top and filled with jam, poppy seeds, or another sweet filling) consumed on Purim.

It happened in 1946. Jewish scholars gathered at the Hillel House at the University of Chicago for a critical inquiry into a question of grave import: "*Latkes* or *hamantaschen*?" Ponderous academic rigor and arguments based on research served both teams. As one might imagine, they did not achieve consensus regarding the weighty problem at hand.

Since then, the debate has become a beloved tradition at that university and at other universities around the United States. Jewish scholars use it to discover and reveal their "inner clown." The event is organized as a serious symposium in which a panel of speakers grapple with that question of existential import: Which traditional, calorie-laden delight is preferable? The biologists hold forth on the chemical makeup of each, the sociologists examine their influence on society, the gender studies specialists assess the oppressive nature of each of the two foods, and the economists present their market value. The finest scholars, among them Nobel Prize winners (such as economists Milton Friedman and George Stigler and physicist Leon Lederman), make great efforts to convince the audience of the correctness of their arguments and prove that the potato pancake is superior to the *hamantaschen* or vice versa. Generally, at the end of the deliberation both foods are served to those present, allowing them to examine the question in an empirical fashion and form their own impressions. Ruth Fredman Cernea has devoted an entire academic book to this debate.[11] In her introduction she relates that the original event took place at a time when Jewish academics were hesitant to display their Jewishness in public, sensing that they should keep their identity private. The festive public debate offered them a rare opportunity to expose their hidden Jewishness and at the same time to introduce a light note into the stuffy seriousness of academia.

These are some of the arguments that have been made for each of those sweet, calorie-rich foods:

LATKES

Its round shape symbolizes eternity.

It has no beginning and no end, and symbolizes life's cyclical nature.

It is egalitarian because its side is always equidistant from the center.

Its Hebrew name, *l'vivah*, seems to stem from *lev*, "heart," and "the Merciful One desires the heart" (*Zohar, Ki Teitzei* 22:108).

HAMANTASCHEN

The triangle is the most stable shape.

It aspires higher, with a form that symbolizes progress.

The triangle is reminiscent of the saying of Shimon HaTzadik, "The world stands on three things: Torah, worship, and acts of kindness" (*Mishnah Avot* 1:2).

The Hebrew term is *ozen Haman*, "Haman's ear," and the ear reminds us of the call, "Hear, O Israel" (Deuteronomy 6:4).

Hamantaschen, or *oznei Haman* as they are called in Israel, are Ashkenazic treats for Purim. They are triangle-shaped cookies traditionally filled with poppy seeds. Many people may have heard that this was "Haman's purse" or "Haman's ear," but the real origin of the name of this cookie stems from the fact that in Yiddish, *haman* means "the poppy."

The debate took place in the best traditions of both rabbinic and academic cultures, of profound deliberations whose goal is to uncover the deepest meanings of things and ferret out the truth. At the same time, it is an accepted tradition in the yeshivah world to crown someone "Rabbi Purim" (here, perhaps, "Professor Purim") and to conduct a parody of pseudo-rabbinic give-and-take on humorous topics. Cernea adds that the debates take place on university campuses shortly before the end of a semester, just when the stress and anxiety of final exams are approaching their peak, and the debate plays an important role in lowering the level of tension for the students.

A few years ago, my American rabbinical students in Jerusalem also decided to hold such an event; I was privileged to be present and was amazed at the debate over whether the latke or hamantaschen should prevail. The debaters presented graphs, statistics, philosophical arguments, and sophisticated analyses—all, of course, in a spirit of levity intended to show the lighter side of the Jewish tradition.

In Israel, we do eat potato pancakes on Chanukah, but primacy among Chanukah foods undoubtedly belongs to the *sufganiyah*. One can only wonder what the nature of the debate would be if it were aligned with the Israeli pattern and the oily doughnut with a hidden center of sweet jam were to go head-to-head with the *hamantasch*. Moreover, it would be interesting to consider what possible arguments might be mustered if we were to bring onto the stage the Moroccan *sfinj*—that marvelous ring without beginning or end, head or tail—or the Dutch *oliebollen* or the Italian *bomboline*.

> The name *sufganiyah* is mentioned as far back as the Mishnah. To be more precise, the plural form *sufganin* appears (Mishnah Challah 1:4–5), in reference to a baked item made from dough. Medieval sources describe the *sufganin* as having been fried in oil. The Mishnah's *sufganin* have come a long way to become today's *sufganiyot*, and it may be that the original *sufganin* were something like a flat wafer cookie rather than a baked treat that rises.

Prayer of the Month

Dedication of a Home (*Chanukat HaBayit*)— Not Just for When You Move In

ON A RECENT FRIDAY, we put together a magnificent coat closet. From now on, anyone coming into our home will see before them a well-organized space, with mirrors on the doors—and not a hodgepodge pile of rumpled coats, scarves, backpacks, and gym towels. This step lifted the mood of everyone in the family, and we sat down for our Shabbat meal in a particularly celebratory atmosphere. As modest and minor an effort as it was, even putting together that IKEA cabinet was a kind of home dedication. In our tradition, the creation of the world took place over six days but never really came to an end; the blessing *Yotzeir Or* in the morning service thanks God for "renewing each day the work of Creation"; Creation continues ever since then in a divine-human partnership. So too, the dedication of a private home does not have to be a one-time event.

When a new baby is born, when a son or daughter is drafted into the armed forces or goes to college or moves away from home, when the family overcomes some personal, interpersonal, or other sort of crisis—each of these is an opportunity to rededicate our home. Renewing the interior—whether that means putting in a new kitchen or reorganizing those pesky junk drawers—is also an excellent occasion for a celebration. Chanukah, which is such a home-oriented holiday, is a good opportunity to think about *chanukat habayit*.

"May this house be built with wisdom and established with understanding" (Proverbs 24:3).[12] This verse emphasizes the fact that a house is not just four walls, but everything that is built and created within it over time. Building a lasting home requires wisdom and understanding, patience, and infinite love. And as in many of life's special moments, the Jewish tradition helps us mark the dedication of a home with blessing and ceremony.

The primary blessings at a *chanukat habayit* are those for affixing a *mezuzah* on the doorpost—"Praise to You, Eternal our God, Sovereign of the universe, who hallows us with mitzvot, commanding us to affix the *mezuzah*"—and the familiar *Shehecheyanu* blessing, which we say when we come to a holiday or have the opportunity to perform an infrequent mitzvah—"Praise to You, Eternal our God, Sovereign of the universe, for giving us life, sustaining us, and enabling us to reach this season." However, one can add to these two blessings many readings and songs. Here are a few suggestions of things to say at a *chanukat habayit* and at moments when a home is renewed.

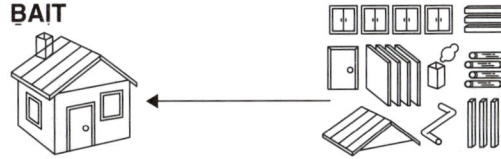

A Blessing for the Home: Four Options

א

Within this gate	בְּזֶה הַשַּׁעַר
may there be no hate.	לֹא יָבוֹא צַעַר.
Into this home	בְּזֹאת הַדִּירָה
may no trouble come.	לֹא תָּבוֹא צָרָה.
Through this door	בְּזֹאת הַדֶּלֶת
may rushing be no more.	לֹא תָּבוֹא בֶּהֱלֵת.
In this dwelling	בְּזֹאת הַמַּחְלָקָה
may there be no yelling.	לֹא תָּבוֹא מַחֲלֹקֶת
In this place	בְּזֶה הַמָּקוֹם
May blessing and peace fill all space.¹³	תְּהִי בְּרָכָה וְשָׁלוֹם.

ב

May this home be a place of ease	יְהֵא זֶה הַמָּקוֹם נָוֶה,
wherein all who come find peace.	מִשְׁכָּן לְשָׁלוֹם.
May contentment here abide,	פֹּה תָּנוּחַ לָהּ שַׁלְוָה,
with friendship by its side.	כָּאן תִּדְרֹךְ הָאַחֲוָה.
Tranquility and joy will mesh	פֹּה יִפָּגְשׁוּ נַחַת וְשִׂמְחָה
with blessing and success.	עִם בְּרָכָה וְהַצְלָחָה.
Under this home's canopy	בְּצֵל זֹאת הַקּוֹרָה
may Torah's song sound happily.	יִתְרוֹנֵן קוֹל תּוֹרָה.
In every corner of this place	בְּזֶה הַמָּעוֹן, בְּזוֹ הַפִּנָּה
may *Shechinah* fill all space.	תְּהֵא שְׁרוּיָה הַשְּׁכִינָה.

ג

May it be Your will, Eternal our God and God of our ancestors, caring and merciful Ruler, that You be filled with compassion for us and guide our efforts, and those of all who dwell in this home, toward success. May all of us be blessed in every way with everything good. Save us from all misdeeds, illness, and misfortune, and may this home filled with all manner of bounty. May it be successful and blessed—for us and for our descendants. So may it be Your will, and let us say: Amen.¹⁴

יְהִי רָצוֹן מִלְּפָנֶיךָ יְיָ אֱלֹהֵינוּ וֵאלֹהֵי אֲבוֹתֵינוּ וְאִמּוֹתֵינוּ, מֶלֶךְ רַחוּם וְחַנּוּן, שֶׁתִּתְמַלֵּא רַחֲמִים עָלֵינוּ וְתַצְלִיחַ מַעֲשֵׂינוּ לָנוּ וּלְכָל בְּנֵי בֵיתֵנוּ הַדָּרִים בַּבַּיִת הַזֶּה. נִהְיֶה כֻּלָּנוּ מְבֹרָכִים בַּכֹּל מִכֹּל כֹּל, תַּצִּילֵנוּ מִכָּל חֵטְא וּמִכָּל חֳלִי וּמִכָּל צָרָה, וְיִהְיֶה בַּיִת זֶה מָלֵא כָּל טוּב, מֻצְלָח וּמְבֹרָךְ – לָנוּ וּלְזַרְעֵנוּ, כֵּן יְהִי רָצוֹן וְנֹאמַר אָמֵן.

ד

רִבּוֹן הָעוֹלָמִים, הַשְׁקִיפָה מִמְּעוֹן קָדְשֶׁךָ,
וְקַבֵּל בְּרַחֲמִים וּבְרָצוֹן אֶת תְּפִלַּת בָּנֶיךָ וּבְנוֹתֶיךָ וְתַחֲנוּנָם,
אֲשֶׁר הִתְאַסְּפוּ כְּדֵי לַחֲנֹךְ אֶת הַבַּיִת הַזֶּה,
וּכְדֵי לְהַבִּיעַ בְּפָנֶיךָ אֶת תּוֹדוֹתֵיהֶם
עַל כָּל הַחֶסֶד וְהָאֱמֶת אֲשֶׁר עָשִׂיתָ עִמָּהֶם.
אָנָּא, חַסְדְּךָ מֵאִתָּם אַל יָמוּשׁ, וּבְרִית שְׁלוֹמְךָ אַל תָּמוֹט.
הָגֵן עַל בֵּית מְגוּרֵיהֶם, שֶׁלֹּא תְאֻנֶּה לוֹ רָעָה,
וְכָל נֶגַע וָצַעַר לֹא יִקְרַב אֵלָיו, וְלֹא יִשָּׁמַע בּוֹ קוֹל צְוָחָה.
זַכֵּה אֶת בְּנֵי הַבַּיִת שֶׁיֵּשְׁבוּ בְּמִשְׁכָּנָם בְּאַחֲוָה וּבְרֵעוּת,
לְאַהֲבָה וּלְיִרְאָה אוֹתְךָ וּלְדָבְקָה בָךְ, וְלַהֲגוֹת בְּתוֹרָתֶךָ וּלְקַיֵּם מִצְוֹתֶיהָ.
וְכֵן יְהִי רָצוֹן, וְנֹאמַר אָמֵן.

Sovereign of all worlds, look out from Your sacred abode
and accept, willingly and lovingly, the prayers and supplications of Your children
who have gathered here to dedicate this house
and to express to You their thanks
for all the kindness that You have extended to them.
May Your care for them never waver, and may the covenant of Your peace
   never falter.
Protect their home so that no misfortune befall it
and no plague or disaster approach it, and may no cries of distress be heard
   from it.
Enable the members of this household to dwell in their home in close kinship
   and friendship,
in love and awe of You and closeness to You, speaking of Your Torah and keeping
   its commandments.
So may it be Your will, and let us say: Amen.[15]

The dedication—or rededication—of a home can be an excellent opportunity for conversation and reflection about what home, establishing a home, and life within our homes means to us.

The Torah describes how a priest (*kohein*) purifies a house that has been defiled by an outbreak of disease in its walls (Leviticus 14:33–57). It is interesting to ponder how a house can suffer from what is in humans a skin disease, *tzaraat*. What can *tzaraat* mean in the case of a house? What is that like? When does a house become sullied by impurity or struck by illness? How does a house get purified or healed? How can we guard the health of our homes?

Tishrei   Marcheshvan   Kislev   Tevet   Sh'vat   Adar   Nisan   Iyar   Sivan   Tammuz   Av   Elul

"A Psalm for the Dedication of the House" (Psalm 30)

It is puzzling that Psalm 30 (like many other chapters) is attributed to King David. After all, David did not build the Temple; his son Solomon was given that privilege. A midrash explains that the intention to do a good deed is what matters most, and that is why the "dedication of the House" is here attributed to David, even though in practice he did not get to build it (*Midrash T'hillim* 30).

> 1 A psalm: A dedication-song for the House
> Of David:
> 2 I will raise You high, Eternal,
> For You have pulled me up,
> And You have not let my enemies rejoice over me.
> 3 Eternal my God,
> I cried out to You—and You healed me!
> 4 Eternal, You brought me, body and spirit,
>   up from Sheol;
> You have kept me alive that I should not
>   plunge into the Pit....
> 12 You have turned my wail into a waltz for me!
> You've untied my tatters, You've girded me
>   with joy—
> 13 So that Glory may sing a psalm to You,
>   and spare the silence, the silence of blood;
> Eternal my God, my thanks I give to You forever![16]

This psalm describes the moment of salvation from impending disaster. It includes words of thanksgiving to God, who redeemed the Psalmist—David, according to the Psalm—from Saul and did not let him remain in trouble. He admits that for a brief moment he was frightened when he thought God had abandoned him ("You hid Your face—I was terrified!" [v. 8]) but was instead present in divine salvation. Later, the Psalmist turns to the "profitability" of God's salvation ("What profit is there in my blood, in my plunging into the Pit? Can dust praise You? Can it declare Your truth?" [v. 10]), asserting that both the Psalmist and God will benefit from the Psalmist being saved. Psalm 30, "a dedication-song for the House," appears in morning prayers from the seventeenth century onward. There are some who claim that its inclusion in the daily worship service was a mistake and that originally it was only meant to be read during the days of Chanukah (since the Hebrew word for dedication is *chanukah*); after being printed in several prayer books without those specific instructions, it began to be recited every day. Another possible (perhaps retroactive) explanation is that the understanding of the synagogue as a *mikdash m'at* (lesser temple) is what led to this psalm being recited daily.

TEVET

Zodiac Sign: Capricorn | Tribe of the Month: Asher
Breastplate Stone: Beryl/*Tarshish*

The name Tevet is taken from the Babylonian name Teveitu. The word's origin is uncertain, but some argue that it is close in meaning to the Hebrew verb *tava*, meaning "drown," since in the rainy winter months of Tevet we often find ourselves sunk into mud.

The name of the month appears in the Book of Esther, one of the later books of the *Tanach*/Hebrew Bible, dated to the Second Temple time, alongside its more ancient numerical name: "Esther was taken to King Ahasuerus, in his royal palace, in the tenth month, which is the month of Tevet, in the seventh year of his reign" (Esther 2:16).

KAVANAH: A MEDITATION FOR TEVET

"ALL THAT YOU HAVE SAID was spoken out of a true heart, and there is no one who can deny your words. Today is not the first time your wisdom has been shown, but from the beginning of your life all the people have recognized your understanding, for your heart's disposition is right." (Judith 8:26–27)

> May the One who blessed Sarah with vigor and joy
> bless us with the ability to renew ourselves at every age.
> May the One who blessed Rebekah with a voice that was heard
> bless us with an environment attentive to our desires.
> May the One who blessed Leah with fertility
> bless us through the fruits of our labors.
> May the One who blessed Rachel with love
> bless us with the ability to love ourselves.
> May the One who blessed Judith with wisdom and leadership
> bless us with courage and with the ability to remove obstacles from our path.
>
> *Havayah*, the One whose name is Being—bless us with joy in our being.
> *Ein HaChayim*, Source of life—bless us with a constant flow of wisdom and knowledge.
> *Shechinah*, Presence—be present among us
> and endow us with love and togetherness, peace and friendship.[1]

During the month of Tevet, which begins with the shortest days and longest nights of the year, it is good to recall that "there will not be a victory of light over darkness as long as we do not recognize the clear and simple truth that we must enhance the light rather than fight the darkness" (A. D. Gordon, 1856–1922).[2] Even a small candle can expel great darkness.

Tishrei   Marcheshvan   Kislev   Tevet   Sh'vat   Adar   Nisan   Iyar   Sivan   Tammuz   Av   Elul

At the Gates of Tevet

The month of Tevet begins with the end of Chanukah, with a full menorah filling the room with darting, flickering light. After Chanukah comes to an end early in the month, Tevet has no additional holidays other than the tenth day, which is marked by a minor fast memorializing the beginning of the siege of Jerusalem by the Babylonian Empire in the waning months of the First Temple. Tevet comes as winter is in full force in Israel (and elsewhere in the Northern Hemisphere). It is the very heart of winter, and at the same time, Tevet marks the beginning of the days growing longer, a phenomenon that will reach its zenith in the heart of summer. It is similar to reaching the bottom of a deep body of water, and pushing off the ground to propel oneself back toward the air and light; we know light is coming, even in this darkest of months. After all, it is always darkest before the dawn.

This chapter on Tevet deals with traditions both ancient and forgotten, new and renewed. The first two *iyunim* dive into Rosh Chodesh Tevet from a feminine perspective. One explores the Festival of the Women, observed by many North African Jewish communities, and also the bravery of Jewish women more generally. The second relates the story of Regina Jonas, the first woman in the world to have been ordained as a rabbi. A third *iyun* examines the fast of the tenth of Tevet and other fast days that were once observed during this month but have been forgotten. The twenty-first of Tevet is Hebrew Language Day, so the fourth *iyun* explores the revival of the language. The Prayer of the Month is the *Sh'ma* recited at bedtime, which is said not only in Tevet, of course, but throughout the year. Nonetheless it is an appropriate subject to consider during this very "nocturnal" month. As the Poems of the Month, I have chosen two night poems by Lea Goldberg.

Poems of the Month

Lailah ("Night") and *Mizmor Lailah* ("A Night Psalm")

This time of the year, the coldest and darkest, can be used to ponder those aspects of our lives that belong to the nocturnal, the personal, and contemplative. I chose to share here two "nocturnal" poems by Lea Goldberg.

The literary scholar Lea Goldberg (1911–70) worked as a translator, journalist, and illustrator, but above all she is remembered as a beloved poet. Both poems below describe the night not only as a period of time, but as a spiritual condition. The night may be felt as a lonely time, it may provoke fear and anxiety, but it also invites us to contemplate and be present in a way that darkness and the solemnity of the night fully allows.

The poem *Mizmor Lailah* ("A Night Psalm") describes desperation in the face of utter darkness, which is gradually replaced by confidence that the light will shine. In the poem *Lailah* ("Night") Goldberg talks about a gift—a "basket full of stars"—similar to a harvest basket in which the pilgrims brought their first fruits to the Temple. Using very few (albeit powerful) words, the poem describes the excited beating of the heart as one approaches the steps of the beloved one (or maybe—God). In Hebrew, "heartbeat" and "step" are the same word (*paam*), suggesting a synchronization of rhythm and an increase of excitement toward a desired meeting.

Night	לַיְלָה
Lea Goldberg	לֵאָה גּוֹלְדְּבֶּרְג
A basket full of stars,	טֶנֶא מָלֵא כּוֹכָבִים,
the fragrance of whispering grass,	רֵיחַ דְּשָׁאִים דּוֹבְבִים,
deep	עָמֹק
deep in the dew	עָמֹק בַּטַּל
my heart beats.	פּוֹעֵם לְבָבִי.
Now your footsteps come near.	הִנֵּה פְּעָמַיִךְ קְרֵבִים.
A myriad of droplets tremble.	הִרְעִידוּ רִבּוֹא רְבִיבִים.
Deep	עָמֹק
deep in the dew	עָמֹק בַּטַּל
my heart beats.[3]	פּוֹעֵם לְבָבִי.

A Night Psalm
Lea Goldberg

מִזְמוֹר לַיְלָה
לֵאָה גּוֹלְדְּבֶּרְג

The crescent moon is draped in black,
all the stars are hidden from sight,
from the North to far Yemen
there is not a single ray of light.

אֶת כָּל הַכּוֹכָבִים טָמַן,
אֶת הַסַּהַר עָטַף בִּשְׁחוֹר
מִצָּפוֹן וְעַד תֵּימָן
אֵין קֶרֶן אוֹר.

And morning, faithful widower,
clutches a grey sack tight,
from the North to far Yemen
not a single ray of light.

וְהַבֹּקֶר אַלְמָן נֶאֱמָן,
שַׂק אֵפֶר עַל מָתְנָיו יַחְגֹּר
מִצָּפוֹן וְעַד תֵּימָן
אֵין קֶרֶן אוֹר.

O please, light a white candle
in the black tent of my heart,
from the North to far Yemen
let there be light.[4]

הַדְלִיקָה נָא נֵר לָבָן
בְּאֹהֶל לִבִּי הַשָּׁחוֹר,
מִצָּפוֹן וְעַד תֵּימָן
יִזְרַח הָאוֹר.

Rosh Chodesh Tevet: The Festival of the Women

ON THE FIRST DAY OF TEVET, as the Chanukah lights were burning, in Tunis and other Jewish communities in North Africa the women would gather together. They were in the habit of celebrating every Rosh Chodesh, but they observed Rosh Chodesh Tevet with particular festivity. It was known in Arabic as Id Al-banaat—Festival of the Women, Women's Holiday, or perhaps Rosh Chodesh for Women. The customs for observing this day varied depending on where it was celebrated. In some locations the holiday was observed only by unmarried girls, and in other places it was a holiday for women of every age and stage of life. As the Chanukah lights shone, they ate holiday foods, sang songs, danced, and received blessings from a rabbi.[5]

We do not know the reason the Festival of the Women was established during Rosh Chodesh Tevet. One theory about this timing is that on "the first day of the tenth month" (Ezra 10:16), Ezra the Scribe called on the people of Judah who had returned from Babylon to divorce their foreign wives. This explanation asserts that in response, the Israelite women celebrated the departure of their rivals. We have no evidence, though, that this story is true. I prefer the idea (no less impossible to prove) that the Festival of the Women is connected to Queen Esther, the savior of her people, who was taken to the house of King Ahasuerus "in the tenth month, which is the month of Tevet" (Esther 2:16). The Book of Esther is also the only place in the Hebrew Bible in which the name of this month is mentioned.

There are some who have linked the holiday with Judith's brave deeds, but one could link the stories of at least two other special women to the Festival of the Women—Jephthah's daughter and Mattathias's daughter. These two women's stories are so dramatic, and yet we never learn their names; simply mentioning them is like erecting a monument by which they can be remembered. These stories are traditions of solidarity and sisterhood. We present them now to you.

Judith

The Book of Judith is one of the books of the Apocrypha; it was written in Jewish circles and for Jewish readers, but it did not enter the canon of the Hebrew Bible. The book tells a story of the clever machination and bravery of the beautiful widow who rescued her people and slew Holofernes, the Assyrian military commander who had laid siege to the city. Some consider the book the world's first historical novel. As the people and its leaders are sunk in confusion and despair, Judith goes to the enemy's encampment and requests political asylum from Holofernes. Her cover story proves convincing—she relates that she knows her people are about to lose and that she is interested in joining the winning side. The commander is impressed by her beauty and her wisdom, and he invites her to consort with him. Judith pretends to accede to the ruler's wishes. She offers an impassioned prayer for success in her undertaking, and then she approaches his bed, takes the drunken Holofernes's sword in hand, calls out, "Give me strength today, O Eternal, God of Israel!" and, with a double blow on his neck, severs his head (Judith 13:9–11). The commander's death sows despair and confusion among the Assyrian troops, and the Jews win a tremendous victory.

She said in her heart, "O Eternal, God of all might, look in this hour on the work of my hands for the exaltation of Jerusalem. Now indeed is the time to help Your heritage and to carry out my design to destroy the enemies who have risen up against us." (Judith 13:7–8)

There is no certainty that Judith's story took place at Chanukah time, nor is there any proof that these events actually occurred. Nevertheless, our tradition attaches Judith's story to Chanukah. Indeed, Judith's character mirrors Judah Maccabee. Their names are similar, and both are symbolic representatives of the Jewish people. Judith's heroism is seen as echoing that of Judah, and the figures of the sword-bearing Judah and of Judith with a sword in one hand and the severed head of Holofernes in the other adorn many *chanukiyot* beginning in the sixteenth century. On Rosh Chodesh Tevet, women would recount Judith's bravery and join together to eat cheese-based foods, based on the medieval tradition that Judith refused to eat nonkosher meat in Holofernes's camp and fed him cheese patties to put him to sleep—just as Yael lulled Sisera to sleep with milk (Judges 4:17–21, 5:24–27). (See pp. 134–35.)

Jephthah's Daughter

We know almost nothing about the young maiden described in our sources only as the daughter of her father and murderer, or about her brief life.[6] All we know is that her father vows, before going out to war against the king of the Ammonites, "Whatever comes out of the door of my house to meet me on my safe return from the Ammonites shall be the Eternal's and shall be offered by me as a burnt offering" (Judges 11:31). Jephthah does indeed emerge victorious from that battle, and to his (and our) horror, what comes out first to greet him upon his return is none other than his only daughter, who greets her father with drums and dance. Jephthah goes into mourning, but he does not renounce his vow to God; in fact, his daughter encourages Jephthah to keep his vow, asking only, "Let me be for two months, and I will go with my companions and lament upon the hills and there bewail my maidenhood" (v. 37). After he grants his daughter the time she asked for, we read that "he did to her as he had vowed" (v. 39). The *Tanach* cannot bear to express in explicit terms the horrific deed done to the young woman, but the Rabbis did not "spare the rod" in dealing with Jephthah:

> And the Holy Spirit cries out: Would I ask for you to sacrifice human beings to Me? "... That which I never commanded, never decreed, and that never came to My mind" (Jeremiah 19:5), and I did not tell Jephthah to sacrifice his daughter to Me! (*Tanchuma Buber, B'chukotai* 7)

The Bible reports on an ancient observance by Israelite women, established in memory of Jephthah's daughter: "So it became a custom in Israel for the maidens of Israel to go every year, for four days in the year, and chant dirges for the daughter of Jephthah the Gileadite" (Judges 11:40).

Rabbanit Rivkah Lubitch, the rabbinical court "pleader" who works for the Center for Women's Justice, whom we encountered in our exploration of Tishrei (pp. 37–38), sought to rescue Jephthah's daughter from her anonymity and grant her a name: Tanot, based on an ancient name given her in Apocryphal literature. She explained the name in her original modern midrash:

> And why was she called "Tanot"? Because it is written, *And so since long ago, the daughters of Israel go to wail (le-tanot) for the daughter of Jephthah the Gileadite, four days a year* (Judges 11:40). And they said, Tanot does not mean "wailing" but is the name of Jephthah's daughter. And what does she do? She sits in heaven and listens to the stories of the earthly daughters of Israel, and then sits by the Shekhinah and bewails their sorrows in Her ear, prays for them, and pleads their righteousness.[8]

Tanot appears in other midrashim by Lubitch as an advocate for Jewish women, a sort of female parallel to the prophet Elijah.

The story of Jephthah's daughter became associated after the fact with Rosh Chodesh Tevet. The fourteenth-century Spanish commentator on Jewish liturgy Rabbi David Abudarham wrote that it is dangerous to drink water at the transitional times between the four seasons (see pp. 77–78), meaning Rosh Chodesh of the months of Tishrei, Tevet, Nisan, and Tammuz. The reason he gives for why water is dangerous at the beginning of Tevet is "because at that time Jephthah's daughter was slaughtered and all the waters turned to blood."[7] This explanation serves as an epitaph and a memorial to Jephthah's daughter and her horrific fate.

The stories of Judith and Jephthah's daughter, both linked to Rosh Chodesh Tevet, display a wide range of feminine behaviors and female fates, from brave victor to victim. On the surface, the two stories share very little in common: the latter is given a few verses in the Bible, with the protagonist remaining unnamed, while the former, whose protagonist's name is like that of her people, occupies an entire book in which her voice is heard clearly. One takes bold action; the other is forcefully acted upon. One is put to death because she innocently emerges from her home; the other brings redemption for Israel because she deliberately and purposefully emerges from her home straight to the enemy's camp. Despite the differences between their stories, a closer look reveals surprising similarities between Judith and Jephthah's daughter. Both their stories are marked by horrible violence: one is murdered because of her father's haughty pride and the other kills in order to save her people. Both step onto the stage of history for a brief moment and were later kept from it: one loses her youthful life, while the other returns to the anonymity of her home, and the book that recounts her exploits did not make it into the Jews' sacred canon.

The two of them—Jephthah's daughter and Judith—acted within a system that allowed them only a very narrow range of activity. One accepted her fate: "'Father,' she said, 'You have uttered a vow to the Eternal; do to me as you have vowed'" (Judges 11:36), asking only for a delay to mourn her lost life with her friends; the other took advantage of her beauty and craftiness in order to entice a military commander, who lost his head in more than one sense in response to her seduction. Both of them once stood at the center of public events and in our days have been returned to the stage of history and remembrance—one by Jewish maidens, who bewail a lost maidenhood, and the other by an entire people, who celebrate her wisdom and her savvy.

Mattathias's Daughter

A medieval midrash tells of a third woman whose story helps explain the Festival of the Women—the daughter of Mattathias the High Priest. Here the connection to Chanukah is direct and explicit, since Mattathias was a leader of the Maccabean rebellion. Hidden, unexpected threads connect her story and those of the two women mentioned above:

> When the Greeks saw that the people Israel did not feel the sting of their edicts, they declared a bitter, dark edict: that no bride on the first night of her marriage should proceed from her wedding canopy other than into the home of the local ruler. When the Jews heard this, their hands went slack and their strength ebbed, and they refrained from declaring any engagements. Jewish girls would mature and grow old and still remain virgins . . . and the Greeks would harass and assault Jewish virgins, and this practice went on for three years and eight months, until the daughter of Mattathias the High Priest married a Hasmonean man named Eliezer. When her day of celebration arrived, he sat her in a palanquin. . . .
>
> When they sat down for a banquet, Hannah, Mattathias's daughter, stood up from the palanquin, clapped her hands together, ripped apart her purple cloak, and stood undressed before all the Jews, and before her father and mother and father-in-law. When her brothers saw this, they were embarrassed and turned their faces to the ground and tore their clothes, and they approached her in order to kill her. She said to them, "Hear me out, brothers and uncles! Because I stood naked before righteous men, having committed no [other] transgression, your zealotry is directed at me. But you have no such zealous anger about turning me over to an uncircumcised man to assault me?! . . . Ruler of the universe, if You will have no mercy on us, have mercy on the sanctity of Your great name by which we are called, and take vengeance for us today!"
>
> . . . At that moment, her brothers were stirred with zealotry. . . and took counsel.
>
> . . . And the Holy Blessed One provided great salvation for them.[9]

The story of Mattathias's daughter is a story of courage and resourcefulness—not before the enemy but before her relatives, and not on the battlefield but in her own home. She bares herself on her wedding night, knowing that is the only way she will succeed in shocking her brothers, who had remained indifferent to the knowledge that the local ruler would defile her on her wedding night. She does indeed shock them, so much so that they want to murder her. The midrash criticizes the fact that the brothers tolerated the violence that their sister was about to suffer but are outraged at her violation of social norms of modesty. Once they hear their sister's plea, they gather up their courage and fight the enemy.

We have no historical information about a "first night decree" regarding Jewish brides nor any historical evidence of such a protest by Mattathias's daughter. It is fascinating, though, that the midrash explains the Hasmoneans' brave exploits and their war of liberation as stemming from the brave act of a lone, defenseless young woman. Perhaps this story contains a *tikkun* (repair) to the story of Jephthah's daughter: Mattathias's daughter does not accept the decree that she should be sacrificed, and in a brave act of rebellion she calls her male relatives to action. Her path is different from that of Judith, but both women act shrewdly, leading their people to victory. Even so, it is sad to discover that women who succeeded in rescuing their people were forced to do so by compromising their sexuality and risking what was most dear to them. We need new stories of women's bravery, stories that empower women and celebrate their wisdom and wit in a positive way.

Even if these three women's stories are not literary traditions created for ideological and educational reasons, their cultural value is great. Each of them, and the combination of all three, enrich our understanding of the holiday of Chanukah and of the Festival of Women as well.

May these brave, clever women—and like them, brave Jewish women across the ages—inspire us to revive ancient and new traditions, including the Festival of the Women. May this be a day on which we can celebrate the courage of women not only in extreme situations but also in the struggle for daily existence—a day of celebrating life and liberty, female solidarity, and collective human responsibility.

A Candle for Rabbi Regina Jonas

IN THE MIDST OF THE DARKNESS that descended upon European Jewry during the days of Nazi rule, a special candle was lit on Rosh Chodesh Tevet in the Hebrew year 5596 (December 27, 1935). On that date, for the first time in Jewish history, rabbinic ordination was bestowed upon a woman—Rabbi Regina Jonas. Jonas, who was ordained in Germany and murdered in the Holocaust, was also the first person in our people's history who argued, on the basis of a systematic halachic inquiry, for equal rights for women in Judaism, including ordaining them as rabbis.[11]

"Can Women Serve as Rabbis?"

Regina Jonas was born in 1902, lived with her mother in a poor neighborhood in Berlin, and was never married. From a young age, she served as a teacher in the Jewish school in Berlin. She continued her studies at Berlin's Hochschule für die Wissenschaft des Judentums, completing them in 1930. That was not enough, though, and she strove to obtain rabbinic ordination at a time when ordaining women was unthinkable. As part of her efforts, she wrote a thesis entitled "Can Women Serve as Rabbis?" That question, which many today would see as trivial, was unprecedented at the time. Jonas presented many arguments from rabbinic literature in moderate, measured language in order to prove that women can be ordained as rabbis.

In her thesis, Jonas addressed, for example, the argument that men and women sharing work would lead to "sexual misdeeds." She compared, among other things, the permission granted to unmarried men or widowers to serve as teachers in settings in which they would be exposed to female coworkers and showed it does not lead to improper behavior. Therefore, she argued, women can also fill leadership roles without causing concern. At the conclusion of her thesis, Jonas wrote, "All things considered, and taking into account all the matters discussed above, it is not so revolutionary or un-Jewish to see that in practice there is no impediment to [a woman] serving as a teacher of Judaism or as a rabbi."[12]

Jonas did not regard herself as a revolutionary. She was, in fact, a rather traditional woman. Her goal was to prove, from within the sources themselves and using classical halachic tools, that there was no reason to prevent women from obtaining rabbinic ordination. I don't know whether she would define herself as a feminist, but she was undoubtedly a pathbreaker, and today she serves as an inspiration to many women.

Rabbi Leo Baeck (1873–1956), who stood at the head of German Jewry at the time, refrained from publicly declaring his support for Jonas and her demand for the ordination of women, but he apparently gave her encouragement and quiet support. Baeck kept in touch with her during all the years of her activity, and he and his wife kept up a friendly correspondence with her for many years. After a tenacious struggle, Jonas received private rabbinic ordination from Rabbi Max Dienemann, one of the most prominent liberal rabbis in Germany (who moved to Palestine in 1938). As a rabbi, she taught Judaism, worked as a chaplain in a hospital, an old-age home, and an institution for the blind, served as lecturer and sermonizer around Germany, and published articles on academic and theological subjects.

"Fähigkeiten und Berufungen hat Gott in unsere Brust gesenkt und nicht nach dem Geschlecht gefragt. So hat ein jeder die Pflicht, ob Mann oder Frau, nach den Gaben, die Gott ihm schenkte, zu wirken."

"God planted skills and duty in our hearts and did not ask about our sex. Therefore, every woman and man has the duty to fulfill what God has given them." (Regina Jonas)[10]

Rabbi in Troubled Times

Jonas did not abandon her work even when evil befell German Jewry. In 1942 she was deported, along with her mother, to the ghetto at Terezin (Theresienstadt), and there too she continued to work as a chaplain (*Seelsorger*) alongside Viktor Frankl, the well-known psychiatrist and postwar author of *Man's Search for Meaning*. She took on the difficult task of greeting the Jews who arrived by train at Theresienstadt and helping them adjust to the difficulties of the life that had been imposed on them. Jonas continued to lecture and arrange classes, theater presentations, and shows in an attempt to ease the lives of those interned in the camp and distract them from the daily atrocities. Her many surviving lectures include discourses on keeping Shabbat and mitzvot under camp conditions. Despite some individuals' opposition to her service as a rabbi, there is evidence that her lectures and sermons were delivered to rooms filled to capacity and that many listeners stood at the door and in the street in order to listen to her. Her words touched their tortured hearts.

A short time before she was deported to Theresienstadt, Jonas deposited her personal papers for safekeeping in the archive of the Berlin Jewish community. Found among those papers was her thesis, which she had presented to the Hochschule (which was closed by the Nazis in 1942). Jonas and her mother were sent to the Auschwitz death camp in the last days of 1944, where she was murdered a short time later.

Memory Lost—or Suppressed?

In the early 1990s, after the fall of the Berlin Wall and the reunification of Germany, previously closed archives were opened to the public. As a result, a wealth of surprising information about German Jewry in recent generations became available. Among the documents preserved in the archive of the Berlin Jewish community, held then at Potsdam, was an envelope containing Jonas's papers, which had until then been all but forgotten. In the envelope were Jonas's groundbreaking rabbinic thesis on the ordination of women, a few pictures of her, and her ordination certificate from 1935.

Regina Jonas's story had disappeared not only because of her cruel murder and because many of the people whom she assisted were murdered as well, but also because of an incomprehensible and inexplicable silence that surrounded her and her activities. Some of the prominent personalities among German Jewry and the majority of

---

In a letter to the philosopher and scholar Martin Buber in 1938, Regina Jonas wrote about her work, saying, "I give spiritual guidance to patients in hospitals and to the residents of nursing homes. I also lecture at the synagogue, I've presided over funerals, and I give sermons at the synagogues of the nursing homes."

Further on in the letter, Jonas asks Buber to help her move to Palestine, but in the end she was unable to leave her mother and remained in Germany: "I have come to believe that in the Chasidic community, there is more freedom and less prejudice against women. I had hoped to find in you an understanding for the ideal that I could not find with all my teachers; the 'question of women' is as complex as the 'Jewish question' in the Diaspora. I do not want to leave my profession; I must work. Maybe this is a possibility in the Land of Israel."[13]

the survivors of Theresienstadt who knew Jonas and her work did not make memorializing Regina Jonas a priority, and much of her work was forgotten for more than a generation. I—a rabbi myself—did not know a thing about Jonas until a few years ago; I thought that women were first ordained as rabbis in the United States in the 1970s.

The reasons for this "public amnesia" remain hidden. We can only speculate and can certainly not judge Holocaust survivors for their memories of those dark years or what they chose to share afterward. Now, we have the obligation and privilege of bringing to light the name of the person who gave so much light to her people during a time of great darkness, and to ensure that the heritage of Regina Jonas, murdered by our enemies, will no longer be forgotten. For me, Rosh Chodesh Tevet—Id Al-banaat, the Festival of the Women—is now also the holiday of Regina Jonas, a distant, brave sister.

Women in the Rabbinate

In 1972, Sally Priesand was granted rabbinic ordination by Hebrew Union College–Jewish Institute of Religion, the Reform Movement's rabbinical seminary. That was the first institutional ordination of a woman as a rabbi. Since then, hundreds of women have been ordained by non-Orthodox movements and serve as communal leaders in Jewish institutions around the world.

In recent years, some Orthodox communities have created opportunities for women to be ordained and to serve as rabbis in congregations, as teachers of halachah, and more. A few institutions have responded to the efforts of these women and have begun to prepare and ordain women for the rabbinate in Israel and the Diaspora. For example, Rabba Sara Hurwitz was the first woman to be ordained as a rabbi by an Orthodox seminary in the United States. In Israel, there are currently six Orthodox rabbinical institutions for higher halachic (legal) education that work to empower women, either through ordination or other programs.

Tishrei   Marcheshvan   Kislev   Tevet   Sh'vat   Adar   Nisan   Iyar   Sivan   Tammuz   Av   Elul

A Fast (or Fasts) during Tevet and the Danger of Translation

The tenth of Tevet marks the beginning of the end of the First Temple. On that day, Nebuchadnezzar, king of Babylonia, laid siege to Jerusalem. At the end of the siege he destroyed the city:

> And in the ninth year of his reign, on the tenth day of the tenth month, King Nebuchadnezzar moved against Jerusalem with his whole army. They besieged it and built towers against it all around. (Jeremiah 52:4; see also II Kings 25:1)

The tenth of Tevet was declared a fast day, one of the four fasts marking events connected to the destruction of the First Temple. In addition to the fast in Tevet, we mark the seventeenth of Tammuz, the day the walls of Jerusalem were breached during the siege; the ninth of Av, the day that our tradition asserts that both the First and Second Temples were destroyed and on which other disastrous events occurred; and the third of Tishrei, the Fast of Gedaliah, which marks the murder of Gedaliah son of Achikam, governor of Judah, after which the remaining Jewish inhabitants of Judah scattered and the Jewish community of the First Temple era was no longer.

In the State of Israel, the fast of the tenth of Tevet took on additional significance when, in 1951, the chief rabbinate declared it the General Day of Mourning for Holocaust victims whose date of death is unknown. Although this was intended to provide surviving families an opportunity to formally mourn, most of the Israeli public observes Yom HaShoah on the twenty-seventh of Nisan (see pp. 193–97).

"And Darkness Came Over the World for Three Days"

An ancient tradition speaks about not one fast day in Tevet but three in a row! *M'gillat Taanit Batra*, a composition from the time of the *Geonim* (i.e., the centuries after the completion of the Talmud), lists the fast days observed in each month:

> On the eighth of Tevet [because] the Torah was written in Greek in the time of King Ptolemy, and darkness came over the world for three days; on the ninth of the month, [but] our rabbis did not write down what it was for; on the tenth [because] the king of Babylonia arrived at Jerusalem to lay waste to it.[14]

Tevet, as we have noted, is the month that begins at the darkest time of the year. Here, tradition describes difficult events that brought three days of darkness upon the world, and so fasts were established on those three days. Two are explained—the fasts on the eighth and the tenth of Tevet—but the fast on the ninth of Tevet remained unexplained, its origins undocumented. We have a tradition that was preserved without anyone at all remembering why it was established.

The mystery was solved by the *piyut* known as *Ezk'rah Matzok* ("I will recall the distress") by Yosef ben Avitur, a Spanish poet of the tenth century. The poem as it has been preserved speaks of "three blows" endured during the month of Tevet, of which it is said, "The month of Tevet—I was much whipped during it," and a fast was declared for each. In addition to the eighth and tenth of Tevet, the poet says "the eloquent speaker ... was ripped away" on the ninth of Tevet—that is to say, Ezra the Scribe died on that date. Over time, the fasts of the eighth and ninth of Tevet were forgotten. The fast of the tenth of Tevet itself is relatively short, since it lasts from dawn until evening during a time of year when daylight is already short, so the day's emotional impact is not like that of the Ninth of Av.

"The King of Greece Forced Me to Write the Law in Greek"

It is easy to understand why a fast day was declared on the day that symbolizes the beginning of the fall and destruction of Jerusalem, and one can understand as well why it would be appropriate to mark the day when Ezra the Scribe—one of the heads of the community of Jews who returned from Babylon—passed away. But why should the translation of the Torah into Greek be regarded as a disaster worth marking with an annual fast day? The tractate *Sof'rim*, which deals with the laws of writing a Torah scroll, tells us about two events connected to Ptolemy Philadelphus, king of Egypt in the third century BCE. The first is that he instructed the Jewish sages to translate the Torah into Greek; the second is that a miracle occurred for the seventy-two elders whom the king gathered, and though each one translated the Torah independently, they all produced the exact same translation. In addition, each of the scribes went so far as to change the simple contextual meaning of the Torah in thirteen places in order to prevent any misunderstandings; this was done without any coordination, in exactly the same way.

We would expect that the day the Torah was translated with agreement and unity among the elders would be a day of celebration: the wellsprings of Torah would be spouting forth and anyone—Jews unfamiliar with Hebrew and non-Jews, anyone with a thirst for knowledge—could come, learn, and imbibe the waters of the Torah. However, that is not how things unfolded. In *Sof'rim* we read, "That day was as difficult for [the people] Israel as the day the Golden Calf was made," and in *M'gillat Taanit Batra* we also learn that as a result of the translation, "darkness engulfed the world for three days." Why did the Torah, which is light, cause the world to be darkened? Because the Greek translation made the Jewish people's sacred Scripture into everyone's property. The Torah, which had been transmitted as a private matter expressing the intimate relationship between the people Israel and God, was wrested away from them, and henceforth anyone who wanted could come and do with it as they wished. And indeed, this proved to be the case; there are instances when Christians used biblical verses as proof texts for their faith, and over time some used the text of the Hebrew Bible to attack the Jews. This explains why the Oral Torah was not set down in writing for many generations.

Beyond the danger inherent in translating the Torah, Tractate *Sof'rim* tells us that "the Torah could not be sufficiently translated." This raises an essential question: is

---

It once happened that five elders wrote the Torah for King Ptolemy in Greek, and that day was as ominous for Israel as the day on which the Golden Calf was made, since the Torah could not be accurately translated.

It also happened that King Ptolemy assembled seventy-two elders and placed them in seventy-two [separate] rooms without telling them the reason for which he had assembled them. He then went to each one of them and said to him, "Write for me [a translation of] the Torah of Moses your master." The Eternal inspired them and the mind of all of them was identical, so that each on his own wrote the [same translation of the] Torah, introducing [the same] thirteen alterations. (*Sof'rim* 1:7–8)

Rabbi Eliezer Yehuda Waldenberg (1915–2006), an influential Jerusalem rabbi, identified a causal relationship between the three disasters that took place during the month of Tevet. In his view, the translation of the Torah into Greek was the spiritual cause of the death of Ezra the Scribe, who was the embodiment of Torah study in its purest form, and his death in turn eventually brought about the destruction of the Temple (*Tzitz Eliezer* 13:56).

it possible to accurately translate from one language to another? In my work, I sometimes want to translate a text into another language. I learn over and over again that there is no such thing as an "exact translation" or a "literal translation"—a translation that preserves the language's flexibility, the meaning of each word, the inherent music of the words, and the richness of their world of images. Most often, a translation cannot preserve the multiplicity of meanings that are in a text. I repeatedly tell my students that translation is not a science but an art. Perhaps the mourning engendered by the translation of the Torah is that in the process of translation, the Torah's flexibility and the multiple facets of its words are removed. There is a reason that our sages compared the day of the Torah's translation to the day of the worship of the Golden Calf (which they date as the seventeenth of Tammuz): on those two days, both of which became fast days, the words of the living God were exchanged for a form that is static and inanimate.

Translation as a Bridge

On a trip to South America after my army service, I visited the city of Cochabamba in Bolivia. There I saw an improvised workshop of linguists and church people trying to translate the Bible into a few indigenous Latin American languages, some of which had had no written form until recently, and in some cases an alphabet had been created specifically for this project. While it is true that in some cases translation misses some of the meanings, translation also makes it possible for disparate cultures and faiths to encounter one another. A true dialogue can take place only if there is a shared language for the exchange of ideas.

The Torah is a foundational text sacred to two religions—Judaism and Christianity. While Christianity created what it calls the New Testament and the writings of the Church Fathers, Judaism continued the process of Oral Law with rabbinic literature: the Mishnah, the Babylonian and Jerusalem Talmuds, and collections of midrash—a constant flow of interpretation that has continued through our own time, with no sign of slowing down. The Torah, which in the past was used for interreligious confrontation, attempts at conversion, or to inflame antisemitism, has become, among a growing circle of readers, an important instrument in interreligious dialogue whose purpose is not persuasion or argument, but rather understanding and friendship.

> For all the peoples may walk, each in the name of its gods,
> and we shall walk in the name of the Eternal our God forever and ever.[15]
> (Micah 4:5)

Hebrew, Revived—Part I

A WAR TOOK PLACE in Jerusalem in 1913, though not a shot was fired and no one lost their life; rather, this was a "War of Language," involving strong beliefs, passions, and emotions. This "war" was over the struggle to use Hebrew as the language of instruction and speech in educational systems and public life. Hebrew Language Day, observed on the twenty-first of Tevet, provides a special opportunity to think about this language.

When he was young, my grandfather Moreno Levi was on the "wrong" side in the language war. He went to the Lemel School in Jerusalem, which was then under the auspices of "Ezra," the German Jewish community's philanthropic organization, and the language of instruction was, of course, German. As a very young child, my grandfather liked the school, the teachers, and the warm meal they provided each day, and so he remained loyal to the school's position and its language. His older brothers, though, were enthusiastic partners in the struggle for instruction in Hebrew. Today, some people forget that the opposition to Hebrew did not necessarily stem from anti-Zionist positions. Even at Lemel, after all, some subjects were studied in Hebrew. But the school's teachers and principal, Ephraim Cohen-Reiss, never imagined that one could teach mathematics, biology, and other sciences in Hebrew. At the time, there were no Hebrew textbooks, no Hebrew pedagogic traditions, and no Hebrew technical terms. How could one teach algebra or explain the process of photosynthesis, they wondered, in the language of the Torah? Can one blame them for having such doubts?

The students had a chance to rebel during the celebration of Kaiser Wilhelm II's birthday. Diplomats and religious notables were present at the well-attended ceremony, where German flags were flown and the German national anthem was played—but the students refused to stand and participate in the singing. They walked out in protest, tore their German-language notebooks, and scattered the pages along the route to the German consulate, all the while singing and chanting slogans in favor of Hebrew education in Palestine.

The struggle for Hebrew gained momentum and prevailed. Very quickly, my grandfather joined in the excitement of the pro-Hebrew camp. In fact, my family tells the story that even in the middle of a heated family argument, he would stop and correct errors in his children's speech. Hebrew won!

Do You Believe in Miracles?

Visiting Barcelona, I have been asked more than once by scholars, teachers, and cab-drivers (some of whom I did not suspect of harboring excessive love for Jews), with a hint of admiration, about the secret of the revival of the Hebrew language. Why, in Catalonia, are they having such difficulties reviving the Catalan language, while in Israel a handful of immigrants managed to breathe life into an ancient language that had ceased to be spoken almost two thousand years earlier?

First, we have to admit that the rumors of Hebrew's demise were exaggerated. Over all the centuries in which Hebrew was not a spoken language, it never ceased to exist. Every Jewish boy (though, sadly, not every Jewish girl) learned at least how to read Hebrew. Jews prayed in Hebrew, read the Torah in Hebrew, and studied religious law and customs in Hebrew. They even communicated with Jews in other communities using the holy language. Hebrew's vitality was also expressed in Hebrew prayers, poems, and *piyutim*. Hebrew never stopped being present; it was simply not used in daily speech or for everyday life.

Still, transforming Hebrew into a new language is an expression of revolution and, at the same time, of continuity. It is a protest against the past but also a profound commitment to tradition. The practical reason for Hebrew's success stems from the fact that Zionism was (and still is) a mass undertaking of people from the four corners of the earth, who spoke a myriad of languages and dialects, and there was a need for a common language for them all. The renewal of Hebrew as a spoken language that would meet the needs of modern life in the Land of Israel was a necessity—there simply was no other shared language.

> Many people took part in the effort to revive Hebrew. The task was accomplished only thanks to their dedicated efforts. More than any other individual, though, Eliezer Ben-Yehuda (1858–1922) is identified with the revival of Hebrew. Ben-Yehuda's birthday, the twenty-first of Tevet, was selected to be Hebrew Language Day in Israel.

Even so, the transformation of an archaic sacred language into a language in which people naturally love and argue, delight and hurt, evade, philosophize, and curse is no small accomplishment. It cannot be explained in sociological or political terms alone. Even learned scholars who study the revival of Hebrew as a spoken language admit that it is difficult to explain its sweeping success in strictly scientific terms. Hebrew's success in piercing through centuries of silence and overcoming the hesitancy even of some of the most passionate Zionists in a process that was complex and public, yet still subtle and secret—such a success is something that is difficult to explain. Would it be an exaggeration to call the revival of Hebrew a miracle?

The Academy Becomes Approachable

The Academy of the Hebrew Language is the State of Israel's senior institution responsible for the Hebrew language. The Academy has coined tens of thousands of words in every aspect of life: medicine, politics, economics, sports, and more. Ronit Gadish, the Academy's veteran academic secretary, has counted 128,000 words that the Academy has thus far invented or approved. Many of those terms have been accepted into general use, but there have also been words that were rejected by the public. Sometimes a word has enjoyed a late blossoming and come into use long after it was first created.

In the past, there has been some tension between the "popular will" and the **Academy of the Hebrew Language**. Sometimes the experts and linguists of the Academy invented words that were deemed unnatural (although, to be fair, almost no word is "natural" before it is accepted by people's minds, and only after use does it become "natural"). For example, the word *gerev* for "sock" sounded to some like the name of a skin disease, and the word *iparon* for "pencil" was considered, for some reason, particularly ugly. Many of the Academy's innovations have been neglected and forgotten, but many others eventually made their way into today's spoken Hebrew. A nation's intentional direction of its language's development is not a simple matter. It requires a great deal of flexibility and attentiveness, along with determination and adherence to clear criteria. The Academy has sometimes been an object of criticism

From Time to Time → Dalia Marx

for not always recognizing spontaneous and organic linguistic developments. Sometimes the Academy has given its stamp of approval only after the words achieved widespread use. For example, the word *yisum*, "application," was approved by the Academy in 1982 (after being rejected in 1968), since it had gained widespread acceptance, especially in the armed forces. *Yisum* means application in the abstract sense—as in "application of a program" or "application of knowledge"—but as time changed, so did the word's meaning, and *yisum* lent itself to the word *yisumon*, a computer "app."

In recent decades, the Academy has opened its doors to the public. Its attractive website and the public inquiries service that it offers, have proved to be efficient, effective, and user-friendly. The Academy even solicits the public's assistance in determining new words. In some fields, people working in the field have preceded the Academy in coining new terms for new technological developments. So, for example, most of the terms related to computer science, whether hardware- or software-related, were suggested by people in that field. The Academy members gladly adopted many of those suggestions, creating a partnership between the Academy and the public in an effort to make Hebrew a living, breathing, developing language (for more on the revival of the Hebrew language, see "Hebrew, Revived—Part II" on page 229).

The Less Bright Side of the Hebrew Revival

These days, people sometimes get involved in debates about Zionism and just how successful it has been. It seems that there is one fact, though, about which there is general agreement: not only is the success of the Hebrew language ensured, but its accomplishments have exceeded all expectations. Its status today is so strong and stable that not even those who denounce it most harshly can ignore how it is alive and kicking. Even the debates over whether the language has been debased and disrespected are conducted in fluent, passionate Hebrew.

I recall our amazement in elementary school when we first heard the "Song of the Partisans" sung in Yiddish. We had sung it—in Hebrew, of course—each Holocaust Memorial Day: "Never say that there is only death for you / Though leaden skies may soon reveal a sky of blue." Hearing it in Yiddish made us wonder: who would have wanted to translate it into Yiddish? It never occurred to us that the poet, Hirsh Glick, who was murdered not long after he composed the lyrics, wrote it in his native language, Yiddish. The Hebrew language shone so brightly on the young State of Israel that everything created before its renewal was left behind in darkness. We grew up with disdain for "jargon" and the languages of the Diaspora, never imagining the beauty of the cultural treasures we were missing out on.

The time has come to take notice of this not so bright side of the revival of Hebrew. The effort to make Hebrew the sole language spoken in Israel entailed the aggressive suppression of languages and dialects spoken by Jews over many generations in Diaspora communities. Yiddish, Ladino, and Judeo-Arabic dialects are just the more widely

The Academy of the Hebrew Language was established through the Supreme Hebrew Language Institute Law, enacted by the Knesset on August 27, 1953. The Academy was the heir to an earlier institution, Vaad HaLashon HaIvrit, the self-appointed Hebrew Language Committee.

The law states that the Academy's task is "to guide the development of the Hebrew language on the basis of research in the language in its various periods and branches." Two sections of the law establish the new institute's status: "Decisions of the Institute as to matters of grammar, spelling, terminology, or transliteration, published by the Minister of Education and Culture in *Reshumot* [the official publication for government decisions], shall be adhered to by educational and scientific institutions, by the Government and its departments and agencies, and by local authorities" (section 10); "The contribution of the State to the budget of the Institute shall be included in the budget of the Ministry of Education and Culture" (section 11).

(See pp. 229–31 on surprising new words in Hebrew.)

When I first met my husband Roly's grandmother in Buenos Aires, she tried to speak with me in Yiddish. I didn't expect that, so I was perplexed and didn't quite know how to respond. To my astonishment, his grandmother burst into tears. She refused to believe that I was Jewish, because I didn't speak Yiddish. My father-in-law tried to explain that I'm from the Land of Israel and I speak Hebrew. She held her ground, asking what kind of Jew this is who doesn't know how to speak Yiddish. (The very name of the language means "Jewish.") It took some time before she could be convinced that there are Jews who do not speak Yiddish.

A lovely example of **the renewal of a Jewish language** comes from the group that calls itself "the New Babylonians," which started on Facebook. While it is still active online, there are now many other groups and events that occur entirely outside the virtual world. Some relatives of mine, women who came from Iraq, are active in the group, which numbers over seventy thousand members, who call themselves "the preservers." They seek to preserve the culture and language of Iraqi Jews, arranging gatherings with lectures and performances in Iraqi Judeo-Arabic, and they even create and maintain cultural ties with figures in the worlds of culture and humanities in the "old country."

known examples of languages rich in culture, emotion, and creativity that were effectively delegitimized in the new Jewish state. Our great love for Hebrew does not have to erase the memory of the other **rich and complex languages** in which Jews spoke and created over many generations and that were forgotten or suppressed upon arrival in Israel. The rigid insistence of those who advocated for Hebrew as the national language uniting all the Diaspora communities is understandable, but now the time is ripe for correcting the effort to eradicate the other languages.

Today, when we understand the cost of the melting-pot approach that erases the uniqueness of the citizens' identities, it is important that the State of Israel learn how to include the different Jewish languages and cultures. Over the past few years, groups and publications—academic and nonacademic—have taken up the cause of Yiddish, Ladino, Jewish Aramaic (originally spoken by the Jews of Zakho, Iraq), and various Judeo-Arabic dialects. This embrace of older Jewish dialects even extends to a popular Facebook page on which the outstanding products of Israeli culture are translated into . . . Aramaic.

Prayer of the Month

Bedtime *Sh'ma*

When my late father came back from the Yom Kippur War in 1973, he brought with him a tiny book of Psalms. This little book—with its green plastic cover and first-page dedication by the chief rabbi of the time to "our brave fighters"—went from drawer to drawer and shelf to shelf for a few years until it came into my possession. The careful reading of the book of Psalms has become a standard practice for me before going to sleep. Equally lovely is the bedtime *Sh'ma*, printed in tiny letters at the back of the book. The bedtime *Sh'ma*—along with a private *t'chinah* (a prayer of supplication) that I added when I was in the sixth grade on a Passover hike with the Scouts—became one of my favorite prayers.

On the first day, God created the light and separated it from the darkness. But before Creation, darkness and light were intermingled, forming a complete whole known as *tohu vavohu* (the primordial chaos from Genesis 1). Creation separated day from night, but it seems that the two still have a tendency to mix (if only in human consciousness). Precisely for this reason, it was important for the Rabbis to create a barrier between the two dimensions of existence—the day and the night—and to mark them with clear boundaries.

The ritual boundary markers surrounding sleep on both ends are the bedtime recitation of *Sh'ma, K'riat Sh'ma Al HaMitah*, said when going to sleep, and the dawn blessings, *Birchot HaShachar*, said after waking up. Those two prayers stand like border guards placed between the realms of day and night, but they also highlight the connection between the two realms and the fact that day and night define each other.

The bedtime *Sh'ma* is recited by an individual at home in a liminal moment—between day and night, between public and private, between wakefulness and sleep. This is the reason why over generations, verses, psalms, and *t'chinah* supplications have been added; they express the heart's hidden feelings, worries, and hopes. The variation among them is not only among different Jewish ethnic groups' rites—Ashkenazic, Mizrachi, Chasidic, and the like—but also among prayer books of the same rite. In some of those traditions we find psalms, confessions, *t'chinot*, passages from classical texts, and more—all added to the *Sh'ma*. The order of the component parts is also different from version to version.[16]

Here are the principal parts of the short version of the bedtime *Sh'ma* according to the Ashkenazic rite, which is relatively brief and follows the order of the components of the prayer as they appear in the Talmud (except for the first part, "I Hereby Forgive," which developed in the sixteenth century under the influence of Lurianic Kabbalah):

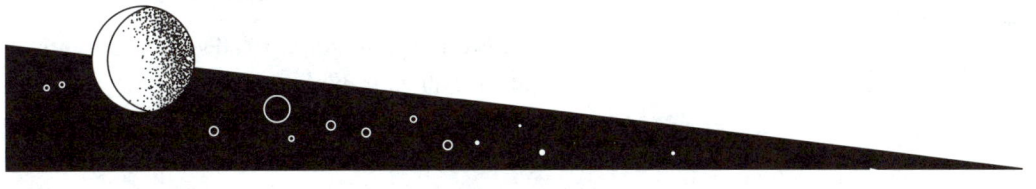

Tishrei Marcheshvan Kislev *Tevet* Sh'vat Adar Nisan Iyar Sivan Tammuz Av Elul

A T'chinah—
Prayer for the Bedtime *Sh'ma*
Rabbi Chen Ben Or Tsfoni

Hear my whispers at bedtime,
let the cords of sleep cover my eyes,
You who don light as a garment.
Caress my eyes until their lights go out,
cover me with Your heavens,
with a thin, delicate azure cloth.
Shed light on my sleeping world with
   Your Presence,
and may no one by punished on my account.[17]

הָרַבָּה חֵן בֶּן אוֹר צְפוֹנִי
שְׁמַע לִחִישׁוֹתַי שֶׁעַל הַמִּטָּה,
הַפֵּל עָלַי חַבְלֵי שֵׁינָה
עוֹטֶה אוֹר כַּשַּׂלְמָה.
לַטֵּף אִישׁוֹנֵי עֵינַי עַד שֶׁיִּכְבּוּ,
כַּסֵּה אוֹתִי בִּשְׁמֶיךָ,
בִּירִיעַת תְּכֵלֶת דַּקָה וְרַכָּה.
הָאֵר עוֹלָמִי הַיָּשֵׁן בִּכְבוֹדֶךָ
וְלֹא יֵעָנֵשׁ שׁוּם אָדָם בִּסְבָתִי.

The "I Hereby Forgive" passage is somewhat similar to the short statement said before reciting *Kol Nidrei* at the beginning of Yom Kippur:

> With the consent of the Almighty and
>   consent of this congregation,
> in a convocation of the heavenly court,
> and a convocation of the lower [human]
>   court,
> I hereby grant permission
> to pray with transgressors.[18]

In this passage too, we find the obliteration, if only briefly, of the distinction between sinners and those who, it appears, have not sinned and a renunciation of the right to be angry. This is a unique openness of heart undertaken at an important moment during the holiest day of the year. While it is true that the bedtime *Sh'ma* is meant to be said privately and daily, while the prayer above is said publicly and openly at an emotional peak moment, both share the intent to release the one who prays from anger and resentment. Both are said in moments of transition—one from wakefulness into sleep and the other from the everyday routine into the sanctity of Yom Kippur. (See pp. 19–21.)

I Hereby Forgive הֲרֵינִי מוֹחֵל\מוֹחֶלֶת

I hereby forgive anyone who made me angry or annoyed
or who committed an offense against me,
whether against my person or my financial assets,
or my honor, or anything I own,
whether forced to do so or having done so willingly,
whether in error or intentionally,
whether in speech or in action,
and let no person be punished on my account.

The tendency to get angry is a malignant, destructive quality that can overpower and harm us. In order to enter a mindset that will lead us into relaxed sleep with our souls intact, it is good to deal with the feelings of anger and hostility that have gathered inside us over the course of the day. As part of the process of relaxing, the *Sh'ma* prayers begin with a formula in which we individually extend forgiveness to anyone who harmed us, made us angry or annoyed, or even committed an actual offense against us—even if the offender has not asked for forgiveness. This is based on a Talmudic description of the practice of Mar Zutra (a Babylonian teacher of the fifth century), who, when going to bed, would say, "I forgive anyone who caused me trouble today" (Babylonian Talmud, *M'gillah* 28a). It seems even then it was known how hard it is relax and fall asleep in the grip of anger. Forgiving others helps us shed feelings of anger and along with it our desire to wield power over others and satisfy our own egos, so we may achieve the tranquility needed for sleeping.

Entering the realm of sleep means relinquishing control and awareness. Forgiving others and purifying oneself from anger is a necessary first step on the path to giving up control. This is the transition that the bedtime *Sh'ma* makes possible and even creates—the symbolic parting from the world through sleep should be done through reconciliation and relaxation.

Sh'ma Yisrael

שְׁמַע יִשְׂרָאֵל, יְיָ אֱלֹהֵינוּ, יְיָ אֶחָד.
Sh'ma Yisrael, Adonai Eloheinu, Adonai Echad!
Hear, O Israel, Adonai is our God, Adonai is One!
בָּרוּךְ שֵׁם כְּבוֹד מַלְכוּתוֹ לְעוֹלָם וָעֶד.
Baruch shem k'vod malchuto l'olam va-ed.
[*Quietly:*] Blessed is God's glorious majesty forever and ever.

You shall love the Eternal your God with all your heart, with all
   your soul, and with all your might.
Take to heart these instructions with which I charge you this
   day. Impress them upon your children.

Recite them when you stay at home and when you are away,
when you lie down and when you get up.
Bind them as a sign on your hand and let them serve as a symbol on
your forehead;
inscribe them on the doorposts of your house and on your gates.

It is impossible to exaggerate the importance of *k'riat Sh'ma*, "the recitation of *Sh'ma*," in Jewish consciousness through the generations. At times these were the only words of prayer remembered by Jews who lived in distant places, words they heard their parents and grandparents intone; these words impart a feeling of home. Those lines were on the lips of many Jews who departed from this world—from Rabbi Akiva, whose soul left him as he came to the word "One/*Echad*" in the *Sh'ma*, to the victims of the Holocaust, many of whom called out these words declaring God's oneness and uniqueness with their last breath.

During the bedtime *Sh'ma*, the first paragraph of the *Sh'ma*—commonly called the *V'ahavta* ("You shall love")—is recited (although in some versions, all three paragraphs of the traditional *Sh'ma* are recited). This passage, and especially the verse *Sh'ma Yisrael . . .* , "Hear, O Israel . . . ," is a kind of concentrated essence of faith, commitment, and belonging, because of both its content and the status it has acquired over time among the Jews. Therefore, the halachah states that if a person focuses their intention properly even for just the first verse of *Sh'ma*, the obligation to recite the entire *Sh'ma* liturgy is fulfilled.[19] What could be more fitting, then, than this passage for recitation before going to sleep? Our tradition offers those headed to bed an opportunity to renew their covenant with the Jewish people (since, after all, the lead verse is addressed to us, the people Israel) and with God. Reciting these verses can also be calming, reassuring, and comforting when we have anxieties about entering the realm of sleep.

Naming the Angels	קְרִיאָה בְּשֵׁם הַמַּלְאָכִים
In the name of the Eternal, God of Israel,	בְּשֵׁם יְיָ אֱלֹהֵי יִשְׂרָאֵל,
to my right—Michael,	מִימִינִי מִיכָאֵל
to my left—Gabriel,	וּמִשְּׂמֹאלִי גַּבְרִיאֵל
and before me—Uriel,	וּמִלְּפָנַי אוּרִיאֵל
and behind me—Raphael,	וּמֵאֲחוֹרַי רְפָאֵל
and above my head—the Presence of God.	וְעַל רֹאשִׁי שְׁכִינַת אֵל.

Here we call the names of the benevolent angels. Those going to sleep surround themselves with the beneficent presence of four angels—Michael, Gabriel, Uriel, and Raphael—and above them all, *Shechinat El*, God's immanent Presence.

"Who Casts Sleep" Blessing

Blessed are You, Eternal our God,
    Sovereign of the universe,
who casts cords of sleep on my eyes
    and slumber on my eyelids.
May it be Your will, Eternal my God
    and God of my ancestors,
that I lie down in peace
    and rise up in peace.
Prevent dark thoughts
    and bad dreams from disturbing my slumber.
Make my sleep perfect and whole,
and enlighten my eyes
    lest I sleep the sleep of death.
Blessed are You, Eternal,
    who illuminates the entire world
with glory.[20]

בָּרוּךְ אַתָּה יְיָ אֱלֹהֵינוּ
מֶלֶךְ הָעוֹלָם,
הַמַּפִּיל חֶבְלֵי שֵׁנָה עַל עֵינָי
וּתְנוּמָה עַל עַפְעַפָּי.
וִיהִי רָצוֹן מִלְּפָנֶיךָ יְיָ אֱלֹהַי
וֵאלֹהֵי אֲבוֹתַי וְאִמּוֹתַי,
שֶׁתַּשְׁכִּיבֵנִי לְשָׁלוֹם
וְתַעֲמִידֵנִי לְשָׁלוֹם,
וְאַל יְבַהֲלוּנִי רַעְיוֹנַי
וַחֲלוֹמוֹת רָעִים,
וְהִרְהוּרִים רָעִים,
וּתְהִי מִטָּתִי שְׁלֵמָה לְפָנֶיךָ,
וְהָאֵר עֵינַי פֶּן אִישַׁן הַמָּוֶת,
בָּרוּךְ אַתָּה יְיָ,
הַמֵּאִיר לָעוֹלָם כֻּלּוֹ
בִּכְבוֹדוֹ.

"Concluding Poem" is probably the last lyric poem written by the major Israeli poet Natan Alterman (1910–70). It can be seen as a sort of optimistic ethical will. Here are the last words of the poem's third section:[21]

The body that shuts its eyes
has no fear as sleep arrives,
as land and sky depart
    the way the soul might leave
      the heart.
For they return as they went out,
in great mercy, with great trust.

הַגּוּף הָעוֹצֵם עֵינַיִם
אֵינוֹ יָרֵא בִּנְפֹל שֵׁנָה,
בִּהְיוֹת אֲדָמָה וְשָׁמַיִם
נִלְקָחִים מִמֶּנּוּ כִּנְשָׁמָה.
כִּי אֵלָיו יַחְזְרוּ יֵשׁ מֵאַיִן,
בְּחֶמְלָה רַבָּה, בֶּאֱמוּנָה.

The "who casts sleep" blessing is worded entirely in the first person singular. In this way, it is different from almost all other blessings in Jewish liturgy, even the most personal, which are generally worded in the plural ("Praise to You, Eternal, *our* God . . ."). It opens with vivid word-pictures—God "casts cords of sleep on my eyes and slumber on my eyelids"—which might calm even sleep-resistant young children, and it continues with a general request, "May it be Your will . . . that I lie down in peace and rise up in peace." After that are three requests making the general request for sleep even more specific and detailing the desired manner of sleep—"perfect and whole"—and rising. At the heart of night, the blessing concludes with hope and faith that we will see the light that God is to provide for the world: "Blessed are You, Eternal, who illuminates the entire world with glory."

The bedtime *Sh'ma* is a prayer whose words are sweet and beloved. It has been and still is the lullaby for millions of Jews from childhood through old age across the generations.

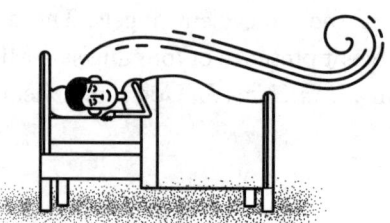

SH'VAT

**Zodiac Sign: Aquarius | Tribe of the Month: Joseph (representing Ephraim and Manassah)
Breastplate Stone: Lapis Lazuli/*Shoham***

Sh'vat received its name from the name of the Babylonian month Shabbatu, which may mean "to strike" (reminiscent of the Hebrew term *sheivet* for a scepter or a rod intended for use to strike as punishment), and may be related to the strong rains of this month.

KAVANAH: A MEDITATION FOR SH'VAT

May we be "like a tree planted beside streams of water" (Psalm 1:3);
may we yield our fruit in season, may our foliage never fade,
  and may whatever we produce thrive (Psalm 1:3);
may we have mercy on everything planted, growing, and seeking life;
may this mercy expand and extend to the four corners of the earth;
may we recognize the pain and fear of every living being on earth,
    multiplying good and being a blessing;
may we recall at all times how pleasant and praiseworthy is all that God created;
May we know that if we spoil and destroy, God forbid,
  there is no one to set things right after us.
—based on *Kohelet Rabbah* 7

AT THE GATES OF SH'VAT

THE ALMOND TREES at the side of the road to Jerusalem are wearing festive white dresses, and the sun is breaking through the Israeli winter. This is the promotional video or the movie trailer for spring, which is just outside the door. Winter is still here, but the days are getting longer, the nights are getting shorter, and the almond trees are starting to blossom. When the moon is full, we will celebrate the New Year for Trees. Tu BiSh'vat reminds us that all of us—people, animals, and plants—are part of creation and all of us are in need of kindness. Sh'vat is a month of song—the song of the grasses and of all of nature, the song of our family (Family Day is observed in Israel during Sh'vat), and the song of a special Shabbat, Shabbat Shirah, "the Shabbat of Song," on which we read two of the great songs of our ancestors, the Song at the Sea and the Song of Deborah.

The first *iyun* in the chapter explores the growth of Tu BiSh'vat from its first appearance on the calendar through our own time. The second *iyun* brings up questions about the nature of our connection to the Land of Israel and the land on which we live through the prism of Tu BiSh'vat, inviting us to investigate the holiday's ecological and environmental potential. The third *iyun* draws a connection between winter's Tu BiSh'vat and summer's Tu B'Av holidays, which divide the year into two equal parts. The fourth *iyun* explores song and its role in the Hebrew language and in Israel, since Sh'vat is the month during which we observe Shabbat Shirah. Israel's Mother's Day—which has morphed into Family Day—falls during Sh'vat and is the focus of the fifth *iyun* of the chapter. The Poem of the Month, Kadya Molodowsky's *Efnt dem Toyer*, "Open the Gate," invites us to celebrate family and reflect on the meaning of the Jewish family today. Our Prayer of the Month is a series of special prayers written by Rabbi Chaya Rowen Baker especially for Family Day.

Tishrei   Marcheshvan   Kislev   Tevet   Sh'vat   Adar   Nisan   Iyar   Sivan   Tammuz   Av   Elul

POEM OF THE MONTH

Efnt dem Toyer ("Open the Gate")

Kadya Molodowsky / *Kadye Molodovski*

Open the gate, throw it wide open,	*Efnt dem toyer, efnt im breyt,*
Though it must pass a chain that is golden:[1]	*s'vet do durkhgeyn a goldene keyt:*
Papa	*der tate,*
And Mama,	*di mame,*
Brother	*der bruder,*
And Sister,	*di shvester,*
And among them, a bride and groom,	*khosn-kale*
happy and gay,	*in mitn*
Riding upon a golden sleigh.	*af a goldenem shlitn.*
Open the gate, throw it wide open,	*Efnt dem toyer, efnt im breyt*
Through it must pass a chain that is golden:	*es vet do durkhgeyn a goldene keyt:*
Grandpa	*der zeyde*
And Grandma,	*di bobe,*
Uncle,	*der feter,*
And Aunt,	*di mume,*
And among them, the grandchildren,	*di eyniklekh*
happy and gay,	*in mitn*
Riding upon a golden sleigh.	*af a goldenem shlitn.*
Open the gate, throw it wide open,	*Efnt dem toyer, efnt im breyt*
Through it must pass a chain that is golden:	*es vet do durkhgeyn a goldene keyt:*
A pear	*a bar*
And an apple,	*un an epl*
A cup filled with honey.	*un honik a tepl,*
and a yellow ginger cake	*un a lekekh a geler*
Set upon a golden plate.[2]	*af a goldenem teler.*[3]

From Time to Time → Dalia Marx

In the beginning there was dancing in preschool. To the sound of accordion music, the golden chain—that is, we children, pair by pair—passed by, holding hands under the watchful eye of the teacher, who took care to ensure that the "gate"—that is, the two tallest children in the class—was open wide and that the gatekeepers not give in to the temptation to trap one of the couples passing through as a golden chain. My children's preschool teachers did not sing this particular song very much with the children, since new songs had appeared and pushed aside the old ones. Perhaps such is the way of the world, but the gate is still open for Saba and Savta (Grandpa and Grandma), uncles and aunts, grandchildren, great-grandchildren, and all the generations that walked the path before us and the path that we pave for our own descendants.

During the month of Sh'vat, we mark Family Day: the nuclear family in the poem's first stanza and the extended family in the second are the "golden chain" that must not be broken, passing from past to future in a magical carriage. The poem calls for the gate to be opened wide and for many families to pass through, each one with its own ways of doing things and with its own customs.

Tu BiSh'vat: A Growing Holiday

CAN YOU PICTURE a festive celebration on the day that begins the tax year? Tu BiSh'vat was originally a day like that. The Mishnah established the fifteenth of Sh'vat for the purpose of calculating tithes from fruits that grow on trees, a kind of income tax day based on tithes. Over the years, the holiday's celebrations expanded, taking on new forms as old ones dropped away—not unlike a tree that changes again and again with the seasons.

The first mention of the fifteenth of Sh'vat is in the Mishnah, which enumerates four *rosh hashanah* (new year) days throughout the year, each for a different purpose. The New Year for Trees is the fourth of these new years, and since it is the day on which taxation of the fruit of the tree begins, every single fruit that a tree bears beginning on the sixteenth of Sh'vat is to be calculated for the tithe in the following year. Classical halachah did not set up any special requirements for marking the fifteenth of Sh'vat, and the sixteenth-century law code *Shulchan Aruch* does not say any more than that the daily penitential prayers known an *Tachanun* are not said on that date. But although halachah has little to say about Tu BiSh'vat, our tradition is rich in customs, traditions, and interpretations of Tu BiSh'vat. Actually, it is precisely the absence of mandatory practices that enabled Tu BiSh'vat, the New Year for Trees, to develop in multiple directions. Let us examine seven stops along the route of the holiday's development.

The First Stop: Even before the Israelites entered their land, they were commanded, "When you enter the land, you shall plant any tree for food" (Leviticus 19:23)[4]; perhaps we should go back even further, to the task given to humanity in the story of Creation: "Then, out of the soil, God Eternal grew trees alluring to the eye and good for fruit. . . . So God Eternal took the man, placing him in the Garden of Eden, to work it

Liturgical poets (*pay'tanim*) in the Land of Israel composed poetic versions of the blessings of the *Amidah* for special occasions, which were recited (or sung) in place of the usual prose versions of the prayers. Such *piyutim* are called *k'rovot* (singular: *k'rovah*). Here is part of a special *k'rovah* for Tu BiSh'vat, written by Rabbi Y'hudah HaLevi son of Rabbi Hillel, who lived in the Land of Israel in the ninth century. The text was discovered in the Cairo Genizah, the great repository of discarded sacred documents from the city's medieval Jewish community that was rediscovered at the end of the nineteenth century. Each of the eighteen stanzas of this *k'rovah* is itself a blessing that reflects one of the traditional eighteen blessings of the *Amidah*. The closing formula of each stanza is that of the traditional blessing, but the body of each stanza of the *piyut* develops the blessings' theme in the context of Tu BiSh'vat. In addition, each stanza includes the name of a tree or plant in alphabetical order. As was the custom with prayers in the Land of Israel, before the closing formula of each blessing, a biblical verse is cited that is thematically connected to the blessing. The following are the first three blessings from HaLevi's *piyut*:[5]

Bring down strong saving rains for My many followers.
Make the walnut tree [אֱגוֹז, *egoz*] blossom for my dainty ones.
On the New Year for Trees
strengthen my faithful ones,
"For the Eternal is sun and shield" (Psalm 84:12).
Praise to You, Eternal, Abraham's Shield.

God will shine light for those God guides,
a bright cypress [בְּרוֹשׁ, *b'rosh*] God will illuminate for those God has saved.
On the New Year for Trees
bless the land of the living with saving rains,
"For the one who finds Me finds life" (Proverbs 8:35).
Praise to You, Eternal, who revives the dead.

Great and praised and exalted above all gods,
the grapevine [גֶּפֶן, *gefen*] likened to God's own vineyard.
On the New Year for Trees
enhance joy for those who say, "There is none like God,"
"For great in your midst is the Holy One of Israel" (Isaiah 12:6).
Praise to You, Eternal, the holy God.

and keep it" (Genesis 2:9, 15). Here there is no mention of taxation of anything that grows on trees, nor is a date mentioned at all, but we do find the requirement to "work and keep," to till and tend, what grows from the soil—to plant and raise trees that yield food, in order to make life on earth possible.

The Second Stop: The Mishnah is where we first encounter the term "the new year for trees":

> There are four new year days: on the first of Nisan is the new year for kings and [the order of] the Festivals; on the first of Elul is the new year for the tithe of cattle (Rabbi Elazar and Rabbi Shim'on say: on the first of Tishrei). On the first of Tishrei is the new year for [counting] years, for [calculating] Sabbatical years and Jubilee years, for planting [trees], and for vegetable [tithing]. And the first of Sh'vat is the new year for trees in accordance with Beit Shammai; but Beit Hillel say: [it is] on the fifteenth [of Sh'vat]. (*Mishnah Rosh HaShanah* 1:1)

As with many issues, there is a debate regarding the timing of the new year for trees that can be traced back to the schools of thought of Hillel (Beit Hillel) and Shammai (Beit Shammai). As usual, Beit Hillel's verdict—that the new year for trees falls on the fifteenth of Sh'vat—is established and followed. The Rabbis legislated the details of the various "gifts for the poor"—*leket*, *shich'chah*, and *pei-ah*, which are the overlooked or intentionally ignored parts of the seasonal harvest that became a kind of tax paid by land and property owners. The goal was to engage the entire populace, not only those who owned land, in benefiting from the land's yield. Thus the new year's day for trees, the date for beginning the tithe year, serves to advance the cause of social justice.

The Third Stop: After the destruction of the Temple, when most Jews no longer lived in their own land, Tu BiSh'vat became a day marking our connection with the Land of Israel. Eating fruit was a way to connect to the land, to its tastes and its textures. Jews in the Diaspora tried to eat fruits from the Land of Israel on Tu BiSh'vat to express their longing for and connection to the land. In addition, special *piyutim* were written in the Land of Israel in honor of Tu BiSh'vat. Those poems reflect the desire to endow the day with a festive character and to mark it liturgically.

The Fourth Stop: This stop is the *tikkun* (repair) established by the kabbalists of Safed, students of Rabbi Isaac Luria (known as the ARI), sometime in the sixteenth–seventeenth centuries. According to the Kabbalah, the world was in disarray as the result of Adam's sin and banishment from the Garden of Eden. The kabbalists took it upon themselves to repair that situation (an act also called *tikkun*) through innovative ceremonies, among them *Tikkun Tu BiSh'vat*. On that night the kabbalists sought to approach the Garden of Eden, taste its fruits, and repair the damaged parts of creation.

The kabbalists' *tikkun* created an elaborate ceremony that included instructions to eat various fruits, which they divided into three categories: (1) fruits whose outer layer is discarded and the inner part eaten, such as pomegranates and nuts, which represent the realm of *asiyah*, the "physical" and lowest of the realms described by Lurianic Kabbalah; (2) fruits whose seeds are not eaten, such as olives and dates, which represent the next realm of *y'tzirah*, the "emotional"; and (3) fruits eaten in their entirety, such as grapes and figs, which represent *b'riah*, the "mental" realm. According to this schema, the highest and "spiritual" realm of *atzilut* is too pure to be represented by any fruit. The kabbalists' innovation was in the very act of granting Tu BiSh'vat cosmic theological significance. Through a series of religious ceremonies, they intended to repair the entire world.[6]

The Fifth Stop: This stop celebrates the Jews' return to the Land of Israel at the beginning of modern Zionism. Starting in the late nineteenth century, teachers steered Tu BiSh'vat into the role of a tree-planting holiday, which was part of a larger effort to make the land lush and productive. Through this newly reshaped holiday, the pioneers hoped to become rooted in the soil of the land and counter the feeling that they were floating, untethered and rootless, like a Jew in a Marc Chagall painting.

The historian and teacher Rabbi Ze'ev Yavetz held the first Tu BiSh'vat planting ceremony with his students from the school in Zichron Yaakov in 1890, just a few years after his arrival in *Eretz Yisrael*. A year later, he wrote that the reason for the new custom was this:

> In order to inculcate affection for the plants that the Eternal planted for our ancestors, that they might be sated by those plants' bounty and enjoy their beauty, the school should make a holiday of the day designated among the people Israel since ancient times as the New Year for Trees, arranging the trees, the plants, and lilies and the flowers in an attractive fashion, as is done in the countries of Europe on the first of May.[7]

That custom became established among the teachers, and in 1908 the teachers' union, Histadrut HaMorim, declared Tu BiSh'vat a planting holiday for children. Tu BiSh'vat thus took on a national, Zionist significance. Its Zionist meaning became even more pronounced when Tu Bish'vat was chosen as the day of the establishment of the Knesset.

The book *Chemdat Yamim* first appeared in print at Izmir, Turkey, in 1731. It included a Tu BiSh'vat seder created by the kabbalists. Some suspect that the author, whose identity is unknown, came from the ranks of the Sabbateans, the followers of the false messiah Shabbetai Zvi. Nonetheless, the Tu BiSh'vat seder presented in the book influenced the kabbalists' seders. The following is part of the prayer to be said before eating the fruit:

> The earth is sated from the fruit of Your work" (Psalm 104:13), so one may "eat of its fruit and be sated by its bounty" (paraphrasing Jeremiah 2:7). From [the fruit], every living soul is enlivened through the spiritual power that is in them, [which is] the fruit of the mouth of Your holy angels who guard its fruit. "From Me your fruit is found" (Hosea 14:9), the reward of children. "Its fruit is food and its leaves a source of healing" (Ezekiel 47:12)....
>
> May it be Your will, Eternal our God and God of our ancestors, that through the sacred power of eating fruit, which we are now eating and blessing—while reflecting on the secret of their supernal roots, upon which they depend—their supernal sap will be aroused, so that *shefa* [overflowing bounty], favor, blessing, and bounty be bestowed upon them. May the angels appointed over them also be filled by the powerful *shefa* of their glory; may it return and cause them to grow a second time, from the beginning of the year until its end—for bounty and blessing, for good life and peace. And fulfill for us the word that You promised us through Malachi, Your seer, "And I will banish the devourer from among you and they will not destroy the fruit of your earth and the vine of your field will not miscarry, says *Adonai Tz'vaot*" (Malachi 3:11). (*Chemdat Yamim* 3:14)

Chemdat Yamim also instructs us to think about the secret of the root, or origin, of each of the fruits before consuming it, because speech can arouse the forces of the upper world.

The Sixth Stop: This stop broadens Tu BiSh'vat once again, beyond the national story into a more universal and general message of *tikkun olam*, repairing the world. Beginning in the 1970s, climate scientists began to issue warnings about the dangers inherent in the brutal and destructive exploitation of nature. Jews used Jewish language to inspire a commitment to nature, and many Tu BiSh'vat seders began to exhibit an ecological character. The "Ecological Confessional [*Vidui*]" written by Rabbi Moti Rotem provides an example of the inclusion of environmental content in Tu BiSh'vat seders. Like the confessional prayers of Yom Kippur, this prayer is also a Hebrew alphabetical acrostic:

אָפַפְנוּ	We enveloped Your world in fog, smoke, and soot.
בִּזְבַּזְנוּ	We wasted natural resources that we received in trust.
גָּזַלְנוּ	We stole the vast expanse of the horizon with ugly construction.
דִּלְדַּלְנוּ	We carelessly reduced the population of wild animals.
הֵפַרְנוּ	We violated the covenant of balance between humans and nature.
וִתַּרְנוּ	We abandoned the promise of a good quality of life for our children.
זִהַמְנוּ	We polluted seas, lakes, and rivers with the poison of our greed.
חוֹרַרְנוּ	We pierced the ozone layer that embraces our planet.
טִמֵּאנוּ	We sullied fresh living water with our own effluent waste.
יָצַרְנוּ	We made mountains of trash and garbage in our yards and in the wilderness.
כָּרַתְנוּ	We cut down forests for short-term profits.
לִכְלַכְנוּ	We polluted nature and landscapes, beaches, paths, and peaks.
מִשְׁכַּנּוּ	We casually mortgaged the future of Your world for lack of vision.
נִצַּלְנוּ	We fully exploited nature's gifts, in our self-centeredness.
סִכַּנּוּ	We endangered the world's very existence with nuclear weapons.
עָקַרְנוּ	We uprooted birds from their nesting areas and migration routes.
פָּצַעְנוּ	We injured mountainsides with stone quarries.
צִעַרְנוּ	We distressed You and Your children through our irresponsibility.
קָטַפְנוּ	We picked wildflowers that no longer exist.
רָמַסְנוּ	We trampled heights, fields, and furrows.
שָׂרַפְנוּ	We burned trees from the forest on the altar of our hate.
תִּעַשְׂנוּ	We industrialized at the cost of air and water quality.

For all these, God of forgiveness, forgive us and pardon us and grant us atonement. We exploited Your treasures, and it has not been worth it.

Open our eyes to Your presence in nature, make our hearts cling to the mitzvah of guarding Your world, unite our hearts to accept our limits and find our place in Your world.[8]

Like the kabbalists before them, those who work to protect the environment have concerns that encompass the entire world. The former sought to influence the worlds above by using their ceremonies to repair the sin of the first human, Adam. The latter try to correct what is wrong through their concern for this world. With a broad mission to repair what has gone wrong, a variety of contemporary organizations hold events designed not only to repair the earth, but also to strengthen solidarity between the two peoples—Israelis and Palestinians—who now share the same harsh, beloved land. During these events, the goal expands beyond planting trees and includes building understanding between two peoples through a shared commitment to planting where there has been uprooting, and to nurturing understanding where there has been hostility.

Perhaps **a seventh stop** can be added along the route of the holiday's development; this stop moves Tu BiSh'vat from the general to the more personal, and places the human being at the center. This stop is self-*tikkun*, for which "self-improvement" is a pale translation. Lately, we have heard interpretations according to which everything that happens in the world or in nature can serve as a reflection of an individual's physical, spiritual, and emotional situation. If, in the past, sermonizers and kabbalists compared the world and its phenomena to a human being, today the comparison is drawn in the opposite direction. Nature and all its phenomena are enlisted to explain the experience of the individual "I" in a confusing world. In one Tu BiSh'vat seder which I attended, the sorting of the fruits into three types was explained as representing three types of people. The fruits of the realm of *asiyah*, whose outer shells are not consumed, represent people who close themselves off from their surroundings, who bind themselves up in their selfhood and are not open to others. The fruits of the realm of *y'tzirah*, whose core is not eaten, represent those whose "bellies are full" (as we say in Hebrew) of difficult experiences in the past, traumas and wounds that they are unable to digest or swallow. The fruits of the realm of *b'riah*, which are eaten in their entirety, represent people who have difficulty setting boundaries and hold themselves back from reality. The experience concluded with the teaching that every one of us has in our personalities something of all three types of fruit, all three realms, and so we are all called to perform *tikkun*.

Each of the stops along Tu BiSh'vat's route builds upon earlier meanings and creates new ones. And so, over the course of generations, various and complementary Jewish values have been expressed: a commitment to social justice, to *tikkun* of the cosmos and to *tikkun* of the self, to the revival of our people and our homeland, and to the world in which we live.[9]

On the eve of Tu BiSh'vat, thousands of seders take place in Israel and abroad, in which families, communities, schools, and youth groups sing, study, and eat, celebrating together their love of the Land of Israel and their commitment to the earth on which we all dwell. The seder format is influenced by those of the kabbalists, sometimes without their mystical elements and instead adopting a contemporary Jewish or Israeli feel. In the morning in Israel, people will take saplings and seedlings in hand to be planted throughout the country; Jews everywhere will participate in countless activities and lessons on Tu BiSh'vat that address our commitment to the land—which, according to Genesis, includes working and protecting it.

The fifteenth day of Sh'vat, a date on the Hebrew calendar that originally related to technical aspects of taxation and tithes, has come to be filled with profound religious meanings, changing form again and again over the ages. One explanation for Tu BiSh'vat does not negate any other; rather, the insights complement to each other, enriching the holiday. Tu BiSh'vat is an example of religious creativity and ritual innovation constructed over many generations, one level at a time.

They Didn't Try to Kill Us, So How Can We Celebrate?

Tu BiSh'vat, the New Year for Trees, provides an excellent opportunity to ask from which tree Adam and Eve ate. What was that tempting, forbidden fruit of the Tree of Knowledge? As we know, the Torah does not reveal the precise fruit. Many people assume that it was an apple, but that idea cannot be found in Jewish sources (it comes from Christian beliefs, actually). The fact that we do not know what the fruit of the Tree of Knowledge was invites us to use our imagination.

> Our Sages asked: What was the fruit of the Tree of Knowledge from which Adam and Eve ate? Four rabbis suggest four different answers: "Rabbi Meir said: It was **wheat**.... Rabbi Y'hudah bar Ilai said: It was **grapes**.... Rabbi Abba of Akko said: It was an **etrog**.... Rabbi Yosei said: It was **figs**" (*B'reishit Rabbah* 15:7). (See pp. 227–28.)
>
> We hold a slice of bread or another baked food made of **wheat** in our hands, take a bite, and say, "As we eat this bread naturally and with enjoyment, we remember those whose bread is thin, those who break bread in sorrow for the members of their household. As we eat this bread, we express our commitment to end poverty and heal the gaps in our society."
>
> We hold raisins or **grapes** in our hands, take a bite, and say, "As we taste the fruit of the vine, we say that just as the tendrils of the grapevine entwine themselves around whatever they encounter, never letting go, so must we embrace the ill, the elderly, the injured, and the exhausted members of our society and not let them go."
>
> We hold a **fig** in our hands, take a bite, and say, "'Everyone shall sit under their grapevine or fig tree with no one to disturb them,' says the Eternal of Hosts who spoke" (Micah 4:4). As we eat the fruit of the fig tree, we remind ourselves of our commitment to enable all human beings to live in tranquility in their homes and to support themselves by their labors, and of our responsibility to rise up against anyone who disturbs the home, land, or property of others."
>
> We hold in our hands a citrus fruit that stands for the **etrog**, take a bite, and say, "Citrus fruits symbolize a person who has both learning [torah] and good deeds [see *Vayikra Rabbah* 30:12]. As we eat this citrus, we remind ourselves that it is not study that ultimately matters, but action [Mishnah Avot 1:17] and that it is not enough to simply believe in justice; one must work diligently to achieve it."
>
> As we eat from the foods that some of our ancient Sages identified as the fruit of the Tree of Knowledge, we bring to mind the bounty of creation, its beauty, and its fullness. We recall that human beings, as such, are the crown of creation, and we remind ourselves that it is our task to preserve the soil, to tend it and till it, and to make our own country into a blessing for all its inhabitants and all those who love it.
>
> Praise to You, who has graced us with the fruit of knowledge.

AN OLD JOKE HAS IT that Jewish holidays share the same pattern: "They tried to kill us. They didn't succeed. Now let's eat!" So it is with Chanukah, Purim, and Passover. The gloomier flip side of the joke is that other holidays are built on the opposite model: "They tried to kill us. They succeeded. Let's fast." So it is with the Ninth of Av. Tu BiSh'vat is different. It does not mark any threat or any rescue. No enemy rose up against us to destroy us, we were not forced to fight for our lives—and yet we sit down to a meal?! Well, okay—that's always a good idea.

Sometimes we sink so deeply in the travails of the present that we forget to notice the continuing miracle we are privileged to observe: the Jewish people's renewal in its land. The Jews went into exile from their land and were separated from its terrain, scents, winds, and tastes. The people's spirit survived and even flourished over the centuries, but its palpable reality was restricted and narrowed during that time. For many Jews, the return to Zion symbolized a return to a healthy and natural life, both as individuals and as a nation.

But what is the meaning of the return of Jews to their soil in our time when most of us live distanced from nature and are not directly involved in working the land? It seems that Tu BiSh'vat can serve as an alarm clock awakening us to pressing contemporary questions. That is largely how the holiday has functioned over the course of many generations.

The absence of any halachic basis for Tu Bish'vat observance resulted in each generation renewing and enriching it (see pp. 123–27). Here I will examine more deeply one of those "stops" along the route of its development—the one that links Tu BiSh'vat to the preservation of nature and the environment. In recent decades a new melody has crept into Tu BiSh'vat and the seders celebrating it. Today many people understand that neglecting the environment is just part of a larger worrisome picture in our world: when the pursuit of profit leads to our skies being filled with ugly towers, when sewage pollutes

From Time to Time → Dalia Marx

the water sources and causes damage to animals and plants, when air pollution breaks new records, and when fruit trees continue to be uprooted, concern for the environment is not perceived as the caprice of some eccentric hippies but rather an urgent matter—universal and very Jewish at the same time—for us all.

Tu BiSh'vat is increasingly becoming a day on which we take note of our commitment to the good earth and to those who tread upon it, to the preservation both of the trees and of humankind. This does not mean, of course, that the other meanings of the holiday are no longer valid. Quite the opposite: our responsibility to protect human life and our planet is an addition to the holiday "seder plate" and enhances it. Tu BiSh'vat, then, is not just a day of celebration but also a day to recognize the enormity of our responsibility for the environment in which we live. This year on Tu Bish'vat, let us look around in love and concern. Let us be careful not to destroy our world, and let us commit ourselves to preserving both *adam* (humanity) and *adamah* (the earth).

Tu BiSh'vat does not mark a day on which "they tried to kill us," but it does mark a close and very real existential danger to us all. If we are not vigilant in defending the land upon which we live, we will hasten our own end. In that way, all of us on earth are in the same boat.

Appropriately, then, a midrash tells us that God called to Adam and warned him:

> When the Blessed Holy One created Adam, God took him and led him around all the trees the Garden of Eden and said, "Look at My works! How beautiful and praiseworthy they are. Everything that I have created, I created for you. Take care not to damage and destroy My world, for if you damage it, there is no one to repair it after you."
> (*Kohelet Rabbah* 7)

Maybe, if we are careful about this warning, it can be an appropriate *tikkun*—corrective—for our wrongdoing against the earth upon which we all dwell.

🐦 The Connection between Gardening and Parenting

WHAT IS THE CONNECTION between Tu BiSh'vat, the fifteenth of the month of Sh'vat marked as the new year for trees, and Tu B'Av, the fifteenth of the month of Av, known as the festival of love, on which ancient Israelite women would dance in the vineyards in a giant annual matchmaking event (see pp. 321–24)? Both are celebrated mid-month (the middle of a lunar month, at the time of the full moon), and each represents a different but complementary world: Tu BiSh'vat represents the renewal of nature and its fruits, and Tu B'Av relates to romantic and marital relationships and the creation of new families and the "fruits" they will bear. If we draw an imaginary line between them, they seem to split the year into two equal parts, and by doing so they instruct us about the annual pendulum that swings between fruits and vegetative growth at one end and fertility and love at the other.

The connection between the fertility of the land and human fertility was already made long ago by our forebears:

> Your spouse shall be like a fruitful vine within your house;
> Your children, like olive saplings around your table. (Psalm 128:3)

In his description of Tu BiSh'vat customs, Rabbi Chayim Palachi (1788–1868) of Smyrna (Izmir) cites the verses from Psalms that appear here. According to the custom he describes, each member of the family had a role at the holiday meal and in the blessings for consuming the different fruits:

> The evening of Tu BiSh'vat marks the new year of trees, and in most Jewish communities around the world it was the custom to arrange a table of as many of the tree fruits and fruits that grow from the ground that one could acquire, and each person would recite the blessing over one of the fruits.
>
> The **man** of the house says the blessing on wheat, after the promised [divine] blessing of food, "God satisfies you with choice wheat" (Psalm 147:14), so that he should have food in abundance.
>
> The **woman** of the house says the blessing on products of the grapevine, in accordance with the verse "Your wife shall be like a fruitful vine within your house" (Psalm 128:3).
>
> And the **son** says the blessing on olives, ". . . your sons, like olive saplings around your table" (Psalm 128:3).
>
> The pomegranates and the nuts are assigned to the **daughters** . . . (these being fruits whose inner parts are consumed, perhaps a reference to feminine modesty).
>
> Honey and apples are for the **young children**, as it is written, "Under the apple tree I roused you" (Song of Songs 8:5) and "Honey and milk are under your tongue" (Song of Songs 4:11).[11]

The psalmist chose to describe the blessing of family life through images of agricultural abundance. In the same spirit, a familiar Zionist song, *Mal'u Asameinu Bar*, describes in one breath agricultural abundance and family abundance: "Our silos are filled with grain and our vineyards with wine, / Our homes hum with babies, and our cattle are fertile."[10] Indeed, it is common to speak of parenting in Hebrew using language also used for agricultural endeavors: sowing seeds (*zera'im*—sometimes, as in the verse from Psalm 126, with tears); nurturing children (*l'hashkot*, also used of irrigation); and removing figurative stones from their paths (hearkening to the literal stone-clearing, *sikul avanim*, that takes place in the fields). We help them grow and hope to see the fruits of the labor we invested in raising them. Raising children does in fact require investing, believing, and having infinite stores of love—very much like the requirements for working the land, in terms of huge commitments of heart, hand, and soul. Parents and farmers: each group approaches its creative labor as a daunting, sacred task, but a task done with love; each group knowing that much depends on them and what they do, but at the same time recognizing so much is out of their control. Both groups do not know what the future will bring or what fruit their decisions might bear.

Like the rain that the farmer needs to make a living, so the secrets of fertility are not in our hands and are often a riddle. Asking for the gifts of both rain and fertility is present in the

From Time to Time → Dalia Marx

midrash about Rabbi Yochanan, who places them on the same keychain, as it were:

> Three keys the Blessed Holy One blessed has retained in God's own hands and not entrusted to the hand of any messenger, namely: the key of rain, the key of childbirth, and the key of the revival of the dead. (Babylonian Talmud, *Taanit* 2a)

Let's examine two of those keys—the key of rain and the key of childbirth. Both are on the "divine keychain," beyond the reach of human beings.[12] The similarity ends there, though, since the key of rain and the key of childbirth do not open the same gates. Good farmers know which fruit to hope for. They can evaluate what a good return on their efforts would be. They may have questions and doubts, but the general rule is simple: the greatest possible output at the lowest possible cost. Farmers may "fall in love" with their output, but their main concern is achieving quantity, quality, and a good price.

Good parents, however, do not know exactly what "good fruit" to expect, nor do they seek to minimize the real and symbolic "costs" of their labors. Parents hold a lovely apple in their hands and know that there are myriad apples like it in the orchard—but has a child ever been born like this tiny baby we cradle softly in our arms, in amazement? Will another child just like our little child ever be born?

All parents hope that their children will be healthy and talented, loved and happy, just as all farmers hope their fruits will be large, juicy, and good, but is there a formula for success in child-rearing? When we bring children into the world, we give them whatever we can to meet their needs, give them the conditions in which to grow up happy and confident, make it possible for them to achieve their dreams—but unlike farmers, we do not have clear criteria for determining whether they are "successful" or "good."

These things apply not only to child-rearing, since in our days the accepted criteria to determine who is successful have been undermined. We have the good fortune to live in an era when expected gender roles are changing. Many women participate in the workforce and regard their work as fulfilling and expect to find meaning and purpose in it; many men are no longer willing to give up their part in accompanying their young children on their first steps in the world. The way parents divide child care and home management, which was clear in the past, is no longer obvious. It is also not always clear how much we should prod our children to get ahead and how much space we should give them for dreaming, how much to give in to their desires (and whims) and when to set boundaries. We are uncertain about the practical meaning of the call to "train a youth according to their own way" (Proverbs 22:6), how much to allow children to follow

> When [Rabbi Nachman and Rabbi Yitzchak] were about to part, [Rabbi Nachman] said, "Pray master, bless me."
>
> He replied, "Let me tell you a parable: To what may this be compared? To a man who was journeying in the desert; he was hungry, weary, and thirsty and he came upon a tree the fruits of which were sweet, its shade pleasant, and a stream of water flowed beneath it. He ate of its fruits, drank of the water, and rested under its shade.
>
> "When he was about to continue his journey, he said, 'Tree, O Tree, with what shall I bless thee? Shall I say to thee: May your fruits be sweet? They are sweet already. That your shade be pleasant? It is already pleasant. That a stream of water may flow beneath you? Lo, a stream of water flows already beneath you; therefore [I say], 'May it be God's will that all the shoots taken from you be like you.'
>
> "So also with you. With what shall I bless you? With [the knowledge of the Torah?] You already possess [knowledge of the Torah]. With riches? You have riches already. With children? You have children already. Hence [I say], 'May it be God's will that your offspring be like you.'" (Babylonian Talmud, *Taanit* 5b–6a)

Rabbi Uri of Strelisk taught: "A person is like a tree. If you stand in front of a tree and watch it incessantly to see how it grows and to see how much it has grown, you will see nothing at all. But tend to it at all times, prune the runners, and keep the vermin from it, and—all in good time—it will come into its growth. It is the same with a person: all that is necessary is to overcome obstacles, and growth and success will come. But it is not right to examine every hour to see how much has been added to the growth."[13]

their own paths, and how much to accompany and even direct them in an increasingly hostile and alienating world.

Many times, the ones who pay the price for parental confusion and embarrassment are the little seedlings—the children. It seems, though, that they also benefit from seeing their parents working toward a decision along with them. With regard to which path to take, children are exposed to a variety of types of family, parenting styles, and levels of intimacy. In recent years, many parents have been exposed to new and innovative models of family life. The multiplicity of options can sometimes be confusing, but it is also liberating and exciting.

At the end of the month of Sh'vat in Israel we observe Family Day. The thirtieth of Sh'vat is the *yahrzeit* of Henrietta Szold, who was born in 1869 and died on that Hebrew date in 1945 (see p. 139). She had no children of her own, but was still a mother to many.

In Sh'vat, the month of budding and blooming in the Northern Hemisphere, we mark the new year for trees and the beginning of nature's rebirth after its winter sleep, and we can look across to the other side of the calendar, to Tu B'Av, and its hopes for creating and sustaining families.

Shabbat Shirah—The Shabbat of Song

I never studied Spanish in an organized fashion, but I love the sound of the language and its lilting intonation. Since I met my husband Roly, who is originally from Argentina, learning Spanish has become a necessity. His parents speak neither English nor Hebrew. Other than my husband, my Spanish teachers have been songs. All the basic grammatical forms and verb conjugations, along with my earliest vocabulary, were entirely absorbed from the songs in Spanish that I memorized. With *Gracias a la vida*, Mercedes Sosa taught me how to express myself in the past tense, and with his blazing tangos, Carlos Gardel taught me some essential expressions in Argentinian Spanish.

There's something about songs that allows us to learn deeply in a different way—to gain knowledge not through intellectual effort but through natural and pleasant absorption and exposure. Songs teach and transfer knowledge joyously and simply. Songs can be comforting and can relieve bitter feelings. Songs can make their way into a pained heart and heal it no less than the finest, most elaborate explanations and logical arguments. Studies have shown the healing properties of song and of music in general—for, among others, Alzheimer's patients. "With what should one sweeten the days," asked the great Israeli poet Natan Zach, "if not with *shirim*?"[14] *Shirim*, in Hebrew, means both "poetry" and "songs."

Serving God in Joy and Gladness

The Talmud asks, "What is the service [of God] that is [made] with joyfulness and gladness of heart? You must say: It is song" (Babylonian Talmud, *Arachin* 11a). I belong to a generation of students who were forced to learn chapters of Bible by heart back in our school days. We complained a good deal about the pointlessness of it, but in retrospect it is clear to me that my efforts at memorization were worthwhile. My friends and I used to add melodies to those chapters, making their study not only more pleasant but also easier. Additionally, the melodies that we paired with the chapters awakened the musicality within the texts. Sometimes I am sorry that my children were not asked to learn selected chapters by heart.

The Torah is sung, or chanted, with particular notes, and so are the selections from the Prophets that we call the haftarah. The Five Scrolls (Song of Songs, Ruth, Lamentations, Ecclesiastes, and Esther) have special melodies as well: a joyous one for Esther, a sad one for Lamentations, and a festive one for Ruth, Song of Songs, and Ecclesiastes. Chanting those texts according to the *t'amim* (cantillation marks, or trope) is designed to aid the reader in remembering the text, as does the tradition of reading the Mishnah or Psalms with musical intonation. When we read from our Scriptures with the *t'amim*, they become songs that enter the heart in special ways.

On a Shabbat during the month of Sh'vat, we read the Torah portion from Exodus known as *B'shalach* (Exodus 13:17–17:16). This Shabbat is known as Shabbat Shirah, the Shabbat of Song. It draws its name from two great and ancient songs chanted in the synagogue. The first is *Shirat HaYam*,

> The Talmud tells of six oaths that the Blessed Holy One made to the people Israel. The last of them is "that they not reveal the secret to outsiders" (Babylonian Talmud, *K'tubot* 111a). Rashi identifies one of these "secrets" as "the secret of the biblical *t'amim*." The text of the Torah is available to everyone, but according to this interpretation, the secrets of how we read and chant it aloud in synagogue remains hidden from foreign ears.

the Song at the Sea, sung by the liberated Israelites after crossing through the Sea of Reeds on dry land as the Egyptian army chased after them (Exodus 15). Of all the stirring events in the week's Torah reading, it was this song that gave its name to Shabbat Shirah. An interesting midrash explains the uniqueness of *Shirat HaYam*:

> From the day that the Blessed Holy One created the world until the Israelites stood at the edge of the sea, we find no one who offered a song to the Eternal other than Israel. God created Adam, but he [Adam] offered no song. God rescued Abraham from the fiery furnace, but he offered no song. Similarly, [God rescued] Isaac from the knife, but he offered no song. Similarly [God rescued] Jacob from the angel, and from Esau, and from the people of Shechem, but he offered no song.
>
> When the Israelites came to the sea and it was torn asunder for them, right away they offered a song to the Blessed Holy One, as [Scripture] says, "Then Moses and the Israelites sang this song [to the Eternal]" (Exodus 15:1).
>
> . . . Said the Blessed Holy One, "From these people I would expect that." (*Sh'mot Rabbah, B'shalach* 23)

One of the customs that has become attached to Shabbat Shirah *is putting out food for the birds. Many explanations have been given for this custom (which has also encountered some opposition). According to one explanation, Shabbat Shirah, the Shabbat of Song, is an appropriate time for thanking those winged creatures for their singing.*

The Song at the Sea is also read on the seventh day of Passover in memory of the passage through the Sea of Reeds. According to tradition, the splitting of the sea occurred at this time of year, seven days after the Exodus.

Shirat HaYam actually appears every day in the morning service (Shacharit) as part of the preliminary section, P'sukei D'Zimrah. In that way, the great, foundational miracle of the splitting of the sea and the rescue of the Children of Israel is made real and present in our daily lives.

According to this midrash, the Israelites were the first to sing praises to God. Not Adam and none of the three Patriarchs or the four Matriarchs sang to their Creator when they were saved from serious danger. It was the Children of Israel, the slaves who had been set free, who responded in unison (according to this midrash) to the miracle that had been performed for them, and "right away they offered a song." This spontaneous public song we read in *B'shalach*—the Song at the Sea, *Shirat HaYam*—gave a name to this special Shabbat: Shabbat Shirah.

The second song recited on Shabbat Shirah is in the haftarah portion for the week: *Shirat D'vorah*, the Song of Deborah, which Deborah the prophetess sang in the wake of the victory she led against the army of Sisera, the Canaanite general. Like Moses and Miriam singing in *Shirat HaYam*, Deborah sings a song to the God of Israel: "Hear, O kings! Give ear, O potentates! I will sing, will sing to the Eternal; will hymn the Eternal, the God of Israel" (Judges 5:3). This too is a song of victory, relief, and faith. The story of Deborah's victory over Sisera's army appears in narrative form in chapter 4 of the Book of Judges, and immediately afterward, in chapter 5, the same events are related in poetic language that gives the events a more festive and exalted character.

Singing Women

Shabbat Shirah's two songs—the Song at the Sea recited in the Torah reading and the Song of Deborah recited in the haftarah—are both connected to women. Some have suggested that most of the biblical songs were **written by women**. For our purposes this is particularly significant, because today some believe that hearing a woman's voice in song is an immodest act, and there are even those who try to prevent women from singing in public. The advocates of banning women's singing voices base their view on a radical interpretation that takes out of context a statement by a lone Babylonian Talmudic sage, Sh'muel: "A woman's voice is erotic provocation" (*B'rachot* 24a). Sh'muel made this statement in the context of a discussion about the conditions under which one should not recite the *Sh'ma*, since the liturgical recitation of *Sh'ma* requires unique concentration and intention.

In response to the claim against hearing the voices of women singing, we can point to the great singing women in our tradition, Miriam and Deborah, and go back to the male lover's words to his female beloved in Song of Songs: "O you who linger in the garden, a lover is listening; let me hear *kolech* [your voice]!" (Song of Songs 8:13). When Israeli Orthodox women established a religious women's forum in 1998, they called it *Kolech*—Your Voice— borrowing directly from this verse in Song of Songs, which invites the woman who "linger in the garden" to make her voice heard.[17]

Israeli Song in Hebrew

Poetry and song have always been an important part of Jewish tradition in all communities, from the poetic passages of the Bible and the songs of the Levites in the Temple, through the *piyutim* written in the Land of Israel in late antiquity and the traditions of singing *piyutim* of various genres, all the way down to our own day. Rabbi Nachman of Bratzlav, an influential Chasidic leader in the late eighteenth and early nineteenth centuries, said about the unique characteristics of song, "Tears open gates; song makes walls collapse." Indeed, when people sing together, they find that they share a special unity of spirit. This quality of song brings us to the Hebrew songs of contemporary Israel. The pioneers of the nineteenth century who left the traditional Jewish world and disdained many of its expressions still continued the tradition of group singing. Even though the content of these song sessions—both then and now—has not always been classically religious, they nonetheless have a unifying communal dimension reminiscent of synagogue life and even a distinctly religious dimension of connection to the sublime. The late, great Israeli songwriter Naomi Shemer is quoted as saying:

> We are a small, familial public, which actually came from the synagogue, as if throwing out the synagogue but dragging it around. . . . We are really a community, a tribe; we are in search of togetherness, maybe so we can strengthen each other, maybe so we can

Midrash *Shiru*
Rabbi Tamar Duvdevani

"Then Moses and the Children of Israel sang this song to the Eternal, and they spoke, saying, I shall sing to the Eternal, for God has triumphed gloriously"

"Then Miriam the prophet, Aaron's sister, picked up a hand-drum, and all the women went out after her in dance with hand-drums. And Miriam called out to them in response, 'Sing to the Eternal, God has triumphed gloriously; horse and driver God cast into the sea'"[15] (Exodus 15:20–21).

Why is it written, "Miriam called out to them **in response**"? For song had already burst forth from Moses's lips, as it is written, "I shall sing to the Eternal," whereas Miriam knew a song that was unknown to Moses. What is the song of Moses? "I shall sing [*ashirah*, in the singular] to the Eternal." This is a song of one voice that does not join with a chorus of voices and melodies. Moses sought to bring forth from each person's heart and to redeem each person's song. But the song of redemption was not complete.

And what is the song of Miriam? "Sing [*shiru*] to the Eternal"— "sing" in the plural. Miriam taught, "The Eternal spoke these words to your entire assembly at the mountain out of the midst of the fire, the cloud, and the opaque darkness, with a great voice, which did not cease" (Deuteronomy 5:19).

What is the meaning of "a great voice"? It means that it contains within a multitude of voices, accents, languages, and sounds. For the voice is the voice of God, and the image is the Image of God—made up of each person, each unique in form and thought. Thus she sang, "Sing [*shiru*] to the Eternal"—for this collects and unites all voices, and includes each personal "I shall sing/*ashirah*" in the multifaceted shared song.

Miriam said to them, "Sing [*shiru*] to the Eternal," and they recalled the image of God that was within them, made up of seventy faces and seventy tongues and seventy melodies. "Sing to the Eternal, praise God's name" (Psalm 96:2). When you sing to God, you praise God's name.[16]

> **When Miriam Sang**
> Esther Shkalim
>
> "And Miriam chanted for them, 'Sing to the Eternal, for God has triumphed gloriously'" (Exodus 15:21).
>
> "When the Blessed Holy One gave the Torah, not a bird took flight, not a bull bellowed" (*Sh'mot Rabbah, Yitro* 29).
>
> When Miriam the prophet sang
> at the sea,
> Moses uttered no rebuke,
> Aaron did not take flight,
> the pillar of fire did not burn,
> and the whole people triumphed gloriously:
> Let us be silent
> and hear.[18]
>
> כְּשֶׁמִּרְיָם הַנְּבִיאָה
> שָׁרָה
> עַל הַיָּם,
> מֹשֶׁה לֹא גָּעַר
> אַהֲרֹן לֹא פָּרַח
> עַמּוּד הָאֵשׁ לֹא שָׂרַף
> וְכָל הָעָם גָּאֹה גָּאָה:
> בְּחֶסֶה
> וְנִשְׁמַע

express ourselves.... This is our natural means of expression, it's our skin, you can't separate it from the body.[19]

Shemer describes singing in groups as a natural, almost biological, need. The secular Jews left the synagogue, but the void it left in them had to be filled. Singing together with others expresses essential spiritual and national needs, and it is an expression of what Shemer calls "togetherness."

Contemporary Hebrew songs have an interesting and rich set of interconnections with Jewish content, in at least four different modes:

- **Traditional Jewish Music with New Words:** This is how a melody composed by Shalom Charitonov of the Chabad Chasidism for the Yom Kippur *piyut* "Like Clay in the Hand of the Potter" took on new words in the Zionist lullaby *Sh'chav B'ni* ("Lie Down, My Son"), written during the Arab riots in Palestine in 1929 by Emmanuel HaRussi. Both express longing and faith.

- **New Music for Traditional Texts:** This mode is exemplified by the melodies composed for Israel's annual Chasidic Song Festival, held from 1969 to 1992. Those compositions provided contemporary melodies for lines from classic texts. One well-known example is Nurit Hirsch's melody for *Oseh Shalom*. A similar phenomenon exists in the United States when musicians such as Debbie Friedman create new music for traditional liturgies.

- **Musical Settings for "Secular" Hebrew Poetry with a Connection to the Sublime:** This mode highlights what appear to be secular poems but whose contents can be understood as prayers that have a profound connection to the sacred and sublime. An example is Lea Goldberg's "Songs of the End of the Road," some of which have been set to music.

- **Newly Composed Songs That Challenge the Distinction between Poetry and Prayer:** An example of a new prayer-song that has become almost canonical since it was first recorded in 2001 by singer Sarit Hadad is the song "When Your Heart Cries" (*K'shehalev Bocheh*), with words by a popular lyricist Yossi Gispan and music by Shlomo Elbaz. It begins: "When your heart cries / only God hears. / The pain rises from your soul. / A person falls before they sink down / in a small prayer that slices the silence."[20] In addition, the artist and singer Kobi Oz has written:

> Over the last few years, I've soaked my soul in the warm marinade of Judaism, and the result, *Psalms of the Perplexed*, is an [album] that includes brand new songs that move in a gray zone that is neither "religious" or "secular." ... We're not talking about something "spiritual," naïve, or kabbalistic, but rather Hebrew songs that would put a smile on the shining faces of our old rabbinic sages.[21]

In recent years we have witnessed a greater willingness to grapple with sacred texts, rereading them and singing them, in addition to writing and composing sacred songs. May we be privileged to increase song in our world, for, as Rabbi Y'hoshua ben Levi said, "Whoever utters song in this world shall be privileged to do so in the next world too" (Babylonian Talmud, *Sanhedrin* 91b).

 # Family Day

I ONCE HEARD A SERMON given by a rabbi who spoke in praise of the Book of Genesis. He claimed that it is a guidebook for proper family life. Our ancestors, he said, presented us with examples of how to conduct our relationships as couples, parents, and siblings. I sat listening in amazement. Were the first families of Genesis really families to emulate? What can we learn from the example of a man who rises up against his brother and murders him? Or from a man who passes his wife over to another man for his own advantage? Or from a parent who puts his children's lives in danger? Or from a man who steals the birthright from his brother through trickery and then connives with his mother to defraud his old, weak father? Or from brothers who sell another brother into slavery and tell their grieving father that he'd been killed by a wild animal? Or from a son who suggests to his father that the father kill the son's two sons (the father's grandsons) if the son fails to retrieve his brother from captivity—and the captor is none other than the brother who had been "killed by a wild animal," disguising himself? The Bible, and primarily the Book of Genesis, provides extreme and troubling models of family life. This doesn't mean, though, that we cannot learn from the Torah's narratives.

First, the Bible's stories teach us without fuss about the complexity of the institution called "family." A family can be a warm, protective nest from which we emerge to face the difficulties of our existence and deal with whatever life throws at us, but it can also be a damaging place, one that is unfair and leaves us scarred. The Book of Genesis does not seek to hide the difficulties inherent in family life, and it doesn't reduce them to anything shallow. In fact, it portrays them in full force. In most cases, one brother does not attack another with the intent to kill, but feelings of envy and anger among siblings—and sometimes even hostility and hatred—are nevertheless part of the fabric of family relations and something to be addressed. The Bible, unlike Hollywood movies, does not supply us with saccharine depictions of imaginary families in which no one raises their voice and no suppressed emotions poison the atmosphere.

Genesis includes difficult, problematic descriptions of families, but there is a dimension of comfort as well. It ends with an atmosphere of reconciliation and closeness. The brothers described at the end of the Book of Genesis, Ephraim and Manasseh, are not embroiled in struggle. The book that follows, Exodus, depicts extended cooperation among three siblings: Moses, Miriam, and Aaron.

Along the path that transforms Jacob's descendants into a nation, we observe a process of development and refinement. Our forebears were sometime plagued by difficult and damaging family relationships, but nevertheless—here we are! The Jewish people lives on, and the Jews are even known among the

Ephraim and Manasseh, the first brothers in our history not enmeshed in struggle and competition with one another, are also the ones we mention in the blessing of children that is customary in many households on Friday nights. It is customary for parents to place their palms on the head of each child and recite:

For sons: May God inspire you to live like Ephraim and Manasseh. (Genesis 48:20)

For daughters: May God inspire you to live like Sarah, Rebekah, Rachel, and Leah. (based on Ruth 4:11)

For every child:
May God bless you and keep you.

יְבָרֶכְךָ יְיָ וְיִשְׁמְרֶךָ:

May God's light shine upon you, and may God be gracious to you.

יָאֵר יְיָ פָּנָיו אֵלֶיךָ וִיחֻנֶּךָּ:

May you feel God's Presence within you always, and may you find peace. (Numbers 6:24–26)

יִשָּׂא יְיָ פָּנָיו אֵלֶיךָ וְיָשֵׂם לְךָ שָׁלוֹם:

And in my family—inspired by Marcia Falk's *The Book of Blessings*—we add for each child:
  Be who you are—and may you be blessed in all that you are.[22]

Melodies / *Nigunim*
Fania Bergstein

You planted melodies in me, my mother and
 my father
Melodies, forgotten hymns.
Seeds, seeds my heart carried—
Now they rise and grow.

Now they sprout offshoots in my blood,
Their roots intertwine in my arteries,
Your melodies my father, your songs my
 mother,
Awaken and reverberate in my pulse.

Here I listen to my distant lullaby,
Chanted from mother to daughter.
Here will sparkle in tears and laughter
"Lamentations" and Sabbath tunes.

Each sound is hushed and each note is stilled.
It's within me that your faraway voices teem.
My eyes I'll close and I am with you
Above the darkness of the abyss. [23]

שְׁתַלְתֶּם נִגּוּנִים בִּי, אִמִּי וְאָבִי,
נִגּוּנִים מִזְמוֹרִים שְׁכוּחִים.
גַּרְעִינִים; גַּרְעִינִים נְשָׂאָם לְבָבִי –
עַתָּה הֵם עוֹלִים וְצוֹמְחִים.

עַתָּה הֵם שׁוֹלְחִים פֹּארוֹת בְּדָמִי,
שָׁרְשֵׁיהֶם בְּעוֹרְקַי שְׁלוּבִים,
נִגּוּנֶיךָ, אָבִי, וְשִׁירַיִךְ אִמִּי,
בְּדָפְקִי נֵעוֹרִים וְשָׁבִים.

הִנֵּה אַאֲזִין שִׁיר עַרְשִׂי הָרָחוֹק
הִבִּיעַ פִּי אֵם אֱלֵי בַת.
הִנֵּה לִי תִּזְהַרְנָה בְּדֶמַע וּשְׂחוֹק
"אֵיכָה" זְמִירוֹת שֶׁל שַׁבָּת.

כָּל הֶגֶה יִתַּם וְכָל צְלִיל יֵאָלֵם
בִּי קוֹלְכֶם הָרָחוֹק כִּי יֶהֱמֶה.
עֵינַי אֲעַצֵּם וַהֲרֵינִי אִתְּכֶם
מֵעַל לְחֶשְׁכַּת הַתְּהוֹם.

other nations of the world as a particularly family-oriented people. There may be a reason to feel not only consolation, but also hope and optimism.

The Family as Microcosm

The family is a living laboratory, a microcosm, a world complete unto itself. Within it we learn to function both as individuals and as part of a system. A baby discovers the world through a connection with its parents, present and attentive to its needs. When the baby has grown a bit, they are exposed to other members of the family, immediate and more distant, before going out into the world. The sounds, aromas, first touches we come to know—all these define our relationship with the world and the people with whom we come into contact. Those of us who had the good fortune to grow up in a supportive family defined by relationships of trust are able to take the security and warmth to other relationships and into the families we will establish. Those who grew up in more strained and difficult families in which cold and judgmental relationships prevailed need to do a considerable amount of work in order to create different families and relationships that are more accepting and supportive.

We do emerge from our families into the world, but to tell the truth, that's not a precise description. We never really emerge from our families; we never actually leave them behind. Every family changes its form, over time. A family with small children is not the same family when the children have reached their teen years or have moved out. The dynamics in a family keep changing. The parent who cradled a little baby in their arms becomes the sworn enemy of a teenager, and then a friend and confidant of the young adult, and finally the parent—in need of assistance and support—becomes dependent on the child. At the same time, there are some things in a family that do not change. We will always be someone's children, someone's little brother, twin sister, older sibling. Even after our parents have gone to their rest, we carry them with us in our memories, in our resemblance to them, in the experiences we have internalized, in the fear that we have become too much like them, and in the concern that maybe we've strayed too far from them . . .

The Thirtieth of Sh'vat—Mother's Day or Family Day

In the beginning there was Mother's Day. In preschool we drew pictures for *Ima* (Mom), we overbaked cookies, and we woke her up in the morning with a special kiss. Israel's Mother's Day was established in pre-independence Palestine in 1947, on the anniversary of Henrietta Szold's death, the thirtieth of Sh'vat. Szold, who was dubbed "the Children's Mother," had no children of her own, but she raised many children as a result of her intensive involvement with the undertaking known as Youth Aliyah (Aliyat HaNoar). The intent of the day's founders was to offer praise to mothers for their hard, sometime Sisyphean work and at the same time to enhance expectations that women would continue to be the pillar of the home as trusty homemaker, faithful companion, and model mother.

In the 1980s the day became Family Day, dictated by social and cultural changes in Israel. Mothers are no longer perceived as the ones who—unaided and with their own two hands— keep the whole family operating, give support, feed, wipe away tears, and make the best of every situation. What underlies the decision to transform Mother's Day into Family Day was the feeling that the entire family should be celebrated. Some did regret that Mom's special day was taken away and would have preferred to leave it as it was and supplement it with a parallel Father's Day (as is celebrated in the United States, for example).

An Opportunity to Think about Family and Families

Family Day is an opportunity to give some thought to the topic of families, to different ways of sharing tasks and roles, and to the changing gender roles within a family. More and more women find satisfaction in work, not just as extra income for the family but to develop careers of their own, and reciprocally, more and more men are discovering the joy of a more significant presence in the family realm and in child-rearing.

At the same time, we are becoming aware of varying models of families. The model of the nuclear family—father, mother, and children—took shape in the wake of the Industrial Revolution and mass migration into cities that began in the eighteenth century. The nuclear family was the most efficient arrangement for urban living in relatively small apartments and far from one's extended family.

Today, with longer life expectancies and the loneliness experienced by many in the urban jungle, people are reflecting on the price we have paid for moving to the nuclear family framework. I do not know many who advocate for a return to the full tribal model of the extended family, but thought needs to be given to how we can adopt some aspects of what Israelis lovingly call the *chamulah*, from the Arabic word for extended families. These larger groups could be actual blood relatives, or it could be a "chosen family" that creates a supportive community in which each and every individual can express their own needs. Young couples, for example, could place babies and toddlers with older family members while spending time on their studies and building their careers. Grandchildren could spend more time with grandparents while parents are at work. Older folks would not be alone, and children would receive attention and care from addi-

Henrietta Szold, educator, thinker, and activist, was a central figure in the Zionist movement. Szold made *aliyah* from the United States in 1929, at the age of sixty. She had been one of the founders of Hadassah, the Women's Zionist Organization, in 1912 and later helped lay the foundation for the health and welfare systems of what became the State of Israel. She also headed Youth Aliyah, which brought Jewish children to Palestine from Nazi Germany. Szold was the daughter of a Conservative rabbi, Benjamin Szold, and the first woman to study at New York's Jewish Theological Seminary (although not for rabbinic ordination).

Henrietta Szold is well known for her insistence on saying Kaddish for her mother. In a touching letter to a male friend who offered to take on that responsibility for her, she wrote, "My mother had eight daughters and no son. . . . When my father died, my mother would not permit others to take her daughters' place in saying the Kaddish, and so I am sure I am acting in her spirit when I am moved to decline your offer. . . . You understand me, don't you?"[24]

tional loving adults. Two sets of single-parent families could decide to move into one home together, sharing expenses, childcare, and household tasks. If such a plan were implemented with sensitivity and empathy, everyone could benefit from the *chamulah* design.

In recent years, we are increasingly witnessing new models of families: single parents, families with two parents of the same sex, blended families, and multigenerational families. It is an important societal challenge to include these many models and to make space for varied expressions of family life. And by the way, we need to consider not only new family structures, but also new forms of living. For example, in the past, kibbutzim had children's houses where the children lived (and these were the only "houses" on a kibbutz; adults lived in a "room"), while today more and more elderly people live in nursing homes or assisted-living units intended for senior citizens.

The thirtieth of Sh'vat, Family Day, is an excellent opportunity to look around at the people sitting at our tables, give thanks for what is, and hope for even better things to come. Family Day gives us a chance to reflect in a fresh new way on what family actually is and to consider how we can be less dogmatic, more inclusive, and more enabling—it is a positive challenge and opportunity to live according to our values.

PRAYER OF THE MONTH

Prayers for the Welfare of Our Families

MY FRIEND RABBI CHAYA ROWEN BAKER has composed a series of prayers to be recited on the thirtieth of Sh'vat, Family Day. The first prayer is read out loud in unison, and those that follow are read quietly by each worshiper, according to the individual's family situation.[25]

Recite in unison:
   My God,
   I offer thanks to You for the great kindness You have bestowed upon me,
   for my family members who are always with me.
   Please instill among us friendship, mutual responsibility, health, and peace.
   Instruct me in Your ways and may we follow Your paths,
   and may this verse be true in our lives:
   "How fair are your tents, O Jacob, your dwellings, O Israel" (Numbers 24:5).

Individually, quietly:
[For a spouse:]
   Master of peace,
   Grant peace between me and my husband/wife/spouse.
   Grant me the ability to be attentive and sensitive to his/her/their needs,
   to grow together with him/her/them and to be a loyal friend to him/her/them.
   Help us to deal with difficult times
   and to help each other in times of crisis and sorrow,
   and may we be privileged to live as the wise King Solomon advises:
   "My beloved is mine, and I am my beloved's, who browses among the lilies"
                                                               (Song of Songs 2:16).

[For parents:]
   Grant me patience and love to observe the mitzvah "Honor your father and your
      mother" (Exodus 20:12)
   at any moment when I am called upon to do so.
   Bless me with the ability to fulfill that responsibility as a privilege and not a burden,
   out of love and not compulsion, in joy and satisfaction and not impatience.
   Bless me with the privilege of learning from my parents and from all the
      generations that came before me.

[For siblings:]
   Uproot from my heart all envy and competitiveness
   and make my heart ready to receive my brother(s)/sister(s)/sibling(s) in kindly
      manner
   and to assess him/her/them generously.

Rabbi Oshrat Morag has composed a blessing to be said on Friday nights, in addition to the traditional blessing for children or in its place:

A Blessing for Children and Families

May it be Your will, Adonai our God, God of our ancestors, to protect our family, today and every day. May happiness and love dwell amongst us, and may You protect us from all hurt and wounds, sorrow and disappointment, whether by our own doing or by those seeking to harm us. Merciful nurturing Parent, out of the mouth of babes and nursing infants You have ordained strength (Psalm 8:3). Please, guide our children (names of child/children), so they may never lose their way. Brighten their day, let smiles always adorn their faces, and protect them from all trouble and distress, from all affliction and evildoers. Bring them back to us always safe and joyous. Praised are You, Adonai, who brings joy to parents and children.[26]

Banish any disagreements and strife that may come between us,
and enable us to accompany each other supportively and lovingly through life's vicissitudes,
because we are, in fact, "our brother's keeper" and, like Joseph, "in search of my brothers" (Genesis 37:16), we seek each other's well-being.

[For children:]
Grant me the patience and wisdom to educate my children with understanding and openness.
Bestow my heart with the understanding needed to raise them to love God and to love human beings,
to a life of Torah and good deeds.
Bless my children with the privilege of living long, bountiful, joyous lives.

[For grandchildren and great-grandchildren:]
Endow me, in Your grace, with good years of satisfaction and patience,
so that I might be privileged to see descendants
and to watch them grow and flourish,
loving God and loving human beings,
studying Torah and doing good deeds,
and may this verse be true in our lives:
"May you see your children's children, peace for Israel" (Psalm 128:6).

Recite in unison:
Bless our homes with joy, song, merriment, and delight,
Love and companionship, peace and friendship,
And let us say: Amen.

To these lovely blessings we might add others for additional family members, for chosen family members, and perhaps for those who are the caretakers for our relatives, young and old—dear ones whom we have come to view as members of the family, even if they are not part of our biological family.

ADAR

Zodiac Sign: Pisces | Tribe of the Month: Benjamin
Breastplate Stone: Jasper/*Yashfeh*

The name Adar appears in the Book of Esther, at the beginning of chapter 9. Its origins are apparently the Babylonian month Addaru. It is likely that the source is the Akkadian verb *addaru*, which means "to be sad" or "to be fearful" and may also mean "to be dark" or "to be hidden." It is not clear whether there is a semantic connection between the verb and the name of the month, which clashes with the Jewish tradition's call to increase joy during the month of Adar. It could be that the emphasis on joy is a response to the dark nature of the month, which falls during the winter in the Northern Hemisphere. In any case, the meaning of "to be hidden" fits well with the Book of Esther, the *m'gillah* (scroll) that is all about what is hidden.

Kavanah: A Meditation for Adar

Purim, the festival of the concealed and concealing, teaches us about the courage to accept what is invisible, to believe in miracles. A daring midrash relates that the Torah was forced upon the people Israel at Sinai: "Rabbi Avdimi bar Chama bar Chasa said: . . . [A verse in the Torah] teaches that the Blessed Holy One upended the mountain above the Israelites like a tub and said to them, 'If you accept the Torah, excellent, and if not, there will be your burial.'" However, further on in the text, Rava adds that in the end Israel chose the Torah: "Rava said: Even so, they again accepted it willingly in the time of Ahasuerus, as it is written: 'The Jews ordained, and took upon themselves . . .' (Esther 9:27), and he taught: The Jews ordained what they had already taken upon themselves [earlier, under duress]" (Babylonian Talmud, *Shabbat* 88a). This midrash indicates how daring it is—and how vital—to accept the Torah specifically as a choice and personal decision, and not because of being forced to do so. Purim, then, is a festival of choice, a celebration of the joy of choosing.

> May it be that we always know how to choose and to renew ourselves, to change forms but to preserve our inner essence.
>
> May it be that we seek and find meaning in the hidden moments, the moments of concealment.
>
> May it be that we believe in the possibility of miracles even in the face of chaos and despair.

At the Gates of Adar

"From the time that Adar begins, we increase joy" (Babylonian Talmud, *Taanit* 29a). Is this a description of an existing situation? Is it an instruction? A command? A recommendation? During Adar we celebrate Purim, the most jolly and lighthearted of all the Jewish holidays. It is indeed a happy holiday, but that does not mean it lacks a serious side. Purim raises interesting questions about the meaning of happiness, about the sources of happiness, and about whether to summon happiness if it doesn't just come to us naturally.

The first *iyun* we will explore in this chapter is called "Must We Be Happy? Always?" It asks whether we are really required to be happy and what is even intended by saying "to be happy." There we will pay some attention to a relatively new branch of psychology called "positive psychology." The second *iyun*, "The Joy in Incompleteness," addresses how we grapple with fears and hopes in an uncertain world. The third *iyun*, "The Faces of Janus," looks at two days of struggle related to women's rights that fall in Adar. The fourth *iyun* addresses the question of the meaning of a doubled Adar in Hebrew leap years and asks about the connection between a leap year (in Hebrew, literally "a pregnant year") and pregnancy in general. A fifth *iyun* examines the custom of dressing up in costume on Purim, especially in the context of gender and gender identity. The final pages explore the dozens of local "Purims" that Jewish communities have declared for themselves. The Poem of the Month is the upbeat *Shir Samei-ach* ("A Happy Song"), and the Prayer of the Month explores the ways Esther does *t'shuvah*—or at least, how others wish she does *t'shuvah*.

Tishrei   Marcheshvan   Kislev   Tevet   Sh'vat   Adar   Nisan   Iyar   Sivan   Tammuz   Av   Elul

Poem of the Month

Shir Samei-ach ("A Happy Song")

A Happy Song
    Yaakov Orland

שִׁיר שָׂמֵחַ
יַעֲקֹב אוֹרְלַנְד

Even if our head is bowed
and sorrow is all around us—
let's catch on fire and shout out loud
the happiness that's found us.

אִם גַּם רֹאשֵׁנוּ שַׁח
וְעֶצֶב סוֹבְבָנוּ –
הָבָה וְנִתְלַקַּח
מִן הַשִּׂמְחָה שֶׁבָּנוּ.

Hey, hey,
let's fill up
with joy and glee so fine.
Hey, hey,
sing: up and up!
Rise up in flame, O wine!
Rise up in flame, O wine!
Hey, hey . . .

הֵי, הֵי,
הָבָה וְנִתְמַלֵּא
שִׂמְחָה, שִׂמְחָה כִּמְלֹא הָעַיִן,
הֵי, הֵי,
שִׁירוּ: עֲלֵה, עֲלֵה!
עֲלֵה וּבְעַר הַיַּיִן!
עֲלֵה וּבְעַר הַיַּיִן!
הֵי, הֵי . . .

Rise up and burn like fire
and ignite our power!
Woe to one who lacks desire;
tonight's a joyous hour!

עֲלֵה וּבְעַר כָּאֵשׁ
וְהַדְלִיקֵנוּ כֹּחַ!
אֲבוֹי לַמִּתְיָאֵשׁ,
הַלַּיְלָה יֵשׁ לִשְׂמֹחַ!

Hey, hey,
tonight we'll be free
and everyone alive,
Hey, hey,
all of us, you will see,
have a spark to make them thrive!
Have a spark to make them thrive![1]

הֵי, הֵי,
הַלַּיְלָה יִגָּאֵל
כָּל מִי, כָּל מִי שֶׁנְּשָׁמָה בּוֹ,
הֵי, הֵי,
כָּל אִישׁ בְּיִשְׂרָאֵל –
נִיצוֹץ שֶׁל נֶחָמָה בּוֹ!
נִיצוֹץ שֶׁל נֶחָמָה בּוֹ!

The story of *Shir Samei-ach* is unusual. In the wake of a terrorist attack on a bus at Maaleh Akrabim in the northern Negev on March 17, 1954, in which eleven Israelis were killed—at the time, the worst such attack since the War of Independence (1947-49)—the atmosphere in Israel was dark and depressed. Days later, Moshe Sharett, who had just become prime minister, ran into the poet Yaakov Orland and the composer Mordechai Zeira at a Purim party at the Milo Club in Tel Aviv. The story is told that Sharett "locked them up" in the club's little kitchen (which was filled with goodies) and told them they couldn't come out until they had written a song to raise everyone's spirit. Not long after, the pair emerged with a song, written on a paper napkin, that opens with a nod to the prevailing gloom: "Even if our head is bowed." The two performed the song, with its upbeat Chasidic melody, for the customers at the club. Sharett—who was also gifted with musical talent—took out a clarinet and accompanied them.

Very soon the song gained wide popularity. When you hear the uplifting melody and its encouraging words, it is hard to imagine that the origin of "A Happy Song" is in a collective national trauma.

As we approach the month of Adar, I would like to give some thought to the happiness that I seek for myself and my loved ones. Ideally, joyful behavior is something that should be praised, but it cannot stand on its own; it must be tempered by responsibility and meaning. When I look for simple, modest happiness that comes from within and not from the superficial images of broadcast commercials, I think of Orland and Zeira's "A Happy Song." The basic assumption of the song, written in such dark times, is that happiness lies within us (although I could do without the imagery of catching on fire). The spark of comfort is the one through which we can touch the good and hope for redemption—even if it is only partial redemption. This idea may be a bit naïve, but it is also true.

Rabbi Nachman of Bratzlav is said to have put such an emphasis on happiness because he himself suffered from "melancholy." Rabbi Nachman (1772–1810), great-grandson of the founder of Chasidism, the Baal Shem Tov, was an original and profound thinker and leader, and he devoted a great deal of thought to the topic of sadness and despair. One of his most widely quoted statements is "It is a great mitzvah to be happy at all times." When we examine the context in which this was said, we see that for Rabbi Nachman, happiness was not self-evident:

> It is a great mitzvah always to be happy, and to make every effort to determinedly keep depression and gloom at bay. . . .
>
> The principle is that a person must be very determined and put all their strength into being nothing but happy at all times. For it is human nature to draw itself to gloom and depression on account of life's pains and misfortunes. And every human being is filled with suffering. Therefore, a person has to exercise great effort and force happiness at all times. . . .
>
> And though broken-heartedness is very good, nevertheless it must be only for a brief period. It is right to set aside for oneself some time in the day for feeling remorse and speaking one's piece in the presence of the Blessed One, as is cited in our works. But the entire day one needs to be happy. (*Likutei Moharan* 2:24)

The happiness about which Rabbi Nachman is speaking is not lighthearted nor an escape from sadness, but rather an emotion constructed in awareness of life's pain and sadness, and also from a choice—a decision that each individual must make in this complex world.

Two superb entertainers,
two who are known to be great,
two of the greatest comedians—
a Jewish comic and fate.
They enter a duel
with not one moment's rest.
And still—What? We go on?
We go on!
My friend, you're the best!
—**Natan Alterman**[2]

Must We Be Happy? Always?

"Read this book," "drink that drink," "take this course," "speak with that trainer," "try this pill" . . . everyone wants to sell us happiness and a happy life. Even with the recent global challenges of the past number of years, there is still an emphasis on happiness and optimism. Our culture tells us that we need to be happy, that we *must* be happy, that our success in the world is measured by how happy we feel (or at least, how much happiness we project on social media) and that we evaluate everything we do based on the enjoyment it brings us. From the time that Adar begins, we "increase joy." But why? What kind of happiness are we talking about? Why is happiness good, and must we really be happy? Always?

When Judaism Met the West and They Both Met the East

When the individualistic Western ethos—whose primary aspiration is to focus on oneself and one's self-actualization—encounters the Jewish ethos—according to which our actions must be directed toward *tikkun olam* and additional lofty goals—a connection is made that is not self-evident. When the two of them together meet the teachings of the East—that we must be focused on the present and live each moment in its fullness—sometimes a strange hybrid is formed that would want nothing more than for us to feel good, avoid whatever causes suffering, and remain always happy.

The search for personal happiness is not a local phenomenon. It is part of a wider phenomenon connected to the New Age theories that developed in the West. The "feel good" culture seeks to block out sadness and sorrows that stand between us and the achievement of our goals. What is our highest goal, according to this culture? To be happy. In Israel, we have an additional ingredient spicing up our search for happiness: we must forget the pioneers who drained the swamps, who were consumed by malaria by day and by unrequited love by night; we must say goodbye to self-sacrifice in battles of the few against the many; we eschew the temporary humble dwellings, deprivation, and making do with little. Israelis today want to be happy, and they are not embarrassed about it. Israeli professors disseminate theories of happiness in the world's universities and in the hidden recesses of ashrams. From Zion shall go forth the Torah of positivity.

The Crooked Smile of Alienated Narcissism

Aspiring toward personal happiness—when it is disconnected from social context and justice and instead rooted in self-absorption without relating to the wider world—is vacuous; it will likely lead precisely to a feeling of sadness and suffering—our own and that of others. Furthermore, one should not underestimate the importance of sadness as an essential state of mind that enables us to learn about ourselves, or the value of frustration or deprivation as leverages toward action. Sometimes one must dwell for a time in those emotions and not give in to the "instant" culture that urges us to find a quick way out of them. I should emphasize that I do not think that there is a positive value in suffering or advantage in misery. I'm asking instead about what moves us to act: Is it the search for meaning and wholeness in the confusing world in which we live? Or is it striving for a saccharine happiness with no cares, no need to grapple with anything? What is the real happiness we're after—the relaxed cheerfulness of painlessness or the joy of creativity and *tikkun*?

Positive Psychology

Despite everything said earlier, happiness is a serious and very important matter. The amount of happiness and satisfaction in our lives is an important component of the quality of our existence, our life expectancy, and our ability to handle what life throws at us. Until recently, the vast majority of studies in the field of clinical psychology dealt with human pathologies such as mood or personality disorders. A new branch of psychology proposes to focus on the people's strengths and not only their challenges. The researchers and clinicians who work with this approach, known as positive psychology, offer to look at "the part of the glass that is half full," not out of a denial of the "half empty" part, but from an understanding that even a person who is thirsting and suffering can quench their thirst from the full half.

Professor Martin Seligman, an American Jewish psychologist (b. 1942), has discerned three types of happiness. The first type is happiness deriving from pleasure and enjoyment. A second type comes from a life of doing and flowing with what is important to that individual (family, work, love, or a hobby), since when we do something we love, we are so invested in it that time goes by unnoticed. The third type is happiness that comes from a life of meaning and purpose, a life of devotion to a cause, working for a higher goal; this type of happiness is not necessarily always connected to pleasure. That third type, Seligman claims, is the most profound and enduring of the three and the primary contributor to fulfillment in life.[4] It is in direct contradiction to what we might call "happiness lite," which is the sort of happiness that advertisers offer us. Seligman's third type of happiness is not the happiness of forgetting our troubles and ignoring our difficulties, but rather the opposite—the happiness of involvement and contribution.

The call in the Book of Psalms to "rejoice with trembling" (Psalm 2:11) contains the meaning of proper happiness: we should be happy and rejoice with meaning and commitment. It encourages us to live a life of "trembling," but with joy and fulfillment. Happy people are healthy, creative, and active. Psychological well-being and happiness are tools that enable us to create, act, and do good in the world.

The month of Adar calls us to increase joy. May it be true, inclusive joy that—in the phrase we use in Hebrew—"comes from the heart and enters the heart."[5]

Here is an example. In the book *Badulina* (first published in Hebrew in 1999), Israeli journalist Gabi Nitzan describes a small imaginary kingdom whose name is the title of the book, and it is headed by a charming royal couple whose entire job is "to serve as role models for people, reminding them of their right and obligation to live in wealth and contentment forever." How so? People must put politics out of their minds, and forget whatever seems to threaten their existence and whatever brings them sorrow. The kings of Badulina even visit Israel, where they try to teach the anxiety-ridden Israelis "that their fundamental obligation in this world is not ideological or nationalistic, but personal: to be happy." One can understand the secret of the magical attraction that made the book so popular that it became one of the best-selling books in the history of Israeli publishing.[3]

The Joy in Incompleteness

LITTLE SHOP OF HORRORS is a 1986 film adapted from an off-Broadway musical (which was itself adapted from a 1960 film) that portrays a strange and mysterious plant that comes from another planet into a second-rate flower shop.[6] At first, the plant appears harmless, and it brings the flower shop considerable additional revenue, but young Seymour—the film's main character, who is lacking in self-confidence—quickly learns that the plant is murderous: it lives only on human blood! In order to satisfy the finicky plant, Seymour is dragged into acts of violence that grow more and more horrific—even committing murder. In the end he succeeds in overcoming the plant and subduing it. The final scene shows Seymour and his beloved Audrey married, enjoying happiness and even wealth, living the American dream in a prosperous suburb. At first, this seems like a classic Hollywood happy ending, but then the camera pans out from the house to show the manicured lawn and lovely garden, in which, to our great horror, is a small and cute plant that is the very likeness of the murderous plant from the shop! That movie reminds me more than anything of the Purim story. The *M'gillah*, as we like to call the Book of Esther, portrays a dramatic, exciting, surprising rescue of the Jews of Persia due to the clever actions of Esther and Mordechai. But like the small murderous plant growing in the manicured suburban garden, the question remains: What will happen next? Who will stand up for those whose doom was decreed and who were then rescued—this time—from great travails? Who can guarantee that in another generation or even the very next year, another enemy like Haman won't arise? How can anyone be sure that while they are celebrating, the very plant that tried to do them in is not growing in their own garden? Furthermore, who can guarantee that the "plant" of murder and cruelty didn't sprout within their own heart, threatening to destroy them from within?

Like Passover, Purim is a holiday of rescue, or redemption. The rescue in the city of Shushan, though, is essentially different from the **rescue of the Israelites from Egypt**. Israel's deliverance from Egypt brought a tribe of slaves out to freedom and into a long journey through the wilderness, during which they coalesced into a nation and in the end were prepared to enter the Promised Land. The Exodus from Egypt is a national, historic rescue operation whose significance is eternal. The story of the rescue of the Jews of Persia, in contrast, is a local story of a rescue limited in place and time. God's involvement in the two events is also very different. In one, God takes Israel out of Egypt with a mighty hand and an outstretched arm that is visible to all, strikes Egypt with plagues and defeat, and splits the sea. In the other, God acts secretly, behind the scenes, and is never explicitly mentioned. The Jews in Shushan remained in the same situation, without changing their location or varying from their ways and customs. They remained in the Persian Diaspora, which for the most part provided a comfortable and prosperous life. Did they learn anything from the murderous threat and the rescue that came their way? It seems they did not. And if we ask ourselves honestly, what could they have learned?

In the exhibit hall at the Majdanek death camp, there is a display of shoes,

---

The Exodus from Egypt is one of the foundational events in the history of the Jewish people. This is evident from the fact that the number of references to the Exodus in the prayer book is about the same as the number of references to the creation of the world. For example, in the *Kiddush* for Friday evenings, we mention that Shabbat is "a reminder of the work of Creation" and immediately afterward that it is "a reminder of the Exodus from Egypt." Just as Creation marks the birth of the world, so does the Exodus mark the birth of the Israelite nation. Both have a fateful cosmic significance.

Purim, though, is a holiday of temporary deliverance, a rescue that did not change the course of history in the long run. In this sense, it represents many of our life experiences.

From Time to Time → Dalia Marx

glasses, and other items that belonged to the victims. Among those items is a Hebrew Bible opened to the Book of Esther. Visitors who can read Hebrew notice right away which words are visible there: "Haman then said to Ahasuerus, 'There is a certain people, scattered and dispersed among the other peoples in all the provinces of your realm, whose laws are different from those of any other people and who do not obey the king's laws, and it is not in Your Majesty's interest to tolerate them. If it please Your Majesty, let an edict be drawn for their destruction, and I will pay ten thousand talents of silver to the stewards for deposit in the royal treasury'" (Esther 3:8–9). The curators of the display chose that passage in order to show the viewers the ongoing insecurity of Jewish life as a people scattered and dispersed among the other peoples.

Purim directly addresses the experience of living in the Diaspora. In fact, the Land of Israel is not mentioned at all in the *M'gillah* except in the verse describing Mordechai's lineage, where we learn that he is a descendant of Kish, "who had been exiled from Jerusalem in the exile-community that had been carried into exile along with King Jeconiah of Judah, which had been driven into exile by King Nebuchadnezzar of Babylon" (Esther 2:6). In this lone verse, which includes just one mention of the Land of Israel, the word "exile" appears four times. Indeed, Purim is the holiday of "exile," a holiday of living in a foreign place (even if that foreign place is generally comfortable and easy). But what does exile really mean, in its most profound sense?

Many infer from the Book of Esther that only in the Land of Israel can Jews be truly secure. I, on the other hand, believe that more than anything, Esther teaches that we *all* live in a world we cannot control. Exile can be a psychological or existential state, it can be felt within one's family or in the workplace, and not just a geographical location. What we can know, most essentially, is that we cannot know—that we live and function in a reality in which there is, by definition, no complete security. Maybe there is an optimistic side to the understanding that we are at once both at home and wandering and to the recognition that we are living with both security and uncertainty—that to some extent we are always a little bit strangers, living in a state of exile of the soul, no matter where we are. Perhaps such recognition can liberate us from the need to be in control of our lives all the time and at any price.

Foreignness as a Historical and an Existential Situation

We have been commanded to drink to excess on Purim, to actually get drunk—not simply drink to attain the lightness that a cup or two can provide, but to drink *ad d'lo yada*, "until one cannot know the difference between 'cursed be Haman' and 'blessed be Mordechai'" (Babylonian Talmud, *M'gillah* 7b). This commandment makes the holiday widely popular, but if we examine it deeply we find that its purpose is to allow us to taste the lack of knowledge, uncertainty, and bitterness of impotence, of being drunk—that is, to intensify and emphasize the sense of vulnerability and lack of control over the unstable reality of our lives. Being in a situation where you can no longer discern between disaster and rescue is a moment of the Jews standing at the crossroads before the miracle occurred for them. One path is the path of light and joy and gladness and honor, the path of rescue, while the other path—the one the heroes of the *M'gillah* were saved from having to take—is Haman's path, one of hatred and destruction. Standing like that, inebriated, without being able to tell the two apart, is standing at the precipice. It reveals the fear that hides behind the supposedly lighthearted tale. Standing *ad d'lo yada*, "until one cannot know," emphasizes the happy ending but also reminds us that the end could have been completely different.

The Book of Esther is one of the only two books in the Hebrew Bible in which God's name is not mentioned (the other is Song of Songs). This is the *M'gillah* of blind fate. It is the text of God's hidden face, which reveals the situation of the homeless Jew who is in perpetual exile. Even when life in exile offers comfort and opportunity, unexpected dangers remain. The rescue of the Jews in Persia is dramatic, surprising, and exciting—but as we have said, it is not a rescue for all time and does not bring about an essential change in the life of the Jews.

Purim is often compared to Chanukah. Both are called "minor holidays"—that is, they are not present in the Torah—and therefore there are no prohibitions against labor on those holidays. On both holidays we supplement the *Amidah* and the Grace after Meals with *Al HaNisim* ("For the Miracles") in memory of the miraculous rescues that occurred. Unlike Chanukah—during which we recite *Hallel*, a series of psalms of praise and complete joy—*Hallel* is not recited on Purim. That might well engender some surprise and wonderment, since the story of Purim is mentioned in the *Tanach* but Chanukah does not appear in the Hebrew Bible at all. In the Talmud, Rabbi Yitzchak explains that we do not say *Hallel* on Purim "because no song is said for a miracle that occurred outside the [Holy] Land." Rabbi Nachman reminds him that the miracle of the Exodus occurred outside the Land of Israel, and in response he is told that "before Israel entered the [Holy] Land, all the lands were considered fit for song to be said [if a miracle had occurred within their boundaries]; once Israel entered the Land, no other countries were considered fit for song to be said" (Babylonian Talmud, *Arachin* 10b). This exchange between sages underscores the fact that Purim is a holiday of exile, while Chanukah is about the rededication of the Temple at the center of Jerusalem.

Some regard our tradition's reservations about Purim as revealing some hesitation about the comforts of life in the Diaspora. I feel grateful that I live in the State of Israel, despite of all the difficulties here. Yet, I remind myself that life in our world—regardless of where we happen to live—is life in exile, even if we live happily in the land for which our ancestors longed. Exile is first and foremost a psychological state of uncertainty and insecurity—and maybe these days that is true even more than it was in the past. We can easily access our email inbox, view social media, and read our newspaper from anywhere in the world or speak with our loved ones on the other side of the planet. We are in so many places at once that sometimes we feel we are everywhere but home. We have the collective DNA of the experience of not being home—in other words, of exile. In the Talmud we read the familiar sentence "From the time that Adar begins, we increase joy." These words have been set to music and are sung far and wide, and they hang on the walls of schools in bright, festive signs

---

The Hallel prayer is composed of six festive chapters of the Book of Psalms that are recited or sung, with a blessing both at the beginning and the end. Its point is to express praise and glorification of God. The full *Hallel*, which stands for complete joy, is said on Sukkot, Sh'mini Atzeret/Simchat Torah, Chanukah, Shavuot, and the first day of Passover. On the other days of Passover and on Rosh Chodesh, two of the passages are skipped; this is referred to as the "partial Hallel," indicating that the joy is not complete. For example, our redemption from Egypt celebrated during Pesach meant devastation for the Egyptians and the death of their firstborn children, which partially decreases our joy.[7]

In many congregations today it is customary to recite *Hallel* on Yom HaAtzma-ut (Israel Independence Day) and Yom Y'rushalayim (Jerusalem Day). Opinion is divided over whether the full or shortened version of *Hallel* should be read on those days, and whether blessings should be said with it. (See the prayers for the month of Iyar, p. 236.)

illustrated with hamantaschen and smiling masks. It appears that we would prefer to forget that that sentence was added on to an earlier statement and cited in the Talmud in the name of the Babylonian *Amora* called Rav: "Just as with the beginning of Av we curtail joy, so with the beginning of Adar we increase joy" (Babylonian Talmud, *Taanit* 29a). As we enter Adar and its increased joy, we know that its time is limited and that only five more months will pass before we have to curtail our joy during the month of Av, in memory of the terrible destruction of the Temple. But the sadness of the month of Av will itself yield to Elul, the month of mercy and forgiveness. The feelings of joy and sadness are the experiences of a full life, each one containing awareness of the other.

The Book of Esther teaches us the art of incompleteness, of partiality (as opposed to wholeness), the joy of letting go of doubts, the thrill of victory in this round and hope for the next round. Indirectly it reminds us that even if right now the situation is tough, we should hope for better things to come. It reminds us of the "not knowing" undercurrent of our lives. But it also invites us to enjoy our lives, to love, to feel, to have mercy, to live a life of kindness—not despite the uncertainty but precisely because of it.

The Faces of Janus

PURIM IS A HOLIDAY of human activism, and especially female activism. God may be working in the Purim story, but behind the scenes and hidden. Perhaps for this reason, Purim invites a fight against injustice on two adjacent days, both of which are connected to women: International Agunah (chained woman) Day, observed on the Fast of Esther (the thirteenth of Adar), and International Women's Day on March 8, which often falls in the month of Adar.

International Women's Day was established in the aftermath of demonstrations held by female textile workers in New York City on March 8, 1857. The women were protesting long working hours, low wages, and deplorable working conditions. In solidarity with their struggle, the day became an established institution. It was marked with particular festivity in the former Soviet Union as Heroic Working Women's Day and even today remains popular. In 1975 the United Nations established Women's Day as a formal observance, and today it is observed and celebrated in many countries, including Israel.

International Agunah Day is, on the other hand, a distinctly Jewish calendar event. *Agunah* is a Jewish legal term describing a woman whose husband is lost or missing or simply refuses to grant her a *get*, a Jewish bill of divorce; thus, she is "anchored," metaphorically chained, and unable to break free of a marriage that is effectively over. When a husband—the only person who is empowered to grant a divorce according to the strictest interpretation of Jewish law—refuses to do so, the woman is impacted not only because she cannot remarry, but also because she has been rendered powerless over her own life and future. Withholding a *get* is a form of domestic abuse and unfortunately is an ongoing problem for many Jewish women. The day of struggle for the rights of such women was first observed in 1995 on the Fast of Esther, with a public call to free those women from the bonds of unwanted matrimony.

At first glance it would seem that Women's Day is worldwide and embraces all, while Agunah Day is only about Jewish women held captive in an difficult marital bond. However, both of these days contain a double meaning—one for all humankind and one that is particularly Jewish. The date for each was carefully chosen, combining past and present, tradition and innovation. Thus, the date for Women's Day is based on modern events, while the date for Agunah Day is based on the ancient story of Queen Esther, who declared a fast to create solidarity in the face of her problem. Since it is possible to see a connection between the suffering of *agunot* and Esther's suffering, contemporary Jewish women chose to place on the communal and religious agenda the misery of those chained women by granting new meaning to the ancient observance of the Fast of Esther.

Some people have suggested both International Agunah Day and International Women's Day have a special connection to Purim, even if Women's Day is observed according to the civil calendar. Seeing this connection is not surprising; the symbol of Purim and its main character is a woman, Esther, who strides along the pages of the *M'gillah* and the carpets of Ahasuerus's palace. At first, she appears as "shapely

---

The Book of Esther describes Mordechai asking Esther to intervene with her husband, the king, on behalf of the Jews. Esther, committed to the task but filled with anxiety that her actions will be ineffective and might even lead to her death, fasts for three days and nights and asks the Jewish community to do the same. Over time, it became a custom to remember Esther's heroism and the salvation of the Jewish community by observing the Fast of Esther, Taanit Esther, from sunrise to sundown on the day before Purim.

and beautiful" (Esther 2:7) and is related to as an object, a silent woman who—even when asked a question—does not answer: "But Esther did not reveal her kind or her people" (Esther 2:20). By the end of the story, though, she has become a crafty heroine who cleverly arranges to save her people. The empowerment of women, their presence, and their voices are heard—this is the goal of Women's Day. Additionally, Purim marks the relief and deliverance of the Jews from a threat of destruction due to their Jewishness, so it is an appropriate time to note our commitment to the weakened and vulnerable elements of society.

Women's Day is an international observance, its date set by the civil calendar, but it has clear resonances with Jewish concerns. The constant Jewish demand for justice finds expression on this day. Any struggle for people's trampled rights must be a Jewish struggle. The Torah expresses concern for the welfare of orphans, strangers, and widows, and the Jewish people has carried this spirit for generations. It is no wonder that Jews stood—and still stand—at the forefront of the feminist struggle, just as they stood and still stand at the forefront of many struggles for human rights and for the recognition of the divine image in all those marginalized and weakened by society.

Like Janus, the two-faced god from Roman mythology, Purim has both a yearning face that notes suffering and existential angst, and also a face that celebrates activism and victory. Feminism is the same way: one side is anguished by women's suffering and fights for their rights, and the other side calls for women's creative expression and empowerment. So too are the two days that we have discussed here: Agunot Day marks the suffering of women chained to a marriage that is nonexistent or without love and mercy, and protests the failure of the religious leadership to help them; International Women's Day symbolizes women's struggle for equality of rights and power and celebrates women's vitality and creativity. Another international day of observance that in most years occurs during the month of Adar is the International Day of the Elimination of Racial Discrimination. This observance is held on the vernal equinox, March 21. The United Nations established this day after an event in 1960 in which South African police opened fire on people protesting apartheid in the town of Sharpville, killing sixty-nine protesters. Symbolically, the day that emphasizes equality between people was scheduled for the day on which there is an equal number of hours of both daylight and darkness. (See pp. 76–79.)

International Women's Day on March 8 also marks the struggle against domestic violence, including violence against women. The silence that so often accompanies crimes committed within a family led Rabbi Naama Dafni-Kellen to compose the following prayer:

A Prayer for the Elimination of Violence against Women

Our God and God of our ancestors, help us to strengthen the broken voice, the silent outcry, of those for whom the protective family walls have become prison walls. There are those who pray that we respond to their suffering, and they cry out:

Put my tear in your bag as well. Let us hear the call of the blood of our brothers and sisters that screams, reminding us that we are created in Your image. For about You it is said: I hear silence as well as a voice.

Help us reveal within ourselves a genuine willingness to help them start anew. May they find the enormous courage to cry out, not to hide, and the hope to create a better future. May we be with them as they reveal incredible inner resources and as they choose life.

To the women who withstand domestic violence, we call out with our whole hearts: Open for me, my sister, raise your voice with power, have no fear. There is reward for your labor. Shed tears like a torrent. I have seen your tears.

You are our sister, you are our sister, you are our sister. May you grow into thousands of myriads.

Our God in heaven, pleqse hear the cry of the poor and rescue them, create in them and in us a new soul, and bring us salvation and life.

Praised are You, Adonai, who in goodness renews daily the purity of the human soul.

Praised are You, Adonai, who strengthens our hands in establishing a society in which all people have the right to live lives full of respect and love.

Please, O God, please heal us.[8]

A Matter of Time: Adar I

We are time's captive, sometimes embraced by it closely, sometimes held more loosely. Time: sometimes it flies, sometimes it moves along slowly, sometimes it actually comes to a halt. That is, of course, how we sense it. Time is relative; different people perceive it differently. My beloved Argentinian sister-in-law looks at the clock hanging on the kitchen wall just as I—with my partly *Yekke* (German Jewish) roots—do, but when we set a time for a family meal, it is clear that the way we each read the clock produces very different results!

We are time's captive, but sometimes time is our captive—up to a point, at least. We try to transcend that point by stuffing an infinite number of activities into every minute of every hour of the day. It sometimes seems that all human activity is a war against time. Then comes Adar I, that modest month that arrives and gets squeezed in and makes our year a month longer; its arrival presents a picture of reconciliation, a portrait of coexistence between heaven and earth. But how?

The lunar year, in which we count the months of the year in the Hebrew calendar, is 11 days shorter than the solar year of 365 days (and a few hours). Were we to rely solely on the lunar calendar, the Jewish holidays would "float" along the whole length of the annual calendar. That is precisely what happens with the Muslim calendar, which relies only on the moon: over time, the Muslim holy month of Ramadan falls in different seasons. For the Jewish calendar, this is a particularly significant point for the holiday of Passover. The Torah tells us to observe the Passover feast in the month of *Aviv*, which means "spring": "Observe the month of Aviv and offer a Passover sacrifice to the Eternal your God, for it was in the month of Aviv . . . that the Eternal your God freed you from Egypt" (Deuteronomy 16:1). Following a strict lunar calendar would gradually distance Passover from the spring season, and we would be celebrating the holiday at the wrong season. To solve this problem, our ancestors devised a calendar that integrates the lunar cycle and the solar cycle, which leaves the seasons at their proper times. To enable the holidays not to "move backward" from their designated seasons, once every few years we add a month at the end of the year—of the biblical year, that is, which begins with the month of Nisan and ends with the month of Adar. And so, as Elul approaches, the aromas of autumn reach our noses (again, in the Northern Hemisphere), and in Nisan, we observe the spring buds.

The extra Adar—Adar I—added to the annual calendar is a modest reflection of the "real" Adar, called Adar II in leap years. All the events of the month—including Purim, Moses's birthday and the anniversary of his death (both on the seventh of Adar), and even birthdays—are marked during Adar II, not Adar I. In some ways, Adar I is a sort of phantom month. Even so, it is in every way a real month, one that we announce on the preceding Shabbat and celebrate as it begins.

The adjustment of the calendar by adding an extra month on a regular basis is a human action designed to deal with two cosmic arrays, two systems for marking time: the lunar, according to which we mark the months and the holidays, and the solar, according to which we mark the seasons. This is a delicate balance that serves to reconcile the cosmic time of nature and the time humans define and establish. The

From Time to Time → Dalia Marx

calendar adjustment is not an act against nature (or against God), but rather an act of cooperation. This is what stood as the foundation of the Sages' concept of time. Time, as we experience it, is a combination of divine and human action. In a midrash on the verse "These are the fixed times of the Eternal, sacred occasions, which you shall call them . . . My festivals, each in its appointed time" (Leviticus 23:2) . . . they relayed the following:

> If the year had to be adjusted, and the [Sages in the court / *beit din*] sat and deliberated and were unable to proclaim "It is adjusted" until after [after] it happened [that is, after it was clear that an adjusted year—a leap year—had already begun], is the year adjusted? It is, therefore, written, "You shall call them—My festivals." If *you* call them, they are My festivals. If not, they are not My festivals.
>
> In another case, the year should not have been adjusted, yet they adjusted it perforce or unwittingly or mistakenly—whence is it derived that it is (nevertheless) adjusted? From the verse (Leviticus 23:4) "These are the fixed times of the Eternal, the sacred occasions, which you shall celebrate [them] each in its appointed time": "them" [אתם, *otam*]—even unwittingly; "them"—even mistakenly; "them"—even under duress; if it is "you" [אתם, *atem*] who called them, they are "My fixed times," and if you did not, they are not My fixed times. (*Sifra, Emor* 9:9)

The midrash playfully reads the three-letter word *alef-tet-mem* (אתם) with different vowels, changing it from *otam* (them) and making it *atem* (you, masculine plural). This gives us the message that the festivals become hallowed only if "you," the people Israel, call them festivals. Even if the *beit din* were to mistakenly adjust a year that should not include an added month of Adar or neglect to add the month when necessary, that year will still be as the Rabbinic court said it should be, rather than as the cosmic, astronomical considerations would have indicated it should be.

The process of **adjusting the calendar year** was secret, known only to the well-informed Sages in the Land of Israel, who would deliberate on this matter:

> When our Sages adjusted the year, ten learned elders would enter the *beit midrash* together with the *av beit din* [the senior judge, head of the court], lock the doors, and discuss the matter the whole night. At midnight they would say to the *av beit din*, "We desire to adjust the year so that it shall have thirteen months. Do you concur with us?" To which he would reply, "Whatever your decision, I accept it." At that moment, a light would proceed from the *beit midrash* and come toward them. They thus knew that God was pleased with them. (*Sh'mot Rabbah* 16:20)

This midrash paints a lovely picture of how the Blessed Holy One sent out light from the *beit midrash* as proof of God's approval of the Rabbis' intercalation. Setting up the calendar is a cooperative undertaking of heaven and earth, a partnership between the Divine and the human.

For many generations, the astronomical considerations behind the calendrical adjustment were known to the Sages of the Land of Israel

---

Before the calendar was fixed by established rules, according to which we can know in advance when a "pregnant" or "leap" year is anticipated, the decision about the length of the calendar year was made every year by the Sanhedrin, the supreme Rabbinic court, on the basis of the moon's position. However, there was not universal agreement about the calendar: in the Second Temple period, there were Jewish sects that calculated the calendar according to a fixed, unchanging cycle. The apocryphal Book of Jubilees, for example, describes a calendar according to which the year is fixed and divided into four equal segments, each of which has thirteen weeks and begins with a special day. This calendar may have been entirely theoretical, or it may have reflected a cultic calendar of a Dead Sea sect:[9]

> On the first of the first month, the first of the fourth month, the first of the seventh month, and the first of the tenth month are the days of remembrance and the days of the seasons. At the four divisions of the year they are written down and ordained as an eternal testimony. . . . All the days of the commandments are fifty-two weeks of days, a complete whole year.
>
> Now you, command the Children of Israel to observe the years according to this number: 364 days. It is a complete year. It will not corrupt its proper time, from its days or its festivals. (Jubilees 6:23–32)

The sectarian calendar was not accepted by the Jewish people, and some claim that it was only theoretical and never actually observed. Either way, this calendar presents a fixed and static picture determined by heaven and unaffected by human actions, unlike the Rabbinic calendar, in which God and people join together to establish the patterns of time.

Tishrei   Marcheshvan   Kislev   Tevet   Sh'vat   Adar   Nisan   Iyar   Sivan   Tammuz   Av   Elul

and was kept a secret ("the secret of calendrical adjustment"). Since the middle of the fourth century, the calendar has been fixed by predetermined rules. Therefore, there is no longer a need to establish the time of the new moon's appearance on the basis of witness testimony, and we can know which years will have thirteen months even a century in advance. And yet, the affirmation of time bears in its DNA the ancient method reflecting collaboration of heaven and earth.

"I'm About to Lose Control, and I Think I Like It"

The addition of the month of Adar and the adjustment of the year teach us an interesting lesson: in order to influence the world and act with, within, and maybe even beyond time, one must first accept time, the changes in the year, and the changes in one's life. We have to understand that we have no real control over our lives and our time, nor are we able to understand them fully. Despite the arbitrary nature of time and its changes—or maybe precisely because of them—we have a good deal of freedom and choice. And before we enter the great joy of Adar II, the "real" Adar, let us pause for a moment during that human invention, the time tunnel known as Adar I, and give some thought to the passage of time and the changes it brings about in us—may they be for the better!

"Pregnant" Years and Pregnant Women

It may be surprising to discover that the term the Rabbis gave for the addition of a month to the year is the very same term that they used for pregnancy—*ibur*. The baby gestating in a **"pregnant" year** is the additional month of Adar.

The shared term is no accident. Many cultures noted a similarity between the cosmic cycle of the moon and women's menstrual cycle. Both last about twenty-eight days; both are processes of growth, fullness, and contraction. This is how Rabbi Moshe ben Yitzchak of Vienna (1180–1250) describes it in his book *Or Zarua*:

> Know that each month a woman is renewed and immerses [in a ritual bath] and returns to her husband as dear to him as on their wedding day. Just as the moon is renewed at each Rosh Chodesh and all are eager to see it, so it is with a woman: when she is renewed each month, her husband is eager for her and she is as dear to him as a new woman, as it were. And that is why Rosh Chodesh is a holiday for women. (*Or Zarua*, Rosh Chodesh, 453)

Rabbi Moshe ben Yitzchak draws a comparison between the renewal of the moon and a woman's monthly renewal. (Note that the Hebrew term for "month," *chodesh*, is from the same root as the term for "new," *chadash*.) He also mentions that the similarity between the two phenomena lead to Rosh Chodesh being understood as a women's holiday.

In many languages there is a linguistic connection between the words for the two cycles—the lunar and the feminine. For example, the term

---

In addition to declaring years "**pregnant**," the Rabbis of classical Judaism also declared months "pregnant." The timing of Rosh Chodesh was decided on the basis of witness testimony on the "birth" of the moon as it began to wax. Whoever spotted the new moon in the sky would come before the Rabbinic court and give testimony. The testimony of all the witnesses would be accepted after careful examination. This is how the Mishnah depicts the examination of the witnesses:

> How did they examine the witnesses? The pair that arrives first they examine first. They bring in the elder of the two, and they say to him, "Tell us how you saw the moon: Facing the sun or turned away from it? To the north or to the south? How high was it? To which side was it leaning? And how broad was it?" . . . Rabban Gamliel had pictures of the shapes of the moon. . . . These he used to show to the unskilled and say, "Did you see it like this or like that?" (*Mishnah Rosh HaShanah* 2:6, 8)

Once the court confirmed the testimony, the head of the court would announce that the thirtieth day since the last month began was now consecrated as the first day, the Rosh Chodesh, of the next month (and the previous month had been one of twenty-nine days, not thirty). But if the testimony was insufficient or the moon had not been visible (because of clouds, for example), the month that was ending was considered "full"—that is, a thirty-day month, and the next day would be Rosh Chodesh of the next month. This was a procedure fraught with tension, as the Rabbis knew—whoever controls time, controls the conversation! (See *Mishnah Rosh HaShanah* 2:8–9.)

From Time to Time → Dalia Marx

in English for women's monthly cycle, "menstruation," as with Romance languages, is derived from the Latin term for "month," *mensis*. However, it is also possible to see a connection between the lunar cycle and the cycle of human life as a whole. Our ancestors lived close to nature. The lunar cycle symbolized and expressed for them the entire circle of life: birth, youth, ripeness, old age, death, and rebirth. The lunar cycle teaches us a lesson in humility and in optimism. The full moon, whole and shining, will grow smaller and draw into itself; so too our lives, in which peak periods of progress and flourishing are not eternal. That is the way of the world. But the moment is never far off in which the moon (and in the same sense, our lives) will again begin to fill up.

Let us return to the idea of pregnant years. The process of determining which year is a leap year and therefore needs the additional thirteenth month is described in Rabbinic literature as something intimate and secret. In the same way, the act of human conception is private and shrouded in mystery. The former is about the secrets of the universe, and the latter is about the hidden human aspects of relationship and choice. In a way, the adjustment of the calendar is also about a couple—the sun and the moon—and their relationship: their unique interactions as together they set the calendar and create time. Perhaps there is a kind of relationship between the human realm and the cosmic one, too, which together shape our perception of time.

According to tradition, women received Rosh Chodesh as a special festive time unique to them because they did not take part in the sin of the Golden Calf, "and the Blessed Holy One gave them their reward in this world: they observe Rosh Chodesh more than men do" (*Pirkei D'Rabbi Eliezer* 45:4). There is evidence that in the past women would celebrate Rosh Chodesh together. The *Shulchan Aruch* designates the custom of women resting on Rosh Chodesh as a "good custom" (*Shulchan Aruch, Orach Chayim* 417:1).

In recent decades, many women have renewed the tradition of women's Rosh Chodesh celebrations. Groups of women meet for study, prayer, artistic creation, and shared conversation on Rosh Chodesh. For years, I have been a member of a Rosh Chodesh group in which we customarily open each meeting with a candle-lighting ceremony. Each woman lights a candle, presents herself along with her female family lineage (in my case, for example: Dalia Sara, daughter of Yael, daughter of Sarah, daughter of Miriam; granddaughter of Ruth, daughter of Yente), and recites a short prayer in anticipation of the new month. In that way we invoke the presence of our mothers' foremothers at our gathering and add to its sanctity.

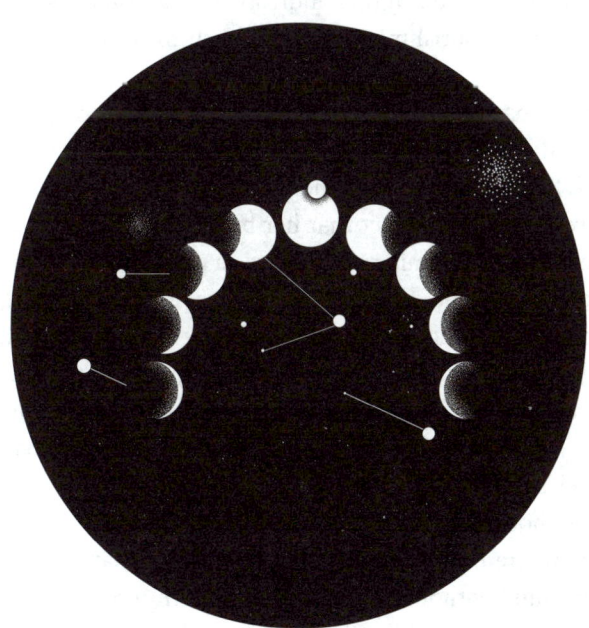

Tishrei Marcheshvan Kislev Tevet Sh'vat *Adar* Nisan Iyar Sivan Tammuz Av Elul

"Everything Turned Upside Down: Switching Gender on Purim

WE ARE NOT THE ONLY ONES who dress up in costume on Purim. The Purim story itself dresses up in costume: it is full of hidden moves and switched roles. The *M'gillah* contains the Purim watchword, *v'nahafoch hu* ("and it was turned upside down" [Esther 9:1]). Accordingly, among the various disguises in the *M'gillah*, instances of gender role reversal stand out. One example is the eunuchs, who play a key role in shaping the story and enabling Esther's victory. The eunuchs guarded the women while they prepared for their encounter with King Ahasuerus, and simultaneously cared for them, providing them with everything they needed. In a way, the eunuchs had their own unique gender role. They are men who underwent castration. As a result, they could approach government officials (something women could not do) and they could also be alone with women (something men could not do). They are referred to in the masculine, yet are immersed in a feminine world.

Another example is none other than Mordechai, who adopted his relative, young Esther, as a daughter when she was orphaned and who saw to all her needs. A midrash attributed to Rabbi Yudan relates the story of a miraculous gender switch that happened to Mordechai:

> Once, [Mordechai] went looking and searched among all the wet nurses but did not find a wet nurse for Esther, so he nursed her himself. (*B'reishit Rabbah* 30:8)

Mordechai's concern for his infant relative was so great that he diligently went searching high and low for a wet nurse, and when he found no other solution, his own body began to lactate and he nursed her. In this midrash, Mordechai physically transforms so as to provide the baby's nourishment. The midrash provides a complex view on gender roles.

Unlike the amazing change Mordechai was privileged to undergo, another midrash depicts what the Rabbis consider to be a monstrous reversal that happened to Queen Vashti. In the Babylonian Talmud, her refusal to appear before the king and the feast he held is explained by the fact that her beauty had been corrupted and her body disfigured. According to the midrash, this was a punishment for treating Jewish women cruelly. In one midrashic description, she broke out in *tzaraat*, the biblical skin ailment; according to another, "[the angel] Gabriel came and made her a tail" (Babylonian Talmud, *M'gillah* 12b). What is the meaning of Vashti's tail? On the one hand, it moves her from the human realm and transforms her into an animal. On the other hand, "tail" may be a euphemism here for "penis" (as it is in many languages, including German and Yiddish).

Why did our Sages choose this particular interpretation of Vashti, making a laughingstock of the tragic figure of a bold woman who dared to say no to the whims of her drunken husband—and without any hint of such an interpretation in the source material? It seems to me that they identified her strong-willed, assertive behavior as "masculine" and consequently "punished" her by attacking her beauty and femininity. In this way, perhaps the Rabbinic interpretations participate in the concern of the people of Shushan that women might show too much independence.

Another figure, one who does not appear in the Book of Esther but whose characteristics and whose story are "in dialogue" with it, is Judith (see p. 101), a wondrous character whose book did not make it into our biblical canon but remained in the Apocrypha. In order to save her people from the conqueror Holofernes, Judith changed out of her widow's clothing to make her beauty visible. With her clever mind and unflappable demeanor, she first tricked Holofernes into thinking she supported his military endeavor and was also ready to submit to him sexually, before reversing her role and beheading him. In using her status as a woman yet transcending gender expectations, she succeeded in leading the people Israel to a brilliant victory.

Judith's character and actions integrate qualities that were generally understood as masculine—leadership, assertiveness, a coolheaded nature, even cruelty, alongside those understood as feminine—modesty, submissiveness, and seduction, all of which she employs wisely and prudently. The story of Judith served as a kind of correction for that of Esther: Judith did not give herself over to the foreign king but instead murdered him, thus heralding defeat for Israel's enemies.

We see in Judith's story, as in the Purim story, gender fluidity and unclear gender identities. What can this literary blurring of gender roles and identities teach us about Purim for our time and about our lives?

To answer that, let us return for a moment to the Torah's prohibition against cross-dressing: "A woman must not put on man's apparel, nor shall a man wear woman's clothing; for whoever does these things is abhorrent to the Eternal your God" (Deuteronomy 22:5). The Rabbinic reasons given for this command are the avoidance of licentiousness and a concern for preserving social norms. Despite this prohibition (or perhaps because of it?), there is a widely known custom of dressing in gender-crossing costumes on Purim.

The custom of going in costume on Purim is first documented in thirteenth-century Italy, apparently under the influence of the carnival in Christian society. As early as the fourteenth century, we find reference to gender-crossing costumes. In his book *Even Bochan* (c. 1322), Rabbi Kalonymus ben Kalonymus describes the custom he was familiar with:

> On the fourteenth day of the month of Adar,
> Jewish lads from near and far
> make merry with grandeur and glory;
> it's a wild and raucous story.
> They recall the wonders and make miracles known
> wearing anklets and bangles that women own....
> One wears a woman's dress and necklace,

It seems that gender and the division of gender roles were on the minds of Kalonymus ben Kalonymus and his contemporaries; elsewhere Kalonymus writes about the gloomy state of affairs of being male in this world. The suffering man is pained by his fate and envies women. He cannot be consoled about that "immutable deformity" that he believes marks him as a man.[10] His lament about being a man ends with his frustrated acceptance that he must recite the traditional blessing that thanks God "for not having made me a woman."[11]

> God in heaven
> who did miracles for our ancestors with fire
>   and water:
> You transformed the fire of Ur of the Chaldees
>   so it would not burn [Abraham].
> You transformed Dinah [to a girl] in the
>   womb of her mother [Leah].
> You transformed the staff [of Moses] to a
>   snake before a million eyes.
> You transformed [Moses's] hand to
>   [diseased] white
> and the Sea of Reeds to dry land
> and the sea floor into solid and dried-up
>   earth.
> You transformed the rock into water,
> hard flint to a fountain.
> Who would then transform me from a man
>   to woman?
> Were I only to have merited this being so
>   graced by goodness
> I could have now been the lady of the house,
> exempt from military service!
> What shall I say?
> Why cry or be bitter?
> If God in heaven has decreed upon me
> and has maimed me with an immutable
>   deformity,
> then I do not wish to remove it.
> The sorrow of the impossible is a human pain
>   that nothing will cure
> and for which no comfort can be found.
> So I will bear and suffer until I die and wither
>   in the ground.
> Since I have learned from our tradition
> that we bless both, the good and the bitter,
> I will bless in a voice hushed and weak:
> "Blessed are You, Eternal, who has not made
>   me a woman."[12]

 another pretends to be wild and reckless.
With drumming and dancing and joy they regale,
these with those, male with female.[13]

What Will Become of Modesty?

In the *Shulchan Aruch* by Yosef Karo (1488–1575), which codifies Sephardic practice, the custom of dressing up in costume on Purim is not mentioned, leading us to believe that among Sephardic Jews this custom was not known in his time. However, Rabbi Moshe Isserles (1520–72), known as the Rema, whose addenda to the *Shulchan Aruch* describes Ashkenazic customs, says:

> And as for the custom of wearing masks on Purim, and men wearing women's dresses and women wearing men's clothes, no prohibition is violated by doing so, since the purpose is just for simple joy. ... And some say that it is forbidden, but the prevailing custom is according to the prior opinion. (gloss to *Orach Chayim* 696:8)

For Isserles, wearing gender-crossing clothing is permitted on Purim, since its purpose is to express holiday joy, to be happy and rejoice. The permission to dress up may have been retroactive: a reluctant accommodation to reality, and an acceptance of the principle that "it is better that people sin unwittingly than that they do so intentionally." Since the Jews living in the Christian world may have been influenced by the Christian custom of dressing in costume for carnival, it is possible that Isserles and his contemporaries believed the Jewish practice of wearing costumes had become so popular that it would be difficult to decree against it. It is also possible they actually saw value in this type of dressing up.

However, even in the Rema's time, there was opposition to his opinion. His statement even stirred up a debate among the experts in halachah, with some permitting the practice and others warning about the dangers involved in gender-crossing costumes on Purim. In granting permission to experiment with dress on Purim, some saw the danger of violating accepted gender norms. Others believed this "controlled experimentation" served as a kind of bulwark against further experimentation within society's prescribed gender boundaries. Then there were those who regarded gender-crossing costumes as an exercise intended to enable everyone to experience a variety of identities, thus allowing them to find their own unique identity. I will end with the words of the Talmud:

> One who sees a multitude of Israelites says:
> "Blessed is the Holy One who discerns secrets,
> for the mind of each is different from that of the other,
> just as the face of each is different from that of the other."
> (Babylonian Talmud, *B'rachot* 58a)

Many cultures have customs of dressing in costume and assuming different identities—for a limited time. One well-known example is the Christian institution of carnival, marking the beginning of the liturgical season of Lent that precedes Easter. Known throughout the world by various names, the carnival celebrations create a challenging alternative to the social order. Differences of age, gender, and status are erased, and power becomes the butt of humor and derision. Venice's carnival of masks, which lasts for two weeks, is especially well-known, as is Mardi Gras in New Orleans. Hiding their faces behind masks, the residents of the city could mix freely with one other. Perhaps there is really nothing at all frivolous about that frivolity. Carnival often acted as a pressure valve for the people of the lower classes. It enabled them to remove the proverbial yoke off their back for a predetermined period and let them do wild and disrespectful things precisely so that for the rest of the year they would accept their social status without protest.

In using language like "gender-crossing" and "cross-dressing," we are referring to the ancient context in which the Rabbis and following generations were writing. Many in contemporary society no longer believe that clothing has gender—women can wear pants and men can wear dresses without seeing themselves as "cross-dressers." This language of "crossing" is meant to highlight the ways our tradition has shown examples of transcending gender norms and expectations. (Rabbi Ariel Tovlev)

Purim Sheini: A Second Purim

Rabbi Purim, Rabbi Purim,	רַבִּי פּוּרִים, רַבִּי פּוּרִים,
won't you tell me why,	אֱמֹר נָא לִי מַדּוּעַ,
why Purim doesn't come	מַדּוּעַ לֹא יָחוּל פּוּרִים
twice in every week?[14]	פַּעֲמַיִם בַּשָּׁבוּעַ?

The question asked in the stanza from a children's song (*Ani Purim*) by Levin Kipnis is based on an assumption that is not entirely accurate. Local "Purim" celebrations have been celebrated throughout the year in various Jewish communities. The educator and folklore scholar Yom Tov Levinsky (1899–1973) counted ninety such "Purim" days—approaching an average of two a week—spread across the entire year that were celebrated among Jews in various places around the world.[15] These days are known as Purim Sheini, a "second Purim," which commemorates the rescues and miracles that occurred to a whole community or to a family.

Purim, like other Jewish holidays, is celebrated at the same time in the month of Adar by all Jewish communities. (The only exception is Shushan Purim, when Purim is celebrated a day late in walled cities such as Jerusalem.) Taken as a whole, the year's Jewish holidays and observations reflect an awareness, albeit a bit idealized, that at one time we were together as one and experienced the foundational experiences of our people. All of us received the Torah at Mount Sinai (and according to a midrash, the souls of future Jews-by-choice were there as well). We all experienced the destruction of the Temple, and the danger in Haman's decree threatened all Jews. In truth, though, already at a very early stage the Jews were dispersed into a variety of locations around the world, and their basic experiences were very different, depending on the time and place in which they lived. The existential experience of a Jew in Fez in Morocco was quite different from that of a Jew in Venice, a small town in Bavaria, or a village in the Cochin district of India. The life history of a Jew in Toledo during the Golden Age of Spanish Jewry was quite different from that of a Jew living in Toledo during the period of the Inquisition. The "Second Purim" days took shape in response to the unique life and communal experiences of each community.

These special days were established by communities in the West and East alike, and they were observed for many centuries, from the Middle Ages to the Holocaust. Sometimes a Second Purim was still celebrated by the émigrés from a particular community even after they left it.

"Anyone for Whom a Miracle Occurred"

Rabbi Avraham Danzig (1748–1820), who was active in Vilna, formulated the guiding principle of a Purim Sheini. He explained, "Any individual for whom a miracle occurred, and all the more so a town or city, can institute, by agreement and with a ban [for nonobservance] on them and all that come after them, to observe that Purim day. And it seems to me that the meal they make in honor of the miracle is a required meal [*s'udat mitzvah*] and not just a festive banquet." And as an example he describes a rescue incident his own family experienced:

Tishrei   Marcheshvan   Kislev   Tevet   Sh'vat   **Adar**   Nisan   Iyar   Sivan   Tammuz   Av   Elul

> And so we do regarding the miracle performed for us in the year 5064, on the night before the fifteenth of Kislev [in mid-December 1303], when there was a mass death in the courtyard where I live because of a fire that broke out from the *polver* [gunpowder] and a few of the houses in the courtyard came down, including one of my own . . . and the wall fell on my daughter Vitke until there was only a brief step between her and death, and my wife was injured in the face. . . . And of all the members of my household, including me, there was not one who didn't lose at least a few drops of blood. And the Eternal, may [God] be praised, in . . . mercy and kindness considered that blood as a sacrifice of atonement, and [God] saved us, and all of us remained alive, although I did sustain great damages, a few hundred reds [a type of coin] God exchanged in kindness, money [*damim*] in place of blood [*damim*].[16]

Rabbi Danzig describes being rescued from a fire that seems to have been sparked by an explosion of gunpowder. No one was injured, and the "reds" (coins of blood-red color) were spilled rather than blood, to cover the cost of the damages. To mark that familial miracle, Danzig adds, he took it upon himself and his household to mark their rescue for all generations:

> I accepted upon myself and my descendants, without a formal vow, the day of the fifteenth of Kislev, which is in any case, in many communities in our district, a fast day for the G'milut Chasadim Society, to make it into a day almost half of which is given over to the Eternal, and in any case anyone who is able will fast, and that night they will gather together right after the *Maariv* prayers and light candles as is done on festivals and recite *Shir HaYichud* [a *piyut* in praise of God] pleasantly and slowly, and *Shir HaKavod* [another *piyut* in praise of God] in song, and after that some psalms are to be recited slowly. . . . And after that, they should have a festive meal for those who study Torah, anyone who can be there, and give *tzedakah* in whatever amount they can, as the Eternal has blessed them. May the Eternal heal the people's ailments.[17]

It is interesting that the day the Danzig family was saved comes as the continuation of a special fast for the G'milut Chasadim Society. Danzig specifies explicit religious practices that he took upon himself to observe on that day, such as lighting candles, "as is done on festivals," and singing *piyutim*, as is customary on Shabbat.

Surprising Religious Audaciousness

In a few communities, poems and scrolls (*m'gillot*) were composed to commemorate the local miracle. In Casablanca, Morocco, for example, the teacher Asher Hassin composed a text in 1943 called *M'gillat Hitler*, which offered thanks for the rescue of Moroccan Jewry by the Allies and expressed sorrow for the disaster befalling European Jewry. The "Hitler Scroll" opens with these words:

> And it was in the days of Hitler the painter, he being the corporal dictator over all Germany, seventeen provinces. In those days, this villain sat on the throne of his government in Berlin the capital. . . .

It concludes:

> It is upon us to establish this day of salvation in its time, on the eleventh of November, like the days when the Jews rested from Haman, and the month turned from sadness to joy for us, to make it a day of feasting and joy and gifts to the needy. . . .

> Cursed be Hitler! Cursed be Mussolini! Cursed be Tojo! Cursed be Himmler! Cursed be Goering! Cursed be Goebbels! Cursed be Hess! . . . Cursed be all the evil ones![18]

This *m'gillah*, in the style of *M'gillat Esther*, instructs the Jews of Casablanca to make a "Hitler Purim," a day of drinking and rejoicing and gifts to the poor. It is interesting to note that the *m'gillah* begins with a sort of blessing for reading it: "Blessed are You, *Avinu*, who constantly has mercy upon us, crushes our enemies underneath us, and grants us the privilege of reading this *m'gillah*." This is not a complete liturgical blessing—it lacks some of the requisite "Blessed are You, Eternal our God . . ." formula—but it no doubt fulfills the religious function (if not to the halachic standard) of a blessing. In other places the religious indicators of the Second Purim were even more explicit, and they included—in addition to the recitation of a *m'gillah* describing the events of the day—the *Al HaNisim* (For the Miracles) prayer composed especially to mark the event, as well as the recitation of *Hallel* (Psalms 113–118). The custom of reciting *Hallel* is particularly interesting, given that on Purim itself, *Hallel* is not recited (see p. 152).

The Second Purim observances reflect religious and cultural creativity. They opened the door to ritual and liturgical innovation, engendered a great deal of creativity, and sometimes even displayed audacity regarding Jewish law. In the lively polemics that took place within religious Zionism during the establishment of the State of Israel (which, to a large extent, continue to this day) about the religious character of Yom HaAtzma-ut (Israel's Independence Day), for example, it might have been possible to cite the dozens of instances of communities that had not hesitated to establish new holidays of a clearly religious character on their annual calendar.

Perhaps the concept of a Second Purim can be broadened even further. Maybe it would be appropriate to celebrate more holidays for individuals, families, and communities. In this manner, the general national holiday sends out a sort of secret internal hint or message to individuals, families, and communities to personalize the holiday and give meaning to important events in their own history. For example, perhaps we could imagine celebrating a "Second Passover," not necessarily in its biblical sense but rather as a commemoration of individuals or families going out into symbolic or actual freedom. Maybe it would be appropriate to celebrate a "Second Shavuot" to mark the time when we had a life-changing insight, a sort of personal "giving of the Torah." Many of us observe a personal Yom Kippur (even if we don't call it that) on which we remember a particular soul-searching or a commitment to self-improvement that we've undertaken. We might even relate to our birthdays and those of family members and loved ones as a personal Rosh HaShanah.

Yom Tov Levinsky notes that in certain cases, some fast days were even canceled in order to observe a communal Purim Sheini. Rabbi Yonatan of Fulda, in Germany, for example, made the fast of the seventeenth of Tammuz into a Second Purim to commemorate his community's escape from danger, and in Morocco the Fast of the Firstborn was canceled on the day before Passover in order to commemorate the rescue of the community, transforming a fast day into a festive occasion. According to Levinsky, in some places Jews even refrained from work on Purim Sheini, meaning they gave it the status of an actual traditional and ancient festival.[19]

Prayer of the Month

Esther Does *T'shuvah*

GOD'S NAME IS NOT MENTIONED in the Book of Esther, apparently quite deliberately. Esther and Mordechai do not act the way some believed Jews should act. Their names are foreign. There is no evidence at all in the *M'gillah* that they lived according to Jewish practices. The book's story takes place outside the Land of Israel, and there is no hint that any of the protagonists long for Zion. Worse than that, Mordechai pushed young Esther into the arms of the foreign king. All these elements led the Rabbis to waver on the question of whether to include Esther in the biblical canon. Among the biblical books found among the Dead Sea Scrolls there was not one copy of Esther, and some scholars have ventured to say that the people of the Qumran community had qualms about the book's daring secular nature.

According to Rabbi Sh'muel bar Y'hudah (a Babylonian sage who move to the Land of Israel), Esther herself came and stood before the Rabbis, demanding of them, "Set me in place [to commemorate me] for [all future] generations! . . . Write an account of me for [all future] generations!" (Babylonian Talmud, *M'gillah* 7a). The Book of Esther did in fact enter the Jewish canon of twenty-four biblical books, but it still causes discomfort. In order to counter the permissive, if not assimilationist, character of the *M'gillah* and to justify its place in the canon, some readers have searched for evidence of divinity hidden between the lines.

Some have claimed that within the book there is a profound but hidden religious stance, which is why it is sometimes referred to not as *M'gillat Esther* but rather *m'gillat hahester*, "the scroll of concealment." They argue that God is at work throughout the scroll, but concealed behind the scenes. There is a scribal tradition to write out the *M'gillah* in such a way that at the top of each column, the same word appears: *hamelech*, "the king." The king in the story is Ahasuerus, but that scribal trope hints that the "King who is the Ruler of rulers," not the flesh-and-blood king of Persia, truly rules over the events in the scroll. Another method used to address the challenges posed by the Book of Esther is to juxtapose it with an alternative text that rights its perceived wrongs, such as what we find in the Book of Judith, which was written during Second Temple times. Judith was considered a proper, modest Jew, who brought her people victory not by submission to the ruler but by heroically killing him. The ways of biblical canonization are hidden: Esther entered the Bible while pure; praiseworthy Judith did not.

Additions to the Book of Esther in the Septuagint

The fact that God's name is not included in the Book of Esther caused questions about the sanctity of the book and its inclusion in the biblical canon.[20] One of the most ancient attempts to manage these challenges are the additions made to it during the Second Temple era that have been preserved in the Septuagint, the Greek translation of the Hebrew Bible (see pp. 108–10). The additions to the book were apparently originally composed in Hebrew, but the only evidence we have are their Greek translations. These additional passages reflect a religious viewpoint attributed to Esther and Mordechai, including a prayer by each of them in turn. Here, for example, is Esther's prayer and the preparations she makes before prayer as she approaches King Ahasuerus:

> Then Queen Esther, seized with mortal anguish, fled to the Eternal. She took off the garments of her honor and put on the garments of distress and mourning, and instead of costly perfumes, she covered her head with ashes and dung, and she utterly humbled her body; every part that she loved to adorn she covered with her tangled hair. (Esther 14:1–2 in the Septuagint)

After she makes these painstaking preparations, including donning mourning clothes, covering herself in ashes, and fasting, we read, "She prayed to the Eternal God of Israel and said. . . ." The prayer opens with praise for God's acts of kindness and a recognition of her own sins and those of her people. In that way she hopes to arouse God's mercy. And she continues:

> O my Eternal, You alone are our Ruler; help me, who am alone and have no helper but You, for my danger is in my hand. . . .
>
> And now we have sinned before You, and You have delivered us into the hands of our enemies because we glorified their gods. . . .
>
> O Eternal, do not surrender Your scepter to what has no being, and do not let them laugh at our downfall, but turn their plan against them and make an example of him who began this against us. . . .
>
> You have knowledge of all things, and You know that I hate the splendor of the lawless and abhor the bed of the uncircumcised and of any alien. You know my trouble, that I abhor the sign of my proud position that is upon my head on days when I appear in public . . . and I do not wear it on the days when I am at rest. And Your servant has not eaten at Haman's table, and I have not honored the king's feast or drunk the wine of libations. Your servant has had no joy since the day that I was brought here until now, except in You, O Eternal God of Abraham. O God, whose might is over all, hear the voice of the despairing and save us from the hands of evildoers. And save me from my fear! (Esther 14:3–19 in the Septuagint[21])

In this version of the story, Esther says she became queen not from a personal desire but from a lack of any other alternative, and that she detests her situation and the king to whom she is married. She promises that despite her life in the palace, she has observed the commandments of Judaism, has not eaten unkosher food or drunk unkosher wine. She also did not wear her crown on Shabbat, so as to avoid violating the prohibition against carrying things from place to place. In her prayer, Esther mentions that she is an orphan and alone, and she places her hope in God. She concludes the prayer with a request for her people's salvation ("hear the voice of the despairing") and for herself as well ("and save me from my fear").

This prayer as well as other additions to the book are placed in Esther's mouth so as to allay any suspicion that the *M'gillah* was unworthy to enter the Holy Scriptures. Their purpose is to testify that the characters' intentions were for the greater glory of God.

Tishrei   Marcheshvan   Kislev   Tevet   Sh'vat   Adar   Nisan   Iyar   Sivan   Tammuz   Av   Elul

During the pandemic, my dear mentor Professor Avigdor Shinan and I had a conversation about Esther and how little the biblical story tells us about her feelings, hopes, and fears. I don't remember who had the idea, but we ended up writing a play about Esther that tells the story of Purim in her own words. It is an attempt to uplift Esther, give her a voice, and open a window to her experiences, emotions, anxieties, wishes, and joys. This brief excerpt shows Esther remembering her childhood and the times Mordechai taught her to read and write—something that until recently was quite rare for women but in her case is documented in the Bible (Esther 9:29). Her empowerment then empowered others:

> Twilight falls in Lat. I rest my quill next to my parchment on my writing desk. My servant rushes with a sort of holy anxiety to pack the writing tools in a gold box, roll up the parchment, and lock it in a drawer. She gives me the key, so that I may hide it away.
>
> She loves to look at me as I write, her eyes shining and her head moving unknowingly, following the movement of my hand as I write words on the parchment. In her eyes, this is something magical—a woman and a writer. Worlds are created by the quill, but who will ever understand?
>
> I reflect on my old life, before I was brought to the king's palace, thinking about my life with Mordechai ben Yair. After dinner, Mordechai would draw the curtains tightly closed. Tired and drained from a day of intrigue, he would pull out old quills and parchment and place them on the table before me. I never understood why my cousin bothered to teach me . . . [but] the gift of reading and writing rescue me from boredom and meaningless existence in the palace.[22]

It seems that when each generation reads *M'gillat Esther*, there is a new urgency to address perceived absences in the original story. In our time, it means searching for and amplifying Esther's own unique voice, perspective, and experience.

Esther Prays in Ladino

Modern reworkings of the Book of Esther have also sought to give it a heightened religious dimension. One of those is a musical play in Ladino entitled *Esther*. The words were written in 1932 by Shlomo Reuven Mordejai, who was born in Thessaloniki, Greece, in 1908, moved to the Land of Israel in his youth, and lived there until his death in 1984. The melodies were composed by Isaac Sion (d. 1943). The musical includes a wealth of prayers and supplications in the face of the travails of the Jews, as well as thanks and praise following their rescue. *Esther* was written one year before the Nazis' rise to power in Germany and about a decade before the expulsion of Thessaloniki's Jews to Auschwitz, where most of them were murdered. This difficult historical context makes the play's prayers for rescue particularly poignant.[23]

Most of the prayers are recited with passionate concern by a chorus that accompanies the characters through the events of the play. This is the prayer of the chorus when Haman's murderous plan becomes known (act I, scene 2):

Dió, porké abandonarmos?	My God, why do You abandon us?
Oh, siente muestra orasión!	Hear our cry and come hence!
Dió santo! Kómo salvarmos?	Holy God, rush to save us!
Kómo salvarse tu nasión?	Rush to Your people's defense.
Amán el negro, el potente	That evil Haman
Kiere la fin de Israel.	A decree for our death has penned.
Deshas tu vinir la muerte	Will You stand by and watch as we die?
Para tu puevlo eternel?	Is this to be Israel's end?
Dió, porké abandonarmos?	My God, why do You abandon us?
Oh, siente muestra orasión!	Hear our cry and come hence!
Dió santo! Kómo salvarmos?	Holy God, rush to save us!
Kómo salvarse tu nasión?[24]	Rush to Your people's defense.

Throughout the ages, the Jewish tradition has sought ways to make Esther into the "ideal" Jewish woman. Sadly, chapter 10, the final chapter of the Scroll of Esther, speaks exclusively about Mordechai and neglects to mention Esther. This is a task we have—to give voice to the silenced. In this case, the silenced one is Esther. In doing so, we follow Jewish culture and lore ascribing great importance to Esther, the Jewish queen who reigned over 127 provinces, through literature, art, and popular culture. What Esther really felt and thought is up to each one of us to imagine and to envision her in her lofty—yet dangerous and challenging—role.

From Time to Time → Dalia Marx

NISAN

Zodiac Sign: Aries | Tribe of the Month: Reuben
Breastplate Stone: Ruby/*Odem*

The name Nisan, which came to the Land of Israel with the returning exiles from Babylon, appears only in the later books of the Hebrew Bible—those that took shape during the early Second Temple period (Esther 3:7; Nehemiah 2:1). The meaning of the name is "bud," like the Hebrew *nitzan*, and indeed in the Middle East it is the month of budding and flowering. Other names include "the month of the *aviv*," with *aviv* referring to ripened grain in the field, and "the first month," of which Exodus 12:2 famously says, "This month shall mark for you the beginning of the months; it shall be the first of the months of the year for you." There are traditions according to which one uses ruby as an amulet for a woman giving birth, perhaps because its deep color resembles the shades in the human flesh or because the Hebrew word for *ruby* is derived from the Hebrew word for *red*. How appropriate it is, then, that this stone from the priestly garments is identified with Reuben, firstborn of the tribes, and with Nisan, the month in which the Jews were born as a people.

Tishrei   Marcheshvan   Kislev   Tevet   Sh'vat   Adar   Nisan   Iyar   Sivan   Tammuz   Av   Elul

KAVANAH: A MEDITATION FOR NISAN

THE PASSOVER HAGGADAH tells us, "As in every age and generation, the task is ours: to see ourselves as if we had come out of Egypt."[1] In every generation, we should identify with our ancestors' troubles and rejoice in their rescue. An additional meaning of this precept is that we should think about our own lives within that framework. We need to remember that every one of us has a personal Egypt that we must leave again and again; that there will be a frightening crossing of the Sea of Reeds through which we must be continually reborn; that we must walk a long way through a threatening wilderness in order to arrive at our destination.

Every Person Needs an Egypt
    Rabbi Amnon Ribak

כָּל אָדָם צָרִיךְ מִצְרַיִם
הָרַב אַמְנוֹן רִיבְּקָה

Everyone should have some kind of Egypt in their lives,
To find Moses within themselves,
To struggle out, and strive.
To have to fight,
With a hand of might
Or with gritted teeth to seek the light,
To walk through darkness, and survive.

כָּל אָדָם צָרִיךְ שֶׁתִּהְיֶה לוֹ
אֵיזוֹ מִצְרַיִם,
לִהְיוֹת מֹשֶׁה עַצְמוֹ מִתּוֹכָהּ,
בְּיָד חֲזָקָה,
אוֹ בַּחֲרִיקַת שִׁנַּיִם.

Everyone should have some kind of Egypt in their past:
The dream, the dread,
The bond, the hand that they can always trust.
To learn to cast their sore eyes heavenwards —
Every person needs a prayer, one, to know by heart.
Every person should, for once at least, be bowed,
Everyone should have a shoulder, to lean on in the crowd.

כָּל אָדָם צָרִיךְ אֵימָה וַחֲשֵׁכָה גְּדוֹלָה,
וְנֶחָמָה, וְהַבְטָחָה, וְהַצָּלָה,
שֶׁיֵּדַע לָשֵׂאת עֵינָיו אֶל הַשָּׁמַיִם.
כָּל אָדָם צָרִיךְ תְּפִלָּה
אַחַת,
שֶׁתְּהֵא שְׁגוּרָה אֶצְלוֹ עַל הַשְּׂפָתַיִם.
אָדָם צָרִיךְ פַּעַם אַחַת לְהִתְכּוֹפֵף –
כָּל אָדָם צָרִיךְ כָּתֵף.

Everyone should have some kind of Egypt in their gears,
To go forth, at the mid of night, into the desert of their fears,
Redeem themselves from a house of bondage,
March straight into the sea,
And see the waters part before them, as if by decree.
Everyone should have a shoulder, calm, and firm, and strong,
On which to carry, through the desert, the remains
    of Joseph's bones.
Everyone once bowed should walk tall and free and proud.

כָּל אָדָם צָרִיךְ שֶׁתִּהְיֶה לוֹ
אֵיזוֹ מִצְרַיִם,
לִגְאֹל עַצְמוֹ מִמֶּנָּה מִבֵּית עֲבָדִים,
לָצֵאת בַּחֲצִי הַלַּיְלָה אֶל מִדְבַּר הַפְּחָדִים,
לִצְעֹד הַיָּשֵׁר אֶל תּוֹךְ הַמַּיִם,
לִרְאוֹתָם נִפְתָּחִים מִפָּנָיו לַצְּדָדִים.
כָּל אָדָם צָרִיךְ כָּתֵף
לָשֵׂאת עָלֶיהָ אֶת עַצְמוֹת יוֹסֵף,
כָּל אָדָם צָרִיךְ לְהִזְדַּקֵּף.

Everyone should have some kind of Egypt cross their ways,
And Jerusalem in their prayers,
And a journey, long and hard
To remember in their heart
And with their feet until the end of days.[2]

כָּל אָדָם צָרִיךְ שֶׁתִּהְיֶה לוֹ
אֵיזוֹ מִצְרַיִם.
וִירוּשָׁלַיִם,
וּמַסָּע אָרֹךְ אֶחָד,
לִזְכֹּר אוֹתוֹ לָעַד
בְּכַפּוֹת הָרַגְלַיִם.

At the Gates of Nisan

Our ancestors, crafting a midrash on the word *Nisan*, gave it additional meanings appropriate to the month in which Passover occurs. For example, Rabbi Pinchas HaKohein, an eighth-century poet who lived in the Land of Israel, wrote a *piyut* in a genre known as *Kiddush Y'reichim* (Sanctification of the Month); the following lines are about the month of Nisan:[3]

> Spring for salvation and liberty has been stored
> since the people were then saved by the Guardian.
> Nisan—its joy is in the past, and to raise it like a banner [*l'nos'san*] in the future,
> Named for their miracle [*nisan*], it is called Nisan.

> אָבִיב לְיֵשַׁע וּדְרוֹר חֻסַּן
> בְּהִוָּשַׁע עַם בּוֹ בְּמַחְסָן
> נִיסָן – גִּילוֹ לְשֶׁעָבַר וְלַבָּא לְנוֹסְסָן
> דִּבּוּר לְשֵׁם נִסָּן נִקְרָא נִיסָן.

In the Hebrew, Rabbi Pinchas rhymes these four lines and includes wordplay, perhaps to create a sense of play and joy. After all, this month is one of joy and celebration, both because of the past redemption from Egypt and the future redemption of Israel, which the Babylonian Talmud tells us will also take place in Nisan: "In Nisan they were redeemed; in Nisan they will again be redeemed" (Rosh HaShanah 11a). The poet provides two interpretations of the name "Nisan," both based on the Hebrew noun *neis*, which has two definitions—banner and miracle. In the month of Nisan God will raise up Israel as one raises a banner and waves it in display; in the month of Nisan God will once again, as at the Exodus, perform miracles for God's people. Rashi too, in his Talmud commentary, offered a similar derivation of the name of the month: "Because of the miracles [*nisim*], the month is called Nisan" (Rashi to Babylonian Talmud, B'rachot 56a).

ISN'T IT INTERESTING to wonder what our year would look like if it began in spring, with the new growth of leaves and blossoms and birdsong as the days grow longer and longer, rather than with taking stock of our lives in Tishrei, as the days grow shorter and shorter and the darkness grows longer and longer? What if the year started with thinking about Exodus and redemption, about new beginnings, instead of days of beating our fists against our chests as we confess our sins? What might Judaism look like had the month of Nisan remained the first month of the year, as it is in the biblical calendar? "This month shall mark for you the beginning of the months; it shall be the first of the months of the year for you" (Exodus 12:2).

In this chapter we will explore the many dimensions of the month of Nisan, especially the holiday of Passover that starts mid-month. In the first *iyun*, I will explore the redemption that we experienced in Nisan and its place today. Nisan is the birth month of the people Israel, and in that context, the second *iyun* of the chapter deals with questions of Jewish peoplehood through the story of the ten lost tribes. The third *iyun* looks at women and gender aspects of Passover, along with some practical suggestions for the seder. The fourth *iyun* introduces the post-Passover Mimouna festival, its origins, and its place in contemporary Israeli life. The fifth *iyun* moves us from Passover to Holocaust Memorial Day, asking how we should memorialize the Shoah. The sixth *iyun* deals with *S'firat HaOmer* (Counting of the Omer) and suggests some ways to mark it in our lives today.

The Poem of the Month is a spring *piyut* by Mosheh ibn Ezra, *Kotnot Pasim*, and alongside it a contemporary Israeli response by songwriter Yoram Taharlev. The Prayer of the Month is *T'filat Tal*, the Prayer for Dew, which is said beginning on Passover and with which we mark the end of the rainy season and the beginning of the dry season.

From Time to Time → Dalia Marx

Poem of the Month

When Taharlev Met Ibn Ezra: *Kotnot Pasim Lavash HaGan*
("The Garden Donned Coats of Many Colors")

THE POET AND THINKER Moshe ibn Ezra (1055–1140), one of the poets of the Golden Age of Spanish Jewry, wrote a poem about spring and liberty called "Kotnot Pasim Lavash HaGan" ("The Garden Donned Coats of Many Colors"). The poem—brief but rich in content—extends its branches into rich and fascinating worlds of meaning.[4]

The Garden Donned Coats of Many Colors
    Moshe ibn Ezra

כְּתָנוֹת פַּסִּים לָבַשׁ הַגַּן
מֹשֶׁה אִבְּן עֶזְרָא

The garden donned coats of many colors,	כְּתָנוֹת פַּסִּים לָבַשׁ הַגַּן
and its grass garments were like robes of brocade,	וּכְסוּת רִקְמָה מַדֵּי דְשָׁאוֹ
every tree dressed in a checkered tunic,	וּמְעִיל תַּשְׁבֵּץ עָטָה כָל־עֵץ
and showed its wonders to every eye.	וּלְכָל־עַיִן הֶרְאָה פִלְאוֹ
Each new blossom came forth in honor of time renewed,	כָּל צִיץ חָדָשׁ לִזְמָן חֻדַּשׁ
came gaily to welcome.	יָצָא שׂוֹחֵק לִקְרַאת בּוֹאוֹ
But at their head advanced the rose,	אַךְ לִפְנֵיהֶם שׁוֹשָׁן עָבַר
ruler of them all, for his throne was set on high.	מֶלֶךְ כִּי עַל הוּרַם כִּסְאוֹ
It came out from among the guard of its leaves	יָצָא מִבֵּין מִשְׁמָר־עָלָיו
and cast aside its prison clothes.	וַיְשַׁנֶּה אֶת בִּגְדֵי כִלְאוֹ
Whoever does not drink their wine upon the rose bed—	מִי לֹא יִשְׁתֶּה יֵינוֹ עָלָיו
that person shall bear guilt!	הָאִישׁ הַהוּא יִשָּׂא חֶטְאוֹ

Nature's awakening in the spring is described in the poem in lyrical terms—the garden, with its lawns and its trees, is revived; it puts on new, invigorating clothing. Each full line in Hebrew ends with an "o" rhyme, perhaps best read in a tone of amazement, the speaker bedazzled by the spring.

At the center of the poem, the ruler is portrayed as a rose, whose blooming from its bud is described as a release from prison ("out from among the guard of its leaves"). Just as Joseph, the original owner of a "coat of many colors," came out of Pharaoh's dungeon and changed his clothes en route to freedom, so did the rose—representing the spring—"cast aside its prison clothes."

Who's the King Here?

The most obvious way of identifying the ruler whose "throne was set on high" is that the ruler is God, sovereign over the universe as affirmed by nature. It seems to me, though, that it is no less accurate to claim that the ruler is a human being—any human being. After all, every person is—or can be and deserves to be—the ruler in their own garden. This understanding emphasizes that the poem does not consider freedom to

> The phrase *k'tonet pasim* brings us back to Joseph and the garment Jacob made for him out of his special love for his son (Genesis 37:3). It is usually translated into English as "a coat of many colors"—a translation made famous by the King James Version of the Bible. Modern Hebrew understands *k'tonet pasim* as a "striped" coat. Ibn Ezra's use of the term may be influenced by the way earlier *piyutim* referred to Temple priests as *lovshei pasim*, "those who wear colors." Apparently, this epithet indicated not a garment of many colors or even of stripes, but rather a garment with sleeves. One who wore such long-sleeved garments—such as priests—signaled their membership in a high social class, since long sleeves did not allow one to do manual labor.

mean going out from among a hostile population. Bondage is not necessarily an external force. Chains can be internal, a form of self-imprisonment.

This approach comports well with modern liberation theology: all individuals must remove the bonds that they have placed on themselves in order to flourish from within. The redemption in Nisan is national but also individual, and everyone must emerge from their own bud—"out from among the guard of [their] leaves"—to freedom.

The poem also contains a warning to us—rulers in our own gardens—to be wise in drinking the juice of our lives. Maybe the poet is winking at us merrily and calling on us to rejoice and have a drink, and whoever does not "shall bear guilt" and miss their destiny. The harsh phrase "bear guilt," which casts a surprising glance toward the one who does not celebrate and drink wine, is taken from a verse in the Book of Numbers about the punishment imposed on someone who does not offer the Passover sacrifice: "that person shall bear their guilt" (Numbers 9:13). It is as though the poet's call to us to rule our lives, enjoy them, and take pleasure in them—with that warning that we are guilty if we do not—almost gives it a religious character. It calls on us to fully embrace the life given us. The connection between the phrase "that person shall bear guilt" and the Passover holiday is explicit, and the poet's command to drink wine evokes the seder; this strengthens the religious character of poem, even though at first read one might fairly classify it as a drinking poem.

> The term translated here as "rose," *shoshan*, is often translated as "lily" or as a generic term for a pretty flower. Midrashists and poets used the term in its feminine form, *shoshanah*, as a code name for the people Israel. For example, when the male lover in the Song of Songs describes his beloved five times with the clause "Like a *shoshanah* among thorns, so is my darling among the maidens," it was understood as referring to the uniqueness of the people of Israel among the nations.

Old Wine in New Bottles

The poem *Kotnot Pasim* found new life in the twentieth century, when it made its way into many kibbutz Haggadot. Those Haggadot show Passover as, above all, the holiday of spring, and the first cup that one drinks at the seder is dedicated, in many kibbutz Haggadot, to the season's blooms and blossoms. My kibbutznik friends tell me that this *piyut* is one of the most popular parts of the kibbutz seder and is sung with particular enthusiasm. In this way, the old wine of Ibn Ezra's poem is poured into new containers.

Nature and Culture from Another Angle

The depictions of nature in the poem are filled with religious meaning, such as the **clothes of the High Priest** in the ancient Temple. This weaves nature into the particular culture of the Jewish people. The anthropologist Claude Lévi-Strauss (1908–2009) stated that human consciousness is built on awareness of binary contrasts, such as the contrast between day and night, between hot and cold, between being clothed and being naked, between life and death, etc. Underlying all those pairs, he contended, is the basic contrast between nature and culture. Lévi-Strauss claimed that humankind's task was to elevate the natural into the cultural, to transcend nature and make it into something governable and cultural—to treat raw food by cooking it, to clothe the naked body, and to sanctify sexual relations through marriage.[5]

Kotnot Pasim suggests a somewhat different way of grappling with the question of the relationship between nature and culture. Nature (the flowering garden) and culture (the High Priest and his elaborate costume) are not in competition with one another, but instead complement and teach one another. They are not set into a hierarchical relationship: nature is not governed by culture, nor is it subservient to culture. Nature is described using terms from the world of the sacrificial cult and the Holy Temple, which in turn are illuminated and explained using terms from the botanical realm. The relationship between nature and culture is reciprocal in this poem. It is as though the poet has said that the High Priest's garments are as natural as nature awakening to life in the spring, and reciprocally, nature is sacred and exalted in the very same way as God.

A New Middle East

Another layer of the "robe of brocade" of Ibn Ezra's poem are the lyrics written by an immensely popular Israeli poet, lyricist, and author, Yoram Taharlev (1938–2022), in his song *Rei-ach Tapuach Odem Shani* ("Scent of Apple, Red of Scarlet"). This is a spring love song whose speaker calls his beloved—sometimes described as a little bird and sometimes a gazelle—to return to his blossoming, fragrant garden. The poem's language is almost identical to the male lover's words in the Song of Songs:

> For now the winter is past,
> The rains are over and gone.
> The blossoms have appeared in the land,
> The time of pruning has come;
> The song of the turtledove
> Is heard in our land.
> The green figs form on the fig tree,
> The vines in blossom give off fragrance.
> Arise, my darling;
> My fair one, come away.
> (Song of Songs 2:11–13)

Even though there are no explicit references to the Land of Israel in the lyrics, the images from the Song of Songs transport us to Israel's countryside and its fragrances. The lyrics conclude with the male lover inviting his beloved to "the gazelle's bed" (*eres hatzvi*). This seems to be an erotic invitation from the male gazelle to his lover, but the phrase *eres hatzvi* is a near-homonym for *eretz hatzvi*—"Land of the Gazelle" or "beautiful land"—one of the biblical names for the Land of Israel (Daniel 11:16, 41). Taharlev's female gazelle, then, naturally belongs in the Land of the Gazelle, the Land of Israel, and its Mediterranean landscapes.

Taharlev wrote the poem as lyrics for a melody written earlier by composer Nachum Heiman (1934–2016), which is set in 7/8 time, a Mediterranean rhythm. Approaching

---

We read in the Torah about the **garments of the High Priest**, "These are the vestments they are to make: a breastpiece, an ephod, a robe, a fringed tunic, a headdress, and a sash" (Exodus 28:4), and many of these Hebrew terms appear in the poem's description of the "clothing" worn by the garden. Ibn Ezra's "robes of brocade" (*k'sut rikmah*) also allude to the High Priest's clothing, of which we read, "You shall make the sash of embroidered work [*maaseih rokeim*]" (Exodus 28:39). In the poem, the Hebrew word *tzitz* means the blossoms and leaves that renew each season and shine with joy: "Each new blossom came forth in honor of time renewed,/ came gaily to welcome." Ibn Ezra engages in wordplay with *tzitz*, alluding to the *tzitz* that is part of the High Priest's outfit, worn on his forehead: "You shall make a *tzitz* of pure gold" (Exodus 28:36), with the Hebrew noun variously translated as "frontlet" or "diadem" or, because of its floral sense, "rosette." The descriptions of the High Priest in the poem are set in the context of nature's reawakening in the spring and highlight the relationship between nature—the world of Creation—and the culture of the people Israel—specifically the Tabernacle and, later, the Holy Temple. In fact, the Torah itself includes fascinating parallels between the creation of the world and the construction of the Tabernacle. For example, the end of the process of Creation is reported with the words "On the seventh day, God had completed [*vay'chal*] the work that had been done" (Genesis 2:2), and at the very end of the erection of the Tabernacle we read, "Moses had completed [*vay'chal*] the work" (Exodus 40:33). The Rabbis also attempted to show that every detail of the world's creation had its parallel in the work of the Tabernacle. For example, a midrash equates the light of Creation with the light that the priests kindled in the Temple (*Sh'mot Rabbah* 34:2).

the task of writing lyrics for this melody, Taharlev wanted to express something local and Mediterranean. Looking for inspiration, he turned to the oldest Mediterranean poems he knew—the Hebrew poems of the Golden Age poets in Spain. The one poem that served as his main example was none other than *Kotnot Pasim*. Like Ibn Ezra, Taharlev describes the arrival of spring as a garment worn by nature: "The fields have all donned a garment of dew." And like Ibn Ezra, Taharlev makes poetic use of the cup: here the cup is filled with the wine of love, red like the setting sun's reddish cast that promises the pleasures of love.

Scent of Apple, Red of Scarlet
Yoram Taharlev

רֵיחַ תַּפּוּחַ אֹדֶם שָׁנִי
יוֹרָם טְהַרְלֵב

Come back, little bird, the wind at your wing,
the buds in my garden already are grown.
The perfume of lemon, the buds of the apple,
the rains have all passed and the winter has flown.

שׁוּבִי צִפּוֹרֶת עַל כְּנַף הָרוּחַ
כְּבָר בְּגַנִּי פִּתַּח הַסְּמָדָר
בֹּשֶׂם לִימוֹן נִצַּת הַתַּפּוּחַ
גֶּשֶׁם הָלַךְ וְחֹרֶף עָבַר.

Who is it who'll bring you the news in this message?
Who will invite you, O bride, to my garden's bed?
I've built you a nest here on branch and on treetop;
the apple is fragrant, and of a scarlet so red.

מִי לָךְ יָבִיא אֶת זוֹ הָאִגֶּרֶת
מִי יִשָּׂאֵךְ כַּלָּה אֶל גַּנִּי
קֵן לָךְ אֶבְנֶה עַל בַּד וְצַמֶּרֶת
רֵיחַ תַּפּוּחַ אֹדֶם שָׁנִי.

Come now, yes, come, gazelle of such beauty,
the fields have all donned a garment of dew,
already red are the spring and the sunset,
and in our cup—wine that's reddish in hue.

בֹּאִי נָא בֹּאִי צְבִיַּת הַחֶמֶד
בֶּגֶד שֶׁל טַל לָבְשׁוּ הַשָּׂדוֹת
כְּבָר הֶאֱדִימָה עַיִן וָשֶׁמֶשׁ
וּבִגְבִיעֵנוּ יַיִן אָדֹם.

Who is it who'll bring you the news in this message?
Who will invite you, O bride, to my garden's bed?
I've built you a nest here on branch and on treetop;
the apple is fragrant, and of a scarlet so red.

מִי לָךְ יָבִיא אֶת זוֹ הָאִגֶּרֶת
מִי יִשָּׂאֵךְ כַּלָּה אֶל גַּנִּי
קֵן לָךְ אֶבְנֶה עַל בַּד וְצַמֶּרֶת
רֵיחַ תַּפּוּחַ אֹדֶם שָׁנִי.

Come now, come back, for the winter is over,
a new dawn is here at the summer's behest.
Return to your nest, little bird, from your roving,
come back, my doe, to gazelle's place of rest.

בֹּא שׁוּבִי כִּי תַם הַחֹרֶף
שַׁחַר חָדָשׁ הַקַּיִץ הֵבִיא
שׁוּבִי אֵלַי קִנֵּךְ הַצִּפּוֹרֶת
שׁוּבִי צְבִיָּה אֶל עֶרֶשׂ הַצְּבִי.[6]

🔺 Why Is This Night Different— and What Is Still the Same?

SLAVES WHOSE SPIRITS are battered and whose bodies are bent and beaten from arduous, meaningless work lift their eyes from their daily toil and go out free. The Israelites embark on the journey of their lives into the unknown. They head toward the land their ancestors cherished, which had been remembered through the generations. They raise hesitant, tearful eyes toward an unfamiliar homeland. The journey to the Land of Israel is a journey for a life of meaning. It is a long journey whose results we may not live to see, but the path itself is very beautiful too. Every time we seek a life of meaning, we are marching toward a homeland hidden in our hearts, in search of redemption.

Because of the days of mourning and remembrance—both ancient and new—that are spread across the Jewish calendar, we are likely to miss the important fact that Judaism is filled with abundant optimism. Judaism is a religion and culture swathed in hope and the belief that evil is not a necessity, that things can be other than they are. Jewish optimism is reflected in the belief that it is always possible to do *tikkun*, repair, and that even if "everything is foreseen, free will is given" (*Pirkei Avot* 3:19), and we have the power to change this dynamic world and our dynamic lives. We believe that we have the ability to repair what we have broken. We have not come into this world to live helpless lives or to repeat our mistakes over and over. We are not random visitors to this world, puppets on a string acting a predetermined role only to be piled lifeless in the puppet master's box of props at the end of the show. No! Our actions have meaning. We write the story of our lives, as individuals and as a people, and it is within our power to be redeemed even from difficult and disheartening situations. We can—and therefore we must—leave our best fingerprint on the world.

> "Wherever I go, I am going to the Land of Israel." This statement, attributed to Rabbi Nachman of Bratzlav, has been interpreted in many ways. I understand it as the belief that going toward the Land of Israel—literally or metaphorically—is a journey toward all that is good and beautiful, a statement asserting a belief in the possibility of redemption, a belief that has great hope.[7]

The month of Nisan invites us to recall the redemption from Egypt—the complete redemption, the emergence from slavery into freedom, from subjugation to a life of choice. It invites us to think too about hope for the future. Rabbi Y'hoshua says, "In Nisan they were redeemed; in Nisan they will again be redeemed" (Babylonian Talmud, *Rosh HaShanah* 11a). Nisan connects us by thin but strong strands both to the past we cherish and to the future we hope for.

"For It Will Surely Come"

The belief that the world is essentially good and that goodness is possible gave Jews strength even in the most difficult times. This principle of faith forced them to believe that even when good was not visible or palpable, redemption would still arrive: "Even if it tarries, wait for it still; for it will surely come, without delay" (Habakkuk 2:3). In the Jewish tradition, many have read this verse as a prophecy of the coming of the Messiah, who will bring solutions to the suffering of individuals, the Jewish people, and the world. There are some who believe in the coming of a flesh-and-blood Messiah and even suggest the signs that will indicate their impending arrival. Others understand this statement to be an expression of the idea that absolute good is the anticipation and direction of the future, knowing that the perfect good is an aspiration to hope for. Some ask only for a modest redemption, knowing it is up to them to act with all their energy in full awareness that the results will sometimes be only partial, faded versions of the ultimate goal they hope to reach.

In my view, life with an expectation of good things is a life of commitment to action. The knowledge that the Messiah, by definition, is always in the "will surely come" (someday) category propels us into activity that knows no end. We might think that if our efforts toward redemption and *tikkun olam* are met and our goals accomplished, then our work would be done. Conversely, failure—when our efforts do not match our dreams or result in any changes—might make us despair. But neither of these approaches is true; regardless of what we achieve and work toward and heal and create, there is always more to do. Striving to do good is endless, eternal—not just for one societal rupture but for all. We should not despair at this; instead, we should strengthen our commitment to action.

Indeed, striving for redemption is not—and should not be—a passive expectation of help from heaven. Such a striving is embodied in a life of commitment and action. When we live a meaningful life, we connect to the divine image within us. In the *Aleinu* prayer, we declare that it is up to us "to perfect the world [*l'takein olam*] under the rule of God." I understand that exhortation as a call for *tikkun olam*, repairing the world, as a demand that we actualize the potential good in the world, thus becoming junior partners with God in the ongoing process of Creation (see pp. 291–92). Even though we are flesh-and-blood creatures, we are not merely sojourners passing through this world; we are not guests here. We have a role to play in healing the ruptures and repairing the world—our private worlds, our community, our country, and so on in ever-expanding circles.

My Pure Soul

The first blessing that the Talmud directs us to say upon awakening (Babylonian Talmud, *B'rachot* 60b), which even now is one of the first blessings said in the morning, is the blessing on the restoration of our soul after sleep. It begins with these words:

My God, the soul You have given me is pure.	אֱלֹהַי, נְשָׁמָה שֶׁנָּתַתָּ בִּי טְהוֹרָה הִיא.
You created it, You shaped it,	אַתָּה בְרָאתָהּ, אַתָּה יְצַרְתָּהּ,
You breathed it into me	אַתָּה נְפַחְתָּהּ בִּי,
and You protect it within me.[8]	וְאַתָּה מְשַׁמְּרָהּ בְּקִרְבִּי.

Just after waking up, we declare that our soul is pure, that God created it and planted it within us. The words "the soul You have given me is pure" are a declaration before God—and no less so before ourselves—that we are fundamentally good. For me, the *Birkat N'shamah* (Blessing of the Soul) is a call to follow a good, worthy path throughout the day. It reminds us that there is a pure soul within us. We may do something bad, but at the most basic level we are good. Moreover, even if we have done something bad or strayed from the path, we are able set things right. Every morning we are given the full potential to do good. A fresh new page is spread before us, even if yesterday's page is stained and creased. This approach is quite different from other religions that describe human beings as shameful vessels whose existence is based on awareness of sin.

The belief in our essential goodness and our ability (and therefore obligation) to do good is mobilizing. Indeed, throughout the centuries many Jews have lived lives of dedication and commitment. Even when external conditions were not easy, many of them stood out as repairers of the world. The proportion of Jews among human rights activists, activists for women's right, fighters for social justice, and environmental activists is far greater than the proportion of Jews in the population at large (at least, in the Diaspora). What all these struggles have in common is action, mobilization, and commitment to right wrongs by doing good. It sometimes seems that an ancient code, seared into our culture, leads Jews to refuse to accept things as they are and to act for *tikkun olam*, each person in their own way and on their own path.

It is doubtful whether there have been many periods like ours in the history of the Jews, in which our visions of how to right the world's wrongs are so varied and contradictory. There are those who seek universal redemption for all humankind. There are others who are concerned about Mother Earth, our planet. Some worry in particular about the most disenfranchised among us, including people of other religions and nations. Others seek to realize the dream of a Greater Israel from the Jordan to the sea. Some put their energy into the lives of their communities, be they small or large. Some look for redemption by joining one group or sect after another, and some look for personal redemption of their inner world by joining body and soul. The list goes on and on . . . But the pursuit of all these paths share a basic dissatisfaction with human existence, the belief that things could be better, and a desire to act on behalf of *tikkun*.

Our memory of the past ("in Nisan they were redeemed") and our hope for the future ("in Nisan they will again be redeemed") are intended to bolster both our spirits and our attachment to life in the here and now, rather than wallow in nostalgia for a remote past or engage in pipe dreams about a wondrous distant future. Memory of the past and hope for the future call us to focus on what is in front of us and on our commitment to make our lives more meaningful and responsible, wherever we are and whatever we do!

Commitment to *tikkun olam* stems first and foremost from an understanding that reality is flawed and fragile. The foundation of this commitment is a recognition that in order to create change, there is a fixed and unflagging need to educate and be educated, to doubt and to learn. It is this recognition that stands at the center of the seder night, all of which flows from one question and our attempts to answer it: *Mah Nishtanah?* Why is this one different? Behind the door of that question hide deeper, more vital questions, whose answers are much less clear: What will we make different? What will we change? What must we change in our lives in order to make them more meaningful and better?

> The poet Yehuda Amichai (1924-2000) has written about his father's deathbed charge. The last words of direction his father gave him were "Thou shalt not change" and, immediately following that, "Thou shalt change. You will change." These two principles—the need to preserve an existing tradition alongside the need to renew and change it—are the cornerstones of every culture.⁹

The poet Rachel Bluwstein—whose work is published under her first name alone—used poetry to express the commitment to practical change and to warn against the mistake of harboring utopian dreams: "Not nebulous tomorrow," she demands, but "today materialized in the hand."

Here on Earth
Here on earth—not in high clouds—
On this mother earth that is close:
To sorrow in her sadness, exult in her meager joy
That knows, so well, how to console.

Not nebulous tomorrow but today: solid, warm, mighty
Today materialized in the hand:
Of this single, short day to drink deep
Here in our own land.

Before night falls—come, oh come all!
A unified stubborn effort, awake
With a thousand arms. Is it impossible to roll
The stone from the mouth of the well?[10]

כָּאן עַל פְּנֵי אֲדָמָה – לֹא בֶּעָבִים, מֵעַל –
עַל פְּנֵי אֲדָמָה הַקְּרוֹבָה, הָאֵם;
לְהֵעָצֵב בְּעַצְבָּהּ וְלָגִיל בְּגִילָהּ הַדַּל
הַיּוֹדֵעַ כָּל כָּךְ לְנַחֵם.

לֹא עַרְפִלֵּי מָחָר – הַיּוֹם הַמֻּמָּשׁ בַּיָּד,
הַיּוֹם הַמּוּצָק, הֶחָם, הָאֵיתָן:
לִרְווֹת אֶת הַיּוֹם הַזֶּה, הַקָּצָר, הָאֶחָד,
עַל פְּנֵי אַדְמָתֵנוּ כָּאן.

בְּטֶרֶם אָתָא הַלֵּיל – בּוֹאוּ, בּוֹאוּ הַכֹּל!
מַאֲמָץ מְאֻחָד, עַקְשָׁנִי וָעֵר
שֶׁל אֶלֶף זְרוֹעוֹת. הַאֻמְנָם יִבָּצֵר לָגֹל
אֶת הָאֶבֶן מִפִּי הַבְּאֵר.

O Brother, Where Art Thou?

TO PARAPHRASE a famous Israeli song from the sixties (*Shir Baboker Baboker*, written by Amir Gilboa), "Suddenly some tribes wake up in the morning and feel like they're a people and start walking."[11] They are told, "You go free on this day, in the month of Aviv" (Exodus 13:4), and they leave. In the month of Nisan, Israel is created as a people. Jacob had thirteen children—twelve sons and a daughter. They came to Egypt with their children and all their descendants. Ten of the sons have a tribe with tribal land named for them, and one son, Joseph, has two tribes named for him, or rather for his sons Ephraim and Manasseh.

The twelve tribes left Egypt and became a nation. According to tradition, there are only two remaining tribes from the original twelve—Judah and Benjamin, along with part of the tribe of Levi (which didn't get its own share of the Land). The rest of the tribes were "lost" after the Assyrian Empire conquered the northern Kingdom of Israel in the eighth century BCE.

What became of the ten tribes? Where did they go? What happened to them? These questions, suffused with longing for those lost brothers, have ignited the Jewish imagination throughout the ages. The Rabbis of old wondered what befell the lost tribes, speculated about their fate, and asked whether they might ever return. One ancient tradition asserts that they are living beyond a miraculous river named Sambatyon (*B'reishit Rabbah* 11:5, 73:6). The unique character of the Sambatyon is a hindrance to those who want to reunite with the ten tribes: during the week the river hurls rocks at anyone who approaches it, and on Shabbat when the river is calm, one is halachically forbidden to cross it.

The myth of the ten lost tribes stirred many people—Jews and non-Jews alike—to search for them, to set out on treks to far-off lands and try to identify them. What motivated at least some of these seekers was the belief that the lost tribes' return would herald the coming the Messiah and the era of redemption.

I want to dedicate this *iyun* to a man who claimed to have found every last one of the ten lost tribes: the amazing traveler Eldad HaDani. Eldad lived in the ninth century and claimed, as his name indicates, to be descended from the tribe of Dan. He claims that he came from an independent Jewish state, "ancient Havila, where the gold is," which is found "across the rivers of Kush" and on the other side of the Sambatyon. Eldad said that the tribe of Dan left the Land of Israel just before the split into the two kingdoms of Israel and Judah, in an effort to avoid participating in the civil war between the two kingdoms.[12]

Eldad claimed that aside from the people of his tribe, Dan, people from the tribes of Gad, Naphtali, and Asher also lived in his country. The claim that there existed Jewish sovereignty outside of the Land of Israel is astounding. Eldad appeared before the elders of the community of Kair-

Jacob's daughter Dinah did not get to be the mother of a tribe. However, a midrashic tradition recounts that Joseph married her daughter, and therefore two tribes were born of that union. (Though an uncle marrying his niece may strike the modern reader as odd or inappropriate, this was considered an advantageous marriage according to ancient and Rabbinic standards.) The additional tribe that came from him is a hidden representation of the silent sister (*Yalkut Shimoni*, *Vayeishev* 146). Thus, according to this midrash, justice was achieved for Dinah.

After the death of King Solomon in the tenth century BCE, his empire split into two: the Kingdom of Judah, populated mainly by the tribes of Judah and Benjamin, and the Kingdom of Israel, where the other tribes lived. The Kingdom of Israel is also known as Ephraim, after the largest of its tribes, or the Kingdom of Samaria (after its capital). It was conquered by the Assyrian Empire in the eighth century BCE. Its inhabitants—the people of those ten tribes—were exiled to other places in the Assyrian Empire, where they assimilated. The residents of the Kingdom of Judah were also exiled in the year 586 (or 587) BCE, after Jerusalem fell into the hands of Nebuchadnezzar, king of Babylon. A few of the Judahite exiles returned to Judah fifty years later, under the aegis of Cyrus, king of Persia, but by this time the people of the ten tribes were lost. Over the centuries, the disappearance of the ten lost tribes gained attention and raised the hope that their descendants might be found and welcomed into the embrace of their people, just as some of the Judahites came back to Zion after the fall of the Babylonian kingdom.

ouan, in Tunisia, bringing them some of the laws and customs practiced by those tribes. Eldad told his spellbound audience about the time he was shipwrecked and fell into the hands of cannibals, only to escape a horrible fate after being redeemed by a wealthy merchant of the tribe of Issachar. Eldad followed the merchant of Issachar to his country, located in "the mountains of the seacoast," whose people are learned in Torah and rich in property, and in which "there is not . . . any oppression or robbery," and where there are "leaders of armies but they fight with no one." From there he continued to the land of the people of Zebulun, "encamped in the hills of Paron," and from there to the tribe of Reuben, who live near them. Eldad continues to describe his visits with the tribes of Ephraim, Manasseh, and Simeon. He also told of another tribe known as the tribe of Janus, who "fled from idolatry and cleaved to the fear of God." Throughout the ages, there were many traditions about that tribe, whose members were all redheads. Yom Tov Levinsky observes that the traditions about the "*roite Yiddalakh*" ("the red Jews," in Yiddish) gained a prominent place in the exiled Jewish people's dreams of redemption.[13]

Stirred by those strange stories, the sages of Kairouan wrote to the *Gaon* Rabbeinu Tzemach in Babylonia and asked him how they should respond to Eldad HaDani's tale, which obviously raised eyebrows but was amazingly consistent and detailed. The *Gaon*'s reply was hesitant: "The words of Eldad—some of them appear to be like what our sages say and some seem exaggerated." He adds that it may be that Eldad erred, that he "made a mistake and switched things around because of the great suffering he endured and the difficulty of the journey, which afflicts a person's body."[14] Eldad HaDani told no fewer than thirteen stories to the people of Kairouan and later to the people of Spain. In his book, first published in 1480, there are also many innovations in Jewish law—such as the laws of slaughter—observed in Eldad's country.

In recent decades we have witnessed an unprecedented phenomenon of a growing number of individuals who desire to become part of the Jewish people. A North American friend in his seventies told me that in his lifetime, Jews, who used to be an extremely hated and denigrated group, had become a desired one (despite ongoing antisemitism). Sometimes this is done through conversion. Sometimes it is by laying claim to an ancient connection to the Jews, such as the people or groups that regard themselves as descendants of the ten tribes or of Iberian crypto-Jews. There are also those who become a part of Jewish communities with no intention to convert but out of a desire to be truly connected to the people Israel, such as non-Jewish spouses of Jews.[15]

Was Eldad HaDani telling the truth? Was it truth mixed with fiction, or did he make it all up? We may never know the answer, but in my view this matter is important because it illustrates that such stories are quite common. A tradition about the continued existence of the ten tribes and their dwelling place across the River Sambatyon is found in Jewish literature of all sorts—*piyut*, midrash, Chasidic tales, and halachic responsa. Those stories had many iterations over the generations. At times, Jews were hesitant about expressing a longing for the ten tribes, in part because Christians were also searching for them, since they believed the return of the ten lost tribes would presage the impending return of their Messiah. Nevertheless, these legends excited Jewish hearts and aroused a longing for redemption in the dark places of their hardships.

In our time, we continue to encounter tribes and ethnic groups whose members declare themselves descendants of the ten tribes, such as the B'nei Menashe of the Kuki, Chin, and Mizo tribes in northeastern India. Some have claimed that other ethnic groups—such as the Pathan (or Pashtun) tribes in Afghanistan (ironically the same tribe from which the Taliban emerged)—are also of Israelite descent. Today there are genetic tests that attempt to prove that one group or another is of Jewish descent. Sometimes wishful thinking, political agendas, and romantic fantasies mix with bits of fact when it comes to identifying the ten tribes, encouraging their return to Judaism, and bringing them to Israel. Unfortunately, we must be cautious because there are some who take advantage of this romantic folklore. They make members of these "lost tribes" dependent on charismatic religious leaders and use them as pawns in contemporary Israeli politics. If we have a desire to meet our long-lost "family members," we must ensure their independence and empowerment.

Jewish Peoplehood

The month of Nisan, the month of our birth as a people, is an excellent time to examine the issue of Jewish peoplehood. In comparison to other peoples and religions, Jews are a people, a nation, a tradition, a religion, and a culture all at the same time. It is rare to find secular Catholics or Presbyterians of no religion, but relatively common to meet secular Jews and even atheists who are fervently Jewish. Jewish identity is not defined solely by religion, but rather by peoplehood. In fact, God's first promise to the first Hebrew Abraham, after telling him to leave his land, his native setting, and his father's house, is connected to peoplehood, not religion: "I will make of you a great nation" (Genesis 12:2). The promise is not that Abraham will be a great religion but rather a great nation or people. And it is precisely that people who will see blessing: "I will bless you; I will make your name great, and you shall be a blessing" (12:2). This blessing is a great call to us all, urging us to be a blessing: "And all the families of the earth shall bless themselves by you" (12:3).

In our day, it seems that a symbolic Sambatyon river roils more fiercely than ever, dividing Jews who live in Israel from Jews of the world, and threatens to separate us from each other. Today's Sambatyon flows in two directions: not only are the Jews of the Diaspora in a profound sense inaccessible to us Israelis, but to a great extent we Israelis lie "beyond the Sambatyon" for them—and unfortunately, it seems that too many Israelis want to make the Sambatyon even wider! An important task that faces us is to make sure that the river remains passable and that no stones are thrown at those who wish to approach its banks.

Women at the Seder: Speaking Out of Order?

PASSOVER SONGS, the taste of *charoset* made with a special family recipe, the bickering over whether we like our matzah balls to sink or float, teasing whoever had to read the part about the wicked child, the open door for Elijah, and many other family traditions—all these are among many Jews' earliest childhood memories. The Passover Haggadah is the most common religious text among Jews in both Israel and the Diaspora. While it is true that more people attend synagogue on the Days of Awe than on Passover, the seder is the event in which the largest number of Jews participate—and actively! Passover is celebrated at home—where most of us cannot rely on trained professionals, cantors, and rabbis, to run the seder for us—responsibility for organizing and conducting the seder rests entirely on members of the family.

Gathering together, the family atmosphere, the special texts, and the different flavors all contribute toward making seder night so central. Invisible strands link those seated at the table to our people's historical past, to the unique traditions of each family and community, and to the private history of each person present. Therefore, on this night it is particularly important to ensure that each and every participant is given an appropriate place.

In the Babylonian Talmud, we read the words of Rabbi Y'hoshua ben Levi: "Women are obligated to [drink] those four cups [of wine], since they too took part in that miracle" (*P'sachim* 108a–b). That is a statement of principle equating women and men in the requirements of the seder, because all of them experienced the miracle of the Exodus from Egypt. But does everyone really take part in the celebration?

Kulanu M'subin: Are All of Us Reclining Tonight?

The Four Questions (or rather the four answers to the one question "What is different tonight?") highlight the uniqueness of the day—one of them says that "on this night all of us recline," *kulanu m'subin.* In the Jerusalem Talmud we find an explanation for the requirement to recline: by reclining we remind ourselves of our release from slavery and being free people (*P'sachim* 10:1 [37b]). The Rabbis of the Talmud observed that wealthy Romans ate in relaxation while reclining, and on this night they wanted all the Jews to be like the relaxed rich. "Reclining" is generally understood to be a position of half-sitting, half-lying on one's left side and doing so together, as at a party. After all, there are two ways to understand the phrase *kulanu m'subin*: in Hebrew, it can be translated as "all of us recline" or, conversely, "all of us gather together."

What does "all of us recline" really mean? "All of us," the Mishnah teaches, "even the poor person among the people Israel" (*Mishnah P'sachim* 10:1). However, the Babylonian Talmud shares this caveat: "In her husband's presence, a woman is not obligated to recline, but if she is an important woman—she must recline" (*P'sachim* 108a). All those who come to seder,

---

The Four Questions insist that "all of us recline," the way free people do . . . but then why are **women exempt** from that requirement?

Three primary reasons for this exemption have been suggested. Rashbam (Rabbi Sh'muel ben Meir, in twelfth-century France) explained that a married woman is exempt from reclining because "she is in awe of her husband."[17] Rav Acha Gaon (in eighth-century Babylonia) explained that it is not customary for women to pour wine or to recline.[18] Rabbeinu Manoach (in thirteenth-century Provence), in his commentary to Maimonides, wrote, "She is not obligated to recline, since she is busy preparing and serving the food."[19] Each of these commentators approach the exemption differently. While Rashbam holds that it would be unseemly for a woman to recline next to her husband, Rav Acha expresses concern for the woman's honor and perhaps her modesty, and Rabbeinu Manoach is practical: after all, someone has to set the table and serve the food . . .

The exemption from observing this ritual—and all other commandments that are time bound—might, at first glance, seem to make things easier on women, since their lives and time are not constrained by religious observance. In practice, however, this exemption excludes women from participation in an important dimension of the holiday and does not enable them to have a place at the table.

For many generations, Ashkenazim continued the custom that women do not recline, while Sephardim adopted the position of the medieval tosafists, that "all of our women are considered important," and so they reclined.[20]

From Time to Time → Dalia Marx

then, are obligated to recline as do free people, except for married women unless they are "important women." What is the significance of the fact that most married women did not recline—that they did not sit like free people on the Festival of Freedom? Does that indicate that their status as free people was not self-evident? Are women not included in "all of us"? A few halachic authorities found that exemption problematic and tried to address it.

Rabbi Mordechai ben Hillel HaKohein (1250–98), of Germany, solved the problem by citing the tosafists (Talmud commentators in the generations after Rashi, starting in the twelfth century): "All of our women are considered important" and thus are required to recline. No woman is unimportant, and so none is exempted from the requirement. Rabbi Moshe Feinstein (one of the foremost American halachic authorities of the twentieth century, diverged from this position by writing that there is no need to claim that all women have actually become "important." Rather, "one must show them respect even as the way of the world," meaning that one must respect women because they are by their very nature equal, and the issue is not connected to whether they are considered distinctly important people or not.[16]

Women's Solidarity

Many women sense that elements of Jewish tradition leave them mute and unrepresented. We cannot deny the exclusion of women from the public realm over the course of far too many generations, but if we take a close look at the events that form the basis of the Passover holiday, we will find that strong, active, and optimistic women occupy a central place in the narrative. This is an important precedent for women in our time who are looking for their place in Jewish tradition. The story of the redemption from Egypt began and was made possible by dint of the actions of dedicated women who refused to give in to despair.

The Hebrew women refused to knuckle under to Pharaoh's murderous order and continued to bring life into this world. Jochebed, Moses's mother, is one of them; she gave birth and protected her son from Pharaoh's decree. Her daughter, Miriam, hid the newborn in a basket of reeds and set him floating on the Nile. The midwives who attended Jochebed also chose the path of rebellion and showed mercy to the Hebrew babies. Who were those midwives? Pharaoh called them "the Hebrew midwives" (Exodus 1:15). It is possible to read this and understand they are "Hebrew midwives," but it is also possible to read the phrase as "the midwives of the Hebrews," meaning that they themselves were not Hebrews but bravely cooperated with the women of the enslaved nation to keep the newborn boys alive. Pharaoh's daughter herself refused to take part in her father's murderous plans. When she saw the helpless baby brought to her by the Nile, her human compassion overruled her social and class attachments. A midrash calls Pharaoh's

---

Rabbi Avira (third-century Rabbinic scholar) spoke about the power of the women in Egypt, whose merit led to the redemption of the Israelites. In poetic language, he described how the women displayed ingenuity and initiative. They understood that slavery and hard labor ground down their spouses and banished any thought of conjugal relations and birthing a new generation. They tried to deal with this situation, and the Eternal helped them out:

> Rabbi Avira expounded: As a reward for the righteous women who lived in that generation, the Israelites were delivered from Egypt. When they went to draw water, the Blessed Holy One, arranged that small fishes should enter their pitchers, which they drew up half full of water and half full of fishes. They then set two pots on the fire, one for hot water [for washing] and the other for the fish, which they carried to their husbands in the field, and washed them, anointed them, fed them, gave them drink, and had intercourse with them. [They became pregnant and gave birth, and the Eternal personally attended the births of the women and cared for and fed the babies.] . . . At the time the Blessed Holy One was revealed at the sea, they [the children] recognized the Holy One first, as it is said: "This is my God whom I will praise" (Exodus 15:2). (Babylonian Talmud, *Sotah* 11b)

According to this midrash, the Holy One helped those who wanted to help their people and served as a loving caretaker for the children born to the Hebrew slaves. Those children were also the first to recognize the Eternal at the crossing of the Sea of Reeds.

daughter "Bityah" (see Babylonian Talmud, *M'gillah* 13a), and she has been regarded by the Jewish tradition as a righteous woman and even a Jew-by-choice. Miriam then ensured that Jochebed, her mother, would be the one to nurse Moses in Pharaoh's house, so that he would imbibe—both literally and figuratively—his first human experiences in the arms of the people Israel.

Reading Jewish sources with a fresh eye makes it possible for women to demand their rightful place. This is not a mere act of intellectual sophistication, nor is it bending the texts to one's own will. Just the act of reading the sources anew is liberating. It gives expression to multiple pure voices that have been suppressed and silenced—and after all, liberation is one of the central themes of Passover.

Many people are now attempting not only to make the place of women equal to that of men at the seder table, but also to find special ways to highlight their function and role in the story of the nation and the family. The following are some customs that are becoming increasingly widespread among Jewish families. They are just a few examples that serve to express our commitment to the preservation and renewal of the traditions of our ancestors.

New Symbols and New Meanings

Miriam's Cup: Miriam's cup is a cup of clear water added alongside Elijah's cup, which symbolizes her role in the story of Passover. According to tradition, Miriam's miraculous well accompanied the Israelites on their journey through the wilderness and provided water to slake the people's thirst. Legend has it that Miriam's well continues to pop up from time to time, and it heals anyone who immerses in its waters (*Vayikra Rabbah* 22:4).

In egalitarian congregations, Miriam's place in the redemption from Egypt and the song she sang at the sea are mentioned when we add Miriam's name alongside that of Moses, not only on Passover but also in the *Mi Chamochah* prayer said as one of the blessings that follows the *Sh'ma*: "Moses and Miriam and all Israel sang to You together, lifting their voices joyously."[21]

An Orange on the Seder Plate: This custom, which is becoming commonplace in many households, has more than one explanation. The most widely known of them tells the story of a woman who asked a well-known rabbi, "Why can't women read from the Torah in synagogue?" The rabbi replied jovially, "A woman's place on the bimah in the synagogue is like an orange's place on the seder plate." Some say the custom originated as a symbol against the exclusion of gay and lesbian people from Jewish life.[22] Today many families are in the habit of adding an orange to their seder plate to express their commitment to pluralism and acceptance of everyone in the family and the nation. The orange has even been mentioned on a few Israeli television series, such as the show *Arab Labor*. This custom invites discussion and makes it possible for those seated (or reclining) at the seder table to ask with honesty, "Why is this night different?" It thus advances the story of the Exodus from servitude to freedom, a process that underlies the entire seder night.

New and Alternative Texts: In many Haggadot, new texts that emphasize the role of women in the Exodus have been added to the traditional text of the seder. Among other things, a number of alternative versions of the "Four Sons" passage have been composed. Many Haggadot bring women into the picture and make their voices heard.

Reviving Old Symbols

Fish on the Seder Plate: The tradition of adding a food to the seder table in order to note the role of women preceded the orange and the feminist revolution by centuries. Rabbi Eliezer of Worms (thirteenth-century Germany) explained that the egg and the shank bone on the seder plate represent Moses and Aaron and added, "And there are those who place another cooked food in memory of Miriam."[24] The third type of food alongside the egg and the shank bone is fish, as a symbol of the Leviathan, the sea creature that the righteous will feast upon in the Garden of Eden in times to come. The fish lives in water, another powerful symbol for Miriam. It was on water that Miriam set her brother Moses afloat when he was a baby, and it was with water from her well that she quenched the Israelites' thirst. The connections among the three foods brings to mind the unique contributions of the three siblings—Moses, Aaron, and Miriam—to Israel's redemption.

The Four Cups for the Four Mothers: Rabbi Yeshayahu Horowitz (seventeenth-century Eastern Europe and Palestine), author of *Sh'nei Luchot HaB'rit*, explains that the three fundamental mitzvot of the holiday—the *pesach* sacrifice, matzah, and bitter herbs—stand for the three Patriarchs, while the four cups of wine stand for the four Matriarchs:

> **Sarah** is [represented by] the first cup, [with] the blessing "who has chosen us from among all peoples," because just as Abraham chose from among the nations and converted the men, so Sarah converted the women; **Rebekah** is [represented by] the cup at the *Magid* section, [where we] "begin with shame and conclude with praise," [since] she began . . . with Esau and concluded with Jacob. . . **Rachel** is [represented by] the cup at the Blessing after Meals, because her son Joseph provided food for the whole

The midrash on the four sons is one of the oldest—and most beloved—passages in the Haggadah. In recent decades, many people have felt a need to bring women to the fore in telling the story of the Exodus. Among other efforts, dozens of versions of "Four Daughters" have been created to be recited alongside the "Four Sons" passage. Here is a version written by me and my friend Rabbi Tamar Duvdevani. In place of the evil son, we have invited the angry daughter, recognizing that there are no bad children . . .

The Torah spoke of four daughters:
One wise, one angry, one simple, and one who knows not how to enquire.

The wise one, what says she?
What are the meanings of the testimonies, the statutes, and the ordinances, which our fathers and mothers passed down to us? Then you shall tell her: "Testimonies"—for our mothers, too, witnessed that same miracle. "Statutes"—for statutes were given to us to walk in their shade and to meditate in them, as it is said: "And I will meditate in Your statutes" (Psalm 119:15). "Ordinances"—for words, poetry, regenerating interpretation, betterment, and *tikkun*, to which we are committed.

The angry one, what says she?
What do you mean by this service?
You spread your arms toward her and say: You, too, have part in this night of exodus, as it is said: "As the reward for righteous women . . . were the Israelites delivered from Egypt" (Babylonian Talmud, *Sotah* 11b); and therefore you deserve to have your voice heard rejoicing in the song of freedom, as it was said about Miriam the prophetess: "And all the women went out after her with timbrels and with dances" (Exodus 15:20).

The simple one, what says she?
What is this?
And you say to her: "In every generation a person must regard themself as if they came out of Egypt." "Person"—each person, as it is said: "Male and female created God them . . . and called their name *adam*" (Genesis 5:2). "Themself," why? As each and every one of us has an Egypt, which we are ordered to recognize, which we are ordered to exit, which we are ordered to expel from within us.

The one that does not know how to inquire:
You open and tell her: "Lift up your voice with strength; lift it up, be not afraid" (Isaiah 40:9), "for sweet is your voice, and your countenance is comely" (Song of Songs 2:14). Our power is diminished and our conversation less worthwhile without you. "We will go with our young and with our old, with our sons and with our daughters, with our flocks and with our herds we will go; for we must hold a feast unto the Eternal" (Exodus 10:9), as we are all party to the Exodus.

May we, in the joy of our freedom, be attentive to the voices of all people of the world.[23]

House of Israel, and she was a homemaker . . . **Leah** is [represented by] the blessing over the *Hallel* song, the fourth cup. . . . One says the Great *Hallel*, all sorts of praise did she offer, having said, "This time I will praise the Eternal" (Genesis 29:35), and from her came . . . our master Moses, may peace be upon him.[25]

As Rabbi Horowitz sees things, the Matriarchs accompany us throughout the entire seder night.

Old Symbols and New Meanings

In some early Ashkenazic Haggadot there is a drawing of the *av haseder* (the seder leader) pointing to his wife and saying, "These bitter herbs," as a tasteless chauvinist joke. Some new Haggadot instead make a connection between the bitter herbs and the bitterness that has all too often been part of women's experiences and to express a commitment to correcting that situation.[26]

We are privileged to live in a generation in which women can make their voices heard and find new roles in many different places, including the story of this holiday. We should not forget, however, that the struggle for equality and freedom—in the context of gender and in other contexts—is far from over. Passover is an excellent opportunity to express a commitment to sanctify the divine image and finding it in the world.

🔺 Lots of Flavors of Mimouna

My grandfather, Moreno Levi—who has already been mentioned earlier in this book—liked to tell the story that on the eve of Passover, the women of his Jerusalem neighborhood would march over to their Muslim neighbors and with great celebration present the women with all the bread, flour, and *chameitz* (leavened foods) from their houses. At the end of the holiday, those same neighbors would come with their households, bringing the Jewish families their first *chameitz*—fresh bread, cakes, and cookies—and everyone would feast together. The intersection of these two moments—before the holiday and after it—were an opportunity for one joyous neighborhood gathering of two peoples and two religions. This act of friendship became a cherished local custom for my grandfather and his neighbors.

Among the Jewish communities of Morocco, however, the custom of hosting and being hosted at the end of Passover gained a status nearly equal to that of a holiday; they called it Mimouna (pronounced mee-MOO-nah). During Passover, Moroccan Jews would remain in the *melach*—the Jewish neighborhood—and confine themselves together. When the festival ended, they opened the neighborhood gates and joyfully greeted their Muslim neighbors.

Much is still unknown regarding the origin of this holiday, and it is not clear when the Jews of Morocco began to celebrate it. The name "Mimouna" appears for the first time at the beginning of the nineteenth century, in the words of Rabbi Avraham Halfon, who actually lived in Libya.[27] However, it is possible that Mimouna customs are far more ancient than that reference.

As someone who did not grow up with Mimouna, I have tried to learn and understand Minouna's traditions, and from my conversations with friends I have discovered an abundance of customs that differ from family to family. These customs include presenting a live fish in a bowl of water; setting out five dates, five golden bracelets in a bowl of dough, five silver coins, five precious jewelry items, and five full fava bean casings wrapped in dough; decorating with flowers; and sharing foods with milk and butter sweetened with honey, jam, and sugar, dried fruits, semolina balls, and *moufletas*, thin crepes made from water, flour, and oil, which have become, in many people's view, the symbol of Mimouna. All of these symbolize fertility, abundance, and blessing. There are families in which it is customary to jovially "whip" the other members of the household with branches of vegetation as a sign of blessing and success. The traditional blessing for the holiday offered in Moroccan Judeo-Arabic to anyone who enters one's house is *tirb'chu v'tisadu*, meaning "may you be fortunate and successful."

What Is Mimouna?

Many explanations and interpretations have been offered for the name and origin of Mimouna. This proliferation of meanings may be indicative of the fact that the celebration was well-known and deeply rooted in the communities that observed it, and the explanations were offered only after it was well established.[28]

A few explanations begin with the name "Mimouna" itself, such as the suggestion that the word derives from the Hebrew noun *emunah*, "faith": the Israelites, redeemed from Egypt in Nisan, faithfully await their future redemption in Nisan despite its ongoing delay. Celebrating Mimouna, then, expresses hope for redemption and faith that it will indeed arrive. Another explanation is that Mimouna is named for Rabbi Maimon, father of Moses Maimonides (which means "son of Maimon"), or for Maimonides himself. Since news of Maimonides's death arrived just as Passover came to an end, some have suggested the Mimouna feast is a communal reenactment of the meal made for mourners after they return from a burial and begin their week of mourning.

Still others have claimed that Mimouna—celebrated on the evening and day just after the Passover holiday—serves as a *m'laveh malkah*, a meal customarily held on Saturday night so as to "accompany the queen" (that is, Shabbat, or in this case, the festival) as it departs. Mimouna is thus another celebration, loaded with the *chameitz* that was forbidden over Passover, and a ceremony of transition designed to assist a gradual return back to routine from sacred holiday time. It also expresses the hope for being able to do a proper pilgrimage to the Temple in Jerusalem when the next holiday comes around.

Other explanations connect Mimouna to local Moroccan Muslim celebrations, and some claim that the holiday originates in pre-Muslim Berber traditions—for example, that Mimouna is named for Maimon, king of the demons, and the celebration is intended to appease the demon so that he would not harm people and the season's crop. Some think that Mimouna is the female equivalent of Maimon and refers specifically to the wife of the king of the gods, Lala Mimouna, who was a local goddess of good fortune adopted, it is claimed, by the Jews. The Israeli historian Yigal Bin-Nun has cited (and translated into Hebrew) one of the songs that the celebrants used to sing to that great Mimouna:

> Here she comes, the great Mimouna;
> here she comes, who fortune greets.
> Old and young rejoice:
> Mimouna brings many treats.
> Here come sweets and sweet fried dough,
> here are cups that overflow.
> Here is strength, here long life,
> here is joy and pleasure, not strife.
> O Mimouna, dear great lady of powers,
> your sun brings bright and healing hours.
> Come each year in beauty and laughter,
> bring us each year blessing ever after.[29]

The words of the song indicate that Mimouna is indeed a female, but not that she is a demon who needs to be appeased. In any case, this illustrates that there is a feminine emphasis in the celebration of Mimouna with a female figure at its center.

Professor Aharon Maman understands the call *leilat l'mimuna* (the night of Mimouna) as "the night of the fortunate woman" and identifies the fortunate woman as a girl for whom a husband is found. On Mimouna night, many families would conclude marriage arrangements between their children, and some of the holiday evening's neighborly visits included visiting the newly engaged young woman. As one woman described, "With us, the real celebration of Mimouna night took place at the home of the girl who got engaged. I recall that when I got engaged, all the neighbors came over to our house, the meal was full of good things, a real royal feast, and every neighbor brought green lettuce and offered a *mazal tov* blessing."[30]

A few of the customs of Mimouna—eating sweet foods, gifting live fish, and going down to a spring to dip one's feet in water—are all wedding customs as well among Moroccan Jews.

Other traditions emphasize the role of women, who with great fanfare prepare enormous amounts of cakes and cookies and serve them on Mimouna night. The celebration is *their* celebration. The centrality of women can be found in many aspects of the celebration of Mimouna, and one can only hope to see that aspect of the holiday undergo further development.

The Mimouna celebration is intimately bound up with the home, whose doors are opened to all, and with the life lived within. It even happens sometimes that the doors are literally taken off their hinges and used as long tables for friends, acquaintances, neighbors, and relatives. In Morocco (and other communities, as mentioned above), the evening was also a celebration of good relations between Jewish and Muslim neighbors.

In Israel in the 1980s, Mimouna became a public event celebrated in parks with tens of thousands of people. In addition to this massive picnic and its celebration of togetherness, the events were known for the prominent presence of politicians. They made sure to appear on these occasions and have their photo taken with the traditional holiday food like a dripping *moufleta* (honey crepe), flashing a smile dripping with honey. In place of the original home- and family-centered holiday, Minouna became, in many instances, a show of power by officials and politicians. Many in the Moroccan community observed this change with sorrow. To them, their homey, easygoing holiday had become a hollow political show. Recent years have seen Mimouna return to the family setting.

Over the last few years, communal Mimouna celebrations and even joint celebrations of Mimouna for Jews and Muslims have been undertaken. The purpose of reviving these celebrations—once symbolizing the bond between these two religious groups—is to break down the barriers that have arisen between these two groups and their cultures. A few years ago, Al Akhawayn University in Ifrane, Morocco, established a "Mimouna Club." The members (who are not Jews) seek to research and experience Moroccan Jewish culture and understand that the culture of the Jews was an important part of the larger cultural fabric of Morocco. To get to

At Home or in a Park (or on Zoom)

One of the important tasks of holidays in general and Mimouna in particular is intergenerational transmission of knowledge and heritage—in this case, primarily passing women's knowledge from generation to generation. Among many Jewish ethnic groups in Israel, the Moroccan community among them, this transmission often skipped a generation, and it is now grandmothers who are teaching their granddaughters. My friend Rabbi Rinat Safania Schwartz, who holds a Mimouna celebration for many people at her home each year, writes:

> Nine years ago, I went to see my *mamou* [Moroccan word for "grandma"] Denise and asked her to teach me to make cookies for Mimouna. "Really?!" she asked, "You want to make Mimouna?" . . . And then we sat, she and I and her caretaker Rinako, and she started to explain to me how to make marzipan. . . . She didn't understand what it was that I didn't understand. She explained to me how to make coconut cookies (she already couldn't remember how many times she had told me to add sugar . . . but the more sugar, the better . . .). And that is how I spent a full day with my *mamou*, talking, laughing, and I learned something of her magic from her. . . . It has been nine years now that, as I see it, I have been performing some of my grandmother's magic. For several years now, thanks to the Mimouna I have been doing, I get to spend quality time with my mother. We sit, talk, make cookies, and think about "home," each of us and her own home. This year I will not get to tell my *mamou* on the phone about my Mimouna. . . . This year she will look down on us from above and be happy that her magic continues among her grandchildren. *Tirb'chu v'tisadu*—Mimouna is on its way.[31]

In spring of 2020 we were in the first COVID-19 lockdown and could not celebrate the festivals as we used to. Yet, one of the silver linings of the pandemic was the creation of new ways of celebrating apart but together. Many online *moufleta* classes took place via Zoom and other hosting sites. We could not physically be together, but the distance could not interfere with our efforts to connect.

know their own heritage, they needed to become familiar with the heritage of the Jews who once lived among them.

Just for Moroccan Jews, or for All Israelis?

Is Mimouna a holiday that belongs only to the Jews of Morocco, or should it become a general Israeli holiday, in which Israelis en masse adopt the traditional customs of Mimouna? If the general public adopts the holiday as its own, the holiday's values and symbols enter the public sphere; however, this might also obscure the unique and special nature of Mimouna as a holiday of the Moroccan community.

Perhaps it would have been a good idea to preserve Mimouna's special nature as a day when members of the Moroccan community invite their neighbors and friends from other communities to celebrate with them, which could serve to demonstrate what the modern *pay'tan* (poet) David Buzaglo wrote about the festival: "For Jews and Arabs one table is laid / as they raise their spirits with music played. / With Jewish women in Arab garb."[32] That poem, written more than forty years ago, can serve now as a prophetic platform for a desired reality.[33]

This tension between private and public celebration applies not only to Moroccan Mimouna but also to the holidays and customs of the various Jewish groups that comprise Israeli Jewish society. In fact, it exists in any country whose immigrants desire to retain part of their unique cultural identities. Early Irish immigrants to the United States shared their Saint Patrick's Day celebrations, which have changed and adapted over time to include the larger American community. Canada's Asian community shared Chinese New Year celebrations, which have also grown to include the larger Canadian populace. American Jews share their love for and connection to Israel by hosting a "Celebrate Israel" parade in New York City close to Israel's Independence Day, which draws tens of thousands of Jewish and non-Jewish participants. Other Israeli examples include Saharena—celebrated by Kurdistan émigrés on Sukkot or the end of Passover—and Sigd (see pp. 63–66)—the communal holiday of Ethiopian Jews observed in the month following the Days of Awe—which is in the process of securing a place in Israeli culture, within the school system and community celebrations. There are also holidays not connected to the Hebrew calendar, and not even Jewish in origin, that Jews have brought to Israel from various Diaspora communities, such as Novy God (New Year), celebrated by Jews from the former Soviet Union on the night of December 31. This same community brought May 9's Victory Day celebrations, which memorialize Germany's surrender as World War II drew to a close.[34] Recently, my friends who made *aliyah* from North America have suggested establishing the United States' Thanksgiving in Israel as a sort of American Mimouna.

And what is to become of the holidays of those who came from Poland? From India? What about the German Jews, known jocularly as *Yekkes*? Those from Iraq? There is much to do . . . someday. Israel, like many other countries, is filled with variety and made up of many different groups of people, bringing together East and West, North and South. May these many faces of our identity always be enriching.

How (and Where) Are We to Remember the Holocaust?

THE JEWS are a people who remember. I have counted more than three hundred words—not including nouns!—in the Hebrew Bible from the root *zayin-khaf-reish*, meaning "remember." Dozens more words with this Hebrew root appear in the siddur, the Jewish prayer book. The belief that God remembers and commands us to remember the past is the foundation upon which our present is built and from which emerges our hope for the future. Jews' feelings of identification and solidarity with generations past are immersed in memory and find expression in prayer and in Jewish texts, and the command to remember is perceived to be a religious commandment, a mitzvah in the full sense of the term.[35] In every generation, one should regard oneself as actively living through and participating in the people's history. Each year the weekly Torah portions invite us to experience the creation of the world, the birth of the Patriarchs and Matriarchs, the descent into Egypt, and slavery's suffering and cruelty. They call on us to join in the Exodus from Egypt, to wander in the wilderness, to stand at the edge of the Promised Land. Every year we break free from the Seleucid conquerors at Chanukah, tremble at hearing our adversary's decree on Purim, and receive the Torah on Shavuot. The pace of Jewish life is formed from memory of the past interwoven with anticipation of the future. For example, when we recite *Kiddush* over wine on Shabbat, two foundational events are mentioned—the universal Creation, marking the birth of the world, and the particularistic Exodus, marking the birth of the people Israel: "You made the holy Shabbat our heritage as a reminder of the work of Creation. As first among our sacred days, it recalls the Exodus from Egypt."

The Holocaust's Double Uniqueness

It is hard to imagine a historical event more embedded in the people Israel's memory and marked more intensively and with as much diversity as the Shoah, the planned and organized campaign for the mass murder of millions of Jews with the explicit goal of exterminating the Jewish people from the face of the earth. The Holocaust—called the Shoah in Hebrew—is presented in countless literary works of poetry and prose, in films, stage plays, the visual arts, in academic research, and in memorial ceremonies observed by governments, institutions, communities, and individuals. Trips to Poland by high school students from Israel and around the world organized by March of the Living have over time taken on the status of pilgrimage. With light and shadows, these all testify to the centrality of the Holocaust in the Jewish experience.

A few songs written in memory of the Holocaust have attained the status of actual prayers. One of the most outstanding is *Ani Maamin*, "I Believe." In an Israeli culture still in formation, newer and less "religious" songs have also attained sacred status, such as Hannah Senesh's *Halichah L'Keisariyah* (known by its opening line, *Eili, Eili*).

Ani Maamin/I Believe

I believe with full faith
in the Messiah's coming,
and even if the Messiah is delayed
I will wait day by day.[36]

אֲנִי מַאֲמִין בֶּאֱמוּנָה שְׁלֵמָה,
בְּבִיאַת הַמָּשִׁיחַ,
וְאַף עַל פִּי שֶׁיִּתְמַהְמֵהַּ,
עִם כָּל זֶה אֲחַכֶּה לּוֹ בְּכָל
יוֹם שֶׁיָּבוֹא.

The melody of this song, derived from the twelfth of Maimonides's thirteen principles of faith (see pp. 317, 351), was composed by Reb Azriel David Fastag, a Modzitzer Chasid, on a train to the death camp at Treblinka. There are several versions of the story. According to one, Fastag promised half of his place in the world-to-come to anyone who would deliver the melody to Rabbi Shaul Yedidya Elazar Taub, the Modzitzer Rebbe (1886–1947). One young man jumped off the train, was saved, and succeeded in bringing the melody to the rebbe. As the story is told, the rebbe declared that the melody, which accompanied Jews into the Nazi crematoria, would be sung again when the Messiah comes. And even though the song does not touch directly upon the Shoah, it has become an established memorial song—identified with this horrific period more than any other.

Tishrei Marcheshvan Kislev Tevet Sh'vat Adar **Nisan** Iyar Sivan Tammuz Av Elul

The Jewish Life Calendar

Siddurim, Jewish prayer books, have served for generations as the daily life calendars of the Jews. The synagogue was the main institution that housed the people's feelings, sufferings, disappointments, and hopes. Perhaps part of the uniqueness of the Shoah is that, unlike other central events enshrined in Jewish memory, its memorializing takes place not primarily inside synagogues but outside them. Relatively few prayers and elegies have been written in response to the Holocaust, and those have not gained much of an audience in Israel. To illustrate the uniqueness of the Holocaust in this regard, let us compare the ways the Holocaust appears in the synagogue and in prayer to that of another harsh and traumatic period that occurred much earlier—the Crusades, and the First Crusade in particular.

According to some estimates, during the disturbances and riots known in Hebrew as "the Disasters of [4]866," referring to 1096 CE, some twelve thousand Jews were murdered. The impact of those massacres on Jewish consciousness in Europe (and beyond) was profound and lasting. The memory of the marauding attacks of the Crusaders of the First Crusade led to the formation of many religious customs: noting the anniversary of Adam's death (his *yahrzeit*), setting aside a *Kaddish* prayer specifically for mourners, the addition of special *Yizkor* prayers on the pilgrimage festivals and Yom Kippur, and the regular recitation on certain Shabbatot of *Av HaRachamim*, a memorial prayer for the martyrs of 1096 (including a call—to God, not other humans!—to avenge their blood), the custom of lighting a candle in memory of the departed, and more. In addition, a wealth of *piyutim* and *kinot* (elegies) were written to memorialize these events. The disaster that befell the Jews of the Rhine Valley—victims of the attacks by First Crusade warriors—remained seared into Jewish consciousness through the ages, because it was given concrete expression. Some of those customs were preserved among only a few communities; others became standard practice throughout Ashkenazic Jewry, such as reciting *Yizkor* prayers; others still became standard practice among all Jewish communities, such as lighting a *yahrzeit* candle and observing the anniversary of a death with the recitation of *Kaddish*. This horrendous period in the history of the Jewish people has been woven into the fabric of Jewish prayer and the life of the synagogue.

Prayers in Memory of the Holocaust

Unlike the strong presence of the memory of the Crusades-era disasters in Jewish prayer and ritual, the Holocaust—in which six million Jews were murdered and many more millions injured—has not received a great deal of liturgical attention. A notable exception is the different versions of the *El Malei Rachamim* prayer ("God, full of mercy")—generally accepted in the Ashkenazic world (in parallel to the Sephardic *Hashkavah* liturgy)—composed to perpetuate the memory of the victims of the Holocaust. They detail the horrors of murders and the cruelty directed at the victims. A few *kinot* (elegies) have been written to mourn the victims of the Holocaust, and in

---

The Disasters of 1096

The First Crusade set out in 1096, in response to Pope Urban II's charge to the faithful at the Clermont Council of 1095 to rise up and redeem the Church of the Holy Sepulchre in Jerusalem from the Muslims. His call fell on responsive ears, and as a result what became known as the First Crusade began.

On their way to Jerusalem, the Crusaders inflicted harsh attacks and massacres on the Jewish communities in the places through which they passed—mainly the Rhine Valley cities of Worms and Mainz—and presented the Jews with the choice of being baptized or being killed. Many Jews chose death. Chronicles and *piyutim* from those days tell of mass suicides by entire families, and of parents who killed their own children so that they would not fall into the hands of the Crusaders.

some communities they are recited on Tishah B'Av and sometimes even on Yom HaShoah (Holocaust Martyrs' and Heroes' Remembrance Day), but none has achieved canonical status. The Holocaust is mentioned in some liberal prayer books, like *Mishkan HaNefesh*, on Yom Kippur, alongside the *piyut Eileh Ezk'rah*, which describes the ten Rabbinic victims of Roman persecution who gave their lives to sanctify God's name and forms the core of the Martyrology section of the day's liturgy.[37]

Many Passover Haggadot, such as various kibbutz Haggadot, also refer to the Holocaust. Since national memory is a primary motif on seder night with its multigenerational family meal, it makes sense that sharing personal memory, such as personal experiences of the Holocaust, occur then as well. In addition, Passover—the Festival of Freedom—is an opportunity to give thought to the darkest period in the history of the Jewish people, in which so many people were murdered and Jews' freedom was denied them just because they were Jews. Professor Avigdor Shinan of the Hebrew University composed a liturgical work called *The Shoah Scroll*, which is intended to be read on Yom HaShoah and has been translated into several languages, including English.[38]

Aside from the handful of examples mentioned here—very few of which have gained widespread attention—not many prayers have been composed that are intended to memorialize the Holocaust.

How can we explain the fact that despite the centrality of Holocaust memory in Jewish and Israeli consciousness, the Holocaust gets little if any representation in formal prayers? Why are there not more prayers in memory of that darkest period in the history of the Jews and of humankind as a whole?

This piercing question has more than one answer. First, the sheer dimensions of the Holocaust are beyond our ability to grasp. It unfolded over the course of years, across a vast geographical expanse, and decimated a huge number of communities. It is difficult to find one focused mode of expression that appropriately marks it. In addition, the Holocaust is still very close to our own time, and it may be that not enough years have passed for us to process the terror into words of prayer—although after previous disasters the liturgical responses followed closely after the events. Third, in the past Jews took responsibility for the disasters that befell them, claiming they were a result of their own sins. For example, in the *Musaf* prayer for the Pilgrimage Festivals, the Jews' exile is explained with these words: "Because of our sins, we were exiled from our land." In the case of the Holocaust, however, most Jews did not agree to take upon themselves the blame for the horrid suffering (although in certain circles, inflammatory accusations can be heard against other groups of Jews who were allegedly responsible for what transpired).[39] On the contrary, the Shoah catapulted many Jews into a crisis of faith and raised the question of where God was during the Holocaust and whether it is still possible to pray to a God who did not halt the annihilation.

Another explanation for this dearth of liturgical innovation may stem from the resistance of many contemporary Jewish circles to changing the existing liturgy in any way, even by adding *piyutim* or prayers that do not impact the traditional liturgy. Such

---

Rabbi Haim Sabato (b. 1952) wrote a *kinah* (elegy) for Holocaust victims that I find especially touching. Sabato was born in Egypt and his family was unscathed by the Shoah, but in his childhood years in the Mazmil transit camp (in today's Kiryat HaYovel neighborhood of Jerusalem), he met many survivors and heard their stories. His poem is a call for empathy and mercy for the victims' suffering. Here are its opening lines:

How My Brothers

Oh, how my brothers' fate was decided and never repealed!
With seals of mud and blood it was cruelly sealed.
A nation rose up against them 'til blooded, they reeled
and like corpses they were dragged from home to field.
Can the land atone for their blood, still unconcealed?[41]

a concern was nonexistent among the halachic authorities and poets in premodern Judaism. Rabbi Joseph B. Soloveitchik (1903–93 North American Orthodox rabbi) expressed his opposition to creating new *kinot* for Tishah B'Av that memorialize those lost in the Holocaust this way:

> Of course the six million deserve to be eulogized on Tish'ah be-Av. But we do so within the frame of reference of the *kinot* we already recite on that day. Instead of Vilna, we mention Worms or Mayence. It does not make much difference, because the scenes described and the words of despair, mourning, and grief are the same.[40]

In their day, the *piyutim* in memory of the Jews of Worms and Mainz were an innovation, but Rabbi Soloveitchik perceived them as already being a fixed and integral part of the tradition. And while medieval rabbis did not hesitate to add new *piyutim* and *t'chinot* (supplicatory prayers), today one finds in many quarters a rejection of new prayers or *piyutim*.

Moreover, there seems to be no agreement about what precisely is to be remembered. Should we concentrate on the horrors perpetrated by the Nazis and their henchmen, or on the dangers of antisemitism, or perhaps on the evils of racism and hatred of the foreigner in general? Should we concentrate on personal stories or on the stories of communities, on the infrastructure of the destruction, on Nazi ideology or on the world's silence, on the everyday acts of bravery or on the partisans' struggle? These questions about "the lessons of the Holocaust" and the values learned as a result—especially in a religious context—remain to this day unprocessed and unsolved.

The Holocaust and Prayer—Has the Time Come to Widen the Net?

The gap between the memory of the Holocaust and its presence in Jewish discourse, on the one hand, and its glaring absence from synagogue life, on the other, may be more indicative of the shrinking role of the synagogue than of anything about Holocaust memory. The positive aspect of this phenomenon is that it has expanded the canvas of Jewish life: memory is no longer exclusive to the synagogue but instead finds expression in new and sometimes unexpected cultural spaces. It is not only the cantor's pulpit, the holy ark, and the worshipers' pews in the synagogue that are sites for holiness, but also the community center auditorium, the theater stage, the public square, the youth movement's field, the schoolyard, not to mention Zoom and social media. In Israel, many organized programs—some of which began spontaneously, like the project "Memory in the Living Room" (*Zikaron BaSalon*), in which Holocaust survivors or, as the years go by, their descendants tell their stories on Yom HaShoah as guests in private homes—share Holocaust memory to new audiences among the second, third, and fourth generations of survivors' descendants and among those whose families were not directly harmed during the Holocaust.

The more difficult aspect of this gap between perception and the synagogue's limited role in responding is a concern that the synagogue is losing its vitality as an institution that enables Jews to commemorate their history and create meaning in their lives. There is a nagging feeling that synagogue prayer—the most vital and purified vehicle for expressing Jewish historical consciousness and marking both communal and personal events is losing much of its power. Some might make peace with this development and regard it as a natural thing, but I see a need to revitalize the synagogue as an institution that is responsive to the needs of today's generation, as an institution that expresses popular sentiment, travails, and hopes of the Jewish people, just as it did until the modern era. If this revitalization occurs, the synagogue—an institution that has come to be seen as alien and unwelcoming by so many—will again serve as a *syn*-agogue (a place for being *with* others), a *beit k'neset* (a place of assembly), a place where people gather during happy or times, a place to study, hear a lecture, pray, celebrate a milestone in one's life, gather with others or find solitude . . . and experience the heartbeat of Jewish life.

"They Must Be Whole"— *S'firat HaOmer* / The Counting of the Omer

FOR SEVEN WEEKS, the Torah tells us, we are to count the time between Passover and Shavuot:

> And from the day on which you bring the sheaf of elevation offering—the day after the sabbath—you shall count off seven weeks. They must be complete: you must count until the day after the seventh week—fifty days; then you shall bring an offering of new grain to the Eternal. (Leviticus 23:15–16)

S'firat HaOmer begins on Passover, the festival of the "bread of affliction," and ends just before Shavuot, when the first of the new harvest's bread is eaten at the Temple with an "offering of new grain." The period of counting occurred in tandem with the agricultural season of ancient Israel: it started with offering a sacrifice of one omer-measure of barley, which was harvested in an impressive ceremony and brought to the Temple, and it ended with the sacrifice on Shavuot, the festival of the wheat harvest.

Perhaps this was intended as a lesson on the process of purification and refinement: barley is a coarse grain generally intended for animal consumption, while wheat—with which the counting period ends—is a fine grain; similarly, Jews moved from Passover's physical rescue from slavery to the spiritual culmination of receiving the Torah on Shavuot. One can also discern this process in the different ways the holidays' respective sacrifices were offered: the omer sacrifice was simple barley flour mixed with oil, but the bread sacrifice was two loaves of wheat bread, which require kneading, rising, and baking. The sacrifice at the beginning of the counting period is simple with little preparation, while at the end, the sacrifice demands investment and attention.

The nature and meaning of *S'firat HaOmer* are not entirely clear from the Torah, but over the generations many explanations have been offered. Some have emphasized the agricultural dimension of the period. Nogah Hareuveni (1928–2007), the founder of the biblical botanical preserve Neot Kedumim, explained that each of the "seven species"—the plants for which the Land of Israel is known—is tied in some way to the Omer period: the olive tree and the grapevine flower during this time, while the pomegranate and date trees form buds; the figs, as yet unripe, appear on the branches, and the barley and wheat stalks burst with grain. The fate of each of these species is determined during these seven weeks, even though their individual needs are sometimes at odds with one another. For all these plants to flourish, a delicate balance has to be maintained among different forces of nature. The Omer count, then, comes during tense days of worry about the success of the year's produce and expresses the need to address times of uncertainty.[42]

Some commentators have explained *S'firat HaOmer* as a time for spiritual preparation for receiving the Torah. If a week symbolizes the creation of the world—six days of activity followed by Shabbat—then a nation of slaves fleeing Egypt was in

---

Apart from *S'firat HaOmer*, in Jewish tradition there are other counts of seven weeks, or forty-nine days. The Temple Scroll, the longest of the Dead Sea Scrolls, describes a holiday celebrated forty-nine days after Shavuot: the Festival of the New Vintage (Bikurei Tirosh) celebrates the product of pressing the first grapes to be harvested in season. After that celebration, another forty-nine days are counted until the Festival of the New Oil (Bikurei Yitzhar). These two holidays were not preserved in Rabbinic tradition and are not celebrated today, but it seems that they were celebrated in ancient times among certain groups. Similarly, Sigd—the holiday of the Jews of Ethiopia—is celebrated seven weeks after Yom Kippur (see pp. 63–66).

From Time to Time → Dalia Marx

need of seven weeks of preparation for the encounter at Mount Sinai. We too need preparation and purification as Shavuot—the holiday on which we renew the covenant—approaches.

Mourning Customs during *S'firat HaOmer*?

During *S'firat HaOmer*, there are several mourning customs observed by many Jews, such as not listening to live instrumental music, not getting a haircut or shaving, and not attending weddings. When were mourning customs introduced as part of *S'firat HaOmer*? There is no hint of these traditions in the Torah or in the Mishnah. We first encounter an explicit description of this custom a few centuries later during the Talmudic era, during which disasters befell the Jews:

> It was said that Rabbi Akiva had twelve thousand pairs of disciples, from Gevat to Antipatris; and all of them died at the same time because they did not treat each other with respect, and the world was desolate. . . . A *Tanna* taught: All of them died between Passover and Shavuot. Rabbi Chama bar Abba or, it might be said, Rabbi Chiya bar Avin said: All of them died a cruel death. What was it? Rabbi Nachman replied: *Askarah*. (Babylonian Talmud, *Y'vamot* 62b)

According to this tradition, it was the disrespect displayed by Rabbi Akiva's many students that brought about their cruel deaths. Rabbi Nachman explains that the cause of death was *askarah*, a word that some understand to refer to a plague and others take to mean a military defeat (*asqariya* is the Arabic word for an army). Some think that the Rabbis are deliberately using code words here, speaking of "students" to refer to soldiers in the army of revolt let by Bar Kochba.

We hear much later, in Geonic literature, about specific mourning customs for *S'firat HaOmer*. Rav Natronai explained the custom of not holding engagement ceremonies or weddings during the period of the Omer through Shavuot, insisting that the custom's origin is not an actual prohibition but rather a sign of mourning because of the disaster that befell Rabbi Akiva's students.

How Are They to "Be Whole"?
Torah Study during *S'firat HaOmer*

The seven weeks of *S'firat HaOmer* are intended to prepare the people Israel for receiving the Torah, and even today these days are considered days of *tikkun hanefesh*—repairing and preparing the soul—that prepare us each year for Shavuot, the Festival of the Giving of the Torah. Perhaps because of

Although the Mishnah contains no mention of observing mourning customs during *S'firat HaOmer*, it does address the severe character of these days of the year. When the Sages discuss the question of how long evil people are on trial in *Geihinom*, they answer "twelve months." But the Mishnah also records the opinion of Rabbi Yochanan ben Nuri, according to whom the difficult trial's length is "from Passover to Shavuot" (*Mishnah Eduyot* 2:10). This is the earliest reference to the period of the Omer as a difficult time.

The destruction of the Second Temple by Roman forces in 70 CE left the Jewish community reeling. Bitter feelings about Roman rule never decreased, and many of the early rabbis and other communal leaders agitated for rebellion. Shimon bar Kozva—later given the moniker Bar Kochba, "son of a star," by the great Rabbi Akiva—led a major uprising against Rome in approximately 132 CE. He was successful in creating an independent Jewish state until the Romans overcame them once again in approximately 135 CE. This was the last time Jews had any kind of sovereignty in the Land of Israel until 1948; this alone is evidence that the results of the Bar Kochba revolt were devastating for the Jewish community of Judea. In addition, Jews were forced into exile and prevented from entering Jerusalem. Countless Jews died in warfare or from hunger and disease. The outcome and trauma of the Bar Kochba revolt also had an impact on Jewish history and theology, such as altering the celebration of Chanukah and spiritualizing Jewish messianism. Interestingly, Rabbinic sages who lived after the revolt referred to him as Shimon bar Koziva, because they considered him to be a liar (*kazav* means "lie"). (*Eichah Rabbah* 2:4)

Rav Natronai Gaon, who was head of the yeshivah at Sura in Babylonia during the ninth century, wrote:
> You asked why one does not conduct betrothal ceremonies or the ceremony of bringing the bride into her new home between Passover and Shavuot and whether or not it was because of prohibitions: Know that it is not because of any prohibition but because of the custom of adopting mourning practices, because the Sages have stated that Rabbi Akiva had twelve thousand pairs of students, all of whom died between Passover and Shavuot . . . and ever since then the early authorities in those days had the custom not to hold weddings during that time. (*Shaarei T'shuvah*, §278)

this, Jews developed special traditions of study and learning connected to *S'firat HaOmer*. What these traditions all have in common is that the study is not exclusively intellectual, but also carries psychological and emotional significance; the study is a matter of self-*tikkun* and preparation in advance of the Festival of the Giving of the Torah. Here are seven of those customs, one for each of the seven weeks:

1. *Pirkei Avot* is read on Saturday afternoons during *S'firat HaOmer*. Rather than focusing on Jewish law, *Pirkei Avot* contains many pithy sayings on ethical instruction and general worldview, such as "Who is rich? One who is happy with one's lot" (4:1). This small tractate originally had five chapters, to which a sixth chapter—known as *Kinyan Torah* ("Acquiring Torah")—was added, in order to provide a chapter for each Shabbat during the counting period. Perhaps this custom's intention is to show that in order to receive the Torah, we must first of all be decent human beings, for as we read in *Pirkei Avot* 2:2, "Fine is the study of Torah along with *derech eretz* [common decency]."[43]

2. **Psalm 67** is recited during *S'firat HaOmer*. Psalm 67 is known as "the Menorah Psalm" because of the custom of writing it in the shape of a seven-branched menorah; it appears this way on prints that hang like large amulets in many synagogues. The psalm begins with the superscription *Lam'natzei-ach binginot* ("For the leader, with instrumental music"), which appears on several occasions in prayer formulas. Perhaps most importantly for the period of the Omer, Psalm 67 comprises forty-nine words, and the middle verse comprises forty-nine letters. Therefore, it is customary to recite this psalm after counting the Omer, concentrating each night on a different word in the text and a different letter in the middle verse.

3. In some communities, it is customary to recite the chapters of the **Song of Songs** during *S'firat HaOmer*. In some Jewish communities, they used to read the Book of Proverbs during the *Minchah* service on Shabbat, dividing it into six parts for each Shabbat of the Omer.[44]

4. The last chapter of *Pirkei Avot* (the added chapter "Acquiring Torah") includes a list of **forty-eight things by which the Torah is acquired**. This is how the Mishnah details them:

> The Torah is acquired by means of forty-eight qualities, which are: study, attentive listening, articulate speech, intuitive understanding, awe, reverence, modesty, joy, purity, ministering to the sages, closeness with colleagues, sharp discussion with students, deliberation, [knowledge of] Scripture, Mishnah, limited business activity, limited sexual activity, limited pleasure, limited sleep, limited conversation, limited laughter, slowness to anger, a good heart, faith in the sages, acceptance of suffering, knowing one's place, being happy with one's lot, making a protective fence around one's personal matters, claiming no credit for oneself, being beloved, loving the Omnipresent, loving [God's] creatures, loving righteous ways, loving justice, loving reproof, keeping far from honor, not being arrogant with one's learning, not enjoying halachic decision-making, sharing one's fellow's yoke, judging one favorably, setting one on the truthful course, setting one on the peaceful course, thinking deliberately in one's study, asking and answering, listening and contributing to the discussion, learning in order to teach, learning in order to practice, making one's teacher wiser, pondering over what

one has learned, and repeating a saying in the name of the one who said it. (*Pirkei Avot* 6:6)

Some people have a custom of delving deeply into one of those items each day, either through meditation, study, or simply pondering its meaning, and on the forty-ninth day repeating them all.

The Torah is acquired by means of forty-eight qualities, which are:

16 Nisan, **study**
17 Nisan, **attentive listening**
18 Nisan, **articulate speech**
19 Nisan, **intuitive understanding**
20 Nisan, **awe**
21 Nisan (seventh day of Passover), **reverence**
22 Nisan, **modesty**
23 Nisan, **joy**
24 Nisan, **purity**
25 Nisan, **ministering to the sages**
26 Nisan, **closeness with colleagues**
27 Nisan (Yom HaShoah), **sharp discussion with students**
28 Nisan, **deliberation**
29 Nisan, **[knowledge of] Scripture**
30 Nisan (Rosh Chodesh), **[knowledge of] Mishnah**
1 Iyar (Rosh Chodesh), **limited business activity**
2 Iyar, **limited sexual activity**
3 Iyar, **limited pleasure**
4 Iyar (Yom HaZikaron, Israel's Memorial Day), **limited sleep**
5 Iyar (Yom HaAtzma-ut), **limited conversation**
6 Iyar, **limited laughter**
7 Iyar, **slowness to anger**
8 Iyar, **a good heart**
9 Iyar, **faith in the sages**
10 Iyar, **acceptance of suffering**
11 Iyar, **knowing one's place**
12 Iyar, **being happy with one's lot**
13 Iyar, **making a protective fence around one's personal matters**
14 Iyar, **claiming no credit for oneself**
15 Iyar, **being beloved, loving the Omnipresent**
16 Iyar, **loving [God's] creatures**
17 Iyar, **loving righteous ways**
18 Iyar (Lag B'Omer), **loving justice**
19 Iyar, **loving reproof**
20 Iyar, **keeping far from honor**
21 Iyar, **not being arrogant with one's learning**
22 Iyar, **not enjoying halachic decision-making**

23 Iyar, **sharing one's fellow's yoke**
24 Iyar, **judging one favorably**
25 Iyar, **setting one on the truthful course**
26 Iyar, **setting one on the peaceful course**
27 Iyar, **thinking deliberately in one's study**
28 Iyar, **asking and answering, listening and contributing to the discussion**
29 Iyar, **learning in order to teach**
1 Sivan (Rosh Chodesh), **learning in order to practice**
2 Sivan, **making one's teacher wiser**
3 Sivan, **pondering over what one has learned**
4 Sivan, **repeating a saying in the name of the one who said it**.]

Of course, it is possible to count and divide the list differently, but the real power of this list is its ability to help us direct our hearts toward the Revelation at Sinai and the reacceptance of the Torah on Shavuot.

According to Kabbalah, there are ten *s'firot*, which are ten modes of divine action in the world. These ten dimensions, such as *Chochmah* (Wisdom), *Tiferet* (Beauty), *Chesed* (Loving-Kindness), and *G'vurah* (Might), are the ways humanity meets with the Divine.

The *s'firot* system is patterned like a tree, with trunk, roots, and branches, or like the image of a person. According to the kabbalists, the world of the *s'firot* is the upper world, which is parallel to and reflected in the human world. The divine and human worlds are in relationship and have mutual influence over one another. The three highest *s'firot*—*Keter* (Crown), *Chochmah* (Wisdom), and *Binah* (Intelligence)—are part of the world of *atzilut* (emanation) and are considered wholly divine and inaccessible to humans. The seven lower *s'firot* can be accessed by humans, and the lower the *s'firah*, the closer it is to human experience.

Kabbalistic thought is focused on the possibility of a partnered and balanced union with God. The lowest *s'firah*—sometimes called *Malchut* (Sovereignty) and sometimes called *Shechinah* (Indwelling Presence of God)—has distinct qualities that make it more accessible to humans. It receives the *shefa* (divine emanations) that flow through the other *s'firot* and makes those emanations accessible to our own world.

Of course, it is impossible to explain the worldview of the kabbalists in just a few sentences.

(Dr. Melila Hellner-Eshed)

5. According to kabbalistic traditions, each of **the seven lower *s'firot*** (the "building *s'firot*," from *Chesed* to *Malchut*) corresponds to one of the days of the week, and each of them also corresponds to one of the seven weeks of *S'firat HaOmer*. Each day, then, is a unique concurrence of two *s'firot*, inviting one to study and self-refinement. The day before Shavuot is "*Malchut* in *Malchut*," also known as *Shechinah*, the immanent presence of God in the world; it follows that the next day we celebrate the Festival of the Giving of the Torah. (See the table at the end of this section.)

6. Among Chabad Chasidim, it is customary to study one page a day of the **Talmudic tractate *Sotah***, which has forty-nine folio pages, during *S'firat HaOmer*. Tractate *Sh'vuot* also has forty-nine pages, but there is no known custom of studying it during *S'firat HaOmer*.

7. In recent years, I have seen a few customs that highlight a different female **biblical figure** on each day of *S'firat HaOmer*. Attention is concentrated on her character and her merits as part of the preparation for Shavuot.[45] Here is my (experimental) list of female biblical figures. Most are Israelites; a few are not. Some of them are well-known, while others are more obscure, and sometimes even their name is unknown to us. One can concentrate on each of them during *S'firat HaOmer*, learn about them, and thus make them present in the Jewish story:

16 Nisan, **Eve** (Genesis 2–4)
17 Nisan, **Adah and Zillah** (Genesis 4:19–23)
18 Nisan, **Sarah** (Genesis 11–23)
19 Nisan, **Lot's wife** (Genesis 19:26)
20 Nisan, **Lot's daughters** (Genesis 19:30–38)
21 Nisan (seventh day of Passover), **Hagar** (Genesis 16 and 21)

22 Nisan, **Keturah** (Genesis 25:1–3)
23 Nisan, **Rebekah** (Genesis 24–27)
24 Nisan, **Leah** (Genesis 29–33)
25 Nisan, **Rachel** (Genesis 29–35)
26 Nisan, **Zilpah** (Genesis 29–30)
27 Nisan (Yom HaShoah), **Bilhah** (Genesis 29–30 and 35)
28 Nisan, **Deborah, Rebekah's wet nurse** (Genesis 35:8)
29 Nisan, **Dinah** (Genesis 34)
30 Nisan (Rosh Chodesh), **Tamar** (Genesis 38)
1 Iyar (Rosh Chodesh), **Asenath** (Genesis 41:45–51)
2 Iyar, **Serach, daughter of Asher** (Genesis 46:17)
3 Iyar, **Shiphrah and Puah** (Exodus 1:15–21)
4 Iyar (Yom HaZikaron, Israel's Memorial Day), **Jochebed** (Exodus 2:1–10)
5 Iyar (Yom HaAtzma-ut), **Miriam** (Exodus 2 – Numbers 20)
6 Iyar, **Pharaoh's daughter** (Exodus 2:5–10)
7 Iyar, **Zipporah** (Exodus 2, 4:24–26)
8 Iyar, **Mahlah, Noah, Hoglah, Milcah, and Tirzah**, daughters of Zelophehad (Number 27)
9 Iyar, **Rahab** (Joshua 2)
10 Iyar, **Achsah, daughter of Caleb** (Joshua 15:16–17)
11 Iyar, **Deborah the Prophet** (Judges 4–5)
12 Iyar, **Jael, wife of Heber the Kenite** (Judges 4–5)
13 Iyar, **Jephthah's daughter** (Judges 11:29–40)
14 Iyar, **Hannah** (I Samuel 1–2)
15 Iyar, **Peninnah** (I Samuel 1:2–4)
16 Iyar, **Abigail** (I Samuel 25)
17 Iyar, **Michal** (I Samuel 18–19; II Samuel 6:16–23)
18 Iyar (Lag BaOmer), **Bathsheba** (II Samuel 11; I Kings 1:11–31)
19 Iyar, **Tamar, daughter of David** (I Samuel 13:1–22)
20 Iyar, **the wise woman of Tekoa** (II Samuel 14:1–24)
21 Iyar, **the wise woman of Abel of Beth-maacah** (II Samuel 20:16–22)
22 Iyar, **Abishag** (I Kings 1:1–4)
23 Iyar, **Pharaoh's daughter, Solomon's wife** (I Kings 3)
24 Iyar, **the Queen of Sheba** (I Kings 10)
25 Iyar, **the woman of Zarephath** (I Kings 17:8–24)
26 Iyar **the woman of Shunem** (II Kings 4:8–37)
27 Iyar, **Huldah the Prophet** (II Kings 22:14–20)
28 Iyar, **Gomer, daughter of Diblaim** (Hosea 1)
29 Iyar, **the Shulamite woman** (the beloved in the Song of Songs)
1 Sivan (Rosh Chodesh), **Vashti** (Esther 1:9–22)
2 Sivan, **Queen Esther** (Esther)
3 Sivan, **Naomi** (Ruth)
4 Sivan, **Orpah** (Ruth 1:4–14)
5 Sivan, **Ruth** (Ruth)

The list of women is arranged by the order of their appearance in the Bible, the last of them being Ruth, the righteous Jew-by-choice who joined the ranks of the people Israel, and it is she who brings us into the Giving of the Torah.

I am writing these words on the tenth of Iyar, when we recite, "Today is the twenty-fifth day, which makes three weeks and four days, of the [Counting of the] Omer." If I were to complete all the additional customs that I have suggested here, I would also be thinking about the combination of the kabbalistic *s'firah Netzach* with itself, *Netzach*, concentrating on "acceptance of suffering," delving deeply into the word *l'umim* (nations) and the emphasized letter *mem* in Psalm 67, studying page 25 of Tractate *Sotah* (which deals with, among other things, the possibility of clemency even when the law requires taking action), and thinking about Deborah the Prophet. On Shabbat I would be reading the fourth chapter of *Pirkei Avot* and the section beginning with "The wise-hearted person is called discerning" (16:21) in the Book of Proverbs.

Teach us to count our days rightly, that we may obtain a wise heart. (Psalm 90:12)

	Chesed (Loving-Kindness)	*G'vurah* or *Din* (Might or Law)	*Tiferet* (Beauty or Glory)	*Netzach* (Victory or Eternity)	*Hod* (Splendor)	*Y'sod* (Foundation)	*Malchut* (Sovereignty)
Chesed (Loving-Kindness)	1 Loving-Kindness in Loving-Kindness	2 Might in Loving-Kindness	3 Beauty in Loving-Kindness	4 Victory in Loving-Kindness	5 Splendor in Loving-Kindness	6 Foundation in Loving-Kindness	7 Sovereignty in Loving-Kindness
G'vurah or *Din* (Might or Law)	8 Loving-Kindness in Might	9 Might in Might	10 Beauty in Might	11 Victory in Might	12 Splendor in Might	13 Foundation in Might	14 Sovereignty in Might
Tiferet (Beauty or Glory)	15 Loving-Kindness in Beauty	16 Might in Beauty	17 Beauty in Beauty	18 Victory in Beauty	19 Splendor in Beauty	20 Foundation in Beauty	21 Sovereignty in Beauty
Netzach (Victory or Eternity)	22 Loving-Kindness in Victory	23 Might in Victory	24 Beauty in Victory	25 Victory in Victory	26 Splendor in Victory	27 Foundation in Victory	28 Sovereignty in Victory
Hod (Splendor)	29 Loving-Kindness in Splendor	30 Might in Splendor	31 Beauty in Splendor	32 Victory in Splendor	33 Splendor in Splendor	34 Foundation in Splendor	35 Sovereignty in Splendor
Y'sod (Foundation)	36 Loving-Kindness in Foundation	37 Might in Foundation	38 Beauty in Foundation	39 Victory in Foundation	40 Splendor in Foundation	41 Foundation in Foundation	42 Sovereignty in Foundation
Malchut (Sovereignty)	43 Loving-Kindness in Sovereignty	44 Might in Sovereignty	45 Beauty in Sovereignty	46 Victory in Sovereignty	47 Splendor in Sovereignty	48 Foundation in Sovereignty	49 Sovereignty in Sovereignty

PRAYER OF THE MONTH

The Prayer for Dew (*Tal*)

ON THE FIRST DAY OF PASSOVER, the Prayer for Dew is recited in synagogues. That is how we mark off the end of the rainy season and the beginning of the dry season. From this point on, our prayers no longer say, "Grant dew and rain as a blessing over the face of the soil" but instead simply "Grant blessing." Among Jewish communities around the world, special festive *piyutim* have been added here to mark the transition into summer. Here I will present the opening lines of the oldest of them known to us, a *piyut* from the fourth or fifth century CE.[46]

I will sing aloud when the time of the songbird comes, and in song I will declare, **"Go in peace, rain!"**	אַבִּיעָה זְמִירוֹת בְּהַגִּיעַ עֵת זָמִיר וּבְזִמְרָה אַעַן: **לֵךְ לְשָׁלוֹם גֶּשֶׁם.**
On the works of our Rock I will gaze, for they are lovely in their time, and like sweet music I will say, **"Come in peace, dew!"**	בְּמִפְעָלוֹת צוּר אַבִּיטָה כִּי נְעִימִים בְּעִתָּם וּבְנֹעַם אֲמַלֵּל: **בֹּא בְשָׁלוֹם טַל.**
The rain has gone and the fall has passed, and everything was created in proper form. **Go in peace, rain!**	גֶּשֶׁם חָלַף וּסְתָיו עָבַר וְהַכֹּל בְּצִבְיוֹן נוֹצַר, **לֵךְ לְשָׁלוֹם גֶּשֶׁם.**
The mandrakes give off their fragrance in the lovers' garden, and troubles are gone. **Come in peace, dew!**	דּוּדָאִים נָתְנוּ רֵיחַ בְּגִנַּת דּוֹדִים וְחָלְפוּ דְוָיִים, **בֹּא בְשָׁלוֹם טַל.**
The land is crowned with grain and ripe grapes, and every creature shouts, **"Go in peace, rain!"**	הָאָרֶץ עֲטָרָה דָּגָן וְתִירוֹשׁ וְכָל יָצוּר צֹוֵחַ: **לֵךְ לְשָׁלוֹם גֶּשֶׁם.**
And offering a Passover sacrifice at the entrance to the One who released us from bondage and forgives covenant violations: **"Come in peace, dew!"**	וּפוֹסֵחַ עַל פֶּתַח מוֹסֵרוֹת מַתִּיר בִּבְרִית מְוַתֵּר. **בֹּא בְשָׁלוֹם טַל.**

Seed to sow	זֶרַע לַזּוֹרֵעַ
and bread to eat	וְלֶחֶם לָאוֹכֵל
You prepared with the command,	הֲכַנְתָּ בְּצִוּוּי
"Go in peace, rain!"	**לֵךְ לְשָׁלוֹם גֶּשֶׁם.**
To make milk flow	חָלָב לְהוֹרִיד
and nectar drip	וַעֲסִיס לְהַטִּיף
from every mountain and hill,	בְּכָל הַר וְגִבְעָה,
"Come in peace, dew!"	**בֹּא בְּשָׁלוֹם טַל.**

The *piyut* is constructed around an alphabetical acrostic that opens each stanza. The stanzas alternate between bidding a grand farewell to the rain and welcoming the dew with joy. Nature is portrayed as acting in harmony, agreement, and calm. As every farmer knows, this portrayal is not always reality. Perhaps the emphasis on the pleasant joys of nature is intended to convince the rain and dew to appear at the appropriate times and constitute a blessing.

Kibbutz Passover *seders* are characterized by their emphasis on the natural and agricultural aspects of the holiday. In some kibbutz Haggadot, one can find poems influenced by the liturgy of dew, such as this one, whose author I have been unable to discover:

The rain has gone and the fall has passed,	גֶּשֶׁם חָלַף וּסְתָו עָבַר
and everything in its time,	וְהַכֹּל בְּעִתּוֹ, וְהַכֹּל בְּעִתּוֹ נוֹצַר
everything in its time has been created.	לֵךְ לְשָׁלוֹם, לֵךְ גֶּשֶׁם!
Go in peace. Farewell, rain!	דּוּדָאִים נָתְנוּ רֵיחַ בְּגִנַּת דּוֹדִים,
The mandrakes give off their fragrance in	בּוֹא, בּוֹא בְּשָׁלוֹם, בּוֹא טַל!
the lovers' garden,	בּוֹא בְּשָׁלוֹם, בּוֹא טַל!
Come, come in peace. Come, dew!	רוּחַ בְּרָקִים וְצִנּוֹרֵי שַׁחַק
Come in peace. Come, dew!	עָשׂוּ שְׁלִיחוּתָם
The lightning winds and channels in the sky	לֵךְ לְשָׁלוֹם, לֵךְ גֶּשֶׁם!
have performed their tasks.	לֶאֱגֹר בַּקָּצִיר גְּדוּלֵי חָצִיר!
Go in peace. Farewell, rain!	בּוֹא, בּוֹא בְּשָׁלוֹם, בּוֹא טַל!
Store grasses at harvest time!	בּוֹא בְּשָׁלוֹם, בּוֹא טַל!
Come, come in peace. Come, dew!	
Come in peace. Come, dew![47]	

One can see how the ancient *piyut* influenced the kibbutz song. Both share a calm observation of nature in harmony, which moves along wisely, "everything in its time."

IYAR

**Zodiac Sign: Taurus | Tribe of the Month: Simon
Breastplate Stone: Chrysolite/*Pitdah***

The name Iyar, like the names of the other months, came from Judeans returning from Babylonian exile; it first appears in the Mishnah (*Rosh Hashanah* 1:3). Its source is the Babylonian month name Ayyaru, which is apparently connected to the word *chamor* (donkey). The Babylonian month got its name from an ancient Semitic festival that was observed during this time, named for the donkey. It also may be that the name Iyar is related to the Hebrew word for light, *or*.

The month's biblical name is Ziv, meaning "shining" or "brilliance," because the sun shines more and more during this month. This is one of the five biblical month names that we know and appears in the Bible along with a specification of where it is in the order of months: "in the month of Ziv—that is, the second month—in the fourth year of his reign over Israel" (I Kings 6:1).

Tishrei   Marcheshvan   Kislev   Tevet   Sh'vat   Adar   Nisan   Iyar   Sivan   Tammuz   Av   Elul

Kavanah: A Meditation for Iyar

>Pray for the well-being of Jerusalem:
>>"May those who love you be at peace.
>
>May there be well-being within your ramparts,
>>peace in your citadels."
>
>For the sake of my kin and friends,
>>I pray for your well-being;
>>for the sake of the house of the Eternal our God,
>>I seek your good.
>>>(Psalm 122:6–10)

At the Gates of Iyar

The month of Iyar comes between Nisan—the month the Israelites left Egypt, crossed through the sea on dry land, and became a people—and Sivan—the month when, according to tradition, the people Israel received the Torah. Between these two momentous occasions comes Iyar. One could regard this month as a sort of brownout, an anticlimax after the glory of Nisan and before the intensity of standing at Sinai. Indeed, the entirety of Iyar comes during the period of *S'firat HaOmer*, the Counting of the Omer, a time of mourning and restraint.

But is Iyar just a month in between? A month of being in the middle? After all, tradition teaches us that during this month manna began to appear in the wilderness for our ancestors, who had the privilege of being fed during the forty years they spent wandering about in the wilderness from the bounty provided by the Divine. And in our own time, since the establishment of the State of Israel, in Iyar we observe both Yom HaZikaron, Memorial Day for Fallen Soldiers of the Wars of Israel and Victims of Terrorist Attacks, and the following day, Yom HaAtzma-ut, Independence Day. Memorial Day is for remembering those who gave their lives and the heavy price paid to establish and maintain the State of Israel, and Yom HaAtzma-ut is a day for rejoicing over its establishment and continued existence. Toward the end of the month, on the twenty-eighth of Iyar, Yom Y'rushalayim (Jerusalem Day) is observed.

The first *iyun* in this chapter address the difficult period between Yom HaZikaron and Yom HaAtzma-ut. The second *iyun* examines the meaning of memory in Israel's collective mind and traces the history of the armed forces' *Yizkor* prayer. The third *iyun* touches on questions of living in the ancestral homeland versus living with a sense of being in exile, and asks whether one can feel in exile even at home. In honor of Yom HaAtzma-ut, the fourth *iyun* explores the produce that blesses the Land of Israel and asks: What is *the* fruit of Israel? The fifth *iyun* considers an important dimension of Zionism, the revival of the Hebrew language, while the sixth *iyun* discusses the different meanings of Lag BaOmer and its various incarnations up to the present. The Poem of the Month is Israel's national anthem, *HaTikvah*, and the Prayer of the Month is the special the *Al HaNisim* prayer that has actually been proposed, in several versions, as a passage of the *Amidah* for Yom HaAtzma-ut.

Poem of the Month

HaTikvah ("The Hope")

IN THOSE LONG-GONE DAYS when there was just one television channel in Israel, the Israel Broadcasting Authority ended the program day around midnight with a nightly presentation of the now mythic "Verse of the Day" (a moment of highlighting a biblical or Rabbinic text), followed immediately by the national anthem *HaTikvah* ("The Hope"). That was a kind of last call for those still lingering to get up from the couch or the armchair and go to bed. Singing *HaTikvah* marked the end of the ceremonies at school too: in the stifling Iyar sun on the lower sports field, we were arranged by class, each of us in a white shirt with a sticker showing a red cudweed flower—which Israelis call *dam HaMakabim*, blood of the Maccabees—standing at attention while the principal, with a serious look on her face, led us in singing the words that cast their spell over us:

The Hope	הַתִּקְוָה
Naftali Herz Imber	נַפְתָּלִי הֶרְץ אִמְבֶּר
So long as within the inmost heart	כָּל עוֹד בַּלֵּבָב פְּנִימָה
a soul of a Jew yearns,	נֶפֶשׁ יְהוּדִי הוֹמִיָּה
so long as the eye looks eastward,	וּלְפַאֲתֵי מִזְרָח קָדִימָה
gazing toward Zion,	עַיִן לְצִיּוֹן צוֹפִיָּה.
our hope is not lost—	עוֹד לֹא אָבְדָה תִּקְוָתֵנוּ
the hope of two thousand years:	הַתִּקְוָה בַּת שְׁנוֹת אַלְפַּיִם
to be a free people in our land,	לִהְיוֹת עַם חָפְשִׁי בְּאַרְצֵנוּ
the land of Zion and Jerusalem.	אֶרֶץ צִיּוֹן וִירוּשָׁלַיִם.

The expression "our hope is not yet lost" in *HaTikvah* is borrowed from Ezekiel's eschatological vision of the dry bones. When Ezekiel blew the breath of life into the bones of the dead and revived them, the people first uttered words of despair: "Our bones are dried up, our hope is lost. We are doomed" (Ezekiel 37:11). Their stance is one of disbelief in the face of the great miracle of their resurrection. Imber takes their words and reverses them: "Our hope is not yet lost," he writes. In doing so, he asserts that in contrast to the revived bones, we have not yet been redeemed or resurrected, and yet our hope—our ancient hope—is not lost.

Naftali Herz Imber (1856–1909), the author of the national anthem, was a colorful poet who wandered about among the early pre-Zionist Jewish settlements (*moshavot*) in *Eretz Yisrael*, stayed in them as a guest, and after indulging in food and drink, would read aloud from his poems. His flowery, emotionally charged words fell on attentive ears among the residents of the towns and expressed their feelings. Imber wrote *HaTikvah*—or, to call it by its original name, *Tikvateinu* ("Our Hope")—around 1878, even before his own *aliyah*. He continued to rework the text over and over, and they say that in each *moshavah* and each town they knew a slightly different version...

It was the melody, it seems, that firmly established the text. A few melodies were adapted for the lyrics, but the now-familiar melody was composed by a young immigrant from Romania named Shmuel Cohen. There are many theories about the sources and influences of the melody of *HaTikvah*, some of which seem like legends.[1] For our purposes, what is important is the fact that the heart-rending melody and stirring words gave *HaTikvah* a unique status. It was a popular song, beloved among the people of the First Aliyah (wave of immigrants to Israel between 1881 and 1903), and was sung

From Time to Time → Dalia Marx

at gatherings and Zionist Congresses. In the 1920s it became firmly established as the *de facto* anthem of all the world's Zionists.

Of Imber's full text, today we sing only the first two stanzas, and even those have undergone some changes from the version published by the author. The person responsible for the version of *HaTikvah* we know today is Dr. Yehuda Leib Matmon-Cohen (who later founded Gymnasia Herzliyah, the legendary Tel Aviv high school, around 1905). He changed the line "to return to the land of our ancestors, to the city where David encamped"—which refers to Jerusalem, David's royal city (using language borrowed from Isaiah 29:1)—with the phrase "to be a free people in our land, the Land of Zion and Jerusalem." This change retained the expression of longing for Zion but removed its messianic overtone, since according to tradition the Messiah will be born to a descendant of King David. In this way, the song emphasized the people and its longing for its homeland and became appropriate to serve as a national anthem.

And the Winning Anthem Is . . .

Aside from *HaTikvah*, there were other suggestions for Israel's national anthem. One suggestion came from religious leaders who suggested Psalm 126, which expresses the joy on the people's return to its own country; it begins "A song of ascents. When the Eternal restores the fortunes of Zion—we see it as in a dream" (see pp. 309–12). Others preferred the poem *Birkat Am* ("The People's Blessing") by Chayim Nachman Bialik, who was known as Israel's "national poet." In contrast to Imber's messianic idyll, Bialik's poem has more activist imagery, and it was the choice of many people from the Second and Third Aliyot (1904–23). This is the first stanza of the poem:

May the hands of all our comrades who cherish	תֶּחֱזַקְנָה יְדֵי כָל־אַחֵינוּ הַמְחוֹנְנִים
the dust of our homeland wherever they are be strengthened.	עַפְרוֹת אַרְצֵנוּ בַּאֲשֶׁר הֵם שָׁם; אַל יִפֹּל רוּחֲכֶם –
Let not your spirits fall, happy ones who rejoice, come as one to support the people![2]	עֲלִיזִים מִתְרוֹנְנִים בֹּאוּ שְׁכֶם אֶחָד לְעֶזְרַת הָעָם!

HaTikvah was ultimately selected, and singing it marked and still marks important events in our people's history. In a moving BBC recording of *HaTikvah*, for example, one can hear hundreds of Jews liberated from Bergen-Belsen singing it, five days after their liberation, as part of a special *Kabbalat Shabbat* service held at the camp. It is hard not to be astounded by the energy and strength of the liberated prisoners' singing. Three years later, *HaTikvah* was sung at the declaration of Israel's independence on the fifth of Iyar 5708 (May 14, 1948), at the Tel Aviv Museum, and later in the ceremony it was performed by the Israel Philharmonic Orchestra. In another historic recording, we can hear David Ben-Gurion announcing at the end of the ceremony, "The State of Israel is established. This meeting is adjourned." Despite its popular status, *HaTikvah* was not officially accepted as Israel's national anthem until 2004. "The Flag and Symbol Law" was amended to give *HaTikvah* this official designation; the name of the law was also amended to "The Flag, Symbol, and Anthem Law."

HaTikvah is unusual among the world's national anthems because it is in a minor key. It is not a prayer in the technical sense of the term, in that it does not address God. It does, however, have a spiritual and exalted tone and seems to address the transcendental, which lends the anthem a liturgical dimension. There are congregations in which it is customary to sing *HaTikvah* at the end of Yom Kippur. Many cantors use its melody for singing parts of the liturgy, such as some of Rosh HaShanah's *Musaf* prayers, prayers said at the conclusion of the *N'ilah* service at the end of Yom Kippur, and at the end of the reading of the Haggadah on Passover. *HaTikvah* has enjoyed numerous recorded performances, and sometimes it is used for political purposes (as it was, for example, in the televised election campaign broadcasts of the short-lived pro-marijuana Green Leaf party) or religious purposes (such as when singer Amir Benayun recorded the words of *HaTikvah* sung to a melody attributed to the Chasidic rabbi Shneur Zalman of Liady).

In recent years, some people have expressed dissatisfaction with the national anthem. In this view, *HaTikvah* is written from a point of view that ignores the country's non-Jewish citizens ("the soul of a Jew yearns") and is patriarchal (the word *Y'hudi*, for "Jew," is masculine) and Ashkenazic (since the viewpoint is to see Zion from the West: "toward the furthest east, forward"), and thus excludes women, Jews from Sephardic and Middle Eastern backgrounds, and non-Jews. One suggestion among many to address this exclusion is that a stanza be added to the anthem or that other changes be made; so far, none of the suggestions have gained acceptance.

The Twilight Hour: Between Yom HaZikaron and Yom HaAtzma-ut

WHEN DOES THE DAY BEGIN? When is the night over? And what are we to make of that slippery time, twilight, between the sun going down and night beginning? It is a complex period that does not really belong to either the day or the night, but at the same time it belongs to both of them.

In Jewish law there are a few approaches that address the vague and mysterious nature of twilight. Rabbi Yosei said, "Twilight is like the blinking of an eye, and the Sages did not know how to figure it out" (Jerusalem Talmud, *B'rachot* 1:1). In other words, the moment at which day ends and night begins is so quick that it is impossible to capture it. We all know intuitively what is day and what is night, but the elusive time in-between—a favorite time of poets—does not give itself up easily. Among the Rabbinic suggested definitions for this moment in time, Rabbi Tanchuma's unexpected image stands out:

> When is twilight? Rabbi Tanchuma said, "[This can be likened] to a drop of blood on the edge of a sword. That drop is divided between one side and the other—that is twilight." (Jerusalem Talmud, *B'rachot* 1:1)

Why did Rabbi Tanchuma choose the image of a weapon of war and a description of divided blood? Maybe it comes from the fact that at twilight the sky is sometimes as red as a drop of blood. Perhaps blood was chosen because it is a thick liquid that takes a relatively long time to slip down the edge of the sword. It could be that the only liquid a sword typically releases is blood. Or maybe this bloody image was chosen in order to show that the change of regime between day and night is a takeover that involves a kind of symbolic murder. The spilled drop of blood cannot fall on one side of the sword; it is divided between the two sides, although the source is the same—the life lost, never to return. Twilight is the thin moment before the dripping of the blood onto the two sides of the sword, a liminal moment, like the moment of passing over a doorstep: we have exited from one realm but have not yet entered the other, and we are in both at the same time. It is the nature of liminal moments to engender a measure of discomfort and anxiety, but they also have fertile and productive aspects. Being in a liminal moment arouses creative thinking and invites us to examine questions and problems from new angles.[3]

Establishing the exact time of twilight is important in Jewish law so that, for example, one can distinguish between sacred and profane times as Shabbat begins and ends. The month of Iyar provides us with a twilight time of another sort, one that separates Yom HaZikaron from Yom HaAtzma-ut. Between these two days there is a watershed moment that differentiates content and emotion. And though the distinction between the two days is extreme, they not only are mirror images of each other, but also define each other.

Shabbat T'kumah: Shabbat of Restoration

In many Israeli congregations and institutions, the Shabbat after Yom HaShoah and before Yom HaZikaron and Yom HaAtzma-ut is marked by special events—primarily discussions and roundtables dedicated to communal self-searching and stocktaking. Some people call the days between these observances the Israeli Days of Awe (or the Israeli High Holy Days), and they call the Shabbat between them Shabbat T'kumah, "the Shabbat of Revival/Restoration."

In the Talmud, *t'kumah* is the name of a stone women wore around their necks as a kind of amulet for protection of a fetus (Babylonian Talmud, *Shabbat* 66b). Some claim that it was a hollowed-out stone in which another stone rested, giving it the special shape of a pregnant rock. Perhaps the *t'kumah*—the restoration and revival of Jewish sovereignty in Israel—is a kind of ongoing pregnancy, an unfinished process of creating and being created, accompanied by challenging anxieties and immense hopes.

Tishrei   Marcheshvan   Kislev   Tevet   Sh'vat   Adar   Nisan   Iyar   Sivan   Tammuz   Av   Elul

> It is hard to capture the range of emotions that occur between Yom HaZikaron and Yom HaAtzma-ut, but as an American living in Israel I was able to experience them myself. I was moved to tears by the events on Yom HaZikaron: the national siren blast leading to a powerful moment of silence observed by everyone as far as the eye could see; the sense of somber reflection that permeated everyday interactions; special Memorial Day programs that gathered mourners of all ages together; television shows suspended so that the names of the fallen could be recited. The entire day feels heavy, and it also feels that the heaviness is shared by all.
>
> Then, in what feels like the blink of eye, the heaviness disappears and is replaced by celebration. I will never forget walking into Jerusalem's city center in that twilight period between Yom HaZikaron and Yom HaAtzma-ut. When I left my apartment, my steps were slowed by the heaviness of Yom HaZikaron. As I walked to the city center, it felt as though the entire city shook off that heaviness—the sad, somber, serious emotions—and began a party. Fireworks lit up the sky. Song and laughter could be heard from balconies and parks. Inexplicably, children running in small gangs tagged everyone they saw with sprays of canned "snow." These children, who were held tightly by their parents the day before with a fervent, whispered prayer for safety and long life, now ruled the streets with their freedom, exuberance, and glee. I have never experienced such a shift in emotions on a national stage, but I came to learn that this is a deeply Israeli phenomenon. The resilience, determination, and hope that were a requirement to create the modern State of Israel are expressed in every second between the start of Yom HaZikaron and the end of Yom HaAtzma-ut. The tears and the laughter, the memorial candles and the fake snow, the prayers and the songs—they are yearly reflections of that original resilience, determination, and hope. (Rabbi Anne Villarreal-Belford)

From Time to Time → Dalia Marx

"And at the Twilight Hour of Mercy" (Chayim Nachman Bialik)

In the past, I used to think celebrating Yom HaAtzma-ut right after Yom HaZikaron was cruel to the bereaved families. Today, I think that the juxtaposition of the two remains difficult, but perhaps it provides a measure of comfort.

The mysterious and elusive character of twilight, when it is not clear whether the moment belongs to the day that is ending or the one beginning, makes the transition between the two days possible. One's soul needs a bit of time to cross the roiling river between the two days. And like all rivers, this roiling river separates the two banks while at the same time connecting them. According to Israeli law, Yom HaAtzma-ut begins at 8:00 p.m. At that time, the mourning nation sighs, lifts up its head, and bursts out in celebration all at once. But the joy is not disconnected from the sadness. To a great extent, the two days define and shape one another. The sense of relief that the State of Israel exists cannot be severed from the sorrow over the loss of life, or from our angst over the character of its existence both in the present and also into the future.

In the Jerusalem Talmud we read, "If there is no knowledge, how can one make a distinction?" (*B'rachot* 5:2). Indeed, making divisions and distinctions between categories is a basic cognitive ability. At the same time, the ability to distinguish differences is also the ability to observe similarities, to see what joins the separate categories together. For the twilight time between Yom HaZikaron and Yom HaAtzma-ut, the moment that separates mourning from joy is also the moment that joins the two together.

Sometimes it is precisely the mixing of two distinct realms that creates the primal material from which something new may sprout. This can occur not only in the life of a nation but also in the life of an individual. Chayim Nachman Bialik wrote a poem called *L'Achad Ha'am* ("For Achad Ha'am"), dedicated to the Zionist thinker Achad Ha'am, about a twilight hour in the life of the people:

> And every person, with God's light within,
> went in search of his star as the day grew dim,
> at the hour of primeval chaos, the hour of realms intertwined,
> with end and beginning, destroying and building, old age and
>   youth combined.[4]

The people's confusing moment—the "hour of primeval chaos"—when the lamp of God is lit in each person's heart and all are in search of redemption, is, in Bialik's description, a time when opposites are mixed together without any hope of separating them. This is a time of new creation born of *tohu vavohu*, the primeval "welter and waste" before Creation, "the hour of realms intertwined." Here, too, we can see that the image of the blood divided between the two sides of the sword's blade is appropriate: there is the blood of fallen soldiers and of all those who lost their lives in wars, and there is also the blood that is a part of birth, growth, and flourishing that we hope for in the State of Israel.

Some Israeli congregations choose to mark that time with special "transition ceremonies," some modeled after *Havdalah*, the short ceremony conducted at the end of Shabbat to mark the transition from sacred time back into everyday reality. In this case, we mark the transition from one sacred time into another. Those ceremonies pour new wine into old bottles and new nectar into old, trusted containers. Their goal is to enable us to experience the misty moment between Yom HaZikaron and Yom HaAtzma-ut, in order to deepen our understanding of each, instilling in us the ability to cope with the transition, and perhaps create something new.

Hebrew University professor Aviezer Ravitsky, a scholar of Jewish thought, used to say in his classes that the Jewish people knows only two existential states: *chorban* (destruction) and *g'ulah* (redemption). It's one or the other, like the two sides of a coin. The situation in which we find ourselves at present is unprecedented in the consciousness of the Jewish people: we are neither here nor there. And that's the source of our confusion. This is an intermediate state in which light and darkness are completely mixed together: we have left the realm of exile in body (and in spirit?), but we have not yet arrived at the opposite shore, and who knows whether we ever will?

Indeed, twilight is a time that contains a measure of creativity and an opportunity for original thought. The confusing moment that catches us unprepared is a time when preconceptions and concepts could be shattered, but it is also a moment for learning. We can make use of the twilight between Yom HaZikaron and Yom HaAtzma-ut to consider important and penetrating questions that reflect on the distance we have traversed, the achievements that have been attained, and the road that is still open before us—privileged to enjoy independence and be a free people in our land.[5]

The Tel Aviv congregation known as Beit Tefilah Israeli (Israeli House of Prayer) conducts a *Havdalah* ceremony each year between Yom HaZikaron and Yom HaAtzma-ut. At the midpoint comes the recitation of this Havdalah prayer, created by the congregation's leaders:[6]

אֱלֹהַי נְשָׁמָה שֶׁנָּתַתָּ בִּי טְהוֹרָה. הִיא אַתָּה בְרָאתָהּ אַתָּה יְצַרְתָּהּ אַתָּה נְפַחְתָּהּ בִּי וְאַתָּה מְשַׁמְּרָהּ בְּקִרְבִּי וְאַתָּה עָתִיד לִטְּלָהּ מִמֶּנִּי וּלְהַחֲזִירָהּ בִּי לֶעָתִיד לָבֹא.

My God, the soul You have given me is pure.
You created it, You shaped it, You breathed it into me, and You protect it within me, and You will take it from me and return it to me in the future.[7]

כּוֹס יְשׁוּעוֹת אֶשָּׂא וּבְשֵׁם יְיָ אֶקְרָא.

I raise the cup of deliverance and invoke the name of Eternal [Psalm 116:13].

בָּרוּךְ אַתָּה יְיָ אֱלֹהֵינוּ מֶלֶךְ הָעוֹלָם, בּוֹרֵא פְּרִי הַגָּפֶן.
בָּרוּךְ אַתָּה יְיָ אֱלֹהֵינוּ מֶלֶךְ הָעוֹלָם, בּוֹרֵא מִינֵי בְשָׂמִים.
בָּרוּךְ אַתָּה יְיָ אֱלֹהֵינוּ מֶלֶךְ הָעוֹלָם, בּוֹרֵא מְאוֹרֵי הָאֵשׁ.

Praise to You, Eternal our God, Sovereign of the universe, Creator of the fruit of the vine.
Praise to You, Eternal our God, Sovereign of the universe, Creator of varied spices.
Praise to You, Eternal our God, Sovereign of the universe, Creator of the lights of fire.

בָּרוּךְ אַתָּה יְיָ אֱלֹהֵינוּ מֶלֶךְ הָעוֹלָם אֲשֶׁר יָצַר אֶת־הָאָדָם וּבָרָא בּוֹ יָגוֹן וַאֲנָחָה, וְשָׂשׂוֹן וְשִׂמְחָה. בָּרוּךְ אַתָּה יְיָ יוֹצֵר הָאָדָם.

Praise to you, Eternal, our God, Sovereign of the universe, who formed human beings and created within them sadness and sighing, and happiness and joy. Praise to You, Eternal, Maker of the human being.

בָּרוּךְ אַתָּה יְיָ אֱלֹהֵינוּ מֶלֶךְ הָעוֹלָם, הַמַּבְדִּיל בֵּין קֹדֶשׁ לְקֹדֶשׁ, בֵּין חֹשֶׁךְ לְאוֹר, בֵּין יָגוֹן לְשִׂמְחָה, בֵּין אֵבֶל לְיוֹם טוֹב, בֵּין יוֹם הַזִּכָּרוֹן לְיוֹם הָעַצְמָאוּת. בָּרוּךְ אַתָּה יְיָ, הַמַּבְדִּיל בֵּין קֹדֶשׁ לְקֹדֶשׁ.

Praise to You, Eternal our God, Sovereign of the universe, who distinguishes between the holy and the holy, between darkness and light, between sadness and joy, between mourning and festivity, between Yom HaZikaron and Yom HaAtzma-ut. Praise to You, Eternal, who distinguishes between the holy and the holy.

Who Are the Ones Who Remember— and Who Is Remembered?

THE PAINFUL POLEMICS hurled about in 2011 about the text of the military's *Yizkor* memorial prayer are indicative of the complex issue of the Israeli public's attempts to grapple with Jewish tradition and questions of memory and memorialization. First, though, a few words about the prayer. *Yizkor* was originally created in Europe at the beginning of the twelfth century in memory of those killed in the pogroms inflicted by the Crusaders on the Jews of Ashkenaz (Germany and northern France) (see p. 194). Later, *Yizkor* texts were written to memorialize family members and relatives: "May God remember forever my . . . who has gone to their eternal rest." Today, the *Yizkor* passage is recited mostly in Ashkenazic synagogues as part of a memorial service on the last day of each of the Three Pilgrimage Festivals (Sukkot, Passover, and Shavuot) and on Yom Kippur.

"Each Generation Brings Creativity and Innovation"

About seven hundred years after its original composition, in the Land of Israel, a new chapter has opened in the history of the *Yizkor* prayer. Most of the leaders of the Zionist movement left behind the worlds of the *beit midrash* and the synagogue, with their ceremonies and formulas, and sought to establish a new culture—a secular Hebrew culture—for the Jewish people living in its land. Nevertheless, when they felt a need for ceremonies or other formal means of expression, they turned to the Jewish tradition. The pioneers used the Passover seder to express their renewed connection to Zion and their expectations for the people's restoration. They chose Shavuot as the time to rejoice over their work on the land. They celebrated Chanukah as an expression of their anticipation of the political and military revival of the Jews. Another example of this trend is the subversive text composed by Berl Katznelson (1887-1944), one of the leading figures in the labor movement in *Eretz Yisrael*, written in memory of those who gave their lives in defense of Tel Hai in 1920. During the events at Tel Hai, eight of the members of the Zionist militia at Tel Hai were killed, among them the legendary hero Joseph Trumpeldor. The traditional *Yizkor* prayer provided the inspiration for Katznelson's subversive *Yizkor*:

> May the people of Israel remember the pure souls of its sons and daughters:
>
> Shneur Saposnik, Aharon Sher, Devora Drechler, Binyamin Munster, [Wolff] Scharff, Sarah Chizik, [Yaakov] Tocker, Joseph Trumpeldor.
>
> Loyal and brave, men and women of peace and labor, who tilled the land and sacrificed their lives for the honor and glory of the people of Israel and for the Land of Israel.
>
> May the nation remember them and be blessed with such progeny. Let us bemoan the radiant youth, the glorious valor, willing sacrifice, and total dedication that were lost in the heavy battle.
>
> Our mourning shall not cease or abate until the day that Israel redeems its despoiled land.[8]

Instead of asking God to remember the fallen defenders, as in the traditional *Yizkor* formula, Katznelson's *Yizkor* employs the traditional framework to express the Jewish people's obligation to remember them. Berl Katznelson took *Yizkor*'s framework and opening formula and secularized it, without diminishing its lofty tone. This text, even though it does not address or even mention God, is constructed as a prayer, containing a profound expression of the people's hopes and longings over many generations.[9]

The *Yizkor* prayer for the fallen defenders of Israel went through several additional versions. After Israel's War of Independence, during which the small Jewish community of *Eretz Yisrael* lost the unfathomable number of six thousand men and women—about 1 percent of the Jewish population at the time, twenty-four hundred of whom were civilians—a text was needed to memorialize them. Katznelson's *Yizkor* was updated and rewritten to make his tone more generic. The resulting prayer became an important component of government and local memorial ceremonies. Here is the official text of *Yizkor* in its current formulation:

> May the people Israel remember its faithful and brave sons and daughters, soldiers of the Israel Defense Forces, and all the fighters of the underground and combat units in the battles of the nation, and the people of the intelligence, security, police, and prison service communities who sacrificed their lives in the war for Israel's establishment, and all who have been murdered in Israel and abroad by murderers from terrorist organizations.
>
> May the people Israel remember and be blessed by its progeny and mourn the radiance of youth, the passion for heroism, the sanctity of will, and the self-sacrifice that perished in that difficult conflict.
>
> May the victorious fallen soldiers of Israel's battle be sealed in the heart of Israel for all generations.[10]

Berl Katznelson warned against unbridled neglect of tradition. When he heard, in 1934, that members of the Machanot HaOlim youth movement chose to go on a hike on, of all days, the ninth of Av, he published this pain-filled letter in the daily newspaper *Davar*:

> A renewing and creative generation does not throw the cultural heritage of ages into the dustbin. It examines and scrutinizes, accepts and rejects. At times it may keep and add to an accepted tradition. At times it delves into mounds of cast-off junk, recovers forgotten items, removes the rust, resuscitates an old tradition that has the power to stimulate the spirit of the generation of renewal.[11]

That outlook informed Katznelson's approach to *Yizkor* as well. (See p. 308.)

Back to the Future?

The armed forces' *Yizkor* was first published on the front page of a memorial booklet entitled *Yizkor* that was dedicated to those who had died in the War of Independence. It was published by the Ministry of Defense and presented to Israel's president, Yitzhak Ben-Zvi, on November 29, 1955. Rabbi Shlomo Goren, who at the time served as chief rabbi of the Israel Defense Forces (IDF), was furious about the wording. He argued that erasing God from the prayer was a "malicious misrepresentation"; he was so angry that he ripped the page containing *Yizkor* from his book and demanded that it be replaced by the "sanctified version." It should be noted that the name of God was not eradicated from the military *Yizkor*; it was never there in the first place!

In the standard siddur issued by the chief rabbi of the IDF, edited by Rabbi Goren and his successors, the wording was changed to bring it closer to the traditional *Yizkor* prayers.[12] It begins by petitioning God to remember the souls of those who died during their military service:

> May God remember the souls of the soldiers of the Israel Defense Forces who sacrificed their lives to sanctify God's name and fell as heroes in Israel's wars for our sacred land, the City of God, and the site of the Temple. "They were swifter than eagles and stronger than lions" (II Samuel 1:23) in their effort to grant Israel eternal victory. The memory of their binding [on the altar, like Isaac] and their bravery will never depart

from us, and their souls will be bound up in the bond of life with the souls of Abraham, Isaac, and Jacob, and with the souls of all the other heroes and martyrs of Israel, in paradise, and let us say: Amen.[13]

Paradoxically, the "traditional" text in this instance is actually the "secular" version, which began with the words "May the people Israel remember." Rabbi Goren's demand to restore what he regarded as the prayer's lost glory was actually a demand for innovation, since the Zionist-military prayer based on the version by Berl Katznelson never mentioned God's name and was devoid of any references to biblical figures. Still, despite a 1962 order by the chief of staff to adopt the opening formula "May God remember," the "secular" formula, "May the people Israel remember," was not replaced. It should be recalled that along with *Yizkor*, the memorial ceremonies include other traditional religious texts—*Kaddish* and the mourners' prayer *El Malei Rachamim*—creating a certain balance between explicitly religious and more secular texts.

In 2011, the IDF announced that henceforth the 1962 order regarding the text of *Yizkor* would be enforced. The unused "official version" ("May *God* remember the souls of the soldiers of the Israel Defense Forces") would replace the version that had been commonly used until then at public events and in military ceremonies (asking for the *people* to remember). The announcement sparked a storm of public debate. Yehudit Bialer, a bereaved mother whose son—the subject of the popular song "Yoram" by lyricist Eli Mohar—had been killed in action in 1969, published a petition opposing the decision. In it she wrote:

> I am the mother of Yoram Bialer, who was killed on the eve of the Memorial Day for Israel's soldiers, on the fourth of Iyar 5729 [April 22, 1969], in a battle against the Egyptian forces that had crossed the Suez Canal and entered the Sinai Peninsula. It is important for me to know that the nation to which he belonged, and which he loved, will remember him. Neither Yoram nor I have any relationship with God. Therefore, I vehemently oppose the changing of the wording.[14]

A Vibrant Tapestry of Humanity

In addition to the change in wording of the first line of the text, the change that stands out in the IDF's versions of *Yizkor* is mentioning of the identities of the fallen soldiers and specifying how they lost their lives. This change is also reflected in the Memorial Day Law. At first, the wording of the prayer was expanded to include those who died in all of Israel's wars rather than just those who died in the War of Independence, while still mentioning those who died in the War of Independence with additional emphasis. Later, the prayer was again reworded to be more comprehensive and inclusive.

Since the end of the 1970s—years when the prime minister was Menachem Begin, one of the leaders of the pre-state Etzel (a right-wing underground fighting force)—a reference to those who lost their lives in the underground militant groups was added into *Yizkor*. This is the origin of the current phrases "and all the fighters of the underground and combat units in the battles of Israel, and the people of the intelligence, security, police, and prison service communities who sacrificed their lives in the war for Israel's revival."[15]

An additional change was introduced during the 1990s, when the families of the victims of terrorist attacks renewed their 1967 request that their relatives also be memorialized in the *Yizkor* prayer. This is the origin of the current phrase "all who have been murdered in Israel and abroad by murderers from terrorist organizations."[16] Each of these additions reflects a widening of the circle of memory to include groups of people who were not originally mentioned among those who gave their lives in the struggle for Israel's national revival.

In the wake of the media attention in 2011, the military chief of staff at the time, Benny Ganz, appointed a commission to examine the text of *Yizkor*. The commission members included members of bereaved families, academics, spiritual and religious leaders, and the general public. Commission chairman Yishai Beer, a general in the IDF reserves, understood the complexity of the discussion and wrote, "We have before us a discussion that touches upon two exposed nerves of Israeli society: the subject of mourning and bereavement, as well as the subject of relations between religious and secular people."[17] The commission's conclusion was that the chief of staff's order (which was not enforced anyway!) should be changed, leaving in place the opening lines "that [had] become sanctified in the tradition of national memory for an entire generation: 'Let the people Israel remember its sons and daughters.'"

We see then that *Yizkor* is a text still under development: it was created, took shape, and has changed form constantly in the wake of political and social changes, while trying to be sensitive to the public's positions and feelings.

Poet and leader of the Vilna Ghetto uprising **Abba Kovner** (1918–87), who fought in the War of Independence, also "secularized" the text of the *Yizkor* prayer. In the 1950s he wrote a special version of *Yizkor* in memory of those murdered in the Holocaust, in which he changed the form of the verb from *yizkor*—"may *God* remember"—to *nizkor*—"may *we* remember."

In Kovner's poem—which has become one of the basic texts in many memorial ceremonies for Holocaust victims and resistance fighters—God is not addressed, and the text is not a prayer in the traditional sense of the term. Nevertheless, it has a very tangible religious significance for many. Like Katznelson, Kovner includes a personal dimension in his *Yizkor* so that individual, personal memory becomes part of the general, political story. Perhaps that is one of the reasons that these texts touch people's hearts so deeply.

"If God Were Not Full of Mercy"

When Berl Katznelson secularized the *Yizkor* prayer, he did so not out of indifference, naivete, or—heaven forbid—ignorance. He chose to write a version of *Yizkor* precisely because of *Yizkor*'s familiarity and power in

Nizkor
Abba Kovner

May we remember our brothers and our sisters,
the homes in the cities and houses in the villages,
the streets of the town that bustled like rivers,
and the inn standing solitary on the way.

The old man with his etched-out features,
the mother in her shawl,
the girl with her braids,
the children.

The thousands of Jewish communities,
people with their families,
the entire congregation of Jews,
that was brought to the slaughter upon the soil of Europe
by the German executioner.

The man who screamed out suddenly
and died screaming.
The woman who clutched a baby to her breast
arms tumbling down.
The baby whose fingers groped for her mother's nipple
that was blue and cold.
The legs, the legs that sought refuge
and there was no escape.

And they who clenched their hands into fists,
the fists that gripped iron,
the iron that was the weapon of the vision, the despair, and the revolt.
And those with staunch hearts
and those with open eyes
and those who cast away their souls
without being able to offer salvation.

We shall remember the day,
the day in its noon,
the sun that rose over the stake of blood,
the skies that stood high and silent.
We shall remember the mounds of ash
beneath flowering gardens.
The living shall remember their dead
for behold, they are here before us.
Behold as their eyes stare around and about,
so let us not be silent
until our lives are worthy of their memory.[18]

I Recall
Marcia Falk

The poet Dr. Marcia Falk composed her own version of the *Yizkor* prayer. This one is more general, but also more personal, speaking in the first person singular: *ezkor*, "I will recall."[21]

In memory of lives that touched
   one's own

I call her/him to mind and heart,
the texture of her/his life,
   its presence in mine.

Images rise up
   and fall away,
moments in the current of time—

tender, harsh,
   extraordinary,
     mundane,

that which gives pleasure in recollection
and that which hurts, yet resists
   being forgotten.

May the threads of memory be woven
into the fabric of my life
   and bring healing.

אֶזְכּוֹר \ מַרְשָׁה פָלק
לְזֵכֶר נְשָׁמוֹת שֶׁנָּגְעוּ בְּחַיַּי
אַעֲלֶה עַל לִבִּי
אֶת רִקְמַת חַיֶּיהָ/חַיָּיו:
מַרְאוֹת גּוֹאִים
וּנְמוֹגִים,
רְגָעִים
מִתּוֹךְ שֶׁטֶף הַזְּמַן–
עֲנֻגִים, קָשִׁים,
מֻרְבָּנִים, פּוֹגְעִים–
לוּ יִהְיוּ נִימֵי הַזִּכְרוֹנוֹת
שְׁזוּרִים בְּמַאֲרַג חַיַּי
לְרַפֵּא.

Jewish tradition, with which he was very familiar. He hoped to arouse Jewish historical memory and feelings with his words. Many kibbutz *Kaddish* prayers followed suit, working from the basis of the traditional *Kaddish* prayer but infusing them with a new meaning in keeping with kibbutz ethos. They sought to magnify and sanctify the human being who chooses life.[19]

A similar phenomenon can be found in Israeli Hebrew poetry that is sometimes labeled as "secular" (although that adjective, for reasons explained here, is not one I consider appropriate), which makes use of Jewish terms and concepts, sometimes skeptically or even defiantly, and sometimes in actual protest. The most widely known example of that is Yehuda Amichai's *El Malei Rachamim* ("God, Full of Mercy"), in which the poet describes God as being stuffed with mercy and not sharing it with human beings: "If God were not so full of mercy, there would be mercy in the world, and not just in Him."[20] Amichai utilizes a powerful and familiar text, one recited at almost every Ashkenazic funeral and memorial service, and pours new meaning into it. His poem reverses the original intent of the prayer but at the same time gives it a new relationship with reality. Amichai's poem is an example of creating a new midrash, based on tradition, and preserving it while also giving it contemporary relevance. Textual references and midrashim of this sort—even when made in a spirit of defiance—are evidence of a living interaction with our sources.

Here is an example of a secular *Kaddish*, written by Oved Sadeh (1925–2008), one of the founders of Kibbutz Beit Keshet.

Yitgadal v'yitkadash . . .
Magnified and sanctified
be the furrow that collapsed
as the plow split
the hard soil.
V'yithadar v'yitaleh
Glorified and exalted—the leaf
that grew, turned green, then red—and fell.
V'yitromam v'yitnasei
Raised high and lifted up
be the one who carries the burden
and when his path collapsed
my path too was trampled.
Yitbareich v'yishtabei-ach
Blessed and praised
be the lone voice
with the voice of the many.
Yitgadal v'yitkadash
Magnified and sanctified
be the individual in his individuality.[22]

יִתְגַּדַּל וְיִתְקַדַּשׁ
הָרֶגֶב שֶׁקָּרַס
בְּפֶלַח מַחֲרֵשָׁה
הָאֲדָמָה הַקָּשָׁה
יִתְהַדַּר וְיִתְעַלֶּה – הֶעָלֶה
שֶׁלִּבְלֵב, וְהוֹרִיק הֶאְדִּים – וְנָשַׁר.
יִתְרוֹמֵם וְיִתְנַשֵּׂא
הַנּוֹשֵׂא בַּמַּשָּׂא
וּבִכְרֹעַ דַּרְכּוֹ
גַּם דַּרְכִּי נִרְמְסָה.
יִתְבָּרַךְ וְיִשְׁתַּבַּח
קוֹל הַיָּחִיד
עִם קוֹל הָרַבִּים.
יִתְגַּדַּל וְיִתְקַדַּשׁ
הַיָּחִיד בְּיִחוּדוֹ.

The first to secularize the text of *Kaddish* in similar fashion was the Hebrew author Yosef Chayim Brenner, who concluded his message of encouragement to Russia's Jews in the newspaper *HaM'orer* in 1906 with the words "Magnified and sanctified be the Hebrew person."

The Farmer and Chagall's Floating Jews

THE PEOPLE ISRAEL once lived in the Land of Israel. Its sons and daughters worked their land, plowed and sowed, picked and harvested, and inhaled the land's aromas. They planted vineyards, trampled grapes, drank their wine, planted gardens, and ate their produce. Their Jewishness was a palpable, practical matter, something they sensed with all their being. Ancient historical memory recalls the farmers dwelling securely on their land, tithing their produce, bringing sacrifices to their Temple, taking time off from farming every seventh year, giving the requisite parts of their harvests to the poor, looking up at the sky, worrying that there might not be rain. Their lives were not perfect, but they were at home. Ever since the Temple was destroyed (70 CE) and most of the Jews were exiled from their land, they lost the embodied dimension of their Jewishness and became landless, with nothing to hold onto.

Between Heaven and Earth

The story of the sage **Rabban Yochanan ben Zakkai**'s escape from Jerusalem symbolizes the transition from a Judaism of the body to a Judaism of the spirit. The Rabbis tell us that when Rabban Yochanan ben Zakkai understood that Jerusalem's fate was sealed—that is, that the Roman siege would result in the sacking of Jerusalem—he understood that he had to leave his beloved home. But the Roman siege meant that the Romans were not letting a living soul leave. The Romans were not letting the *living* leave Jerusalem, but the dead were allowed to be carried out of the city. On the advice of Abba Sikra, the leader of Jerusalem's zealots, Rabban Yochanan instructed two of his students to carry him out of Jerusalem in a coffin. Only by pretending to be dead could he get out of the city.

After his escape in a coffin, jostled about between heaven and earth, Rabban Yochanan had an audience with Vespasian, the Roman governor. The Talmud relates that the governor was so dazzled by Rabban Yochanan's wisdom that he offered to grant the fulfillment of his wishes; Rabban Yochanan made three requests. The Talmud comments that he did not ask for Jerusalem to be saved, because he was afraid that such a request would make the governor angry and in the end he would receive nothing. Instead, one of his three requests was the town of "Yavneh and its sages." Rabban Yochanan established (or, according to the Talmudic narrative, put on a solid basis) a Jewish center outside Jerusalem. At Yavneh he founded a *beit midrash* that became the model for Jewish institutions of study ever since. He transferred the connection to the Temple, with its power, fragrances, and sights, to spirited deliberation and discussion. The center of Judaism moved from the *Beit Mikdash*, the Temple, to the *beit midrash*, the house of study. Yavneh is the birthplace of the ethos of "the people of the book," emphasizing learning over landholding. In his book *The Talmud and the Internet*, the American writer Jonathan Rosen writes about the dramatic transition from Jerusalem to Yavneh:

> In a sense, [Yochanan] ben Zakkai's journey in his coffin is the symbolic enactment of the transformation Judaism made when it went from being a religion of embodiment to being a religion of the mind and of the book. Jews died as a people of the body, of the

Rabban Yochanan's departure from besieged, desperate Jerusalem and his establishment of the center at Yavneh is the subject of this Talmudic passage:

Abba Sikra was the the head of the zealots in Jerusalem and the son of Rabban Yochanan ben Zakkai's sister. [Rabban Yochanan] sent to him saying, "Come to visit me in secret."

When he came, [Rabban Yochanan] said to him, "How long are you going to carry on in this way and kill all the people by starvation?"

[Abba Sikra] replied, "What can I do? If I say a word to them, they will kill me."

[Rabban Yochanan] said, "Devise some plan for me to escape. Perhaps there will be some small salvation."

[Abba Sikra] said to him, "Pretend to be ill and let everyone come to inquire about you. Bring something putrid and place it by you, so that people will say you are dead. Then let your disciples get under [i.e., carry] your coffin, but no others, so that they shall not notice that you are still light, since they know that a living being is lighter than a corpse."

[Rabban Yochanan] did so.

Rabbi Eliezer went under the coffin from one side and Rabbi Yehoshua from the other.

When they reached the gate [of the city], some men wanted to put a lance through the bier [to ensure he was really dead]. [Abba Sikra] said to them, "Shall [the Romans] say, 'They have pierced their teacher?'"

They wanted to give [the coffin] a push. [Abba Sikra] said to them, "Shall [the Romans] say that they pushed their teacher?"

[The men] opened the town gate and [Rabban Yochanan] got out. . . .

Once Rabban Yochanan escaped Jerusalem, he met the Roman general, Vespasian. After Rabban Yochanan proved his wisdom by solving one of Vespasian's problems, Rabban Yochanan was granted one request. He asked Vespasian to give him the town of Yavneh "and its sages," thus ensuring the future of Rabbinic Judaism. (Babylonian Talmud, *Gittin* 56a–b)

land, of the Temple service of fire and blood, and, in one of the greatest acts of translation in human history, they were reborn as the people of the book.[23]

Perhaps the statement that the Jews "died as a people of the body," as Jonathan Rosen suggests, is exaggerated, and indeed he later writes that he approves that Jews shifted away from their attachment to one particular place. Still, there is something to be learned from the assertion that since the destruction of the Temple, Judaism is no longer an embodied religion. Rabban Yochanan's departure from Jerusalem was a kind of advance exercise, a training course in exile from the country. Once the Jews left the Land of Israel and entered the Diaspora, Judaism became a culture of learning, of textual debate, of distance from the soil. That is the Judaism and those are the Jews that the painter Marc Chagall depicted so well, hovering between heaven and earth.

The early leaders of Zionism heaped criticism on what they perceived as the untethered, rootless Jew. I do not accept that criticism and believe instead that we need to embrace both our attachment to the embodied center of Judaism in Jerusalem and also the ethos of shifting away from this center, as did Rabban Yochanan and Marc Chagall. It is true that Chagall's hovering Jew was uprooted from the soil, but he was solidly planted in a rich, fertile reality—in the flowerbeds of family life, the fields of community life, and the orchards of study and intellectual pursuits. The longing for the land of Zion and Jerusalem has been a kind of chronic pain that Jews carried with them, but it has also been a productive force in their lives. After all, Judaism was never a religion of asceticism or nonattachment; throughout Jewish history, it was a religion that sought out life and vitality. There is no doubt that Israel is a unique place in the Jewish psyche and in the Jewish world, but at the same time there is also vitality and importance and value in living in other places.

Jerusalem and Yavneh

Jerusalem—Yavneh's counterpart, partner, and competitor—never disappeared from the Jewish imagination or spiritual world. Over time, our ideas about Jerusalem have changed: Jerusalem grew in stature and became the repository of the Jews' prayers and hopes, the site of redemption and consolation, a promise of good things yet to come. In difficult times, Jerusalem was a refuge squirreled away between the pages of prayer books. It is mentioned in almost every text, prayer, and collection of blessings connected to the life cycle. In every time and in every place that Jews have prayed—in the home or in the synagogue, when reciting the blessings over a meal or chanting the

Haftarah, when visiting a mourner or dancing at a wedding—they "raised up Jerusalem above all joys" (Psalm 137:6), focused their concern on it, and yearned for its rebuilding (see pp. 313–16).

Yavneh and Jerusalem, the two parallel and necessary representations of Jewish life and thought, have existed side by side. Jerusalem is the eternal city, the dwelling place of longing, but Yavneh proved to be sustainable and created a meaningful Jewish life even without the Temple and a political center. Yavneh brought about a profound change in the essence of the Jewish people, and its influence is still felt today. The Jews became accustomed to functioning on a spectrum with their lived reality on one end and their dreams of a rebuilt Jerusalem on the other.

At the Second Zionist Congress in 1898, Max Nordau (1849–1923), a physician, political activist, and one of Zionist's leaders, coined the phrase "muscular Judaism" (*Muskeljudentum* in German). He called for the creation of a new Jew, strong in body as well as spirit, quick and virile. Nordau dreamed of a Jew who was a kind of photographic negative of Marc Chagall's Jew, whom Nordau described as a rootless, weak, battered, and persecuted intellectual.

In later years, Nordau was the object of sharp criticism for his position. Some called him a self-hating Jew, but despite the criticism his dream came true. Jews returned to the Land of Israel, and today the Jewish population of Israel is the largest Jewish community in the world. The Jewish people have returned to the charms of the Land of Israel, the fragrances of its flowers, the views of its horizons, the feeling of the soil underfoot. The Jew floating between heaven and earth took a hoe in one hand and a submachine gun in the other and went to work in the fields. These are stereotypes, of course, and like all stereotypes they are only partially accurate, with limited applicability, but it cannot be denied that something remarkable changed in the Jewish world. The Jews now have their own government, judicial system, police force, and army. There are also, sadly, more than a few Jewish criminals, which Theodor Herzl foresaw. The Jews have restored, in a way, their corporeal, earthly dimensions of life.

When Jerusalem Met Yavneh: On the Power of Longing

Just as Jews carried Jerusalem with them wherever they went, they also carried within the places in which they found themselves, even when they were no longer there—in fact, even when they were living in the Land of Israel. We cannot understand the Kabbalah of Isaac Luria, for example, if we don't recognize that it was created in a community populated by descendants of Jews expelled from Spain, which had been their homeland for generations. The kabbalists lived in beautiful, mountainous Safed, but they harbored a sense of profound brokenness and loss resulting from the Spanish expulsion. In a certain way, both exiles—from Jerusalem and the glorious Jewish life in Spain—were reflected in the same deep, disturbing existential unease that the Safed kabbalists sought to address. Against this backdrop of brokenness and loss, Luria created his idea of *tikkun*, the repair of the primordial broken vessels.

Think of the millions of Jews over the centuries who have said, "Next year in Jerusalem," and yet they never made it to Jerusalem—neither they, their parents, their children, or their grandchildren. What a powerful yearning that was, to long for a

Tishrei   Marcheshvan   Kislev   Tevet   Sh'vat   Adar   Nisan   Iyar   Sivan   Tammuz   Av   Elul

place loved and missed . . . but beyond reach. This sense of yearning and hope persists today. To a certain extent, Jews became so accustomed to the constant feeling that something was missing that when they committed to renewing life in their ancestral homeland, they had to abandon the enduring feelings of longing and expectation that were so significant and omnipresent in Jewish life and culture. So what now, for us Israelis? We are already here, in the place for which Jews longed for centuries. What shall we yearn for? For what shall we long? Maybe Yavneh? Do we have something to learn from Yavneh today?

Yavneh teaches us to study, inquire, doubt, and recognize nuance. Yavneh demands that we recognize that power—by government or by force—is never sufficient. Perhaps after more than seventy years of sovereignty in Israel, it would be right to take on more "Yavneh."

Jonathan Rosen writes:

> Before [Jerusalem] fell, Yochanan ben Zakkai had himself and a whole way of life smuggled out of the city and transferred to the yeshivah at Yavneh. The remnant has always been a reminder that, rich as the world that grew out of the destruction was, something has always been missing.[24]

Taking on more "Yavneh" means understanding that "something has always been missing" in our lives. We Israelis have begun to understand—not necessarily in the easiest way—that we do not have to obliterate everything that Yavneh stands for in order to live in the Land of Israel. We are learning that there is no need to choose between nationalism and sovereignty, on the one hand, and learning and yearning, on the other. The Judaism of Yavneh and the Judaism of Jerusalem can coexist. They are not hostile to one another, and in fact one cannot exist without the other.

> Next year in rebuilt Jerusalem!
> Next year in rebuilt Yavneh!

How Many Types of Foods Bless the Land of Israel?

The *duchifat* (hoopoe) is the national bird of the State of Israel, and the olive tree is our national tree (and also that of the Palestinians, by the way). In honor of Yom HaAtzma-ut, I would like to explore which produce is their counterpart: what is *the* produce *par excellence*, the alpha produce at the top of the pyramid of produce grown in our country? Can we identify it? There are seven stops along the way. Let's get going.

Who Knows Seven?

In *Parashat Eikev* in the Book of Deuteronomy, we read about seven species of vegetation that bless the Land of Israel. This group of seven includes five fruits—grapes, figs, pomegranates, olives, and dates (the honey referred to in the Bible is date honey)—and two grains—wheat and barley. The fate of each is decided during the period of *S'firat HaOmer* (see pp. 198–204). The flowers of the pomegranate, olive trees, and gravevine open or form buds during this season, unripe fruits form on the fig tree's branches, and the grains of barley and wheat become full. The Talmud says that "the north wind is beneficial for wheat that has reached a third [of its maturity] and harmful for olives in blossom; and the south wind is injurious for wheat that has reached a third [of its maturity] and beneficial for olives in blossom" (Babylonian Talmud, *Bava Batra* 147a). For the seven species to ripen, a delicate natural balance is required. The need for and trust in this kind of balance is also an expression of faith. Perhaps for this reason only the first fruits of these seven species were brought to the Temple.

> For the Eternal your God is bringing you
>   into a good land,
> a land with springs and streams and
>   fountains issuing from plain and hill;
> a land of wheat and barley, of vines, figs,
>   and pomegranates,
> a land of olive trees and honey.
>   (Deuteronomy 8:7–8)

Who Knows Six?

The seven species are not the only group of vegetation characteristic of our land. When Jacob sends his sons off with a gift to Egypt's vizier and food distribution manager during the famine there (without knowing that it was his son who was the recipient), he sends them with six species: "Take from among the land's choice products in your bags, and bring the man an offering—a bit of balm, a bit of honey, some laudanum, mastic, pistachios, and almonds" (Genesis 43:11). Although this list seems clear, we do not really know the accurate translation of all the words for these six species. The translations of the second and sixth terms (*d'vash* and *sh'keidim*, respectively) are clear: honey and almonds. The first Hebrew term, *tzori*, seems to refer to a tree sap. The third, *n'chot*, may refer to beeswax or perhaps even to carobs. The fourth, *lot*, is unclear; it may be jujube. The fifth item, *botnim*, means peanuts in Modern Hebrew, but we know that peanuts originated in the Americas; it is, instead, likely pistachios. Unlike the seven species, these six—except for the almond—do not need cultivation or irrigation. They all grow even in a drought year, like the very year in which Jacob sent his sons down to Egypt.

Tishrei Marcheshvan Kislev Tevet Sh'vat Adar Nisan Iyar Sivan Tammuz Av Elul

Who Knows Five?

The Rabbis counted five kinds of grain: wheat and barley (which are among the seven species), oats, rye, and spelt. There is halachic significance to this list: eating bread made from any of them requires reciting *HaMotzi*, the blessing over bread before a meal, and *Birkat HaMazon* blessings after the meal. Rav and Sh'muel, Babylonian sages of the third century CE, teach that if one consumes food made from "an ingredient from the five species [of grain], the blessing is *borei minei m'zonot* [who creates all kinds of foods]" (Babylonian Talmud, *B'rachot* 36b), and these five grains and their products are what can become the forbidden *chameitz* of Passover.

Who Knows Four?

Four are the four species that one takes in hand on Sukkot. The Torah commands, "Mark, on the fifteenth day of the seventh month, when you have gathered in the yield of your land, you shall observe the festival of the Eternal. . . . On the first day you shall take the product of *hadar* trees, branches of *t'marim*, boughs of *avot* trees, and *arvei nachal*, and you shall rejoice before the Eternal your God seven days" (Leviticus 23:39–40). In Rabbinic literature, it was decided that "the product of *hadar* trees" refers to the citron (Hebrew: *etrog*), *t'marim* is the palm branch (what we call the *lulav*), *avot* is myrtle, and *arvei nachal* is willow. Each of them grows in a different region in the Land of Israel, and according to a familiar midrash, each represents a different kind of person among the Jews; when you gather them together in order to say the blessing over the *lulav*, the four species symbolize *K'lal Yisrael*, the **Jewish people** as a whole.

> "The product of *hadar* trees"—these are [like] Israel. Just like the *etrog* [citron], which has taste and has smell, so too there are those among the **people of Israel** who have Torah and have good deeds.
>
> "Branches of *t'marim* [date palm]"—these are Israel. Just like the date, which has taste but no smell, so too there are those among the people of Israel who have Torah but do not have good deeds.
>
> "Boughs of *avot* trees [myrtle]"—these are Israel. Just like the myrtle, which has smell and no taste, so too there are those among the people of Israel who have good deeds but do not have Torah.
>
> "And *arvei nachar* [brook willows]"—these are Israel. Just like the willow, which has no smell and no taste, so too there are those among the people of Israel who have no Torah and no good deeds.
>
> And what does the Blessed Holy One do to them? To destroy them is impossible. Rather the Blessed Holy One said, "Bind them all together [into] one grouping, and these [the Israelites with Torah or good deeds or both] will atone for those [the Israelites with neither Torah or good deeds]." (*Vayikra Rabbah* 30:12)

Who Knows Three?

We will continue to narrow down the list. The Torah cites three species. The second passage in recitation of the *Sh'ma* offers a shorter list of the crops among the seven species that are especially important to the economy of the Land of Israel:

> If, then, you obey the commandments that I enjoin upon you this day, loving the Eternal your God and serving [God] with all your heart and soul, I will grant the rain for your land in season, the early rain and the late. You shall gather in your new grain and wine and oil—I will also provide grass in the fields for your cattle—and thus you shall eat your fill. (Deuteronomy 11:13–15)

The grain, the wine, and the oil are the shortened list of the types of food among the seven species. Grain is *dagan*, which could be the barley and wheat of the seven species. The term *tirosh* is translated as "wine" and refers to the new vintage after the grapes are pressed. Oil is *yitzhar*, which refers to olive oil. In the verses cited here, these three species represent the blessing the Israelites will receive if they heed God's commandments.

These three species were present in the Temple worship: the showbread was made of semolina—that is, grain; wine was poured out as a libation on the altar; and olive oil was used in the Temple lampstand. Now, after the destruction of the Temple, these three still play a part in our own sacred worship. All of them are on our Shabbat tables, our own miniature Temples: challah (for *dagan*, "grain"), *Kiddush* wine (for *tirosh*), and oil (*yitzhar*) for kindling the lights—though of course now most of us use candles.

Who Knows Two?

Sixteen times in the Torah we find the expression "a land flowing with milk and honey." This is its first appearance:

> I have come down to rescue them from the Egyptians and to bring them out of that land to a good and spacious land, a land flowing with milk and honey. (Exodus 3:8)

The expression "flowing with milk and honey" evokes a Land of Israel that is fertile and rich, a land with no need for backbreaking labor, since it is brimming with abundance that drips with sweetness. Milk and honey are sweet foods and used to be among the first given to very small children. (Today one does not give babies honey, but in the past it was mixed with milk and fed to babies.) Perhaps these two species contain the promise that the land itself will feed (and perhaps nurse?) the Israelites once they arrive. This expression also occurs right before the famous verse *Sh'ma Yisrael*, "Hear, O Israel, the Eternal is our God, the Eternal is One!" (Deuteronomy 6:4). The close proximity of those two verses is indicative of the link between faith in one God and an intimate connection to the Land of Israel.

Who Knows One?

Thus far we have winnowed our list from seven species to only two, and so we will keep going and boil our list down to just one item, one sole species, the purest, most essential, most basic of all. So . . . who knows one? What is the one fruit, the Jewish alpha fruit? I would venture to say it is the fruit of the Tree of All Knowledge, the fruit that is both desired and forbidden. The Torah uses three descriptors for this longed-for fruit (Genesis 3:6): it is tasty ("good to eat"), it is pleasant to look at ("alluring to the eyes"), and it can bestow intelligence ("desirable the insight . . . the tree would bring"). The Torah describes the fruit but does not name it. What exactly was the fruit of the Tree of All Knowledge? A midrash suggests four fruits as candidates to be the one identified as this coveted fruit:

> What was the tree from which Adam and Eve ate?
> Rabbi Meir said: It was wheat stalks. When a person is without knowledge, we say of them, "This person has never eaten wheat bread a day of their life." . . .
> Rabbi Y'hudah bar Ilai said, "They were grapes," as it says, "The grapes for them are poison, a bitter growth their clusters" (Deuteronomy 32:32). Those clusters of grapes brought bitterness into the world.
> Rabbi Abba of Akko said, "It was an *etrog* [a citron]. . . . Go and look to see which tree's wood is eaten like its fruit; you will find it is none but the citron.
> Rabbi Yosei said, "They were figs. . . . When Adam ate from the tree, [God] disturbed him and took him right out of the Garden of Eden, and he went to all the trees and none would accept him. . . . But the fig, because of his having eaten of its

We have already encountered all the candidates that could be the fruit of the Tree of All Knowledge. Three of them—wheat, grapes, and figs—are among the seven species. The fourth, the *etrog*, is among the four species of Sukkot. Wheat is not a fruit in the botanical sense, but according to Rabbi Meir, eating wheat bread is a sign of wisdom and maturity. He talks about an expression used to describe a foolish person: that they have never eaten wheat bread. Grapes are mentioned for bringing bitterness into the world, just as knowledge brought with it pain and bitterness. Figs were chosen because Adam and Eve used fig leaves to make clothes to cover their nakedness.

In Western art—non-Jewish art, that is—the fruit of the Tree of All Knowledge was depicted as an apple. That identification was apparently based on the similarity of the terms in Lain for apple, *mălum*, and for "sin," *mălum*. (See pp. 128–29.)

fruit, opened its door and took him in. Thus we read, "They sewed together fig leaves [and made themselves loincloths]" (Genesis 3:7). (*B'reishit Rabbah* 15:7)

So indeed, who knows one? Having arrived at the one fruit, the alpha fruit that stands at the top of the pyramid, the fruit whose taste is the taste of Eden and that gave us our understanding, we are unable to arrive at a consensus regarding its identity. Perhaps there is an important idea in this: each person has to find their own personal fruit of the Tree of All Knowledge, just as—according to the midrash (*Sh'mot Rabbah* 5:9)—the taste of the manna the Israelites received in the wilderness tasted like what each person most enjoyed to eat.

Knowledge really does have many flavors.

May we be privileged to enjoy the sweetness of the fruits of the Land of Israel and their beauty, and may our fruits be a blessing to everyone in the world.

From Time to Time → Dalia Marx

Hebrew, Revived—Part II

WORDS. Piles and piles of words. Eliezer Ben-Yehuda (1858–1922), the linguist who became the symbol of the Hebrew language's revival, and the others who worked to revive the Hebrew language, created all of these words from their "feverish minds."[25] How does one create a new word in an almost dormant language? How do you create a "mother tongue," which so often is taught to parents by their children? In fact, how do you create a language at all? The month of Iyar, in which we celebrate Yom HaAtzma-ut and the existence of the State of Israel, provides an excellent opportunity to think about the Hebrew language and the amazing ways in which it has been enriched and brought up to date.

The Old Will Be New, and the New Will Be Made Sacred

Those who took it upon themselves to renew the Hebrew language were guided by the principle that new Hebrew words should be based on roots and patterns that already existed in Hebrew. From Eliezer Ben-Yehuda, to Chayim Nachman Bialik, to the members of the Vaad HaLashon HaIvrit (Hebrew Language Committee, which later became Israel's official Academy of Hebrew Language [see pp. 112–13]), these thinkers used their knowledge of traditional Jewish texts to shape how new words were created. Yechiel Michael Pines, one of the first members of the Hebrew Language Committee, said, "The best part of a new word is if it is not actually new at all." Below are some examples.

1. **Old Patterns, New Words:** Biblical Hebrew lists a few diseases, such as *baheret* (Leviticus 13:4), and *tzarevet* (13:23). These words share a similar vowel pattern of ⬜a⬜e⬜et. Rabbi Aharon Meir Mazia (1858–1930) was an ophthalmologist, orchard owner, and chair of the Hebrew Language Committee, and he made many suggestions for illnesses not mentioned in classical Hebrew texts; each of the suggestions follows the ⬜a⬜e⬜et vowel pattern. So, for example, the word for jaundice, which causes the skin to become yellow, takes the Hebrew word for yellow—*TZaHoV*—and transforms it using the ⬜a⬜e⬜et vowel pattern to *TZaHeVet*. Hebrew is a living language full of vitality, and so this same vowel pattern has been used to describe additional "social illnesses." A particularly clever example is *SaGeMet*, which describes the self-importance of newly minted graduates of officers' training, which comes from the acronym *SaGaM* (second lieutenant).
2. **Old Words, New Purpose:** The creators of Modern Hebrew debated what to call a pistol or handgun. Eliezer Ben-Yehuda looked to the *Tanach* and found Isaiah describing a precious stone, which Rashi, the Torah commentator extraordinaire, understood as "a stone that burns like a torch." Ben-Yehuda wrote in his newspaper *HaTzvi* in 1898, "In Hebrew we have a root that means a kind of stone [used to spark fire]. That root is *k-d-ch* . . . and therefore it is our opinion and our sense that we should adopt the term *ekdach*" to describe this firearm.[26] Today, a pistol is *ekdach* in Modern Hebrew.

Tishrei   Marcheshvan   Kislev   Tevet   Sh'vat   Adar   Nisan   Iyar   Sivan   Tammuz   Av   Elul

3. **Compound Words:** Sometimes two words are joined together to create a new word. For example, the Hebrew word *afilu* (even if) is a blend of the words *af* (even) and *ilu* (if). The Israeli public has come up with many innovations of these compound words, some of them adopted after the fact by the Academy of Hebrew Language. An example is *kadursal* (basketball), which like English combines the words for ball (*kadur*) and basket (*sal*) to create a new compound word.

4. **Loan Translations:** A loan translation is the transfer of a term from one language to another, translated literally. For example, the word *gan y'ladim* translates literally as "garden of children" but means, of course, kindergarten (originally a German word that was adopted into English without translation). Similarly, the instrument by which we move the cursor on our computer screens is *achbar*, "mouse," borrowing the English term given because of its shape.

What Language Should Inspire Modern Hebrew?

Today, neither Arabic nor Aramaic is the main language that influences the development of Hebrew. Instead, English has the most influence on Hebrew—but it is adapted according to Hebrew rules. So, for example, "to format" is *l'farmet*, and "to catalogue" is *l'katleg*—words that use the English sounds in a Hebrew verb construct. A wonderful example is the Hebrew term for the syndrome known as jetlag. In 1993, the Academy of Hebrew Language announced the Hebrew word is *ya-efet*—a clever play on a three-letter root that has the dual meanings of "fatigue" and "flight." A simple example is the Hebrew word for "honeymoon," which is *yerach d'vash*, a simple translation. In the original Hebrew version of this book, I tried to steer clear of foreign loanwords. Using the word lists published by the Academy of Hebrew Language, for example, I was able to find a Hebrew term for "stereotype"—*hetpes*, from the root of the term *tipus* ("type"—itself an ancient Greek loanword in Hebrew!).

So far we have seen some techniques for coining new Hebrew words. Now let us look at the languages that served as inspiration for those who worked to renew the language. Those pioneers knew that they needed to make use of other languages to enrich Hebrew, but they did not agree about which language would be the primary inspiration. Eliezer Ben-Yehuda's preference was for Arabic. He even suggested that the Vaad HaLashon should accept all Arabic roots as appropriate for use in Hebrew:

> I suggest that the Vaad HaLashon put out a sort of royal proclamation announcing that all the roots in the Arabic lexicon . . . are Hebrew [roots] as well! . . . Let those roots be our clay and our building blocks to create new words for other concepts by means of true creativity appropriate for the Vaad HaLashon.
>
> And our writers, and in particular our poets, who are so thirsty for words, who are searching high and low for every sound that can better convey their ideas and feelings, will introduce those roots into the language and breathe into them the spirit of life as Hebrew words.[27]

Ben-Yehuda's suggestion was not accepted. Instead, others—foremost among them the educator Eliezer Meir Lifshitz—suggested Aramaic instead. He argued that Aramaic is a Northern Semitic language that "lives" on the same branch of the Semitic language tree as Hebrew. Furthermore, Aramaic, in its various dialects, was already familiar to many Jews, since it is the language of midrash, Talmud, Kabbalah, and even parts of the "Hebrew" Bible. Lifshitz suggested the Aramaic of the Talmuds as the central source for borrowing elements from which new Hebrew words would be coined.

The dispute between Ben-Yehuda and Lifshitz may seem to be over a merely technical matter, but undergirding each of their approaches is a different ideological approach. Should Arabic—a living Semitic language—be the model for the renewal of Hebrew, or should it be Aramaic—a Semitic language no longer widely used but close in character to Hebrew, that has been part of Jewish literature throughout the ages? (Some dialects of Aramaic are still spoken today, but they are not the dialects of Jewish sources.) Ben-Yehuda, who abandoned the world of religion, sought to reject the exilic worldview that he saw in Talmud study and characterized by Aramaic, preferring instead to adhere to a language rooted in in the Land of Israel; Lifshitz, meanwhile, regarded the revival of Hebrew as an act of returning to the people's early sources.

The process of reviving Hebrew has been unique. It is successful beyond measure, with nothing to compare it to among parallel efforts by other peoples. In fact, Hebrew's revival has been the opposite of that of other nations whose national linguistic revival was the creation of a written literature for a spoken language. Hebrew has always existed as a literary language, and the focus of the revival was on returning it to the status of a spoken language.

Lag BaOmer: *Yahrzeit*, Might, and New Light

THE ISRAELI POET Yehonatan Gefen wrote, "When they say radish, you feel the tongue."[28] This provocative image—made stronger in Hebrew because of the similarities between the word for radish, *tz'non*, and tongue, *l'shon*—leads us to wonder: Do words conjure up tastes for you? When you say "Lag BaOmer," do you sense in your mouth the taste of an overbaked potato from the campfire? That is just one of the tastes of Lag BaOmer.

Jewish holidays always have a few flavors—agricultural, historical, national, psychological. Lag BaOmer, the thirty-third day of *S'firat HaOmer* (see pp. 198–204), is on the surface no different from the other days of the Omer; its origin is shrouded in mist. Today, Lag BaOmer is considered a minor holiday associated with cutting one's hair (something forbidden during the Omer period), lighting bonfires, and celebrating weddings (also forbidden during the Omer). Even in communities that do not strictly observe the Omer, there may be outdoor barbeque and bonfire celebrations during Lag BaOmer. In Israel, however, there are many unique aspects to this special day.

It is not mentioned in the Torah, Mishnah, or the Babylonian or Palestinian Talmud. We first encounter Lag BaOmer in the words of Rabbi Avraham HaYarchi of Lunel in Provence (who died circa 1215). Mentioning a custom of refraining from holding weddings during *S'firat HaOmer*, he adds that in France and Provence, the custom applies only up to Lag BaOmer:

> And it is customary not to marry between Passover and Shavuot, but the custom in France and Provence is to marry from Lag BaOmer on. And I have heard it said in the name of Rabbi Zerachiah of Gerona that he found written in an old book that came from Spain that [Rabbi Akiva's students] died from Passover until *p'ros haAtzeret* [and that is Lag BaOmer]. (*HaManhig*, Laws of Betrothal and Marriage, 106)

According to this custom, the term *p'ros haAtzeret* (the spreading out of the Shavuot festival) means sixteen days before Shavuot—in other words, the eighteenth of Iyar, which is Lag BaOmer. Rabbi Avraham quotes an anonymous, lost source claiming that the plague (or military campaign) that struck at Rabbi Akiva's students came to an end on the thirty-third day of the Counting of the Omer (see p. 199). We do not know what that old book that was, but in any case, it supports ending the observance of mourning practices during the days of *S'firat HaOmer* on the thirty-third day.

The *Hilula* of Rabbi Shimon bar Yochai

Rabbi Shimon bar Yochai (known by the acronym Rashbi), one of the sages in the Mishnah, lived in the second century CE, during the period of the Bar Kochba revolt. After the Romans discovered that Rabbi Shimon bar Yochai had spoken against them, he hid in a cave with his son due to fear of punishment. They studied Torah in that cave for thirteen years. Authorship of the *Zohar*, the central and most influential text in

---

Originally, Hebrew did not use numerals. Instead, each Hebrew letter was assigned a number: *alef* was one, *bet* was two, and so on. Sometimes, the alphanumeric system creates new "words," and "Lag" in "Lag BaOmer" is one of these. The Hebrew letter *lamed* stands for thirty, *gimel* is three, and together they combine to form "thirty-three," or ל״ג—which we pronounce as *lag*. Assigning numbers to each Hebrew letter eventually led to a process of textual interpretation called *g'matria*, where connections between two different words with identical numbers create exegetical and mystical insight (see p. 325). The numerical value of the entire *alef-bet* is divided into three sections; letters *alef* through *tet* are single-digit numbers; letters *yod* through *tzadi* are double-digit numbers; letters *kof* through *tav* are triple-digit numbers, as follows:

100 = ק	10 = י	1 = א
200 = ר	20 = כ	2 = ב
300 = ש	30 = ל	3 = ג
400 = ת	40 = מ	4 = ד
	50 = נ	5 = ה
	60 = ס	6 = ו
	70 = ע	7 = ז
	80 = פ	8 = ח
	90 = צ	9 = ט

From Time to Time → Dalia Marx

Kabbalah, is traditionally attributed to him; according to that same tradition, central events in Rashbi's life occurred on Lag BaOmer: he married, was ordained as a rabbi, and died on that date. According to tradition, as his death approached, Rabbi Shimon revealed hidden secrets to his students, which are found in the *Zohar*.

The day of Rashbi's death is mentioned as far back as the *Zohar* as a day of *hilula*—a public celebration held on a great person's *yahrzeit* (anniversary of a person's death)—and was celebrated with great fanfare among the circle of mystics surrounding Rabbi Isaac Luria in sixteenth-century Safed. Luria's student, Rabbi Chayim Vital, mentioned this custom:

> The custom of Jews to go on Lag BaOmer to the graves of Rashbi and his son Rabbi Eliezer, who are buried at Meron, is widely known, and to eat and drink and celebrate there. (*Shaar HaKavanot, D'rushei Pesach* 12)

There were some who opposed the practice of having a *hilula* for Rashbi on Lag BaOmer. The Chatam Sofer (Rabbi Moshe Chayim Schreiber, 1762–1839, a leader of Hungarian Orthodoxy), for example, opposed its observance because it is not mentioned in Rabbinic sources and has no basis in Jewish law.[29] Rabbi Joseph Shaul Nathansohn, a nineteenth-century rabbinical authority in Poland, also objected to the *hilula* of Rabbi Shimon:

> But in truth, here too I am surprised, since on the contrary when a righteous and wise person dies, one should mourn. And we fast at the death of tzaddikim, so how shall we make a celebration at the death of our late lamented great rabbi, Rashbi? . . . And if the *Zohar* called for a *hilula* for Rashbi, it is for [his sake], since it is certainly a great joy to have gone to one's rest, but he left us sighing. In truth, there is much to be said about the fact that they used to burn items of clothing on Lag BaOmer. This is a violation of the prohibition against waste [*bal tashchit*]. . . . And I assure you that if they were to take that same money and use it to support the poor in the Land of Israel, Rashbi would be more pleased, and it would benefit Rashbi and benefit the world.[30]

Rabbi Nathansohn raises a question about the very act of celebrating on the date of death, and he also denounces the custom still practiced today of throwing valuable items into the fire, warning against the unnecessary waste.

Regardless, the *hilula* of Rabbi Shimon bar Yochai continues to take place each year at Meron, at the grave marked as that of Rabbi Shimon. The number of people who come to celebrate is in the hundreds of thousands, apparently making it the largest regular gathering in the State of Israel. The celebrants light bonfires on the night of Lag BaOmer in a traditional ceremony and engage in many traditional practices, one of which is the *chalakah* on the morning of the holiday.

A celebration on the anniversary of a person's death is not an obvious practice. After all, the day reminds us of the person's departure from the world and our parting from them. In the Jewish tradition, though, it has become customary to celebrate the legacy of a rabbi or other leading figure on the date of their death, since once people have gone to their eternal rest we can appreciate the full scope of their personalities and accomplishments. If it is customary to light a *yahrzeit* candle, known in Hebrew as a *ner n'shamah* (candle/lamp of the soul) on the date of someone's death, for Rabbi Shimon we light many bonfires on Lag BaOmer.

By way of contrast, the custom of celebrating birthdays in a Jewish setting is a relatively late practice. For example, the only person in the Bible whose birthday is observed is none other than Pharaoh in the Joseph story: "The third day was Pharaoh's birthday, and he gave a feast for all his officials" (Genesis 40:20).

On April 30, 2021, a crowd crush disaster occurred at the *hilula* of Rabbi Shimon bar Yochai in Meron on Lag BaOmer, claiming the lives of forty-five men and boys and injuring over one hundred more. In response, Rabbi Chaim Kanievsky, the spiritual leader of the Lithuanian ultra-Orthodox stream, was asked, "What should we improve?" The premise of this question is that the tragedy occurred as a punishment for sin. His answer was, "Strengthen commitment to Torah and consistency in fulfilling obligations."[31] He also stated that "women should strengthen their commitment to modesty," indirectly accusing women for their conduct, as the reason for the catastrophic event. This response sparked widespread reaction and resistance in the Israeli public sphere. Many compared it with the rabbinic response to a similar disaster that occurred at the *hilula* of Rabbi Shimon bar Yochai in Meron more than a century earlier in 1911, when about eleven celebrants (the exact number is not known) were killed because a railing on which they were leaning collapsed. In response to the crowd crush of 2021, drastic changes were adopted by the authorities, including limiting the number of visitors to Meron, requiring tickets, and having a robust police and military presence in attendance.[32]

Tishrei Marcheshvan Kislev Tevet Sh'vat Adar Nisan *Iyar* Sivan Tammuz Av Elul

Chalakah: The First Haircut Ceremony

In some Jewish communities, a boy's first haircut takes place around his third birthday; according to some traditions, especially among Chasidim, it should take place on Lag BaOmer during the *hilula* at Meron. The custom seems to be local, as evidenced by its name: *chalakah* is the Arabic word for "haircut." The three-year-olds are brought to Meron with a family entourage. The toddlers, with childhood curls in abundance, are lifted onto their fathers' shoulders in a dance that focuses the celebration on the young child. The ceremony is held at the eastern side of the inner courtyard of the building around Rabbi Shimon's grave. The Chasidic custom is to give relatives and honored guests the honor of shearing off a lock of the child's hair as he sits on his father's lap, until all that is left are the ritual sidelocks called *pei-ot*. The boy's appearance changes all at once from a baby-faced toddler with a long mane of baby-fine hair to a young child with short-cropped hair and *pei-ot*. After shearing off the last strands of babyhood, the young child is considered ready to begin a life of Torah study. Many people weigh the shorn hair and give *tzedakah* to the poor in accordance with the weight. There is also a custom of throwing the shorn hair into the fire burning on the roof of the building, with one lock usually kept as a souvenir.[33]

> The custom of the *chalakah* as we know it is an Israeli version of an earlier Ashkenazic tradition mixed with local adaptations and influences (as its Arabic name indicates). In its present form, it is a fascinating blend of East and West, of local customs and the traditional ceremony of induction into the sweetness of Torah study, a rite of passage from infant and toddler into childhood and, concomitantly, an initiation into "bearing the yoke" of the Torah and its study. (See pp. 262–64.)

In its traditional form, the *chalakah* and other customs associated with entry into the world of Torah study were reserved only for boys, and the event took place only among men. Today we face the challenge of crafting meaningful ceremonies to mark the entry into study by all children regardless of gender, while also giving a significant role to all parents.

"He Was a Hero": Lag BaOmer in Zionism

The leaders of Zionism searched for events and symbols from Jewish tradition that could serve as an example of a life of national pride and military heroism for Jewish children. Just as the heroism of the Maccabees became the central focus of Chanukah for the Zionists, so did the heroism of Bar Kochba become central to the Zionist leaders' embrace of Lag BaOmer. But the **Bar Kochba revolt** as a military model is problematic, since the rebellion ended in a horrific disaster and the loss of any hope for Jewish sovereignty for the next nearly two thousand years (see p. 199). Still, the revolt and the person who led it became a symbol of military resistance.

The Rabbis had reservations about Shimon bar Kochba, or as he signed his letters, "Shimon bar Kosba," and his revolt against the Romans. In Israeli children's songs, though, Bar Kochba is recalled as a hero who "called for liberty" and whom "all the nation loved"—at least in the children's song "Bar Kochba" by Levin Kipnis (1929). Children would run around with bows and arrows—a custom that has faded away in recent decades—and they continue to light bonfires, the bigger and higher the better. The bonfires symbolize (or so my preschool teachers taught me) the signal fires that the rebels used to communicate with one another.

Perhaps because of the connection between Bar Kochba and Lag BaOmer, Lag BaOmer was chosen as the day for the establishment of the Palmach, the elite fighting force of the Jewish community in pre-state Palestine in 1941. Seven years later, after the state had been formally instituted, David Ben-Gurion gave the order establishing the Israel Defense Forces on the same Hebrew date. Lag BaOmer was chosen as target practice day for Gadna (the acronym of *g'dud noar*, "youth brigade"), the IDF's youth program for secondary school students. A few years ago, it also became the date for honoring those who serve in the IDF reserves.

Aside from it being a Zionist holiday that reminds us of the Bar Kochba revolt, Lag BaOmer is also a very earthbound, tangible celebration connected to the soil, the trees, and the effort to start a fire and keep it going. It is a holiday observed in nature and in that way is essentially different from Jewish holidays observed in the synagogue and at home. After Lag BaOmer, the holiday of fire, the next holiday is the holiday of the giving of the Torah—Shavuot—which is considered the holiday of water. (The Torah, after all, was compared to water by the Rabbis.) Unlike Shavuot, Lag BaOmer is not a holiday of words, but a holiday of action, tastes, aromas, and lots of smelly and dirty clothes.

The Witches' Holiday in Early Spring?

A holiday similar to Lag BaOmer is May Day, celebrated in many places in Europe, such as Germany, Sweden, Finland, and Latvia. May Day is an ancient pagan festival that predates Christianity and is celebrated on the eve of the **first of May** (a date close to that of Lag BaOmer). It is characterized by bonfires, celebrations, and dancing around the fire, which symbolizes the end of the winter and the anticipated heat of the summer. Since the Middle Ages and the triumph of Christianity, May Day transformed into Walpurgisnacht, named for Saint Walpurga (or Walburga), who lived in the eighth century and was proclaimed a saint on May 1. The holiday also shifted from the eve to the day of May 1. Today, customs that are a mix of ancient pagan traditions for welcoming spring and Christian celebrations of Walpurga exist side by side. One famous example is the gathering of witches that according to popular belief takes place on the Brocken, the highest peak in Germany's Harz mountain range.

We know of no ancient customs of this sort in Judaism, but Lag BaOmer—the holiday created in the Middle Ages—also pays homage to a saintly figure with the *hilula* for Rabbi Shimon bar Yochai on the anniversary of his death. Similar to May Day and Walpurga, Lag BaOmer is a holiday of being in nature, lighting bonfires, and gathering together.

∾

Even though Lag BaOmer is a relatively "young" holiday, it serves as a respite during *S'firat HaOmer* and brings together many disparate subjects: Rabbi Shimon bar Yochai's *hilula*, the *chalakah* ceremonies for young boys, lighting bonfires, the memory of the Bar Kochba revolt, celebrating Jewish sovereignty, and perhaps also hints of ceremonies celebrating the strengthening sun.

The Jewish longing for redemption in the middle of the second century CE helped foment an organized military **revolt, led by Shimon bar Kochba** (meaning "son of a star"), as he was called by his followers. The Sages of Rabbinic Judaism called him Shimon bar Koziva, because of what they considered to be his falsehoods (*kazav* means "lie, falsehood"). The spiritual leader of the revolt was Rabbi Akiva.

The immediate cause for the outbreak of a rebellion was, apparently, the Roman decree against circumcision and their efforts to remake Jerusalem into Aelia Capitolina, a pagan Roman city. The revolt broke out during Hadrian's reign as emperor in the year 132 CE and was cruelly suppressed over the course of three years of fighting. The revolt's results were grievous. The Romans destroyed many Jewish towns and villages, and they issued many decrees forbidding Jews from observing Shabbat or holidays, practicing circumcision, studying Torah in public, or maintaining their own courts.

May 1 is also the date of a very different observance: International Workers' Day. The holiday was formally declared in the year 1889 in Paris at a gathering of Second International (an organization of socialist and labor parties) as the day marking workers' struggle for social and economic justice. Jewish workers have participated in International Workers' Day events from its inception. In Israel, the day was first observed in 1906. Today, after the fall of the Communist bloc, the day's appeal has faded, but it is still observed in many places. In any case, May 1 is home to two completely different holidays—the pagan festival marking changes in nature and the civic holiday demanding social and economic change.

Tishrei   Marcheshvan   Kislev   Tevet   Sh'vat   Adar   Nisan   Iyar   Sivan   Tammuz   Av   Elul

Prayer of the Month

Al HaNisim for Yom HaAtzma-ut

Professor Eliezer Schweid, the late historian of Jewish thought who was also one of the soldiers who liberated the city of Safed during the War of Independence in 1948, told the story that the rabbi of Safed informed the fighters that the city was saved because of two things: a human deed and a miracle. The human deed was that the people of Safed never stopped praying, and the miracle was that the Palmach forces arrived in time. Schweid added that the rabbi was right, since "the fact that we succeeded in liberating Safed with the arms and the force that we had really was a miracle."[34] This observation raises a penetrating question: Should we regard the establishment of the State of Israel as a miracle? Throughout the years of its existence, there has been an ongoing discussion of whether to grant the establishment of the state a religious status and—if it is granted such a status—how it should be commemorated.

Some have suggested saying the traditional *Hallel* on Yom HaAtzma-ut (see p. 152). Others have advocated a special *Kiddush*, along with the *Shehecheyanu* blessing, which thanks God for giving us life and sustaining us. Still others have suggested a special haftarah reading for the day. In many congregations, special liturgies for Yom HaAtzma-ut are recited on the eve and the day of the holiday; some of them include an *Al HaNisim* ("For the Miracles") passage, parallel to those added to the *Amidah* for Chanukah and Purim. More recently, some Israelis hold *Havdalah* ceremonies to transition between Yom HaZikaron and Yom HaAtzma-ut (see p. 215). Here we will take a look at the *Al HaNisim* prayers composed for Yom HaAtzma-ut.

The Rabbis instructed that for any holiday that is not included in the Torah, such as Chanukah and Purim, one should recite the morning and afternoon *Amidah* prayers and include mention of the holiday's events (*Tosefta B'rachot* 3:10). This "mention" is in the form of an *Al HaNisim* prayer said on Chanukah and Purim in both the *Amidah* and the Blessing after Meals (*Birkat HaMazon*). It is a prayer of thanksgiving to God for the miracles God performed for God's people. The miracles are also detailed within the prayer. The desire to create a version of this prayer for Yom HaAtzma-ut indicates that many people regard the establishment of the State of Israel as being somehow miraculous, on a par with the miracles of Jewish survival associated with Chanukah and Purim.

Is there justification in Jewish law for composing a new *Al HaNisim*, a new prayer of thanksgiving, for Yom HaAtzma-ut? Rabbeinu Tam, Rashi's grandson, who lived in twelfth-century France, is quoted as having said, "In all eighteen blessings [of the *Amidah*] a person can add something new, either related to thanksgiving and prayer, or related to asking for what one needs, and since one is making up something on the same theme as the blessing, that is not considered an interruption" (*Machzor Vitry*, §325). In his view, there is justification for adding new words of thanksgiving about new events to the standard prayer.

However, while the wording for the *Al HaNisim* prayers for Chanukah and Purim are ancient—we know about them from the earliest prayer books that we have—an *Al HaNisim* for Yom HaAtzma-ut requires entirely new wording. Those who set out to create a new text faced an interesting question: Is the establishment of the state truly a miracle, and if it is, how should that be expressed in prayer?

From Time to Time → Dalia Marx

Not everyone agrees that an *Al HaNisim* prayer should be said on Yom HaAtzma-ut, and in practice most synagogue communities in Israel do not recite one. Nevertheless, dozens of versions have been composed in recent decades in a variety of circles—Orthodox religious Zionists, the Masorti/Conservative Movement, the Reform Movement—and among Jews who pray according to a variety of customs and rites. These versions are especially interesting, since each one of them reflects its authors' understanding of the meaning of Jewish sovereignty and the existence of the State of Israel. In all of them we find an expression of thanks for the miracle of the state's establishment, but each of them reflects a unique set of beliefs and opinions, religious temperament, and worldview.

Here, then, is one of the new versions of *Al HaNisim* written for Yom HaAtzma-ut. It was composed by Rabbi Yehoyada Amir:

> We thank You for the miracles, for the redemption, for saving acts and consolations, brought about by You for our ancestors in days past, at this season;
>
> for the miracle of our revival and the rebuilding of our lives in our homeland, the font of our existence, after two thousand years of exile;
>
> for the inner strength of a nation that rose from the depths and struggled until it again achieved independence, self-defense, and upbuilding;
>
> for the bravery of the fighters who risked their lives and bequeathed us life, prosperity, and creativity;
>
> for the ingathering of our exiles from the four corners of the earth and for the rich heritage of our communities and tribes, beliefs and outlooks, traditions and prayers;
>
> for the courage to declare before the nations of the world that our lives will be founded on the basis of freedom, justice, and peace, in keeping with the vision of Israel's prophets;
>
> for the faith and the hope, the striving for peace between the children of Sarah and the children of Hagar, and for the hope and longing for redemption that move us and guide our steps.[35]

To add another layer to our exploration of prayers composed in response to unique situations in Israel: during the horrible summer of 2014, in which the war known in Israel as "Operation Protective Edge" took place, two brave women—each a leader in her own community—came together. One is a Masorti/Conservative rabbi and the other is a Muslim sheikha. Together they composed a prayer giving voice to the mothers. It was published in Hebrew and in Arabic.

An *Al HaNisim* prayer for Yom HaAtzma-ut, from the prayer book of Israel's Italian Jewish community:

> We thank You for the miracles, for the mighty deeds, for the saving acts, and for the wonders and the redemption You brought about for us when You placed in the hearts of the rulers and ministers of the world's nations the decision to establish the State of Israel, and when You imbued Your people with a spirit of bravery and wisdom, supporting them in establishing our state, and when You enabled Your children to prevail over the children of Edom and Ishmael, who threatened to return us to their subjugation, steal from us the product of our labors, and drive us out of our land. In Your great mercy You frustrated our enemies' designs and hindered their plans. You delivered the armed into the hands of the weak, the many into the hands of the few. You fulfilled for us the words of Your Torah, "Five of you shall give chase to a hundred, and a hundred of you shall give chase to ten thousand" (Leviticus 26:8), and You removed the shame of subjugation from those of Your people living in the Holy Land. And just as You performed a miracle for us, so perform for us, Eternal our God, wonders and miracles now and in the future, and we will give thanks to Your great name. Selah![37]

Prayer of Mothers for Life and Peace
Rabbi Tamar Elad-Appelbaum and Sheikha Ibtisam Mahameed

God of Life,
who heals the broken-hearted and binds up their wounds,
may it be Your will to hear the prayer of mothers
for You did not create us to kill each other
nor to live in fear, anger, or hatred in Your world,
but rather you have created us so we can grant permission to one
another to sanctify Your name of Life, Your name of Peace in
    this world.

For these things I weep, my eye, my eye runs down with water:
for our children crying at night,
for parents holding their children with despair and darkness in
    their hearts,
for a gate that is closing, and who will open it before the day
    has ended?

And with my tears and prayers that I pray
and with the tears of all women who deeply feel the pain of these
    difficult days,
I raise my hands to you. Please, God, have mercy on us,
hear our voice that we shall not despair,
that we shall see life in each other,
that we shall have mercy for each other,
that we shall have pity on each other,
that we shall hope for each other

And we shall write our lives in the book of Life.
For your sake, God of Life,
Let us choose Life.

For You are Peace, Your world is Peace and all that is Yours is Peace.
And so shall be Your will, and let us say: *Amen*.[36]

From Time to Time → Dalia Marx

SIVAN

**Zodiac Sign: Gemini | Tribe of the Month: Levi
Breastplate Stone: Emerald/*Bareket***

Sivan got its name from the Babylonian month Simanu, "the brick month," since it was during this time they made bricks for building. The *m* sound in the Akkadian name became in Hebrew a *vav*, similar to what happened with the pronunciation of "Kislev."

The name Sivan appears in the Book of Esther. The decree saving the Jews was written in this month, and both the new name and its older, numerical name are recorded in the biblical verse: "So the king's scribes were summoned at that time, on the twenty-third day of the third month, that is, the month of Sivan" (8:9).

KAVANAH: A MEDITATION FOR SIVAN

THE ARI (Rabbi Isaac Luria) used to say each morning, "I hereby take upon myself the positive mitzvah of 'Love your fellow as yourself' [Leviticus 19:18]."[1]

This is an important reminder to have every day, particularly on Shavuot—the holiday on which we celebrate and sanctify our closeness to the Divine, to the Exalted. It is important to begin with the sanctity of life and the sanctity of the connections between one person and another, since neither can be sustained without the other.

> May the One who answered Ruth, who clung to her mother-in-law in love and built a home in Israel—answer us as well.
>
> May the One who answered Naomi, who returned with nothing to the fields of Bethlehem to begin a new life—answer us as well.
>
> May the One who answered Boaz, whose kindness recognized no boundaries of class or relationship—answer us as well.
>
> May the One who answered those who accepted a poor convert, likening her to Rachel and Leah—answer us as well.
>
> May the One who answered those who have chosen to join the people Israel and find shelter under the wings of God's Presence—answer us as well.
>
> May the One who gave us Torah and made its taste sweet in our mouths and our hearts—answer us as well.

AT THE GATES OF SIVAN

WE CARRY BASKETS woven of straw, each with a round, decorated handle, on our shoulders. In those baskets are fruits that my mom took out this morning from the refrigerator drawer and chose for us. Our heads are crowned with flowers. My own mother had a special method for weaving the flowers into a wreath so that they would remain upright and smiling. I wear a festive white dress and black polished shoes that are too tight on my big toes. It is already nice and warm outside, and the sun is blinding as we come from every corner of the country—that is, the two courtyards of the preschool—carrying our first fruits to the "Temple" that our teacher set up in the corner. Quite a few years have passed since my preschool days, but the feelings of festivity and elation from those early Shavuot experiences have not diminished.

Whether Shavuot is a day when we wander in and out of lectures and classes at an all-night *tikkun* or sing the famous *piyut Akdamut Milin* with great feeling, whether we take pride in our cheesecake or spray our neighbors with water (since Shavuot is, after all, also the holiday of water), Shavuot is a beloved, joyous, and delicious holiday. Shavuot is our shared birthday: we were all there at that moment when we became a people, during the foundational event of receiving the Torah at Mount Sinai.

The Poem of the Month is the song *Saleinu Al K'teifeinu* ("Our Baskets Are on Our Shoulders"), and I hope to point out that what appears to be a simple children's song is actually a political text quite loaded with cultural significance. This month's first *iyun* looks at the history of Shavuot and the many directions it has taken. The second *iyun* examines the mitzvah of bringing the *bikurim*, the "first fruits," to the Temple. Shavuot is known as the festival of dairy foods, and our third *iyun* focuses on questions of proper eating and raises some questions about kashrut for our time. The fourth *iyun* is about conversion to Judaism and joining the Jewish people, from the time of Ruth the Moabite—the prototype of the ideal Jew-by-choice, whose story we read on Shavuot—to our own day. The fifth *iyun* explores personal and communal ceremonies of giving the Torah and ceremonies for introducing children to Torah study on Shavuot. Our sixth *iyun* reflects on the twentieth of Sivan, the fast day that changed forms until it was almost entirely forgotten. The Prayer of the Month brings us the central Sephardic and Ashkenazic *piyutim* for the day of the giving of the Torah.

Poem of the Month

Saleinu Al K'teifeinu ("Our Baskets Are on Our Shoulders")

Saleinu Al K'teifeinu ("Our Baskets Are on Our Shoulders") is a sweet children's song, very widely known in Israel. It is so familiar, in fact, that we are likely to miss its complex and revolutionary message. Levin Kipnis (1894–1990), an immensely popular author and lyricist for children, wrote the song in 1929, after the Vaad Leumi (the National Council that served as an unofficial governing body for the Jewish community in pre-state Israel) and the Keren Kayemet (Jewish National Fund) decided to reinstitute the ceremony of *bikurim*, the first fruits of the early summer harvest, on Shavuot. The song offers a new perception of the ancient rite of bringing the *bikurim* to the Temple. To this day, the song is sung in early childhood settings in Israel and in Jewish communities abroad:

Our Baskets Are on Our Shoulders
   Levin Kipnis

Our baskets are on our shoulders,
our heads are crowned;
from the furthest reaches of the country
   we have come,
bringing our *bikurim*.

From Judea, from Samaria,
from the valley and Galilee,
make way for us,
we carry *bikurim* with us,
beat, beat, beat the drum, play the flute!²

סַלֵּינוּ עַל כְּתֵפֵינוּ
לֵוִין קִיפְּנִיס

סַלֵּינוּ עַל כְּתֵפֵינוּ,
רָאשֵׁינוּ עֲטוּרִים;
מִקְצוֹת הָאָרֶץ בָּאנוּ,
הֵבֵאנוּ בִּכּוּרִים.

מִיהוּדָה, מִיהוּדָה, מִשּׁוֹמְרוֹן,
מִן הָעֵמֶק, מִן הָעֵמֶק וְהַגָּלִיל –
פַּנּוּ דֶרֶךְ לָנוּ,
בִּכּוּרִים אִתָּנוּ,
הַךְ, הַךְ, הַךְ בַּתֹּף, חַלֵּל בֶּחָלִיל!

In every line one can feel an uplifted Zionist spirit. Kipnis wanted children to grow to love the country, with all its various regions and its many fruits. Behind this ostensibly simple, naïve ditty is a careful exposition of the mitzvah of pilgrimage to Jerusalem on the festival and the bringing of the traditional first fruits:

> When you enter the land that the Eternal your God is giving you as a heritage, and you possess it and settle in it, you shall take some of every first fruit of the soil, which you harvest from the land that the Eternal your God is giving you, put it in a basket, and go to the place where the Eternal your God will choose to establish the divine name. (Deuteronomy 26:1–2)

Today, the Festival of the First Fruits (Chag HaBikurim) is one of the names by which Shavuot is known, but the phenomenon and the holiday are not seamlessly connected. Farmers report that at the beginning of Sivan, there is little ripe produce to be offered as first fruits. The principal time for pilgrimage to the Temple with *bikurim* was "from Atzeret to HeChag [the Festival]" (*Mishnah Bikurim* 1:6)—that is, Shavuot to Sukkot—which bookended a sort of fourth pilgrimage period.

Bringing the first fruits became connected to Shavuot because the Torah says that on Shavuot the ancient Israelites would bring the bread offering made of the first wheat harvested (Numbers 28:28), known also as *minchat habikurim*.

The link between Shavuot and the bringing of *bikurim* became strong and explicit in modern times, especially due to the new *bikurim* ceremonies established by kibbutzim.

Kipnis's poem can be read as a modern midrash on the Mishnah's depiction of the bringing of first fruits. Here is the first part of that passage:

> How do they set apart the first fruits? When a person goes down into their field and sees that a fig has ripened or a cluster of grapes has ripened or a pomegranate has ripened, they bind reed-grass around it and say, "These are first fruits." . . .
>
> How do they take up the first fruits [to Jerusalem]? [The people of] all the smaller towns that belong to the district gather together to the [central] town of the district and spend the night in the open place of the town and do not come into the houses. And early in the morning the officer [of the district] says, "Come, let us go up to Zion, to the Eternal our God!" (Jeremiah 31:6).
>
> Those who are near [to Jerusalem] bring fresh figs and grapes, and those that are far off bring dried figs and raisins. Before them goes an ox, its horns overlaid with gold and a wreath of olive leaves on its head. The flute is played before them until they draw close to Jerusalem. [Then] they send messengers ahead of them, and they bedeck their first fruits. The rulers and the prefects and the treasurers [of the Temple] go out to greet them. According to the [level of] honor due to those arriving, they would go forth. And all the craftsmen in Jerusalem would rise up before them and greet them, saying, "Our kinspeople, from such-and-such a place, welcome!"
> (*Mishnah Bikurim* 3:1–3)

Both the Mishnah and *Saleinu Al K'teifeinu* include a description of a festive gathering of the excited pilgrims with joyful playing of instruments (drum and flute). These similarities are strong, but the differences between the two texts is even stronger. The Mishnah goes into great detail about the arrival of the pilgrims in Jerusalem, and the mishnayot that follow also describe the bringing of the *bikurim* to the Temple; in contrast, the song concentrates entirely on the festive gathering itself. Note that in the Mishnah, it is the head of the ox that is topped with a garland, while in the poem—and in preschool settings in Israel and abroad—it is the children's heads that are adorned.

Like the Torah, the song emphasizes the value and privilege of living in the Land of Israel. Kipnis diverged from the Torah's message by expunging the religious significance of the bringing of the *bikurim*, describing it instead as a reflection of national pride. The Land of Israel has become the protagonist of the event. The Torah emphasizes bringing the *bikurim* "to the place where the Eternal your God will choose," but the song does not mention exactly where it is they are to be brought. Kipnis, however, describes the places they are brought from: the valleys and mountains, east to west, north to south. Later in the song he offers a poetic portrait of the pioneers' celebrations: "How good are their circles!" This is an interpretive reading of the biblical verse "How fair are your tents, O Jacob, your dwelling places, O Israel!" (Numbers 24:5), which is part of the *Mah Tovu* prayer recited upon entering a synagogue.

At the *bikurim* celebration in Haifa in 1912, Menahem Ussishkin, chairman of the Keren Kayemet (Jewish National Fund), thanked the children who had brought the first fruits, but he added in a didactic tone:

> You, Jewish children, have brought the very first fruits of your land, the fruit of your labors, to the highest national institution dedicated to the redemption of the soil of our ancestors. But did you know that the form of bringing *bikurim* today is not the proper form that was the practice of our ancestors two thousand years ago? They brought their *bikurim* not to Haifa, the city of the future, but to Jerusalem, the eternal city. Not to Mount Carmel but to Mount Moriah. And those fruits they used to give not to the Jewish National Fund but to the Holy Temple.[3]

Just a few years before the song was written and composed, a sharp dispute about how to celebrate the holiday of the first fruits broke out in Israel's Jezreel Valley. In 1924, three settlements—Ein Harod, Geva, and Kfar Yehezkel—celebrated the holiday with a parade, singing, and dancing. A year later, the members of Ein Harod invited all the Jewish settlements in the area to participate, and it appeared that the *bikurim* celebrations in the valley were becoming a tradition. But the religious leadership of the area was opposed to what it perceived as a public desecration of the holiday, which they claimed violated the religious restrictions on many types of activities. Rabbi Y. L. Fishman-Maimon wrote:

> They celebrate the holiday of the first fruits and make the [religious] people's celebration into mourning. . . . They celebrate their holiday, and our holiday they desecrate. The festival of Shavuot, the season of the giving of our Torah, they brazenly dared to desecrate with gatherings of thousands of Jews . . . and they publicize their activities widely, in the newspapers available to everyone.[4]

This was one of the first and most fierce controversies over the nature of the Jewish public sphere in Zionist Palestine. The continued opposition from religious figures bore fruit, and in 1928 when the central Zionist institutions withdrew their support for the celebration, it ceased occurring in its original form. Apparently, Kipnis wrote the song only a short time before the outbreak of Arab riots in late 1929, which reminded everyone that land is not just fields, gardens, and beautiful, fruit-laden vineyards, but also the focus of deep and sometimes murderous enmity.[5]

The Torah and the Mishnah regard the *bikurim* as a religious commandment. In Kipnis's song lyrics, there is a different kind of devotion and emphasis—a nationalist, Zionist dimension. What the two have in common is the joy over the produce of the land and gratitude for the privilege of living in our land and enjoying its richness.

"And If a Person Has Ripened"

Another fascinating reading of the *bikurim* is this poem by Rabbi Tamar Duvdevani, PhD:

First Fruits

A person goes down into their field	בִּכּוּרִים
a person goes down	יוֹרֵד אָדָם אֶל תּוֹךְ שָׂדֵהוּ
into	יוֹרֵד אָדָם
and if a person has ripened,	אֶל תּוֹךְ
and if they are a field	וְאִם הִבְכִּיר אָדָם,
and they go down into	וְאִם שָׂדֶה הוּא
go down to God	וְהוּא יוֹרֵד אֶל תּוֹךְ
and the fig of their heart sees,	יוֹרֵד אֶל אֵל
that they have already become round and swelled	וּתְאֵנַת לִבּוֹ רוֹאָה, שֶׁכְּבָר עָגַל וּכְבָר תָּפַח
and are soft at the core,	וְיֵשׁ בּוֹ רֹךְ,
blessed be they.[6]	יְהֵא בָּרוּךְ.

Duvdevani interprets the mishnah instructing us how to set apart *bikurim*—"When a person goes down into their field and sees that a fig has ripened or a cluster of grapes has ripened or a pomegranate has ripened, they bind reed-grass around it and say, 'These are first fruits'" (*Mishnah Bikurim* 3:1)—as a personal invitation to each of us to go deep into our cores, to the inner workings of our personalities, to look inside and examine whether the field of our lives has ripened.

> What shall we carry on our shoulders, in our baskets?
> What will be the first fruit of our field?
> How will the fig of our own heart look?

Shavuot: It Grows on You

SHAVUOT is one of the **three *r'galim*** (pilgrimage festivals) that the Torah commands us to observe:

> Three times a year you shall hold a festival for Me: You shall observe the Feast of the Unleavened Bread—eating unleavened bread for seven days. . . and the Feast of the Harvest, of the first fruits of your work, of what you sow in the field; and the Feast of Ingathering at the end of the year, when you gather in the results of your work, from the field. Three times a year all your males shall appear before the Sovereign, the Eternal. (Exodus 23:14–17)

The Torah commands the Israelites to make a pilgrimage to the Temple three times a year, but we must assume that it was not possible for many people to do so. Many could not leave their homes, their livestock, and their fields and set out three times a year on a long, expensive, tiring, and dangerous journey. Perhaps only those who lived close to Jerusalem could fully observe this commandment. There are scholars who think that for most Jews in ancient times, fulfilling the mitzvah of pilgrimage was a once-in-a-lifetime event, like the Muslim pilgrimage to Mecca. Incidentally, the command that "three times a year all your males shall appear before the Sovereign, the Eternal" is unusual; it is one of very few mitzvot that applies explicitly to males. However, entire families would make the pilgrimage and celebrate the festival together, and individual family members would offer the personal sacrifices that they were obligated to give, such as a mother's sacrifice after giving birth.

What makes a holiday a regel, *a pilgrimage festival? Rav Nachman, a Babylonian sage cited in the Talmud, presented a list of conditions for a* regel. *These include a priestly lottery used to divide tasks, a special blessing for the occasion, a unique sacrificial requirement, and particular psalms and blessings (Babylonian Talmud,* Sukkah *47b–48a).*

Two, Three, or Four: How Many *R'galim* Are There in a Year?

The Torah speaks of three pilgrimage festivals, but the Rabbis asked themselves whether Sh'mini Atzeret, the day after Sukkot, is a *regel* in its own right. And if so, then there are four *r'galim*.

On the other hand, some see only two of those *r'galim* as primary—Sukkot and Passover—since they divide the year into two equal parts (see pp. 76–78), the rainy season and the dry season. Both are observed for seven days, and their celebrations begins at mid-month, when the moon is full. Each entails two special mitzvot: the four species (*lulav* and *etrog*) (Leviticus 23:40) and dwelling in a sukkah on Sukkot (Leviticus 23:42), and eating matzah (and of course, refraining from consuming *chameitz*) (Exodus 12:15) and the commandment to "tell your children" (Deuteronomy 6:20) on Passover.

Shavuot is different from both: it is just one day long (though various Diaspora communities observe two days) and is devoid of biblical description. The Torah prescribes no traditional practices for Shavuot, other than the day's sacrifices. Since the destruction of the Temple, it has no special mitzvot of its own. The Torah does not even specify its exact day of observance, other than to say, "And from the day on which you bring the sheaf of the elevation offering—**the day after the sabbath**—you shall count off seven weeks. They must be complete: you must count . . . fifty days; then you shall bring an offering of new grain to the Eternal" (Leviticus 23:15–16). Establishing

From Time to Time → Dalia Marx

the date of the holiday on the basis of this passage was a point of contention between the Pharisees and the Sadducees in the Second Temple period.

Shavuot has none of the experiential and emotional elements that are so evident in the other two *r'galim*—the scent of Sukkot is that of the myrtle and *etrog*, its texture is that of the *lulav*, and its sound is the rustling of the wind through the branches on the roof of the sukkah. The taste of Passover is the taste of matzah and *charoset* sampled on the sly before seder night, and its feeling is of family gathering on a night full of meaning, memory, and emotion. Shavuot is different. As we have said, there is no particular mitzvah associated with it and no central ceremony to give it a unique flavor. (Yes, there is the cheesecake—but eating dairy on Shavuot is only a custom, rather than a mitzvah.) Shavuot, a holiday that is a bit lacking when it comes to basic content, has come to include different elements over the course of generations. And that is the way tradition works: it cannot make peace with emptiness. Cultural voids must be filled, and ideas that have no other expression will eventually fill them. The four main names of Shavuot are indicative of four worlds of meaning that have been given to it, sometimes after the fact:

> The Pharisaic and Sadducean sages—leaders of the two largest Jewish sects of the Second Temple—had different understandings of the phrase "the day after the sabbath" in this verse. The Sadducees interpreted it as **the day after the Shabbat day** and thus ruled that the day of bringing the omer of grain as an elevation offering (*t'nufah*) and beginning of *S'firat HaOmer* (the Counting of the Omer) is on the first Sunday after the Passover festival, and Shavuot too would always fall on a Sunday. The Pharisees, however, understood the phrase "the day after the sabbath" to mean the day after the sacrificial ritual of the paschal lamb, and by this reckoning Shavuot would not occur on the same day of the week each year.

- **The Harvest Festival** (Chag HaKatzir): Like the other two *r'galim*, Shavuot has an ancient agricultural basis; it marked the beginning of the wheat harvest.
- **The Festival of the First Fruits** (Chag HaBikurim): This name symbolizes the Jewish people's special connection to the Holy Temple. Although the bringing of first fruits was not originally connected to Shavuot, the two became linked in the popular consciousness, perhaps because of the mitzvah of offering "two loaves of bread" (Leviticus 23:17) made of new wheat at the Temple.
- **The Festival of the Giving of the Torah** (Chag Matan Torah): This name symbolizes the unbreakable triple strand of connection between God, the people Israel, and the Torah. In the link between the Blessed Holy One and the people Israel, the Torah functions like a *ketubah*, a Jewish marriage contract, and a testimony to an unbreakable bond. In fact, sometimes the Torah is described as Israel's bride.
- And of course, **the Festival of Weeks** (Chag HaShavuot): Shavuot marks the conclusion of counting fifty days from the end of the first day of Passover, and it was also understood to be the conclusion of the weeks-long process the Israelites undertook in preparing to receive the Torah.

"The Old Will Be Made New, and the New Will Be Made Sacred"

Over the course of time, each of the stories undergirding the different names of the holiday has been enriched and enhanced by the addition of new strata of meaning. As Rabbi Abraham Isaac Kook taught, "The old will be made new, and the new will be made sacred."[7]

The celebration of **the wheat harvest** reminds us of the Book of Ruth, which takes place during the beginning of the harvest. Ruth is considered the ideal Jew-by-choice, adamantly remaining with her beloved mother-in-law, with no intention or expectation of any material gain from joining the Jewish people: "Wherever you go, I will go; wherever you lodge, I will lodge; your people shall be my people, and your God my God" (Ruth 1:16). Today during Shavuot, it is common to take note of the people who have chosen to become Jewish—especially those who have chosen to live in the State of Israel, when their paths are not always strewn with roses.

The Festival of the First Fruits took an interesting turn in the Zionist movement with the return to *Eretz Yisrael* and the renewed connection to the land and its cultivation. Farmers, including kibbutz members, have attributed particular significance to the holiday, and it is celebrated in many kibbutzim with great fanfare and large gatherings, including a grand procession of "bringing in" the first produce of the season from the field, the orchard, and the factory. The adorable capstone of this procession is when parents enter with babies in their arms, since the children born during the previous year are counted among the *bikurim*.

The Safed mystics saw the **Festival of the Giving of the Torah** as an opportunity to mend the broken tablets of the Ten Commandments and to symbolically renew the acceptance of the Torah. The kabbalists developed a special, ceremonial study, which they considered a *tikkun*, a "repair." The purpose of the *Tikkun Leil Shavuot* was to prepare one's heart to receive the Torah. The Lurianic kabbalistic origin of this *tikkun* was the effort to achieve spiritual reunification of the world. According to their cosmology, part of the creation of the world included a cosmic event called *sh'virat hakeilim*, "the breaking of the vessels," which spread God's essence to all parts of Creation. Despite its tragic nature, *sh'virat hakeilim* led to the creation of the world and gave Jews their unique mission—to repair (*tikkun*) the brokenness that is part of the world. *Tikkun* on Shavuot is also "adornment": one's study on Shavuot is meant to adorn the "bride"—Torah—as she approaches her wedding to the groom—the people Israel. Another explanation of the name *Tikkun Leil Shavuot* is that it can repair the Jewish people's misdeeds as the Torah was being received: in the tumult of the tremendous experience, they fell asleep, so the kabbalists stayed awake and studied all night. The *Tikkun* for Shavuot was originally a mystical ceremony reserved only for those indoctrinated in esoteric secrets. Over the past few decades, the evening or late-night *Tikkun Leil Shavuot* has become much more widespread. Such *Tikkun* gatherings are something the Jewish community has come to enjoy as countless institutions, synagogues, and centers offer study on various subjects—not just those of the kabbalists—on Shavuot night. The local sport in Jerusalem is to try to attend as many different *Tikkunim* and as many different classes as possible on Shavuot night.

In medieval Ashkenaz, Shavuot observance included a ceremony of

---

Sidebar notes:

The Book of Chronicles tells the story of a mass pilgrimage to Jerusalem in the third month (i.e., Sivan) and the covenantal renewal ceremony that was held: "They entered into a covenant to worship the Eternal, the God of their ancestors, with all their heart and with all their soul" (II Chronicles 15:12).

During the ceremony, a festive public oath was taken by the people concerning God, and the author emphasizes the joy and true intentions of all the participants: "So they took an oath to the Eternal in a loud voice and with shouts, with trumpeting, and with blasts of the horn" (II Chronicles 15:14).

This event took place during the reign of King Asa in the third month, which is when the Torah was given to the people at Mount Sinai (Exodus 19:1). This indicates there may have been a connection between this covenantal renewal holiday with its mass oath taking and the holiday of Shavuot. Chronicles' covenantal renewal celebration is described as only occurring once, but it is also possible that it is a description of an annual celebration of the renewal of the covenant with the Giver of the Torah.

A midrash compares the Torah to water: "Words of Torah are said to be like water" (*Midrash Tannaim* to Deuteronomy, 11). In North Africa, it became the custom for people in synagogue to spray water on the Torah reader and on each other. According to this custom, anyone who got wet on Shavuot would suffer no harm all year. Not everyone approved of this custom, but children delighted in splashing water on each other and on passersby as they reveled in the holiday spirit.

From Time to Time → Dalia Marx

initiation into Torah for small children, a sort of personal "Giving of the Torah." In the nineteenth century, Western European Jews began to celebrate Confirmation on Shavuot as a kind of covenant renewal for teenagers, during which they publicly affirmed and celebrated their choice to belong to the Jewish people on the holiday. (See pp. 264–65.)

Interlaced Strands

We have seen a few of the paths that Shavuot has taken in its development over many generations and especially more recently. These multiple directions and expressions are not confusing; instead, they strengthen the power and meaning of the holiday. Thin strands of connection link the various incarnations of the holiday. On the holiday of the giving of the Torah, we all **stood together** and received the Torah at Sinai. This is the event at which we became a people, and a midrash relates that even the souls of future converts to Judaism were present (*B'midbar Rabbah* 13:16). The memory of that foundational event is an appropriate occasion to celebrate the decision made by those who have chosen to become part of the people Israel and adopt its Torah.

Another strand connecting the multiple meanings of the holiday is the ancient and new link to the Land of Israel, which finds expression in the first fruits celebration. This special connection reminds us that things in Israel and in our world are not always perfect and that the world is in need of repair. *S'firat HaOmer*, of which Shavuot is the crescendo, reminds us that our lives are always in flux and our lives are continually in process. These interlaced strands hold the holiday's many aspects together and make it rich and complex.

Perhaps we need to qualify the assertion that **all of us stood** at Mount Sinai, or at least reconsider it.

Who is really included as part of the Israelite community that experienced Revelation at Sinai?

When Moses commanded the people to refrain from sexual relations before the giving of the Torah, he said, "Be ready for the third day: you should not go near a woman" (Exodus 19:15).

Judith Plaskow, in her book *Standing Again at Sinai*, asks where the women were during this momentous gathering.[8] She insists that according to this verse, the "people" commanded to prepare to receive the Torah refers only to Jewish men. They are the ones addressed by Moses. The Torah does not say that it is forbidden for men and women to approach one another; rather, women are the ones whom it is forbidden to approach. At this critical juncture of the creation of the Israelite nation, the women are invisible.

If we believe that Sinai is eternal, we are still able to correct this inequity and to choose in our own lives an inclusive and egalitarian approach to our Judaism.

🕯️ First Fruits, Many Words

Six verbs from the same root of *bet-vav-alef*—meaning "come" or "bring"—appear in the *bikurim* declaration passage: "When you come into the land" (v. 1), "which you bring in from your land" (v. 2), "you shall come to the priest (v. 3), "I have come into the land" (v. 3), "bringing us to this place" (v. 9, at the pinnacle of the process), "wherefore I now bring" (v. 10). Rabbi Elchanan Samet divides these six verbs into two groups: three refer to coming into the Land of Israel, and three address the bringing of the *bikurim*.[9]

The thinker Martin Buber (1878–1965) notes the verbs from the root *nun-tav-nun*, "give," another central root in the *bikurim* declaration. He shows us that this root occurs seven times in the passage. The first three—"the land that the Eternal your God is giving you" (v. 1), "that the Eternal your God is giving you" (v. 2), and "that the Eternal swore to our ancestors to give us" (v. 3)—and the last three—"and giving us this land" (v. 9), "which You . . . have given me" (v. 10), and "you shall rejoice . . . in all the bounty that the Eternal your God has given you" (v. 11)—all refer to the divine gift to Israel. The middle one—"they imposed [literally "gave"] heavy labor upon us" (v. 6)—is about "emphatically establishing the negative background to the divine gift," namely enslavement in Egypt.[10]

DO WE ALWAYS REMEMBER to offer thanks for the abundance we have been given? For the goodness and kindness we have been privileged to receive? Many mitzvot remind us of the fact that this goodness and abundance are not to be taken for granted; so too, modern scholars teach us that gratitude can rewire the brain with positive results.

The Torah commands the bringing of *bikurim*, "some of every first fruit of the soil" (Deuteronomy 26:2), as an expression of thanks for the abundance and bounty with which we have been blessed, "to the place where the Eternal your God will choose" (26:2), meaning the Temple. In addition, the Torah commands those bringing first fruits—farmers all—to read a special text called "the *Bikurim* Declaration," which is an abbreviated narrative of the history of the people Israel from its inception until the moment the farmer stands with a basket facing the priest by the altar.

> **The *Bikurim* Declaration (Deuteronomy 26:1–11)**
> 1 When you come into the land that the Eternal your God is giving you as a heritage, and you possess it and settle in it, 2 you shall take some of every first fruit of the soil, which you bring in [harvest] from the land that the Eternal your God is giving you, put it in a basket, and go to the place where the Eternal your God will choose to establish the divine name. 3 You shall come to the priest in charge at that time and say to him, "I acknowledge this day before the Eternal your God that I have come into the land that the Eternal swore to our ancestors to give us."
>
> 4 The priest shall take the basket from your hand and set it down in front of the altar of the Eternal your God.
>
> 5 You shall then recite as follows before the Eternal your God: "My father was a fugitive Aramean. He went down to Egypt with meager numbers and sojourned there; but there he became a great and very populous nation. 6 Egyptians dealt harshly with us and oppressed us; they imposed heavy labor upon us. 7 We cried out to the Eternal, the God of our ancestors, and the Eternal heard our plea and saw our plight, our misery, and our oppression. 8 The Eternal freed us from Egypt by a mighty hand, by an outstretched arm and awesome power, and by signs and portents, 9 bringing us to this place and giving us this land, a land flowing with milk and honey. 10 Wherefore I now bring the first fruits of the soil which You, Eternal One, have given me."
>
> You shall leave it before the Eternal your God and bow low before the Eternal your God. 11 And you shall rejoice, together with the [family of the] Levite and the stranger in your midst, in all the bounty that the Eternal your God has bestowed upon you and your household.[11]

The Personal and the Historical

The Torah describes in minute detail the ceremony for bringing *bikurim* to the Temple, and in rather rare fashion it brings us a specific liturgical text for the public to say. The farmer stands in front of the priest and declares, "I acknowledge this day before

From Time to Time → Dalia Marx

the Eternal your God that I have come into the land that the Eternal swore to our ancestors to give us" (Deuteronomy 26:3). Through these words, the pilgrims from faraway villages or nearby settlements embody Jewish history in their very being. In every generation, farmers are to view themselves as landless wanderers—if only for a moment. We step onto the stage of history for the first time as refugees, not as kings and rulers. Reviewing this not-so-complimentary history is designed to ward off the hubris that can come with being a landowner.

Bringing the *bikurim*, those earthly products of agricultural labor, is an experience of entering the realm of the sacred: "The priest shall take the basket from your hand and set it down in front of the altar of the Eternal your God" (Deuteronomy 26:4). The ceremony takes place inside the Temple, close to the altar—a place that ordinary Israelites do not regularly approach. The farmer then retells the history of the people, starting with "my father was a fugitive Aramean," through the story of their suffering in Egypt, concluding with the redemption they have been privileged to enjoy. Five verses encompass the history of the nation of Israel. It is also interesting to note what is not included in the *bikurim* declaration: the figure of Moses, the Revelation at Sinai, the giving of the Torah, or any explicit mention of Jerusalem or the Temple. The declaration ends at the dramatic moment when the farmer stands with their basket of first fruits before the priest. The people's entire history is directed toward the foundational moment when the farmer brings the first produce of the land.

We might expect the *bikurim* declaration to include some expression of gratitude for the fruits or possibly a request for a successful future harvest, as do similar texts from other cultures. Instead, we have an expression of thanks for God's acts in history. The farmer presents personal story as bound and woven into the story of the people, and tells the people's story as an entirely personal experience. Perhaps the intent of this narration is to sear the memory of once being weak, landless refugees into our minds, now that the experience has receded into the past. Maybe the intent is to demand that we remember our origins even as we live our lives in the present.

The national is personal; history is personal biography. Sound familiar? After all, we say on Passover, "As in every age and generation the task is ours: to see ourselves as if we had come out of Egypt,"[12] and we are called upon to experience the history of our people with our own bodies. Here the picture is even more complex: the farmer who reads the *bikurim* declaration is an active character—the latest in the chain of protagonists in our national history. By reciting the *bikurim* declaration, the farmer learns their role in the plot and is called upon as someone who personally came into the Land of Israel. The farmer does not thank God for having brought their *ancestors* to the Land of Israel; instead the famer experiences it directly. When this rendition of the story of the people's history is completed with the words "Wherefore I now bring the first fruits of the soil which You, O Eternal One, have given me" (Deuteronomy 26:10), the farmer's self-portrayal is like that of a movie character who bursts out from the screen into the present reality. The farmer is both part of the story and also its realization.

Indeed, each year the farmer learns that the last chapter (so far) in the people's story is taking place at this very moment, the moment in which the *bikurim* are being offered before the priest in the Temple. This statement stands out even more than the call to the participants in the Passover seder to regard themselves "as if" they had gone out of Egypt. Those who bring the first fruits are called upon to see themselves not "as if" they have entered the land, but as the ones who have in fact entered the land, pure and simple.[13] Year after year, the farmer testifies to the privilege of being able to say, "I have come into the land." The experience of offering the *bikurim*—and even more so the recitation of the *bikurim* declaration—testify to that miracle. The philosopher Martin Buber (1878–1965) makes it clear that the farmer is unable to "give" anything of his produce, since the land in all its fullness belongs to God. Only God can give. All that the farmer can do is bring the produce received by divine grace.[14]

The Mishnah gives us a detailed and tangible description of the pilgrimage to Jerusalem and the bringing of the *bikurim* as an impressive shared public act (see p. 244). Those first fruits are brought when the farmer's crops have ripened, and according to the Mishnah, the period of ripening stretches from Shavuot to Sukkot: "from Atzeret to the Festival, one brings [the *bikurim*] and recites [the declaration]" (*Mishnah Bikurim* 1:6). Bringing the *bikurim* presents an interesting dialectical stance: the requirement applies to the individual, but the experience of coming to the Temple is something the individual experiences as part of a collective. And again, the full performance of the mitzvah is an act of the lone farmer, but those farmers recite a text in which they express faithfulness and belonging to the history of the Jewish nation, to being part of the people, and express their thanks for the land given to them and their people.

Just Imagine

The *bikurim* declaration is a bold text that contains a (double) requirement of guided imagery. The Israelites wandering in the wilderness are landless, and they are told to imagine themselves as farmers living securely on their own land. At the same time, the farmers living on the land are told to remember their days of wandering in the wilderness, which necessitates thinking about the fragility of their lives. It reminds the nomads in the wilderness that the day will come when they will arrive at their secure haven, and precisely then they will have to remember the wilderness wandering and be reminded that they are not the owners of the land on which they dwell.

Absent but Present

The mitzvah of bringing *bikurim* is unusual in that it entails another mitzvah—reciting the *Bikurim* Declaration. The recitation of the text in the Temple offers a festive opportunity to consider and examine questions of identity, identification, and peoplehood. We have noted the equality and sharing that characterized the trip to Jerusalem with the first fruits; on that ceremonial occasion, all are equal. The simple farmer and the king himself both load up their baskets and stand before the priest as one. This raises the obvious question: Is everyone really equal in the performance of this mitzvah? Up to this point, I have referred to the farmer being called to go up to Jerusalem, and that farmer has historically always been a "he"; therefore, we need to ask about the role of women in the mitzvah of *bikurim*.

The Rabbis distinguished between the obligation to bring the first fruits and the obligation to recite the *bikurim* declaration. Not everyone required to do the first was required to do the second. The discussion in the Mishnah opens with a principled distinction:

> There are those who bring the *bikurim* and recite,
> [there are] those who bring [them] and do not recite,
> and there are those who do not bring [them].
> (*Mishnah Bikurim* 1:1)

The Mishnah goes on to explain that someone who is able to recite the *bikurim* declaration is someone for whom the text reflects their actual life. Converts, according to the Mishnah, bring the *bikurim* but do not recite the declaration, since they cannot speak of "the land that the Eternal swore to our fathers to give us" (Deuteronomy 26:3), since their ancestors were not Israelites. Women are also counted among those who "bring but do not recite," but for a different reason. The Mishnah reminds us that the original division of *Eretz Yisrael* did not include women among those who received land, so they "cannot say 'the soil which You, Eternal One, have given me' [Deuteronomy 26:10]" (*Mishnah Bikurim* 1:5). Women are partners, then, in the *bringing* of the first fruits, but not in the mitzvah of the *bikurim* declaration, whose purpose is to stimulate thought and identify personal biography with the people's history.

While it is disappointing to see this non-egalitarian position, we need to look at the broader context, which includes the reality that women *were* equal in the obligation to make pilgrimage and bring the first fruits! They stood before the priest in the midst of the Temple and took part in the sanctity along with the rest of Israel. Although this may be counterintuitive for us, it appears that women were included in the realm of sanctity in the Temple era, and the measure of equality between them and Israelite men was even greater than in some quarters of the Jewish community in our own times.

The exclusion of Jews-by-choice from reciting any liturgical formula referring to our ancestors, such as "our God and God of our ancestors," was canceled as far back as the Jerusalem Talmud. Particularly moving is Maimonides's letter to Obadiah the Proselyte, in which he writes, "Yes, you may say all this [the liturgical passages referring to 'our ancestors'] in the prescribed order and not change them in the least," even though a convert's biological parents were not Jewish.[15] As for the exclusion of women from the realm of the sacred, well, that is apparently a task for our generation . . .

Ancient Texts Don't Die

Ever since the Temple was destroyed, the bringing of *bikurim* has become moot, but the *bikurim* declaration has not. It has enjoyed a renaissance ever since the Sages of the Mishnah included it in the Passover seder night ritual that they instituted.

And so we read in the Mishnah about the seder night: "One begins with disgrace and ends with glory; and one expounds from 'My father was a fugitive Aramean' until one finishes the entire passage" (*Mishnah P'sachim* 10:4). However, our Haggadot do not actually contain "the entire passage"—only its introduction. Its dramatic ending—which actually establishes its meaning—is absent. The last verse of the *bikurim* declaration, "Wherefore I now bring the first fruits of the soil which You, Eternal One, have given me," which is the reason for reciting the passage, is not included in the Haggadah, which speaks only about the Exodus from Egypt but cuts the story short before the people's arrival in Canaan. The kibbutz Haggadot, and Israeli progressive religious Haggadot as well, have added in the verse that speaks about the people's arrival in the Land.

In addition, the *bikurim* declaration has enjoyed a renaissance in our own time. Some recite it in its entirety at ceremonies or prayer services on Yom HaAtzma-ut, with the full intention of establishing "this place" and "this land." The recitation of this declaration on Yom HaAtzma-ut forms a sort of completion and refinement of the opening section of Israel's Declaration of Independence, which begins, "The Land of Israel was the birthplace of the Jewish people," and which is devoid of any reference to Jewish life outside the Land of Israel.

Of course, many Jews have lived meaningful and full lives outside of Israel for centuries and many continue to do so even today. It seems that even for those who live elsewhere, the Land of Israel can still be significant for them. I have observed that even when Jews are unhappy with what happens in the State of Israel today, even this dissatisfaction indicates a special connection. Still, the *bikurim* declaration calls us to think about our lives in the Land of Israel and its special meaning and the connection we might have to the Land of Israel no matter where we live.

"Honey and Milk Are under Your Tongue": Food for Body and Soul

I LOVE SHAVUOT. It's not just the baskets on our shoulders and our crowned heads that I enjoy; it's not just receiving the Torah, the white clothes, the ripe grain in the field, and Ruth the Moabite. All of these speak to me, but so does the fact that this is a holiday of dairy foods. As a longtime vegetarian, this custom has always felt pure and clean to me, and also I simply like the taste! There are many flavors to the custom of eating dairy foods on Shavuot, one of which is that our Torah is a Torah of life, and when we celebrate receiving it, it is appropriate to eat food that doesn't require any killing.

> My vegan friends point out to me that dairy foods too entail cruelty to animals. I am forced to agree with them, and so I try to minimize my consumption of those items. Nonetheless, I see a fundamental difference between consuming dairy and eggs and consuming meat.

Torah as Food

The poetic line "Honey and milk are under your tongue" (Songs of Songs 4:11) has been interpreted in the Jewish tradition as referring to the taste of Torah. The Torah has been likened to two basic comfort foods—milk, which satiates babies and sustains their lives, and honey, whose sweetness is nutrient-rich and easy to digest. The Torah can be this way for us too—sustaining, nourishing, and comforting.

Both in the Near East and in Ashkenazic communities (see pp. 262–64), it is an accepted custom to let little children, when they begin to study Torah, lick honey from slates or boards on which the letters of the *alef-bet* are written or to delight them with sweet baked goods in the shapes of the letters. The idea behind these customs is the desire to lead the youngsters to enjoy Torah study and literally make it sweet in their mouths. But the reason for this custom runs deeper than making the Torah sweet. Through it, children learn that they are expected to internalize the Torah; as they "consume" the sweet letters of Torah, they make Torah a vital part of their spiritual existence no less than their physical existence.

Food as Torah

Food is a central component of human cultures, bearing many meanings, and Jewish culture is no exception. Food is a critical component of our holidays, family gatherings, and life-cycle ceremonies. We are obsessed with the precise details of new recipes, ask our friends about their food customs, and try to recall our grandmothers' special recipes. Judaism pays a lot of attention to prohibitions related to food, asking what is permitted and what it forbidden, what is appropriate as food and what is not. It also pays attention to the way food offers comfort. Identifying Torah with foods that are pleasing to the palate invites us to reflect on food—both on food itself and on the question of what is appropriate—kosher—to eat.

The basic principles of kashrut are enumerated in the Torah, and they were developed and expanded in halachah over the ages. The classic example is the command "You shall not boil a kid in its mother's milk," which appears three times in the Torah (Exodus 23:19, 34:26; Deuteronomy 14:21). This prohibition, which speaks about a particular act and is phrased in very focused language, was understood more broadly as a prohibition against the mixing of meat and milk, and that included separate sets of dishes and discussions about how long one must wait between eating meat and eating dairy, and on and on.

In our generation, some people are becoming more strict and extreme about the laws and limitations of kashrut. (Now you can even find kosher poison!) Stringencies of various kinds earn praise, while those who offer leniencies often garner disdain. Extra-special kashrut certifications divide relatives and friends, preventing them from eating together—not because of questions of actual kashrut, but because of questions of particular kosher certifications. This entire situation is symbolized by the fact that kashrut symbols on food packaging have doubled in size in recent years.

The original meaning of the term "kosher" (pronounced *kasher* in Sephardic and Israeli Hebrew) denoted something fitting or proper. If we look around, we will see that many of the people and organizations addressing questions of kashrut have forgotten the true nature of their work. Compared to the business of issuing kashrut certifications, which is only expanding, dealing with kashrut itself has been reduced to something technical, empty, and without inner meaning.

Despite the extreme and exacting positions regarding the political and technical aspects of kashrut and kashrut supervision, it is encouraging to see the first signs of increasing attention to the appropriateness—kashrut in its original and profound sense—of our food in a spiritual, social, and value-driven sense.

A Torah of Life and a Kashrut of Life

The biblical commentator Rabbi Yitzchak Abravanel (Portugal, 1437–Italy, 1508), following Maimonides, explained the great **longevity** of early characters in the Bible as being the result of, among other things, "natural cause"—moderation in food and drink:

> They had good practices in food and drink, [consuming] according to need without extras. For in their generation, they did not eat meat and they did not drink wine. All that began in the time of Noah. They, however, made do by eating plants and vegetation and drinking water. And it is known in medical books that the simpler the food one consumes, the longer one lives. (Abravanel on Genesis 3:5)

In recent years, more and more people are asking what kashrut really is, and what it should be—what makes food proper, ethical, and appropriate for consumption. Is fast food, loaded with fat and cholesterol and injurious to our **health** and well-being, really kosher—even if it is certified as kosher? Can food that was produced by children laboring in conditions of slavery really be kosher? Are animals that were raised cruelly and killed brutally (even with careful attention to halachic detail) kosher for us to eat? Does frozen food that has been warmed and served without thought to children staring at a screen count as kosher? Our Torah is a Torah of life. The food that we consume to nourish our bodies and bring us enjoyment should also be in keeping with a kashrut of life.

Conscious eating is essential. What we put into our bodies becomes what we are. We should therefore take great care with our food. Lately we hear more and more about new methods of examining the kashrut of a product: eco-kashrut, ethical kashrut, the "slow food" movement, and so on. More and more people are looking for a fair-trade label or "social kashrut" labeling no less than other established kashrut certifications.

How Do I Know If It's Kosher?

The Torah, it is said, has seventy faces (the *g'matria* for the Hebrew word for cheese, *g'vina*—one of the stars of the holiday—is seventy). So in honor of the holiday I would like to suggest an experimental list of criteria for testing the kashrut of food. This list is not intended to replace existing kashrut rules, but rather to supplement them with

From Time to Time → Dalia Marx

a dimension of attention. They all emerge from the basic requirement to live a life of *k'dushah*, of holiness: "You shall be holy, for I, the Eternal your God, am holy" (Leviticus 19:2).

1. **Social justice, concern for the have-nots:** "to share your bread with the hungry" (Isaiah 58:7).
2. **Protecting nature, avoiding waste:** the principle of *bal tashchit*, based on Deuteronomy 20:19, "When in your war against a city . . . you must not destroy its trees."
3. **Proper attitude toward animals:** "You shall not boil a kid in its mother's milk" (Exodus 23:19).
4. **Fair employment practices:** "You shall not defraud your fellow. You shall not commit robbery" (Leviticus 19:13).
5. **Health and care for one's body:** "For your own sake, therefore, be most careful" (Deuteronomy 4:15).
6. **A feeling of gratitude:** "Let all that breathes praise the Eternal. Halleluyah!" (Psalm 150:6).
7. **Family and community:** "How good and how pleasant it is that siblings dwell together" (Psalm 133:1).
8. **Attentiveness and consciousness:** "Let the living take this to heart" (Ecclesiastes 7:2).
9. **Taste and enjoyment:** "Honey and milk are under your tongue" (Song of Songs 4:11).
10. **Moderation:** "If you find honey, eat only what you need, lest, surfeiting yourself, you throw it up" (Proverbs 25:16).

Some of these criteria supplement each other, while some are in tension with each other or are even mutually contradictory. For example, "fair trade" goods are likely to be more expensive and thus more problematic from the perspective of social equality. Similarly, what do we do if, for example, a company that produces organic food hires workers under unfair conditions—is it still kosher? The list of examples goes on. That's right: for the essential questions of the appropriateness of what we put in our mouths in our time there are no simple solutions. These are not questions that have decisive answers from rabbis and authority figures. But even if we do not have clear and decisive answers to these questions, and even if—as we read in *Pirkei Avot* 2:21—"the task is not ours to complete" on these issues, "neither are we free to desist from the task"; we must still wrestle with the questions.

> When the Blessed Holy One created the first human,
> God took them and led them round all the trees of the Garden of Eden and said:
> "Look at My works, how beautiful and praiseworthy they are!
> And all that I have created—it was for you that I created it.
> Pay attention that you do not corrupt and destroy My world,
> because if you corrupt it, there will be no one to repair it after you."
> (*Kohelet Rabbah* 7:1)

Kashrut is the system of determining which foods are appropriate to eat, originally based on the Torah. Through the centuries, additional laws and strictures have been added both in response to changing agricultural and livestock production and in reaction to trends in the outside world. For example, some major kashrut organizations have determined that plant-based pork products can never be kosher—not because the food is inherently inappropriate to eat like real pork, but because of concern for "sensitivities to the [kosher] consumer."[16]

Eco-kashrut is a movement that expands on the existing guidelines for kosher certification to address ecological, social, and ethical issues. Eco-kashrut is sometimes called ethical kashrut. Social kashrut is a subgroup of the eco-kashrut movement, but its primary focus is on the way food impacts people—particularly historically oppressed communities within the Jewish community, such as Jews of Color or LGBTQ+ Jews.

Ruth and Joining the Jewish People

LOVE. Not theological argumentation, not religious awareness, and not even an attraction to the mitzvot. It was love that led Ruth the Moabite to join the Jews. It was her love for the people Israel that brought her under the wings of the *Shechinah*, God's protective presence. For her, the Jewish people had a very clear face—the face of Naomi, her mother-in-law. That love, which was a source of consolation and identity for Ruth, would not allow her to turn her back on her mother-in-law in their time of shared grief. Ruth's love led her to plead with her mother-in-law, uttering one of the most moving poems our tradition has known:

> Do not urge me to leave you, to turn back and not follow you.
> For wherever you go, I will go;
> wherever you lodge I will lodge;
> your people shall be my people,
> and your God my God.
> Where you die, I will die, and there I will be buried.
> Thus and more may the Eternal do to me
> if anything but death parts me from you.
> (Ruth 1:16–17)

It is possible that the Book of Ruth was written in response to Ezra and Nehamiah's removal of foreign wives and their children, as a kind of polemic against the separatist approach reflected in this mass expulsion effort. In Rabbinic literature and Jewish literature that followed, different approaches to conversion and converts can be discerned. There have been those who were more stringent and those who were more lenient, those who pushed away potential converts and those who drew them near. Particularly well-known are the stories of the opposite responses of Hillel and Shammai, two of the earliest Rabbinic figures, to the appeals of non-Jews who came to them and asked to convert to Judaism.

The following story provides a sharp example of the different approaches of various sages to converts and the desire to become Jews:

> It happened that a certain non-Jew came before Shammai.
> He said to him, "Convert me on condition that you teach me the whole Torah while I stand on one foot."
> Shammai pushed him away with the builder's cubit that was in his hand.
> When he went before Hillel, he said to [the potential convert], "What is hateful to you, do not do to your neighbor. That is the whole Torah, and the rest is commentary. Go and learn it." (Babylonian Talmud, *Shabbat* 31a)

Shammai understood the non-Jew's request to learn "the whole Torah while he stood on one foot" as an indication of an insulting, dismissive attitude toward Judaism, and so Shammai forcibly sent him away. In contrast, Hillel took the man seriously and taught him the principle—seemingly so simple—that he should not do to someone else what he himself despised. "That is the entire Torah," he said, "now go and delve deeply into it."

The Talmud presents the two positions without saying which one is "right," but the text highlights Hillel's reaction in response both to the non-Jew's request and to Shammai's response, and it seems that the Talmud sides with Hillel. Indeed, this is in line with the fact that in the many disputes between the two sages, it is Hillel's position that is usually accepted.

And so it is across the many generations up to our own: some express hesitation and even opposition to conversion, while some halachic authorities show great appreciation for those who join and rejoice in the enlarged numbers and strength of the Jewish people. Responding to the words of Isaiah, "And strangers shall join them and cleave [*nisp'chu*] to the House of Jacob" (Isaiah 14:1), the Talmudic sage Rabbi Chelbo says, "Converts are as difficult for Israel as a scabbed-over wound [*sapachat*]" (Babylonian Talmud, *Y'vamot* 47b). This is generally understood to mean that converts are like a chronic illness on the Jewish people's skin, although it can be interpreted differently. Rabbi Chelbo's statement, which

From Time to Time → Dalia Marx

appears four times in the Talmud, expresses concern about the social problems that converts may bring to the people Israel. One of the opponents of this view was none other than Rabbi Berechyah, Rabbi Chelbo's star student. The younger sage arrives at the opposite conclusion with his midrashic interpretation of the same verse. In his view, the converts' "cleaving" to the Jews and Judaism is a blessing, and their descendants will be privileged to join the priests' status in the Temple (*Sh'mot Rabbah* 19:4). His view is strengthened by the fact that the root of the word *sapachat* means "to join." And indeed, Jews by choice enrich and inspire the larger Jewish community they have joined and make our people more diverse and inclusive.

The Rigid Version in Israeli Policy

It is troubling that many of the rabbinical court judges involved with official state-sponsored conversion in the State of Israel take a very stringent and demanding stance on this issue. Over the course of the state's existence, discordant voices have been heard regarding converts to Judaism. Those sounds have become especially disturbing since the great immigration from the former Soviet Union (FSU) in the 1990s. More than three hundred thousand people from the FSU live in Israel today who are not categorized as belonging to any religious group. This may not seem odd in other countries, but in Israel our religious identity is part of our official population registry. This has an impact on the immigrants from the FSU, because many are the descendants of Jews and they live as typical Jewish Israelis in the State of Israel, but are not Jewish by the definition of Orthodox halachah. They all arrived in Israel under the state's Law of Return, but the state that brought them and welcomed them has not lived up to the national challenge of embracing them and offering them an accessible path toward conversion. At the present time, only a few thousand of the FSU immigrants convert to Judaism each year. In my role as a rabbi I have met quite a few people who encounter one obstacle after another, and occasionally injustice, in their efforts to gain an official acceptance by Jewish people.

> The Law of Return (1950) grants automatic Israeli citizenship to any Jew who comes to Israel and asks to settle in the country. This does not include instances in which the applicant presents a security risk or has a serious criminal record or the like. The basic assumption underlying the Law of Return is that the State of Israel is the state of the entire Jewish people and any Jew can find a home in it.

Over the years, ultra-Orthodox circles have cast harsh doubts over not only the legitimacy of conversions conducted under the auspices of the Reform and Conservative rabbis, but even some conversions in the IDF carried out by the military chief (Orthodox) rabbinate, and by other Orthodox rabbis. These approaches make Judaism some sort of exclusive club to which one may be admitted only after miserable hazing. This radicalization regarding conversions has even resulted in some ultra-Orthodox rabbis calling for the nullification of a conversion of someone who does not observe Torah and mitzvot in an Orthodox manner.

These unprecedented demands by the official government conversion authorities, the chief rabbinate, and ultra-Orthodox rabbis are an expression of a negative attitude toward conversion of people who don't commit themselves to Orthodox observance.

The idea of nullifying an individual conversion was something almost unheard of in Jewish history, yet today we are facing the automatic reversal of hundreds of conversions by disqualifying the judges who supervised them. In the 1990s a few individ-

On the prohibition against causing suffering or embarrassment to a Jew-by-choice or reminding them of their past, the following passage occurs in a discussion of *onaat d'varim*, verbal mistreatment:

> If one is the child of converts, they must not be taunted with "Remember the deeds of your ancestors." If one is a convert and comes to study the Torah, one must not say to them, "Shall the mouth that ate unclean and forbidden food, abominable and creeping things, come to study the Torah, which was uttered by the mouth of the Almighty?" (Babylonian Talmud, *Bava M'tzia* 58b)

ual conversions were nullified on grounds of nonobservance; in recent years there has been a significant rise in the nullification of completed conversions. Some major Chareidi rabbis emphasized that would-be converts who did not accept the responsibility to perform mitzvot (according to the Chareidi understanding, of course) are "complete non-Jews." This ruling constitutes an *ex nihilo* reform, made without precedent or parallel in the history of halachic rulings. It even contravenes the existing halachah that states that one may not remind a convert of their previous life.

The Festival of the Giving of the Torah and the Festival of the Seekers of Torah

Questions related to conversion in Israel reveal not only the relationship toward Jews-by-choice but also the way in which those who facilitate the conversion—in this case, Israeli society—understand themselves. The limits of this gateway, its boundaries and borders, indicate the way we understand our lives as Jews in our own sovereign state. Would Ruth, the young widow who is considered the ideal Jew-by-choice, be considered a Jew by the powers that be today? Or would King David's great-grandmother and progenitor of the dynasty that tradition tells us will beget the Messiah be forced to experience the kind of suffering imposed in Israel today on those who seek to convert to Judaism?

There is a powerful, subversive message communicated by our tradition in the choice to read the Book of Ruth on Shavuot. At the celebration of the giving of the Torah, we read a story that contains a violation of the Torah. The Torah teaches us, "No Ammonite or Moabite shall be admitted into the congregation of the Eternal" (Deuteronomy 23:4), and yet here in the Book of Ruth, Boaz marries Ruth—a Moabite woman. While it is true that the Rabbis read the Torah's words narrowly, interpreting the male language in the verse as referring to Moabite men but not Moabite women, the fact that the story requires this restrictive interpretation attests to its boldness. The narrator of the book continues to call Ruth "the Moabite" until she marries Boaz. The choice to read this challenging text on Shavuot may have a message for us about the requirement that each generation interpret the Torah anew and read it with fresh eyes.

This describes the overall situation in Israel, but the process for conversion in many places in the Diaspora may be more accommodating and sensitive. In fact, there are a number of organizations whose primary goal is to make the conversion process smooth and ensure a feeling of welcome for people who convert to Judaism. While there is not a standard conversion procedure, most people in the United States and Canada who wish to convert begin with an "Introduction to Judaism" class, which is sponsored by many synagogues or other community institutions. Conversion also usually requires regular meetings with the sponsoring rabbi and regular attendance and participation in the synagogue, concluding with meeting with a *beit din*, ritual immersion, and other rituals. In some communities, Reform and Conservative rabbis work together to support Jews who choose Judaism, and most synagogues make a special effort to ensure Jews-of-choice feel welcome. Perhaps this example should inspire those of us in Israel to reevaluate the strict boundaries and borders currently in place for those who approach the gateway to conversion. In fact, the Reform and Masorti movements in Israel have already taken this approach, and they—along with other groups—work to ease the process and path of conversion in Israel.

Shavuot is the holiday of the giving of the Torah, and no less the holiday of accepting the Torah by those who seek it and choose to celebrate in its light. This is the

From Time to Time → Dalia Marx

wedding anniversary of our covenant with the Torah and with its Giver. Shavuot is also a holiday marking the choice to join the Jewish people and convert to Judaism and the responsibility of those of us who welcome converts to place reliable, sensitive sentries at the entry gates of our people. Ensuring that Jews-of-choice feel welcome past these entry gates is part of our efforts to make Judaism a big tent that includes all.

📖 "And the Torah in One's Mouth Shall Be Sweet"— Rites of Initiation into Torah Study

ONE OF THE THINGS that has set the people Israel apart throughout the ages and in many Diaspora settings was their knowledge of reading and writing. Jews, or at least male Jews, stood out from the general population in that all read and wrote at some level, whether they were in the East or West, rich or poor, Torah scholar or craftsman or simple worker. This was true even when Jews lived in places where the art of reading and writing in the general populace was in the hands of only a few. Reading and writing served first and foremost the goal of Torah study, a mitzvah of the highest order. The Rabbis said, "The study of Torah is equivalent to them all" (*Mishnah Pei-ah* 1:1), meaning that the ability to study includes and makes possible all the other mitzvot.

Introducing small children to the study of Torah was a complex process. The youngsters, sometimes as young as three years old, left their warm and protective homes for a fascinating but also demanding and sometimes quite inflexible school setting. It was necessary to sweeten this transition, quite literally, so that the experience of study would be associated with pleasure and enjoyment. In various Jewish communities, special ceremonies were created for the special day on which a child (meaning, until modern times, a male child) would begin to study Torah.

Yehoshua Sobol's poem, so well-known in the musical setting composed for it by Shlomo Bar, describes the lad as an actual bridegroom and the ceremony of initiation into study as a kind of wedding, a wedding with the Torah.

> Making sure to **teach** children Torah is one of the obligations placed upon a father: "The father is required, with regard to his son, to circumcise him, redeem him, teach him Torah, take a wife for him, and teach him a craft" (Babylonian Talmud, *Kiddushin* 29a). In our day, we would extend this sentiment to apply to mothers as well as fathers, and (except for circumcision) to daughters as well as sons.

A Personal Receiving of the Torah

In some communities, an initiation ceremony took place on Shavuot as a sort of giving of the Torah, writ small. Here is a description given by Rabbi Eleazar of Worms, a halachic authority and kabbalist active in the twelfth and thirteenth centuries, of the ceremony customary among the Rhine Valley Jewish communities:

> It is the custom of our ancestors . . . to sit the children down to study [the Torah for the first time] on Shavuot because that is when the Torah was given. . . . The boys are brought [on Shavuot morning] at sunrise, according to (the verse): "[On the third day,] as morning dawned, there was thunder, and lightning" (Exodus 19:16). He is covered with a cloak on the way from their house to the synagogue or the teacher's house, according to [the verse]: "and they took their places at the foot [or: nether part] of the mountain" (Exodus 19:17). The child is placed on the lap [literally, bosom] of the teacher who sits them down to study, according to [the verse]: . . . "Carry them in your bosom as a nurse carries an infant" (Numbers 11:12); [and according to the verse]: "I have pampered Ephraim, taking him in My arms" (Hosea 11:3).[18]

Dr. Ivan Marcus of Yale University has researched these ceremonies, and he thinks that they are designed as a process of symbolic birth.[19] The father would cover the son with his coat and carry him hidden on his chest in a sort of male pregnancy, and the child would be reborn, as it were, in the synagogue or at the rabbi's home. If his actual birth was natural birth, this was a cultural birth—into the culture of Jewish literacy. The first was in the realm of the feminine; this one was in the realm of the masculine. The child would be greeted warmly by the rabbi, who played the role of male nursemaid—a sort of additional parent—and he would lead the child through a series of ceremonial acts. The child would repeat after the rabbi a series of verses on the subject of the giving of the Torah and its study—letter after letter, word after word. In the course of this reading, the child would lick honey that had been spread over the letters of a writing tablet and eat sweet cake and an egg, upon which words of Torah were written. The aim of all this was to make the experience of entering Torah study sweet and to create a connection between the sweetness in the child's mouth and the sweetness of the Torah:

> They bring over the tablet on which is written [the alphabet forwards, beginning] *alef, bet, gimel, dalet*; [the alphabet written backwards, beginning] *tav, shin, resh, qof*; [and the verse] "When Moses charged us with the Torah as the heritage of the congregation of Jacob" (Deuteronomy 33:4); [the phrase] "May the Torah be my occupation"; [and the first verse of Leviticus, beginning,] "The [Eternal] called to Moses..." (Leviticus 1:1).
>
> The teacher recites aloud each letter of the alphabet [forwards], and the child [recites them] after him; [then the teacher recites] each word of *tav, shin, resh, qof*, and the child does so too; similarly, [they both recite the verse beginning] "When Moses charged us with the Torah..." (Deuteronomy 33:4); [the phrase beginning] "May the Torah be..." and likewise [the verse beginning] "The [Eternal] called Moses..." (Leviticus 1:1).
>
> And [the teacher] puts a little honey on the tablet, and with his tongue, the child licks the honey which is on the letters.
>
> After this, they bring over the cake kneaded with honey on which is written, "The [Eternal] gave me a skilled tongue, to know how to speak timely words to the weary. Morning by morning, [God] rouses, [God] rouses my ear to give heed like disciples. The [Eternal] God opened my ears, and I did not disobey. I did not run away" (Isaiah 50:4–5). The teacher recites aloud each word of these verses, and the boy [repeats] after him.
>
> After this, they bring over a cooked egg which has been peeled and on which is written, "as [God] said to me, 'Mortal, feed your stomach and fill your belly with this scroll that I give you.' I ate it, and it tasted as sweet as honey to me" (Ezekiel 3:3). The teacher recites aloud each word and the boy [repeats] after him.
>
> They feed the boy the cake and the egg because it is good for opening the heart.[20]

The design of the entire ceremony is also reminiscent of the Exodus from Egypt and the Revelation at Sinai. Artwork depicts the procession passing by the river the morning of the ceremony, a reminder of crossing the Sea of Reeds; standing in the rabbi's home is like standing at the foot of the mountain at Sinai; the rabbi who teaches the child his first lesson in Torah is like Moses, who brought the Torah to the people

In Our Village of Tudra
Yehoshua Sobol

In our village of Tudra
in the heart of the Atlas Mountains
they would take the boy
when he reached the age of five.
A crown of flowers would be made for him
in our village of Tudra,
a crown they would place on his head
when he reached the age of five.
All the children on the street
would make a big celebration for him
when he reached the age of five
in our village of Tudra.

And then the "groom" of the celebration
who had reached the age of five,
in our village of Tudra,
would be brought into the synagogue.
And they would write on a wooden board
in honey, from *alef* to *tav*,
all the letters in honey,
and say to him, "My friend, lick it up!"
And the Torah in his mouth
was sweet like the taste of honey
in our village of Tudra
in the heart of the Atlas Mountains.[17]

אֶצְלֵנוּ בִּכְפַר טוּדְרָא
יְהוֹשֻׁעַ סוֹבּוֹל

אֶצְלֵנוּ בִּכְפַר טוּדְרָא
שֶׁבְּלֵב הָרֵי הָאַטְלָס
הָיוּ לוֹקְחִים אֶת הַיֶּלֶד
שֶׁהִגִּיעַ לְגִיל חָמֵשׁ.
כֶּתֶר פְּרָחִים עוֹשִׂים לוֹ
אֶצְלֵנוּ בִּכְפַר טוּדְרָא,
כֶּתֶר בָּרֹאשׁ מַלְבִּישִׁים לוֹ
שֶׁהִגִּיעַ לְגִיל חָמֵשׁ.
כָּל הַיְלָדִים בָּרְחוֹב
חֲגִיגָה גְּדוֹלָה עוֹרְכִים לוֹ
שֶׁהִגִּיעַ לְגִיל חָמֵשׁ.
אֶצְלֵנוּ בִּכְפַר טוּדְרָא.

וְאָז אֶת חֲתַן הַשִּׂמְחָה
שֶׁהִגִּיעַ לְגִיל חָמֵשׁ.
אֶצְלֵנוּ בִּכְפַר טוּדְרָא
מַכְנִיסִים לְבֵית הַכְּנֶסֶת.
וְכוֹתְבִים עַל לוּחַ שֶׁל עֵץ
בִּדְבַשׁ מֵאָלֶף וְעַד תָּו,
אֶת כָּל הָאוֹתִיּוֹת בִּדְבַשׁ,
וְאוֹמְרִים לוֹ: חֲבִיבִי לַקֵּק!
וְהָיְתָה הַתּוֹרָה שֶׁבְּפִיו
מְתוּקָה כְּמוֹ טַעַם שֶׁל דְּבַשׁ
אֶצְלֵנוּ בִּכְפַר טוּדְרָא
שֶׁבְּלֵב הָרֵי הָאַטְלָס.

Israel.[21] Rabbi Eleazar emphasizes that those ceremonies took place on Shavuot, as a sort of private Festival of the Giving of the Torah for the child commencing his studies. Throughout France and Provence, similar ceremonies took place without a connection to any event on the calendar. Instead, they were timed according to the children's readiness to enter into the world of study.

It appears this particular ceremony fell into disuse during the Middle Ages, but it served as an inspiration for many other ceremonies, such as the *chalakah* that takes place at Meron on Lag BaOmer (see p. 234).

Confirmation Ceremonies

Many centuries after the ceremony described by Rabbi Eleazar of Worms was no longer practiced, a different Jewish ceremony was born; this ceremony was also created in Germany, was also about initiation into Torah, and also usually took place on Shavuot. However, while the Rhine Valley initiation ceremonies were intended for young children when they began their formal education, the modern ceremonies were intended for older children in their teens. I am referring to the confirmation ceremonies for young Jews that took place beginning in the nineteenth century in Europe. Confirmation is a **ceremony to renew the covenant**, since the main part of these ceremonies is for Jewish teens to declare their commitment to Judaism in the presence of their congregation.

The first **confirmation** ceremony for girls was held in Berlin in 1817. This was how it was reported in the Jewish magazine *Sulamith*:

> The ceremony was held in a most festive atmosphere. The synagogue was full from wall to wall with four hundred people, who were in tears. The excellent sermon, the festive confirmation ceremony, the shining candelabra, and the two girls, first among Israel to be confirmed, lifted the attendees' spirits. The girls were exceedingly successful in passing their examination. In short, all those components made the event a most lovely ceremonial event.[23]

Jewish confirmation ceremonies were held in the synagogue with great fanfare and large crowds. The young people, usually sixteen or seventeen years old, were examined regarding their knowledge and understanding of the Jewish heritage. The ceremonies included special prayers and uplifting sermons, and they became central events in the lives of individuals and communities. Over time, these ceremonies replaced bar mitzvah ceremonies in many communities, since educators believed that children of twelve or thirteen were too young to understand the magnitude of the commitment and the power of the public ceremony.

Another important matter related to confirmation ceremonies is that they allowed gender equality between boys and girls. About one hundred years before the first bat mitzvah ceremony was held in the United States of America, girls participated in confirmation ceremonies throughout Europe. The participation of girls was natural and required no difficult debate or decisions, since the Jewish educational institutions and confirmation preparation courses welcomed boys and girls alike.

Among many non-Orthodox Jewish communities in North America, confirmation ceremonies are held as a matter of course, in addition to bar/bat mitzvah[22] ceremonies, when older teens can graduate from Jewish school as a group. Rabbis and educators value the confirmation ceremony as a means to preserving the synagogue's connection with the young people and their families and as a meaningful educational opportunity.

I must admit that I originally felt an aversion to these ceremonies, since I regarded them as a sort of imitation of Christian confirmation services (and indeed Jews did draw cultural inspiration from Christian confirmation ceremonies when designing

Jewish ones). After attending a few, though, I was convinced that confirmation is an authentic Jewish educational and spiritual experience.

Jewish confirmation ceremonies invite us to consider intercultural connections and cultural borrowing. If they are done in a conscious, controlled fashion, there is nothing wrong with them. On the contrary, they can enrich our spiritual and religious experience. The Jewish people's activity takes place in a larger world—both influencing and being influenced by its surroundings. So it has been throughout the ages. For example, the holiday of Shavuot itself that was apparently originally modeled on ancient agricultural festivals developed over time into the Festival of the Giving of the Torah. Only a frozen culture does not maintain contact with its surroundings. A mature living culture can allow itself to be influenced, if the influence is done in a controlled way and there is no fear of the culture being swallowed up or losing its uniqueness and its identity.

In every generation, we must accept the Torah anew. The kabbalists knew this, and so did various Jewish communities over the centuries. For Israelis, we also need to consider **developing ceremonies** similar to the confirmation ceremonies, such as a religious ceremony to mark the receipt of one's first government ID card at age sixteen, or one at the end of one's high school studies to add a spiritual dimension to the period of matriculation exams (*b'chinot bagrut*) and preparation for military service. Jewish communities throughout the world have created ceremonies for the ever-lengthening adolescent period, such as rituals when a girl begins to menstruate, "car mitzvah" ceremonies when a teen becomes a licensed driver, and so on. In our time, it seems fitting to include Jewish rituals to mark these milestones in the lives of Jewish young people on their way to maturity.

The proclivity to create significant **childhood ceremonies** for older children is not new. The *b'rit milah* circumcision ceremony—required by the Torah—takes place when children are tiny infants and still unable to understand what is happening or its significance. (This ceremony is reserved only for boys; today there are also B'rit Banot ceremonies to welcome girls into the covenant.) In the Middle Ages, ceremonies of initiation into formal education were added for toddlers who are developing into young children, when they can understand and also remember the ceremony. These initiation ceremonies did not replace the circumcision ceremonies, but rather added to and enhanced the meaning of the circumcision ceremony. Later, in the fifteenth century, we first hear about formal bar mitzvah ceremonies, held when children become adolescents. At that point, bar mitzvah became the central ceremony of childhood (parallel to an infant's circumcision), a status that remains today. At age thirteen, when young people are even more prepared, they can stand before a congregation and begin their lives as Jewish adults. In the nineteenth century, the central childhood ceremony was moved even later, with confirmation ceremonies celebrated at ages sixteen or seventeen, on the assumption that at this older age, young people (who now also included girls) understood the importance and power of a ceremony marking a choice to be counted among the Jewish people.

Tishrei   Marcheshvan   Kislev   Tevet   Sh'vat   Adar   Nisan   Iyar   Sivan   Tammuz   Av   Elul

🕎 The (Forgotten) Fast of the Twentieth of Sivan: Three Stops on the Journey of Mourning

THE ANTHROPOLOGIST Ronald L. Grimes describes doing therapy with a child suffering from depression whose daily routine had been completely upended because he would spend his days crying. As therapy, the psychologist instructed him to cry each night between 7:00 and 8:00 p.m. For that hour, he was to close himself up in his room and cry. All other activity was forbidden. At a certain point, the sadness was channeled from the full day into that hour of crying in the evening, and the child began to understand that he could fill the rest of the hours of the day with other activities. He was freed from the need to be sad during the whole course of the day, because he knew there was a special hour of the day that would contain his sadness and concentrate it, even if it would not erase it or make it disappear from his life. Gradually, even that lone hour was no longer needed.[24]

In the Jewish calendar too, there are days of sadness, days that channel sorrow and suffering, days that make room for all of our other emotions to fill the rest of our time. Over the generations, these days have drawn in the observance of new disasters that have come upon the Jewish people. The following paragraphs are devoted to the twentieth of Sivan, a fast day that has taken on multiple forms and discarded them a few times, before being nearly totally forgotten in our day.

Blood Libel in Beautiful Blois

The twentieth of Sivan was first set as a fast day in memory of the blood libel accusations against the Jews of Blois, a small community of a few dozen families in what is today central France. On that day in the Hebrew year 4931 (1171 CE), thirty-two Jews were murdered in Blois because of a false accusation that they had murdered a Christian boy. This was one of the first blood libels—claims by Christians that Jews had committed a ritual murder.

It seems that a Christian horseman saw a Jew throwing something into a river and thought (in error) that it was the body of a Christian boy. The claim was brought before the local ruler, Count Thibaut V, whose inclination was to be merciful toward the Jews. The rumor was that he had a Jewish lover named Pulcellina. The horseman's story would have been forgotten if not for the countess, who had an account to settle with the Jews because of her husband's infidelity. She enlisted the aid of a monk who made efforts to convert the Jews to Christianity. In the end, the local Jews were imprisoned in their synagogue and burned alive. Tradition tells us that during their last moments, the Jews of Blois sang the *Aleinu* prayer—the prayer of great faith originally composed for the *Musaf* prayers of Rosh HaShanah—which led to the recitation of *Aleinu* in our daily prayers.

A blood libel is a false accusation that Jews have murdered Christian children to use their blood in religious rituals. The most common accusation is that the blood of Christian children is required for the baking of matzah, though other rituals and accusations of poisoning wells or desecrating the host were also included. Blood libels were common in the Middle Ages and sadly persist today. The result of the medieval blood libel accusations was often the mass murder of a town's Jewish community, leading to mourning of communal losses and fear of further attacks. Over time, the term "blood libel" was used to describe any false accusation against the Jews and its resulting attacks. Ephraim of Bonn wrote this *s'lichah*, a penitentiary *piyut*, in memory of the Jews' disasters. It particularly laments the blood libel and disaster that came upon the Jews of Blois:

Woe unto us, for we have been robbed and set on fire,
the lovely, dainty community of Blois, placed on a pyre,
those who came together for Torah, its honor their desire.
oh, how the blaze divided and devoured as it grew higher!
Our enemies spread lies all around:
"You have killed a gentile in the river so the corpse would not be found."
You have imprisoned them, their bodies together bound,
Tortured and beaten them, demanded they declare a different God crowned.
They withstood all the trials, the fire and the flame,
"This is the ritual of the burnt offering on the altar" (Leviticus 6:2) they did exclaim.[25]

From Time to Time → Dalia Marx

The disaster that befell the Jews of Blois touched the hearts of Jews even in distant communities. Rabbeinu Tam (1100–1171) called the communities of Jews in France and the Rhine Valley to observe the twentieth of Sivan as a fast day. Rabbeinu Tam, who died shortly after the incident, said of the twentieth of Sivan, "This fast day will be greater than the Fast of Gedaliah, because it is a Yom Kippur."[26]

A Day of Curses and Maledictions

Over time, the memory of the Blois catastrophe dimmed, and new troubles made the Jews forget earlier ones. But nearly five hundred years later, the memory of the bloodshed on the twentieth of Sivan was connected to the disasters of 1648–49 (known by the acronyms for the Hebrew years of 5408 and 5409, as *G'zeirot Tach V'Tat*), when Cossacks led by Bogdan Chmielnicki attacked the Jews of Poland and Ukraine, murdering thousands of Jews, including men, women, and children. These pogroms continued for a sustained period over a broad area, but on the twentieth of Sivan, the Jewish community of Nemirov was destroyed. To mark this terrible event, the Council of the Four Lands (the Jewish leadership body in the four "lands" that constituted Poland at the time) declared the fast of the twentieth of Sivan as a memorial to the community of Nemirov, as well those whose destruction had until then not been commemorated.

Rabbi Shabbetai Cohen (1622–63), who was exiled from his town during the pogroms, relates that the pogroms began on the twentieth of Sivan, which was a Wednesday (or as we Israelis call it, *yom r'vi-i*, "the fourth day"). He saw a dark connection between the fourth day of Creation—when the heavenly lights (*m'orot*) were created—and the fourth day of the week—the day of these accursed events (*m'eirot*).[27] That midrash makes a horrid inversion: instead of the sun and moon's lights, the Jews saw only darkness. The author wrote, "Therefore I have set for myself and my descendants, my children and their children, a day of fasting and mourning and elegies on the twentieth of the month of Sivan . . . since this day was the beginning of the disasters and miseries and awful, persistent maladies."[28]

> In addition to the elegies and *piyutim* written by Rabbi Shabbetai Cohen and others, some believe that the touching Ashkenazic memorial prayer *El Malei Rachamim* ("God, full of mercy"), which calls for the souls of the dead to be bound up in the bond of life, was composed in the wake of the Chmielnicki massacres.

The Holocaust in Hungary

The fast of the twentieth of Sivan was observed among Ashkenazic communities until the Holocaust. It seems, though, that the destruction and devastation brought about by the Holocaust blunted the ability to remember smaller disasters. Furthermore, the memory of the Shoah has itself not taken on a permanent form among the Jewish public (see pp. 193–97). Nevertheless, in 1946 immediately after the Holocaust, Orthodox rabbis in Hungary—where the fast of the twentieth of Sivan had never been observed—chose that date as the memorial day for Hungarian victims of the Nazis. This choice surely stems from the fact that in the terrible summer of 1944, the height of the deportations of Hungarian Jews to the death camps fell on the twentieth of Sivan. This decision by the Hungarian rabbis aroused a great deal of opposition, both because of the timing of the fast day and the fact they created a new memorial day—at least for the Hungarian community—on the Hebrew calendar.[29]

Tishrei   Marcheshvan   Kislev   Tevet   Sh'vat   Adar   Nisan   Iyar   Sivan   Tammuz   Av   Elul

A Day When "Travails Have Been Redoubled"

To summarize, the disaster that befell the Jews in the small community at Blois made waves in France, Germany, and beyond and led to the establishment of a fast day. Later, the fast day was expanded to include memorializing the Jews of Ukraine and Poland, and later still it was suggested as a memorial day for the destruction of Hungarian Jewry in the twentieth century. In Sephardic and Middle Eastern Jewish communities, the twentieth of Sivan was never observed as a memorial day. That day channeled, as it were, sufferings and disasters that occurred for different Jewish communities in Europe, not only on that day but on other days as well. The same dynamic may have been at work here as with Tishah B'Av, a day on which "travails have been redoubled" (see pp. 305-8), and so it took on the memory of additional pogroms and riots that occurred for different Jewish communities in Europe, over the course of centuries at different times of year. In most Diaspora communities, the twentieth of Sivan is not observed in our time, although there are some who refrain from holding weddings on that day. Some Chasidic communities observe the fast, though its nature is communal and local.

Geographical dispersion and changing conditions from era to era and country to country mean that in addition to the holidays and observances that are common to the whole Jewish people, various Jewish communities have marked off special days to recall both disasters and the memory of happier events (such as Purim Sheini; see pp. 163-65).

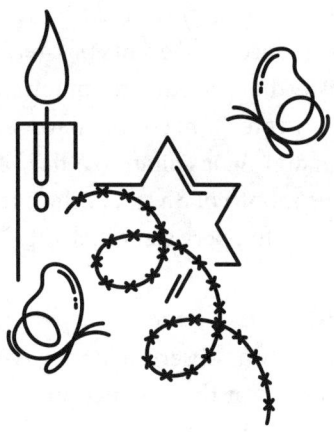

Prayers of the Month

The weekly recitation of the Torah in the synagogue is a spiritual and symbolic reenactment of the Revelation at Sinai.[30] As the Torah is taken out of the holy ark and portions of it are chanted aloud in public each week throughout the entire year, we return to the encounter at Mount Sinai and the astounding Revelation witnessed by the entire people. On Shavuot, this ceremony is particularly central, since this is the day we both read about the Revelation (Exodus 19–20) and observe the anniversary of standing at Sinai. Jewish communities created special *piyutim* to be recited just before reading the Torah's own account of the giving of the Torah.

In the eyes of many, the two *piyutim* below stand at the center of the religious experience of Shavuot. In Ashkenazic communities it is customary to recite the poem *Akdamut Milin* by Rabbi Meir ben Rabbi Yitzchak, and Sephardic communities have the custom of singing the *ketubah* for Shavuot composed by Rabbi Yisrael Najara. Both these *piyutim* are intended to be said at the peak moment of the Shavuot festival. It is interesting to compare what the Ashkenazic poet and, five hundred years later, his Sephardic comrade chose to emphasize about this pivotal event.

Akdamut Milin

Rabbi Meir ben Rabbi Yitzchak, the prayer leader of Worms, wrote the *piyut* known by its opening words, *Akdamut Milin*, in 1095. The poem is written in Aramaic and was intended as a *r'shut* asking the community's assent for the person about to recite the Aramaic translation of the day's Torah reading. In the past, Jewish communities had interspersed an Aramaic translation into the Hebrew recitation of the Torah, since Aramaic was the vernacular language of Middle Eastern Jews for many centuries. That custom appears as far back as the biblical era, when Ezra the Scribe returned to Zion after the Babylonian exile. Later, after Aramaic was no longer widely spoken, most Jewish communities abandoned the custom of reciting the Aramaic translation, but the *piyut* remained in place.

Akdamut Milin could not have been written any later than it was. In 1096, just a year after Rabbi Meir composed it, Crusaders en route to the Holy Land attacked the Rhineland's Jewish communities. The *piyut*'s portrayal of entreating gentiles was replaced by real-world murderous violence. To a certain extent, *Akdamut Milin* marks the conclusion of an era in Jewish-Christian relations in Europe.

Here we cite a small part of that *piyut*, which spans ninety lines, all of which end in the syllable *-ta*. The first forty-four lines are a double *alef-bet* acrostic formed by the initial letters of each line: two beginning with *alef*, two beginning with *bet*, and so on. At the end of the *piyut* is an acrostic spelling out the author's name and a wish that he be blessed with Torah and good deeds.

Akdamut Milin begins with a specific *r'shut* followed by an extended statement of God's greatness, which is beyond the power of human beings to describe.

Piyutim of the *r'shut* genre are poems chanted by a prayer leader before certain prayers in which formal permission is requested from the congregation or God for the prayer leader to stand before the congregation and lead them in prayer. *Akdamut Milin* is a *r'shut* preceding the Aramaic Targum of the Torah. Perhaps the need to receive permission stems from the length of the statements or praise that follows. It may also be that on the Festival of the Giving of the Torah, the poet feels a particular need for permission to translate the Torah into another language.

I shall introduce the reading of the Ten Commandments with a brief introduction,
in which I ask your leave to express myself openly.
I begin nervously, choosing to compose my thoughts along two or three separate lines,
to speak of the Creator of all and the Protector of all Creation for all time.
God's strength is eternal and can never be adequately described,
even if the sky were made of parchment and the forests of the world were planted solely with reeds I could use as pens,
even were the oceans and, indeed, all bodies of water to be made of ink
and all the world's citizens were scribes and secretaries.

אַקְדָּמוּת מִלִּין וְשָׁרָיוּת שׁוּתָא
אוֹלָא שָׁקֵלְנָא הַרְמָן וּרְשׁוּתָא
בְּבָבֵי תְּרֵי וּתְלַת דְּאֶפְתַח בְּנַקְשׁוּתָא
בְּבָרֵי דְבָרֵי וְטָרֵי עֲדֵי לְקַשִּׁישׁוּתָא
גְּבוּרָן עָלְמִין לֵהּ וְלָא סְפֵק פְּרִישׁוּתָא
גְּוִיל אִלּוּ רְקִיעֵי קְנֵי כָּל חוּרְשָׁתָא
דְּיוֹ אִלּוּ יַמֵּי וְכָל מֵי כְנִישׁוּתָא
דָּיְרֵי אַרְעָא סָפְרֵי וְרַשְׁמֵי רַשְׁוָתָא

Now the poet moves on to describe the angels praising God, which, marvelous as the angels and their praises are, cannot equal the grandeur of Israel, who are even more beloved by God. The rulers of the world's nations see Israel in its troubles and try to entice Israel into joining them. Note that in this selection you can see the last two verses of the alphabetical acrostic with the letter *tav*, followed by the four lines whose first letters spell "Meir," the author's first name.

Meanwhile, the nations gather relentlessly, like the waves of the sea,
brazenly demanding proof of Israel's status.
"Where and who is your beloved God, O most comely of nations,"
they ask derisively,
"that God for whom you would die in a lion's den?"
How loving and fitting it would be, O God, if You would love us openly!
We would gladly do Your will then, in every place possible.

תָּאִין וּמִתְכַּנְּשִׁין כְּחֵזוּ אִדְוָתָא
תְּמֵהִין וְשָׁיְלִין לֵהּ בְּעֵסֶק אָתְוָתָא
מָנָן וּמָאן הוּא רְחִימָךְ שַׁפְרָא בְּרֵוָתָא
אֲרוּם בְּגִינֵהּ סָפֵית מְדוֹר אַרְיָוָתָא
יְקָרָא וְיָאָה אַתְּ אִין תְּעָרְבִי לְמַרְוָתָא
רְעוּתִיךְ נַעֲבֵד לִיךְ בְּכָל אַתְרְוָתָא

The suitors—the other nations—try to entice lovely Israel into being romantically interested in them and to abandon their devotion to God. They employ persuasion rather than threat, but Israel spurns their invitations. The greatness of the would-be lovers is minuscule, even negligible, compared to what awaits when salvation arrives. Israel offers an extended description of the reward for this fidelity and the banquet of the righteous that Israel's true lover, God, will spread out at the time of their nuptials:

> Righteousness God will bring to the beloved folk possessed of the greatest merit.
> The greatest joy will God bring to Israel, and the purest of vessels,
> when the exiles are brought back to the holy city of Jerusalem.
> Divine glory will be spread over it day and night,
> and the Temple, the divine *chupah*, will be rebuilt there as well, a people's ultimate act of divine praise.
> The clouds of glory will serve as the most ideal tent. . . .
> [The people] dance together in Jerusalem before the Temple that houses God's Divine Presence on earth. . . .
> [God] will make of [the behemoth and the leviathan] a great feast,
> a festive meal, for the righteous.
> They will be seated around tables studded with rubies and gems,
> a river of balsam flowing right through them.
> They will be delighted with overflowing cups
> of the wine God has been storing in great wine casks since the very days of Creation.

> צִדְקָתָא לְעַם חָבִיב וְסַגִּי זַכְוָתָא
> חֲדוּ שְׁלֵמָא בְּמֵיתֵי וּמָנָא דַכְוָתָא
> קִרְיָתָא דִירוּשְׁלֵם כַּד יְכַנֵּשׁ גַּלְוָתָא
> יְקָרֵהּ מַטִּיל עֲלֵהּ בְּיוֹמֵי וְלֵילְוָתָא
> גְּנוּנֵהּ לְמֶעְבַּד בָּהּ בְּתוּשְׁבְּחָן כְּלִילָתָא
> דְּזֵהוֹר עֲנָנַיָּא לְמִשְׁפַּר כִּילָתָא . . .
> מְטַיְּלֵי בֵּי חִנְגָּא לְבַהֲדֵי דִשְׁכִינְתָּא . . .
> אָרִסְטוֹן לְצַדִּיקֵי יְתַקֵּן וְשֵׁרוּתָא
> מְסַחֲרִין עֲלֵי תַכֵּי דְכַדְכּוֹד וְגוּמַרְתָּא
> נָגִידִין קָמֵיהוֹן אֲפַרְסְמוֹן נַהֲרָתָא
> וּמִתְפַּנְּקֵי וְרָווֹ בְּכָסֵי רְוָיָתָא
> חֲמַר מְרַת דְּמִבְּרֵאשִׁית נְטִיר בֵּי נַעֲוָתָא

In conclusion, the poet turns his camera, as it were, from the feast of the righteous in the Garden of Eden to those seated in the synagogue—the actual intended audience of the speech—and promises that the faithful too will be privileged to sit among "that righteous assembly":

O righteous ones, just as you have now listened to this song of praise,
so may you all be privileged to be among that righteous assembly.
And may you all merit being seated in the very first row
so that you will be able to hear the words that come forth from the majestic presence of God.
God was exalted in hoariest times and shall be so exalted at the end of days.
God desired and chose us, then bestowed the Torah upon us.[31]

זַכָּאִין כִּי שְׁמַעְתּוּן שְׁבַח דָּא שִׁירָתָא
קְבִיעִין כֵּן תֶּהֱוֹון בְּהַנְהוּ חֲבוּרָתָא
וְתִזְכּוּן דִּי תֵיתְבוּן בְּעֵלָּא דָרָתָא
אֲרֵי תְצִיתוּן לְמִלּוֹי דְנָפְקִין בְּהַדְרָתָא
מְרוֹמָם הוּא אֱלָהִין בְּקַדְמְתָא וּבַתְרַיְתָא
צְבִי וְאִתְרְעִי בָן וּמְסַר לָן אוֹרַיְתָא

Originally, the Torah reading for Shavuot proceeded in this order: First, the *kohein* or the first person reciting the blessings over Torah would be called to ascend the bimah. After the blessing was recited, the first verse of Shavuot's Torah portion—"On the third new moon after the Israelites had gone forth from the land of Egypt, on that very day, they entered the wilderness of Sinai" (Exodus 19:1)—was chanted. Then, the Torah reading was interrupted and *Akdamut Milin* recited, immediately followed by the Aramaic translation of the first verse of the Torah reading, which had been chanted. After most congregations stopped the practice of reading the Aramaic Torah translation, the recitation of *Akdamut Milin* was moved so that it was read before the Torah reading began.

Akdamut Milin is a fascinating *piyut*, but also quite long at ninety lines, and its Aramaic is foreign to today's worshipers. In many synagogues its recitation is wearying and little understood, and many prayer leaders hopelessly flub the Aramaic. Many people have suggested either abridging the *piyut* or replacing it entirely.

Ketubah for Shavuot: "My Beloved Went Down to His Garden"

The poet Rabbi Yisrael Najara (1555–1628) was part of the group of kabbalists centered around Isaac Luria. He lived in Safed and in Damascus and later served as rabbi of Gaza, where he died and was buried. His *piyut* is known as "the Shavuot *Ketubah*," because at its center is a marriage contract between the Blessed Holy One and the people Israel. In it the "groom"—God—spells out his responsibilities toward his "bride"—Israel. The two lovers express their love and devotion to each other. Their *ketubah* is the Torah, which is received with great celebration on this festive occasion. Sometimes, it seems that the couple comprises Israel as the groom and the Torah as the bride. This translation uses gendered language to emphasize the author's assumed genders of the bride and groom.

The poet Levin Kipnis wrote a song for Shavuot sung to the same chant as the *piyut*:

**Matan Torah
(The Giving of the Torah)
Levin Kipnis**

No breeze was felt, not a gust was heard,
not a chirp or tweet from any bird;
no cow gave forth a moo, repeating,
not a single lamb's melancholy bleating;
no single bud became a flower,
the waters were silent at that hour;
the angels above ceased singing praise—
no "Holy! Holy" with voices raised.
every being to its breath held fast;
the one sound heard was the shofar blast.
The Eternal then granted us the Law, inspiring us to holiness, purity, and awe.[32]

אָז כָּל רוּחַ לֹא רְחָפָה,
צִפּוֹר שָׁמַיִם לֹא צִפְצְפָה;
פָּרָה בָּאָחוּ לֹא גָּעֲתָה
כִּבְשָׂה בָעֵדֶר לֹא פָּעֲתָה;
שׁוֹשָׁן וָפֶרַח לֹא פָּרְחוּ,
וּמֵי הַיָּם שָׁקְטוּ וְנָחוּ;
מַלְאֲכֵי מָרוֹם לֹא שָׁרוּ,
קָדוֹשׁ! קָדוֹשׁ! הֵם לֹא אָמְרוּ;
כָּל הָעוֹלָם כֻּלּוֹ שָׁתַק לוֹ,
וְקוֹל שׁוֹפָר הָלַךְ חָזָק לוֹ,
אָז נָתַן אֵל אֶת הַתּוֹרָה
זוֹ הַקְּדוֹשָׁה, זוֹ הַטְּהוֹרָה!

The *piyut* is constructed in stanzas of three lines each; the third line is a biblical quotation, usually from the Song of Songs, or a line from the traditional *ketubah*. Here are the first stanzas of the *piyut*:

My Beloved went down to His garden, to His bed of spices,
to delight in the princess, and to spread over her the canopy of His peace;
"King Solomon made himself a palanquin" (Song of Songs 3:9).

Seraphim and *Ophanim* [kinds of angels] He abandoned, and His
  horseman and chariot,
and with the beloved doe, He observed His banquet;
"On His wedding day, on His day of bliss" (Song of Songs 3:11).

My beloved, My doe, come with Me to My chamber, My hall,
for your sake I have left all the legions above, and their host;
"And I will espouse you forever" (Hosea 2:21–22).

Said the Awesome One, You who from the time of love I have heard,
and I love Him with an eternal love,
"Let Him give me of the kisses of His mouth" (Song of Songs 1:2).

To go to the wedding canopy the dance of the camps agreed,
and for her, "We will do, and then obey" (Exodus 24:7),
merited six hundred thousand crowns;
"On the third new moon after the Israelites had gone forth from the
  land of Egypt" (Exodus 19:1).[33]

יָרַד דּוֹדִי לְגַנּוֹ לַעֲרוּגַת בָּשְׂמוֹ,
לְהִתְעַלֵּס עִם בַּת נָדִיב וְלִפְרֹשׂ עָלֶיהָ סֻכַּת שְׁלוֹמוֹ,
"אַפִּרְיוֹן עָשָׂה לוֹ הַמֶּלֶךְ שְׁלֹמֹה" (שיה"ש ג, ט).

שְׂרָפִים וְאוֹפַנִּים נָטַשׁ וּפָרָשָׁיו וְרִכְבּוֹ,
וּבֵין שִׂמְחַת אַיֶּלֶת אֲהָבִים שָׁם מְסִבּוֹ,
"בְּיוֹם חֲתֻנָּתוֹ וּבְיוֹם שִׂמְחַת לִבּוֹ" (שם ג, יא).

רַעְיָתִי, יוֹנָתִי, בֹּאִי אִתִּי לִדְבִיר וְאוּלָם,
כִּי לְמַעֲנֵךְ אֶעֱזֹב כָּל הֲמוֹנֵי מַעֲלָה וְחֵילָם,
"וְאֵרַשְׂתִּיךְ לִי לְעוֹלָם" (הושע ב, כא-כב).

אָמְרָה אֲיֻמָּה אֶת שִׁמְעַת דּוֹד שְׁמַעְתִּיהוּ,
וְאַהֲבַת עוֹלָם אֲהַבְתִּיהוּ,
"יִשָּׁקֵנִי מִנְּשִׁיקוֹת פִּיהוּ" (שיה"ש א, ב)

לַחֻפָּה נִתְרַצְּתָה מְחוֹלַת הַמַּחֲנַיִם,
וּכְנֶגֶד נַעֲשֶׂה וְנִשְׁמָע לָקְחָה שִׁשִּׁים רִבּוֹא עֲדִי עֲדָיִים,
"בַּחֹדֶשׁ הַשְּׁלִישִׁי לְצֵאת בְּנֵי יִשְׂרָאֵל מֵאֶרֶץ מִצְרַיִם" (שמות יט, א).

Rabbi Menachem Yehudah de Lonzano, a contemporary of Najara, was **harshly critical** of the erotic descriptions in the *piyut* and said that the poet "permitted himself to say to the Eternal, may God be blessed, everything that adulterers say to one another."[34] He also criticized Najara for using the rhyme pattern and rhythm of erotic Arabic poetry.

In this way, Najara's *piyutim* resemble the songs and melodies (*nigunim*) of many Chasidim, whose melodies are based on the songs of Ukrainian or Polish shepherds. Using secular, common melodies for sacred purposes was part of what the Chasidim called "elevating the sparks of holiness" found in the melodies.

I find the sensitive, poetic descriptions of love in the poem (for which the author received **some criticism** for his bold frankness) beautiful. I am particularly fond of the fact that Najara gives voice to the bride, Israel. She expresses her feelings before her beloved.

It need not be pointed out that the *ketubah* for Shavuot is rather different from traditional *ketubot* signed at actual wedding ceremonies, which are written in a dry, legal style. The *ketubah* that Najara composed is lyrical and descriptive, and he includes extensive quotations from Song of Songs, the scroll of love whose songs were interpreted as love songs between the Blessed Holy One and Israel. In the biblical book, however, the lovers do not ever meet, while in this *ketubah* they meet and consummate their love.

These Shavuot *piyutim*—*Akdamut Milin* and "My Beloved Went Down to His Garden"—are both about the giving of the Torah at Sinai, yet they each interpret this event differently. Perhaps their different contents reflect the unique experiences of Jews in different communities and teach us something about the way they each connected to the giving of the Torah. Today there are congregations that integrate parts of both *piyutim* into their liturgy. What is the place of the Torah, which we celebrate on Shavuot, in today's society? We must remember that **the Torah is everyone's**. Perhaps it is more accurate to say that the Torah belongs to all those who choose to study it, love it, and regard it as the revelation of the generations and of the exalted, regardless of their individual beliefs and opinions, regardless of their lifestyles and traditions. No one owns the Torah exclusively, and no one can claim to have its one legitimate interpretation. The Torah is not acquired but gives itself over to those who love it, sometimes easily and sometimes with great effort, and its facets are new each day.

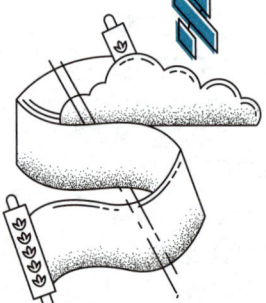

The initiative known as "929: Tanakh Together," started and maintained by Rabbi Dr. Benny Lau (with journalist Gal Gabai working on the first cycle), is a wonderful example of **the Hebrew Bible belonging to everyone**. Here is the project description on its website (929.org.il):

> On Chanukah 5775, December 21, 2014, the first cycle (ever!) of the joint reading of Tanakh began. Every day, at midnight, the daily chapter on the 929 website changes and the next chapter appears, along with interesting information, brief explanations, video clips, pictures, and even narration of the text, for those who prefer to listen.
>
> The lively discourse surrounding the chapter of the day takes place both on social media and in study groups, encounters, and events in the real world. Taking part are Israel's leading academics, cultural icons, public figures, artists, and writers, both men and women. 929 offers all participants the chance to open their eyes and be curious about new and varied approaches. 929 calls on you to rediscover the riches of the bestselling book in history—to listen to it, converse with it, find ourselves within it and it within us, and uncover what Tanakh has to offer us, here and now.

The second cycle introduced an English website, and the third cycle continues this important work.

From Time to Time → Dalia Marx

TAMMUZ

Zodiac Sign: Cancer | Tribe of the Month: Judah
Breastplate Stone: Turquoise/*Nofech*

The name Tammuz is taken from the Babylonian month Tammuzu (in Sumerian, Dummuzi), which is named for the god of vegetation, fertility, and food. The Babylonians believed that each year Tammuzu would go down into the netherworld at the beginning of the month of Tammuz, so festive funerals were held for him. In his absence during the dry season, it is as if nature is dead. According to the Babylonians' belief, Tammuzu returns to life in the autumn, when the plants start to grow again.

Tammuz is mentioned in the Book of Ezekiel, when the prophet speaks about "the women bewailing Tammuz" at the gate of the Temple (Ezekiel 8:14). As the name of the month, though, its first appearance in Jewish sources is in the Mishnah (*Taanit* 4:5–6).

In the Bible, the month is called "the fourth month," following the biblical pattern of counting the months from Nisan.

Kavanah: A Meditation for Tammuz

The Mishnah reports the many calamities that took place on the seventeenth of Tammuz:

> Five things befell our ancestors on the seventeenth of Tammuz, and five on the ninth of Av. On the seventeenth of Tammuz the tablets [of the Ten Commandments] were broken, and the daily burnt offerings [at the Temple] ceased, and the city [wall of Jerusalem] was breached, and Apostomus [a Syrian general] burned the Torah [scrolls], and an idol was set up in the Sanctuary. (*Mishnah Taanit* 4:6)

Our *kavanah* for the month of Tammuz is a request for a *tikkun*, a correction or repair, of each of those calamities:

> May the tablets of life that were broken be held in gentle hands.
> May the daily routine that was interrupted be guarded in beloved compartments of the soul.
> May new life burst forth from within the walls that were breached.
> May the sanctity that burned in flames light our paths from above.
> May hollow idols give way to honor and values.
> May what befell our ancestors and us find *tikkun* in our own chosen paths.

> Thus said the Eternal of Hosts: The fast of the fourth [month], the fast of the fifth [month], the fast of the seventh [month], and the fast of the tenth [month] shall become occasions for joy and gladness, happy festivals for the House of Judah; but you must love honesty and integrity. (Zechariah 8:19)

AT THE GATES OF TAMMUZ

During the month of Tammuz, when the heat of June and July is at its most oppressive, when nature is thirsting for rain and the plants are withering from the dry weather, the summer season—*t'kufat Tammuz*, including Tammuz, Av, and Elul—begins. These three months occur at the peak of summer and bring us to fall's Rosh HaShanah. The summer solstice, the longest day of the year (usually June 21), occurs during Tammuz (see pp. 286–87). From that point on, the days get shorter, and sunlight is slowly diminshed.

The seventeenth of Tammuz is a fast day that marks the breaching of the walls of Jerusalem by the Babylonians in 586 BCE. This begins a period of semi-mourning that lasts three weeks, a time called "between the straits" (Lamentations 1:3), and ends at Tishah B'Av, the day commemorating the destruction of the Temple. In Israel's public sphere, the seventeenth of Tammuz does not draw much notice, perhaps because it comes during the time of year when the school system is not in session.

Indeed, those who do not share that sense of doom and sorrow of Tammuz are the students, who are enjoying their summer vacation. The first *iyun* in this chapter offers some thoughts about the importance of vacations—or more precisely, the importance of being idle. The second *iyun* asks questions about strangeness and intimacy, alienation and authenticity, all of which are part of the core fabric of the month of Tammuz. The third *iyun* examines ancient myths about Tammuz and explores what they teach us about life, death, and rebirth. The fourth *iyun* looks at the social protest movements in Israel and beyond and uses them to examine the tendency toward revolution that is deeply rooted in many Jews. The poem of the month is *Atanu L'cha*, a *piyut* for the seventeenth of Tammuz, and the prayer of the month is a new *t'chinah* (prayer of supplication) for the well-being of students starting their summer vacation.

From Time to Time → Dalia Marx

Poem of the Month
Atanu L'cha ("We Have Come before You")

Atanu L'cha ("We Have Come before You") is a *piyut* of the *s'lichah* genre, a penitential poem, written for recitation on the seventeenth of Tammuz. The poem is an alphabetical acrostic and recounts the people's sins and the hardships imposed upon them. Each stanza concludes with the words "for on the seventeenth of Tammuz" and a reference to one of the disasters that took place on that date. The *piyut*'s list of disasters is based on *Mishnah Taanit* 4:6 (see above). The last stanza is different. Instead of recounting something from the past or describing the present, there is a plea for the future when the seventeenth of Tammuz will be transformed into an occasion for joy and gladness. Here are the first five stanzas, listing the disasters that took place on that date, and the last stanza, with its prayer of hope for the future:

We Have Come before You

We have come before You, Creator of the breath [of all flesh]
heavily sighing with the multitude of our iniquities,
and lamenting sorely because of the hard decrees,
for on the seventeenth of Tammuz the holy tablets were broken.

We were exiled from Your chosen Temple,
and the light was darkened for us;
our sentence was sealed, and the decree was carried out,
for on the seventeenth of Tammuz the holy Torah was burnt.

Our enemies had overthrown the Temple,
the Divine Presence fled from the interior of the holy palace,
and we were betrayed into the hands of the wicked to be consumed,
for on the seventeenth of Tammuz an idol was placed in the Temple.

We were scattered from city to city,
and the old and the young were taken captive;
our city was destroyed, and a fire was kindled therein;
for on the seventeenth of Tammuz the city was broken up.

The destroying enemy acted with callousness toward our sanctuary,
bride and bridegroom were stripped of their ornaments;

אֲתָאנוּ־לְךָ

אֲתָאנוּ־לְךָ יוֹצֵר רוּחוֹת
בְּרֹב עֲוֹנֵינוּ כָּבְדוּ אֲנָחוֹת
גְּזֵרוֹת עָצְמוּ וְרַבּוּ צְרִיחוֹת
כִּי בְּשִׁבְעָה עָשָׂר בְּתַמּוּז
נִשְׁתַּבְּרוּ הַלּוּחוֹת.

גָּלִינוּ מִבֵּית הַבְּחִירָה
דִּינֵנוּ נֶחְתַּם וְנִגְזְרָה גְזֵרָה
וְחָשְׁכָה בַּעֲדֵנוּ אוֹרָה
כִּי בְּשִׁבְעָה עָשָׂר בְּתַמּוּז
נִשְׂרְפָה הַתּוֹרָה.

הָרְסוּ אוֹיְבֵינוּ אֶת־הַהֵיכָל
וּבָרְחָה שְׁכִינָה מִזָּוִית הֵיכָל
וְנִמְסַרְנוּ בְּיַד זֵדִים לְהִתְאַכֵּל
כִּי בְּשִׁבְעָה עָשָׂר בְּתַמּוּז
הָעֳמַד צֶלֶם בְּהֵיכָל.

זֹרוֹנוּ מֵעִיר אֶל־עִיר
וְנִלְכַּד מִמֶּנּוּ רַב וְצָעִיר
חָרְבָה עִירֵנוּ וְאֵשׁ בָּהּ הַבְעִיר
כִּי בְּשִׁבְעָה עָשָׂר בְּתַמּוּז
הָבְקְעָה הָעִיר.

טָפַשׂ בְּמִקְדָּשֵׁנוּ צַר הַמַּשְׁמִיד
וְנִטַּל מֵחָתָן וְכַלָּה אֶצְעָדָה וְצָמִיד

Tishrei   Marcheshvan   Kislev   Tevet   Sh'vat   Adar   Nisan   Iyar   Sivan   **Tammuz**   Av   Elul

because we provoked You to anger we were given up to destruction; on the seventeenth of Tammuz the daily offering ceased. Turn unto us, O You who dwell on high, and gather our dispersed from all the corners of the earth. Say unto Zion, arise; and convert the seventeenth of Tammuz into a day of salvation and comfort for us.[1]	יַעַן כִּעֲסַנוּךָ נִתַּנּוּ לְהַשְׁמִיד כִּי בְּשִׁבְעָה עָשָׂר בְּתַמּוּז בָּטַל הַתָּמִיד. **שְׁ**עֵנוּ בְּשִׁמְךָ שֹׁכֵן רוּמָה וְקַבֵּץ נְפוּצוֹתֵינוּ מִקַּצְווֹת אֲדָמָה **תֹּ**אמַר לְצִיּוֹן קוּמָה וְנָקוּמָה וְשִׁבְעָה עָשָׂר בְּתַמּוּז הֲפוֹךְ לָנוּ לְיוֹם יְשׁוּעָה וְנֶחָמָה.

The topic of the following modern *piyut* is similar to that of *Atanu L'cha*, above, but it addresses the question of guilt and responsibility from a different direction. The author writes that the *piyut* is intended "for situations in which there is a need to be cleansed of the past, of guilt or depression, and 'turn a new leaf.'"[2] He recommends adding a personal prayer or combining this *piyut* with an immersion ritual or a personal act for marking their separation from the event that brought about the rupture or crisis.

Confession: A Prayer for Repair of the Tablets **Rabbi Ofer Sabath Beit Halachmi**	**וִדּוּי-תְּפִלָּה לְתִקּוּן הַלּוּחוֹת** **הָרַב עֹפֶר שַׁבָּת בֵּית הַלַּחְמִי**
God of the Covenant— intimate of the heart, creator of the world: Gaze from Horeb, and forgive. Through Your love, send healing, and mend the cracks within me caused by the senselessness of serving idols. Forgive the shards I left scattered on my path— broken bits of body, pieces of soul— for it all happened by mistake, the result of human frailty. Forgive and, through Your hidden love, send to the shattered tablets a mystical repair of acceptance and light. And send me strength, my God to stand before You.[3]	אֵל אֱלֹהֵי הָעֵדוּת. יוֹדֵעַ לֵב וּבוֹרֵא עוֹלָם, הַבֵּט מֵהַר חוֹרֵב, וּסְלַח וּשְׁלַח בְּחַסְדְּךָ מָזוֹר וְתַקָּנָה אֶל הַסְּדָקִים שֶׁנִּפְעֲרוּ בִי מֵהֶבֶל עֲבוֹדָה זָרָה. סְלַח עַל הַשְּׁבָרִים שֶׁהוֹתַרְתִּי בְּדַרְכִּי, שִׁבְרֵי הַנֶּפֶשׁ אוֹ שִׁבְרֵי הַגּוּף כִּי בְּשׁוֹגֵג הָיוּ כָּל אֵלֶּה וּמֵחֻלְשַׁת אֱנוֹשׁ. סְלַח וּשְׁלַח, בְּחַסְדְּךָ הַנֶּעֱלָם תִּקּוּן שֶׁל קַבָּלָה וָאוֹר, אֶל רְסִיסֵי לוּחוֹת. וּשְׁלַח הַכֹּחַ לַעֲמֹד, אֶל מוּל פָּנֶיךָ אֵל.

From Time to Time → Dalia Marx

On the Importance of Taking a Break

Pippi Longstocking, the freckled girl with braids that stick out sideways, who lives alone with a horse and a monkey, was one of my childhood heroes.[4] Her bravery and bravado enchanted me, but more than her dancing with pirates, outwitting robbers, or sailing to the South Sea, what really touched my heart was a somewhat overlooked part of the book. Pippi discovers that as someone who isn't in school, she doesn't get a winter vacation, and she is very frustrated. All the "normal" children, the ones who populate the rows of seats in school, get a vacation, and only she is left out. On the surface, this unfettered girl lives her whole life in endless vacation, but there's no way to take time off when there's nothing to take time off from. Pippi grasped this truth very clearly. In her wisdom, she understood that a vacation without a beginning and an end is not a vacation, so she decided to join her friends and become a student (an experiment that did not go particularly well . . .).

The lesson Pippi learned is an important one, but my impression is that today many people need to learn the opposite lesson—that in order to work and function properly, one needs to know how to stop. Especially in a world that proceeds at a feverish pace, we need to demand rest for ourselves. However, the force of our need for rest and time spent doing nothing is matched by the difficulty of actually stopping. As far back as the seventeenth century, the French philosopher and mathematician Blaise Pascal wrote, "I have discovered that all the misfortunes of men arise from one thing only, that they are unable to stay quietly in their own chamber. [People seek adventure and diversion only] because they cannot remain with pleasure in their own homes."[5]

On the twentieth of June, Israeli students in middle and high schools begin their summer vacation, followed ten days later by elementary school students and some of the children in kindergarten and preschool. Students in Israeli colleges and universities come out from under the yoke of studies and exams a bit later, and the babies in infant day care are without their usual program from sometime in August. Tammuz, beginning with the school and day care vacations, is a good time for considering the importance of occasionally stopping our regular activities.

Frederick the Great, Father of the Long Summer Vacation

The long summer vacation afforded to students was not originally intended to provide rest and recharging, but to enable children to help with agricultural work and domestic chores. Another consideration was to prevent children sweating through their studies in oppressively uncomfortable classrooms during the summer heat. The Prussian king Frederick the Great (1712–86), known for his advanced social policies, was the first to create a general elementary school system and apparently also the originator of summer vacation from school. The schoolchildren left their classrooms to help their parents with the harvest, which required the work of many hands.

When Jewish communities in the Land of Israel began their education systems, summer break was intended for the same purpose.[6] The question of what Israelis today

The Hebrew terms *shiamum* (boredom) and *batalah* (idleness) belong to the same semantic field, but the difference between them is great. *Shiamum* refers to an annoying, unpleasant feeling of passivity and inactivity, and many times it is accompanied by mild depression and a feeling of worthlessness. *Batalah* is also a condition of inactivity but refers to a conscious choice to refrain from work or other activities. In other words, *batalah* is refraining from activity, and *shiamum* is a name for the feeling that might accompany extended *batalah*. As the Mishnah tells us, "*Batalah* leads to *shiamum*" (Mishnah K'tubot 5:5).

The word *shiamum* apparently derives from the root *ayin-mem-mem*, with an added prefix. This root means "darkness," so *shiamum* may refer to melancholy or depression. The word first appears in the Mishnah when Rabban Shimon ben Gamliel says that even the wealthiest woman should be required to perform some sort of labor, because "*batalah* leads to *shiamum*" (Mishnah K'tubot 5:5). Rashi, commenting on this passage, understands it to mean "insanity."

Boredom as a human and social phenomenon appears rather late in human culture. The French term *ennui* comes into use, it appears, during the reign of Louis XIV at Versailles (1643–1715), which was a gathering point for many members of the nobility with plenty of money and free time. Reports on those gatherings describe an aristocracy with plenty of time on their hands, few tasks, and being waited on by others. In contrast, the English term "boredom" enters the lexicon around the nineteenth century. Apparently, the English were busy until then.

call "the big vacation" was taken up the by Teachers Union at its meeting in Gedera in 1904. There was agreement about the need for a vacation, but not about its timing. The Galilee settlements of the north were reliant on field crops and needed the children's help with harvesting in the summer. The Jewish settlements in the southern area of Judea, though, preferred that the long vacation be scheduled over Tishrei, in the late summer and early fall. Only in 1920 was agreement reached on one uniform set of dates for Israel's summer vacation. Today, even though most children are not pressed into helping on a family farm and every year there are calls to shorten the two-month vacation, it has withstood all pressure for change, and children impatiently count down the days until it arrives. The same trend is true for students in North America. Most school systems preserve the summer break, despite the fact that the original reasons for the time off no longer apply. Some schools have experimented with year-round school to greater or less effect, but the summer break seems to be here for students for good.[7]

Is Idleness the "Mother of All Sin"?

I carefully watch my dog, Simchah. She can lie on the porch in existential bliss for hours at a time. She does not appear to suffer from boredom. Animals out in the wild are certainly never bored. People who lived in the world before the Industrial Revolution were also not bored, and similarly those who live in poverty today. They all were and are consumed with finding food, protecting themselves, organizing their lives, and raising their children. Boredom is a relatively new phenomenon. It belongs to a world with abundant resources.

Gotta Stop

When I was a child, every boy and girl went to one or maybe two after-school activities a week. Today the situation is quite different, and many children have a weekly schedule replete with after-school groups, activities, and lessons that come one after the other, right after the school day. Children's fast-paced schedule includes homework, extended school programs, and a variety of activities at other venues. As a mother, I noticed a difference in the load placed on my oldest child and that of his nine-years-younger sibling. And if the kids have a heavy load, the grownups are even more burdened. We are crumbling under the weight of professional assignments, parenthood, social obligations, communal responsibilities, and so much more. Our lives supply us with endless stimuli and a never-ending to-do list. To maintain our physical and psychological health, we have to stop.

Here we should mention one of the greatest gifts the Jewish people brought to the world's culture—Shabbat, the day when it is forbidden to work, the day when rest is an actual religious commandment. Anti-Jewish Hellenistic authors during the Second Temple period accused the Jews of laziness, spending one-seventh of their lives in uncreative idleness. However, this wonderful stop, Shabbat, allows our bodies and souls to pause with relief from rush of the weekdays, to be recharged with renewed energy. It prepares our hearts for the new week of work and productivity. Shabbat is idleness in the best sense of the term, as are holidays. However, Shabbat and the Festivals are not devoid of content or activities that bring us blessing, so in addition to them we need periods of complete time-out.

It was once thought that industrialization and mechanization would provide humanity with many more hours of free time, but that did not happen. In many places, the hours of work just keep getting longer. It sometimes seems as though we are running like mice on a wheel, running without stopping for a moment so we can actually reflect on the reasons we are running in the first place. A disturbing thought has slowly started to percolate within me. Are we *really* that busy? Do we *really* not have free time for anything, or are we creating busy, stressful lives for ourselves in order to avoid interrupting the rat race and asking ourselves existential questions? Questions like "Am I happy with my life? Am I satisfied with the person I have become? Is my work meaningful?" There is not time to think—we are just too busy!

Even those who love their work and derive meaning and blessing from it would benefit from stopping for a bit, like a painter stepping back from his work only to return to it fresh and aware. A "time-out" is important not only as rest from one's work, but as an important part of the work itself. When I am writing an article and take a break, I discover after I return to writing that in many instances the article continued to be written in my head even when I wasn't actively thinking about it at all. The version of the article after my break is much better. Distance from work is not simply a standstill; it is a time of processing and ripening.

But, as we have said, not every break is a real rest. There is passive time off and there is active time off. With passive time off, we fill our free time with "noise" of all types—scintillating screens, phone calls, social media—in part to avoid the quiet. This is time off in which there is no work, but neither is there any rest. Active time off is a readiness to create real quiet, to engage in relaxed thought and observation, to have a conversation that's not about accomplishing anything. It is a situation in which we do not manufacture noise. Active time off is not at all easy for people in our time, who sometimes seem unable to come to a stop. I see active time off as a very worthy goal, but one that in many cases I find difficult to reach. With all the distractions around us, we not

The lockdowns of COVID-19 seemed to both intensify and alleviate **some of these problems**. On the one hand, all extracurricular activity suddenly stopped, freeing up time on the calendar and lessening the manic rush so many experience on a daily basis. On the other hand, people were suddenly faced with the responsibility of shifting their entire lives online. Parents whose children's schools were closed or moved entirely online were faced with having to become full-time teachers, and working parents no longer had reliable care. Perhaps this is the reason so many parents—the vast majority of them women—stepped out of the workforce during the years of the pandemic.[10]

The **Shabbat** afternoon *Minchah* service is recited before the end of the day, after we have rested and regained our strength. The words of *K'dushat HaYom* (Sanctity of the Day) blessing in the *Minchah Amidah* returns over and over to the gift of rest:

You are One and Your name is one,
and there is none like Your people Israel, a people unique on earth.
A garland of glory have You given us, a crown of salvation,
a day of rest and holiness.
Abraham and Sarah rejoiced in it,
Isaac and Rebekah sang,
Jacob and Rachel and Leah and their children were refreshed by
  its rest.
A rest of love freely given,
a rest of truth and faithfulness,
a rest of peace and serenity, tranquility and security,
a perfect rest which You so desire.
May Your children come to know that this sacred rest links them
  to You,
and through their rest they sanctify Your name.
Our God and God of our ancestors, be pleased with our rest.
Sanctify us with Your mitzvot, and grant us a share in Your Torah.
Satisfy us with Your goodness and gladden us with Your salvation.
Purify our hearts to serve You in truth.
In Your gracious love, Adonai our God, grant as our heritage Your
  Holy Shabbat,
that Israel who sanctifies Your name may rest on it.
Praise to You, Eternal, who sanctifies Shabbat.[11]

It is interesting to see how rest is perceived in this blessing as a spiritual or religious act, and moreover, an act of *kiddush HaShem*, "sanctifying God's name."

The Land Rests

"When you enter the land that I shall assign to you, the land shall observe a sabbath of the Eternal" (Leviticus 25:2).

It is not only humans who are called to stop and rest, but the land as well. The biblical Sabbatical year (*Sh'mitah*, which means "release") is observed every seventh year. It is a year when we release control of the land and its produce, a year of rest for the soil and for those who till it. It is not always natural to let go, to open our closed hand and release what we have been grasping, and to let go of the need to work, to till, and to control. In recent years, the practice of *Sh'mitah* has expanded to include people who are not agricultural workers. For example, some people make conscious choices to refrain from buying new books or clothes during *Sh'mitah* years or to increase charitable giving so as to enable debt relief.

only find it difficult to be present in just one place; we find it difficult to be present at all.

Just as it is impossible to do strenuous physical training for many hours without taking a break and relaxing, so it is impossible to keep studying or working without a recess. This is a basic, well-known truth. Why, then, is it so hard to internalize that message? When I lived in Europe, I saw that people turn off their phones and their computers on Friday at the end of the workday and don't turn them on again until Monday morning. "Whatever happens, happens," people would say, or "Let the world blow up!"—or whatever expression people use in their own language. Their weekends were devoted to family and friends, rest, reading, taking walks, sitting on the porch lost in thought and counting the passing birds. Complete rest, and let the world be damned.

I have recently come to the conclusion that idleness is a lot like vitamins. Sure, we will continue to live even if we suffer from a vitamin deficiency, but we will not be our best, healthiest selves. Without the right balance of vitamins in our body, we will feel weak and be more vulnerable to illness; so too will we be restless and bothered if we don't get enough healthy rest.[8]

Famed Israel Poet Chayim Nachman Bialik (1873–1934) wrote a poem (which later became a widely known song) called *Shir HaAvodah V'HaM'lachah* (of praise to labor and productivity), whose refrain is:

Whom do we thank? Whom do we bless? Labor and work![9]	לְמִי תּוֹדָה? לְמִי בְּרָכָה? לָעֲבוֹדָה וְלַמְּלָאכָה!

In response, I say:

Whom do we thank? Whom do we bless? Labor—and also rest!	לְמִי תּוֹדָה? לְמִי בְּרָכָה? לָעֲבוֹדָה וְגַם לַמְּנוּחָה!

To Die in Tammuz: Some Thoughts on Alienation and Identity

SHALOM JACOB ABRAMOVICH (1836–1917), known by his *nom de plume*, Mendele Mocher Sforim, opened his novel *Fishke the Lame* with a fascinating description taken from shtetl life during midsummer, or more specifically, the fast of the seventeenth of Tammuz:

> The sun's scarcely begun to shine, and sweet summer's in the land, and folks have got so they are feeling newborn and glad-hearted, for seeing God's good earth looking fair again—well, don't you know but that's just when our somber season sets in, and the time comes for Jews to start mourning and shedding tears in earnest. For it's then the whole roster of sad observances must be got through. . . . And it's then that I, mind you, Reb Mendele the Book Peddler, have my work cut out and come into my own, making the circuit of Jewish towns with my cartload of stock, from which I furnish the kindred with all the rueful necessaries of the rites of weeping. . . . Because, you see, whilst Jews are sorrowing everywhere and grieve the livelong summer away, wearing the season out with weeping, I do business and ply my living. But I've got off point.
>
> I remember once of a midsummer morning, on the Fast of Tammuz, I was out on the road betimes, and seated on my perch in the driver's box, wrapped in my prayershawl and phylacteries, and keeping a light hand on the whip, as well, to kind of prod the jade along now and then, and—well, in a word, looking to all the world quite Jewish, as you may say. So anyway, there I was: deep into my sunrise devotions, with my eyes closed, and making very certain to keep them shut so the cheery light of day shouldn't interfere with Fastday observance, you see. Well, sir, Satan, as we know, is never idle; and that day he had got Nature all tricked out and frilly, and looking devilish handsome and nice, and pretty as a picture she was, too; and she had so beguiled me by now, that I'd got this powerful hankering to have myself a quick look. Oh, only the tiniest, fleetingest glimpse, to be sure. Well, I can tell you, for a while there I had me quite a struggle over it. I mean with myself. Because on one hand, you see, there was my Good Side (that's the one on the side of the Angels, you know), saying: ". . . Oh but really, Mendel, you *mustn't*," and on the other hand, there's my Bad Side (my hankering, that is), which is goading me on with, "Pooh! Get an eyeful, why don'tcha . . . Go on, have a gander—*Enjoy!*" And he kind of prises open one eye then, just a wee bit. So I look. Well, Glory be! if I'm not about dazzled by what I see. For, as though for spit, what greets this one eye of mine is Nature at her primy best: this gala prospect that is so near perfect, it fair flattens me, and clean takes my breath away. Yes sir, it was that lovely! Upland I saw fields and fields, flecked with pinkish-white buckwheat blossoms, looking like snowdrops . . . and downland a piece, there's a grassy glen that's verged on either side with stands of nutwood trees, thickets of pine and walnut; and in the middle, a crystal pool of dancing sunlit water, which is sparkling and winking with spangles of silver and gold. And from where I sit, the cattle and sheep grazing in the pasture below look to be only mere dots, dark bitty points of tawny brown and red, and—"*Oh, for shame, Mendel!*" . . . Now this was when my Good Side starts getting preachy on me again.[12]

The storyteller portrays himself as he struggles between his desire to look at the beauty of nature and his knowledge that because of the fast day, such enjoyment is forbidden. This passage, suffused with self-deprecating humor from one of the pioneers of both

Mendele Mocher Sforim (1836–1917) lived during the period of Chibat Tziyon, the pre-Herzlian movement to promote *aliyah* to the Land of Israel and the first years of political Zionism. He was a prolific writer in both Yiddish and Hebrew during a time when it was rare to focus on both languages. One of his major innovations, aside from writing fiction in Hebrew, was that he wrote vivid descriptions of nature in Modern Hebrew. Mendele also translated books about animals and plants into Hebrew. In addition, he edited an edition of *Perek Shirah*, a midrashic composition that describes how everything in the world, animal or vegetable, praises the Blessed Holy One.

modern Hebrew and Yiddish literature, manages to present three different tensions, three riveting paradoxes that shed light on Eastern European Jews, and perhaps on Jews in general, or maybe even on human nature and culture at large.

The tension between nature and culture: Nature in its glory is revealed to Mendele with all its colors, scents, and marvelous myriad appearances, distracting his attention from the fact that the day is one of mourning for the Jews, who are supposed to be "mourning and shedding tears in earnest." Religious law, which demands that he be sad about the events that led to the destruction of the Temple, clashes with the law of nature, which is revealed in its flourishing vitality, affirming life. Mendele is critical here of Judaism and its disconnection from life's vivacity.

The tension between natural, spontaneous feeling and institutionalized religiosity: The days of summer are days of tears and mourning for the Jews, as Mendele points out. During the time of "between the straits," from the seventeenth of Tammuz to the ninth of Av, the destruction of the Temple is recalled, joined by the memory of the troubles and sorrows that the people Israel experienced and the personal anguish of each and every individual Jew. On the other hand, for the bookseller's business, these were good times, since Jews needed books of lamentation, *piyutim* (*kinot*), vernacular prayers (*t'chines* in Yiddish), and other sorts of religious necessities that he supplied. Mendele seems to be critiquing the religious functionaries, who sometimes appear to be working against the original feelings behind the practices he depicts.

The tension between the climates of the Middle East and Europe: Israeli readers will no doubt raise an eyebrow at Mendele's descriptions of the flora of the month of Tammuz: the fields in full blossom, grasses, pools of pure water... Maybe it's that way in Europe, but in Israel, nature closes in on itself, wilts and withers, hopes for the rain that will end the heat of July and August. And perhaps we Israeli Jews, who are privileged to live in the land our ancestors yearned for and dreamed of, can take Mendele's words and learn from them that our basic existential experiences—both as individuals and as people who live in the Jewish nation—establish our consciousness.

These three tensions discernible in Mendele's vivid depiction are at the foundation of questions of religious behavior and religious feeling in general: every culture puts its stamp on nature and every culture relates to nature, sometimes from a desire to conquer and rule it and sometimes from a desire to merge and melt into it. The tension between religious feeling and institutionalized religion is the tension between an individual's emotional, passionate prayer—like Hannah's at Shiloh (I Samuel 1)—and the requirement to perform some normative halachic behavior, such as the ritualized worship by the priests in the Temple. This tension exists in every culture and is very much present in Jewish culture. Another tension is intercultural: those three weeks of "between the straits" mark Israel's mourning for its lost Temple, but underlying them may have been earlier calendar events that were observed in the ancient Near East and are now largely forgotten.

The summer solstice—when daylight hours are longest and night is shortest—

From Time to Time → Dalia Marx

falls during Tammuz. From solstice on, summer's strength wanes, days get shorter, and nights get longer. In the cultures of the ancient world, they marked the solstices (in December and June) and the equinoxes (in March and September) as holidays or, alternatively, as days of mourning. The ancients dedicated particular attention to changes in nature and regarded them as significant. (See pp. 76–78.)

The summer solstice stands out less in the Jewish calendar, but it is easy to see how the mourning over the seasonal "death" of nature and fertility was translated into mourning over culture, meaning the destruction of the Temple. It is natural that the "blues" our ancestors experienced at the annual "death" of nature in the summer somehow connected with the national and religious mourning over the destruction of the Temple. Perhaps akin to the hope and faith that nature would be renewed and rise again from its destruction, our predecessors believed that the Jewish people would also rise to renewed life after its destruction. It is also possible to see that this seasonal mourning might appear pagan and so took on a form that emphasizes the unity and singularity of God.

Perhaps these paradoxes do not represent actual contradictions or polar opposites, but are instead part of one complex system, a variegated range of cultural and emotional traits and expressions within which we function.

☀ Crying Over You, Tammuz

DID ONLY THE NAMES of the months come from Babylonia and make themselves at home in Jewish culture, or did something of their content also "make *aliyah*" along with the names? This question is most poignant with regard to Tammuz, a month named for the Babylonian pantheon's god of vegetation and animals. The worship of Tammuz gets an oblique reference in one of the prophecies of Ezekiel, who describes how God brought him to the northern gateway of the Temple "and there sat the women bewailing Tammuz" (Ezekiel 8:14). It is not clear whether Ezekiel is describing a scene that in fact took place at the northern entrance to the Temple in Jerusalem or whether he is projecting scenes he witnessed from where he lived in Babylon. Either way, the pagan reference is clear.

Tammuz and His Wife: An Unconventional Couple

Tammuz (in Sumerian, Dummuzi)—the god of vegetation, fertility, and food—played an important role in Babylonian worship, alongside his wife, the goddess Inanna (later, Ishtar), the queen of the heavens. Inanna was a marvelous, powerful character and the most important goddess among all the goddesses of Sumer (a culture that sprung up about five thousand years ago in what is today Iraq). This is her story, in brief:

> The great goddess Inanna came down from her royal throne in the heavens and headed for the underworld. (The object of her journey was apparently seizing control there from her sister, Ereshkigal.) She did so dressed in glory and jewels, on her chest a pendant on which was the following bold inscription: "Come, man, come!"
>
> Inanna was not received well in the underworld. She had to cross its seven gateways, at each of which the guard of the underworld stripped her of one of the trappings of royalty, glory, and authority. Inanna's protests were ineffectual, her authority being useless in the kingdom into which she had trespassed. As she stood before her suffering sister, Ereshkigal, the judges of the underworld killed her, and she became "a corpse, a hunk of rotten flesh, and the corpse was hung up on a hook."
>
> When Inanna's faithful maidservant, Ninshubur, saw that her mistress had not returned from the underworld, she tried to enlist the aid of the gods, but only Enki, the god of wisdom and sweet water, agreed to come to her assistance. He took grime that had accumulated under his fingernails and made two little creatures, whom he endowed with lifesaving powers. The two creatures succeeded in making their way into the underworld and ingratiating themselves with Ereshkigal, Inanna's sister, by identifying with her and showing empathy for her pains. Ereshkigal offered to reward them for their assistance, and they asked—as Ninshubur had instructed them—to revive Inanna. And so it was, but the joy was incomplete. In place of the goddess who came back to life, the judges of the underworld demanded another living creature. Inanna agreed to hand over to them her husband, Dumuzzi (Tammuz), the god of fertility. This was an act of revenge for his failure to come to her aid when she had been in trouble.

Sidebar:

The Hebrew poet Shaul Tchernichowsky (1875–1943) expressed this feeling in his poem "The Death of Tammuz," the last stanza of which reads as follows:

Go forth, O ye daughters of Zion, lamenting
This grief-stricken world whence magic is fled!
This grief-stricken world whose soul is eclipsed—
For Tammuz, the radiant Tammuz, is dead![13]

Tchernichowsky interprets the sorrow at the death of Tammuz as sadness over "a world whence magic is fled," or, to render the Hebrew more literally, "a world immersed in an absence of miracles." But like the mythical phoenix that burns to ash but rises to life again and again, one can assume that the world without miracles will arise from its ruins and be reborn.

> Dumuzzi's sister, Geshtinanna, could not be consoled over the death of her younger brother and offered herself in his place. Inanna, Dumuzzi's wife, agreed to let Geshtinanna share the underworld with her husband, so that Dumuzzi would spend six months a year there—the dry season—and his sister would take his place in the land of the dead for the other six months. When she would arrive, Dumuzzi would go free.[14]

This myth is a story of renewal and death, of despair and hope in eternal life and in human life. It is connected to the cycle of nature and agriculture and deeply rooted in the Middle East, where the summer is a parched season of drought. The story also teaches us, though, about the forces within human beings, with their cycles of ascents and descents.

Let us focus on just one aspect of this complex story—the relationship between Tammuz/Dummuzi and Inanna. In this context, Inanna is the strong, active one who takes initiative, while Dumuzzi is dependent on her; perhaps he is even happy to be liberated from his dominant wife when she is trapped in the underworld. The deal that allows Geshtinanna to take the place of her brother, Dumuzzi, in the underworld allows Dumuzzi to be present in the world for only six months a year. Nature is alive, then, only half of the year, as are the marital relations between Dumuzzi and Inanna. This may soften the gap between life and death and touch on the existential angst of the people who lived in Mesopotamia, who were dependent on nature's fertility cycles for their sustenance.

A Girl Who Died and Was Born Again

The story of Inanna is a painful story of descent into the netherworld, death, and return. In the end, it is an optimistic tale of a tragic fall, which is sometimes necessary in order to rise higher. Similar stories of seasonal death and a return to life are known throughout world cultures. Literature scholar Yael Renan adds to our understanding of the story of Inanna and Dummuzi, reading it in the context of partnership: "Dummuzi and Inanna are satisfied with one another half the time, and that in itself is not a bad achievement. What this means is that for the rest of the time they have to live with feelings of loneliness, rejection, disappointment, insult, or anger. They draw out the best and worst of what is hidden within them."[15] Thus the story transforms from being a creation myth to being a story that describes a couple's relationship.

A similar myth can be found in the Greek story of Persephone, daughter of Demeter, goddess of the soil. Persephone, an innocent, naïve girl who picked flowers in the meadow, was kidnapped by Hades, the god of the underworld, to be his wife. In protest and grief, her mother Demeter suspended the produce of the soil. Demeter's mourning destroyed the land and brought about severe famine—the land yielded no crops, and the cows gave no milk. In the end, the gods succumbed to Demeter's siege and set Persephone free. However, before she emerged from the underworld, the girl swallowed some pomegranate seeds. Those seeds determined her fate, and from that point forward she was allowed to spend the spring and the summer with her mother on the land, while each autumn she was gathered into the soil to stay with Hades until the end of the winter, in an eternal cycle. In this way the Greeks provided themselves with an explanation of winter's "death of nature" and its rebirth in the spring.

Tishrei Marcheshvan Kislev Tevet Sh'vat Adar Nisan Iyar Sivan Tammuz Av Elul

It is interesting to note that in the Babylonian myth, summer is the time of nature's death. For those who live in a hot, dry climate like Israel, the summer represents a stop to vitality. In Greek mythology, by way of contrast, it is the winter that represents death, while the spring and summer represent life. Indeed, geography is the determinant of consciousness.

Simona Matsliah-Chanoch, who wrote about myths of death and rebirth, summarizes the tale of Persephone with these words: "There once was a little girl. She died, and she was reborn." These stories explain not only the change of seasons and the secrets of nature, says Matsliah-Chanoch, but also address deep psychological processes.[16] In the symbolic deaths of these stories, she sees an expression of attempts to deal with periods of depression, which is akin to death, and interprets them as forces of healing. A downfall is not the end of the story; instead, it is something like a pregnancy from which one may be reborn. Matsliah-Chanoch reads ostensibly simple children's tales, such as "Snow White" and "Little Red Riding Hood," in similar fashion, shaking off their luster and revealing that they too contain a similar process: these myths and tales are deep parts of our collective subconscious, encouraging us to derive strength, comfort, and primarily hope from them.

And so the story of Inanna and Tammuz/Dummuzi is, in the end, a story of hope. Even if its pagan context is foreign to us, it still has the power to shed light on deep processes in the natural world and on the nature of human beings.

# Long Live the Protest!

In the summer of 2011, a social protest movement dubbed "the cottage cheese protest"—in part because of the skyrocketing price of this food staple—swept through Israel. Tents lined Rothschild Avenue in Tel Aviv and filled Jerusalem's parks, and the Israeli public was swept up in feelings of altruism and sharing. Both before and after these protests, the world has seen social protest movements sweep through our countries and towns. North America had a protest similar to the cottage cheese protest in the fall of 2011 with Occupy Wall Street, and the Arab Spring protests against authoritarianism started in 2010. More recently, protests for racial justice have swept the globe, as have protests urging global leaders to more forcefully address climate change. **In 2023**, Israel's streets were once again filled with hundreds of thousands of protesters as they fought to protect Israel's judicial system from government reforms.

It is difficult to measure the impact of these protests. Were they one-time events, or did they address something basic in our societies and somehow change them? This question remains unanswered, but it does raise other questions: What is a protest? What is the connection between Jews and protests, and why are Jews some of the most famous protestors in the world?

The First Protest

In a way, the creation of the world was a protest—a protest against primeval chaos. It established order and meaning in the midst of that chaos and differentiated realms in order for life and meaning to be possible in a complex reality. If Creation was an act of revolution, then the first revolutionary is none other than the Blessed Holy One, who bequeathed to us—those created in the divine image—the gnawing sense of dissatisfaction that propels us to take action, change and fix things, and so take part in Creation.

At the foundation of the Jewish ethos stands the belief that the world was not only created but continues to be created anew each day, that **Creation is ongoing** and without end. The world is renewed each and every day, and we who live in it have an active role: we are not observers but participants in Creation. This understanding encourages us to regard the world as eternally fresh and dynamic and young. It also teaches us that the world is not perfect, that it suffers from flaws and damage, and

In many ways, the scope of the protests of 2011 pale in comparison to the protests of **2023**. Israel's prime minister, Benjamin Netanyahu, formed a right-wing coalition, and one of its main goals was labeled "judicial reform." The government coalition asserted that Israel's High Court of Justice had overstepped and become an "activist court," with many in the coalition referring to it as "judicial dictatorship." Their proposed initiatives included empowering the Knesset (Israel's parliament) majority to have the ability to overturn court decisions and determine the court's nominees. Undoubtedly, any discussion on these "reforms" cannot be separated from the enduring and existential debate over Israel's identity as a Jewish and democratic state. Protestors asserted that these changes would undermine Israel's democracy by eroding checks-and-balances and placing too much power in the governing coalition while neutralizing the judiciary. They also argued that Netanyahu would personally benefit from the judicial overhaul, since he was facing a corruption trial. People felt so strongly about ensuring Israel's democracy that they took to the streets on a daily basis, and sometimes these protests numbered in the hundreds of thousands. Israel's president, Isaac Herzog, warned that the judicial changes could lead to civil war.

The extent of the protests expanded to an unprecedented level in the months after the coalition announced their plan, as evidenced by not only the number of participants in the protest, but also their diversity and significance. Regular Israelis were joined by university leaders, law professors, thousands of lawyers, all the largest law firms in the country, the heads of high-tech industry, hundreds of senior economists, thousands of academics, military reservists, retired military officials, leaders in combat units, and experts in security. Additional pressure also came from international leaders, including US president Joe Biden and secretary of state Antony Blinken, members of the United States Congress, European heads of state, and leading world economists. As of the writing of this chapter, the final future outcome of these judicial changes is still unknown. What we do know is that this period has had a significant impact on the hearts of so many Israelis and Jews around the world; on Shabbat, when we recite the prayer for the State of Israel, eyes fill with tears as we remember that this is our country—and that we passionately want it remain so.

> During the morning Shacharit service, the idea of **Creation continuing** each day is mentioned in the Yotzeir Or blessing, in which we say, "In Your goodness You daily renew Creation." The world is renewed each day, and we, created beings, are called upon to take part as actual junior partners in Creation. (See pp. 317–20.)

that many things need improvement. Our task here on earth is to be partners in the work of Creation. Life in this world, then, is a life of recognizing the brokenness of existence and at the same time a life of commitment to repair and improvement. In the *Aleinu* prayer that closes each service during the day, we proclaim that we are expected "to repair the world by divine sovereignty."

If God was the first protestor, then Abraham was the first human protestor. According to the postbiblical Book of Jubilees, Abraham recognized the greatness of the one God who created the world on the eve of Rosh HaShanah, and he prayed to that God. God's answer was the awesome command "Go forth from your land, your birthplace, and your father's house, to the land that I will show you" (Genesis 12:1). A well-known midrash recounts that Abraham smashed the idols of his father's shop (*B'reishit Rabbah* 38:13)—a protest against his father and his culture. Even the plain text of the Torah indicates Abraham's unwillingness to accept things as they are, when he bargains with God over saving the righteous residents of the city of Sodom, with what seems to be a healthy amount of chutzpah.

Abraham, our ancient ancestor, was known as "the Hebrew" (*HaIvri*; Genesis 14:13), a name that stems from his origin "across [*mei-eiver*] the river" (referring to the Euphrates, in Mesopotamia; Joshua 24:3). However, Rabbi Y'hudah reinterpreted the term *ivri* midrashically: "The whole entire world was on one side [*mei-eiver echad*], and he was on the other side [*mei-eiver echad*]" (*B'reishit Rabbah* 42:8). Abraham "crossed over" by situating himself as an opponent of his present reality and its uncaring, nonchalant flowing along. He made an important transition ("crossing over") in his life. Opposition to the norm and independent thought define Abraham and us, his descendants, as well.

Don't Ever Be Satisfied!

To be a Jew means, in a certain sense, to be dissatisfied. To be a Jew means never to be entirely happy with things, but rather to look at reality with some discomfort and a desire to change it. Unlike other cultures, Judaism doesn't seek nirvana and tranquility. In fact, it calls on us to oppose our current reality in all its aspects, sometimes even offering forcible resistance. This may not be the most comfortable idea, but it is based on the profound understanding that our lives have meaning and our actions have a purpose. This is an approach that mobilizes and arouses us, as in the popular Israeli song by Ehud Banai, who summons us to believe that "if you have messed up, you can set things right" (it has a better ring to it in the Hebrew: *Im kilkalta, atah yachol am l'takein*).[17]

In light of all this, perhaps it is no wonder that there are so many Jewish activists and leaders in movements for all kinds of social change: minority rights, women's status, protecting the environment and nature, and so on. In human and Jewish history, there have been people who created new spiritual paradigms, who founded a state, who established monumental and impressive projects both spiritual and material. Yet even small, simple acts have great importance. One should not disdain the everyday and seemingly mundane acts. The Talmud tells us that "people should always regard themselves as though they were half guilty and half meritorious: if they perform one precept, happy are they for tilting the balance toward the side of merit; if they commit one transgression, woe to them for tilting the balance toward the side of guilt" (Babylonian Talmud, *Kiddushin* 40a–b). Our Rabbis are teaching us here the importance of action in everyday life. Each act we take is significant, and a single mitzvah can shift the balance. Responsibility is placed not only on rulers and heads of state, but on each and every person, and each one of us can "tip the scales" of the very delicate system that is our world.

Berl Katznelson (1887–1944), a Zionist leader and thinker, expressed a profound religiosity in his thought and leadership. Commenting on this Talmudic statement, he said:

> [We have inherited] the ancient Jewish view that the entire world is continually weighed on a scale, and each of us and each of our deeds can tip the scale, and every moment is that critical moment.[18]

On his ninetieth birthday, the late Shimon Peres (1923–2016), former president and prime minister and one of the greatest leaders of the State of Israel, said:

> I am proud to be a member of a dissatisfied nation. Dissatisfaction drives a commitment to progress. I look at where we started and where we are today. And I think to myself: to be an optimist is so logical.[19]

Katznelson, who played such an important part in dramatic moments in the life of the people in its old-new homeland, emphasizes the importance of each and every act and the fact that every moment is critical. It is not only great moments and grand eras such as the one that led to the establishment of the State of Israel—a period in which Katznelson was an active participant—that matter, but regular everyday moments as well, in which people dutifully perform their everyday tasks loyally, out of a sense of duty. Berl adds, "If you think you have fulfilled your obligation, know that the obligation has no defined measure and is never fulfilled." That is, rather than resting on one's laurels, one should strive higher and always move forward and never think that the tasks of our lives can ever be fully completed.

"Yours is not to complete the work" is the calming observation of Rabbi Tarfon, a first-century sage, but in the same breath he adds, "but neither are you free to desist from it" (*Pirkei Avot* 2:21). This lesson is important for understanding the tension between having a commitment that is eternal and total, and the simultaneous awareness that our ability is limited, since there are still only twenty-four hours in a day. We will never manage to do everything. Our obligation to do *tikkun* (repair) is an important principle, and it means that we have an assignment in this world. We are not passersby who are born, live, and die. Our actions in this world have significance. We are not leaves driven by the wind, passing from this world as though we had never been in it. We have the power to change and mend our world. And if we can do such *tikkun*, then it is our obligation to work for that to happen.

Since the establishment of the State of Israel, we must ask if the Jews, as a moral force acting for *tikkun olam*, continue to be such a people now that we are no longer the weak and oppressed "other." It is not easy to be empathetic and attentive to the world's problems when we ourselves are weak and weakened, but it is actually more difficult to do so when we are strong and sated. Of course, Israel's strength is tempered by the reality that it is surrounded by countries who are enemies, many of whom have leaders who would love to see Israel no longer exist. This is the challenge that we face:

to continue to fight for social justice and *tikkun olam* even when we hold strength and power, and not only when we feel vulnerable.

The Jewish tradition calls on us to enjoy life and to see the beauty in it. It instructs us to live a life of connection and intimacy, to love, to live in a good community, to derive enjoyment from what is beautiful and good in the world. Tendencies toward asceticism and refraining from the joys of life earn contempt in Jewish literature. It is precisely our focus on this world, with all its anguish and beauty, that directs us to work for its continued existence through correcting the evil and injustice that exist in it. The Jewish tradition calls us to struggle for life and its meaning, rather than run away from it.

The cottage cheese protest of the summer 2011 melted into autumn, and after that came winter, but it seems that among the Israeli public the fruits of that summer continue to be felt in Israeli discourse. The same is true for the ongoing impact of racial justice, climate change, and other protests that continue to take place throughout the world; these global movements continue to bear fruit of justice and repair. May these fruits ripen into a new society, one that is more just, aware, and directed toward *tikkun* of the world.

Prayer of the Month

Prayer for the Welfare of Schoolchildren on Vacation

WHAT SHALL WE WISH FOR children starting their summer vacation? What should be desire for them as they put down their notebooks and go out for the adventures that the vacation holds for them? Here is a special new prayer written for those schoolchildren. It was composed for the unaffiliated Tel Aviv congregation Beit Tefilah Israeli, one of the most original prayer communities that have sprung up around Israel in recent years. This is an example of the commitment to renew and reinvigorate Judaism. In Israel, *hitchadshut Y'hudit* ("renewing Judaism" or "Jewish renewal") is marked by a commitment to tradition blended with a desire for innovation and inclusion. The metaphor I like to use is that *hitchadshut Y'hudit* pours old wine into new vessels and at the same time pours new nectar into old vessels.

One of the tasks that the people who are involved with this kind of renewal have taken upon themselves is to create new prayers that speak to the lives of Israeli Jews, and as part of that effort they composed a prayer for schoolchildren, their parents, and their teachers as they start their summer break. The prayer is recited with pomp and celebration at the Shabbat service before the long summer vacation. All the children about to start the vacation from school are called to the front of the bimah, a large tallit is spread over their heads, and the entire congregation recites the prayer.

> ***Mi Shebeirach* Prayer for Schoolchildren Starting Summer Vacation**
> May the One who blessed our ancestors Abraham, Isaac, and Jacob, Sarah, Rebekah, Rachel, and Leah, bless all the children in Israel beginning their annual school vacation and all their teachers and parents who are completing the school year with them.
> May it be Your will that You lead them in peace and well-being, guard their well-being, and bring them to the coming school year rested and with renewed vigor.
> May the One who is good and beneficent to all creatures grant them discernment and knowledge to continue to grow, to be inquisitive, to learn, and to explore the world at their own pace, continuing to discover the world's beauty through eyes filled with wonder and hearts filled kindness.
> May God bless you and keep you.
> May God's light shine upon you, and may God be gracious to you.
> May you feel God's presence within you always, and may you find peace.[20]

The sentiments in this prayer are very appropriate for the end of a period of study. May we all be blessed with never-ending learning and teaching, deepening our understanding and drawing wisdom from our always nourishing sources.

AV

Zodiac Sign: Leo | Tribe of the Month: Issachar
Breastplate Stone: Sapphire/*Sapir*

The name Av came from Babylon with those who returned to Zion from exile. It apparently comes from Akkadian, where the word *abbu* means "stalks" or "reeds," because this was a month of harvest. A second explanation for the name is "fire," which would be a reference to the high heat of this summer month. Another possible meaning, and a surprising one, is that the word *abbu* in Akkadian means "hill." The Babylonians believed that a particular hill was the entranceway to the world of the dead, and during this month the Babylonian holiday of the dead was observed.

In the Middle Ages, the month receive a prefix: M'nachem, meaning someone who consoles or comforts a person in distress or mourning. Adding that word emphasizes the people Israel's hope for consolation, and it expresses faith that the Messiah will be born on the ninth of Av.

In the Bible, the month is known by its place in the count of months: "the fifth month," counting from Nisan.

Kavanah: A Meditation for Av

> For just a moment I will stop to consider
> the mountains of memories
> the false hopes
> the insults seared deep
> the moments of lost holiness.
> This time I won't rush
> I will stop—even if just for a moment—
> I will stop at the narrow place
> until another feeling sprouts.
> And it will sprout within me, without delay
> and I will know that anything is possible.
> I will know that anything is possible.

At the Gates of Av

THE MONTH OF AV invites us to take a dive into deep water, until we reach the bottom out of breath; only then can we push off the bottom with our feet and start to rise above the waves. Returning to the surface can only happen if we've made it to the depths, to that frightening place without breath. That is how it is with the Jewish tradition: the profound mourning of Tishah B'Av becomes meaningful precisely because of the consolation that follows. Our lives are lights and shadows, low tides and high tides, since in the lives of an individual, a people, and the world there are dark and difficult times. In the end, though, Jewish tradition teaches us that life is good and the world is a place full of hope, since "the world is judged with goodness" (*Pirkei Avot* 3:19).

Tishah B'Av gives the month its gloomy character and is the focal point of a structured period of time spread over ten weeks: the three weeks of "between the straits," from the seventeenth of Tammuz through Tishah B'Av, followed by seven weeks of consolation, from the end of Tishah B'Av through Rosh HaShanah. The three weeks before Tishah B'Av are built of concentric circles of mourning that seem to close in, growing in intensity. They begin on the day the walls of Jerusalem were breached, the seventeenth of Tammuz. The mourning customs intensify starting at Rosh Chodesh Av, from which time, the Mishnah teaches, one reduces joy and celebration (*Mishnah Taanit* 4:6). The gloomy atmosphere sharpens on Shabbat Chazon, the Shabbat before Tishah B'Av, and reaches its crescendo on the day the First and Second Temples were destroyed. From that point on—actually, from the *Minchah* prayer on the afternoon of Tishah B'Av—winds of consolation begin to blow. If you visit the Kotel, the Western Wall of the Temple Mount in Jerusalem's Old City, at the end of Tishah B'Av, you will find books of *kinot* (poems of lamentation) abandoned by worshipers who were there earlier. This custom expresses the hope that by next year's Tishah B'Av, redemption will have arrived and there will be no more use for those *kinot* books. A week after

Tishrei   Marcheshvan   Kislev   Tevet   Sh'vat   Adar   Nisan   Iyar   Sivan   Tammuz   Av   Elul

The lion, king of beasts and the zodiac sign for the month of Av, is also the symbol of the tribe of Judah, since Jacob blessed his son, "Judah is a lion's cub" (Genesis 49:9). In Jewish tradition, the image of the lion only expands from there. It becomes the symbol of Jerusalem, Judah's capital city. Later, the people as a whole are likened to a lion: "Lo, a people that rises like a lioness, leaps up like a lion" (Numbers 23:24). Rabbi Yosef Karo calls on us to be lions when he offers this guidance at the beginning of the *Shulchan Aruch*: "One should take on strength like a lion to arise in the morning in the service of the Creator."[1]

Even God is sometimes compared to a lion—in particular, a suffering lion: "At each watch [of the night] the Blessed Holy One sits and roars like a lion and says, 'Woe to the children, on account of whose sins I destroyed My house and burnt My temple and exiled them among the nations of the world'" (Babylonian Talmud, *B'rachot* 3a). Like the lion, the month of Av is regal and noble and at the same time sad and pensive.

Tishah B'Av is Tu B'Av, the Jewish day of love, which continues to garner a renewed presence in the Jewish world.

Here is what the month of Av brings in this book. In the first *iyun* we will explore the power of memory in Jewish tradition, and I will also ask about the relevance of Tishah B'Av today. The second *iyun* focuses on the saddest psalm—Psalm 137, which begins "By the waters of Babylon"—and asks how it came to be recited at dining tables along with its happy "sibling," Psalm 126, which we recite on Shabbat and holidays. The third *iyun* examines the presence and significance of the Temple even two thousand years after its destruction. The fourth *iyun* is rather fraught: Messiah and messianism in Jewish culture, in which I will offer my own understanding of the belief in the coming of the Messiah. The fifth *iyun* traces the history of the Jewish love festival, Tu B'Av (the Fifteenth of Av), which is similar to Valentine's Day in that it is a celebration of love, but its origins, nature, and expression are very different. The Poem of the Month is a *piyut* by Rabbi Abraham ibn Ezra, *Eish Tukad B'kirbi* ("A Fire Is Kindled within Me"), customarily sung on Tishah B'Av. The Prayer of the Month, in honor of Tu B'Av, is the *Sh'ma*, which is all about the promise of love and a command to love.

Poem of the Month

Eish Tukad B'kirbi ("A Fire Is Kindled within Me")

The comparison between then and now, between an unfortunate present and a longed-for idealized past (whether it was really good or whether we just remember it that way), underlies our concept of mourning Jerusalem's destruction. In *Eish Tukad B'kirbi* ("A Fire Is Kindled within Me"), this is reflected in the painful contrast between the present feeling of being distant from God, of God's face being hidden, and the Israelites' youthful days and sense of closeness that once prevailed between Israel and its heavenly parent. Stanza after stanza, in alphabetical order, the poet compares the Exodus from Egypt and its rescue and redemption with "the Exodus from Jerusalem" and its destruction and exile.

The poem is attributed to Rabbi Abraham ibn Ezra and is sung in both the Ashkenazic and Sephardic traditions on Tishah B'Av. It is written in a way that allows us to experience the destruction as a very personal event. The poem's title is borrowed from a biblical verse, "A perpetual fire shall be kept burning on the altar, not to go out" (Leviticus 6:6). The poet invites us to sense in a concrete, palpable way the fire within us, burning even as Jerusalem and the Temple are destroyed. Here are some stanzas from the beginning and end of the poem (according to the Sephardic and Ashkenazic versions).

A Fire Is Kindled within Me
Abraham ibn Ezra

A fire (of joy) is kindled within me as I think (of the time)
    When I departed from Egypt.
But I will raise (my own) lamentations as I recall (the time)
    When I departed from Jerusalem.

Then Moses sang, a song unforgettable,
    When I departed from Egypt.
But Jeremiah mourned and wailed with bitter lamentation,
    When I departed from Jerusalem.

My House was established and the cloud abode (thereon),
    When I departed from Egypt.
But the wrath of God lay upon me like a (dark) cloud,
    When I departed from Jerusalem.

The waves of the sea roared and piled themselves like walls,
    When I departed from Egypt.
But proud (waters) overwhelmed and flowed over my head,
    When I departed from Jerusalem.

Food (fell) from heaven and the rock gushed forth water,
    When I departed from Egypt.
But there was wormwood, gall, and water of bitterness,
    When I departed from Jerusalem.

Round about Mount Horeb (I exulted) morning and evening,
    When I departed from Egypt.
But (I) was summoned to mourning at the rivers of Babylon,
    When I departed from Jerusalem.

. . . .

The singing cry of victory and the fanfare of trumpets (I heard),
    When I departed from Egypt.
But wailing of infants and groans of the wounded,
    When I departed from Jerusalem.

The Table, the Candlestick, and Whole burnt-offerings and incense (were established),
    When I departed from Egypt.
But idols, abominations, graven images and (heathen) pillars,
    When I departed from Jerusalem.

[*The Sephardic and Middle Eastern tradition continues:*]
The Torah, the Testimony, and the Order of (Temple) service
(were taught to me),
    When I departed from Egypt.
But an absence of students [of Torah] and the suspension of the daily sacrifice [occurred],
    When I departed from Jerusalem.

Divine, God of the [heavenly] hosts, showed us wonders,
    When I departed from Egypt.
And [God] will return the Divine Presence and [sacrificial] worship,
    To the midst of Jerusalem.

[*The Ashkenazic tradition continues:*]
The Torah, the Testimony, and the precious [Temple's] Implements [were brought along],
    When I departed from Egypt.
May (I obtain) gladness and joy, and let sorrow and sighing flee away,
    When I return to Jerusalem.[2]

אֵשׁ תּוּקַד בְּקִרְבִּי
אַבְרָהָם אִבְּן עֶזְרָא

אֵשׁ תּוּקַד בְּקִרְבִּי בְּהַעֲלוֹתִי עַל לְבָבִי,
בְּצֵאתִי מִמִּצְרָיִם.
וְקִינוֹת אָעִירָה לְמַעַן אַזְכִּירָה,
צֵאתִי מִירוּשָׁלָיִם.

אָז יָשִׁיר מֹשֶׁה שִׁיר לֹא יִנָּשֶׁה,
בְּצֵאתִי מִמִּצְרָיִם.
וַיְקוֹנֵן יִרְמְיָה וְנָהָה נְהִי נִהְיָה,
בְּצֵאתִי מִירוּשָׁלָיִם.

בֵּיתִי הִתְכּוֹנָן וְשָׁכַן הֶעָנָן,
בְּצֵאתִי מִמִּצְרָיִם.
וַחֲמַת אֵל שָׁכְנָה עָלַי כַּעֲנָנָה,
בְּצֵאתִי מִירוּשָׁלָיִם.

גַּלֵּי יָם הָמוּ וְכַחוֹמָה קָמוּ,
בְּצֵאתִי מִמִּצְרָיִם.
זֵדוֹנִים שְׁטָפוּ וְעַל רֹאשִׁי צָפוּ,
בְּצֵאתִי מִירוּשָׁלָיִם.

דָּגָן מִשָּׁמַיִם וְצוּר יָזוּב מַיִם,
בְּצֵאתִי מִמִּצְרָיִם.
לַעֲנָה וְתַמְרוּרִים וּמַיִם הַמָּרִים,
בְּצֵאתִי מִירוּשָׁלָיִם.

הַשְׁכֵּם וְהַעֲרֵב סְבִיבוֹת הַר חוֹרֵב,
בְּצֵאתִי מִמִּצְרָיִם.
קָרוֹא אֵלַי אֵבֶל עַל נַהֲרוֹת בָּבֶל,
בְּצֵאתִי מִירוּשָׁלָיִם.
. . . .

רִנָּה וִישׁוּעָה וַחֲצוֹצְרוֹת תְּרוּעָה,
בְּצֵאתִי מִמִּצְרָיִם.
וְזַעֲקַת עוֹלָל עִם נַאֲקַת חָלָל,
בְּצֵאתִי מִירוּשָׁלָיִם.

שֻׁלְחָן וּמְנוֹרָה וְכָלִיל וּקְטוֹרָה,
בְּצֵאתִי מִמִּצְרָיִם.
וֶאֱלִיל וְתוֹעֵבָה וּפֶסֶל וּמַצֵּבָה,
בְּצֵאתִי מִירוּשָׁלָיִם.

[נוסח ספרד ועדות המזרח:]
תּוֹרָה וּתְעוּדָה וְסֵדֶר הָעֲבוֹדָה,
בְּצֵאתִי מִמִּצְרָיִם.
וְחֶסְרוֹן הַתַּלְמִיד וּבִטּוּל הַתָּמִיד,
בְּצֵאתִי מִירוּשָׁלָיִם.

אֵל אֱלֹהֵי הַצְּבָאוֹת יַרְאֵנוּ נִפְלָאוֹת,
בְּצֵאתִי מִמִּצְרָיִם.
וְיָשִׁיב שְׁכִינָתוֹ אֶל צִיּוֹן וַעֲבוֹדָתוֹ,
לְתוֹךְ יְרוּשָׁלָיִם.

[נוסח אשכנז:]
תּוֹרָה וּתְעוּדָה וּכְלֵי הַחֶמְדָּה,
בְּצֵאתִי מִמִּצְרָיִם.
קוֹל שָׂשׂוֹן וְשִׂמְחָה וְנָס יָגוֹן וַאֲנָחָה,
בְּשׁוּבִי לִירוּשָׁלָיִם.

    This descriptive *piyut* presents two poles, starkly worded: one attracts consolation, the other mourning. Its regular, repetitive structure invites us to think in two great paradigms: the redemption from Egypt is the prototype of all redemption, and the destruction of the Temple represents all destructions and disasters.

    One could, of course, learn from *Eish Tukad B'kirbi* that our lives as Jews (and perhaps simply as human beings) are lives of "either/or," either redemption or exile, either black or white, two sides of one coin. I suggest, however, that we read it in exactly the opposite way, viewing the *piyut*'s extremes as indicative of the broad spectrum between rescue and destruction, which then leads us to recognize that life is always drawn in shades of gray. Some may think that this "gray" encourages a gray of indifference and passivity, but in my view it actually demands action. It requires us to recognize that

I found it interesting—and a little sad—to come across a modern *piyut* built on the model of the medieval *Eish Tukad B'kirbi*. This one was written around the time of the establishment of the State of Israel by Rabbi Shalom Raddai (1912–84), who had come to Israel from Yemen, and it reverses the original poem. Here are some lines from Raddai's poem, which also begins with the phrase "A fire is kindled within me as I think of the time when I. . .":

A fire is kindled within me when as I think of the time	when I was in Yemen;
My soul murmurs, so horrified,	when I came to Zion.
Jews so precious, renowned, and praiseworthy	when I was in Yemen;
The Shulamite sets no boundaries on dross	when I came to Zion.
To awesome God praise [was offered] daily	when I was in Yemen;
Diligent in their labor, but God they do not worship	when I came to Zion.
Every day and night were Torah times	when I was in Yemen;
Just the "Torah" of the body prevails above all	when I came to Zion.
Schools for teachers taught the faith of Moses	when I was in Yemen;
The children rejoiced at there being no lessons	when I came to Zion.
The count is infinite: how much I lack	[of] what was in Yemen.
May the One who lives and perseveres restore us, and guide us justly	as in times of old in Zion.³

everything we do can bring goodness closer and reminds us that there is always a danger that we will fall to the side of destruction. It seems that the *piyut* is actually warning us about extremes, about "either/or" situations, which carry with them the danger of extremism and fundamentalism. Most of the Jewish people's days have not been ones of calm repose, but they have also not been days of destruction and disaster. In that in-between space, every action bears great significance. The people Israel is a people of transition. We live in between—between a historic, often painful past and our hope for the future, between foreignness and a sense of being at home, between a sense of loss and a feeling of satisfaction.

This range was well understood by Abraham ibn Ezra, to whom this *piyut* is ascribed. He spent his first fifty years in thriving, Golden Age Spain, but he was forced to leave when a radical, murderous Muslim sect known as the Almohads ascended to power. He was very familiar with life between the spectrum of fear and comfort, exile and blessing, and he succeeded in functioning within it.

The Jewish people knows the meaning of "small mercies," of grappling with complex situations rather than Hollywood-style scripts. The poem *Eish Tukad B'kirbi* is a fine reminder of the reality brought on by past disaster, of the gap between dreams and reality. A reminder, and an incentive to address the dangers—external and especially internal—that we face today as a society and as a country.

Let me conclude with the wish of the prophet Isaiah (35:10) alluded to in our *piyut*: "gladness and joy, and let sorrow and sighing flee"—and it is really only up to us!

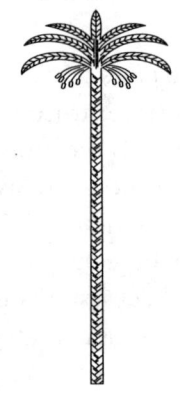

"The Face of Tishah B'Av": The Tenacity of Memory

THE STORY IS TOLD that Napoleon was walking one day in the streets of Paris when he heard the sound of wailing and weeping coming from a synagogue that he was passing. When he asked why the Jews were crying, someone in his entourage told him, after a quick investigation, that they were mourning the destruction of their Temple. "What Temple? When was it destroyed? Why wasn't I informed?" Napoleon asked in surprise. When it was explained to him that the Temple had been destroyed more than seventeen hundred years earlier, he exclaimed, "A people that mourns its lost Temple for so many generations will surely get to go back and rebuild it."

Whether or not this story contains a kernel of historical truth, it does indicate the important role of memory in Jewish culture. Memory of the past is the force that moves us forward toward the future, and we are better able to soar toward the future when we are strongly rooted in the past. When we observe our holidays, we not only remember on an intellectual level the past events that led to their establishment; we actively experience them anew. We feel the joy of the festival pilgrims, we leave Egypt again every year, and every year we again receive the Torah. The Torah commands us, "Remember the days of old, consider the years of ages past. Ask your parent, who will inform you, your elders, who will tell you" (Deuteronomy 32:7). In his book *Zakhor*, which deals with historical consciousness among the Jews, Yosef Hayim Yerushalmi points out that the Jews are the only people for whom the instruction to remember is an actual religious commandment that applies to the entire people.[4]

Tishah B'Av is not unusual in this regard. The day that marks the destruction of the Temple is the saddest day on the Jewish calendar, and sometimes it has been referred to as "the black fast" (to distinguish it from Yom Kippur, "the white fast"). Over the course of three weeks, Jews prepare their hearts for Tishah B'Av. The three weeks "between the straits," starting with the fast on the seventeenth of Tammuz, when Jerusalem's walls were breached, through Tishah B'Av, when the Temple was destroyed, are a time of ever-increasing heaviness, mourning, and sadness.

A Sponge for Sorrows

Other days of mourning in the Jewish calendar have absorbed the memory of additional disasters, but none more so than Tishah B'Av; this day has absorbed the memory of many disasters other than the destruction of the First and Second Temples as the centuries passed:

> Five things befell our ancestors on the seventeenth of Tammuz, and five on the ninth of Av.
>> On the ninth of Av it was decreed against our ancestors that they should not enter the Land [of Israel], and the Temple was destroyed the first and

---

In English, if we see someone walking around looking gloomy or sad, we might say that someone is "down in the mouth" or has "a face like a wet weekend." In Hebrew, the phrase used is *partzuf shel Tishah B'Av*—the "face of Tishah B'Av," which illustrates the emotional weight and lasting impact of the Ninth of Av.

Individual and National Mourning: Alike and Opposite

Mourning the destruction of the Temple is similar to personal mourning over the death of someone close to us. But in one important respect they are opposites. Individual mourning begins at the peak of its harshness with the death and burial of a relative, after which the mourner enters ever-wider circles of mourning marked by decreasing severity: the seven-day period of *shivah* with its intensive mourning customs, the thirty days (*sh'loshim*) of less-demanding mourning practices, the full year of mourning, followed by an annual *yarhzeit* observance in memory of the departed. In contrast, national mourning over the destruction of Jerusalem builds slowly, gaining in intensity until it reaches its peak. Perhaps the process was designed this way because the rabbis knew that unlike the spontaneous and unmediated sorrow over a personal loss, consciousness of national mourning is a gradual process that increases in severity because it comes less naturally for the individual; our ancestors wanted to create an intensification of the experience, after which, in a sudden shift, comes the relief of seven weeks of consolation.

the second time, and Beitar was captured, and the city [of Jerusalem] was plowed up. (*Mishnah Taanit* 4:6).

According to the Mishnah, then, there were five disasters that occurred on the ninth of Av: First, the generation of the wilderness who left Egypt in the Exodus was given the penalty of not being able to enter the land of the Canaan because of the sins of the ten spies; that entire generation died in the wilderness. Second and third, both Temples were destroyed—the first in 586 BCE and the second in 70 CE. Fourth, about seventy years after the destruction of the Second Temple, the town of Beitar—the last rebel stronghold of the Bar Kochba revolt—fell to the Romans and was destroyed. Finally, Jerusalem was completely destroyed by the Romans.

When Jews gather for prayer on the night of Tishah B'Av, we sit on the ground and recite *kinot* in low voices, recalling not only the destruction of the Temples, but also all the travails that our people has endured. Among these poems of lamentation for Tishah B'Av, one can find many written during the Middle Ages that describe the sufferings, disasters, murderous prosecutions, and acts of martyrdom (or *kiddush HaShem*, "sanctification of God's name") of the Jews in their various locations.

Throughout the course of history, additional tragic events beyond the five listed in the Mishnah have been absorbed by Tishah B'Av. Some may not have occurred on the ninth of Av but were later reported to have occurred then; others simply seemed appropriate for commemoration on that date. So, for example, we have this list:

> I have already mentioned that I am a veteran Jerusalemite; on my mother's side, I belong to the tenth generation. I've lived in Jerusalem most of my life, and today my home is just a few kilometers from where the Temple once stood. Tishah B'Av has a lot of meaning for me, even though I personally do not hope that the Temple will be rebuilt. Nevertheless, the most meaningful Tishah B'Av experience I have had was actually in Berlin, praying at the rebuilt synagogue—originally largely destroyed during World War II—on Oranienburger Strasse. As we sat by candlelight in the gigantic, barren courtyard where the impressive structure once stood, chanting Lamentations and singing *kinot*, I thought about destruction in its most fierce manifestation. As our voices echoed in the darkness, sorrow over the destruction of the Temple combined with sorrow over the subsequent destructions of the sacred throughout our history.

On the ninth of Av in the year 5050 [1290], the Jews of England were expelled.

On the ninth of Av in the year 5066 [1306], the Jews of France were expelled.

On the ninth of Av in the year 5252 [1492], the Jews of Spain were expelled.

On the ninth of Av in the year 5430 [1670], the Jews of Austria were expelled.

On the ninth of Av in the year 5674 [1914], World War I broke out.

On the ninth of Av in the year 5701 [1941], the Jews of Poland were sent to ghettos.

On the ninth of Av in the year 5702 [1942], the Warsaw Ghetto was wiped out.[5]

Obviously, not all these disasters took place precisely on the ninth of Av, but the Jewish people understood that it is impossible to live through a calendar year with a constant sense of destruction and horror, so it concentrated many of its disasters into one day. Not long after becoming prime minister of Israel in 1977, Menachem Begin sought to move Holocaust Memorial Day to Tishah B'Av, thus placing the Holocaust in the continuum of destruction and exile and perhaps seeking to prevent it from casting too dark a shadow over the State of Israel. His suggestion was not accepted, of course, because Holocaust Martyrs' and Heroes' Remembrance Day (Yom HaShoah) on the twenty-seventh of Nisan, which was established in 1959, had already attained sufficient status and importance in the minds of the Israeli people. (Some Ultra-Orthodox groups do memorialize the Holocaust on Tishah B'Av, as this is the day dedicated to commemorating destruction and loss.) In addition, it may be that the summer timing of Tishah B'Av—when schools are not in session—helped determine the outcome of Begin's proposal.

Is Tishah B'Av Still Relevant?

Must we still mourn and wail over the destruction of the Temple? This question is not at all new; it was first posed twenty-five hundred years ago, "in the fourth year of King Darius"—that is, around the year 518 BCE—two years after the construction of the Second Temple had begun. A delegation came to Jerusalem "to entreat the favor of the Eternal" (Zechariah 7:2) and also to inquire as to whether one still needed to mourn the destruction of the First Temple: "Shall I weep and practice abstinence in the fifth month, as I have been doing all these years?" (7:3). That is, is the mourning over the destroyed Temple during the fifth month—meaning Av—still in force, even in a time when the Second Temple was being rebuilt? Are the four fasts in memory of the Temple appropriate in a time when the air resounds with expectations for building the new Temple? Must one still mourn the Temple that was destroyed?

Underlying this question is the need to clarify whether, in principle, the fast was intended to be permanent or only temporary. Must the destruction be recalled even when the people's situation changes radically, or should the fast be canceled? Zechariah does not give a direct reply, instead focusing on a future when it will not be just the fasts that are canceled:

> Thus said the Eternal of Hosts, "The fast of the fourth month, the fast of the fifth month, the fast of the seventh month, and the fast of the tenth month shall become occasions for joy and gladness, happy festivals for the House of Judah; but you must love honesty and integrity." (Zechariah 8:19)

Zechariah makes it known that the fasts are temporary, while the values of truth and peace are eternal, mitzvot that will stand for all time. Perhaps he is suggesting that if we know how to love honesty and integrity, we will be privileged to enjoy these days as occasions of joy and gladness.

Many generations later, another leader wondered about the place of Tishah B'Av in his era. It is told that Rabbi Y'hudah HaNasi (second to third century), the redactor of the Mishnah, sought to "uproot Tishah B'Av" (Jerusalem Talmud, *Taanit* 4:6 [69c]). Despite his stature and influence, his effort was unsuccessful, since the text immediately reports, "but they did not let him." It seems that the editors of the Jerusalem Talmud were a bit shocked by Rabbi Y'hudah HaNasi's initiative and were quick to cite another version of this story, according to which he asked "to uproot Tishah B'Av when it falls on Shabbat," rather than canceling the entire observance.

The question of whether the fast should be the eternal or ephemeral was asked

---

Approximately eighty thousand American children attend Jewish summer camps each year,[6] and a Tishah B'Av observance has become an important part of camp's informal Jewish education experience. Special camp programs on topics such as antisemitism, senseless hatred, and creating shelters of peace occur on Tishah B'Av, along with more traditional commemorations. I remember one summer at a camp in Wisconsin, when the campers spent days lovingly building a model of the Temple, and then on Tishah B'Av they destroyed it to demonstrate in a small way the emotional impact of the Temple's destruction. In addition, despite the summer's heat and a full camp schedule, many campers and staff observe the fast day.[7]

King Solomon built the First Temple in the tenth century BCE, which was then destroyed by the Babylonians in 586 BCE. The Second Temple was built by the Jews who returned from Babylonian exile and inaugurated around 518 BCE. The Second Temple was destroyed by the Romans in 70 CE. The Rabbis of the Talmud asked, "Why was the Second Temple destroyed?" (Babylonian Talmud, *Yoma* 9b). They ask a similar question about the destruction of the First Temple, but their answer for was fairly straightforward: "idol worship, forbidden sexual relations, and bloodshed" led to the destruction of the First Temple. However, they argue that during the Second Temple period, people were engaged in the study of Torah, fulfilled the commandments, and performed acts of kindness, so there should have been no reason for God to destroy the Temple. Then they answer their own question: "The Temple was destroyed because of sinat chinam [senseless hatred]."

When Berl Katznelson, a member of the Second Aliyah (1904–14), heard in 1934 that one of the youth movements chose to go on a hike on Tishah B'av, he was horrified. He did not expect them to observe the day in a halachic sense, but he was nonetheless saddened by their ignorance. "It is inconceivable that someone did this deliberately. However, this ignorance in itself should awaken thoughts of longing." The ability to remember and mourn, he claimed, is a strength that allows us to grow. "The creators and great ones of our people," he added, established the day so the people of Israel could "mourn the destruction through the generations on the day of memory, with all the intensity of feeling of someone whose dead is lying before them, of someone who has lost their freedom and birthright."[10] Only those who love with all their hearts can mourn that way. Love of life, freedom, and homeland are bound up with a consciousness of their fragility.

From Time to Time → Dalia Marx

again in the Babylonian Talmud. Rav Papa, a fourth-century Babylonian sage, divided reality into three possible situations: "When there is peace, they [i.e., the fasts] shall be for joy and gladness; if there is persecution, they shall be fast days; if there is no persecution but also no peace, then those who desire may fast and those who desire need not fast" (Babylonian Talmud, *Rosh HaShanah* 18b). The exception is Tishah B'Av, "because several misfortunes happened on it." In his view, the fasts on the other dates are flexible and depend on the people's situation at that time. In other words, Rav Papa believes that the people's perception of its present situation is what matters most.

Tishah B'Av in Our Time

In modern times there have also been some who wished to assign a completely different meaning to Tishah B'Av. Some leaders of classical Reform Judaism related to Tishah B'Av as an actual festival, a day marking the Jewish people's emergence from its oppression and becoming a worldwide "kingdom of priests and a holy nation" (Exodus 19:6), whose task is to disseminate prophetic ethics throughout the world.[8] This approach to Tishah B'Av was eventually rejected by the Reform Movement, which—since the middle of last century—has discovered (gradually, it should be said) the significance of historical Zion and the modern State of Israel. Today, the Reform Movement decisively identifies itself as a Zionist movement, though of course not every Reform Jew agrees with everything that happens in Israel today.[9] Some Religious Zionist voices in Israel have also expressed the desire to eliminate the fast of Tishah B'Av. These voices rose particularly in the years after the Six-Day War, but the idea has never been widely accepted.

What is it that people actually do on Tishah B'Av? There are those who fast all night and all day, read the Book of Lamentations, and say special *kinot* prayers. There are others who choose to fast only half the day, to recognize the uniqueness of living in a period of Jewish sovereignty in the Land of Israel. Still others devote the day to study groups, prayer, and lamentations. And there are some who seek to demonstrate unconditional love and kindness (ahavat chinam). All of these practices share a commemoration of the destruction that once was and a commitment to avoid any future destructions. The active memory of Tishah B'Av is an expression of loyalty to the people's past and hope for a better future. Tishah B'Av is a day on which I give thought to the holy site that was destroyed, the sanctity that was violated, and the suffering of innocents among the Jews and in the family of humankind at large. The darkness can be dispelled with light, but there are times when it is important for a little darkness to remain. Even if most of the time our faces are filled with light that we seek to shine on others, on this day we may allow ourselves to wear what in Hebrew we call "a Tishah B'Av face."

By the Rivers of Babylon, We Were Like Dreamers

"BY THE RIVERS OF BABYLON, there we sat, sat and wept as we remembered Zion" (Psalm 137:1)—an unusual opening for an unusual psalm. The saddest chapter of the Book of Psalms is printed in many prayer books for reciting before *Birkat HaMazon* (Blessing after Meals) on weekdays. This placement emphasizes the bitter taste of exile and stresses our devotion to Zion. Unlike warriors who hang up their weapons during times of peace, the Levites hang up their lyres in times of crisis and refuse to use them to sing songs of Zion. The psalm also includes the powerful oath "If I forget you, O Jerusalem, let my right hand wither; let my tongue stick to my palate if I cease to think of you, if I do not keep Jerusalem in memory even at my happiest hour" (137:5–6), which to this day we say at a wedding as the glass is broken and also at many baby-welcoming ceremonies (both *b'rit milah* and *simchat bat*).

At the end of a meal, when the body's needs have been satisfied, tradition invites us to recall Jerusalem in ruins. In this way individuals tie their fate to that of the people and swear allegiance to the place that unites all of Israel—Zion. Even during festive and personal moments—such as a wedding or the birth of a child—when the focus is on our personal happiness, we are called upon to pause and express our devotion to Zion and Jerusalem.

On Shabbat and festivals, it is customary to precede *Birkat HaMazon* with another psalm, quite different in tone: "A song of ascents. When the Eternal restores the fortunes of Zion, we will be like dreamers" (Psalm 126:1). The mourning, tears, and self-restraint of Psalm 137 are replaced by the joy of those returning to Zion. The custom of reading one of these two psalms before *Birkat HaMazon* develops quite late; it appears for the first time in the book *Seder HaYom* by Rabbi Moshe ben Machir, printed in Safed in 1599. However, the instruction to remember the destroyed Holy Temple after enjoying food on weekdays, as well as to express our hopes for redemption on holidays and Shabbat, appears as far back as the *Zohar*.[11]

Two Cries, Two Laughs

Psalms 137 and 126 meet in the prayer book as two sides of the same coin, opposites in every possible way—sadness and despair versus hope and joy. It is surprising, then, to find stylistic, linguistic, and conceptual similarities between them.[12]

Psalm 137

א עַל נַהֲרוֹת בָּבֶל שָׁם יָשַׁבְנוּ גַּם־בָּכִינוּ בְּזָכְרֵנוּ אֶת־צִיּוֹן.

1 By the rivers of Babylon, there we sat, sat and wept, as we remembered Zion.

ב עַל־עֲרָבִים בְּתוֹכָהּ תָּלִינוּ כִּנֹּרוֹתֵינוּ.

2 There on the poplars we hung up our lyres,

ג כִּי שָׁם שְׁאֵלוּנוּ שׁוֹבֵינוּ דִּבְרֵי־שִׁיר וְתוֹלָלֵינוּ שִׂמְחָה שִׁירוּ לָנוּ מִשִּׁיר צִיּוֹן.

3 for our captors asked us there for songs, our tormentors for amusement: "Sing us one of the songs of Zion."

ד אֵיךְ נָשִׁיר אֶת־שִׁיר־יְיָ עַל אַדְמַת נֵכָר.

4 How can we sing a song of the Eternal on alien soil?

ה אִם־אֶשְׁכָּחֵךְ יְרוּשָׁלָ͏ִם תִּשְׁכַּח יְמִינִי.

5 If I forget you, O Jerusalem, let my right hand wither,

ו תִּדְבַּק־לְשׁוֹנִי לְחִכִּי אִם־לֹא אֶזְכְּרֵכִי אִם־לֹא אַעֲלֶה אֶת־יְרוּשָׁלַ͏ִם עַל רֹאשׁ שִׂמְחָתִי.

6 let my tongue stick to my palate if I cease to think of you, if I do not keep Jerusalem in memory even at my happiest hour.

Psalm 126

א שִׁיר הַמַּעֲלוֹת בְּשׁוּב יְיָ אֶת־שִׁיבַת צִיּוֹן הָיִינוּ כְּחֹלְמִים.

1 A song of ascents: When the Eternal restores the fortunes of Zion, we will be like dreamers.

ב אָז יִמָּלֵא שְׂחוֹק פִּינוּ וּלְשׁוֹנֵנוּ רִנָּה אָז יֹאמְרוּ בַגּוֹיִם הִגְדִּיל יְיָ לַעֲשׂוֹת עִם־אֵלֶּה.

2 Then our mouths shall be filled with laughter, our tongues with songs of joy. They shall say among the nations, "The Eternal has done great things for them."

ג הִגְדִּיל יְיָ לַעֲשׂוֹת עִמָּנוּ הָיִינוּ שְׂמֵחִים.

3 The Eternal will do great things for us and we shall be happy.

ד שׁוּבָה יְיָ אֶת־שְׁבִיתֵנוּ כַּאֲפִיקִים בַּנֶּגֶב.

4 Restore our fortunes, O Eternal, like watercourses in the Negev.

ה הַזֹּרְעִים בְּדִמְעָה בְּרִנָּה יִקְצֹרוּ.

5 They who sow in tears shall reap with songs of joy.

ו הָלוֹךְ יֵלֵךְ וּבָכֹה נֹשֵׂא מֶשֶׁךְ־הַזָּרַע בֹּא־יָבֹא בְרִנָּה נֹשֵׂא אֲלֻמֹּתָיו.

6 Though he goes along weeping, carrying the seed-bag, he shall come back with songs of joy, carrying his sheaves.

In both psalms—the "sad" one and the "happy" one—the term "weep" occurs: "there we sat, sat and wept" (137:1) and "though he goes along weeping" (126:6). There is joy and laughter in both as well—in one, the taunts of the captors (137:3); in the other, "our mouths shall be filled with laughter, our tongues with songs of joy" (126:2). Both psalms mention the reaction of the non-Israelites to Israel's situation: in Psalm 137 it is their arrogant, inconsiderate demand to "sing us one of the songs of Zion" (137:3), and in Psalm 126 it is astonishment at the miraculous deliverance of Israel: "They shall say among the nations, 'The Eternal has done great things for them'" (126:2). Both psalms refer to bodies of water: the mighty "rivers of Babylon" (137:1), into which are mixed the tears of the Judean exiles, and the request to restore Israel "like watercourses in the Negev" (126:4). Both poems use verbs from the overlapping roots *shin-vav-bet* ("return," "restore") and *shin-bet-hei* ("take captive"). Bible scholar Professor Yair Zakovitch suggests that the connection between these two psalms existed long before they were both linked to *Birkat HaMazon*, realized already within the biblical text. The psalm of rejoicing, he suggests, was written in response to the psalm of lament.[13]

In many prayer books the two psalms appear side by side, but it seems that each of them reveals a different subtext that is quite unexpected. Psalm 137, the plaintive "By the rivers of Babylon," reveals the fact—even if obliquely—that no matter where Jews live there can be consolation and relief. Some who sit by the mighty, fertile waters of a foreign land may not long for the drought-prone Land of Israel—including many Jewish exiles in Babylon, whose lives of comfort and success overruled their desire to return to Israel. By the same measure, the request for Zion's fortunes to be restored like dry riverbeds in the Negev in Psalm 126's "song of ascents" may also mask some trepidation about the sudden and powerful rush of water that is so often destructive and dangerous and that can just as suddenly become dry and empty. (Unfortunately, we have often been made aware of the disastrous consequences of a wadi that is suddenly and without warning engulfed in rushing water.)

The connection between these psalms—two different sides of the same coin—reminds us that there is no sadness without a measure of hope, just as there is no joy without some anxiety. Another similarity is that in both psalms, because of the ambiguous nature of Biblical Hebrew verbs, it is unclear which tense is intended. In Psalm 137, the speaker adopts an odd turn of phrase, describing the "rivers of Babylon" as "there," even though the speaker is supposedly sitting right by them. In Psalm 126, it is not clear whether the return to Zion is happening before the speaker's eyes or in memory of the past. In both psalms, then, there is a certain virtual atmosphere of reality blended with a dream. And while Psalm 126 is sung in many homes with joy and delight after meals on Shabbat and holidays, few actually recite Psalm 137 on weekdays. Perhaps that reticence comes from lack of time on a workday, or maybe it is a subconscious refusal to take part in the psalm's despair or in its plea to take cruel revenge on the enemy—including their infant children (137:9). However, even though Psalm 137 is not recited often, it still appears in many prayer books alongside its upbeat counterpart. Over the generations, these two psalms came to stand like two memorial pillars, one commemorating destruction and devastation, the other, redemption. One stands for the travails of existence and survival, the other for hope for the future, which we have a taste of on Shabbat.

Jewish Yin, Jewish Yang

What is our reality today? Are we in the harsh reality of "the rivers of Babylon" or in the excitement of the "song of ascents"? It seems that neither situation adequately captures our lives today. Many Jews in the Diaspora feel at home, while quite a few Israeli Jews feel like strangers in their own land. Do these psalms still relate to our lives as representing two sides of the same coin? Or is it better to relate to the concepts of exile and redemption as defining a range within which our lives take place—somewhere between the far reaches of both? Or perhaps they portray something like the yin-yang of Chinese philosophy, meaning they are opposites that are somewhat intermixed, and neither has an independent existence without the other. (See pp. 301–306.)

The days "between the straits" that end at Tishah B'Av invite us to think about our existential situation then and now. The dynamism and indeterminacy of our current situation—a complex mix of light and shadows, tears and smiles—are precisely what allow us to read these psalms creatively and what impel us to act so that our world will become better and more just.

From Time to Time → Dalia Marx

Jewish Phantom Pain: On the Temple That Was Destroyed

PEOPLE WHO HAVE LOST A HAND or foot sometimes continue to experience phantom pain in their absent limb. For many generations, Jews have suffered phantom pain from their missing Temple in Jerusalem, even though it was destroyed nearly two thousand years ago and the Jewish people created a robust religious life without a Temple or even access to Jerusalem. Longing for the Temple is not phantom pain for a missing limb, but pain for what was once the nation's heart—its spiritual, cultural, and economic center. How can a people survive in the absence of what was once its vital, beating heart? The fact is, despite all predictions to the contrary, the Jewish people have done exactly that. We have survived and even flourished without the Holy Temple.

As a Jew born in Jerusalem, the lively capital of a sovereign State of Israel, I have been privileged to live in unusual conditions as measured by Jewish history. For many long years, living in Jerusalem was the Jews' unattainable wish. They mentioned it in prayers and supplications, and it shaped their inner language and hopes for redemption—even if it was not a physical part of their lives. Generation after generation of worshipers asked to see it, and to see it rebuilt, but were not privileged to do so. The Temple's centrality was inseparable in the mind of our ancestors from the centrality of the Land of Israel and Jerusalem.

> "Just as a navel is set in the middle of a person, so the Land of Israel is the navel of the world.... The Land of Israel sits at the center of the world; Jerusalem is in the center of the Land of Israel; the sanctuary is in the center of Jerusalem; the Temple building is in the center of the sanctuary; the Ark is in the center of the Temple building; and the foundation stone, out of which the world was founded, is before the Temple building" (*Tanchuma, K'doshim* 10).
>
> According to this tradition, the world comprises concentric circles that, as one travels inward, center on the stone—*even hashtiyah*—that is the foundation of the entire world.

Representing the Temple in the Absence of a Temple

Even before the destruction of the Second Temple in the year 70 CE, the Pharisees moved Temple religious commandments outside the Temple. For example, they insisted on eating meat that had not been set aside for ritual use at the Temple in the manner that the meat of sacrifices was consumed. This level of practice was instituted precisely because of the great importance attributed to the Temple, but paradoxically what emerged was the understanding that it is possible to live a meaningful Jewish life outside the Temple as well.

The sights, scents, and sounds of the Temple—as well as the feelings of those who passed through its gates—came to a sudden halt when the Temple was destroyed, but in a way they were preserved in sustainable alternatives. Here I will mention a few of the alternatives to Temple worship and sacrifices.

***Talmud Torah* (Torah Study) as Temple Worship:** The carefully measured words of the Mishnah about the Temple were intended to absorb the experience of the Temple, its worship, and its role as a center of pilgrimage. Instead of actively offering sacrifices, Jews busied themselves with studying the sacrifices. The focus shifted from place and action to words and learning. What previously could only have been done at the Temple in Jerusalem, and only by descendants of the priest Aaron who had received the appropriate training, could now be done metaphorically by every Jew (although, until modern times, generally only by a male Jew) at any time and in every place.

The Mishnah's tractate *Pei-ah* begins with a statement of principle regarding the status of *talmud Torah*:

> These are things for which no limit is prescribed: *pei-ah* [leaving the edges or corners of fields, orchards, and vineyards unharvested, so the poor may harvest them], first fruits, the festival offerings [i.e., pilgrimage to Jerusalem], deeds of loving-kindness, and the study of Torah.
>
> These are things that are limitless, of which a person enjoys the fruits in this world while the principal remains in the world-to-come: honoring one's father and mother, performing deeds of loving-kindness, making peace between one person and another; and the study of Torah is equal to all. (*Mishnah Pei-ah* 1:1)

Torah study is included in the first part of this mishnah with mitzvot connected to the Temple, such as offering first fruits or observing pilgrimage festivals. The second part of this mishnah places Torah study alongside the other mitzvot whose rewards endure for a person into the next world, and thus suggests that study and scholarship make all the other possible.

***G'milut Chasadim* (Acts of Loving-Kindness) as Temple Worship:** Rabbi Yochanan ben Zakkai, who left Jerusalem on the eve of its destruction in order to establish the *beit midrash* at Yavneh, became the father of the Rabbis' major revolution. He offers "another atonement" as a substitute for offering sacrifices—acts of loving-kindness (see pp. 221–22). He elevated *g'milut chasadim* to the level of Temple worship, indicating the great importance of acting in the world with kindness and concern. This also paves the way for understanding that all the mitzvot that are not connected solely to Temple are equal in value to those that are.

The Dining Table as an Altar: The Jewish home—and the family life maintained there—became a site of sanctity, a kind of substitute for the Temple. Rabbi Yochanan and Rabbi Elazar teach, "While the Temple still stood, the altar made atonement for a person, but now that the Temple no longer stands, a person's table makes atonement for them" (Babylonian Talmud, *M'nachot* 97a). A home's dining table could provide atonement for the members of the household, just as the Temple altar once did. A family's routine life became as sacred as what was performed in the Temple itself. About a millennium later, the Sephardic commentator on Jewish liturgy Rabbi David Abudarham (fourteenth-century Spain) explains the mitzvah of washing one's hands when rising from bed in the morning by saying that a person at home is like the High Priest and the home is like the Temple, so one must wash one's hands to attain purity before morning prayers.[14]

Prayer in Place of Temple Worship: Prayer indeed existed before the destruction and in parallel to the Temple worship. However, in the Rabbis' consciousness, it came to be seen as a worthy and sufficient replacement for offering sacrifices. "Is there such a thing as service [of God] in one's heart?" the Rabbis ask regarding the demand to serve God "with all your heart" (Deuteronomy 11:13), and they reply, "It is prayer" (Jerusalem Talmud, *B'rachot* 4:1 [29a–b]). According to this approach, prayer—the service of God that one performs in one's heart—is not just a substitute for the sacrifices, but rather it is the actual, proper performance of the biblical commandment.

That being said, there is no central prayer service in Jewish worship that does not include a request for the rebuilding of Jerusalem. In the *Amidah*, the haftarah blessings, and *Birkat HaMazon*, we mention the rebuilding of Jerusalem. The Passover Haggadah and the Yom Kippur liturgy end with the call "Next year in rebuilt Jerusalem!" At life-cycle events, we also remember Jerusalem. Before a glass is broken at a wedding ceremony, this verse is recited: "If I forget you, O Jerusalem, let my right hand wither; let my tongue stick to my palate if I cease to think of you, if I do not keep Jerusalem in memory even at my happiest hour" (Psalm 137:5–6). Sometimes at a baby-welcoming ceremony (*b'rit milah* or *simchat bat*), a parent will recite those verses. Even when we offer words of consolation to mourners, some people will include the personal consolation as part of the consolation of the entire city, as one does in the Ashkenazic tradition: "May the Ever-present comfort you among the mourners of Zion and Jerusalem."

In the Middle Ages, the custom of breaking a glass at a wedding was connected to mourning the destruction of the Temple. On their day of joy, the couple remember the destruction of Jerusalem and their commitment to its remembrance, accompanying that act of memory with breaking the glass. In medieval times, this was understood as a symbolic reenactment of the destruction of the Temple.

T'shuvah (**Repentance**) **as Sacrificial Worship:** Rabbi Y'hoshua ben Levi, a Talmudic sage of the Land of Israel, praises the person "who sacrifices their [evil] inclination and confesses [their sin] over it" (Babylonian Talmud, *Sanhedrin* 43b). He continues:

> When the Temple was in existence, if a person brought a burnt offering, they received credit for a burnt offering; if a meal offering, they received credit for a meal offering; but one who was humble in spirit, Scripture regarded them as though they had brought all the offerings, for it is said, "True sacrifice to God is a contrite spirit" (Psalm 51:19). And furthermore, their prayers are not rejected, for it is written [continuing the same verse], "God, You will not discard a contrite and crushed heart."

In the first part of this midrashic homily, Rabbi Y'hoshua compares personal humility to the sacrificial service, and in the second part he teaches that "one who is humble in spirit" has a higher status than a person who brings a sacrifice—and is considered as one who offered all the sacrifices. Prayer, states Rabbi Y'hoshua, is preferable to the sacrifices, because it is not "discarded."

HaTikvah: "As Long as in the Heart Within . . ."

Jews who did not enjoy the privilege of seeing the holiness of Jerusalem with their own eyes wove it and the Temple into their inner emotions both at moments of crisis and of happiness—during any transition in their lives. They turned toward the Temple Mount when praying and kept the dream of the Temple alive. Siddurim, Haggadot, *ketubot* (wedding contracts), sukkah decorations, challah covers, bread knives for slicing challah, *Kiddush* cups, amulets for mothers giving birth and for their babies, and so on—all of these have borne the visual image of the Temple or of the Temple Mount. In many Jewish homes one finds on the wall facing in the direction of Jerusalem a decorative *mizrach*, marking the direction of Jerusalem, toward which one faces while praying. It serves as a sort of permanent compass indicating the direction of Zion. It is called a *mizrach*, meaning "east," even if Jerusalem is not actually to the east of the person who hangs it.

Today, many Jews are privileged to live in the sovereign State of Israel, and many

> Wherever they are in the world, **Jews face Jerusalem** when they pray. Thus, even when we are located far from one other, all of us face the one eternal center; in this way, we are together even when we are spread out to farthest reaches of the globe:
>
> If one is in the east—one should turn one's face to the west;
> if in the west—one should turn one's face to the east;
> if in the south—one should turn one's face to the north;
> if in the north—one should turn one's face to the south.
> In this way all Israel will be turning their hearts toward one place.
>
> (Babylonian Talmud, *B'rachot* 30a)

of us see its upbuilding as the fulfillment of an ancient dream, even if we are not longing for the rebuilding of the Temple. In fact, many of us observe efforts to build a Third Temple with trepidation and concern. The Temple has not been completely eradicated, though. We see signs of it everywhere: the image of the Temple menorah is stamped on our government ID cards and passports and is the official emblem of Israel. Judaism changed from being a religion centered on its Temple to a decentralized religion in which the Temple is remembered in absentia but whose sanctity still finds expression in many places and forms.

At the beginning of this section, I compared the presence of the absent Temple to the phantom pain experienced by someone who has lost a limb. One of the methods for treating phantom pain is called "the mirror cure." In this approach, a mirror is placed in front of the place of the missing, painful limb, and treatment is applied to the existing, healthy limb that is reflected in the mirror. This sometimes provides relief from the phantom pain.[15] Mirror therapy is somewhat similar to various approaches suggested through the years for addressing the absence of the destroyed Temple. In place of the Temple itself, Jews have creative "reflections" of the Temple in both individual and public observance. In the eyes of some, these reflections serve as an interim solution until the rebuilding of the Temple, while for others—myself included—these reflections represent respect for the past Temple in a reality that no longer desires or needs an actual Temple.

Our Sages did not regard the destruction of the Temple as the end of the special relationship between God and the people Israel. They found other expressions for that connection: Torah study, *g'milut chasadim*, family and community life, *t'shuvah*, and prayer.

We Want *Mashiach* (Messiah) Now?

LIKE A SHEET OF PAPER held so that both edges meet, the mourning over the greatest destruction in Jewish history (and other destructions that have been attached to it over the years) directly meets our longing for redemption. The month's monosyllabic name Av took on the additional name M'nachem, which is one of the names of the Messiah; according to tradition, the Messiah will be born on Tishah B'Av. On that date, it is only fitting to deal with the subject of the Messiah and messianism.

The belief in the coming of the Messiah became established as a central tenet of Judaism when Maimonides counted it among his Thirteen Principles of Faith. But even he, "the Great Eagle" (as he is known in traditional literature), recommended refraining from concentrating too much on messianic matters:

> No one should ever occupy oneself with the legends [about the conditions and time of the Messiah's arrival] or spend much time on midrashic statements bearing on this and like subjects. One should not deem them of prime importance, since they lead neither to the fear of God nor to the love of God. (*Mishneh Torah*, Hilchot M'lachim 12:2)[16]

Maimonides even stated that the Messiah arrival will change nothing in how the world works. Indeed, alongside longing for the age of Messiah, one also finds in Judaism a cautious approach toward excessive excitement about messianism. A teaching of Rabban Yochanan ben Zakkai (see pp. 221–23) teaches us the proper approach in this regard: "If you have a sapling in your hand and they tell you 'The Messiah is coming!' first plant the sapling and then go to greet them" (*Avot D'Rabbi Natan* B, 31). That is, our current lives and taking care of the actual future take precedence over fulfilling our messianic wishes. First one should sow and plant, and only afterward can one be free to greet the Messiah.

In our liturgy we find the clearest expression of Jews' beliefs and hopes, and there we find the hope for Messiah expressed over and over again. In the weekday *Amidah*, for example, the fifteenth blessing is devoted to "a sprout from [the line of] David," which refers to the Messiah, who will be a descendant of King David. The belief in a messianic age appears in *Birkat HaMazon*, the Passover Haggadah, and many prayers and *piyutim* for Shabbat and holidays.

"To Repair the World [*L'takein Olam*] by Divine Sovereignty"

The belief in a Messiah or, alternatively, a messianic age, is a belief in what is good and proper. It is a faith that in the future the world will be a better place than it is now and that the people Israel will be privileged to be saved. It is no surprise, then, that precisely at times of sorrow and suffering, Jews concentrated on the expected arrival of the Messiah, who would redeem the world—and they even believed that their own actions could hasten the coming of the Messiah. A belief in the Messiah is central to Christianity as well, but unlike Christians, who believe that their Messiah has already come in the past and will return at the end of days, Jews believe that the Messiah has not yet arrived.

In the Bible, there are clear expressions regarding redemption and descriptions of "the day of the Eternal," when all humankind will be subject to judgment. The idea of the Messiah, though, does not appear in explicit fashion in the Bible, although there are some who point to what they consider to be hints, such as Isaiah's prophecy about "a shoot [that] will grow from the stump of Jesse," who will reign during a time of complete redemption (Isaiah 11:1–15). The belief in a person who will appear at the end of days as God's messenger, fight Israel's enemies, and make the world into a good and proper place appeared in Judaism during the Second Temple period. Messianic hopes find broad expression in Rabbinic literature from the outset, and from then on these hopes have been considered an established element of Judaism.

Hope for a redeemed future was, over the centuries, the motivating force that drew people to the belief that what has been damaged can be repaired. This belief is deeply connected to the idea that our role on earth is to take action to bring redemption closer, as the *Aleinu* prayer reminds us "to repair the world by divine sovereignty" (see p. 294). Perhaps this is part of the reason so many Jews are active in social justice movements and struggles for *tikkun olam* (more on that below).

> The term **tikkun olam** appears in classical Rabbinic literature, but the sense in which it is used today borrows from Lurianic Kabbalah. In that view, the creation of the world was marred by the shattering of the vessels, that is, the *s'firot* that could not contain the tremendous divine light. As a result of the shattering of the vessels, good and bad were intermixed (or, in the language of the Kabbalah, the sparks of holiness and the shells were mixed together). Our role in the world is to gather the sparks of holiness, to repair the damage, and to gather up the good.

The foundation of our hope for a repaired, just world is the belief that good can exist, that it is within our power to create change, and that we are forbidden to take our time about bringing this change about. As Yaakov Rotblit writes in his widely popular song *Shir LaShalom* ("Song for Peace"), "Don't say 'the day will come.' Bring on that day!"[17] These words reflect a longing for and commitment to the good, express faith that we have a role in the world, and assert that we can and must bring about change in our world. This understanding also explains the need to distinguish between the constructive and creative commitment to create a just and well-ordered world and the dangerous and destructive expressions of messianic beliefs.

"Any Messiah Who Arrives Is a False Messiah"

A person's attitude toward the Messiah and their level of eagerness for the Messiah's arrival indicate both that person's ideological and social affiliation and their religious temperament. Within Judaism, there are those who are proactive in striving to bring a messianic age, those who long for the arrival of a flesh-and-blood Messiah, and those who even actively try to identify the Messiah.

> The poem *Ani Ma'amin* ("I Believe"), written by Shaul Tchernichowsky in 1892, expresses a profound faith in the spirit of humankind as a redemptive and beneficent force that is able to foster a new and better reality. Here are the poem's first two stanzas:
>
> Rejoice, rejoice now in the dreams,
> I the dreamer am the one who speaks.
> Rejoice, for I'll have faith in humankind,
> for in humankind I believe.
>
> For my soul still yearns for freedom
> I've not sold it for a calf of gold,
> for I shall yet have faith in humankind,
> in its spirit great and bold.[18]
>
> שַׂחֲקִי, שַׂחֲקִי עַל הַחֲלוֹמוֹת,
> זוּ אֲנִי הַחוֹלֵם שָׂח.
> שַׂחֲקִי כִּי בָאָדָם אַאֲמִין,
> כִּי עוֹדֶנִּי מַאֲמִין בָּךְ.
>
> כִּי עוֹד נַפְשִׁי דְּרוֹר שׁוֹאֶפֶת
> לֹא מְכַרְתִּיהָ לְעֵגֶל-פָּז,
> כִּי עוֹד אַאֲמִין גַּם בָּאָדָם,
> גַּם בְּרוּחוֹ, רוּחַ עָז.

Zionism's various trends reveal clear messianic elements that appear in different forms and with unique emphases. Secular Zionism has often seen itself as heralding a universal human redemption. In religious Zionism, there has always been a pronounced tension between political action and profound faith that we, by our actions, bring the Messiah. This faith was particularly strong in the circles around Rabbi Tzvi Yehudah Kook (1891–1982) and his students. In Chareidi (ultra-Orthodox) Judaism, an especially strong messianic fervor can be seen among Chabad Chasidim. The messianic faction of that movement continues to see the last Lubavitcher rebbe, Rabbi Menachem Mendel Schneerson (1902–94) as the Messiah and does not recognize his death. These moves toward a messianic extreme have aroused, and continue to arouse, strong opposition among secular and religious groups, strengthening the trend toward refraining from any talk about the Messiah and the messianic age. In the Reform Movement's prayer books, requests for the coming of an individual flesh-and-blood Messiah have been replaced by requests for a messianic age. Instead of seeking a redeemer (*go'eil*), expectation of redemption (*ge'ulah*) is emphasized. Opposition to the tendency to act to bring the Messiah sooner ("forcing the end" is the Hebrew phrase)

From Time to Time → Dalia Marx

has been heard from thinkers such as Professor Yeshayahu Leibowitz (1903–94), who argued passionately that the essence of Messiah is that the Messiah *will* come—in the future, perpetually. From my childhood memories, I can recall hearing Leibowitz, a sharp-tongued believer who loved to speak with young people. He used to wag his finger and say, "Messiah is someone who is always going to arrive." And then he would raise his voice, adding, "Any messiah who actually arrives is a false messiah."

To Be or Not to Be

While religions of the East focus on *being*, Judaism, in its many manifestations, seeks *becoming*. It concerns itself not only with presence and the present but also with commitment to action and to the future. The proportion of Jews around the world who work to "repair the world" seems high. Jews have stood out, and still stand out, for lending their hand to many struggles, among them the struggle for equal rights and racial justice in the United States and in South Africa, and they have stood at the forefront of the movements for women's rights, workers' rights, environmental justice, and more. As a rule, one can find Jews among the outstanding activists in all the struggles for human rights and social justice. Many Jews look to the future, do not settle for the present situation, are not satisfied with the present reality, seeking instead to right the world's wrongs. The United States Supreme Court justice Ruth Bader Ginsburg expressed it this way: "Dissents speak to a future age. It's not simply to say, 'My colleagues are wrong and I would not do it this.' But the greatest dissents do become court opinions and gradually over time their views become the dominant view. So that is the dissenter's hope: that they are writing not for today, but for tomorrow."[19]

The belief in the end of days, in redemption, kept Jews going in difficult times; during especially tough times there was a resurgence of interest in messianism and in calculating when the end-time would arrive. (This is characteristic not only of Judaism, of course.) This belief has come to include a variety of worldviews, hopes, and desires that sometimes oppose each other. The Messiah of the West Bank settlers' movement and of the young radicals who have settled on hilltops in the disputed territories, for example, is not the Messiah of the religious peace movement or of environmental activists. Attitudes toward messianism are shaped by beliefs and opinions and no less by personal temperament and character. In this lies the fertile power of the belief in redemption: the power to dream can include narratives and desires that are different and even contradictory. Today, when we live in a sovereign Jewish state, we need to be careful with these beliefs, because what was once a distant, harmless fantasy could come true today in a way that is harmful and dangerous. Therefore, it is up to us to be that much more responsible in our hopes for redemption.

"And Even Though the Messiah May Tarry"

In Maimonides's list of the Thirteen Principles of Faith he writes, "I believe with full faith in the coming of the Messiah, and even though the Messiah may tarry, nonetheless I will await the Messiah's arrival each day." I would like to propose that we understand the messianism of Maimonides's statement this way: We should not attempt to grasp the Messiah's heels or crown any individual, period of time, or idea with the crown of Messiah. As Professor Leibowitz said, the Messiah is an expectation regarding the future; the Messiah is always coming and is never fully here. This concept of the Messiah who is perpetually on the way accompanies a belief in the good and a commitment to the future. Recognizing that the absolute good is something to strive for, the "yeast in the dough" that motivates us to act and to strive for the good, even as we understand that it will never be fully realized.

That is how I understand the concept of messianism—as a process and not an outcome, as the belief that it is possible (and therefore necessary) to maximize goodness, to fix what is broken in our personal, familial, professional, communal, and human worlds. Messianism is the striving, not the arriving, the partial and not the complete, and Tishah B'Av is an excellent time to give that some thought.

Tu B'Av (Fifteenth of Av): Celebrating in the Vineyards

YOUNG WOMEN DANCING in the vineyards, their foreheads shining with the perspiration of enthusiasm, white dresses flowing and shining silver in the moonlight, bare feet turning up the soil, hands held tight in a circle. The young women are dancing, and the young men are gathered in clusters at some distance, watching them bashfully and longingly. The looks from the young men stir the young women's enthusiasm, but the women continue to dance by themselves in an endless circle, even as some of them steal furtive glances at the men. It is harvesttime in the vineyards, and the village is celebrating the grape harvest, happy with the productivity of the good soil.

Tu B'Av is a rural agricultural holiday, a celebration of fertility and youth, creativity and sensuality. It reflects an ancient culture, perhaps one that predates the people Israel. Its origins are unknown to us, but there are indications of an ancient myth still bubbling up to the surface. All we know about Tu B'Av is the vivid description in the Mishnah. Rabban Shimon ben Gamliel, president of the Sanhedrin at the end of the Second Temple period, equates it with Yom Kippur, the holiest day of the year, on which white clothes are worn as an indication of a desire to be purified:

> Rabban Shimon ben Gamliel said, "There were no happier days for Israel than the Fifteenth (Tu) of Av and Yom Kippur, for on them the daughters of Jerusalem used to go forth in white garments, and these were borrowed, so as not to embarrass anyone who did not have any. . . . And the daughters of Jerusalem went forth to dance in the vineyards. And what did they say? 'Young man, lift up your eyes and see, what would you choose for yourself? Set not your eyes on beauty. Set your eyes on family.'" (*Mishnah Taanit* 4:8)

Was Tu B'Av observed over the course of Jewish history? And if so, how? We cannot know, but in modern times it sparked the imagination of the pioneers in the Land of Israel, who described it as a secular folk festival, a holiday of nature for a people living securely on its land, enjoying its fruits and satisfied with their lot. Tu B'Av, known these days to Israelis as the holiday of love, is not a Jewish version of Valentine's Day. There is no exchange of cute cards, saccharine emojis, or overpriced chocolates in red heart-shaped boxes. But if we were to ask about the image of Tu B'Av in Israeli life, we would have to admit that other than being a popular date for a few music festivals and for booking weddings, it has not yet attained much of a form.

The Festival of the Waning Sun

Tu B'Av, like its sibling Tu BiSh'vat, is not a holiday based in the Torah. We first read about both occasions in the Mishnah. The two holidays divide the year into two equal parts, and both take place at mid-month, when the moon is full. Some have claimed that the ancient origin of these two holidays is connected to sun worship: during the six months from Tu BiSh'vat to Tu B'Av, the sunlight gets progressively stronger, fertilizing the soil and helping it yield its produce, and so Tu BiSh'vat was established as the New Year for Trees.

In contrast to that, "from the fifteenth of Av onward the strength of the sun grows less," and for the following six months "they no longer felled trees for the altar"

The Sages of Rabbinic Judaism sought to explain how Tu B'Av is comparable to Yom Kippur—the holiest day of the year, the day of pardon and forgiveness. They provide six possible reasons (all found in the Babylonian Talmud, *Taanit* 30b-31):

1. "Rav Y'hudah said in the name of Sh'muel, 'It is the day on which permission was granted to the tribes to intermarry between them.'" Thus did the tribal conception of Israel give way to an inclusive national conception.
2. "Rav Yosef said in the name of Rav Nachman, 'It is the day on which the tribe of Benjamin was permitted to reenter the congregation [of Israel]'" and marry women from other tribes—which was forbidden to them after the scandalous incident of the concubine at Gibeah (Judges 19–21). This reconciliation enabled the banned tribe to survive.
3. "Rabbah bar bar Chanah said in the name of Rabbi Yochanan, 'It is the day on which the deaths [of the generation of Jews] in the wilderness ceased.'" This meant that the period of wandering had drawn to a close and it was possible to enter the Promised Land.[20]
4. "Ula said, 'It is the day on which Hoshea the son of Elah removed the guards that Jeroboam, son of Nebat, had placed on the roads to prevent Israel from going [up to Jerusalem] on pilgrimage . . . so they may go to wherever they wish.'" That is, there was ritual pluralism, with each person deciding for themselves where to go on pilgrimage—Jerusalem, Beth El, or Dan.
5. "Rav Mat'nah said, 'It was the day on which the slain of Beitar were buried.'" In other words, it was the day when the Romans granted permission for those killed at Beitar during the Bar Kochba revolt (see p. 306) to be buried, which they had forbidden as a punishment to the rebels.
6. "Rabbah and Rav Yosef both said, 'It was the day on which they ceased to fell trees for the altar'" in the Holy Temple. Rav M'nashya added that it was called "the day of the breaking of the scythe," meaning the end of the harvest or the end of the season of cutting down trees. From this point on, the trees were left untouched and allowed to rest.

The fact that the Rabbis offer so many explanations for the holiday is an indication that in their time Tu B'Av was not observed and its ancient origins had been forgotten or suppressed.

(Babylonian Talmud, *Taanit* 31a). After Tu B'Av, the soil and trees are at rest. Now that the silos are filled with grain and the vats with wine, it is the land's time to rest and gather strength; similarly, Tu B'Av became the day when young people could rest from their harvesting work, celebrate, and renew their strength (see pp. 281–84). And there is another parallel between the two days: Tu BiSh'vat is observed sixty days before Passover, and Tu B'Av is observed sixty days before Sukkot.

"So as Not to Embarrass Anyone Who Did Not Have Any"

The Mishnah stresses that on Tu B'Av all the barriers of class were removed and no separation was made between the poorer and wealthier young women. During the lively dancing, the weave of the women's clothes should not reveal a young woman's family connections or social status. In this spirit, the Talmud cites a tradition according to which the young women from privileged families would each borrow a dress from someone of lower social status: "The daughter of the king borrows . . . and all Israel borrow from one another, so as not to embarrass anyone who did not have any [white garments]" (Babylonian Talmud, *Taanit* 31a).

The British anthropologist Victor Turner explored rites of passage—ceremonies conducted at a time of a person's passage from one life stage to another. These ceremonies mark the passage, but they also cause the passage to be realized. The goal of the ceremony is to help the participants address significant moments, and move themselves from one realm into another. In the case of the dancers and young men on Tu B'Av, the goal of the ceremony is to assist the participants to move from being single to being in a couple and preparing to begin a family.[21] Turner showed that the liminal stage of transition is characterized by the celebrants belonging to neither their former nor their new status, and at the same time belonging to both. In other words, a person in a liminal situation is in two different states at once but is not really part of either. According to Turner, when people experience a rite of passage, they are uncategorized as to social group, gender, age, or status. They are like unshaped matter that has lost its old form but has not yet taken on a new form. Only at the end of the ceremony will they acquire a clear and stable identity.

The ceremony on Tu B'Av—its different clothing, possibly unrestrained dancing, young women raising their voices in provocative song in front of the young men, the young men gazing unreservedly at the young women—reflects this momentary suspension of social structures. But this violation of norms was actually intended to reinforce the existing order, to undermine it in a controlled fashion in order to strengthen it. This structured violation creates a situation in which those who have been removed from the continuous flow of life are given an opportunity to examine their reality, which is normally unexamined. This is a distinct period of time set aside for reflection and creative thinking.

Lights and Shadows on the Festival of Love

As far as we know, the celebration of Tu B'Av was never conducted with sacrificial offerings or prayers, but instead with this lively, popular celebration. Nevertheless, heavy shadows fall on the image of these young women who are leisurely prancing about in the hidden reaches of the vineyards. As explored above, the Rabbis offered multiple explanations of Tu B'Av. One explanation is that it was set aside as a holiday in order to mark the return of the tribe of Benjamin into the community of Israel. The Book of Judges (chapters 19–21) details the story of the concubine at Gibeah, who was raped, abused, and killed in an unimaginably cruel fashion by the Benjaminites when she entered a town in their territory. This event led to a bloody civil war, in which the people of Benjamin fought the other tribes, and myriads were killed. The war nearly put an end to the members of the tribe of Benjamin, and when the rest of the Israelites decided not to marry off their daughters to men from Benjamin, the tribe was under threat of extinction. Tu B'Av marks the end to that threat. The happy celebration, then, covers up an awful trauma in the life of the young nation. The dances on Tu B'Av may have been created in response to an instruction from the ostracized elders of Benjamin to the members of the tribe to abduct wives for themselves, lest the tribe be wiped out:

> So they instructed the Benjaminites as follows: "Go and lie in wait in the vineyards. As soon as you see the girls of Shiloh coming out to join in the dances, come out from the vineyards; let each of you seize a wife from among the girls of Shiloh, and be off for the land of Benjamin." (Judges 21:20–21)

Dr. Hannah Pinhasi, a scholar of Talmud, contrasts the story of the concubine—who found herself alone in the dark among men who assaulted her—with the women gathered on Tu B'Av—who wore white and danced together, happy and safe in their bodies. Pinhasi suggests that this holiday brings that trauma to the fore and offers a response to it.[22] Her comments on the *tikkun*—the correction and repair—accomplished by Tu B'Av are moving and effective, but there is still a need for further *tikkun* of this holiday. According to the Mishnah's depiction of the Israelite young women's dance, the men are active participants, while the women are passive subjects: men

---

Victor Turner (1920–83), who gained renown for his studies of the Ndembu tribe in Zambia, pointed out that, in a structured manner, rites of passage break structures of thought and behavior of the people who experience them: they have no property or familial or social status. They stand naked in a situation of "sacred poverty"—an egalitarian state shared by everyone in that situation. Turner named this state "communitas." Communitas is a situation of joy, shared identification, equality, and the erasure of difference. One's strong sense of identity by class, gender, or group disappears or becomes irrelevant. This is a moment both in time and outside of it that escapes every effort at definition and stands out in its fluidity against the stability of both the situation that preceded it and the one that will follow, which are characterized by a clear, unchanging structure.[23]

The month of Av ushers in a time of diminished joy and celebration. "But in the olden days," teacher and author Yom Tov Levinsky (1899–1973) explains, "when Israel lived on its land under its grapevine and fig tree, the period of Av was a radiant time in the life of the people.... In the vineyard—the harvest was coming on in full force, and songs and cries of joy over the flagons of new wine arose from the Carmel. The almond harvest also arrived, [with] the carpet of dates drying in clusters, the cooking of dates and pomegranates and the like. The songbirds whose music had halted with the heat of the summer in Tammuz would rise at the morning watch, suffused with morning dew, to offer their sweet songs once again."[24]

observe, women are observed; men choose, women are chosen. For this reason, the full *tikkun* of this holiday will only come, in my view, when young people dance for their own enjoyment, not subject to piercing stares, comments, or—worse—inappropriate actions.

Squelching the Myth That Keeps Popping Up

The Torah speaks about three kinds of produce with which *Eretz Yisrael* is blessed: *dagan* (grain), *tirosh* (fresh grape wine), and *yitzhar* (fine vegetable oil). Wheat and barley are the grains, grapes are the source of the new wine, and olives are the source of the oil.[25] Two of those crops enjoy a pilgrimage holiday close to the time when they are ripe: barley at Passover and wheat at Shavuot, and it is possible that the olive harvest is close to Sukkot. But what about the grapevine, which gives us the fruit that makes wine—the elixir that, in the words of the Psalmist, "cheers a person's heart" (Psalm 104:15)? Why doesn't the grapevine have the privilege of having its own holiday? When Joshua and Caleb came back from their scouting assignment in the Land of Israel, did they not bring with them a gigantic cluster of grapes (Numbers 13:23)? There is reason to think that our sources suppressed traditions of an ancient wine festival, perhaps because it was a holiday of unrestrained passions like the festivals of Dionysus in Greek mythology or the Roman festivals of Bacchus. It may be that Israelite culture extinguished this holiday because it endangered public order and morals. The holiday disappeared, leaving only traces behind.[26]

Now it is up to us to ask what form we would like to give to Tu B'Av—the ancient, newly renewed holiday of love.

It appears that a few verses in the Bible hint at ancient wine celebrations. For example, the Book of Judges describes, "They went out into the fields, gathered and trod out the vintage of their vineyards, and made a festival" (9:27). In the Temple Scroll, one of the Dead Sea Scrolls discovered in the mid-twentieth century, there is also mention of a festival that celebrates the new harvest's fresh wine, celebrated seven weeks after Shavuot. Seven weeks after that, another holiday was observed—the festival of the new oil. We have no evidence of how these holidays were celebrated, nor even of who celebrated them.

Prayer of the Month

Praying for Love

Tu B'Av, the festival of love, falls, of course, during the month of Av—the month of the Temple's destruction. It is also a month of consolation and of faith that a covenant can be maintained even in times of crisis. That is why Av is a good month to think about prayers about love.

The Torah does not command us to love our parents nor to love our children or our spouses, but it does explicitly command us to love God; it even specifies how: "With all your heart, with all your soul, and with all your might" (Deuteronomy 6:5). This begs the question, though—how is it possible to command love? Can one really be required to *feel* something? Perhaps this mitzvah is commanded precisely because it does not come naturally for everyone. It is not simple to have the consciousness of loving God and knowing God in all our ways.

The requirement to love God appears immediately after the best known verse in Jewish prayer: *Sh'ma Yisrael, Adonai Eloheinu, Adonai Echad*, "Hear, O Israel, the Eternal is our God, the Eternal is One!" (Deuteronomy 6:4). If we accept *Adonai*, the Eternal, as our God and believe in God's unity, loving God and all of Creation comes naturally. The traditional Jewish prayer service has wrapped the prayer *Sh'ma Yisrael* in a sort of love sandwich. Before it we recite the blessing known as *Ahavat Olam* or *Ahavah Rabbah*, "the blessing of love," in which the people Israel is promised God's eternal love. After it we recite the lines that follow *Sh'ma*, which command us to love God "with all your heart, with all your soul, and with all your might." Only after God has promised that God loves Israel can God expect Israel to requite God's love with theirs; God does not demand that Israel love God until God has promised to love them.

> *Ahavat Olam*
> Everlasting love You offered Your people Israel
> by teaching us Torah and mitzvot, laws and precepts.
> Therefore, Eternal our God, when we lie down and when we rise up,
> we will meditate on Your laws and Your commandments.
> We will rejoice in Your Torah forever.
> Day and night we will reflect on them
> for they are our life and doing them lengthens our days.
> Never remove Your love from us.
> Praise to You, Adonai, who loves Your people Israel.[27]
>
> ***Sh'ma Yisrael, Adonai Eloheinu, Adonai Echad!***
> **Hear, O Israel, the Eternal is our God, the Eternal is One!**
>
> You shall love the Eternal your God with all your heart, with all your soul, and with all your might.
> Take to heart these instructions with which I charge you this day.
> Impress them upon your children.

The system of *g'matria* assigns each Hebrew letter a numerical value (*alef* = 1, *bet* = 2, etc.). Therefore, the numerical value of the Hebrew word *echad*, "one," is 13, which is also the numerical value of the word *ahavah*, "love." Where there is love between two individuals—*ahavah* + *ahavah* / 13 + 13—the total is 26; this is also the numerical value of the unpronounceable four-letter name of God (the ineffable name of God, the Eternal), which we replace with the Hebrew word *Adonai*. This numerological midrash indicates that true love between two people is a way to bring God's presence into the world. May we be privileged to enjoy the inspiration of divine presence wherever we go.

Recite them when you stay at home and when you are away,
when you lie down and when you get up.
Bind them as a sign on your hand and let them serve as a symbol on your forehead;
inscribe them on the doorposts of your house and on your gates.[28]

(Deuteronomy 11:4–9)

Love is the foundation of the relationship between God and God's people and is not dependent on anything external. God's love for God's people has no rational explanation, which is always the case with love. As Moses said, "It is not because you are the most numerous of peoples that the Eternal set the Eternal's heart on you and chose you—indeed you are the smallest of peoples. But it was because the Eternal loved you" (Deuteronomy 7:7–8).[29] Israel is called upon to return God's love ("You shall love the Eternal your God"), for God loves Israel ("Everlasting love You offered Your people Israel"). The commandment to love God is, as we have said, infinite and absolute—"with all your heart, with all your soul, and with all your might"—and in every situation—"when you stay at home and when you are away, when you lie down and when you get up."

The great Jewish thinker Franz Rosenzweig (1886–1929) argued that God's love for humanity is the command to humankind to love the world. The reverse is also true: humanity's love for God means loving the other.[30] In this spirit, the poet Dr. Marcia Falk (b. 1946, United States) has published her own version of the *Sh'ma* to be recited in a congregation, based on the traditional text and emphasizing the ways to love God:

Sh'ma: Communal Declaration of Faith
Marcia Falk

Hear, O Israel—
The divine abounds everywhere
and dwells in everything;
the many are One.

Loving life
and its mysterious source
with all our heart
and all our spirit
all our senses and strength,
we take upon ourselves
and into ourselves
these promises:
to care for the earth
and those who live upon it,
to pursue justice and peace,
to love kindness and compassion.
We will teach this to our children

throughout the passage of the day—
as we dwell in our homes
and as we go on our journeys,
from the time we rise
until we fall asleep.
And may our actions
be faithful to our words
that our children's children
may live to know:
Truth and kindness have embraced,
peace and justice have kissed
and are one.³¹

שְׁמַע, יִשְׂרָאֵל —
לֵאלֹהוּת אַלְפֵי פָּנִים,
מְלֹא עוֹלָם שְׁכִינָתָהּ,
רִבּוּי פָּנֶיהָ אֶחָד.

נֹאהַב אֶת־הַחַיִּים
וְאֶת עֵין הַחַיִּים
בְּכָל־לְבָבֵנוּ וּבְכָל־נַפְשֵׁנוּ
וּבְכָל־מְאֹדֵנוּ.
יִהְיוּ הַדְּבָרִים הָאֵלֶּה
בִּלְבָבֵנוּ וּבְקִרְבֵּנוּ:
שְׁמִירַת אֶרֶץ וְיוֹשְׁבֶיהָ,
רְדִיפַת צֶדֶק וְשָׁלוֹם,
אַהֲבַת חֶסֶד וְרַחֲמִים.
נְשַׁנְּנָם
לִבְנוֹתֵינוּ וּלְבָנֵינוּ
וּנְדַבֵּר בָּם
בְּשִׁבְתֵּנוּ בְּבֵיתֵנוּ,
בְּלֶכְתֵּנוּ בַדֶּרֶךְ,
בְּשָׁכְבֵנוּ וּבְקוּמֵנוּ.
וְיִהְיוּ מַעֲשֵׂינוּ
נֶאֱמָנִים לִדְבָרֵינוּ,
לְמַעַן יֵדְעוּ דּוֹר אַחֲרוֹן,
בָּנוֹת וּבָנִים יִוָּלֵדוּ:
חֶסֶד וֶאֱמֶת נִפְגָּשׁוּ,
צֶדֶק וְשָׁלוֹם נָשָׁקוּ.

The powerful proclamation of divine love and the demand for love in return has stimulated many people to question about the difficult trials the Jewish people has faced. The poet Eliaz Cohen, one of the shining leaders of the religious poets' group Mashiv HaRuach, wrote a prayer-poem during the difficult days of the Second Intifada, the wave of Palestinian terror attacks in the Land of Israel during the early 2000s. The poem, which is presented as "a *yichud* [a kind of *piyut*] for the Days of Awe," turns the traditional language of *Sh'ma* on its head; instead of demanding that Israel remember that "*Adonai* is our God, *Adonai* is One," the poem demands that God remember God's people Israel and love Israel with all God's heart, and with all God's soul, and with all God's might:

Sh'ma, Adonai / Hear, O Lord
Eliaz Cohen

Hear, O Lord, Israel, Your people, Israel is one

And You shall love Israel Your people

With all Your heart

And with all Your soul

And with all Your might

And these children who are being killed for You
    daily shall be

upon Your heart

And You shall teach them diligently in Your heavens

And You shall talk of them:

When You sit in Your house

And when You walk by the way

And when You lie down and when You rise

And You shall bind them as a sign upon

Your hand (phosphorescent blue numbers) and they
    shall be as frontlets

between Your eyes (like the sniper's shots)

And You shall write them (in blood) on the
    doorposts of Your house

And on Your gates³²

The poem's defiant tone challenging God—for example, in the call to God to take the numbers that the Nazis had tattooed into the arms of Jews ("phosphorescent blue numbers") and make them into *t'fillin*—was shocking to many readers. Some thought that the poem was a sacrilege, while others regarded it as an expression of profound faith, a release of anger, and an expression of feverish expectation of God's self-revelation and love in a pained world.

ELUL

Zodiac Sign: Virgo | Tribe of the Month: Zebulun
Breastplate Stone: Amtheyst/*Yahalom*

The name Elul is borrowed from the name of the Babylonian month Elulu or Ululu. Some believe the name is derived from the Akkadian verb *ululu*, meaning "purify." It may be that the verb originally referred to a Babylonian temple purification ceremony and as such is very appropriate to Jewish tradition, since Elul is a month of preparation for the Days of Awe and the new year.

This month is first mentioned in the Book of Nehemiah, where we read that the rebuilding of the wall around Jerusalem was completed "on the twenty-fifth of Elul" (Nehemiah 6:15).

An additional name for the month is "the sixth month" (Haggai 1:1), according to the count of months beginning with Nisan.

Kavanah: A Meditation for Elul

In moments of great stillness
when we contemplate things which no mouth can utter—
at that hour, let us deepen the insight that we have.
Let us look inward.
Let us lift up our lives as if we were lifting a bucket from a well.
It is incumbent upon us to strive for self-understanding.
It is incumbent upon us to balance the forces working in our souls.[1]

The obligation to do *tikkun*—that is, to foster spiritual correction or healing—was at the heart of the theology of Rabbi Israel Salanter (1810–83), the founder of the modern Mussar movement, the goal of which is to correct—*l'takein*—our moral qualities. He taught that it is not sufficient to perform the mitzvot in a technical manner; instead what matters is our commitment to worship God with honesty and intention (*kavanah*) in thought and inner feeling.

A popular folk story about Rabbi Israel Salanter describes that one day he was walking somewhere in his city late at night when he saw a light shining in one of the homes. When he went in, he saw a tailor bent over his work by the light of a candle about to burn out. The rabbi inquired of the man why he was working at such a late hour and with a light so small that at any moment it could be entirely extinguished; shouldn't he be lying down and going to sleep? The tailor said, "As long as the flame is still burning, one can still fix what's wrong."

Rabbi Salanter was very moved by what he had heard, and he understood the profound truth in it: "The lifebreath of a person is the lamp of the Eternal" (Proverbs 20:27), and when it is burning it is not only *possible* to fix things—we are *obligated* to fix things! According to other traditions Rabbi Salanter met a cobbler rather than a tailor, but regardless, it is said that for many days he walked about in his room, pacing back and forth, repeating to himself, "As long as the flame is still burning, one can still fix what's wrong!"

AT THE GATES OF ELUL

WHEN I SAY THE WORD "Elul," I taste the end of summer, feel the days getting shorter, anticipate the beginning of the school year, and know that it is time to start preparing for the Days of Awe—days of reflection and thought. Elul closes the circle of the Hebrew year, but at the same time it is already anticipating the new year with Rosh HaShanah and Yom Kippur.

Elul is the place schoolchildren come after summer vacation, and amazingly they seem to have grown a year—they're a little taller, their voices have changed, and they look at each other with slight surprise at these changes. Their notebooks are pristine, and their books still have the scent of the printing press. Their hearts are full of promises for the new year, and everything is still open and possible. Elul is a month of preparing one's heart, taking stock of oneself, and doing *t'shuvah* (repentance/return) in advance of the Days of Awe. The month of Elul summons us back home from all the physical and mental places where we may have been and turns us inward toward careful reflection.

According to one midrashic tradition, Adam was created on Rosh HaShanah (*Vayikra Rabbah* 29:1), and according to another, the entire world was created on Rosh HaShanah (Babylonian Talmud, *Rosh HaShanah* 11a). Either way, Elul—the month preceding these events—is like a preparatory course for Creation, the beginning before the beginning. Elul is the end of the year, but it is also a birth canal—the passageway through which the new year begins.

The name "Elul," which "made *aliyah*" from Babylon with the rest of the names of the months, is first mentioned in the Book of Nehemiah (6:15). The name sounds both strange and familiar, odd and intimate, as it rolls off the tongue. Despite the fact that it is not a Hebrew name, our ancestors ascribed a meaning to it. There are several suggestions are some that we read the Hebrew word as an acronym—assigning different words to the four letters of "Elul," א-ל-ו-ל, *alef-lamed-vav-lamed*—that reveals the month's true character and purpose. Here are three of those suggestions.

The most widely known reading of "Elul" as an acronym comes from a verse in the Song of Songs (6:3), the beginning of which is "I am my beloved's, and my beloved's is mine," or in Hebrew, "*ani l'dodi v'dodi li*." (Note that in Hebrew, the *alef* is silent and adopts the sound of its vowel, while the *vav* functions as both a letter making the "v" sound and as a vowel making the "u" sound.) As we know, Jewish tradition regards the Song of Songs as a dialogue expressing the love between God and the people Israel. This interpretation reminds us that the month of Elul, the month of mercy and forgiveness, is a month of unusual closeness between us and the Blessed Holy One. It is as though we stand face-to-face and yearn for renewed closeness and connection, like a renewed love between a couple for whom routine and its challenges have led them to grow distant from one another.

A different approach is suggested by the phrase "to one another and presents to the poor"—*ish l'rei-eihu umatanot la-evyonim*—in Esther 9:22. This chapter of Esther describes the Jews who turned the day of their near deaths into a day of feasting and celebration. These four words from the verse relate to two different kinds of connections (1) those between us and "one another," perhaps the friends and relatives we hurt during the year and (2) between us and "the poor," the weak and needy in our society for whom we are required to provide.

From Time to Time → Dalia Marx

A third verse with a string of words whose acronym is "Elul" is found in Deuteronomy 30:6: "Then the Eternal your God will open up your heart and the hearts—*et l'vavcha v'et l'vav*—of your offspring to love the Eternal." This verse speaks about the role of God, who actively assists in the preparation of our hearts. After all, Elul is the month of preparing our hearts for *t'shuvah*.

These three verses all harbor within them the name of the month in acronym form, and they each symbolize the vast expanse created by the circle of *t'shuvah* that begins in Elul. The dual clauses "I am my beloved's, and my beloved's is mine" in this accepted interpretation refers to our special connection with our heavenly parent. The topic of "to one another and presents to the poor" from Esther refers to our obligation to create fair and caring connections among people. And the verse from Deuteronomy emphasizes the divine favor we enjoy and the work of profound *t'shuvah* that is expected of us.

Elul's soul-searching and *t'shuvah* are individual and personal, but they take place within a larger matrix of mutual responsibility and an effort to seek the face of God and other people. Jewish tradition teaches us that the best way to get to the end is to begin. Elul concludes the Hebrew year, but it also flows into the year to come, as a month of *cheshbon hanefesh* (self-evaluation), doing *t'shuvah*, and preparing our hearts for the Days of Awe, the new year, and its blessings.

The first *iyun* in this chapter is about *S'lichot*, the special prayers said late at night or at dawn (depending on community and individual practice) that prepare our hearts for Yom Kippur. The second *iyun* we will take up is the shofar—that primal blast of sound like the cry of a baby at the moment of its birth—and its unique mysteries. While these first two *iyunim* deal with ancient customs (the shofar sounds go back to the Torah, and we know about *S'lichot* from as early as the eighth century CE), the topic of the third *iyun* is a new custom taking shape in contemporary Jewish life—the celebration of a New Year for Animals on the first of Elul. Psalm 27, which is read in many communities every day from the first of Elul up to the end of Sukkot, is the Poem of the Month. As usual, we conclude the chapter with the Prayer of the Month, but this time it will not be a prayer in the usual sense but rather a reading of the Thirteen Attributes of God that is central to the *S'lichot* prayers.

According to tradition, after smashing the first set of tablets of the Ten Commandments, Moses ascended Mount Sinai a second time on the first of Elul, and he stayed there forty days and forty nights until descending with the second set of tablets. The Hebrew calendar invites us to experience the anxiety and anticipation that our ancestors experienced while Moses remained on the mountain. Those forty days that begin on the first of Elul bring us right to the tenth of Tishrei, to Yom Kippur—the climax of the process of self-evaluation and *t'shuvah*.

The verse from Deuteronomy is taken from the weekly portion *Nitzavim*, which we read at the end of Elul on the Shabbat before Rosh HaShanah. This *parashah* deals with *t'shuvah*, which will lighten the Jews' punishment if they sin:

When all these things befall you—the blessing and the curse that I have set before you—and you take them to heart amidst the various nations to which the Eternal your God has banished you, and you return to the Eternal your God, and you and your children heed God's command with all your heart and soul, just as I enjoin upon you this day, then the Eternal your God will restore your fortunes and take you back in love. [God] will bring you together again from all the peoples where the Eternal your God has scattered you. . . . Then the Eternal your God will open up your heart and the hearts of your offspring—to love the Eternal your God with all your heart and soul, in order that you may live. . . . You will again heed the Eternal and obey all the divine commandments that I enjoin upon you this day. And the Eternal your God will grant you abounding prosperity in all your undertakings, in the issue of your womb, the offspring of your cattle, and the produce of your soil. For the Eternal will again delight in your well-being as in that of your ancestors, since you will be heeding the Eternal your God and keeping the divine commandments and laws that are recorded in this book of the Teaching—once you return to the Eternal your God with all your heart and soul. (Deuteronomy 30:1–3, 6, 8–10)

Many verbs in this passage are derived from the root *shin-vav-bet*, "return," which is also the root of the word *t'shuvah*—one of the central themes of the Days of Awe. The idea is not that we necessarily repent of wrongdoing, but that we can return to a place of goodness—implying that our origins are good. A *t'shuvah* is also translated as "response," so our acts of *t'shuvah* are responses that we believe will be received by someone—in this case, by God. *Parashat Nitzavim* is always read just before Rosh HaShanah, and it helps keep these ideas of *t'shuvah* at the forefront of our minds as we head into the Days of Awe.

Tishrei   Marcheshvan   Kislev   Tevet   Sh'vat   Adar   Nisan   Iyar   Sivan   Tammuz   Av   Elul

Poem of the Month

The Stuff of Which Life Is Made: Psalm 27, "The Eternal Is My Light and My Deliverance"

THE PSALMS are colorful living tissues that weave together the fabric of our lives: security and strength, anxiety and loss, wonder at the amazing majesty of Creation, faith in the likelihood of goodness, love, loneliness, and longing. Not all the psalms include all those things, but the Book of Psalms—the longest book in the Hebrew Bible—bears within it innumerable feelings and human situations. Psalm 27, "The Eternal Is My Light and My Deliverance," is a characteristic example of this rich weave. Many communities recite this psalm from Rosh Chodesh Elul through Hoshana Rabbah, the seventh day of Sukkot, while others recite it year-round.

¹ Of David. the Eternal is my light and my deliverance— from whom should I feel fright? The Eternal is the stronghold of my life— from whom should I feel terror? ² When evildoers approach me in battle to feed on my flesh— my pursuers, my adversaries— they have stumbled, they have fallen down. ³ If a camp encamps against me, my heart will not fear; if a war arises against me, in this I would trust: ⁴ One thing have I sought from the Eternal—how I long for it: that I may live in the House of the Eternal all the days of my life; that I may look upon the sweetness of the Eternal, and spend time in the Palace; ⁵ that God might hide me in God's sukkah on a day of trouble, hide me in the hiding places of God's tent, raise me high upon a rock. ⁶ Now my head rises high above my enemies roundabout, and in God's tent I'll offer offerings to the sound of *t'ruah*. I shall sing and chant praises to the Eternal!	¹ לְדָוִד יְיָ אוֹרִי וְיִשְׁעִי מִמִּי אִירָא יְיָ מָעוֹז־חַיַּי מִמִּי אֶפְחָד׃ ² בִּקְרֹב עָלַי מְרֵעִים לֶאֱכֹל אֶת־ בְּשָׂרִי צָרַי וְאֹיְבַי לִי הֵמָּה כָשְׁלוּ וְנָפָלוּ׃ ³ אִם־תַּחֲנֶה עָלַי מַחֲנֶה לֹא־יִירָא לִבִּי אִם־תָּקוּם עָלַי מִלְחָמָה בְּזֹאת אֲנִי בוֹטֵחַ׃ ⁴ אַחַת שָׁאַלְתִּי מֵאֵת־יְיָ אוֹתָהּ אֲבַקֵּשׁ שִׁבְתִּי בְּבֵית־יְיָ כָּל־יְמֵי חַיַּי לַחֲזוֹת בְּנֹעַם־יְיָ וּלְבַקֵּר בְּהֵיכָלוֹ׃ ⁵ כִּי יִצְפְּנֵנִי בְּסֻכֹּה בְּיוֹם רָעָה יַסְתִּ־ רֵנִי בְּסֵתֶר אָהֳלוֹ בְּצוּר יְרוֹמְמֵנִי׃ ⁶ וְעַתָּה יָרוּם רֹאשִׁי עַל אֹיְבַי סְבִיבוֹתַי וְאֶזְבְּחָה בְאָהֳלוֹ זִבְחֵי תְרוּעָה אָשִׁירָה וַאֲזַמְּרָה לַיְיָ׃

From Time to Time → Dalia Marx

⁷ Hear, Eternal, my voice— I am crying out! Be gracious to me, answer me!	⁷ שְׁמַע־יְיָ קוֹלִי אֶקְרָא וְחָנֵּנִי וַעֲנֵנִי:
⁸ My heart has said to You: "Seek my face." I am seeking Your face, Eternal—	⁸ לְךָ אָמַר לִבִּי בַּקְּשׁוּ פָנָי אֶת־פָּנֶיךָ יְיָ אֲבַקֵּשׁ:
⁹ Do not hide Your face from me. Do not turn Your servant away in anger, You have been my help— Do not forsake me, do not abandon me, God of my deliverance!	⁹ אַל־תַּסְתֵּר פָּנֶיךָ מִמֶּנִּי אַל־תַּט־בְּאַף עַבְדֶּךָ עֶזְרָתִי הָיִיתָ אַל־תִּטְּשֵׁנִי וְאַל־תַּעַזְבֵנִי אֱלֹהֵי יִשְׁעִי:
¹⁰ For my father and my mother have abandoned me, Yet the Eternal gathers me up.	¹⁰ כִּי־אָבִי וְאִמִּי עֲזָבוּנִי וַיְיָ יַאַסְפֵנִי:
¹¹ Make Your path apparent to me, guide me in the upright road because of those up ahead who lie in wait for me.	¹¹ הוֹרֵנִי יְיָ דַּרְכֶּךָ וּנְחֵנִי בְּאֹרַח מִישׁוֹר לְמַעַן שׁוֹרְרָי:
¹² Do not hand me over to the lust of my adversaries— for false witnesses have risen against me, puffing violently!	¹² אַל־תִּתְּנֵנִי בְּנֶפֶשׁ צָרָי כִּי קָמוּ־בִי עֵדֵי־שֶׁקֶר וִיפֵחַ חָמָס:
¹³ Had I not the faith that I would see the goodness of God in the land of life…	¹³ לוּלֵא הֶאֱמַנְתִּי לִרְאוֹת בְּטוּב־יְיָ בְּאֶרֶץ חַיִּים:
¹⁴ Wait with hope for the Eternal fill your waiting with hope in the Eternal; let your heart be strong and of good courage, and wait hopefully for the Eternal.²	¹⁴ קַוֵּה אֶל־יְיָ חֲזַק וְיַאֲמֵץ לִבֶּךָ וְקַוֵּה אֶל־יְיָ:

Why was this particular psalm chosen to be read during this period? The answer is not simple, since the poem's content is complex to the point of being confusing. It includes a declaration of faith, a plea, despair, and hope. Many chapters of Psalms begin with a description of a plight and then continue to describe being saved, but here the process is different: the poem opens with trust in God but moves to a feeling of being alone and orphaned. The question of why Psalm 27 was chosen is underscored by the fact that it does not speak directly to the themes of the Days of Awe, such as forgiveness and repentance. Nonetheless, I will try to explain this far from self-evident choice.

Psalm 27 begins with a declaration of trust, made with a certain bravado: "The Eternal is my light and my deliverance—from whom should I feel fright? The Eternal is the stronghold of my life—from whom should I feel terror?" (v. 1), but as it continues we hear the gnawing fear of the child has of abandonment: "**Do not forsake me**, do not abandon me, God of my deliverance!" (v. 9). Here the appeal is in the second person: the poet speaks *to* God, not *about* God. Even the poet's father and mother may abandon them, but not God, the ultimate parent.

In the middle of the psalm there is longing for a place that is protected and safe: "That I may live in the House of the Eternal all the days of my life" (v. 4). This is the human desire

The memory of impotence and fear as we watched Mom or Dad's back recede into the distance after they dropped us off at a new day care, preschool, or other unfamiliar setting is common to many of us and is carved into our psyche. The words "For my father and my mother have abandoned me" express the most profound sense of aloneness that one can experience.

Indeed, even if it is at a very advanced age, at some point our parents depart from this world. In the end, we are left as orphans. That is the way of the world, and that is how it ought to be—not, heaven forbid, in the opposite order. Nonetheless, the poet's sense of having been abandoned touches our hearts, and it stands in contradiction or opposition to God's eternal kindness: "Yet the Eternal gathers me up."

Even though it seems that Psalm 27 was not composed particularly for the month of Elul and the Days of Awe, some readers have found hints that connect it to these days.

A reference to shofar blowing on Rosh HaShanah is hidden in the words "If a war arises against me" (v. 3), because in war the shofar blasts served to summon the troops and threaten the enemy. And perhaps the sound of those blasts is mentioned in the phrase "I'll offer offerings to the sound of t'ruah" (v. 6), with t'ruah being one of the calls for blowing the shofar.

The grand entry of the High Priest into the Holy of Holies in the Temple on Yom Kippur may be discerned in the words "That I may look upon the sweetness of the Eternal, and spend time in the Palace" (v. 4). Perhaps this connection also underlies the words "Hear, Eternal, my voice—I am crying out! Be gracious to me, answer me!" (v. 7).

The name of the Sukkot festival appears as well: "That God might hide me in God's sukkah on a day of trouble" (v. 5).

Finally, the name of the month, Elul, is encoded in reverse in the first word of the psalm's penultimate verse: "Had I not" in Hebrew is lulé—Elul in reverse! The traditional Masoretic text of the psalm marks the word with a dot over and under every letter— לּוּלֵ֗א —perhaps to point out this connection.

"that I may look upon the sweetness of the Eternal"—that is, to experience a deep and extended divine revelation. And even if at the beginning of the psalm the poet brags about not being afraid of enemies or of those who seek to do harm, the psalm continues by expressing a desire to return to a safe place, perhaps a kind of divine, motherly womb: "That God might hide me in God's sukkah on a day of trouble" (v. 5).

The psalm concludes on a note of hope, without which there is no human existence: "Wait with hope for the Eternal—Let your heart be strong and of good courage, and wait hopefully for the Eternal" (v. 14).

The aggregation of contradictory emotions in the psalm lie at the heart of the human experience, and for that reason our predecessors regarded it as an appropriate psalm for this time of year.

"Finishing without Air"

The Psalmist has their say, and at the critical moment they sound like someone left without words, without air: "Had I not the faith that I would see the goodness of God in the land of life . . ." (Psalm 27:13)—in other words, if I did not believe in seeing God's beneficence, then . . . But the Psalmist does not continue that thought. The possibility of losing faith is too much to bear; it cannot be uttered. Instead, the poet concludes in a festive tone: "Wait with hope for the Eternal. . . . let your heart be strong and of good courage, and wait hopefully for the Eternal" (v. 14).

This long, speech-like psalm ends with deep emotions that cannot really be expressed in words. And so it is with the prayers of the Days of Awe and the days preceding them that help us prepare—the prayers are long and wordy, but what takes place inside the worshipers, and what happens during those prayers, is beyond words. No words can encapsulate this mix of feelings, worries, and hopes. And just as the great drama of the psalm takes place within the soul of the Psalmist, so too the drama, tension, fear, love, and so on all take place within the souls of those praying on the Days of Awe—each one on our own and all of us together.

The psalm's prevailing message is one of hope and tenacious adherence to faith as a power that reinforces us and sustains us. This is a message that encourages you to choose life. From Rabbi Yehodaya Amir I have learned that the last verse of the psalm—"Wait with hope for the Eternal. . . . Let your heart be strong and of good courage, and wait hopefully for the Eternal"—is constructed in a spiral form: first one must choose a stance of hope, and in consequence a process of strengthening one's heart and gaining confidence may occur, which in turn brings us back to the original command, "Wait hopefully for the Eternal," but at a higher level.

Who Knows Sixty?

About 60 of the 150 psalms in the Book of Psalms have entered the liturgy, not including innumerable isolated verses and expressions from psalms that are woven throughout our prayer books. These psalms are recited on many and varied occasions, starting early in the day with *P'sukei D'Zimrah*, a section of psalms that comes at the beginning of the morning service and concludes with the psalm of the day, and ending with the chapters of psalms recited as part of the bedtime *Sh'ma* (pp. 115–18). Various psalms accompany the weekly and annual cycles and appear in *Kabbalat Shabbat*, before *Birkat HaMazon*, in *Hallel*, and on many other occasions. Many people read certain parts of the Book of Psalms each day, completing the entire book each week or month. There is a custom of reading psalms as a petitionary prayer for someone who is ill or as a memorial to someone no longer alive. Many people even keep a tiny copy of Psalms in their wallet or car as an amulet for divine protection.

The Book of Psalms is one of our ancient prayer books that tradition ascribes to King David, who is known as the "sweet singer of Israel." Readers in our time are likely to find some of the psalms' language difficult and the images distant. Nevertheless, this book is a never-ending source for expressing a wide range of feelings, of consolation and empowerment, of empathy and faith. There is a reason the psalms are one of the most fertile sources for the composition of new *piyutim*, Hebrew poems, and the like.

Quite a different expression of faith in the possibility of building a bridge across grave despair—although similar in its "nevertheless" feeling—can be found in this poem written by Rachel Bluwstein in 1923 in Petach Tikva:

In the Garden
Rachel Bluwstein

On an Elul morning the world is pink and azure,
bestowing consolation.
Should I get up, shake off yesterday's dust,
believe in tomorrow's creation?
Should I, humble of heart, welcome the yoke,
for my fate find justification?

Among the rows and furrows, a young lass will arrive,
the faucet will flow.
She sprays droplets of life, not a thirsty stalk
is abandoned, laid low.
Perhaps God's willful heart can be forgiven,
perhaps begin again anew?[3]

An Unapologetic Look at *S'lichot*

If you happen to walk through Jerusalem's busy Machaneh Yehudah shuk on a Friday morning, you will probably hear the word *s'lichah* from the people pushing past you to buy their Shabbat treats. *S'lichah* means "forgive"—in this case, "forgive me for rushing past you to buy my chocolate rugelach!" *S'lichah* is also a liturgical genre of penitential prayers and supplications recited in religious worship at designated times, inviting us for reflection and soul-searching. They are recited particularly before and on Yom Kippur. *S'lichot* (the plural of *s'lichah*) is the name for a particular worship service. Different *minhagim* (customs) dictate exactly when *S'lichot* is recited; typically, Sephardic communities recite it during the entire month of Elul through Yom Kippur, while Ashkenazic communities begin *S'lichot* just before Rosh HaShanah (except on Shabbat and Rosh Chodesh), and in many Reform congregations it is recited on the Saturday evening before Rosh HaShanah. It is customary to offer *S'lichot* during times when the congregation does not normally meet—late at night or at dawn—to invite people to think in a creative way about their lives, choices, and commitments. No matter when it is recited, *S'lichot* is meant to help us concentrate and prepare ourselves for the Days of Awe.

A predawn chill wind blows affectionately over people still bleary from a sleep that has ended too soon; parkas are zipped up in the goosebump chill. It's crowded in the tiny women's section, but there is the scent of a bundle of mint leaves in the hand of the *shamash* (beadle) who patiently welcomes the clusters of schoolchildren who have come on a field trip for a taste of *S'lichot*. The taste of artemisia tea in glasses, poured by one of the kerchiefed women, a comfort for the throat at a Jerusalem autumn sunrise. The wavering voice of the elderly *chazan*, his plaintive tone nearly a sob, and the response of the congregation: "*Yah*, hear Your unfortunates, who seek out Your face. Heavenly God, do not close Your ears to our cries from this place." And on the way out, the feel of the hot pita from the bakery, the taste of zaatar (hyssop) spice . . . And that's it. Time to go home and go back to sleep. After the early morning "*S'lichot* tour," there's no school for the rest of the day. So it was year after year for me, and later, for my children. The memory of *S'lichot* in the picturesque Nachlaot neighborhood of Jerusalem is burned into my hard disk: the irregular time of day, the unfamiliar synagogue, the mysterious text. It was the foreign nature of it all that made the ceremony into something mysterious and interesting. But that is also what kept it a distant experience, something anthropological, a lovely and fascinating folklore that didn't entirely belong to me. During the course of my army service, I came to understand that I had to transform the *S'lichot* ceremony into something meaningful and relevant to my life, rather than a ceremony that I visited but was not a partner in shaping. In our Haifa apartment, my fellow roommates and I would get up (almost) every morning before the first light of dawn, gather in one of the rooms, pray and sing together, and try to connect to that place in the soul that has so much yearning and longing for forgiveness . . .

With Moses on the Mountain

S'lichot services combine prayers, *piyutim*, and biblical verses about confessing sins, requesting forgiveness, and doing *t'shuvah*, but also about remembering the nation's suffering and expression of hope for redemption and for repair of the covenant with God. *S'lichot* prayers are said on fast days and on various occasions during the year, but when we talk about *S'lichot* without additional specification, we mean the special liturgy recited as we prepare for the Days of Awe and during the Ten Days of Repentance between Rosh HaShanah and Yom Kippur. Their purpose is to prepare our heart in a continuing process that leads up to Yom Kippur. At the heart of the *S'lichot* liturgy is the recitation of God's Thirteen Attributes of Mercy (pp. 351–55) and a short alphabetical confessional (*Ashamnu*, *Bagadnu*; see pp. 35–39). The customs of reciting

From Time to Time → Dalia Marx

S'lichot are different from region to region and from community to community. The practice of Sephardic, Middle Eastern, and North African Jewish communities is to begin reciting *S'lichot* the day after Rosh Chodesh Elul—the date on which, according to tradition, Moses returned to the summit of Mount Sinai for a second time after smashing the first set of tablets. We accompany him, so to speak, with the recitation of *S'lichot*. Ashkenazic Jews begin reciting *S'lichot* on the Saturday night before Rosh HaShanah or the previous week's Saturday. Sephardic Jews generally recite an established, fixed liturgy of *S'lichot* every day in Elul (with a longer liturgy during the Ten Days of Repentance), while among Ashkenazic Jews, the liturgy changes day-to-day. Some recite *S'lichot* in the middle of the night, and some recite them very early in the morning. What all the customs and rites have in common is the unique character of the *piyutim* of *S'lichot*. They are about asking for forgiveness and preparing our hearts for Yom Kippur, and are recited or sung at a special time when people are generally not awake or at least not gathered in public.

Standing at the Threshold

Just as we wake up our bodies and our consciousness at an unaccustomed hour (or stay awake very late at night), we teach ourselves to wake up our spirits and our minds in uncharted ways to break out of routine habits of thought and behavior that cause us or others pain, and transform those habits into behavior that will benefit ourselves and others.

S'lichot prayers remove us from our comfort zone in a very physical way, from being snuggled up in our warm beds on those ever-longer autumn evenings out into the chilly outdoor air. Our bodily emergence from this place of comfort is intended to help us emerge from the psychological and spiritual places where we may also be slumbering. When we agree to make this transition, even for an instant, and stand at the threshold—to encounter the world in a manner that clashes with our regular patterns of thought—we find that our minds experience an unfamiliar openness toward learning and experiencing our existence in a unique way.

In order to wake up, one first has to sleep. The human experience of *S'lichot* is an experience of waking up, but also of recognizing that sometimes we fall asleep. Just as when we arouse our sleeping hearts when we beat our chests again and again as we recite the words of the *Vidui* (*Ashamnu, bagadnu . . .*), *S'lichot* also wakes us up. The *piyutim* are there to wake our spirits, our conscience, our feelings. Over and over again, these *S'lichot* prayers repeat the call to rouse ourselves; like a parent addressing a child who refuses to get up in the morning, with patient (and perhaps a little monotonous) insistence, we call on the recalcitrant soul to wake up, and we keep calling and calling until we reach a receptive ear.

The desired awakening is ours—not only ours, but God's as well. Like little children tugging at their sleeping mother's sheets, so do we call out to our God, "Rouse Yourself, why do You sleep, O Eternal? Awaken, do not reject us forever!" (Psalm 44:24).

The *S'lichot* prayers call on us to be attentive. And it is so hard to be attentive, to

The *piyut* titled *Ben Adam, Mah L'cha Nirdam* ("Oh, human being! Why do you sleep?") summons us to wake up and pay attention. It expresses the pressing nature of *S'lichot* ("Wash yourself clean, do not wait for many days to go by"). This *piyut* is sung in most rites of the Sephardic and Middle Eastern and North African communities.

Oh, human being! Why do you sleep? Rise up and voice your pleas!
Pour out your words, seek forgiveness from the Master of All.
Wash yourself clean, do not wait for many days to go by.
Quickly, seek help from the One who dwells beyond, within.
Flee from all wrongdoings and fear their unintended consequences.
God, please hear the prayers of Israel who faithfully call on Your Name.
You are the Source of all that is right; and we are truly humbled.

Rise up, be strong and take courage so you may confess your failings!
Seek God with reverence and find atonement.
In this realm of the spirit wonders never cease.
Every word that is said will be received.
The Compassionate One will have compassion on us as parents do toward their children.
You are the Source of all that is right; and we are truly humbled.[5]

listen—especially in our time, when all those little devices that capture our concerns and connections constantly distract our attention with beeps and notifications. The *S'lichot* prayers call us to listen internally, to hear our world's heartbeat, and to wake up.

Reciting *S'lichot* is a powerful invitation to prepare, clarify, and deepen our minds and spirits. It can take place at home, at work, during study, within community, and even publicly in open spaces. *S'lichot* can also be a tool for deepening the connections and friendships among people who are prepared to open their hearts together in an act of soul-searching. Alongside traditional liturgy, many people are creating new texts and even using modern songs to most accurately express our thoughts and feelings at today's *S'lichot*.[4]

In this chapter about the last month of the year, I wish and hope that we will not be drop-in visitors in our rich, multihued Jewish tradition, but instead be at home in it, each of us in their own way, everyone with their own proper amount—even if it feels strange or a bit embarrassing. This home that continues to be built, generation after generation—all of us are partners in its construction, and each of us needs to feel at home in it, regardless of where we are in the world.

The first line of the *piyut* that appears to the left—except for the phrase "Oh, human being!"—is taken from the biblical Book of Jonah. The prophet Jonah flees from God's instruction to prophesy against the city of Nineveh. Instead, Jonah gets onto a boat on the mistaken assumption that one can flee from God. To chastise him, God summons a great wind "and the ship was in danger of breaking up" (Jonah 1:4). All the sailors take quick action in response to the storm: "and the sailors cried out, each to his own god, and they flung the ship's cargo overboard to make it lighter for them" (1:5). Jonah, however, remains oblivious: "Jonah, meanwhile, had gone down into the hold of the vessel where he lay down and fell asleep" (1:5). Many of us recognize the yearning to get into bed, turn away our faces, and fall asleep in times of trouble, but we also know that running away is not a solution. The captain knows this too; he approaches Jonah and says to him, "How can you be sleeping so soundly! Up, call upon your god. Perhaps your god will be kind to us and we will not perish" (1:6).

The Book of Jonah is read in its entirety on the afternoon of Yom Kippur, toward the end of the day, closing the circle begun weeks earlier at *S'lichot* with this *piyut*. The Hebrew word *adam*, which begins the *piyut*, can be read as beyond a specific gender and is clearly not limited to Israelites. Everyone—every man and woman, every person—needs to wake up, shake themselves off, and look both inside and outward. The captain and his sailors are not part of the divine covenant with Israel, yet all of them together are on the ship being tossed to and fro on the waves of the great tempest of life. The wake-up call from a foreign captain—*Ma l'cha nirdam?* Why do you sleep?—opens the *piyut* and provides its title.

Lamaze for Creation: Shofar during Elul

Crossing a border is a scary moment. I remember the twinge of fear every time I crossed a border on my long trip around South America after my army service. Who knows what new regulation the guards would come up with this time? How long will they delay us? Will they try to pin a false charge of smuggling on us? A drug charge? At one of those border crossings, the border patrol agent had a hard time with a strange twisted object that the person ahead of us in line had brought along in his luggage. The agent turned the object over and looked inside, searching for how it could be activated or something that would explain what it is. The man ahead of me tried to satisfy the guard's curiosity with his broken Spanish and prove that it was not a weapon. The agent closed the suitcase with the shofar inside and signaled the man to pass through. We smiled at each other, "Are you really sure," I asked in whispered Hebrew, "that it isn't a weapon?"

Indeed, the shofar is a powerful method of awakening and touching deep strands of the self that have fallen asleep. Hearing the shofar blasts on Rosh HaShanah is a mitzvah commanded in the Torah, and we actually hear it before the first of Tishrei and the New Year: the Rabbis instituted blowing of the shofar on every weekday of Elul during *S'lichot* or after the morning worship service, with the exception of the day immediately before Rosh HaShanah. With some anxiety and a measure of hope we follow Moses's second ascent to the summit of Mount Sinai to get the second set of divine tablets, and we follow his stay on the mountain for forty days and forty nights—for us, and for Moses, from Rosh Chodesh Elul through Yom Kippur. Blowing the shofar and hearing its blast is one of the ways we do this.

> Unlike the first set of tablets of the Ten Commandments, which were the work of God's hands, the second set of tablets was constructed collaboratively by God and Moses. A midrash attributed to Rabbi Yonatan relates that "the tablets were six handbreadths long and three wide. Moses grasped two handbreadths and the Blessed Holy One grasped two handbreadths, with a space of two handbreadths in the middle" (Jerusalem Talmud, *Taanit* 4:5 [23a]).
>
> The midrash's description of the "two handbreadths in the middle" is that of an interstitial space—the dynamic space of encounter between the human and the Divine and of interpretation and creativity.

Furthermore, since two separate midrashic traditions assign Rosh HaShanah as the day of the world's creation or the day of the creation of the first human being, sounding the shofar during Elul is a kind of Lamaze course to prepare for the world's creation and our creation. Just as women in the last stages of pregnancy focus internally as they prepare to give birth, so Elul is a month of focusing inward, preparing our hearts. Just as pregnant women "nest" at the end of pregnancy by reorganizing and arranging their homes, Elul is an opportunity to reshape the "home" that is our own mind and spirit.

Before the Word Came to Be

What makes the blowing of the shofar so moving, so capable of touching hidden strands of our being? Perhaps it stems from the very fact that the shofar is unusual within Jewish prayer, which is a very word-centered practice. Other religions stress silence, meditation, chanting; Jewish prayer is composed of countless words. In daily prayer, and even more so on holidays, worshipers guzzle pages and pages of blessings, prayers, and supplications. The wordless shofar stands out in its stark contrast to all these words. There are no printed notes for blowing the shofar, and one cannot play along in harmony with it. All we have are the three lengths of blasts: *t'kiah*, *sh'varim*, and *t'ruah*. Like speech, shofar sounds are produced from the mouth. However, its voice is not a human voice but a primal sound that precedes all words, perhaps something like the first cry of a newborn baby. In no other place in the Jewish tradition do we find the use of a musical instrument as the core of a mitzvah.

The shofar sounds also include an element of surprise. We never know just how (or whether) they will come out. (How embarrassing when the shofar blower takes a great big breath, puts the shofar to their mouth, turns red, tries again, but doesn't succeed in producing anything more than a pathetic whistle of air.) The sound of the shofar evokes dim memories of ancient times; it arouses profound feelings about things we cannot name.

Shofar—For Improvement (*Shipur*) or as an Amulet?

Rabbi Saadyah Gaon (who lived in tenth-century Babylonia, Egypt, and *Eretz Yisrael*) listed ten reason for blowing the shofar on Rosh HaShanah. Those reasons can be sorted into two main categories: those that focus on human beings and those that focus on God.[6]

The reasons for the first type show that the sound of the shofar is intended to wake us up and urge us to do *t'shuvah*:

> "The Eternal sounds out the Eternal's voice" (Joel 2:11)—this refers to Rosh HaShanah, when the shofar is blown; "at the head of the Eternal's army" (2:11)—this is the people Israel, who are shaken and quake at the sound of the shofar and return [to God] in *t'shuvah* in order to be acquitted in judgment on Yom Kippur. (*Tanchuma*, Warsaw edition, *Vayishlach* 2)

The sound of the shofar makes us quiver and tremble, playing on unseen chords in the core of our being, and when we hear it, we "are shaken and quake" and do *t'shuvah*. The word "shofar" itself has been interpreted as a call to improve—*shapru*—our behavior (*Vayikra Rabbah* 29:6). These explanations, as we have said, focus on human responses to the shofar.

The other type of reasons given for the shofar focuses on God, based on the assumption that the shofar blasts can influence the heavens and arouse God's mercy for the people Israel. So, for example, in the midrash offered by Rabbi Y'hudah, son of Rabbi Nachman, on the verse "God ascends amidst acclamation; the Eternal, to the blasts of the shofar" (Psalm 47:6):

> When the Blessed Holy One ascends and sits upon the Throne of Judgment, that is in order to do [strict] judgment. What is the reason for this statement? "God ascends amidst acclamation [*t'ruah*, the term used also for the shofar blast]." But when Israel take their shofarot and blow them in the presence of the Blessed Holy One, the Holy One rises from the Throne of Judgment and sits upon the Throne of Mercy—as it is written, "the Eternal, to the blasts of the shofar"—and is filled with compassion for them, taking pity upon them and changing for them the measure of justice to one of mercy. (*Vayikra Rabbah* 29:3)

According to this midrash, absolute and unsparing divine justice is the appropriate nature of judgment for the occasion. However, the shofar blasts influence God to have a change of heart, to move from the Throne of Justice—which God had ascended

Another explanation for the shofar focuses on human emotions. Thus, an unexpected midrash explains that **the sound of the shofar** is like sobbing or wailing. In this context, the midrash mentions the wailing of Sisera's mother referred to in *Shirat D'vorah* (Song of Deborah) in the Book of Judges, who waited in vain for her son—the commander of the Canaanite army that was attacking and harassing the Israelites—to return from the battlefield: "Through the window peered Sisera's mother, behind the lattice she wailed [*vat'yabeiv*]" (Judges 5:28). The empathy shown to Sisera's mother is all the more striking since the text shares her harsh and difficult words about the fate of women of Israel: "A damsel or two for each man, spoil of dyed cloths for Sisera, spoil of embroidered cloths" (Judges 5:30). According to one opinion in the Talmud, the verb used for wailing should be understood as groaning or sighing and, according to another, as sobbing in short bursts (Babylonian Talmud, *Rosh HaShanah* 33b). Making the connection to Sisera's mother is a daring move because it draws a connection between Sisera's belligerence (and his victories) and the wailing of his bereaved mother. This Talmudic passage may be expressing schadenfreude at the fall of an enemy, but it may also be showing empathy toward human suffering—even the suffering of an enemy (or at least the enemy's mother). This, too, is part of the ancient, primal sound of the shofar.

"justly" and appropriately—to the Throne of Mercy and take pity on God's people. Another familiar explanation of the sounding of the shofar is that it reminds God of the binding of Isaac and the ram that was offered in his stead and therefore serves to plead for God's mercy on account of our ancestors' merit.

In another place, Rabbi Yoshiyah explains that **the shofar sound** is a way to entice God, asking, "Don't the nations of the world know how to sound the blast? What a plethora of horns they have! . . . Yet you say, 'Happy is the people who know the sound of the *t'ruah* blast.' It can only mean that they know how to win over the heart of their Creator with the *t'ruah* blast" (*Vayikra Rabbah* 29:4). According to this midrash, it is not the music that is important, since others have plenty of musical instruments of their own, but rather the shofar—that simple and musically unsophisticated instrument—whose mission is to reach the divine throne and somehow appease God. (In another version of the midrash, the shofar attempts to "seduce" God!)

To summarize the two categories of explanations: some emphasize the shofar's unique ability to wake a person up to a psychological process of *t'shuvah*, while others see in the shofar in a magical dimension and believe the goal of blowing the shofar is to encourage God to act kindly and charitably toward us (and thus, there would seem to be no real need for *t'shuvah*). These two views of the shofar represent religious outlooks that are profoundly different but may complement one another.

Blow Shofar First, Ask Questions Later?

Let us digress from our examination of Elul's shofar blowing and instead imagine we are standing under a big window where we can eavesdrop on a conversation that took place on Rosh HaShanah almost two thousand years ago. The discussion is about blowing the shofar on Rosh HaShanah when the holiday falls on Shabbat. In the Mishnah we read:

> If a festival day of Rosh HaShanah fell on a Shabbat, they would blow the shofar in the Holy Temple, but not in the provinces. After the Temple was destroyed, Rabban Yochanan ben Zakkai ordained that they might blow it wherever there was a rabbinic court. (*Mishnah Rosh HaShanah* 4:1)

Until the great destruction, there was a clear distinction in practice regarding blowing the shofar on Shabbat in the Temple, and apparently all of Jerusalem, versus what was done in the "provinces"—the towns outside Jerusalem, where the sanctity of Shabbat prevailed over the mitzvah of blowing the shofar and quashed it. After the Temple was destroyed, **Rabban Yochanan ben Zakkai** changed that rule. What is stated succinctly in the Mishnah is told at greater length in the Talmud:

> Our Rabbis taught: Once Rosh HaShanah fell on a Shabbat [and all the towns assembled], and Rabban Yochanan said to the sons of B'tirah, "Let us blow the shofar."

From Time to Time → Dalia Marx

> They said to him, "Let us discuss the matter."
> He said to them, "Let us blow and afterward discuss."
> After they had blown the shofar, they said to him, "Let us now discuss the question."
> He replied, "The horn has already been heard in Yavneh, and what has been done is no longer open to discussion." (Babylonian Talmud, *Rosh HaShanah* 29b)

These few lines condense a great drama that occurred at Yavneh, the spiritual center of Jewish life after the destruction of Temple. Rabban Yochanan ben Zakkai addresses the "sons of B'tirah," an important family that was involved in the religious leadership of the people, and suggests they blow the shofar even though it was Shabbat—something that until then was contrary to the accepted practice. The sons of B'tirah suggest instead, "Well, let's talk about it first." To make a change of this sort, one would have to conduct a serious deliberation and then make a decision. Rabban Yochanan instead pushes them to go ahead and blow the shofar, convincing them that there would be plenty of time afterward to have that discussion. And indeed, on that Rosh Hashanah that fell on Shabbat, they blow the shofar. However, when the sons of B'tirah ask to have that promised discussion, Rabban Yochanan tells them the horse is already out of the barn: "The horn has already been heard in Yavneh, and what has been done is no longer open to discussion." There is nothing left to discuss; it is a *fait accompli*. Rashi explains, "It would be unseemly for us to besmirch ourselves by saying we made an error."

Rabban Yochanan ben Zakkai lived during the time of the destruction of the Second Temple, and he is the person most identified with Judaism's adaptation to the post-destruction reality (see pp. 221–23). He decreed that mitzvot relating to former Temple worship are "reminders of the destruction," then adapted them to the post-destruction reality of Judaism without a Temple. Memorializing the Temple ensures it remains an important institution for many generations after its destruction, but paradoxically it also makes any practical need for it superfluous.

There will surely be some who claim that Rabban Yochanan's actions were unacceptable and antidemocratic, since he established facts on the ground without discussion and perhaps deliberately deceived his interlocutors. But one can also appreciate the boldness of a leader who made a decision in a crisis; Rabban Yochanan understood that in the absence of a Temple, there was a desperate and urgent need for meaningful worship. There was no time to bury the decision-making process in committee processes, so to speak. Practical commandments were needed to give meaning to life and show that Judaism had not lost its vitality, but had only changed its rituals in order to adapt to a new reality. Despite Rabban Yochanan's boldness, shofar blowing on Shabbat did not become established as the accepted practice, except in many liberal synagogues, where Rabban Yochanan's approach continues to be followed. In our time, we need brave religious leaders unafraid and undeterred by the anticipation of objections—and also willing to engage in deep dialogue and collaboration with any detractors—who will be able to lead a sustainable, rooted Judaism into the future.

Let us return for a moment to the shofar, that instrument with an ancient, primal sound. It is a powerful "weapon" that takes true aim. Whether we aim it at our own hearts, use it to try to entice the Blessed Holy One, or try to make profound social change with it, the shofar takes accurate aim but causes no harm. On the contrary, it is a weapon that empowers and benefits those who use it or hear it during Elul's preparatory course for Creation—our pre–Rosh HaShanah birth-of-the-world Lamaze class.

The First of Elul: Rosh HaShanah for the Animals

Americans Richard Schwartz, PhD, and Aharon Varady were, as far as I know, the first to suggest renewing the New Year for Animals. Schwartz has written a number of books on Judaism and vegetarianism, and Varady is the founder of the online Open Siddur Project, the goal of which is to share prayers, ceremonies, *piyutim*, and liturgical insights from around the world. The New Year for Animals is an example of how Jews from all over use cyberspace to share and disseminate ideas. Varady writes:

> What better way [is there] to begin a month dedicated to humbling ourselves and repairing our relationships than by reflecting first on our relationship with *behemah*—the domesticated animals which depend on us for their care and sustenance. The category of *behemah* includes all animals historically bred by humans as domesticated creatures, both kosher and non-kosher, e.g. cats and cattle, dogs and donkeys, goats, pigs, chicken, and llamas. If we can imagine, empathize, and understand the dependency of *behemah* in our care, how much better can we realize our relationship with the blessed Holy One, and the infinite chain of inter-dependencies uniting all living relationships in reflection of this Oneness.
>
> Once upon a time when the Temple still stood, the [New Year for Animals] celebrated one means by which we elevated and esteemed the special creatures that helped us to live and to work. Just as rabbinic Judaism found new ways to realize our Temple offerings with *tefillot*—prayers—so too the [New Year for Animals] challenges us to realize the holiness of the animals in our care in a time without tithes. The New Year's Day for Animals is a challenge to remind and rediscover what our responsibilities are to the animals who depend on us for their welfare.... [It] is the day to reflect on our immediate or mediated relationships with domesticated animals, recognize our personal responsibilities to them, individually and as part of a distinct and holy people, and repair our relationships to the best of our ability.[7]

In a similar vein, Schwartz writes, "Renewing an ancient, almost completely forgotten Jewish holiday may seem audacious. But it is essential to help revitalize Judaism, improve the health of Jews, sharply reduce the current massive mistreatment of animals, and help move our precious but imperiled planet to a sustainable path."[8]

THEY GUARD OUR HOUSES. They are our children's good friends, and they bring enjoyment to the elderly among us. They produce the song that make our mornings more pleasant. They rejoice in our joy, and worry when we are sad. They light up our lonely times. Some of us feed with their milk or their meat. How can it be that until now Judaism has not devoted a special day to mark our responsibility toward animals? How can it be that it is natural for us to mark a New Year for Trees, but we are silent about the animals, creatures so much like ourselves? How can no one have thought of this before?

Well, they actually did think about this before, but a bit differently. Our Sages designated Rosh Chodesh Elul as "the New Year for the tithe of cattle," the day on which one-tenth the number of beasts was set aside for the purpose of Temple sacrifices. This designation has been forgotten over time, though, in the absence of a Temple to which one would bring the animal tithe. The first of Elul is counted among the four "new years" in the Hebrew year, three of which we have addressed in previous chapters: "On the first of Elul is the New Year for the tithe of cattle. Rabbi Elazar and Rabbi Shimon say: the first of Tishrei" (*Mishnah Rosh HaShanah* 1:1). Our ancestors assumed that by the beginning of Elul, most of the domesticated cattle had already given birth to their young, so from then on, any lambs, kids, and calves born would be considered as belonging to the next year for the purpose of tithing. Rabbi Elazar and Rabbi Shimon consider a later date appropriate, suggesting the first of Tishrei.

How did the day that marks a tax computation year for animal sacrifices (which was apparently not an especially festive occasion) turn into a day for preserving animal species? How did a day originally connected to the Temple worship become a day that can be celebrated anywhere, in any era? This transformation is how the day that marks the tax year for tree fruits became Tu BiSh'vat—a day expressing love and longing for the Land of Israel and reaffirming our commitment to environmentalism (see pp. 123–26). This process of transformation is how tradition works. It can attach new meanings over time. The date exists, along with its name, and all we have to do is fill it with content.

From Time to Time → Dalia Marx

"Let the Soul of Every Living Being Bless"

It seems that we have taken very seriously the divine command to rule over the animals and control them (Genesis 1:28), but we have forgotten the commanded principle "to work [the earth] and keep it" (Genesis 2:15). We are not just tillers, working the land; we are also guardians of the land and all that lives on it, in it, and above it. To remind ourselves of this role, it is a good idea to dedicate one special day to it. And just as the kabbalists of Safed marked Tu BiSh'vat as a day devoted to a *tikkun* (repair) of our relationship with flora and fauna—and through that to *tikkun* of the whole world—so it is appropriate to designate a day for doing a *tikkun* of our relationship with the animal kingdom that shares our world. It is precisely in our time, when so many people are asking themselves what it is appropriate to eat and how we should feed our bodies (see pp. 255–57), that it is important to give some thought to our relationship with the animal kingdom—both domesticated and undomesticated animals, the ones that share our homes and the ones that fend for themselves in the wild.

As we have seen, the Mishnah includes a debate about the specific time to mark Rosh HaShanah for the tithing of cattle and flocks—the first of Elul or the first of Tishrei. What underlies each of these dates, other than the simple zoological consideration? Rabbi Elazar and Rabbi Shimon think that on the first of Tishrei, Rosh HaShanah, "*all* who dwell in the world pass before [God] like sheep" (*Mishnah Rosh HaShanah* 1:2). The simile comparing "all who dwell in the world" to "sheep" (in Hebrew, the word is *kivnei maron*) is a bit opaque, and modern scholarship suggests that it is a misreading—or shall we say, a *creative* reading, as the Rabbis so often do—of a Greek term (with a Hebrew prefix) "as a *noumeron*," meaning a military battalion. The Greek was understood by Jews in Hellenized Judea, but Babylonian Jews living far from the Greek-speaking world made a rather creative reading of the term *noumeron* and "understood" or "interpreted" it quite differently.[9] The shared fate of human beings and animals stands out on Rosh HaShanah, the Day of Judgment on which, according to tradition, the entire world is judged.

The majority of sages in the Mishnah, however, preferred to establish the first of Elul as the beginning of the tithing year, and it seems that the earlier date is in fact more appropriate. The first of Tishrei is already "occupied," and it is hard to imagine that we could free up enough emotional and spiritual space for another ceremony. Elul, on the other hand—the month of mercy, forgiveness, and love, the month of anticipation and readiness—is an appropriate time to arouse empathy and kindness toward those who, like us, are made of flesh and blood and who, like us, are familiar with joy and contentment, sorrow and pain. During the month of Elul, we blow a shofar made from an animal's horn and continue to do so all month. When we hear the wailing of the shofar, it is appropriate to hear the suffering voice of animals and to improve human teatment of them. This is one more example of creating new meaning for the ancient framework—of pouring new nectar into old vessels.

"Human and Animal You Save, O Eternal"

Rosh Chodesh Elul stands like a security guard at the entrance to the cycle of *t'shuvah*, forgiveness, and taking stock of our individual lives. This cycle comes to its peak

Tishrei   Marcheshvan   Kislev   Tevet   Sh'vat   Adar   Nisan   Iyar   Sivan   Tammuz   Av   Elul

Regarding attitudes toward animals, the Books of Jonah and Ecclesiastes present unusual approaches that may even stand in opposition to the general approach found in biblical literature. In many other instances, the Bible presents the human being as the crowning glory of Creation, meant to rule over nature and control its creatures.

The fact that these two works entered the biblical canon—after extended internal debate in the case of Ecclesiastes—indicates how pluralistic the redactors of the Bible were. In Rabbinic tradition many voices were heard, and Talmudic literature makes room for voices of opposition to have central positions. We even hear the voices of sages who were excommunicated (such as Elisha ben Abuyah). This inclusive approach enables readers to read critically, empowering them to claim their own position with the sources.

forty days later, on Yom Kippur. And on the afternoon of Yom Kippur, the most sacred day of the year, we read the Book of Jonah, which includes fascinating references to animals, their role in the world, and our attitudes toward them.

First, the name of the prophet is the name of a bird—in Hebrew, *yonah* means "dove"—the same bird our Sages used to refer to the people Israel. Furthermore, after the prophet arrives at the city of Nineveh (which in Hebrew cleverly includes the letters of Jonah's name) and delivers his prophecy of doom to its people, we are told that humans *and* animals fasted and wore sackcloth. The king of Nineveh decrees, "They shall be covered with sackcloth—human and animal—and shall cry mightily to God" (Jonah 3:8). Perhaps there is a tone of disdain in the words of the king, who demands that animals also fast and mourn. After all, what sin had *they* committed? Does the decree indicate a lack of moral judgment? Or might we instead see in the king's words a recognition of a fate shared by all—great and small, rich and poor, human and animal—who would suffer in the anticipated disaster? In fact, animals also suffer in natural disasters and wars throughout history.

At the end of the book, when God rebukes Jonah for being upset that the prophecy of destruction would not be fulfilled, even though it would have meant huge losses of human and animal life, God sends a plant to grow to provide shade for Jonah. The next day, God destroys the plant and asks Jonah, "Are you so deeply grieved about the plant?" (Jonah 4:9); God is forcing the prophet to take a good look at his own behavior:

> Then the Eternal said, "You cared about the plant, which you did not work for, and which you did not grow, which appeared overnight and perished overnight. And should I not care about Nineveh, that great city, in which there are more than a hundred and twenty thousand persons who do not yet know their right hand from their left, and many animals as well? (Jonah 4:10–11)

In God's view, the shared fate between humans and animals is natural. Both humans and animals will be lost in the arbitrariness of the anticipated punishment. The comparison between the people of the city, about whom we are told that "they do not yet know their right hand from their left," and the animals is immediately obvious. And perhaps it is not only the sinful residents of Nineveh who are similar to the beast; perhaps all human beings live in this world not knowing "their right hand from their left," like an animal of limited intelligence. The comparison may be offensive, but its message—that though we are the crowning glory of Creation, intelligent beings capable of making choices, our existential situation in the world is not all that different from that of animals—is nonetheless important. Thus, the Psalmist says, "Human and beast You save, O Eternal" (Psalm 36:7).

Ecclesiastes's complex and nuanced approach to the question may be useful in understanding this idea:

From Time to Time → Dalia Marx

> For in respect of the fate of humans and the fate of animals,
> they have one and the same fate:
> as the one dies so dies the other,
> and both have the same lifebreath;
> the human superiority over the animal is nonexistent,
> since everything amounts to nothing.¹⁰
> (Ecclesiastes 3:19)

Ecclesiastes begins by distinguishing between "the fate of humans" and that of animals but immediately equates the two: "they have one and the same fate." The members of both sets will die, and their deaths are similar since "both have the same lifebreath." Later, in an interesting dialectical move, Ecclesiastes again separates the human being, who seems to be in a superior position: "the human superiority over the animal," but the verse ends by again equating human and animal: unlike God, they are "mere vapor"—they "amount to nothing." To this we can add that if humans flourish, animals too will flourish, and vice versa. This approach—juxtaposing human uniqueness and humans' role as part of the natural world—should guide us in our attitude regarding our place in our world: perhaps the world was created for us, but we are here both to work it and preserve it, to till it and tend it.

How Shall We Celebrate the New Year for Animals?

Should the first of Elul be celebrated among family, in school, in youth groups, or in the public sphere? How does it compare to other blessings or celebrations for animals, such as those some Christians observe on Saint Francis Day? Many questions remain unanswered right now, waiting for our response. Recently, I observed the first of Elul this year with members of the Rosh Chodesh group in which I take part. We lit candles, studied together, and then recited prayers and a *t'chinah* (supplicatory prayer) with an active participation by Joy, who is our hostess Vicky's dog.

The first of Elul is a new observance, celebrated on a renewed date, without any established traditions. To tell the truth, there is not even agreement on just what it is we are observing! Some people emphasize our responsibility to preserve God's Creation and all God's creatures; others emphasize the shared fate of people and animals. Some insist that our responsibility to all that lives reflects our responsibility toward ourselves and our own fate, while others

Rabbah Gila Caine writes:
The suffering in today's world is great—human suffering and the suffering of all life forms who share this world with us. The source of this suffering is in the carelessness we demonstrate toward life itself, in our feeling that it is OK to waste, in the disjunction between human beings and our world. This is a social and environmental issue. But no less so, it is a religious issue, because our attitude toward living creatures shows how much we have stopped approaching the world with the sense of wonder and amazement appropriate for a place that is so unbelievable in its variety and beauty. This sense of connection is what we celebrate on the first of Elul.¹¹

Here are two examples of texts for marking off the New Year for Animals:
1. The people at Ginger House (Zangwill), the vegetarian community center in Jerusalem, created a seder for Rosh Chodesh Elul along the lines of the Tu BiSh'vat seder. As in a seder for Tu BiSh'vat, appropriate verses and midrashim are read, and there is a progression of four cups of wine:
   The first cup: in honor of fish (aquatic creatures)—white wine.
   The second cup: in honor of amphibians and reptiles (creatures that live in water and on land)—white wine with an admixture of red.
   The third cup: for fowl (creatures that are airborne)—red wine.
   The fourth cup: for mammals (land creatures)—red wine with an admixture of white.¹²
2. Rabbi Jill Hammer and Kohenet Sarah Chandler suggested gathering in a place hospitable to house pets or a place where one can view wild animals to recite blessings of thanks for the animals and to express our responsibility for them. Between blessings a shofar is to be blown. Toward the end of the ceremony, the following blessing is recited, with the intention of celebrating the beauty in the multitude of nature: *Baruch atah Adonai, Eloheinu Melech haolam, m'shaneh hab'riyot.* (Praised are You, O Eternal, who makes [all] creatures different.)¹³

emphasize the need to show kindness to pets and farm animals; still others prioritize defending endangered species. All of those express different dimensions of our responsibility toward the animal world. Taking into consideration the relationship between humans and animals—the harm, consumption, and exploitation of animals by humans—it is even possible to suggest that the first of Elul be a day of confession and chest beating. It seems more proper, though, to use of the first day of the month of *t'shuvah* for reconnecting, taking stock, and recommitting to Creation and all creatures with love and empathy.

Prayer of the Month

The Thirteen Attributes, "Which Do Not Come Back Empty-Handed"

BREATHLESS, I RAN through a certain airport to my gate: nine, ten, eleven . . . I was encouraged—I was already at gate twelve and soon I would be at the anticipated goal: gate fourteen. At the moment of running through the airport, I did not pay attention to the absence of gate thirteen; it was only when I was sitting in my seat on the plane did it hit me that gate thirteen was missing! Indeed, in Western culture the **number thirteen** is a symbol of bad luck. Elevators go from floor twelve to fourteen, airlines sometimes skip row number thirteen, the streets of Florence list house number 12.5 between numbers 12 and 14, and real estate agents report difficulty selling apartments with the number thirteen.

Not so in Judaism. In Judaism, the number thirteen actually symbolizes many important and good things. At age thirteen, children arrive at the age of mitzvot. Rabbi Yishmael created a list of thirteen principles by which the Torah is interpreted (*Sifra* on Leviticus 1), which found its way into the morning worship service. Maimonides enumerated the Thirteen Principles of Jewish Faith. His list also entered our liturgy, and Rabbi Daniel the *dayan* (judge) even turned it into the familiar *piyut* known as *Yigdal*. And of course, there are God's Thirteen Attributes of Mercy, the core of the *S'lichot* prayers.

Emphasizing the number thirteen as a positive number was used during a time of Jewish powerlessness in the Middle Ages as a coping device against the often oppressive Christian ruling powers, in order to poke fun at their discomfort. Beyond that, however, the number has additional meanings: thirteen in *g'matria* (Hebrew numerology) is the sum of the letters in the word *echad* (אֶחָד), meaning "one," and in the word *ahavah* (אֲהָבָה), meaning "love" (see p. 325).

El Melech Yosheiv Al Kisei Rachamim (God, a Sovereign who is . . .), an early *piyut* of unknown authorship that occurs many times in the liturgy for *S'lichot* and the Days of Awe, presents the Thirteen Attributes of God:

> Majestic God, Your throne is mercy; love and kindness Your path.
> Though we wander and stray, Your forgiveness grows, as You pardon our wrongs, one by one—
> doing what is right for every living being.
> In Your mercy and love, do not treat us harshly for the harshness of our deeds.
> The Eternal descended in the cloud, stood with him there, and proclaimed:

Triskaidekaphobia is the name given to a fear of the **number thirteen**. The reason for this fear is not entirely clear. It may be related to northern European mythology, in which there is a story about a feast of gods in which the thirteenth god was not invited and took his revenge for that slight. Furthermore, Christians saw Judas Iscariot, who betrayed Jesus by denouncing him to the Romans, as the thirteenth guest at the Last Supper.

Echad Mi Yodei-a ("Who Knows One?"), the well-known *piyut* that we sing at the end of the Passover seder, builds up to the count of thirteen, paralleling the Thirteen Attributes of God—at least in Ashkenazic editions of the Haggadah. In many Sephardic Haggadot, the count ends after twelve. It appears that the number thirteen was added to distinguish this *piyut* from Christian game songs and perhaps to poke fun at Christians' suspicion of the number.

Tishrei   Marcheshvan   Kislev   Tevet   Sh'vat   Adar   Nisan   Iyar   Sivan   Tammuz   Av   **Elul**

"Eternal, Eternal—
God, compassionate, gracious, endlessly patient, loving, and true;
showing mercy to the thousandth generation; forgiving evil, defiance,
and wrongdoing; granting pardon."[14]

"וַיֵּרֶד יְיָ בֶּעָנָן וַיִּתְיַצֵּב עִמּוֹ שָׁם וַיִּקְרָא בְשֵׁם יְיָ" וְשָׁם נֶאֱמַר:
אֵל מֶלֶךְ יוֹשֵׁב עַל כִּסֵּא רַחֲמִים וּמִתְנַהֵג בַּחֲסִידוּת
מוֹחֵל עֲווֹנוֹת עַמּוֹ מַעֲבִיר רִאשׁוֹן רִאשׁוֹן,
מַרְבֶּה מְחִילָה לַחַטָּאִים וּסְלִיחָה לַפּוֹשְׁעִים,
עוֹשֶׂה צְדָקוֹת עִם כָּל בָּשָׂר וָרוּחַ לֹא כְרָעָתָם תִּגְמֹל.
אֵל הוֹרֵתָנוּ לוֹמַר מִדּוֹת שְׁלֹשׁ עֶשְׂרֵה זְכֹר לָנוּ הַיּוֹם בְּרִית שְׁלֹשׁ עֶשְׂרֵה
כְּמוֹ שֶׁהוֹדַעְתָּ לֶעָנָו מִקֶּדֶם וְכֵן כָּתוּב בְּתוֹרָתֶךָ:

"וַיַּעֲבֹר ה' עַל פָּנָיו וַיִּקְרָא: יְיָ יְיָ, אֵל רַחוּם וְחַנּוּן אֶרֶךְ אַפַּיִם וְרַב חֶסֶד וֶאֱמֶת
נֹצֵר חֶסֶד לָאֲלָפִים נֹשֵׂא עָוֹן וָפֶשַׁע וְחַטָָּאָה וְנַקֵּה."

"And the Eternal passed before [Moses's] face / and [he] called out: / Eternal, Eternal / God, / showing mercy, showing favor, / long-suffering in anger, / abundant in kindness and faithfulness, / keeping kindness to the thousandth [generation], / bearing iniquity, rebellion, and sin / and clearing—no, not clearing (the guilty), calling to account the iniquity of the fathers upon the sons and upon the sons' sons, to the third and fourth [generation]!" (Exodus 34:6–7).[15]

The verses that give us the **Thirteen Attributes** of God present some problems of interpretation. First, who is the subject of the verb we've translated as "[he] called out" at the beginning of the passage? Does Moses call out to God, or is it God saying the words that follow (which is how Jewish tradition understands the phrase)? Second, an ancient tradition refers to the list of God's attributes as "the Thirteen Attributes," but it is not entirely clear how one is to count each of these divine attributes, and one can see different systems of enumerating them. Third, tradition repeats God's attributes only partially, deliberately excising the harsher attributes (such as "calling to account the iniquity… to the third and fourth [generation]!"). The last of the attributes counted among the thirteen, "clearing," is actually just the first part of a longer infinitive verb phrase that in whole expresses the opposite: God does not clear the guilty of responsibility. The Rabbis took foundational biblical texts, then selectively reshaped and redefined them in a new context, thus creating a new narrative based on—and at the same time, independent from—the biblical text.

The line "You teach us to proclaim Your Thirteen Attributes" in this *piyut* relies on a midrash that teaches that after the sin of the Golden Calf, when Moses interceded with God to ask God to show mercy to God's people, God taught Moses the **Thirteen Attributes**. According to the plain meaning of the Torah verses, Moses appealed to God's compassion, but according to Rabbi Yochanan, it was actually God who taught Moses to recite those Thirteen Attributes as a tool for arousing God's merciful nature:

> Rabbi Yochanan said, "Were it not written in the text, it would be impossible for us to say such a thing. This verse teaches us that the Blessed Holy One wrapped in a tallit like the prayer leader of a congregation and showed Moses the order of prayer. God said to him, 'Whenever the Israelites sin, let them carry out this service before Me, and I will forgive them.'" [The verse continues,] "Eternal, Eternal" (Exodus 34:6): I [the Eternal] am present before a person sins, and I am there after a person sins and performs repentance. "God, merciful and gracious": Rav Y'hudah said, "A covenant was made with the Thirteen Attributes that they will not return empty-handed." (Babylonian Talmud, *Rosh HaShanah* 17b)

According to this daring midrash by Rabbi Yochanan, God—wrapped in a tallit like someone leading a synagogue service—taught Moses "the order of prayer" that would be effective in fending off God's anger. The words of Rav Y'hudah, which immediately follow Rabbi Yochanan's, make it clear that the former was speaking about the Thirteen Attributes; these are considered an established "covenant," specifying that one who recites these words "would not return empty-handed," but rather can be confident the words will be effective.

From Time to Time → Dalia Marx

The Thirteen Attributes are central to the liturgy of the Days of Awe, and they are also the focus of the various Jewish communities' *S'lichot* prayers, where they are usually recited three times. They can be recited only when a minyan is present, with particular attention being paid as they are sung in a powerful melody or cantorial mode. At the *S'lichot* service, some communities have the custom of blowing the shofar during the recitation of the Thirteen Attributes of God.

Everyone agrees that there are thirteen attributes mentioned, but what are they exactly? Different commentators and legal scholars have different systems for enumerating those attributes. Here, for example, are three such lists: that of Rabbi Saadyah Gaon, a tenth-century *Gaon*; the list according to the tosafists, the authors of the *Tosafot* commentary on the Talmud, who lived in medieval Germany and France; and the list according to Maimonides, who lived in Spain, Morocco, Egypt, and the Land

	Saadyah Gaon	**Tosafists**	**Maimonides**
יְיָ	Eternal	Eternal	Eternal
יְיָ	—	Eternal	—
אֵל	God	God	God
רַחוּם	showing mercy	showing mercy	showing mercy
וְחַנּוּן	showing favor	showing favor	showing favor
אֶרֶךְ אַפַּיִם	long-suffering in anger	long-suffering in anger	long-suffering in anger
וְרַב חֶסֶד	abundant in kindness	abundant in kindness	abundant in kindness
וֶאֱמֶת	and faithfulness	and faithfulness	and faithfulness
נֹצֵר חֶסֶד לָאֲלָפִים	keeping kindness to the thousandth (generation)	keeping kindness to the thousandth (generation)	keeping kindness to the thousandth (generation)
נֹשֵׂא עָוֹן	bearing iniquity	bearing iniquity	bearing iniquity
וָפֶשַׁע	and rebellion	and rebellion	and rebellion
וְחַטָּאָה	and sin	and sin	and sin
וְנַקֵּה	and clearing	and clearing	and clearing
לֹא יְנַקֶּה	—	—	no, God will not clear

of Israel in the twelfth century.[16]

The Thirteen Attributes make the qualities of the transcendent and infinite God into something that can be measured and counted. This can bring about a feeling of calm, especially at this time of year when we stand before the tremendous realities that have no name. Ending the list of divine attributes with "and clearing" teaches us that the end of the process of *t'shuvah* is cleansing, opening a new page on which we can begin the new year that is just beyond the threshold.

This is a not a prayer in the usual sense of the word. The Thirteen Attributes contain no expressions of pleading or supplication, nor any praise or thanks, but rather just a measured recitation of God's qualities (as it were). Customs of reciting God's names are known in many religions as a meditative tool for religious devotion. Indeed, the recitation of this short list is an opportunity for reflection and concentration on God's attributes and on our obligation to try to be God-like as we travel our own paths in this world.

AFTERWORD

We have come to the end of our journey over the twelve months of the Jewish year. Now that we have traveled through the entire year, it is time to start over—to say farewell to the year that has passed and to welcome the new year and its blessings.

> May we be privileged to walk along the paths of time, over and over, for many long years.
> May the ancient garden paths be pleasant underfoot.
> May we be wise and fortunate in tending that garden, deepening its roots.
> May we know too how to find new routes to follow, responsibly and with unending love.
> And may we be fortunate to have the words of this prayer come true in our lives:

May it be	יְהִי רָצוֹן
that we go out in peace	שֶׁנֵּצֵא לְשָׁלוֹם
and stride in peace	וְנִצְעַד לְשָׁלוֹם
and see blessing in the works of our hands	וְנִרְאֶה בְרָכָה בְּמַעֲשֵׂה יָדֵינוּ
and find grace, favor, and kindness	וְנִהְיֶה לְחֵן וּלְחֶסֶד וּלְרַחֲמִים
in the eyes of God and our fellow human beings.	בְּעֵינֵי אֱלֹהִים וְאָדָם.

May it be	יְהִי רָצוֹן
that the years that await us	שֶׁהַשָּׁנִים הַבָּאוֹת לִקְרָאתֵנוּ
be blessed and good years,	יִהְיוּ בְּרוּכוֹת וְטוֹבוֹת
free of envy and malic	חֲשׂוּכוֹת מִצָּרוּת־עַיִן
and suffused with joy and laughter,	וּרְוִויוֹת בְּשִׂמְחָה וּצְחוֹק
good health of body and mind,	בִּבְרִיאוּת גּוּף, נֶפֶשׁ וְרוּחַ
creativity, growth,	בִּיצִירָה, בִּצְמִיחָה
and love.	וּבְאַהֲבָה

King David said:
I will speak of the sovereignty, greatness, and might of the Blessed Holy One:
that every day a person is formed
and every day a person is born.
Every day a person lives, every day a person dies, every day a person's spirit is taken away
and returned to the One who gave it in trust.
Every day that person is sustained, as is a baby from its mother's breasts, by the fruit of their own deeds. (*Seder Eliyahu Zuta* 15)

GLOSSARY

abba/av: "Father."

adam: "Man," "person."

adamah: "Earth," "land."

agunah: "Chained woman"; a Jewish woman whose husband will not hand over a divorce decree in a Jewish court, thereby preventing her from remarrying, usually considered a form of abuse and coercion.

alef-bet: The Hebrew alphabet.

Al HaNisim: "For the miracles"; the name of the prayer inserted into the *Amidah* and *Birkat HaMazon* for Purim and Chanukah. Many also add it for Yom HaAtzma-ut, Israel's Independence Day (the fifth of Iyar).

aliyah: "Ascent"; this word can refer to both immigration to Israel (making *aliyah*) or rising to read the blessing over the Torah during a liturgical service (having an *aliyah* to the Torah).

Amharic: The vernacular native language of the Beta Israel, the Jews of Ethiopia.

Amidah: A series of blessings that form the centerpiece of Jewish worship services; on weekdays there are nineteen blessings that form the *Amidah*, and on Shabbat there are seven.

Amora: A Jewish sage from the era of *Amoraim*, ca. 250–500 CE, who discussed Mishnaic law and whose teachings became the Gemara.

Ashkenazim (adj. Ashkenazic): The people, customs, or rites originating in Germany (Ashkenaz) that spread through Eastern Europe, Russia, Western Europe, and North America.

asiyah: The world of "action"; one of the four worlds, or levels of being, according to Jewish mystical thought.

atzilut: The world of "emanation"; one of the four worlds, or levels of being, according to Jewish mystical thought.

av/eim beit din: "Father/mother of the house of law"; the highest judicial official in a Jewish court of law.

Avinu: "Our Father"; a common way to refer to God in a more personal, familial tone.

Avinu Malkeinu: "Our Father, Our King"; one of the central prayers of the High Holy Days.

aviv: "Spring."

bal tashchit: "Do not destroy"; one of Judaism's basic ethical principles prohibiting wasteful destruction, usually applied to Jewish environmentalism.

beit (pl. batei) din: "House of law"; a Jewish court of law.

Beit Hillel: The House (school of thought) of Hillel (Jerusalem, first century BCE to first century CE). Hillel was one of the most important Jewish religious figures, whose teachings feature prominently in the Rabbinic literature; he and his school of thought were in perpetual debate with Beit Shammai, and his rulings—considered more lenient than Shammai's—are accepted as authoritative for Jewish law.

beit (pl. batei) k'neset: "House of assembly"; synagogue.

beit (pl. batei) midrash: "House of learning"; both the institution and the space dedicated for Torah study.

Beit Mikdash: The ancient Temple in Jerusalem.

Beit Shammai: The House (school of thought) of Shammai (Jerusalem, first century BCE to first century CE). Shammai was an important Jewish figure, whose teachings are featured throughout Rabbinic literature; he and his school of thought were in perpetual debate with Beit Hillel, and his rulings—considered stricter and more literal than Hillel's—are rarely accepted as Jewish law.

Beta Israel: The Ethiopian Jewish community.

Between the straits (*bein ham'tzarim*): The three-week period of mourning between the seventeenth of Tammuz, marking the breach of Jerusalem's walls by the Babylonian army in 586 BCE, and Tishah B'Av, marking the destruction the First and Second Temples (586 BCE and 70 CE respectively).

bikurim: "First fruits"; the harvest offering that was brought to Jerusalem and the Temple in ancient times.

bimah: "Raised platform"; usually the place where the Torah is read and prayer leaders stand.

Binah: "Wisdom" or "Intuition"; one of the ten *s'firot* of Jewish mystical thought.

Birkat HaMazon: "Blessing after Meals," composed of four blessings and additional verses.

b'riah: The world of "creation"; one of the four worlds, or levels of being, according to Jewish mystical thought.

b'rit milah: "Covenant of circumcision"; the ceremony that formally initiates male babies into the covenant with God through the act of circumcision. Today there are also ceremonies marking the birth of female babies.

chalakah: "Shearing"; the first haircut for a three-year-old child, traditionally for a boy. In Yiddish and among Ashkenazic Jews, it is referred to as an *upsherin*.

chameitz: "Leavening"; a category of food—usually made from grains—that contain leaven or that may be contaminated by leavened products; forbidden to be consumed during Passover.

chanukat habayit: "Dedication of a home."

chanukiyah (pl. *chanukiyot*): The nine-branched candelabra lit on Chanukah; some also refer to it as *menorah* (pl. *menorot*), which technically was the seven-branched candelabra that stood in the Temple.

chatan/kalat B'reishit: "Groom/bride of Genesis"; the person who offers the Torah blessing (*aliyah*) on Simchat Torah, before the Torah cycle begins again with Genesis.

chatan/kalat Torah: "Groom/bride of the Torah"; the person who offers the Torah blessing (*aliyah*) on Simchat Torah before the entire cycle of Torah is completed with the reading at the end of Deuteronomy.

chazan/chazanit: Musical prayer leader, cantor.

cherem: A type of excommunication pronounced by a rabbi or a community.

Chesed: "Compassion/Love"; one of the ten *s'firot* of Jewish mystical thought.

cheshbon hanefesh: "Accounting of the soul"; a spiritual process of self-reflection that becomes the focus during Elul—the month before the High Holy Days—and during the Ten Days of Repentance between Rosh HaShanah and Yom Kippur.

chet: "Sin"; a term used in archery to indicate an arrow that has missed its target, therefore transforming the idea of *chet* from "sin" to "missing the mark."

chiloni: The word commonly used in Israel to describe people who identify as secular.

chodesh: "Month."

chutzpah: Audacity, extreme self-confidence.

dati: The word commonly used in Israel to describe people who identify as religious.

Days of Awe (in Hebrew, *Yamim Noraim*): The period spanning Rosh HaShanah (New Year) and Yom Kippur (Day of Atonement).

Dead Sea Scrolls: A collection of ancient Hebrew and Aramaic manuscripts discovered in caves near Qumran, believed to be hidden by a Jewish sect during the time of Roman rule and Jewish revolt in the first century CE. Some of these manuscripts, now on display at the Israel Museum, are the oldest known versions of Hebrew biblical books.

derech eretz: "Way of the land"; a phrase that means being respectful toward others.

Din: "Judgment"; one of the ten *s'firot* of Jewish mystical thought. Also referred to as *G'vurah*.

dreidel (in Hebrew, *s'vivon*): The spinning top played with during Chanukah.

Eretz Yisrael: "Land of Israel"; specifically, the physical land that was ancient Israel, distinct from the people (*am*) or State (*M'dinat*) of Israel.

Gaon (pl. *Geonim*): The Jewish head of the Babylonian academy from the period ca. 550–1050 CE.

Ge'ez: The ancient holy language of the Beta Israel; used for prayer and for the writing of the *Orit* (the Torah).

Geihinom: The word describing the Jewish concept of hell, derived from the name of a valley (Gei Ben Hinom) south of Jerusalem where a cult devoted to the god Moloch would sacrifice children.

gelt: Yiddish word for gold or coins; now it is usually made of chocolate and given to children on Chanukah.

Gemara: Commentary and expansion on the Mishnah from the second to fifth centuries CE. Together with the Mishnah, it comprises the Jerusalem and Babylonian Talmuds.

geshem: "Rain."

get: Jewish bill of divorce.

g'matria: A type of Jewish numerology wherein each Hebrew letter corresponds to a number; often used as a means for textual interpretation.

g'milut chasadim: "Acts of loving-kindness."

genizah: A depository (usually attached to a synagogue) for damaged sacred texts that cannot be thrown away. Specifically refers to the Cairo Genizah, in which unprecedented wealth of Jewish manuscripts were found (from the sixth to nineteenth century).

g'ulah: "Redemption."

G'vurah: "Strength/Might"; one of the ten *s'firot* of Jewish mystical thought. Also referred to as *Din*.

hachnasat orchim: "Welcoming guests" or "welcoming the stranger."

haftarah: A selection from the books of Prophets (*N'vi-im*) read on Shabbat as part of the Torah service.

Haggadah (pl. Haggadot): "Telling"; the book that contains the blessings, readings, and rituals for the Passover seder.

halachah: Jewish law.

Hallel: "Praise"; the special addition of Psalms 113–118 to festival worship services, sometimes recited in their entirety or in part. There is also the Great *Hallel* (Psalm 136) and the Daily *Hallel* (verses of praise) recited in the morning service.

hamantaschen (in Hebrew, *oznei Haman*): "Haman's purse" (Yiddish) or "Haman's ear" (Hebrew); a triangle-shaped cookie filled with jam, poppy seeds, chocolate, or other ingredients eaten during Purim, named after the villain of the Purim story, Haman.

HaTikvah: "The Hope"; Israel's national anthem.

Havdalah: "Separation"; the ceremony occurring at the end of Shabbat or a holiday marking the separation between sacred time and ordinary time.

hilula: A celebration or commemoration held on the anniversary of the death of a religious leader or a righteous person.

Hod: "Splendor"; one of the ten *s'firot* of Jewish mystical thought.

Id Al-banaat: Arabic term for Festival of the Women/Daughters, a north African Jewish tradition.

IDF: Israel Defense Forces.

ima/eim: "Mother."

iyun: "Study, deliberation, meditation, reflection"; in this volume, an *iyun* signifies a unique section devoted to a particular topic.

Kabbalah: An umbrella term referring to Jewish mysticism.

Kabbalat Shabbat: "Receiving/Welcoming the Sabbath"; the special liturgical ceremony composed of a series of psalms and hymns recited before Shabbat *Maariv* worship.

Karaites: An ancient Jewish sect (still in existence today) that rejected Rabbinic law and focused mostly on biblical law.

kashrut: The system determining which foods are appropriate or fit (kosher) to eat.

kavanah: "Intention"; a *kavanah* is a way to mentally and spiritually prepare for what follows, be it a prayer, an experience, or reading the text that follows.

kes (pl. *kessoch*): Title of the traditional religious leader of the Beta Israel.

Keter: "Crown"; the first of the ten *s'firot* of Jewish mystical thought.

ketubah: A marriage contract.

kibbutz: "Grouping"; a type of communal, cooperative work and living collective, originally agricultural but now including other economic branches, first established by members of the Second Aliyah. Today, many kibbutzim are privatized and no longer cooperative.

kibbutznik/kibbutznit: A member of a kibbutz.

Kiddush: A blessing recited on Shabbat and holidays over a glass of wine or grape juice, marking the sanctification of the day.

kinot: "Elegies," "laments."

kohein: "Priest."

Kol Nidrei: "All vows"; the legal text recited (or chanted or sung) as Yom Kippur begins, releasing members of the community from all the vows they made or will make.

Kotel: "Wall"; specifically, this refers to the Western Wall, one of the walls surrounding the Temple Mount in Jerusalem.

K'riat Sh'ma L'Mitah: "Recitation of the *Sh'ma* at Bedtime"; the collection of prayers recited before going to sleep.

Ladino: A Judeo-Spanish romance language developed by Sephardic Jews; it is still spoken today. Also called Judesmo.

latkes (in Hebrew, *l'vivot*): Potato pancakes fried in oil.

leap month: In the Hebrew calendar, an extra month following Adar (called simply Adar *bet* or Adar II) is added to the calendar every seven out of nineteen years.

leap year: A year with an extra month (Adar II) that adjusts the lunar calendar to the solar calendar. In Hebrew, it is called *shanah m'uberet*, "a pregnant year."

Maariv/Arvit: The evening prayer service.

Maccabees: The fighters who rebelled against Seleucid rule, rededicated the Temple, and created the festival of Chanukah; also the names of the apocryphal books describing these events.

machzor: The prayer book for Rosh HaShanah and Yom Kippur; there is also a special prayer book called *machzor* for Sukkot, Passover, and Shavuot.

Malchut: "Sovereignty"; also called *Shechinah*, the lowest of the ten *s'firot* of Jewish mystical thought. It is considered a feminine *s'firah*.

mashiach: "Messiah."

Matityahu: The Hebrew pronunciation of Mattathias (died in 166 BCE), the scion of the Hasmonaean dynasty and the leader of the Maccabees.

melamed: "Teacher"; mostly used in a *talmud Torah*, a traditional religious (elementary) school.

m'gillah (pl. *m'gillot*): "Scroll"; used to describe the Book of Esther (*M'gillat Esther*) and other books of the Hebrew Bible read on festivals.

midbar: "Desert" or "wilderness."

Mikdash: "Tabernacle, Temple"; usually used to refer to the First or Second Temple in Jerusalem.

mikdash m'at: "A minor temple"; usually used to refer to a synagogue or a home.

mikveh: A pool of water used for ritual immersion for purposes of conversion or ritual purity.

Mimouna: A Moroccan Jewish celebration occurring immediately after Passover ends.

Minchah: The afternoon prayer service.

Mi Shebeirach: "May the One who blessed"; a category of petitionary prayers recited during the Torah service, often used to ask for healing.

Mishkan HaNefesh: "Sanctuary of the soul"; the name of North America's Reform Movement's High Holy Day prayer book (*machzor*), published in 2015.

Mishkan T'filah: "Sanctuary of prayer"; the name of North America's Reform Movement's Shabbat, Festival, and weekday prayer book, published in 2007.

Mishnah: The first major Rabbinic written collection of Jewish law, redacted by Rabbi Y'hudah HaNasi, ca. 220 CE. It is divided into six orders.

mizrach: "East"; can also describe a decorated sign that hangs on the eastern wall of a home or synagogue, directing people toward Jerusalem.

Mizrachi: Jewish communities from the Middle East and North Africa.

m'laveih malkah: "Escorting the queen"; a special meal held immediately after Shabbat ends on Saturday night, in an attempt to more gradually return from the sacredness of Shabbat—often referred to as a queen—to the routine of the rest of the week.

Mount Herzl: The national cemetery of Israel located in Jerusalem; Theodor Herzl and major Zionist leaders are buried there, and it serves as a military cemetery. In Hebrew it is called Har Herzl.

Musaf: An additional prayer service recited on Shabbat, Rosh Chodesh (new month), and holidays, replacing the additional offering brought to the Temple.

Nachman of Bratzlav, Rabbi: An influential Chasidic leader in the late eighteenth and early nineteenth centuries, whose followers are called the Bratzlav Chasidim.

Netzach: "Victory"; one of the ten *s'firot* of Jewish mystical thought.

nigunim: "Melodies"; wordless tunes often used during Jewish prayer or ritual.

olim: "Immigrants" to Israel.

omer: Sheaf of wheat or barley.

Operation Moses: The 1984 mass immigration of the Ethiopian Jewish community to Israel.

Orit: The Torah written in Ge'ez; used by the Ethiopian Jewish community.

parashah: "Portion"; usually refers to the weekly Torah portion. The Torah is divided into fifty-four portions to be read each week, though in some cases two portions are read on the same Shabbat.

pay'tan (pl. *pay'tanim*): "Poet"; late ancient and medieval liturgical Hebrew poets. Today, *payatan* also refers to a liturgical music composer or performer.

pei-ah (pl. *pei-ot*): "Corner, side, edge"; can refer to the corners of one's fields that are left unharvested or unplowed to allow people who are poor to collect food. Another meaning is the unshaven or uncut sideburns worn by Orthodox and ultra-Orthodox men.

Pirkei Avot: "Teaching of the Fathers/Ancestors"; a collection of ethical teachings from Rabbinic sages.

piyut (pl. *piyutim*): "Poem"; a religious poem or hymn sometimes included in the fixed order of a worship service.

pogroms: This usually refers to attacks on Jews in Eastern Europe and Russia in the nineteenth and twentieth centuries, but also refers more broadly to any attack by a majority group against a minority group.

P'sukei D'Zimrah: Aramaic phrase meaning "verses of praise"; the collection of psalms that form the first part of *Shacharit* morning services.

Purim Sheini: "Second Purim"; innovative and local Purim-type holidays that commemorate a personal, familial, or communal redemption.

regel (pl. *r'galim*): "pilgrimage [festivals]," also known as *Shalosh R'galim* or Three Pilgrimage Festivals, referring to Sukkot, Passover, and Shavuot, because their original observance required making a pilgrimage to Jerusalem to offer sacrifices at the Temple.

saba: "Grandfather."

savta: "Grandmother."

s'chach: "Branch, thatch"; the natural material required for the covering of a sukkah.

seder: "Order"; used here to refer to the ritual meal held on the first two nights of Passover.

sefer Torah (pl. *sifrei Torah*): Scroll or book of Torah, written by a special scribe (called a *sofer STaM*) on parchment.

Sephardim (adj. Sephardic): The people, customs, or rites originating in Spain (Sepharad) that spread through the Middle East, Turkey, Amsterdam, South America, and North America after the expulsion from Spain (1492).

seven species: Seven types of food mentioned in the Bible (Deuteronomy 8:8), including wheat, barley, grapes, figs, pomegranates, olives, and honey (most likely from dates).

s'firah (pl. *s'firot*): One of the ten emanations or dimensions of God.

S'firat HaOmer: "Counting of the Omer"; the practice of counting each day of the seven weeks between Passover and Shavuot.

Shacharit: The morning prayer service.

shamash: A synagogue sexton or usher, who generally assists the clergy or acts as the caretaker of the synagogue building.

shaon hakayitz: Daylight saving time.

Shechinah: The feminine, indwelling presence of God; also called *Malchut*, the lowest of the ten *s'firot* of Jewish mystical thought and therefore closest to humanity.

shefa: "Flow"; the divine emanation flowing through the ten *s'firot* of Jewish mystical thought.

Shoah: "Catastrophe"; the Hebrew term for the Holocaust.

siddur: "Prayer book"; the Hebrew words *siddur* and *seder* share the same root letters, reflecting that a prayer book is also a book of the order of the prayers.

Sigd: A communal holiday of covenantal return celebrated by the Beta Israel, on the twenty-ninth of Marcheshvan.

s'lichah: "Forgive"; a category of penitential prayer.

sufganiyah (pl. *sufganiyot*): A fried donut usually filled with fruit jelly or jam, a traditional Israeli food for Chanukah.

sukkah (pl. sukkot): "Booth"; the open-air, open-sided thatched hut erected during the holiday of Sukkot as a reminder of the time the Israelites wandered in the desert.

tal: "Dew."

Talmud: The Rabbinic collection combining the Mishnah and Gemara. The Jerusalem Talmud, or *Y'rushalmi*, was codified ca. 350 CE in the Galilee of the Land of Israel; the Babylonian Talmud, or *Bavli*, was codified in Babylon ca. 550 CE.

talmud Torah: A religious elementary school.

Tanach or **TaNaKH:** The Hebrew Bible, composed of the acronym *Torah* (Five Books of Moses), *N'vi-im* (Prophets), and *K'tuvim* (Writings).

Tanna: A sage from the era of the *Tannaim*, ca. 70–250 CE, whose teachings are codified in the Mishnah and elsewhere.

Targum: "Translation"; usually used to refer to translations of the Hebrew Bible, especially into Aramaic.

Tashlich: A ceremony developed by the medieval Ashkenazic Jewish community during which sins are symbolically cast away into water.

t'chinah (pl. *t'chinot*): A prayer of supplication; originally a prayer genre specifically written for and recited by women, such as the *t'chinah* recited before Shabbat candle lighting.

t'filah: "Prayer."

T'filat HaGeshem: "Prayer for Rain"; recited on Sh'mini Atzeret, the day after Sukkot, which marks the beginning of the rainy season in Land of Israel.

T'filat Tal: "Prayer for Dew"; recited from the first day of Passover through Sh'mini Atzeret, corresponding to the dry season in the Land of Israel.

T'fillat HaAdam: "Prayer of the human"; the name of Israel's Progressive (Reform) Movement's prayer book for Shabbat, Festival, and weekdays (2020; English-Hebrew version, 2022).

t'fillin: "Phylacteries"; black leather prayer boxes attached to the forehead and forearm with dangling leather straps during morning weekday worship, which contain four passages from the Torah, including the first portion of the *Sh'ma* (Deuteronomy 6:4–9).

Tiferet: "Beauty"; one of the ten *s'firot* of Jewish mystical thought, associated with Jacob.

tikkun: "Repair."

tikkun olam: "Repair of the world"; a Lurianic Kabbalistic concept that transformed the Rabbinic phrase into a theology, wherein the fundamental brokenness of the world can be repaired through performing religious deeds when they are combined with spiritual intention and contemplation. Many Jews use this phrase today to refer to social justice efforts and activism.

t'kufah: "Period" or "season." The Rabbinic sages determined that there are four "seasons" in the year: *T'kufat Tishrei*, *T'kufat Tevet*, *T'kufat Nisan*, and *T'kufat Tammuz*. Today, the word *t'kufah* is used more broadly.

tosafists: Talmudic commentators in the generations following the preeminent commentator Rashi, in the twelfth and thirteenth centuries.

t'shuvah: "Return"; the spiritual process of repentance and renewal that is emphasized during Elul and the High Holy Days.

tzaddik (pl. tzaddikim): A righteous or saintly person.

tzaraat: A biblical skin disease, often mistakenly translated as leprosy, that can also infect a home or cloth.

tzedakah: "Righteous giving"; usually translated as "charity," but related to the Hebrew word for righteousness.

Tziyon: "Zion."

Un'taneh Tokef: "Let us proclaim"; this liturgical poem is one of the most central prayers of Rosh HaShanah worship.

ushpizin: Aramaic for "guests"; the ceremony held each night of Sukkot that symbolically invites a male ancestor into the sukkah; new innovations include female ancestors as well.

ushpizot: A contemporary addition to *ushpizin* that invites female ancestors into the sukkah.

Vidui: "Confession"; the long and short fixed confessionary prayers recited specifically on Yom Kippur, but can also be recited daily or at the end of one's life.

wadi: Arabic word for a valley or ravine that is usually dry, except during the rainy season.

yahrzeit: The anniversary of a person's death.

Yekke: A person of German Jewish origin who is stereotyped as being extremely punctual and attentive to details.

Y'hudi: "Jew."

Yiddish: A Judeo-German dialect developed by Ashkenazic Jews; it is still spoken today.

Yizkor: Service recited on Yom Kippur and at the end of each of the Pilgrimage Festivals in memory of loved ones who have passed away.

Yom Tov: "Good day"; a festival or holiday that originated in the Torah. People sometimes say, "Gut/Good *yontif*," an Ashkenazic greeting derived from *Yom Tov*, to wish someone "happy holiday."

Y'sod: "Foundation"; one of the ten *s'firot* of Jewish mystical thought, associated with Joseph.

DIAGRAM OF THE HEBREW CALENDAR YEAR

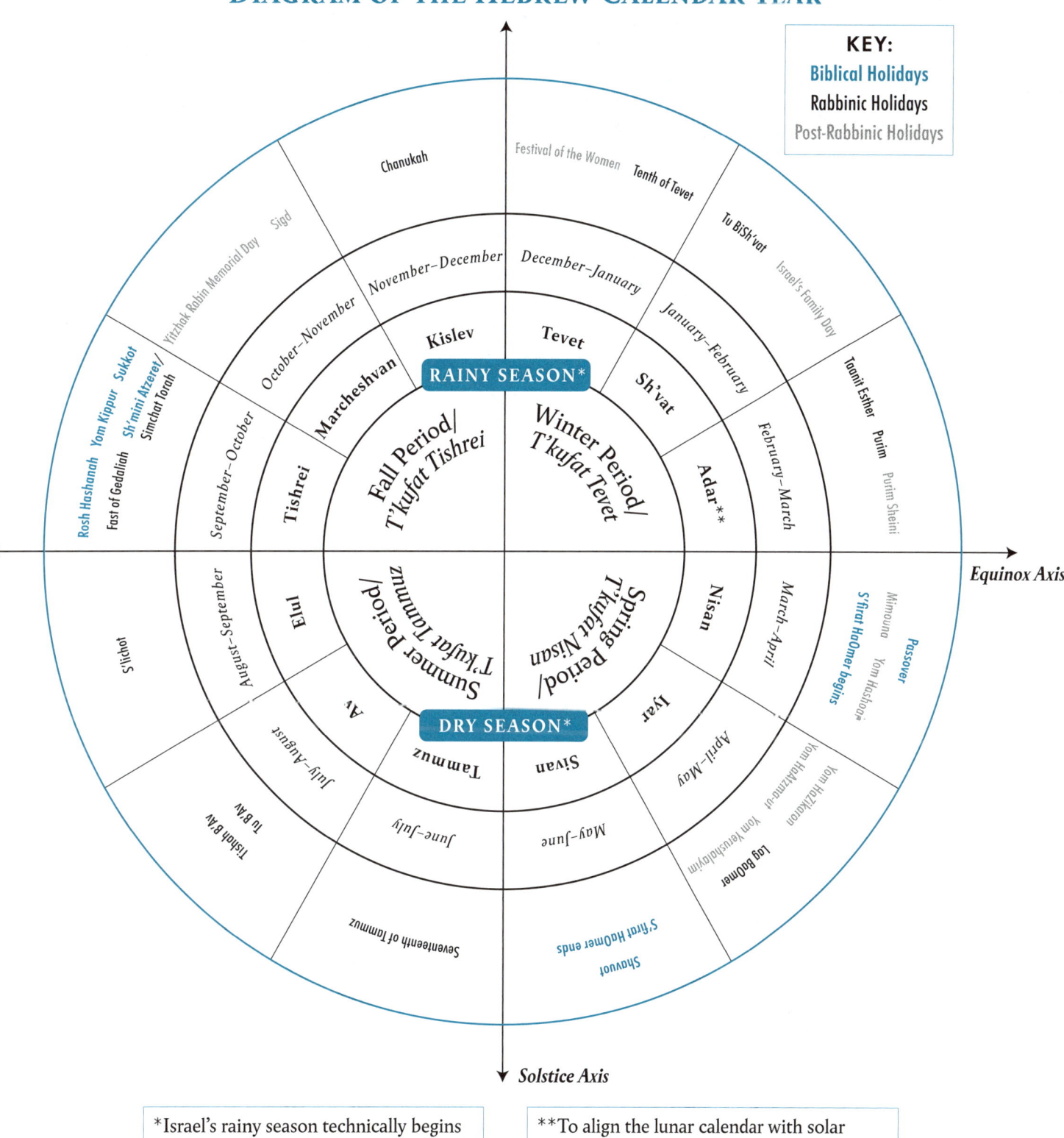

*Israel's rainy season technically begins on Sh'mini Atzeret (22 Tishrei) and ends on the first day of Passover (15 Nisan), when the dry season begins.

**To align the lunar calendar with solar seasons, the Rabbis decreed a leap year occur in seven of nineteen years by adding an extra month, Adar II, into the Hebrew calendar.

SOURCES, PERMISSIONS, AND NOTES

Preface

1. "The Seasons of the Year," from *Hovering at a Low Altitude: The Collected Poetry of Dahlia Ravikovitch* by Dahlia Ravikovitch, translated by Chana Bloch and Chana Kronfeld. Copyright © 2009 by Chana Bloch, Chana Kronfeld, and Ido Kalir. English translation copyright © 2009 by Chana Bloch and Chana Kronfeld. Used by permission of W. W. Norton & Company, Inc.
2. See the classic essay on time by the sociologist Norbert Elias, *An Essay on Time*, ed. Steven Loyal and Stephen Mennell (Dublin: University College Dublin Press, 2007).
3. For example, see Yonah Fraenkel, ed., *Machzor Pesach L'fi Minhagei Ashkenaz L'chol Anfeihem* (Jerusalem: Koren, 1993), 225–34; and Ezra Fleischer, "Studies in *Piyyut* and Medieval Hebrew Poetry," *Tarbiẓ* 39 (1969–70): 19–37 (relevant here: 19–21). See also Rabbeinu Bachya's commentary to Exodus 28:15.

Tishrei

1. "Everything changes…", originally published in German in 1964 as "Alles wandelt sich," translated by Tom Kuhn. Copyright © 1964 by Bertolt-Brecht-Erben / Suhrkamp Verlag. Translation copyright © 2019, 2015 by Tom Kuhn and David Constantine. From *The Collected Poems of Bertolt Brecht* by Bertolt Brecht, translated by Tom Kuhn and David Constantine (New York: Liveright, 2018), 905. Used by permission of Liveright Publishing Corporation.
2. The passage from "My Little Sister" by Abba Kovner, translated by Shirley Kaufman, first appeared in *My Little Sister and Selected Poems 1965–1985* (Oberlin, OH: Oberlin College Press, 1986), 72. © 1986 by Oberlin College and reprinted by permission of Oberlin College Press. Originally published in Hebrew as *Achoti K'tanah* (Tel Aviv: Sifriat Poalim, 1967), 49. © All rights reserved by Abba Kovner and ACUM.
3. Victor Turner, *The Ritual Process* (New York: Transaction Publishers, 1969).
4. On these functions of ritual, see Mary Douglas, *Purity and Danger: An Analysis of the Concepts and Pollution and Taboo* (London: Routledge and Kegan Paul, 1966).
5. Among the occasions on which Rosenblum expressed that concern is one recorded in a documentary film directed by Yehuda Yaniv, *Un'taneh Tokef* (1991), which records the Beit HaShita community's efforts to grapple with the death of so many of its sons in war.
6. I am grateful to Haggai Ben-Gurion of Beit HaShita for information about the composition of Rosenblum's *Un'taneh Tokef*.
7. Matti Friedman, *Who by Fire: Leonard Cohen in the Sinai* (New York: Spiegel & Grau, 2022), 10–11.
8. Ephraim of Bonn, cited in *Or Zarua*, Laws of Rosh HaShanah.
9. *Or Zarua*, Laws of Rosh HaShanah.
10. Adapted by the author from *Mishkan HaNefesh*, vol. 2, *Yom Kippur* (New York: CCAR Press, 2015), 208–16.
11. Pew Research Center, "Jewish Americans in 2020," May 11, 2021, https://www.pewresearch.org/religion/2021/05/11/jewish-americans-in-2020/.
12. Lea Goldberg, *Shirim*, ed. T. Ruebner (Tel Aviv: Sifriat Poalim, 1973), 2:154. © All rights reserved to Hakibbutz Hameuchad Publishing.
13. Lea Goldberg, *Shirei Sof Haderech*, trans. Pnina Peli, in *Kol Haneshamah: Shabbat v'Chagim* (Wyncote, PA: The Reconstructionist Press, 1994), 740. © All rights reserved to Hakibbutz Hameuchad Publishing.
14. Yotam Benziman, *Forgive and Not Forget: The Ethics of Forgiveness* (Jerusalem–Tel Aviv: Van Leer Jerusalem Institute and Hakibbutz Hameuchad, 2008) [Hebrew].
15. Adapted from Dalia Marx, "Wrestling with Forgiveness," ReformJudaism.org, https://reformjudaism.org/wrestling-forgiveness.
16. *Mishkan HaNefesh*, vol. 2, *Yom Kippur*, 18.
17. *Seder Rav Amram Gaon*, ed. Daniel Goldschmidt (Jerusalem: Mosad Harav Kook, 1972), 163.
18. Dalia Marx, "What's in a Bowl? Babylonian Magic Spells and the Origin of *Kol Nidrei*," in *All These Vows: Kol Nidre*, ed. Lawrence A. Hoffman (Woodstock, VT: Jewish Lights, 2011), 26–41.
19. *Mishkan HaNefesh*, vol. 2, *Yom Kippur*, 16.
20. Maimonides, *Guide for the Perplexed* 3:43.
21. Mordecai M. Kaplan, *The Meaning of God in Modern Jewish Religion* (Detroit: Wayne State University Press, 1995), 208–9.
22. Claude Levi-Strauss, *Mythologiques* (4 vols.: *The Raw and*

the Cooked, From Honey to Ashes, The Origin of Table Manners, and The Naked Man), in various editions.
23. Shimshon Gershon Rosenberg, The Remainder of Faith: Postmodern Sermons on Jewish Holidays (Tel Aviv: Resling, 2014), 75–77 [Hebrew].
24. I am grateful to my friend Dr. Anat Yisraeli for directing me to this resource: "Purple Ribbons for Sukkot," Shalom Bayit, https://www.shalom-bayit.org/purple-ribbons-for-sukkot/.
25. Gili Zivan, "The Sukkah as an Expression of the Transient and Permanent in Our Lives," The Jacob Herzog Center for Jewish Studies, https://merkazherzog.org.il/הסוכה-כביטוי-לארעי-ולקבע-שבחיינו/# [Hebrew].
26. Michal Wosner, "Tears of Simchat Torah," Ynet, September 29, 2010, https://www.ynet.co.il/articles/0,7340,L-3960769,00.html.
27. I am grateful to Rabbi Yehoram Maor and to Zeev Kainan for the inspiration for some of these blessings.
28. Mishkan HaNefesh, vol. 2, Yom Kippur, 82.
29. Chayim Nachman Bialik, Letters, vol. 1 (Tel Aviv, 1890), 21 [Hebrew].
30. Hebrew original: Kavanat HaLev: Machzor HaT'filot LaYamim Noraim (Jerusalem: Israel Movement for Progressive Judaism, 1989), 285. Translation: Dalia Marx, "Al Chet in Israeli Culture: Israeli Confessions over Everything," in We Have Sinned: Sin and Confession in Judaism—Ashamnu and Al Chet, ed. Lawrence A. Hoffman (Woodstock, VT: Jewish Lights, 2012), 64. Used by permission of Rabbi Moti Rotem and MARAM.
31. Excerpted from Rivkah Lubitch, "The Confession of the Judge, Version 2007," Ynet, September 17, 2007, https://www.ynet.co.il/articles/0,7340,L-3450317,00.html. Used by permission of Rivkah Lubitch, Center for Women's Justice.
32. Many thanks to Rabbis Ruth Gan Kagan and Nachshon David Carmi for permission to include their prayer here. Their poetic English version, which can be sung to the traditional Ashkenazic melody for the short vidui, is dedicated to their beloved teacher Rabbi Zalman Shachter-Shalomi.
33. First published by Dr. Vered Noam on her Facebook page before Yom Kippur 2013. I am grateful to her for permission to include her Vidui here.
34. Y'hudah Aryeh Leib Alter, S'fat Emet, Genesis vol., sermon for Chanukah 1893.
35. Personal conversation with author, date unknown.
36. Personal conversation with author, date unknown.
37. Mishkan T'filah, 473.

Marcheshvan
1. Rabbi Maya Leibovich in Parashat HaMayim: Immersion in Water as an Opportunity for Spiritual Renewal and Spiritual Growth, ed. A. Lisita, D. Marx, M. Leibovich, T. Duvdevani (Tel Aviv: Hakibbutz Hameuchad Publishing, 2011), 146 [Hebrew]. Used by permission of Rabbi Maya Leibovich.
2. Leibovich, in Parashat HaMayim, 146.
3. In Hebrew, the words for geshem, "rain," and hitgashmut, "realization," share the same root of gimel-shin-mem.
4. Esther Raab, "Geshem," in Poems of Esther Raab, ed. Tzvi Luz (Tel Aviv: Hakibbutz Hameuchad, 1997) [Hebrew]. I am grateful to Ehud Ben-Ezer, the heir to Esther Raab's literary estate, for permission to use her poem and add an English translation. © All rights reserved by Esther Raab and ACUM.
5. Talma Alyagon-Roz, "Geshem B'ito," in HaTikvah Chozeret LaLev: MiShirei Talma Alyagon Roz, ed. Amnon Shiloh (Haifa: publisher unknown, 2003). © All rights reserved by Talma Alyagon-Roz and ACUM.
6. The Ladino scholar Yehuda Hatzvi explained the origin of this aphorism in a personal email correspondence. In reply to my question about it, he wrote, "As far as I know, the origin of the saying is in the Sephardic Jewish community of Jerusalem in the nineteenth century. The 'falakot' are the strikes on the soles of the feet (a practice that still continues in the Middle East). The governor of Jerusalem in those days, whether out of consideration for the Tishrei holidays or whether he wanted the holidays to pass without the shouts and screams of prisoners being beaten in the Kishleh, the Ottoman jail in the Old City, ordered a suspension of the falakot, which were resumed after Sukkot and Sh'mini Atzeret. It is obvious that, over time, the reference to falakot came to mean the hard work and concerns of ordinary workdays."
7. "Birkat HaShanim," in Siddur Rinat Yisrael, ed. Shlomo Tal (Tel Aviv: Moreshet, 1984), 60 [Hebrew].
8. This is a direct quote from the official Prayer for the State of Israel.
9. "Eitan Haber, trusted aide to Yitzhak Rabin, dies at 80," Toronto Star, October 7, 2020, https://www.thestar.com/news/world/middleeast/2020/10/07/eitan-haber-trusted-aide-to-yitzhak-rabin-dies-at-80.html.
10. "Chukim l'zichro shel Yitzhak Rabin," R'shimat Chukim, Knesset, https://www.knesset.gov.il/rabin/heb/Rab_Law2.htm.
11. Yochi Brandes, The Secret Book of Kings, trans. Yardenne Greenspan (New York: St. Martin's Press, 2016), 404–5.
12. "Michtav me'et Omnitsky, David el Chayim Nachman Bialik," The National Library of Israel, accessed March 23, 2023, https://www.nli.org.il/he/archives/NNL_ARCHIVE_AL997009626348605171/NLI.
13. Yosi Ziv, Festival and Holiday in the Ethiopian Jewish Tradition of Beta Israel (Tel Aviv: Makhon Mofet; Jerusalem: Ben Zvi Institute, 2017), 159–160 [Hebrew]. I want to thank Shoshana Ben-Dor for her useful comments on this section.
14. Ziv, Festival and Holiday, 171.
15. I am grateful to Shoshana Ben-Dor for her assistance in

translation and for her permission to use her transcriptions and translations as the basis of material presented here.

Kislev

1. This *kavanah* begins with a translation of the traditional words of the prayer *Al HaNisim*, "For the miracles," recited on Chanukah. The lines following "For the miracles / large and small" are my personal addition.
2. Originally written in the thirteenth century by Mordechai ben Isaac. Translated into the German by Leopold Stein. Translated from German to English by Marcus Jastrow and Gustav Gottheil.
3. William G. Braude, trans., *The Midrash on Psalms* (New Haven, CT: Yale University Press, 1959), 1:279.
4. Ben Zion Dinur's remarks appear in Yom Tov Levinsky, *Sefer HaMoadim* 5:197 (Tel Aviv: Dvir, 1954).
5. Aharon Zeev, "*Anu Nos'im Lapidim*," arrangement by Binyamin Bar-Am (Tel Aviv: Hotza-at HaMerkaz L'Tarbut, 1950). The Hebrew text and links to recordings of the song are available at https://www.zemereshet.co.il/m/song.asp?id=357. © All rights reserved by Aharon Zeev and ACUM.
6. Ely Ben-Gal, *Ke-she-och'lim im HaSatan* (Tel Aviv: Am Oved, 1989), 323.
7. Saturday Night Live, "Weekend Update: Adam Sandler on Hanukkah," December 3, 1994, video, uploaded August 6, 2013, www.youtube.com.
8. Jerry Bodlander, "Kagan Deploys Humor and the Artful Dodge," *Associated Press*, June 29, 2010, video, https://www.youtube.com.
9. The Hebrew text of *M'gillat Y'hudit* and an English translation are available online: https://opensiddur.org/readings-and-sourcetexts/festival-and-fast-day-readings/jewish/hanukkah-readings/megillat-yehudit-for-hanukkah/.
10. Y. Y. Rivlin, "Chanukah among the Eastern Jews," *Machanayim* 54 (1960–61): 66–68 [Hebrew].
11. Ruth Fredman Cernea, ed., *The Great Latke-Hamantash Debate* (Chicago: University of Chicago Press, 2005).
12. Author's translation.
13. The first selection (א) is of a widely circulating prayer in Hebrew. To my chagrin, I have not succeeded in tracing its source, nor the source of the one that follows (ב). Readers able to identify the origin of either are invited to contact me. The translations of selections א and ב here preserve the rhyme rather than the meaning of each line. These two translations are by Rabbi Anne Villarreal-Belford.
14. Selection ג is adapted from a prayer composed by Rabbi Chayim Yosef David Azulai (1724–1806), a Sephardic rabbi who lived in *Eretz Yisrael*. He composed a *chanukat habayit* liturgy that included passages for study, from the Mishnah and the *Zohar*.
15. Selection ז is borrowed from the prayer book of Israel's Masorti (Conservative) Movement, *Vaani T'filati: Siddur Yisraeli* (Jerusalem: Rabbinical Assembly of Israel and the Masorti Movement, 2010), 230.
16. Adapted from Richard Levy, *Songs Ascending: The Book of Psalms in a New Translation with Textual and Spiritual Commentary* (New York: CCAR Press, 2018), 1:108.

Tevet

1. An earlier version of this prayer appeared in Rabbi Gili Zidkiyahu's thesis for rabbinic ordination at Hebrew Union College-Jewish Institute of Religion, and has been reworked and adapted with help from the author for this publication.
2. A. D. Gordon, in a talk at the founding of the Hebrew Writers Association, 1921, https://benyehuda.org/read/6714 [Hebrew].
3. Lea Goldberg, *Shirim*, ed. Tuvia Ruebner (Tel Aviv: Sifriat Poalim, 1973) 2:18 [Hebrew]. © All rights reserved to Hakibbutz Hameuchad Publishing. "Night," quoted from *Lea Goldberg: Selected Poetry and Drama*, trans. Rachel Tzvia Back and T. Carmi (New Milford, CT: Toby Press, 2005), 107 [English]. © 2005. Used with the permission of Koren Publishers Jerusalem Ltd. and The Toby Press LLC. © All rights reserved to Hakibbutz Hameuchad Publishing.
4. Lea Goldberg, *Shirim*, ed. Tuvia Ruebner (Tel Aviv: Sifriat Poalim, 1973) 2:196 [Hebrew]. © All rights reserved to Hakibbutz Hameuchad Publishing. "A Night Psalm," quoted from *Lea Goldberg: Selected Poetry and Drama*, trans. Rachel Tzvia Back and T. Carmi, 107 [English]. © 2005. Used with the permission of Koren Publishers Jerusalem Ltd. and The Toby Press LLC. © All rights reserved to Hakibbutz Hameuchad Publishing.
5. Yom Tov Levinsky, *Sefer HaMoadim*, vol. 5 (Tel Aviv: Dvir, 1954), 59, 277–78.
6. In Biblical Antiquities, an extracanonical work that dates from Second Temple times, Jephthah's daughter is known as Seila, which seems to be a corruption of *sh'eilah*, a Hebrew term for a "request," perhaps reflecting her request to her father for a delay of "two months" to "bewail her maidenhood" and perhaps also because of her father's words in this book, "Rightly is thy name called Seila, that you should be offered for a sacrifice" (Biblical Antiquities 40:1). According to this tradition, Jephthah's daughter willingly accepted her fate.
7. *Sefer Abudarham HaShalem* (Jerusalem: Usha, 1963), 311.
8. Rivkah Lubitch, in *Dirshuni: Contemporary Women's Midrash*, ed. Tamar Kadari (Waltham, MA: Brandeis University Press, 2022), 100.
9. *Midrash Chanukah*, in Adolf Jellinek, *Beit HaMidrash*, vol. 1 (Leipzig: Druck und Verlag von Friedrich Niels, 1853), 132–136.
10. The text quoted here is from a memorial plaque for

Regina Jonas in Berlin on Krausnickstrasse.
11. Elisa Klapheck, *Fräulein Rabbiner Jonas: The Story of the First Woman Rabbi*, trans. Toby Axelrod (San Francisco: Jossey-Bass, 2004).
12. Regina Jonas, *Fraeulein Rabbiner Jonas: kann die Frau das rabbinische Amt bekleiden? – eine Streitschrift*, ed. Elissa Klapheck (Berlin: Hentrich & Hentrich, 1999), 285.
13. See Melody Barron, "The Story of Regina Jonas, the First Female Rabbi," *The Librarians* (blog), The National Library of Israel, November 9, 2017, https://blog.nli.org.il/en/rabbi_regina_jonas/.
14. Shlomit Elitzur, *Wherefore Have We Fasted?* (Jerusalem: World Union of Jewish Studies, 2007), 102-4 [Hebrew].
15. Translation adapted by author.
16. Hebrew readers will find a more extensive exploration of the bedtime *Sh'ma* in my book *When I Sleep and When I Wake: On the Prayers between Day and Night* (Tel Aviv: Yediot Books, 2010) [Hebrew].
17. Chen Ben Or Tsfoni, "T'chinah for Bedtime Sh'ma," *Barchu: Toward a Renewal of Prayer in Israel*, ed. Yehoyada Amir, Mike Nitzan, and Naama Dafni Kellen (Jerusalem: HaT'nuah HaReformit B'Yisrael, 2010), 126 [Hebrew].
18. Author's translation.
19. *Shulchan Aruch*, *Orach Chayim* 60:5.
20. Author's translation.
21. Natan Alterman, "Shir Siyyum," from his collection *Chagigat Kayitz* (Tel Aviv: Hakibbutz Hameuchad Publishing, 1965), 197. © All rights reserved by Natan Alterman and ACUM.

Sh'vat
1. As discussed by Kathryn Hellerstein, the Yiddish *goldene keyt* (golden chain) is a symbol in Jewish lore of the continuity of traditional beliefs and values. I. L. Peretz wrote a famous play called *Di Goldene Keyt*, of which Molodowsky was certainly aware. "Open the Gate" is reprinted from *Paper Bridges: Selected Poems of Kadya Molodowsky*, trans. and ed. Kathryn Hellerstein (Detroit: Wayne State University Press, 1999), 207. © 1999 Kathryn Hellerstein, with the permission of Wayne State University Press.
2. Molodowsky, *Paper Bridges*, 207.
3. This Yiddish transliteration was taken from The Yiddish Book Center: Preserving Jewish Culture website, adapted from *In eynem: The New Yiddish Textbook*, vol. 1, by Asya Vaisman Schulman, Jordan Brown, and Mikhl Yashinsky (Amherst, MA: White Goat Press, 2020), https://www.yiddishbookcenter.org/language-literature-culture/heymarbet-homework/open-gate.
4. Author's adapted translation.
5. The complete *k'rovah* is found in J. Schirmann, "Shirim Achadim L'Ibn Gabirol," in *Leket Shirim U-fiyyutim*, Micha Joseph Schocken bar mitzvah volume (Berlin: privately published, 1936), 14-20.
6. I first encountered this idea in Ari Elon's book *Trees, Earth, and Torah: A Tu B'Shvat Anthology* (Philadelphia: Jewish Publication Society, 1999).
7. Assaf Golan, "Seder Tu B'Shvat: Why and How Is the Holiday Celebrated?" *Israel Hayom*, January 27, 2021, https://www.israelhayom.co.il/article/844609 [Hebrew].
8. I am grateful to Rabbi Moti Rotem for permission to reprint his ecological *vidui* here. This *vidui* was originally published in 1997 by Beit Daniel of Tel Aviv in their version of Tikkun Tu B'Shvat.
9. For more detail, see Elon, *Trees, Earth, and Torah*.
10. Pinchas Elad-Lander (1905-87) wrote the lyrics to the song *Mal'u Asameinu Bar* ("Our Silos are Filled with Grain") in 1932-33, and David Zehavi (1910-77) set them to music that same time.
11. Chaim Pallachi, *Sefer Moed L'chol Chai* (Bnei Brak: Makash, 1997-98), 7:9.
12. The third key in God's hand is the key of the revival of the dead. This topic appears alongside that of rain in the second blessing of the *Amidah*, known as *G'vurot* (God's mighty acts).
13. Martin Buber, *Tales of the Hasidim: The Later Masters* (New York: Schocken Books, 1948), 148.
14. Natan Zach, *Kol HeChalav V'had'vash* (Tel Aviv: Am Oved, 1994-95), 5. © All rights reserved by Natan Zach and ACUM.
15. Kolech's purpose, as it appears on its website (https://www.kolech.org.il/en/), is "to increase public awareness and bring about change in Israeli religious society. It seeks to disseminate the values of gender equality and mutual respect, to encourage equal opportunities for women in the public arena, including the advancement of women's rights in religious and *halachic* spheres. Kolech encourages greater equality for women in matters of personal status, such as marriage and divorce, and is at the forefront of an uncompromising battle against all forms of gender violence."
16. Rabbi Myra Hovav, "Erev Vavoker L'cha V'alecha" (Rabbinic thesis, Hebrew Union College–Jewish Institute of Religion, Jerusalem campus, 2011), 18.
17. Sarit Hadad, vocalist, "K'she-halev Bocheh," by Yossi Gispan, lyrics, and Shlomo Elbaz, music, track 8 on *Ashlayot Metukot*, 2001. © All rights reserved by Yossi Gispan and ACUM.
18. Kobi Oz, "Mizmorei Nevochim," Makom website, August 2, 2009, https://www.mako.co.il/music-Magazine/articles/Article-95277a43e7d9421006.htm.
19. Biblical text translation adapted by the author.
20. Rabbi Tamar Duvdevani, "Midrash *Shiru*." The Hebrew original appears in *Dirshuni: Midreshei Nashim*, ed. Nehama Weingarten-Mintz and Tamar Biala (Tel Aviv: Yediot Acharonot, 2009), 86. Translation by Rabbi Haim Shalom, used by permission of the translator.

21. The Hebrew original is in Esther Shkalim, *Mah Tzericha Isha Lada'at* (Modi'in: Kineret Zmora Bitan, 2017). © All rights reserved by Esther Shkalim and ACUM.

22. Marcia Falk, *The Book of Blessings: New Jewish Prayers for Daily Life, the Sabbath, and the New Moon Festival* (New York: CCAR Press, 2017), 124–25.

23. Sarah Honig, "Another Tack: A Very Israeli Story," *Contextualization* (blog), June 7, 2013, https://sarahhonig.com/2013/06/07/another-tack-a-very-israeli-story/#more-2377. The translation, which was first published in the *Jerusalem Post*, appears with the translator's permission. © All rights reserved by Fania Bergstein and ACUM.

24. Jewish Women's Archive, "Letter from Henrietta Szold," https://jwa.org/node/22356.

25. Chaya Rowen Baker, "Blessings for Family Day," was originally published in the Hebrew version of this book, *Bazman* (Rishon L'Tzion, Israel: Y'diot Achronot, 2018), 147–148. Used by permission of Rabbi Chaya Rowen Baker.

26. Oshrat Morag, "A Blessing for Children and Families," in *Tefilat Ha-Adam: An Israeli Reform Siddur for Shabbat*, ed. Dalia Marx and Alona Lisitsa, trans. Levi Weiman-Kelman and Efrat Rothem (Jerusalem: MARAM, 2022), 208. Used by permission of Rabbi Oshrat Morag and MARAM.

Adar

1. Yaakov Orland, "*Shir Same-ach*." Track 3 on the album *Shimcha Belibi*. Aderet Music Corp., 2006. MP3. © All rights reserved by Yaakov Orland and ACUM.

2. The Hebrew original is from Natan Alterman, "*Esther Ha-Malka*" section of "*Shir HaBadchan*" in *Machazot* (Tel Aviv: Hakibbutz Hameuchad Publishing, 1973), 398–99. © All rights reserved by Natan Alterman and ACUM.

3. Gabi Nitzan, *Badulina*, trans. Sondra Silverston (self-pub., 2019), 36, 28.

4. Martin Seligman, *Authentic Happiness: Using the New Positive Psychology to Realize Your Potential for Lasting Fulfillment* (New York: Free Press, 2004).

5. Like every psychological theory, positive psychology is challenged and criticized. This section offers a valuable suggestion, in my opinion, and a prism through which one can view their life and circumstances, but one should check what is right for them.

6. *Little Shop of Horrors* was an off-Broadway musical from 1982, written by Howard Ashman with music by Alan Menkin. The musical was based on a 1960 film directed by Roger Corman and written by Roger Corman and Charles B. Griffith, and was in turn the basis for a 1986 film version directed by Frank Oz.

7. It is also customary when reading the Haggadah during Pesach to remove ten drops of wine from our cups for each of the ten plagues Egypt endured in solidarity with the suffering of the Egyptians.

8. Rabbi Naama Dafni-Kellen, "A Prayer for the Elimination of Violence against Women," in *T'filat HaAdam: An Israeli Reform Siddur for Shabbat*, ed. Dalia Marx and Alona Lisitsa, trans. Levi Weiman-Kelman and Efrat Rotem (Jerusalem: MARAM, 2022), 401–2. Used by permission of Rabbi Naama Dafni-Kellen and MARAM.

9. We don't know whether this calendar was ever in use or if it was an ideal perception of time. See, for example, Sacha Stern, "Qumran Calendars: Theory and Practice," in *The Dead Sea Scrolls: In Their Historical Context*, ed. T. Lim (Edinburgh: T&T Clark, 2000), 179–86.

10. There have been many different interpretations about this poem. Some read it as a man's unattainable desire to be a woman, others understand it as reflecting complex feelings toward gender identity, and still others read it as mockery against women. For more insight, see Noam Sienna, *A Rainbow Thread: An Anthology of Queer Jewish Texts from the First Century to 1969* (Philadelphia: Print-O-Craft Press, 2019), 78–81.

11. About this particular blessing—men thanking God for not creating them "a woman"—in its context in the Morning Blessings, see Joel Kahn, *The Three Blessings: Boundaries, Censorship, and Identity in Jewish Liturgy* (Oxford: Oxford University Press, 2010).

12. Adapted from the English translation by Rabbi Steven Greenberg, Aharon N. Varadi, Nir Kraukauer, and Isaac Gantwerk Mayer. Published by the Open Siddur Project under a Creative Commons license, https://opensiddur.org/prayers/civic-calendar/international/transgender-day-of-visibility/prayer-of-kalonymus-from-sefer-even-bohan-1322/.

13. The Hebrew original of the complete poem can be found in Jefim Schirmann, *HaShirah HaIvrit BiSfarad UvProvans*, vol. 2 (Jerusalem: Mosad Bialik, 1956), 505.

14. Levin Kipnis, "*Ani Purim*." Track 1 on the album *Shirim L'Yeladim*. Hed Arzi Music, 1990. CD. Originally written in 1932; for more information see https://www.zemereshet.co.il/m/song.asp?id=231. © All rights reserved by Levin Kipnis and ACUM.

15. Yom Tov Levinsky, *Sefer HaMoadim* (Tel Aviv: Dvir, 1955), 6:297–321.

16. Avraham Danzig, *Chayei Adam* (Jerusalem: Shiloh, 2004), 155:41, 421–22.

17. Danzig, *Chayei Adam*, 421–22.

18. The Hebrew original and a translation by Isaac Gantwerk Meyer, excerpted here, are available on the Open Siddur Project under a Creative Commons license, https://opensiddur.org/readings-and-sourcetexts/festival-and-fast-day-readings/jewish/purim-sheni-readings/megilat-hitler-by-prosper-hassine-casablanca-1944/.

19. Levinksy, *Sefer HaMoadim*, 6:297-321.

20. The Rabbis felt uncomfortable with the content of the Scroll of Esther and the fact that the name of God—or any

matters relating to Judaism and Jewish life—does not appear in it, and they debated whether it had to be included in the Hebrew Bible canon. According to a midrashic text, Esther herself appeared before the Rabbis and demanded her inclusion in the Book of Books (Babylonian Talmud, M'gillah 7a).
21. Adapted from the New Revised Standard Version Updated Edition of the National Council of Churches of Christ in the United States as found at Bible Gateway: https://www.biblegateway.com.
22. "*Diary of a Queen,*" Dalia Marx and Avigdor Shinan, Presentation at *Beit Avi Chai*, March 2, 2022, https://www.youtube.com/watch?v=OBf5Sj8WohU [Hebrew].
23. The play was published in Hebrew translation by Dr. Avner Peretz in *L'et KaZot: Machazeh Musikali l'Purim M'Soloniki*, ed. Tamar Aleksander and Shoshanah Vaikh-Shahak (Tel Aviv: Ofir, 1993). The English translation is the work of this book's translator.
24. Ladino transcription uses the orthographic conventions established by the National Authority of Ladino's *Aki Yerushalayim* journal. Special thanks to Bryan Kirschen, PhD, of the Ladino Linguist (https://ladinolinguist.com), for providing this transcription.

Nisan

1. *Mishkan HaSeder: A Passover Haggadah*, ed. Hara E. Person and Jessica Greenbaum (New York: CCAR Press 2021), 96.
2. Rabbi Amnon Ribak, "Every Person Needs an Egypt" ("*Kol Adam Tzarich Mitzrayim*"). English translation by Amnon Ribak. © All rights reserved by Amnon Ribak and ACUM.
3. The Hebrew original is from Shulamit Elizur, *Piyutei Rabbi Pinchas HaKohein* (Jerusalem: World Union of Jewish Studies, 2004), 689.
4. This translation is amended from T. Carmi, ed., *The Penguin Book of Hebrew Verse* (London: Penguin Classics, 1981), 323. © T. Carmi 1981. Reprinted by permission of Penguin Books Limited.
5. Claude Lévi-Strauss, *The Raw and the Cooked* (New York: Harper Torchbooks, 1969).
6. Yoram Taharlev, "*Rei-ach Tapuach Odem Shani.*" Track 1 on the second album of *Arba Acharei Tzohorayim*. United Entertainment, 2012. Apple Music. See also the Taharlev website, http://www.taharlev.com/songs_selection_song_id_19.html. © All rights reserved by Yoram Taharlev and ACUM.
7. Rabbi Nachman of Bratzlav, "L'chol Makom She'ani Holech," *Atar HaPiyut v'HaT'filah*, https://www.nli.org.il/he/piyut/Piyut1song_010345700000005171/NLI.
8. *Mishkan T'filah* (New York: CCAR Press, 2007), 34.
9. Yehuda Amichai, "My Parents' Lodging Place," originally published in Hebrew in *Patuach Sagur Patuach* (Tel Aviv: Schocken Books, 1998), 56. The translation is from Yehuda Amichai, *Open Closed Open*, trans. Chana Bloch and Chana Kronfeld (Orlando: Harcourt, 2000), 59.
10. Rachel Bluwstein, "Here on Earth," in *Modern Hebrew Poetry: A Bilingual Anthology*, ed. and trans. Ruth Finer Mintz (Berkeley-Los Angeles: University of California Press, 1966), 111-12. The original Hebrew can be found here: https://benyehuda.org/read/4339.
11. Amir Gilboa, *Shirim Baboker Baboker* (Tel Aviv: Hakibbutz Hameuchad, 1953).
12. "The Book of Eldad HaDani," in *Kitvei R. Avraham Epstein*, vol. 1 (Jerusalem: Mosad Harav Kook, 1949-50), 1-189.
13. Yom Tov Levinsky, "B'ikvot Aseret HaSh'vatim," *Machanayim* 66 (1961-62): 118-23.
14. Micha Perry, *Masoret Ve-shinuy: Mesirat Yeda Be-kerev Yehudei Ma'arav Eiropa Biymei Ha-beinayim* (Tel Aviv: Hakibbutz Hameuchad, 2010), 49-63.
15. On this phenomenon, see Tudor Parfitt and Netanel Fisher, eds., *Becoming Jewish: New Jews and Emerging Jewish Communities in a Globalized Jewish World* (Newcastle upon Tyne, UK: Cambridge Scholars Publishing, 2016).
16. Rabbi Moshe Feinstein, *Ig'rot Mosheh, Orach Chayim* 5:20.
17. Rashbam on Babylonian Talmud, *P'sachim* 108b.
18. *Sh'eilot de Rav Aha Gaon*, 77.
19. Commentary on *Mishneh Torah, Hilchot Chametz uMatzah* 7:8.
20. See Yaakov Gartner, "Must Women Recline at the Seder," Bar Ilan University, March 23, 2002, https://www2.biu.ac.il/JH/Parasha/eng/pesah/ger.html [Hebrew].
21. *Mishkan T'filah: A Reform Siddur* (New York: CCAR Press, 2007), 156.
22. For a first-person account on the development of the orange on the seder plate, see https://jwa.org/podcasts/canwetalk/episode-73-orange-belongs-seder-plate.
23. This original translation by Orna Meir first appeared on Ritualwell.org as "Four Daughters: Wise, Angry, Simple, and Unable to Enquire," https://ritualwell.org/ritual/four-daughters-wise-angry-simple-and-unable-enquire/. Adapted by author.
24. Rabbi Eliezer of Worms, *Maaseh Rokei-ach* (Bnei Brak: Y. Heilprin, 1982-83), §59, p. 13.
25. Rabbi Yeshayahu Horowitz, *Sh'nei Luchot HaB'rit* (Amsterdam, 1648-89), *Pesachim, Matzah Ashirah*, 156a.
26. See Yael Levin, "Minhagim HaK'shurim B'nashim UvChag HaPesach," *Milin Chavivin* 1 (2004-5): 15-20.
27. Rabbi Avraham Halfon (1735, Livorno Italy-1819, Safed) was a biblical and Talmudic commentator, poet, and leader of the Tripoli Jewish community in the late eighteenth century. He is the author of the book *Chayei Avraham*.
28. Aharon Maman, "Mimouna: Midrash HaShem Uminhagei HaChag," in *Mechkarim B'tarbutam shel Y'hudei*

Tz'fon Afrika, ed. Yissachar Ben-Ami (Jerusalem: Vaad Adat HaMaaravim BiY'rushalayim, 1990–91), 85–95.

29. A loose translation from the Hebrew in Yigal Bin-Nun, "Al Mekoroteha Harishoniyim shel HaMimouna," *Pe'amim* 117 (2009): 154.

30. Maman, "Mimouna," 93.

31. Rabbi Rinat Safania-Schwartz, "MiMimouna MiMorocco L'Yisrael" (Rabbinic thesis, Hebrew Union College–Jewish Institute of Religion, Jerusalem campus, 2017), 4.

32. Rabbi David Bouzaglo, "Shamah Ivrim Va'aravim," as found in David Guedj, "Mimouna in Marrakech 1936," *Moroccon Jewish Heritage*, April 24, 2019, https://moreshet-morocco.com/2019/04/24/גדב--דוד1936-במרקש-מימונה/.

33. I am grateful to Prof. Meir Buzaglo for permission to use lines from his father's *piyut*.

34. Although the Nazi surrender to Soviet forces occurred on May 8, Stalin's announcement came on May 9.

35. Yosef Hayim Yerushalmi, *Zakhor: Jewish History and Jewish Memory* (Seattle: University of Washington Press, 1982), 25.

36. *Mishkan T'filah: A Reform Siddur* (New York: CCAR Press, 2007), 675.

37. See "Etty Hillesum," "Hana Senesh," "Rabbi Regina Jonas," in *Mishkan HaNefesh: Machzor for the Days of Awe, Yom Kippur* (New York: CCAR Press, 2015), 525–29.

38. Avigdor Shinan, *M'gillat HaShoah* (Jerusalem: Schechter Institute, 2003).

39. Pointing the theological finger of blame is unfortunately altogether too common. Some ultra-Orthodox rabbis have claimed that Reform Judaism is to blame, while others point the finger at anti-Zionist Chareidim.

40. Joseph B. Soloveitchik, *The Lord Is Righteous In All His Ways* (Jersey City, NJ: Ktav, 2006), 291.

41. Haim Sabato, *Bo'i Haru'ach* (Tel-Aviv: Aliyat Hagag, 2008), 79–80. Used by permission of Aliyat Hagag.

42. Nogah Hareuveni, *Nature in Our Biblical Heritage*, trans. Helen Frenkley (Kiryat Ono: Neot Kedumim, 1980), 59–60.

43. Elsewhere *derech eretz* (common decency) receives priority, as it says: "*Derech eretz* preceded the Torah" (*Vayikra Rabbah* 9:3, 35:6).

44. Rabbi Tovia Preschel, *Ma-amrei Tuvia*, vol. 5 (Jerusalem: Mosad HaRav Kook, 2006), 314–17.

45. For details on Rabbi Jill Hammer's version, please see https://ritualwell.org/ritual/omer-calendar-biblical-women/.

46. The *piyut Abiah Z'mirot* is part of a wider complex of *piyutim* said as part of the Prayer for Dew. See Ezra Fleischer, "L'kadmoniyut Piyutei HaTal," *Kovets al Yad* 8, no. 18 (1975–76): 91–139.

47. Shai Zarchi, ed., *A Proposal for the Seder: The Passover Haggadah—Tradition and Renewal* (Tel Aviv: Mashkal, 2000), 19 [Hebrew].

Iyar

1. On the musical influences on *HaTikvah*, see Edwin Seroussi, "*Hatikvah*: Conceptions, Receptions and Reflections," *Yuval* 9 (2015), https://jewish-music.huji.ac.il/yuval/22482 [Hebrew].

2. Chayim Nachman Bialik, *Birkat Am* (Tel Aviv: Dvir, 1973). For more details, see https://benyehuda.org/read/3604 [Hebrew].

3. Victor Turner, *The Ritual Process* (New York: Transaction Publishers, 1969), 94–5.

4. Chayim Nachman Bialik, "L'Achad Ha'am" (Tel Aviv: Dvir, 1973). For more details, see https://benyehuda.org/read/7028 [Hebrew].

5. I am grateful to Rabbi Chaya Rowen-Baker, from whom I learned the Talmudic discussion about the hour of twilight in this context.

6. "Havdalah Blessing for Distinguishing between Yom HaZikaron and Yom HaAtzmaut" by Esteban Gottfried from *Et Sefod vEt Rekod* ("Time to Mourn and Time to Dance"), 2007, Beit Tefilah Israeli. I am grateful to Rabbi Esteban Gottfried for permission to reproduce this prayer. The entire ceremony can be viewed at https://ritualwell.org/ritual/havdalah-transitional-ceremony-between-yom-hazikaron-yom-haatzmaut/.

7. This sentence is taken from the traditional version of the blessing over the soul, recited upon awakening in the morning.

8. Berl Katznelson, "Yizkor (1920)" in Eran Kaplan and Derek J. Penslar, eds., *The Origins of Israel, 1882-1948: A Documentary History* (Madison: University of Wisconsin Press, 2011), 216–217. Reprinted by permission of the University of Wisconsin Press. © 2011 by the Board of Regents of the University of Wisconsin System. All rights reserved.

9. Ilana Shamir, "Changes in the Wording of the 'Yizkor'" [Hebrew], *Yizkor*, https://www.izkor.gov.il/9298fd09a3166041529222beeb7930b7.

10. "Yizkor," *Yizkor*, https://www.izkor.gov.il/e8c02cee2cf70ebb6eaf29e8c8d02d17 [Hebrew].

11. Berl Katznelson, "Mekorot Lo Achzav," *Davar*, 14 Av 5694 [July 26, 1934]. The English version here is based in part on a translation in Gil Troy, "The Secular Socialist Zionist Who Insisted on Mourning on Tisha B'Av," *Jewish Journal*, August 4, 2022, https://jewishjournal.com/commentary/opinion/350593/the-secular-socialist-zionist-who-insisted-on-mourning-on-tisha-bav/.

12. Gili Cohen, "IDF Set to Remove 'God' From Text Recited at Army Memorials," *Haaretz*, May 17, 2012, https://www.haaretz.com/2012-05-17/ty-article/special-yizkor-text-to-regain-its-role-next-memorial-day/.

13. "Yizkor Elohim et Nishmot Chayalei Tz'va HaHaganah L'Yisrael," *Siddur T'filot L'Chayal L'chol Shanah* (Tel Aviv: Rubenstein, 1963), 421.

14. Yehudit Bialer, "Yizkor Am Yisrael," *Atzuma*, June 16, 2011, https://www.atzuma.co.il/yizkor.
15. "Yizkor," *Yizkor*.
16. "Yizkor," *Yizkor*.
17. Yishai Beer, "Letter from the head of 'Yizkor' examining team," *Tarbut.il*, July 28, 2011, https://tarbutil.cet.ac.il [Hebrew].
18. Abba Kovner, "Nizkor—Let Us Remember," Yad Vashem, https://www.yadvashem.org/yv/en/remembrance-day/generations-light-the-way.asp (adapted), with no attribution to the translator. © All rights reserved by Abba Kovner and ACUM.
19. See Dalia Marx, "T'filat HaKaddish—Me-emek HaRhein L'emek Yizr'el: T'filat HaAvelim BaT'nua HaKibbutzit," in *Jewish Prayer: New Perspectives* [Hebrew], ed. Uri Ehrlich (Beer-Sheva: Ben-Gurion University Press, 2016), 291–313.
20. Yehuda Amichai, "El Malei Rachamim" in *B'merchak Sh'tei Tikvot* (Tel Aviv: Hakibbutz Hameuchad, 1960).
21. "I Recall/*Ezkor*" by Marcia Falk, from *The Days Between: Blessings, Poems, and Directions of the Heart for the Jewish High Holiday Season* (Brandeis University Press, 2014). Copyright © 2014 Marcia Lee Falk. Used by permission of the author.
22. Zvi Shua and Aryeh Ben Guryon, eds., *Yalkut Avelut* (Kibbutz Beit Hashita, 1990–91), 146. See also Dalia Marx, "From the Rhine Valley to Jezreel Valley: Innovative Versions of the Mourner Kaddish in the Kibbutz Movement," *Between Jewish Tradition and Modernity: Rethinking an Old Opposition; Essays in Honor of David Ellenson*, ed. Michael Meyer and David A. Myers (Detroit: Wayne State University Press, 2014), 123–41.
23. Jonathan Rosen, *The Talmud and the Internet: A Journey between Worlds* (New York: Picador, 2000), 15.
24. Rosen, *The Talmud and the Internet*, 36.
25. Much of this language borrows from the popular children's song called "Eliezer ben-Yehuda," written by Yaron London and Matti Caspi.
26. Eliezer Ben-Yehuda, *HaTzvi*, 6 Tevet 5657 [December 11, 1898].
27. Eliezer Ben-Yehuda, "Mekorot Lemalei HeChaser Bilshonenu," *Zichronot Vaad HaLashon HaIvrit* 4, (1912): 3-16.
28. Yehonatan Gefen, "K'she'omrim," *The Sixteenth Lamb* [Hebrew] (Tel Aviv: Dvir, 1978).
29. Chatam Sofer, *Yoreh Dei-ah*, 2:233 (Pressburg: Anton von Schmidt, 1841), 50–51, https://www.nli.org.il/he/books/NNL_ALEPH002036522/NLI.
30. Rabbi Joseph Saul Nathanson, *Sho-el Umeishiv* (Brooklyn, NY: HaMachon L'Chasidut, 1960), 39.
31. "In the wake of the Meron disaster: Rabbi Kaniewski called on women to become stronger in modesty," *Maariv*, May 4, 2021, https://www.maariv.co.il/news/israel/Article-838363 [Hebrew].
32. Previously published in part in my article "Liturgical Responses to Catastrophe: A Preliminary Outline," *CCAR Journal: The Reform Jewish Quarterly*, Spring 2022.
33. For an analysis of the ceremony and its meaning, see Yoram Bilu, "From Milah (Circumcision) to Milah (Word): Male Identity and Rituals of Childhood in the Jewish Ultraorthodox Community," *Ethos* 31 (2003): 172–203.
34. I heard this story from Rabbi Yehoyada Amir.
35. *T'filat HaAdam: An Israeli Reform Siddur* (Jerusalem: MARAM, 2020), 36. Used by permission of Rabbi Yehoyada Amir and MARAM. (The translator is also grateful to Rabbi Amir for the improvements he suggested, which are incorporated here.)
36. Translation by Rabbi Amichai Lau-Lavie, slightly revised here. Published by the Open Siddur Project under a Creative Commons license at https://opensiddur.org/prayers/collective-welfare/nations/shalom/prayer-of-mothers-for-life-and-peace-by-sheikha-ibtisam-mahamid-and-rabbi-tamar-elad-appelbaum/.
37. Hillel Sermonetta and Angelo Piattelli, eds., *Seder T'filot K'Minhag B'nei Roma* (Jerusalem: printed by the editors, 2014), 381. Used by permission of Angelo Piattelli.

Sivan

1. Rabbi Chayim Vital, *Shaar HaKavanot* (Jerusalem: Yeshivat HaChayim V'HaShalom V'kholel Ateret Mordechai, 1985), 1:1.
2. Levin Kipnis, *Saleinu al K'tafeinu* ["Our Baskets Are on Our Shoulders"], 1929, https://www.zemereshet.co.il/m/song.asp?id=226. © All rights reserved by Levin Kipnis and ACUM.
3. Yom Tov Levinsky, *Sefer HaMoadim*, vol. 3, *Shavuot* (Tel Aviv: D'vir, 1950), 201-2.
4. For more details, see Moti Zeira, *Rural Collective Settlement and Jewish Culture in Eretz Yisrael During the 1920s* [Hebrew] (Jerusalem: Yad Izhak Ben Zvi, 2002), 169.
5. The Arab riots of 1929 took place August 23–29, 1929, as a result of many different tensions and long-standing debates, though access to the Western Wall in Jerusalem was the immediate trigger. This was one of the first major riots against a Jewish presence in British Mandate Palestine and led to the deaths and injury of nearly five hundred Jews.
6. Unpublished original poem, printed here by permission of the author.
7. *Iggeret ha-Rayah*, vol. 1 (Jerusalem: Mosad Harav Kook, 1962), 214 (Letter 164).
8. Judith Plaskow, *Standing Again at Sinai* (New York: HarperCollins, 1991), 25.
9. Elchanan Samet, *Studies in the Weekly Parashah: First Series; Leviticus, Numbers, Deuteronomy* [Hebrew] (Tel Aviv: Miskal, 2009), 388.
10. Martin Buber, *The Way of Scripture* [Hebrew] (Jerusalem: Bialik Institute, 1964), 84.
11. Translation adapted by the author.

12. *Mishkan HaSeder: A Passover Haggadah*, ed. Rabbi Hara E. Person and Jessica Greenbaum (New York: CCAR Press, 2021), 96.
13. Buber, *The Way of Scripture*, 84.
14. Buber, *The Way of Scripture*, 84.
15. From Isadore Twersky, ed., *A Maimonides Reader* (New York: Behrman House, 1972), 475.
16. Rabbi Menachem Genack, CEO of the Orthodox Union's kosher division, as quoted in Jacob Gurvis, "Impossible Pork Is Here, but It Won't Be Certified as Kosher," *Baltimore Jewish Times*, October 31, 2021, https://www.jewishtimes.com/impossible-pork-is-here-but-it-wont-be-certified-as-kosher/.
17. Yehoshua Sobol, "*Etzleinu BiChfar Tudra*," from the play *Kriza* (1976). © All rights reserved by Yehoshua Sobol and ACUM.
18. Rabbi Eleazar of Worms, "The Laws of Shavuot," in *Sefer HaRokei-ach*, 296. Translation from Ivan Marcus, *Rituals of Childhood: Jewish Acculturation in Medieval Europe* (New Haven: Yale University Press, 1998), 26–27.
19. Marcus, *Rituals of Childhood*.
20. Rabbi Eleazar of Worms, as found in Marcus, *Rituals of Childhood*, 27–28.
21. For example, see what is referred to as "The Birds Haggadah," an illustrated Ashkenazic Haggadah from around 1300. It can be viewed at https://www.imj.org.il/en/collections/199815-0.
22. The term "bet mitzvah" can be used as a gender-inclusive term for all Jewish coming-of-age ceremonies celebrated at thirteen.
23. Anonymous, *Aus einem Briefe aus Berlin*, in *Sulamith* 5, no. 1 (1817/1820): 279, found in Klaus Herrmann's "Jewish Confirmation Sermons in 19th-Century Germany," in *Preaching in Judaism and Christianity: Encounters and Developments from Biblical Times to Modernity*, ed. Alexander Deeg, Walter Homolka, and Heinz-Günther-Schöttler (Berlin: Walter de Gruyter, 2008), 103–4.
24. Ronald L. Grimes, *Deeply into the Bone: Re-inventing Rites of Passage* (Berkeley: University of California Press, 2000), 337–40.
25. A. M. Habermann, *Sefer G'zeirot Ashk'naz V'Tzar'fat* (Jerusalem: Tarshish, 1945), 134–35.
26. Rabbi Ephraim ben Jacob of Bonn, "Kaf B'Sivan Hayom Hamar v'HaNimaher," in *Sefer HaZichronot*, by Rabbi Shmuel Abuhav (Jerusalem: Hotzaat Chevrat Ahavat Shalom, 2008), 22–26.
27. Simon Bernfeld, *Sefer HaD'maot* (Berlin: Eshkol, 1926), 135.
28. Shabbetai Cohen, *Megillat Eifah* [Scroll of Darkness], appendix to Solomon ibn Verga, *Shevet Y'hudah* (Hanover: Wiener, 1856), 139.
29. The rabbis of the Neolog movement in Hungary and the rabbis of the independent congregations—the "status quo" congregations—chose to mark the Holocaust of Hungarian Jews on the twenty-fourth of Adar, since on that date (March 19) in 1944 the Nazis conquered Hungary.
30. Ruth Langer, "Celebrating the Presence of the Torah: The History and Meaning of Reading Torah," in *My People's Prayer Book*, vol. 4, *Seder K'riat HaTorah (The Torah Service)*, ed. Lawrence A. Hoffman (Woodstock, VT: Jewish Lights, 2000), 19–28.
31. Translations of *Akdamut Milin* by Rabbi Dr. Martin S. Cohen in *Siddur Tzur Yisrael: Sabbath and Festival Prayers* (Roslyn, NY: Shelter Rock Jewish Center, 2006). Used by permission.
32. Levin Kipnis, "*Matan Torah*" from *Macharozet: Z'mirot Umischakim Liyladim* (Frankfurt-am-Main: Omanut, 1923), 124–25. © All rights reserved by Levin Kipnis and ACUM.
33. Slightly revised from "Shavuot: 'Akdamut' and 'Ketubah,'" Orthodox Union, June 30, 2006, https://www.ou.org/holidays/akdamut_and_ketuvah/.
34. Rabbi Menachem de Lonzano, *Sh'tei Yadot*, 142.

Tammuz
1. Translation by David Asher, *Selichoth for the Propitiatory and Penitential Days, and for the Minor Fasts, to Which Are Added the Selichoth for the Minor Day of Atonement* (London: Valentine, 1912), 184–85; amended by Aharon Varady for the Open Siddur Project, https://opensiddur.org/prayers/lunisolar/commemorative-days/fast-days/shivah-asar-btamuz/ki-bshivah-asar-btamuz-a-selihah-for-the-17th-of-tamuz/, and further amended for this book.
2. Rabbi Ofer Sabath Beit Halachmi, *Bar'chu: Bamah L'hitkadshut HaT'filah B'Yisrael* (Jerusalem: Library of Progressive Judaism, 2010), 91.
3. "A Prayer for Repair of the Tablets" by Rabbi Ofer Sabath Beit Halachmi, previously published in *El Halev: A Collection of Prayers and Blessings for Our Time*, (Jerusalem: Hebrew Union College–Jewish Institute of Religion and the Israel Movement for Reform and Progressive Judaism, 2005), 50 [Hebrew] and in *Bar'chu: Bamah L'hitkadshut HaT'filah B'Yisrael* (Jerusalem: Library of Progressive Judaism, 2010), 91 [Hebrew]. All rights reserved by Rabbi Ofer Sabath Beit Halachmi.
4. Astrid Lindgren, *Pippi Longstocking* (New York: Viking Books, 2020).
5. Blaise Pascal, *Collected Works* (Hastings, UK: Delphi, 2020), 917.
6. I am grateful to Dr. Yoav Silbert, professor of philosophy and the history of education, who shared this information in a personal conversation.
7. James Pederson, "The History of School and Summer Vacation," *Journal of Inquiry & Action in Education*, 5, no.1 (Fall 2012), retrieved from https://digitalcommons.buffalostate.edu/jiae/vol5/iss1/4.

8. Tom Hodgkinson sings the praises of proper idleness in his book *How to Be Idle* (New York: HarperCollins, 2005).
9. Chayim Nachman Bialik, *Songs and Hymns of Children* (Tel Aviv: Dvir, 1933) [Hebrew]. Originally printed in the *Bema'ale* newsletter (Issue 19 [47], October 14, 1932), 5.
10. Megan Cassella, "The Pandemic Drove Women Out of the Workforce. Will They Come Back?," *Politico*, July 22, 2021, https://www.politico.com/news/2021/07/22/coronavirus-pandemic-women-workforce-500329.
11. *Mishkan T'filah: A Reform Siddur* (New York: CCAR Press, 2007), 352.
12. S. Y. Abromovich (Mendele Mocher Sforim), *Tales of Mendele the Book Peddler: Fishke the Lame and Benjamin the Third*, ed. Dan Miron and Ken Frieden, trans. Ted Gorelick and Hillel Halkin (New York: Schocken Books, 1996), 14–15.
13. Shaul Tchernichowsky, "Mot Tammuz" (The Death of Tammuz), translated by Isaac Schwartz in *Kol Shirei* (Tel Aviv: Schocken, 1937).
14. Based on S. Shifra and Jacob Klein, *BaYamim HaR'chokim HaHem: Antologiya Mishirat HaMizrach HaKadum* (Tel Aviv: Am Oved, 1996), 368–91.
15. Yael Renan, *Elot V'giburim: Mitosim al G'vulot HaKoach* (Tel Aviv: Am Oved, 2001), 36–37.
16. Simona Matsliah-Chanoch, *Reversible Death Fairy Tales* (Karkur: Prague, 2009) [Hebrew].
17. "Al Tifchad," lyrics and music by Ehud Banai, track 8 on *HaShlishi*, produced by Yehudah Ravitz, 1992.
18. Yariv Ben-Aharon, *Shorshei Y'nika shel Hagar'in Hachalutzi* (Efal: n.p., 1983), 15.
19. Shimon Peres, "Speech at the Opening Ceremony of the Presidential Conference in Honor of State President Shimon Peres's Ninetieth Birthday," June 18, 2013, Israeli Presidential Conference, https://www.youtube.com/watch?v=G-88NraFwGM.
20. Rabbi Esteban Gottfried, *Siddur Erev Shabbat Umo-eid* (Tel Aviv: Beit Tefilah Israeli, 2013), 126.

Av

1. *Shulchan Aruch, Orach Chayim* 1:1.
2. The translation of the first nine stanzas by Abraham Rosenfeld in *The Authorised Kinot for the Ninth of Av*, 2nd ed. (London: I. Labworth & Co., 1970), 145. The translation does not preserve the AAC/BBC rhyme pattern of the Hebrew.
3. Shalom Raddai, *Rabbi Shalom Raddai v'Chiburav: Ta'aniya Va-aniya, HaAsif, U'Ma'archei Lev*, ed. Moshe Gavra (Bnei Brak: HaMachon L'Cheiker Chachmei Teiman, 1999), 36–37.
4. Yosef Hayim Yerushalmi, *Zakhor: Jewish History and Jewish Memory* (Seattle: University of Washington Press, 1982), 5.
5. *HaAvodah SheBaLev: Siddur T'filot* (Jerusalem: Israel Movement for Progressive Judaism, 1982), 225.
6. Ben Sales, "How Summer Camp Has Become an American Jewish Institution," Jewish Telegraphic Agency, May 22, 2020, https://www.jta.org/2020/05/22/lifestyle/how-summer-camp-has-become-an-american-jewish-institution.
7. "Campopedia: Tisha B'Av," Foundation for Jewish Camp, https://jewishcamp.org/campopedia/.
8. Lawrence A. Hoffman, *Beyond the Text: A Holistic Approach to Liturgy* (Bloomington: Indiana University Press, 1987), 119.
9. Today, all Reform rabbinic, cantorial, and education students must know classical as well as Modern Hebrew and are required to spend their first year of study immersed in Israeli society and exposed to all its diversity while at the Hebrew Union College–Jewish Institute of Religion in Jerusalem, where I am privileged to teach them.
10. Berl Katznelson, "Mekorot Lo Achzav," *Davar*, 14 Av 5694 [July 26, 1934]. The English version here is based in part on a translation in Gil Troy, "The Secular Socialist Zionist Who Insisted on Mourning on Tisha B'Av," *Jewish Journal*, August 4, 2022, https://jewishjournal.com/commentary/opinion/350593/the-secular-socialist-zionist-who-insisted-on-mourning-on-tisha-bav/.
11. *Zohar, T'rumah* 157, 2.
12. Translation of both Psalms are from *Tanakh: The Traditional Hebrew Text and the New JPS Translation* (Philadelphia: Jewish Publication Society, 1999). Adapted by author.
13. Yair Zakovitch, "'Al Naharot Bavel': Tehillim 137—Zikkaron Be-tzel Ha-trauma," in Zipora Talshir, Shamir Yona, and Daniel Sivan, eds., *Homage to Shmuel: Studies in the World of the Bible* [Hebrew] (Beer Sheva and Jerusalem: Ben-Gurion University of the Negev and Bialik Institute, 2001), 203 [Hebrew].
14. *Sefer Abudarham: Shiur Peirush HaB'rachot v'HaT'filot, Seder T'filot HaChol: Birchot HaShachar*, 7.
15. Norman Doidge, *The Brain That Changes Itself: Stories of Personal Triumph from the Frontiers of Brain Science* (New York: Viking, 2007), 186–87.
16. Adapted from Isadore Twersky, ed., *A Maimonides Reader* (New York: Behrman House, 1972), 225.
17. Ya'akov Rotblit, "Shir L'Shalom," performed by Yair Rosenblum, on *The Best of Israeli Folk Songs* (Jerusalem Records, 1995).
18. From Shaul Tchernichowsky, "I Believe," adapted from the translation by Vivian Eden in "Poem of the Week: This Is the Poem That Could Replace 'Hatikvah,'" *Haaretz*, October 13, 2013, https://www.haaretz.com/life/books/2013-10-13/ty-article/.premium/poem-this-could-replace-hatikvah/0000017f-f0cc-d8a1-a5ff-f0ce8a800000. © Vivian Eden. Permission donated in memory of Vivian Eden's cousin, Rabbi Elliot Stevens, *z"l*.
19. Jay Croft, "10 Quotes That Help Define the 'Notorious

RBG' Legacy of Ruth Bader Ginsburg," *CNN Politics*, September 20, 2020, https://www.cnn.com/2020/09/19/politics/best-ruth-bader-ginsburg-quotes-trnd/index.html.
20. The reason a generation of Jews wandered the wilderness for forty years and died there is because of the episode with the scouts (Number 13:25–14:24). When the twelve scouts returned from scouting out the Land of Israel, ten of them convinced the Israelites that they were too weak to conquer the land, and the people lost faith in God and God's promise. As a result, God condemned the entire generation to die in their wanderings. The only exceptions were the two scouts who refuted the claims of the other ten: Caleb and Joshua. According to Rabbah bar bar Chanah, the last of this generation died on Tu B'Av.
21. Victor Turner, *The Ritual Process* (New York: Transaction Publishers, 1969), 94.
22. Hannah Pinhasi, "Chag HaChofesh HaNashi," Ynet, July 23, 2010, https://www.ynet.co.il/articles/0,7340,L-3923818,00.html.
23. Turner, *The Ritual Process*.
24. Yom Tov Levinsky, *Sefer HaMoadim*, vol. 6 (Tel Aviv: D'vir, 1955), 493. Further in the same chapter, Levinsky offers a futuristic look at Tu B'Av celebrations in Israel in the year 2040 (524–26).
25. Nogah Hareuveni, *Nature in Our Biblical Heritage* (Kiryat Ono: Neot Kedumim, 1980), 35–43.
26. I first heard this claim from my student Tomer Dina Ventura, who has researched the sources of Tu B'Av.
27. *Mishkan T'filah: A Reform Siddur* (New York: CCAR Press, 2007), 150.
28. *Mishkan T'filah*, 154.
29. Translation adapted by author.
30. Franz Rosenzweig, *The Star of Redemption*, trans. Barbara E. Galli (Madison: University of Wisconsin Press, 2005).
31. "*Sh'ma*: Communal Declaration of Faith/*Sh'ma*" by Marcia Falk, from *The Book of Blessings: New Jewish Prayers for Daily Life, the Sabbath, and the New Moon Festival* (CCAR Press, 2017). Copyright © 1996, 2017 Marcia Lee Falk. Used by permission of the author.
32. Eliaz Cohen, "*Sh'ma, Adonai*" quoted from *Hear O Lord: Poems from the Disturbances of 2000–2009*, trans. Larry Barak (New Milford, CT: Toby Press, 2010), 15. © 2010. Used with the permission of Koren Publishers Jerusalem Ltd. and The Toby Press LLC.

Elul

1. Based on Martin Buber, from *Avodah SheBaLev* (Jerusalem: Israel Movement for Progressive Judaism, 1982), 85.
2. Richard Levy, *Songs Ascending: The Book of Psalms in a New Translation* (New York: CCAR Press, 2018), 1:97–98, adapted by the author.
3. Uri Milstein, *Rahel: Shirim, Mikhtavim, Reshimot, Korot Chayei-ha* (Tel Aviv: Zemora Beitan, 1985).
4. A range of ideas for *S'lichot* can be found in the booklet *P'tach Lanu Shaar: Asupat S'lichot*, ed. Rabbi Naama Dafni Kellen (Jerusalem: Israel Movement for Progressive Judaism, n.d.).
5. *Ben Adam*, interpreted by Rabbi Nancy Flam, Piyut North America, http://piyutnorthamerica.org/piyutarchive/, adapted by the author.
6. Eliyahu Gelula, "Tafkido shel HaShofar B'Rosh HaShanah V'Ofyah shel HaT'shuvah," *HaMeir LaAretz* annual no. 1 [no. 66] (2004/5): 210–26. Available for download in Hebrew on the site of the Lifschitz Academic College: https://www.lif.ac.il.
7. Aharon N. Varady, "Explanation and Ritual for the Jewish New Year's Day for Animals, Rosh HaShanah La-Behemah on Rosh Hodesh Elul," Open Siddur Project, August 28, 2011, https://opensiddur.org.
8. Richard H. Schwartz, "Restoring and Transforming the Ancient Jewish New Year for Animals: An Idea Whose Time Has Come," *Times of Israel*, August 16, 2022, https://blogs.timesofisrael.com. See also the book by the same name (Woodstock, NY: Lantern Publishing and Media, 2022).
9. Naftali Wieder, *The Formation of Jewish Liturgy in the East and the West* [Hebrew], vol. 1 (Jerusalem: Ben Zvi Institute and Yad Ben Zvi, 1998), 440–47.
10. Translation adapted by author.
11. Rabbi Gila Caine, originally published on the website for the Israel Movement for Progressive Judaism.
12. Jewish Vegetarian Society in Jerusalem, "Haggadah for the Alef b'Elul Seder, the New Year's Day for Animals (Ginger House 2013)," trans. Michael Fraade, Open Siddur Project, August 17, 2014, https://opensiddur.org.
13. Aharon N. Varady, "Kavvanah before Shofar Blowing on Rosh Hodesh Elul for Rosh haShanah la-Behemah (the Jewish New Year's Day for Animals)," Open Siddur Project, August 18, 2016, https://opensiddur.org.
14. *Mishkan HaNefesh: Machzor for the Days of Awe*, vol. 2, *Yom Kippur* (New York: CCAR Press, 2015), 644, adapted by the author.
15. This is an adapted version of the translation in Everett Fox, *The Five Books of Moses* (New York: Schocken Books, 1995), 455.
16. A detailed list of the various enumerations can be found in the *Rosh HaShanah* volume of the Hebrew commentary of Rabbi Adin Steinsaltz to the Babylonian Talmud (Jerusalem: HaMachon HaYisraeli L'Firsumim Talmudiyim, 1997), 72.

ABOUT THE AUTHOR

Rabbi Dalia Marx, PhD, is the Rabbi Aaron D. Panken Professor of Liturgy at Hebrew Union College–Jewish Institute of Religion (HUC-JIR) in Jerusalem. She also teaches at various academic institutions in Israel and Europe and is dedicated to promoting liberal Judaism, religious pluralism, and interfaith understanding. Rabbi Marx, a tenth-generation Jerusalemite, earned her doctorate at Hebrew University and her rabbinic ordination at HUC-JIR in Jerusalem and Cincinnati. She is the author of several books, including *A Feminist Commentary on the Babylonian Talmud: Tractates Tamid, Middot, and Qinnim* (Mohr Siebeck, 2013). She is the chief editor of *T'filat HaAdam*, the Israeli Reform prayer book (MaRaM, 2020), and the coeditor of several other volumes. *From Time to Time: Journeys in the Jewish Calendar* was first published in Israel in 2018 as *Bazman* and has been translated into German, Spanish, and now English. Rabbi Marx and her life partner Roly Zylbersztein, PhD, live in Jerusalem; they have three children.